AFRICAN REGIONAL TRADE AGREEMENTS AS LEGAL REGIMES

African regional trade integration has grown exponentially in the last decade. This book is the first comprehensive analysis of the legal framework within which it is being pursued. It will fill a huge knowledge gap and serve as an invaluable teaching and research tool for policy makers in the public and private sectors, teachers, researchers and students of African trade and beyond. The author argues that African Regional Trade Agreements are best understood as flexible legal regimes, particularly given their commitment to variable geometry and multiple memberships. He analyses the progress made toward trade liberalization in each region, how the Regional Trade Agreements are financed, their trade remedy and judicial regimes and how well they measure up to Article XXIV of GATT. The book also covers monetary unions as well as intra-African regional integration, and examines Free Trade Agreements with non-African regions, including the Economic Partnership Agreements with the European Union.

JAMES THUO GATHII is Associate Dean for Research and Scholarship and Governor George E. Pataki Professor of International Commercial Law, Albany Law School. He is author of *War, Commerce and International Law* (2010) and over 50 articles and book chapters.

CAMBRIDGE INTERNATIONAL TRADE AND ECONOMIC LAW

As the processes of regionalization and globalization have intensified, there have been accompanying increases in the regulations of international trade and economic law at the levels of international, regional and national laws.

The subject matter of this series is international economic law. Its core is the regulation of international trade, investment and cognate areas such as intellectual property and competition policy. The series publishes books on related regulatory areas, in particular human rights, labour, environment and culture, as well as sustainable development. These areas are vertically linked at the international, regional and national level, and the series extends to the implementation of these rules at these different levels. The series also includes works on governance, dealing with the structure and operation of related international organizations in the field of international economic law, and the way they interact with other subjects of international and national law.

Series editors

Books in the series

Trade Policy Flexibility and Enforcement in the WTO: A Law and Economics Analysis
Simon A.B. Schropp

The Multilaterization of International Investment Law
Stephan W. Schill

The Law, Economics and Politics of Retaliation in WTO Dispute Settlement
Edited by Chad P. Bown and Joost Pauwelyn

Non-Discrimination in International Trade in Services: 'Likeness' in WTO/GATS
Nicolas Diebold

Processes and Production Methods (PPMs) in WTO Law: Interfacing Trade and Social Goals
Christiane R. Conrad

African Regional Trade Agreements as Legal Regimes
James Thuo Gathii

AFRICAN REGIONAL TRADE AGREEMENTS AS LEGAL REGIMES

JAMES THUO GATHII

CAMBRIDGE
UNIVERSITY PRESS

CAMBRIDGE UNIVERSITY PRESS
Cambridge, New York, Melbourne, Madrid, Cape Town,
Singapore, São Paulo, Delhi, Tokyo, Mexico City

Cambridge University Press
The Edinburgh Building, Cambridge CB2 8RU, UK

Published in the United States of America by Cambridge University Press, New York

www.cambridge.org
Information on this title: www.cambridge.org/9780521769839

First published 2011

Printed in the United Kingdom at the University Press, Cambridge

A catalogue record for this publication is available from the British Library

Library of Congress Cataloguing in Publication data
Gathii, James Thuo.
African regional trade agreements as legal regimes / James Thuo Gathii.
p. cm. – (Cambridge international trade and economic law)
Includes bibliographical references and index.
ISBN 978-0-521-76983-9 (hardback)
1. Foreign trade regulation – Africa. 2. Africa – Economic integration. 3. Africa – Foreign economic relations. 4. Monetary unions – Africa. 5. Foreign trade regulation. 6. Free trade.
I. Title.
KQC947.G38 2011
343.6′087 – dc22 2011016333

ISBN 978-0-521-76983-9 Hardback

CONTENTS

FIGURES

TABLES

ACKNOWLEDGEMENTS

I would not have been able to write this book without the help of so many people. First, I would like thank my immediate family. My loving wife, Caroline and our two sons, Michael and Ethan, have provided enormous encouragement and loving support to me in so many ways. I am grateful to Dean Thomas Guernsey at Albany Law School for his unwavering support. There are many things that inspired this book. None, however, is more important than my experience teaching short courses at the Trade Policy Training Institute in Africa (TRAPCA), in Arusha, Tanzania. I have now taught at TRAPCA for four years and met a large number of African students who have varied experiences working on trade and investment in the governmental and non-governmental sectors. Teaching these students was as much a learning opportunity for me as it was for them. One thing was clear, though – the continuing need for materials on trade law based on the African experience. This book hopefully goes some way in fulfilling that yawning gap. I would like to extend special thanks to Peter Kiuluku, the Executive Director of TRAPCA and Dr. Caiphas Chekwoti, the Trade Policy Expert at TRAPCA.

Many friends have also encouraged and supported me in this quest, including Kibet Mutui, Ruth Okediji, Makau Wa Mutua, Edward Kwakwa, Obiora Okafor, Joel Ngugi, Sylvia Kangara, Mund Ndulo, Obi Aginam, Benard Sihanya and Ibironke Odumosu.

I benefited from very useful research assistance from the following: Joseph Rogers, Elizabeth Trachy, Asish Nelluvely, Paul Timpone, Dario Arrezio, Rebekkah Weiler, George Hanok and Thomas Lewandowski. The reference librarians at Albany Law School, Mary Wood and Robert Emery, provided invaluable assistance in getting access to everything I needed to complete this project and I thank them for their professionalism. Thanks, too, to Evette Dejesus and Kevin Ramakrishna, for providing important order and support as I wrote the book. At Cambridge University Press, I thank Finola O'Sullivan and her Assistant, Gillian Dadd, for their patience and very helpful assistance.

Parts of this book have been previously published in different form: 'African Regional Trade Agreements as Flexible Legal Regimes', *North Carolina Journal of International Commercial Regulation* (2010) and 'The Underappreciated Jurisprudence of African Regional Trade Judiciaries', *Oregon Review of International Law* (2010). To these journals, I am grateful for providing me with the first stab at exploring the ideas that I explore at fuller length in this book.

Last, but not least, I thank my parents, Joseph and Theresiah Gathii, for their unfailing love and support over the years. I dedicate this book to my late mother-in-law, Mrs. Dorothy Wanjiru Mwangi, whose love and affection is greatly missed.

ABBREVIATIONS

AAMP	African Agricultural Markets Programme
ACP	African, Caribbean and Pacific Group of States
ACTESA	Alliance for Commodity Trade in Eastern and Southern Africa
ADF	African Development Fund
AFC	Administration and Finance Commission
AFCAC	African Civil Aviation Commission
AfDB	Africa Development Bank
AFRAA	African Airlines Association
AFTAR	Africa's Agriculture and Rural Development Unit
AGOA	Africa Growth and Opportunities Act 2000
AMU	Arab Maghreb Union
ANSA	Angola, Namibia and South Africa
ASEAN	Association of Southeast Asian Nations
ASECNA	Agency for Aerial Navigation Safety in Africa and Madagascar
ASYCUDA	Automated System of Customs and Data Management
AU	African Union
AU/AEC/REC	(African Union/African Economic Community) (Regional Economic Communities)
AUC	African Union Commission
AVSEC	Aviation Security
BASA	Bilateral Air Service Agreements
BCEAO	Central Bank of West African States
BEAC	Bank of Central Africa
BEAU	Bank of Central West Africa
BIPPA	Bilateral Investment Promotion and Protection Agreement
BIT	Bilateral Investment Treaty
BLNS	Botswana, Lesotho, Namibia and Swaziland
CAADP	Comprehensive Africa Agriculture Development Programme
CAFTA	US–Central America Free Trade Agreement
CCIA	COMESA Common Investment Area
CCJ	Community Court of Justice

CEAO	Communauté Economique de l'Afrique de l'Ouest
CEMAC	Economic and Monetary Community of Central Africa
CEN-SAD	Community of Sahel-Saharan States
CET	Common External Tariffs
CFA	Colonies Françaises d'Afrique
CIF	cost, insurance and freight
CIP	Payment Incidents Centre
CMT	Committee of Ministers
COBAC	Commission Bancaire de l'Afrique Centrale
COHS	Conference of the Heads of State
CoJ	COMESA Court of Justice
COM	Council of Ministers
COMESA	Common Market for Eastern and Southern Africa
COMESA-CD	COMESA Customs Document
COPAX	Council for Peace and Security in Central Africa
COSCAP	Cooperative Development of Operational Safety and Continuing Air Worthiness Project
CPCM	Conseil Permanent Consultatif du Maghreb
CRTA	Committee on Regional Trade Agreements
CU	customs union
DSB	Dispute Settlement Body
DTI	Department of Trade International (Trade and Economic Development)
EAC	East African Community
EACJ	East African Court of Justice
EAFCA	Eastern African Fine Coffees Association
EALA	East African Legislative Assembly
EAPP	Eastern Africa Power Pool
EBA	Everything but Arms
EBID	ECOWAS Bank for Investment and Development
EC	European Communities
ECCAS	Economic Community of Central African States
EC-GSP	European Commission – Generalized System of Preferences
ECOSOCC	Economic, Social and Cultural Council
ECOWAS	Economic Community of West African States
EC-SADC EPA	Economic Community–Southern African Development Community Economic Partnership Agreements
EDF	European Development Fund
EFTA	European Free Trade Area
EPAs	Economic Partnership Agreements
ESA	Eastern and Southern Africa
ESADA	Eastern and Southern African Dairy Association

EU	European Union
EU-ACP EPA	European Union–African, Caribbean and Pacific Group of States Economic Partnership Agreements
FAA	Federal Aviation Administration
FDI	Foreign Direct Investment
FIFA	International Federation of Association Football
FOCAC	Forum on China–Africa Cooperation
FOMAC	Multinational Peace Keeping Force in Central Africa
FTA	free trade area
FTAg	free trade agreement
GAFTA	Greater Arab Free Trade Area
GATS	General Agreement on Trade in Services
GATT	General Agreement on Tariffs and Trade
GCC	Gulf Cooperation Council
GDP	Gross Domestic Product
GSP	Generalized System of Preferences
HIV/AIDS	Human Immunodeficiency Virus/Acquired immune deficiency syndrome
IBSA	India, Brazil and South Africa
ICAO	International Civil Aviation Organization
ICJ	International Court of Justice
ICT	Information and Communication Technology
IEPA	Interim Economic Partnership Agreement
IGAD	Inter-Governmental Authority on Development
IGADD	Intergovernmental Authority on Drought and Development
IO	Indian Ocean
IOC	Indian Ocean Commission
IOM	International Organization for Migration
IPF	IGAD Partners Forum
IPR	Intellectual Property Rights
IRCC	Inter-Regional Coordination Committee
ITO	International Trade Organization
JCA	Joint Competition Authority
KPA	Kenya Ports Authority
LDC	least developed countries
MARAC	Early Warning Observation and Monitoring System for Central Africa
MC	Ministerial Committee
MEFTA	Middle East FTA
MERCOSUR	Southern Common Market
MFN	Most-Favoured-Nation
MMTZ	Malawi, Mozambique, Tanzania and Zambia

MPA	Millennium Partnership for the African Recovery Programme
NAFTA	North American Free Trade Agreement
NEPAD	New Partnership for Africa's Development
NGO	non-governmental organization
NTB	non-tariff barriers
NTF	Nigeria Trust Fund
OAU	Organization of African Unity
OCA	Optimum Currency Areas
OHRLLS	Office of the High Representative for Least Developed Landlocked Developing and Small Developing Island Countries
OIE	World Organization for Animal Health
ORRC	other restrictive restrictions of commerce
PAIDF	Pan-African Infrastructure Development Fund
PAPED	EPA Development Programme
PCT	Patent Cooperation Treaty
PDCT-AC	Blueprint Consensus on Transport in Central Africa
PLT	Patent Law Treaty
PTA	preferential trade area
RABESA	Regional Approach to Biotechnology and Bio-safety for Eastern and Southern Africa
RATES	Regional Agricultural Trade Expansion Support
RCP	Regional Consultative Process
RICTSP	Regional Information and Communication Technology Support Programme
RISDP	Regional Indicative Strategic Development Plan
RMC	Regional Member Countries
RoO	Rules of Origin
RTA	Regional Trade Agreement
SACU	Southern African Customs Union
SADC	Southern African Development Community
SADCC	Southern African Development Coordination Conference
SARS	South African Revenue Service
SAT3/WASC/SAFE	South Africa/West Africa Submarine Cable/South Africa Far East
SCF	Stabilization and Cooperation Fund
SEACOM	Sea Cable System
SEA-ME-WE	South East Asia-Middle East-West Europe
SERAP	Socio-Economic Rights and Accountability Project
SICA	Automated Interbank Clearing System
SSATP	Sub-Saharan Africa Transport Programme

STAR	Automated Transfer and Settlement System
TDCA	Trade and Development Cooperation Agreement
TEAMS	East Africa Marine System
TIDCA	Trade, Investment and Development Cooperative Agreement
TIFA	Trade and Investment Framework Agreement
TLS	Trade Liberalization Scheme
TMCM	Trade Monitoring and Compliance Mechanism
TRIPS	Trade-Related Intellectual Property Rights
UACC	Upper Air Space Control Centre
UDE	Union Douanière Equatoriale
UDEAC	Union Douanière et Economique de l'Afrique Centrale (Central African Customs and Economic Union)
UEMOA (WAEMU)	West African Economic and Monetary Union
UMAC	Union Monétaire de l'Afrique Centrale
UN	United Nations
UNCTAD	United Nations Conference on Trade and Development
UNESCO	United Nations Economic and Social Council
USAID	United States Agency for International Development
VAT	Value Added Tax
WABA	West African Bankers Association
WAEMU (UEMOA)	West African Economic and Monetary Union
WAHID	World Animal Health Information Database
WAMI	West African Monetary Institute
WAMZ	West African Monetary Zone
WCO	World Customs Organization
WTO	World Trade Organization

TABLE OF CASES

Africa

Campbell and Another v. *Republic of Zimbabwe* (SADC (T) 03/2009) [2009] SADCT 1 (5 June 2009)

East African Law Society and Others v. *Attorney General of the Republic of Kenya and Others* EACJ, Judgment Ref. No. 3 of 2007 (Sept. 2008)

ESCR-Net, Socio-Economic Rights and Accountability Project (SERAP) v. *Federal Republic of Nigeria and Universal Basic Education Commission* Judgment No. ECW/CCJ/APP/0808 (International Network for Economic, Social and Cultural Rights, 2009), available at www.escr-net.org/caselaw/caselaw_show.htm?doc_id$=$1143047

Fick and Three Others v. *Government of the Republic of South Africa and Two Others* (72068/09) [2009] ZAGPPHC (27 Nov. 2009)

Frank Ukor v. *Rachard Lalaye* ECW/CCJ/APP/01/04, (2004)

Gramara (Pvt) Ltd. and One Other v. *The Government of the Republic of Zimbabwe and Two Others* (HC 33/09) [2010] ZWHHC 1 (26 Jan. 2010)

Hadijatou Mani Koraou v. *Republic of Niger* Judgment No. ECW/CCJ/APP/08/08, unofficial translation of Judgment No. ECW/CCJ/JUD/06/08 (27 Oct. 2008)

James Katabazi and 21 Others v. *Secretary General of the East African Community and Another* EACJ, Judgment Ref. No. 1 of 2007 (1 Nov. 2007)

Mike Campbell (Pvt) Ltd. and 78 Others v. *The Republic of Zimbabwe* SADC (T) Case No. 2/2007 [2008] SADCT 2 (28 Nov. 2008)

Mike Campbell (Pty) Ltd. v. *Minister of National Security Responsible for Land, Land Reform and Resettlement* (124/06) [2008] ZWSC 1 (22 Jan. 2008)

Okunda v. *Republic* (1970) E. Afr. L. Rep. 457 (Kenya), affirmed E. Afr. L. Rep. 460

Olajide Afolabi v. *Federal Republic of Nigeria* ECW/CCJ/APP/01/03 (2003)

Prof. Peter Anyang' Nyong'o and Others v. *Attorney General of Kenya and Others* EACJ, Ref. No. 1 of 2006 (30 March 2007)

Von Abo v. *President of the Republic of South Africa* (CCT 67/08) [2009] ZACC 15 (5 June 2009)

International Court of Justice

Iran–US Claims Tribunal

United States v. *Iran*, No. 130-A28-FT, para. 58 (Iran–US Cl. Trib. Rep. 2000)

WTO Dispute Settlement Body

EEC – Import Regime for Bananas, Panel Report, WT/DS38/R, 11 Feb. 1994

European Commission – Conditions for the Granting of Tariff Preferences to Developing Countries, Panel Report, WT/DS246/R, 1 Dec. 2003

European Communities – Conditions for the Granting of Tariff Preferences to Developing Countries, Appellate Body Report, WT/DS246/AB/R, 7 Apr. 2004

Turkey–Restrictions on Imports of Textile and Clothing Products, Panel Report, WT/DS34/R, 31 May 1999

Turkey–Restrictions on Imports of Textile and Clothing Products, Appellate Body Report, WT/DS34/AB/R, 19 Nov. 1999

US – Line Pipe, Panel Report, WT/DS202/R, 8 Mar. 2002

US – Standards for Reformulated and Conventional Gasoline, Appellate Body Report, WT/DS2/AB/R, 29 Apr. 1996

INTRODUCTION

In this book, I discuss the legal framework that undergirds African Regional Trade Agreements (RTAs), both on their own terms as well as in the context of their relationship to the multilateral trading system. I argue that it is important to understand African RTAs on their own terms, because they have contextualizing imperatives grounded in African history, politics and realities that defy being strapped into the straitjacket of European or other non-African experiences. Thus, while African, like other RTAs, must necessarily be evaluated for their consistency or inconsistency with the World Trade Organization's (WTO) non-discriminatory trade rules, this book shows that one cannot overlook the particular nature of African RTAs.

In addition, this book seeks to fill a major gap in the literature on African trading arrangements as legal regimes. While there has been increased attention on Africa in the international trading system, this is one of the first book-length analyses of African RTAs as legal regimes. This book therefore seeks to fill the gap in writing about the legal framework of African RTAs as much as I hope it challenges students and teachers interested in international trade in Africa to carry forward the task of continuing to put into print analysis of the legal framework of African trading systems.

Indeed, a major reason I decided to write this book is because there now is a large and growing market for studying international and regional trade law based on materials specific to Africa. Yet, most teaching and research on trade in Africa continues to rely on materials developed for predominantly non-African audiences in Europe and the United States. While such materials can be a useful starting point, their relevance for African students and researchers seeking to understand African trading relationships may be limited. For example, there are extremely few legal texts prepared for teaching international trade law in Europe or North America that specifically focus on the challenges of livestock agriculture, which forms a significant share of trade for some African countries.

This book is also invariably about the international institutional law that is emerging from African RTAs. As with international institutions, it shows that African regional institutions experience similar issues that other international institutions face. These issues include what to do with Member States who fail to pay their assessed dues; the competence of regional courts to decide cases relating to domestic law; whether RTA judiciaries can make decisions that bind Member States; whether organs of these RTAs may enforce decisions without the cooperation of Member States or take particular actions without the approval of the members, and so on.

As such, this is as much a sourcebook or reference book on the legal framework of African RTAs as it is an analytical examination of these legal arrangements. It advances the claim that African RTAs are not purely or exclusively trade agreements, but rather agreements that encompass a broad set of objectives. Nothing says this better than the Treaty for the Establishment of the African Economic Community, which provides that one of its purposes is to facilitate cooperation 'in every field of human endeavor'. In addition to having an extremely broad range of areas of cooperation, it is a truism that the legal obligations assumed under these treaties are not understood by the leaders as containing punitive sanctions for non-compliance. It seems that African leaders, while eager to make legal commitments in numerous and increasing numbers of treaties, are not equally willing to take responsibility for non-compliance, or indeed to completely surrender certain competencies to the supranational organizations created by these treaties. I develop that argument in full in the first three chapters of the book, which examine three defining features of this flexible understanding of the legal commitments: multiple objectives alongside trade liberalization commitments, variable geometry and multiple memberships.

Chapter I examines how African RTAs have embraced multiple objectives, including a commitment to development that differs from the classic Vinerian laissez-faire trade liberalization model. It examines how these agreements incorporate non-trade objectives including the nestling within them of a variety of projects such as the management of common river basins. Within African RTA treaties, one sees extremely few non-discriminatory commitments such as most-favoured-nation and national treatment, as cornerstones of the liberalization commitments contained in them. This contrasts sharply with the GATT/WTO regime that is in large part premised on these principles of non-discrimination. Chapter II examines variable geometry, according to which RTAs embrace extended time frames for some members to come up to speed in implementing trade liberalization commitments. It also examines the extensive commitment to pay-offs made to countries that lose out from liberalization commitments, as well as preferential allocations of credit and industry to less well off members in trade integration schemes. Chapter III examines the phenomenon of multiple memberships in African RTAs and how this characteristic of open-door membership raises challenges such as those referred to as the *spaghetti bowl*.

The first three chapters of the book demonstrate that African RTAs are not predicated on a vision of market-led integration. Instead, they are largely designed as forums for a variety of initiatives, such as facilitating cooperation around common resources like international rivers and basins among riparian states, and cross-border challenges that include trade, security and health. Rather than simply using the expansion of intra-regional trade as a framework for industrial growth, product diversification and the improvement of the global competitiveness of these products as ways of overcoming small domestic markets, African RTAs were and continue to be seen as frameworks for development cooperation as well. This approach to integration is therefore committed to cooperation at the level of production in the arenas of capital and labour, as well as to coordinated programming and infrastructural development.

As such, African RTAs show a particular preference for multiple objectives that often have little to do with trade and are committed to a vision of development integration that may be regarded to be in tension with trade liberalization grounded on WTO rules of non-discrimination. However, as this book shows, African RTAs explicitly embrace WTO rules, particularly in the area of trade remedies. Indeed, as documented at length, trade integration through regional and bilateral agreements has gained a new momentum not simply to enhance intra-African trade, but rather to promote economic growth, especially because of the small size of individual African economies. In many regions there is an increasing commitment to the view that trade-enhancing rather than trade-protective integration is crucial to achieving long-term economic growth. In addition, such trade-enhancing integration is regarded as being most acceptable when it is consistent with the declared development priorities of African countries.

Regional integration is also regarded as a necessary step for shaking off Africa's external economic dependence and its lop-sided participation in the international trading system through economic self-reliance on a continental level. As I argue, such attitudes towards regional integration reflect the preferences of African governments. Put another way, regional integration as pursued by African governments is pursued in a manner that enmeshes with the preferences of African governments. Among those is a preference not to build strong supranational bureaucracies. This has in turn undermined the achievement of more thoroughgoing intra-regional trade. Indeed, since African governments understand these RTAs as flexible regimes, they regard them less from the efficiency gains that non-discriminatory free trade may offer, than from the benefits that these regimes offer, particularly as forums for integrated development of common resources such as river basins, and in terms of any gains arising from functionally specific objectives that may be nestled within these regimes that do not have to await the long-term horizon which non-discriminatory free trade is likely to offer.

There are eight RTAs, or regional economic communities, recognized by the African Union as pillars of the African Economic Community (AEC). The AEC is expected to be formed in 2027 when these eight RTAs cease operations in favour of the continental AEC. The RTAs are the Arab Maghreb Union (AMU/UMA); the Community of Sahel-Saharan States (CEN-SAD); the Common Market for Eastern and Southern Africa (COMESA); the East African Community (EAC); the Economic Community of Central African States (ECCAS/CEEAC); the Economic Community of West African States (ECOWAS); the Inter-Governmental Authority of Development (IGAD); and the Southern African Development Community (SADC). Each of these RTAs is discussed in greater detail in Chapter V. Chapter VI on the financing of these regional groupings sets out the relationship between these regional economic communities, on the one hand, and the African Union's AEC on the other, while Chapter X addresses relationships these communities are developing among themselves. There are, of course, many other African regional economic groupings, such as the monetary unions discussed in Chapter IX, as well as the offshoots of many of these RTAs discussed throughout this book. Africa's monetary unions as discussed in Chapter IX are the Economic and Monetary Community of Central Africa (CEMAC); the West African Economic and Monetary Zone (UEMOA); and the West Africa Monetary Zone (WAMZ). The fact that African countries belong not only to the above eight RTAs, but also to the monetary unions, not to mention other important groupings in the continent such as the Southern African Customs Union (SACU), the Mano River Union (MRU), the Economic Community of Great Lakes Countries (CEPGL) and the Indian Ocean Commission (IOC), only exacerbates the problem of multiple and overlapping membership in these groupings. As I argue, these downsides must also be seen against certain benefits that countries accrue from one rather than another regional bloc. In Chapter III, for example, I argue that there is an element of forum or regime shifting between different RTAs of which an individual country is a member that these countries regard as tactically defensible. Some countries like Namibia have conducted studies on their multiple memberships and decided to voluntarily withdraw from COMESA as membership was not in its economic advantage. In addition, it is praiseworthy that COMESA, EAC and SADC have decided to negotiate a tripartite free trade agreement (FTAg) that is another step towards rationalization of these multiple memberships. Chapters V and X discuss this planned tripartite FTA.

Chapter VI on the financing of African RTAs shows that promptness in meeting financial obligations is the exception rather than the rule. As such, most of these RTAs have increasingly become reliant on donor funding, which is inconsistent with the declared objective of regionalization as a necessary bulwark against dependence on such external support. From the information I was able to obtain, only SADC seems to have relative financial autonomy. Half, or perhaps more than that, of the EAC's budget is from donors. This, of course, raises questions of ownership of the programmes of the EAC.

This theme is continued in Chapter XI, which examines trade and investment agreements between African and non-African RTAs. A broad range and array of such agreements with European, America, Asian and even Latin American countries is examined. The chapter shows that Africa's external trading partners have invested heavily in negotiating these agreements. The slowdown in multilateral negotiations in the Doha Round has in part spurred the need to negotiate bilateral and regional agreements. In addition, Africa's external trading partners see these regional and bilateral agreements as offering opportunities to negotiate extensive commitments beyond those in current multilateral agreements in areas such as government procurement, services, investment measures, competition and other WTO-Plus commitments. The legacy of these agreements for Africa awaits further critical scrutiny to see whether the promise of mutual gains comes to fruition. At the moment, the mutuality of such gains in many of these agreements is not decidedly on the African side. Yet as the discussion particularly in Chapter IV on the provisions of Article XXIV of the GATT in relation to regionalism in Africa shows, there is much scope for well-founded arguments to justify the kind of extended time frames for meeting commitments African countries have sought in negotiations, as well as the arguments they have advanced on what liberalization of 'substantially all trade' means. There are debatable claims, too, that there is justification for regionalism outside Article XXIV under the Enabling Clause, as more fully discussed in Chapter IV.

Further, in terms of the WTO, Chapter VIII on trade remedy regimes shows that African RTAs have by and large borrowed the trade remedy rules of the WTO. That means that countries like Ethiopia which are not yet members of the WTO, are already subject to WTO disciplines in anti-dumping and countervailing duty law, since COMESA has adopted these rules as its trade-remedy rules.

This book also examines African RTA judiciaries which, to the best of my knowledge, no previous work in book or article form has attempted to do. It shows that African RTA judiciaries entertain a broad range of disputes from an extremely broad category of litigants, unlike the International Court of Justice, for example, which only accepts cases from states that have accepted its jurisdiction. African RTA judiciaries are not simply custodians of the trading arrangements – in fact, they do much less dispute settlement around trade issues compared to the broad range of cases they have assumed jurisdiction over. Many of these judiciaries, as we shall see, have also often entertained cases that are well beyond their treaty-defined jurisdictional bases.

Another feature of African RTA judiciaries that comes out clearly is the boldness of their decisions in relation to the fact that they are relatively new institutions operating in a context in which adherence to notions of national sovereignty is very strong. The East African Court of Justice, for example, has decided cases relating to human rights even though there is no explicit treaty basis for the court to assume jurisdiction over human rights cases that challenge the conduct of Member State governments. For taking such bold steps, the leaders of the EAC amended the Treaty Establishing the East African Community as a statement of the disapproval of some controversial decisions of the East African Court of Justice. Another example is the ECOWAS Court of Justice, whose jurisdiction was expanded in 2005 to allow cases challenging the conduct of Member States with respect to human rights, a jurisdiction it has since not spared in its use.

The examination of African RTA judiciaries shows that they are not sleeping sentinels of the treaties under which they are established. This chapter, like many others, in my view is therefore a call for more attention to be focused on these judiciaries. Ultimately, this book provides a panoramic view of African RTAs that I hope scholars and students will carry forward.

I

African Regional Trade Agreements as flexible legal regimes

A Introduction

Trade integration in Africa is often viewed in light of the European Union and other regional integration arrangements like the North American Free Trade Agreement (NAFTA). From this perspective, integration is regarded as necessarily destined to proceed on a linear path where tariffs and non-tariff barriers are progressively eliminated, the trade regimes of member countries are linked together, and eventually their fiscal and monetary policies are harmonized. In the European experience, trade integration has been the result of a series of treaty commitments that also created a supranational organization to which the states transferred certain types of authority.

Seen in this light, African Regional Trade Agreements (RTAs) contrast sharply with their counterparts in Europe and North America, where there is a much higher commitment to compliance with the legal obligations contained in the treaties establishing them. From this view, African RTAs have not resolved the 'problems of coordination, collaboration or domestic politics' that treaty regimes are argued to remedy.[1] In addition, the treaty commitments in African RTAs do not appear to have raised 'the political costs of noncompliance' such as reputational losses.[2] In short, the existence of regional trade rules and institutions has not done much to change the behaviour of African countries.[3]

1 K. Abbott and D. Snidal, 'Hard and Soft Law in International Governance', *International Organization* 54 (2000) 421, 424. This is a view strongly associated with institutionalists.

2 C. Lipson, 'Why Are Some International Agreements Informal?', *International Organization* 45 (1991) 495, 508 (acknowledging that loss of reputation does promote compliance but does not guarantee it).

3 See S. Krasner, 'Structural Causes and Regime Consequences; Regimes as Intervening Variables', in S. Krasner (ed.), *International Regimes* (Utica, NY: Cornell University Press, 1983), 5–10; see also K. Raustiala, 'Compliance and Effectiveness in International Regulatory Cooperation', *Case Western Reserve Journal of International Law* 32 (2000) 387, 394 (defining effectiveness in terms of the degree to which treaty rules produce 'observable, desired changes in behavior').

The foregoing views are caricatures that are not based on the actual treaty commitments and experiences of African RTAs.[4] This chapter aims to develop a more accurate account of RTAs than existing analyses. This alternative view is based on the types of commitments contained in the treaties, as well as how the RTAs are understood by their members.

These treaty commitments and understandings show that African RTAs are designed as flexible regimes. Flexibility here refers to the following defining features of African RTAs: first, they are regarded as establishing flexible regimes of cooperation as opposed to containing rules requiring scrupulous and rigorous adherence. Second, African RTAs incorporate as a central feature the principle of variable geometry, adopting steps for meeting timetabled and other commitments. Third, African RTAs adopt a broad array of social, economic and political objectives without giving salience to any set of objectives. Fourth, African RTAs demonstrate a particular preference for functionally specific objectives to undertake discrete projects and to serve as forums for the integrated development of common resources, such as river basins that cut across national boundaries. Fifth, African RTAs demonstrate a remarkable commitment to the equitable distribution of gains from trade and a corresponding weakness in the adoption of non-discrimination trade principles and the related objectives of trade liberalization. Sixth, African RTAs are characterized by multiple and overlapping memberships, exemplifying a classic case of the 'spaghetti bowl'.[5] Multiple RTA membership illustrates the flexibility or open-door membership that African RTAs offer.

Understood as flexible regimes, African RTAs therefore contrast sharply with the views of Jorge Dominguez in the Latin American context. Dominguez has argued that trade integration agreements have 'lax implementation' as a 'rule' governing international relations in the Americas.[6]

4 See A. Philip, 'Preface' to F. Kahnert *et al.*, *Economic Integration Among Developing Countries* (Paris: OECD Development Centre, 1969), 9. Four decades ago, it was argued that regional integration in developing countries could not be expected to 'produce spectacular results in the short or even medium term', and that these efforts would subsequently experience 'delays and frequent breakdowns [which] will soon lead to disappointment and discouragement'. *Ibid.*

5 J. Bhagwati, 'US Trade Policy: The Infatuation with Free Trade Agreements', in J. Bhagwati and A.O. Krueger (eds), *The Dangerous Drift to Preferential Trade Agreements* (Washington, DC: AEI Press, 1995), 2–3. A 'spaghetti bowl' is a metaphor used to describe a system in which criss-crossing strands of bilateral trade agreements create a tangled mess of restrictions and regulations, ultimately disrupting rather than promoting free trade. *Ibid.*

6 J. Dominguez, 'International Cooperation in Latin America: The Design of Regional Institutions by Slow Accretion', in A. Acharya and A. Johnson (eds), *Crafting Cooperation: Regional Interdependence in Comparative Perspective* (Cambridge University Press, 2007), 94–5.

According to Dominguez, lax implementation is 'pervasive and long-lasting across issue-areas and time periods, unpunished by co-signatories and generally accepted even when its existence hampered the procedures or organizations that states sought to create'.[7]

Viewing African RTAs as flexible regimes has the advantage of allowing these RTAs to be understood on their own terms, rather than as treaty regimes on a path toward becoming much like their European or North American counterparts. In so doing, it becomes possible to better and more accurately understand the challenges that these RTAs have been designed to address and that have in turn shaped them. As Tiyanjana Maluwa has argued, African countries have preferred informal institutions to the 'bureaucratic strictures and international rule-making or legislative processes of formal international institutions'.[8] Indeed, as this chapter shows, African RTAs are not overseen by powerful supranational bureaucracies, but rather by relatively weak institutions that leave ample sovereignty to their Member States.

Tiyanjana Maluwa in essence alludes to a point that is very important, and often overlooked by pessimists of regional integration in Africa. These pessimists primarily examine the performance of African RTAs based on how well Member States rigorously conform their behaviour to the formally binding trade liberalization commitments found within treaties and similar agreements.[9] While there is clearly merit in assessing these

7 *Ibid.* at 95.

8 T. Maluwa, 'The Move From Institutions? Examining the Phenomenon in Africa', *Proceedings of the Annual Meeting (American Society of International Law)* 100 (2006) 294. Tiyanjana Maluwa used the New Economic Partnership for African Development (NEPAD), as an example of this move away from formal institution-building governed by a treaty or rule system. *Ibid.* at 295. In his view, the design of NEPAD was as a framework of development cooperation and interaction outside the African Union. *Ibid.* Tiyanjana argued that NEPAD reflected a shift 'toward action and results rather than legislation and rule making'. *Ibid.* at 297. In his view African governments are more likely to accede to objective, voluntary and peer evaluation measures than 'punitive and overly prescriptive measures', *Ibid.* at 298. Another example that Maluwa discusses is the African Peer Review Mechanism, a regional effort to have African countries review each other's governance performance. *Ibid.* at 296–7. While the case of Robert Mugabe's Zimbabwe shows some difficulty of voluntary processes, the mechanism has been used in Kenya in 2006 and in South Africa in 2007. See African Peer Review Mechanism, 'Kenya Progress Report on the Implementation of the African Peer Review Mechanism (APRM) National Programme of Action', available at www.nepadkenya.org/Documents/progress_report_jan06.pdf (detailing the progress Kenya has made in implementing changes since its peer review in 2006); African Peer Review Mechanism, 'South African Country Review Report No. 5' (2007), available at www.aprm.org.za/docs/SACountryReviewReport5.pdf (detailing South Africa's progress after implementing the mechanism).

9 See e.g., G.J. Naldi and K.D. Magliveras, 'The African Economic Community: Emancipation For African States or Yet Another Glorious Failure?', *North Carolina Journal of*

rules and institution-building efforts in light of the treaty obligations to which these states have committed themselves, such an approach misses the following crucial insights.

The pessimist approach is based on the false belief, similar to the first generation of African RTAs, that 'integration could be legislated from above, *ex nihilo*', without reference to what was in fact possible on the ground.[10] The failure of first-generation efforts to build RTAs in post-colonial Africa, legislated essentially from above, is in part represented by the collapse of the East African Community in 1977 and by the failure of the Mano River Union economic cooperation arrangement, which had been established in 1973 after its original members, Liberia and Sierra Leone, experienced civil wars.[11] The Mano River Union was revived in 2004.[12] The collapse of the East African Community in 1977 showed the importance of alternative models of cooperation around discrete projects where gains and benefits could be realizable not only in the short term, and where the gains were mutually beneficial to the members as well. In addition, the failure of these first-generation efforts at pan-Africanism showed the limits of ambitious projects driven by the desire to unify in ending colonial rule and apartheid that could not easily be translated into projects of economic cooperation in post-colonial Africa. In fact, long before the collapse of the East African Community in 1977, 'the vision of an African common market in the neo-classical/comparative advantage model had disappeared by 1965'.[13] By the late 1970s, regional

International Law and Commercial Regulation 24 (1999) 601, 603 (concluding that 'the African Economic Community will not succeed without sweeping political, economic and legal reforms', *ibid.*); see also, C. McCarthy, 'Regional Integration in SubSaharan Africa: Past, Present and Future', in A. Oyejide, B. Ndulu and D. Greenway (eds), *Regional Integration and Trade Liberalization in SubSaharan Africa, Vol. 4: Synthesis and Review* (London: Palgrave Macmillan, 1999), 230 (arguing that African countries have adopted over-ambitious regional integration schemes and that this has not been a good policy).

10 J. Ravenhill, 'The Future of Regionalism in Africa', in R.I. Onwuka and A. Sesay (eds), *The Future of Regionalism in Africa* (London: Macmillan Education, 1985), 5, 10.

11 Kahnert *et al.*, *Economic Integration Among Developing Countries*, 67.

12 US Department of State, Bureau of Public Affairs, 'Background Notes: Sierra Leone (06/09)', www.state.gov./outofdate/bgn/s/125195.htm. In 2004, the domestic turmoil began to settle and the first local government elections in 32 years were held in 311 wards nationwide. Sierra Leone along with Guinea and Liberia formed the Mano River Union (Côte d'Ivoire later joined in May 2008). *Ibid.*

13 M.S. Wionczek, 'Introduction – Present Status and Prospects of Economic Integration Movements in Developing Countries: Political Atomization and Economic Backwardness of the Southern Hemisphere', in M.S. Wionczek, *Economic Cooperation in Latin America, Africa and Asia* (Cambridge, MA: MIT Press, 1969), 1, 8–9; see also United Nations Economic Commission on Africa, 'Background Paper on the Establishment of

trade integration in Africa, Asia and the Caribbean was declared to have been in 'various degrees of serious crisis, in states of stagnation or in processes of disassociation'.[14]

In light of such a legacy of failure, economic and political cooperation could therefore hardly be remedied by a regionalism based exclusively on a neo-classical/comparative advantage model and be expected to succeed. Thus, in the second generation of RTAs that followed the collapse of the first wave of African RTAs, the role of treaty commitments became that of providing a framework for initiatives such as joint ventures or initiatives in areas including trade, investment and capital, while also extending further into transport, security, water, electricity supply and labour movement, as well as agreements for the management of common resources such as river basins.[15] Not only were the range of objectives increased, but flexibility was built into these RTAs by allowing functionally specific objectives and incorporating the principle of variable geometry, as outlined above and discussed more fully in Chapter II.

This contrasts sharply with an approach to regional integration that is primarily or solely focused on trade integration and that requires rigorous formal compliance with liberalization commitments within specific time frames. This does not, of course, preclude such treaty commitments having solemnly binding obligations.[16] Indeed many, if not all African RTAs have exactly those kind of commitments.[17] In short, flexibility is not necessarily incompatible with assuming legally binding commitments. Often these obligations are assumed on the understanding that compliance will

an African Common Market', UN Pub. No. E/CN.14/STC/20 (13 Oct. 1963); United Nations Economic Commission for Africa, 'European Integration and African Trade', UN Pub. No. E/CN.14/STC/4 (23 Aug. 1964) (displaying that the vision of African economic integration was a popular theme in the early part of the 1960s).

14 C.V. Vaitsos, 'Crisis in Regional Economic Cooperation (Integration) Among Developing Countries: A Survey', *World Development* 6 (1978) 719.

15 Y. Yang and S. Gupta, *Regional Trade Arrangements in Africa: Past Performance and the Way Forward* (IMF Working Paper 05/36, 2005), 5.

16 See generally A. Chayes and A.H. Chayes, *The New Sovereignty: Compliance with International Regulatory Agreements* (Cambridge, MA: Harvard University Press, 1995). See also H.K. Mutai, *Compliance With International Trade Obligations: The Common Market for Eastern and Southern Africa* (Boston: Kluwer Law International, 2007).

17 See e.g., Art. 47(1) of the Protocol on the Establishment of the East African Community Common Market, signed 20 November 2009, which provides that 'The Partner States undertake to approximate their national laws and to harmonize their policies and systems, for purposes of implementing this Protocol.' Article 47(2) goes on to provide that the 'Council shall issue directives for purposes of implementing this Article', available at www.eac.int/advisory-opinions/cat_view/68-eac-common-market.html (an example of an RTA with binding commitment).

not be stringently enforced because the commitments are balanced against a variety of safety valves, such as the principles of variable geometry and the equitable sharing of the benefits of regionalization.

There are several other examples of flexibility in African RTAs. As noted above, these RTAs adopt flexibility by incorporating rules that provide different obligations between members, as well as differences in timelines to comply with commitments that are based on the varying economic capabilities of their members. For example, in the Treaty for the Establishment of the East African Community, the principle of variable geometry allows the commitments in the treaty to be undertaken at different speeds.[18] The principle of asymmetry allows variations in measures of economic integration, building flexibility right into the framework of RTAs. In the South African Customs Union (SACU), flexibility is achieved in part by allowing protection of new industries from competing goods from SACU and non-SACU countries for a period of no more than eight years for the poorest SACU states.[19] In addition, as noted below, Botswana, Lesotho, Namibia and Swaziland are entitled to tariff assistance for industries of major importance to their economies.[20] Tariffs with regard to such industries may only be decreased with the concurrence of a country that has designated such an industry as being of importance to it.[21] The question

18 See *infra* Chapter III.

19 Section 26 of the South African Customs Union (SACU) Agreement of 2002 provides:

> 1. The Government of Botswana, Lesotho, Namibia or Swaziland may as a temporary measure levy additional duties on goods imported into its area to enable infant industries in its area to meet competition from other producers or manufacturers in the Common Customs Area, provided that such duties are levied equally on goods grown, produced or manufactured in other parts of the Common Customs Area and like products imported from outside that area, irrespective of whether the latter goods are imported directly or from the area of another Member State and subject to payment of the customs duties applicable to such goods on importation into the Common Customs Area. (2). Infant industry means an industry which has been established in the area of a Member State for not more than eight (8) years. (3). Protection afforded to an infant industry in terms of paragraph 1 shall be for a period of eight (8) years unless otherwise determined by the Council. (4). The Council may impose such further terms and conditions as it may deem appropriate.

SACU Agreement, signed 21 October 2002, available at www.sacu.int/main.php?include=docs/legislation/2002-agreement/part5.html.

20 See *infra* Chapter III.

21 SACU Agreement, Art. 26, available at www.sacu.int/main.php?include=docs/legislation/2002-agreement/main.html. Article 26 of the SACU Agreement makes provision for protection of infant industries for Botswana, Lesotho, Namibia and Swaziland. Article 34 provides for the revenue-sharing formula which determines the respective shares of the

of flexibility in the context of variable geometry is addressed in more detail in Chapter II.

RTAs also provide an umbrella within which bilateral and even inter-regional links are formed among a group of countries along functional lines, and whose benefits are often more immediately available than through trade liberalization. This in turn has spurred 'sectoral planning and coordination'[22] which is now a major feature of African RTAs.

This chapter is the first of three that explore this theme of flexibility. It proceeds as follows. First, I discuss how flexibility enmeshes well in the African context, with examples showing how African RTAs have changed the classic Vinerian customs union model, as well as their adoption of multiple objectives. This chapter also discusses how African RTAs act as forums for integrated development and functionally specific projects. These projects are often nestled or nested within the RTAs and they include cooperation on issues relating to security and common river basin management. The chapter ends with another feature of RTAs' enmeshment in the African context – the view that African regionalism is a bulwark for economic self independence. Chapter II discusses how African RTAs have adopted variable geometry as a mechanism for ensuring equality in the sharing of the benefits of trade liberalization and how the prevalence of this concern has back-grounded the commitment to non-discriminatory trade liberalization. Chapter II also discusses at length the highly significant April 2009 East African Court of Justice (EACJ) Advisory Opinion on Variable Geometry and its implications for African RTAs. Chapter III focuses on another important feature of African RTAs as flexible regimes – multiple memberships in RTAs. It begins by reviewing the phenomenon of multiple membership and the advantages it offers African countries with

members of the total customs, excise and additional duties. See also J. Isaken, 'Prospects for SACU After Apartheid', in B. Oden (ed.), *Southern Africa After Apartheid: Regional Integration and External Resources* (Uppsala: Nordiska Afrikainstitutet, 1993), 182. In addition, South Africa may give sympathetic consideration to increasing the customs duty on imports of competing goods as well as to reducing such duty for materials that are used in the production of goods designated as being of importance by Botswana, Swaziland or Lesotho: SACU Agreement, Art. 2 (stating that one of SACU's objectives is to 'facilitate the equitable sharing of revenue arising from customs, excise and additional duties levied by Member States').

22 E.M. Maphanyane, 'SADCC-Future Challenges', in Oden (ed.), *Southern Africa After Apartheid*, 174, 175 (arguing that SADCC initially decided to undertake 'large programmes in agricultures, transport, communications and the energy sector'). Maphanyane further notes that 'the basis of cooperation was the discrete project. This had the effect of making the benefits of cooperation immediate and tangible, and also of building confidence among Member States.' *Ibid.*

such multiple memberships. It then proceeds to examine the resulting 'spaghetti bowl' effect of these multiple RTAs and assesses the transaction costs associated with it.

B Flexibility as enmeshment in the 'African' context

1 Adaptations of the Vinerian model

African RTAs, like others in the Third World, exhibit differences from the classic European market-based customs union integration model.[23] Under the European model, economic integration starts with a free trade area, progresses to a customs union, then to a common market, and finally to an economic union, with a political union as the last stage.[24] This classic integration model associated with Jacob Viner[25] came under serious scrutiny as a model for Third World integration many decades ago.[26] The Vinerian model was developed in an industrial context, while many developing countries were agrarian and raw material producing. The Vinerian model, for example, assumed that trade creation or trade expansion would outweigh trade diversion when trade barriers were lifted.[27] This assumption is often undermined, since a majority of African economies have largely similar products without necessarily having comparative cost advantages between them sufficient to overcome this similarity.[28] The resulting lack of complementary trade in effect undercuts gains in trade.

23 C.A. Cooper and B.F. Massell, 'Toward a General Theory of Customs Unions for Developing Countries', *Journal of Political Economics* 73 (1965) 461, 475.

24 B. Balassa, *The Theory of Economic Integration* (Homewood, IL: R.D. Irwin, 1961).

25 See J. Viner, *The Customs Union Issue* (Carnegie Endowment for International Peace, 1950); see also J.E. Meade, *The Theory of Customs Unions* (Westport, CT: Greenwood Press, 1955); R.G. Lipsey, 'The Theory of Customs Unions: Trade Diversion and Welfare', *Economica* 24(93) (1957).

26 See e.g., Cooper and Massell, 'General Theory of Customs Unions', at 461; R.L. Allen, 'Integration in Less Developed Areas', *Kyklos* 14 (1961) 315; G.M. Meier, 'Effects of a Customs Union on Economic Development', *Social and Economic Studies* (Mar. 1960), 29; R.F. Mikesell, 'The Movement Towards Regional Trading Groups in Latin America', in A.O. Hirschman (ed.), *Latin American Issues: Essays and Comments* (New York: The Twentieth Century Fund, 1961); Robson, *infra* n. 74; R.F. Mikesell, 'The Theory of Common Markets as Applied to Regional Arrangements Among Developing Countries', in R. Harrod and D. Hague (eds), *International Trade Theory in a Developing World* (London: Palgrave Macmillan, 1963) (all criticizing the Jacob Viner integration model).

27 See *infra* Chapter III for an extended discussion.

28 Kahnert *et al.*, *Economic Integration*, at 23. Kahnert notes that the traditional doctrine is based on differences in resource endowments which explain differences in factor prices. However, if one abstracts from natural resources in mining and agriculture, developing countries may not show very different resource endowments. In a general way, scarcity of

Under such conditions, firms in African RTAs end up trading with high cost producers within the region, rather than with low cost producers from outside the region.[29] The small size of most of these economies also means that significant economies of scale are not realizable without enlarging the market through regionalism. This is exacerbated by the fact that economic integration in Africa, even while otherwise enlarging market sizes, does not lead to globally significant increases in productivity, productive area, or purchasing power of the enlarged market relative to productive areas and markets in other regions.[30] In addition, African integration arrangements have often resulted in protecting high cost multinational or local firms that have commanded market share by producing for a segmented market within the individual countries and subsequently within a region.[31]

Some economists therefore argue that African economies need structural changes because they do not exhibit the conditions under which integration can confer benefits on them.[32] This is in part because developing countries tend to trade with developed countries more than they do with each other.[33] In addition, their national outputs are dominated by trade with developed economies, mainly in exporting unprocessed

capital and skilled labour, scarcity of entrepreneurial talent, usually considerable amounts of unemployed unskilled labour, and in many cases even no shortage of land resources, are some of the characteristics of developing countries. *Ibid.* On similarity of factor endowments among developing countries, see *ibid.* at 31–5.

29 One consequence of trade liberalization under regional integration schemes in developing countries is a rise in non-tariff barriers. See Vaitsos, 'Crisis in Regional Economic Integration', at 746.

30 A. Hazlewood, 'Problems of Integration Among African States', in A. Hazlewood (ed.), *African Integration and Disintegration* (Oxford University Press, 1967), 1, 6.

31 See *infra* Chapter II (discussing reasons for adoption of variable geometry); see also Allen, 'Less Developed Areas', at 317–34 (discussing the conditions under which the Vinerian customs union model is feasible).

32 M. Bye, 'Structural Changes Required by Growth', in Harrod and Hague (eds), *International Trade Theory in a Developing World*, 161; see also Vaitsos, 'Crisis in Regional Economic Integration', at 751 (arguing that the traditional theory of integration influenced by Ricardian comparative advantage theory and neo-classical economics did 'not address itself to the issues of major interest on development, namely how the process of integration will dynamically change the structural conditions of production and technology, the process of inter-commodity and inter-activity (rather than simply inter-country) substitution, the dynamics of resource diversification going beyond the questions of specialization, the composition of investments and expectations, the capacity for absorbing externalities, etc').

33 According to Yang and Gupta, 'Regional Trade Arrangements in Africa', at 18. 'For many RTAs, intra-arrangement trade as share of their total external trade remains below intra-African trade as share of total African external trade', *ibid.* at 15.

raw materials.[34] The argument here is that African economies need more than the increase in market size created by a common market because the increase in market size may be marginal relative to other limitations for firms, such as high production costs and very low levels of income that make the effective size of regional markets small.[35]

Thus, as noted in Chapter II, a primary goal of trade integration in Africa became that of promoting large-scale production with a view to shifting trade patterns from external sources.[36] The idea was that such a production shift would in turn result in foreign exchange savings that could then be used to produce what was imported from outside Africa from the newly established production facilities within Africa.[37] In retrospect, this adaptation of the Vinerian model turned out to be pie in the sky – yet it is an idea not wholly abandoned in African RTAs even today.[38]

Import substitution policies were another initial response to this classical customs theory, particularly in the 1960s and 1970s.[39] These policies have increasingly been abandoned through multilateral treaty commitments, particularly since the 1990s.[40] The Vinerian customs union theory was also adapted through a variety of devices to avert unequal integration gains between integrating economies, a theme addressed

34 *Assessing Regional Integration in Africa* (Economic Commission for Africa, 2004), 19 (noting that 'in 1995, primary products accounted for 64% of African exports').

35 Hazlewood, 'Problems of Integration' at 9 (making reference to the view that 'the present cash market of most African countries individually is not larger than that of a moderately sized European town').

36 See *infra* Chapter II.

37 See R.H. Green and A. Seidman, *Unity or Poverty: The Economics of Pan-Africanism* (London: Penguin Books, 1968), 265; S. Linder, *Trade and Trade Policy for Development* (Praeger Series on International Economics and Development, 1967) (suggesting that trade creation would hurt poor economies because it would disrupt the desired country distribution rules and suggesting ways of overcoming such losses through establishment of common industries in the 'least-cost' partner); see also F. Andic, S. Andic and D. Dosser, *A Theory of Economic Integration for Developing Countries, Illustrated by Caribbean Countries*, vol. I (London: Allen & Unwin, 1971).

38 See *infra* nn. 59–79 (discussing functional specificity, RTAs as forums for integrated development of common resources, the equitable distribution of gains from trade and the principle of variable geometry).

39 See Economic Commission for Latin America, 'The Latin American Common Market', UN Pub. No. 59.II.G.4 (New York: UN, 1959).

40 F. Roessler, 'Domestic Policy Objectives and the Multilateral Trade Order: Lessons from the Past', *University of Pennsylvania Journal of International Economic Law* 19 (1998) 513, 516 (discussing the replacement of import substitution policies with trade liberalization via multilateral agreements).

more fully below.[41] Today, while developing countries have largely abandoned import substitution policies, many have yet to fully liberalize their economies under the GATT/WTO obligations they have assumed.[42]

Currently, African RTAs are not based on an approach that focuses on whether countries are complying point by point with regional trade treaty commitments. As such, regionalization grows not only out of formal institutions but independently of them as well. Daniel Bach, for example, has argued that while regionalism focuses on institution building and the conclusion of formal arrangements, regionalization – a much broader concept – arises from 'transactions and interactions' both formal and informal that a variety of state and non-state actors engage in within these regional spaces.[43] In fact, Africa has had its own forms of inter-regional interactions that predate the advent of colonial rule.[44] While these interactions need not be overstated, we also must not lose sight of the manner in which colonial rule created economies that favoured the interests of the various European metropolises at the expense of the colonies,[45] and the

41 See Kahnert *et al.*, *Economic Integration*, at 16 (arguing that the fact that trade theory (in the Vinerian model) 'failed to integrate considerations of income distribution fully into its general framework is a serious shortcoming which invalidates many of its conclusions in terms of political feasibility and even political desirability').

42 World Trade Organization, *Understanding the WTO* (2007), 97, available at www.wto.org/english/thewto_e/whatis_e/tif_e/understanding_e.pdf. The WTO is the only global international organization dealing with the rules of trade between nations. *Ibid.* at 9; see also WTO, GATT and Goods Council, available at www.wto.org/english/tratop_e/gatt_e/gatt_e.htm. The General Agreement on Tariffs and Trade (GATT) covers international trade in goods. The workings of the GATT Agreement are the responsibility of the Council for Trade in Goods (Goods Council) which is made up of representatives from all WTO member countries. *Ibid.*

43 D. Bach, 'Foreword', in D. Bach (ed.), *Regionalisation in Africa: Integration and Disintegration* (Oxford: James Currey, 1999); see generally K. Deutsch, *The Analysis of International Relations* (New Jersey: Prentice Hall, 1988); E. Haas, 'The Study of Regional Integration: Reflections on the Joy of and Anguish of Pre-Theorizing', in L. Lindberg and S. Scheingold (eds), *Regional Integration: Theory and Research* (Cambridge, MA: Harvard University Press, 1971); B. Hettne, 'Globalization, Regionalism and the New Third World', in N. Poku and L. Pettiford (eds), *Redefining the Third World* (New York: St. Martin's Press, 1998) (all providing alternative conceptualizations of regional integration that go beyond the linear paradigm of establishing trade integration through free markets).

44 Economic Commission for Africa, 'Assessing Regional Integration in Africa', at 27 (noting that regional integration 'has been part of Africa's strategy for economic transformation... in some cases for almost a century. The first experiment with integration, the Southern African Customs Union, began in 1910').

45 See Green and Seidman, *Unity of Poverty*, at 127. They note that:

> the existing economies of the separate African states were created under colonial control, the very opposite of the free market conditions which are assumed to be

manner in which independence subsequently restructured these interactions around the ideologies of sovereignty and nationalism.[46]

RTAs today are caught at the crossroads of seeking to overcome the defining features of separate countries whose goals encompass economic, political, social and cultural objectives, in addition to the traditional integration goals of trade liberalization. This is a regionalism tethered by the commitment to separate nations but strengthened by regional connections in trade and other domains among an economically, religiously, socially and politically diverse group of countries. As noted below, perhaps because of this diversity, it is not surprising that objectives such as regional security and the welfare of the citizens are salient within these RTAs. These trade-plus objectives are contextualizing imperatives of African regional integration. From this perspective, African RTA treaties contain a multiplicity of objectives – after all, trade integration cannot be achieved without simultaneously pursuing other objectives. For example, insecurity is a major barrier to trade integration, and any regional integration efforts that do not address insecurity as an objective would be atypical.[47]

Africa is a diverse continent, composed of countries with dramatic differences in their legal regimes, religious and cultural values and norms, economic endowments, political regimes and historical heritage. At one level, this contrasts with the European Union, which was 'built on commonalities of economic interest, politics and culture'[48] and which

> necessary for the best international division of labour. The economic principle of colonial rule dictated government in what was believed to be the best interests of metropolitan capital, in short the operation of a colony as if it were a subsidiary company.

Ibid.

46 Unfortunately, post-colonial nationalism overstated the national state and excluded alternative notions of nationhood that pre-existed the advent of the post-colonial state in Africa and Asia. See e.g., D. Rothchild and R.L. Curry, Jr., *Scarcity, Choice and Public Policy in Middle Africa* (Berkeley: University of California Press, 1978), 228 (arguing that colonialism left 'behind a patchwork of many sovereign states, but the states spawned by this process were themselves artificial entities'); M. Wa Mutua, 'Why Redraw the Map of Africa: A Legal and Moral Inquiry', *Michigan Journal of International Law* 16 (1995) 1113 (arguing that these artificial inherited African states lack moral and legal legitimacy). See generally P. Charterjee, *Nationalist Thought and the Colonial World: A Derivative Discourse* (Minneapolis: University of Minnesota Press, 1993) and B. Anderson, *Imagined Communities: Reflections on the Origin and Spread of Nationalism* (London: Verso, 1991) (both analysing the relationship between nationalism and colonialism).

47 The East African Community Council of Ministers have argued that the East African Community would be an incomplete integration scheme without cooperation on defence and security matters: see http://security.eac.int.

48 J.E. Alvarez, 'How Not to Link: Institutional Conundrums of an Expanded Trade Regime', *Widener Law Symposium Journal* 7 (2001) 1, 15.

also gave primacy to economic integration. In Africa, by contrast, it is important to pursue links across a broad array of indicators to set the context within which trade integration will be successful. Such a broad range of objectives would overcome what Arthur Hazlewood argued was 'a conclusion of despair that mutually beneficial economic co-operation requires close similarity of social and political outlook'.[49] The first generation of African RTAs were narrowly focused on trade integration to the exclusion of other objectives and in so doing underestimated the importance of cooperating on a broad range of objectives.[50]

Thus, today it would be a mistake to simply regard African RTAs merely as 'cognitive representations and formal arrangements'.[51] Rather, African RTAs must be regarded in light of the initiatives and processes including state–society relationships that are cumulatively establishing regionalism in modern Africa.[52] It is apposite to note here that even in the European Union, it would be inaccurate to presuppose that its integration has been achieved solely or purely through legal transformations through the European Court of Justice. As J.H.H. Weiler has argued, 'legal and constitutional structural change' had been crucial to European integration, '*but only in their interaction with the Community political process*'.[53] One African leader put it best: 'The basis of our cooperation, built on concrete projects and on specific programmes rather than on grandiose schemes and massive bureaucratic institutions, must be assured to the mutual advantage of all participating states.'[54]

In other words, looking to concrete projects that are mutually beneficial, as well as the manner in which political and other processes are working towards building of regional integration, is as important as legal and institutional perspectives that focus primarily on states as unitary actors. Joseph Nye cautioned several decades ago that 'scholars studying

49 A. Hazlewood, 'Economic Instrumentalities of Statecraft and the End of the EAC', in C. Potholm and R. Fredland (eds), *Integration and Disintegration in East Africa* (London: University Press of America, 1980), 123, 137.

50 J. Ravenhill, 'The Theory and Practice of Regional Integration in East Africa', in *ibid.*, 37, 51.

51 Bach, *Regionalisation in Africa.*

52 See J.N. Rosenau annd E.O. Czempiel, *Governance Without Government: Order and Change in World Politics* (Cambridge University Press, 1992) (arguing that as in other areas of global governance, non-state actors have become integral in the creation of regionalism in Africa). For more on this, see J.T. Gathii, *War, Commerce and International Law* (Oxford University Press, 2010).

53 J.H.H. Weiler, 'The Transformation of Europe', *Yale Law Journal* 100 (1991) 2403, 2407 (emphasis added).

54 Ravenhill, 'Future of Regionalism', at 217 (quoting Sir Seretse Khama, the first President of Botswana).

integration in Africa must remember the primacy of politics and not be misled by assumptions natural to "developed" societies. It is important to pay attention to social, historical, and economic factors.'[55] That is why this book adopts a multifaceted approach which follows both the legal and institutional efforts being made to build regionalization. It also considers the interactions among national and regional trade officials and non-state actors including business groups, institutions and professionals,[56] examining the extent to which their increased interactions have influenced the realization of regional commitments in trade and related areas.[57] This book therefore explores not only the treaty commitments made in the RTAs, but also other types of instruments containing trade and non-trade agreements between and among African states, such as ministerial declarations and memorandums of understanding.[58] Such informal decisions taken within the context of RTA commitments that are designed to take advantage of regional complementarities help in building and consolidating regional integration initiatives such as infrastructural projects. In doing so, African RTAs have adapted to an environment often

55 J. Nye, *Pan-Africanism and East African Integration* (Cambridge, MA: Harvard University Press, 1965), 250.

56 See International Plant Protection Convention, available at www.ippc.int/index.php?id=1110589&L=0 (follow 'Core Activities' hyperlink then 'Commission (CPM)' hyperlink). Consider, for example, the establishment in April of 2006 of an East African Phytosanitary Information Committee by scientists under the auspices of the International Plant Convention Treaty which, though intended for information-sharing purposes, nevertheless dovetails particularly well with building capacity for phytosanitary trade-related issues. *Ibid.*

57 See H.H. Koh, 'How is International Human Rights Law Enforced?', *Indiana Law Journal* 74 (1999) 1397, 1409–10; H. Koh, 'Transnational Legal Process', *Nebraska Law Review* 75 (1986) 181; H. Koh, 'On American Exceptionalism', *Stanford Law Review* 55 (2003) 1479, 1502 (explaining what Koh terms as vertical internalization or absorption of rules of international law into domestic legal systems). Koh explains that:

> the key to understanding whether nations will obey international law . . . is transnational legal process: the process by which public and private actors – namely, nation states, corporations, international organizations and non-governmental organizations – interact in a variety of fora to make, interpret, enforce, and ultimately internalize rules of international law. The key elements of this approach are interaction, interpretation, and internalization. Those seeking to create and embed certain human rights principles into international and domestic law should trigger transnational interactions, that generate legal interpretations, that can in turn be internalized into the domestic law of even resistant nation states.

Ibid. at 1502.

58 See A. Guzman, 'A Compliance-Based Theory of International Law', *California Law Review* 90 (2002) 1823, 1879–84. Though sometimes regarded as informal relative to the more solemn formal treaty commitments, these types of decisions are now regarded as sources of obligations between states. *Ibid.*

characterized by political instability and inter-country inequality that would threaten a grand scheme of integration that was exclusively based on a Vinerian customs union model.[59]

2 Flexibility as enmeshment in the African context

Flexibility does not make African RTAs any less significant than those agreements in other parts of the world that are thought of as more rule bound. Indeed, highly legalized legal regimes are now not necessarily thought of as superior to those that are not highly legalized.[60] In one context, high legalization is defined by the extent to which obligation, precision and delegation of a formal instrument may serve an important purpose.[61] However, in a different context, such legalization may not necessarily serve the best interests of the parties since it may not 'enmesh' well within the economies, political frameworks and normative commitments of a particular regime.[62] Yet, where parties to formal and informal agreements are continuously reiterating their commitments and making new ones, this contributes to the process of gradually building the regime's norms and rules, as well as the political will and economic investment necessary to give these norms and rules efficacy. For example, the increasing absorption of regional rules into national law of RTA member

59 See Ravenhill, 'Future of Regionalism', at 221–2.

60 See Abbott and Snidal, 'Hard and Soft Law', at 434 (arguing that the choice of soft norms by an international organization may be necessitated by seeking consensus as a way of limiting costs, including contracting costs).

61 See K.W. Abbott *et al.*, 'The Concept of Legalization', *International Organization* 54 (2000) 401. Abbott defines these terms as follows:

> [O]bligation means that states or other actors are bound by a rule or commitment or by a set of rules or commitments. Specifically, it means that they are legally bound by a rule or commitment in the sense that their behavior there under is subject to scrutiny under the general rules, procedures and discourse of international law, and often of domestic law as well. Precision means that the rules unambiguously define the conduct they require, authorize or prescribe. Delegation means third parties have been granted authority to implement, interpret, and apply the rules; to resolve disputes; and (possibly) to make further rules.

Ibid.

62 See C.R. Kelly, 'Enmeshment as a Theory of Compliance', *New York University Journal of International Law and Policy* 37 (2005) 303, 304; see also H. Oh and E. Weiss, 'Strengthening Compliance With International Environmental Accords: Preliminary Observations from a Collaborative Project', *Global Governance* 1 (1995) 119, 124. The two scholars have suggested that the degree to which countries cooperate under a regime such as an RTA will depend upon factors such as 'the character of the activity, the character of the accord, country characteristics, policy, history, leadership, information, the role of... NGOs, actions of other states, and the roles of international governmental organizations'. *Ibid.*

countries, as well as the continual building of a cadre of international trade lawyers with expertise who are increasingly working for RTA members or for the RTAs themselves, are important initial steps in building the efficacy of RTAs as legal regimes.[63] Clearly, though, African RTAs do not eschew legalization even while embracing policy-based integration. Thus, Article 5(3) of the Treaty for the Establishment of the African Economic Community provides for possible sanctions against a Member State that 'persistently fails to honour its general undertakings under this Treaty or fails to abide by the decisions or regulations of the Community'.[64] Article 29(2) of the Treaty for the Establishment of a Common Market for Eastern and Southern Africa (COMESA), gives primacy of the decisions of the COMESA Court of Justice over those of the member countries on questions relating to the interpretation of the treaty.[65] Such primacy is not only unusual among international tribunals, including the International Court of Justice, but also in light of previous decisions of African courts when confronted with conflicting RTA treaty provisions, as I explore more fully in Chapter VII.[66] Notwithstanding these examples, rather than being highly legalized regimes, African RTAs are flexible arrangements. A Southern African Development Coordination Conference (SADCC) report observed that:

> Flexibility does not imply absence of institutions: it creates a need for bodies able to build, modify, and phase out arrangements. What it does imply is avoiding massive, interlocked institutional structures in which the institutional frame (not the content of the programme) becomes the justification of continued cooperation.[67]

63 See L.R. Helfer, K.J. Alter and M. Florencia Guerzovich, 'Islands of Effective International Adjudication: Constructing An Intellectual Property Rule of Law in the Andean Community', *American Journal of International Law* 103 (2009) 1. The efficacy of the intellectual property regime of the Andean Community has been attributed in a large part to a cadre of well-trained legal professionals. *Ibid.*

64 See Treaty for the Establishment of the African Economic Community, Art. 5(3), signed 3 June 1991, 30 ILM 1241 (1991). Such Council-imposed sanctions 'may include the suspension of the rights and privileges of membership and may be lifted by the Assembly upon recommendation of the Council'. *Ibid.*

65 Treaty Establishing the Common Market for Eastern and Southern Africa, Art. 29(2), signed 5 Nov. 1993, available at http://about.comesa.int/attachments/149_090505_COMESA_Treaty.pdf.

66 See *Okunda* v. *Republic* (1970) E. Afr. L. Rep. 457 (Kenya), affirmed E. Afr. L. Rep. 460 (asserting supremacy of Kenyan law over a competing East African Community statute).

67 Ravenhill, 'Future of Regionalism', at 212 (citing Southern African Development Coordination Conference, 'First Steps Toward Economic Integration: Interests, Instrumentalities' (Arusha, Mimeo 1979) 36).

Thus, one significant manner in which African RTAs show a specific enmeshment particular to Africa is that they have focused less on building rigorously formal commitments backed up by sanctions, but rather more on building flexible frameworks of development, coordination and cooperation that give countries their choice of activities that interest them most.[68] In this sense, African RTAs often adopt 'functionally specific'[69] objectives that do not wrestle sovereignty away from national governments, given that it is not always clear if intra-regional trade would

68 *Ibid.* Ravenhill also argues that a

> rigid framework, as was the case with the Treaty for East African Cooperation, makes it impossible for countries to participate selectively in those activities which are of most interest to them . . . [and that] flexibility of institutions and instruments of cooperation is desirable also in that this recognizes that actors' interests do not remain constant. In part this is related to change in the extra-regional economic environment . . . It also anticipates that there will be a continuing rapid turnover of governments in many African states, possibly accompanied by dramatic shifts in policy. Since such transformations have often precipitated the collapse of regional institutions in the past, it is desirable that the framework of cooperation be insulated as much as possible from the consequences of sudden withdrawal of a Member State. Flexible arrangements improve the prospects for projects to be continued with a minimum amount of damage.

Ibid.

69 See e.g., Treaty for the Establishment of the Common Market for East and Southern Africa, Art. 4 (providing for a broad range of undertakings within each of the following areas: trade liberalization and customs cooperation (Art. 4(1)(a)–(f)), transport and communications (Art. 4(2)(a)–(c)), industry and energy (Art. 4(a)–(d)), monetary affairs and finance (Art. 4(4)(a)–(d)), agriculture (Art. 4(5)(a)–(g)) and in the field of economic and social development (Art. 4(5)(a)–(i)); Treaty for the Establishment of the East African Community, chs. 11–27, signed 30 Nov. 1999, available at www.eac.int (click on 'About EAC' tab and follow 'Treaty Establishing the EAC' hyperlink) (providing for a broad range of undertakings within each of the following areas: Chapter 11 (Co-operation in Trade Liberalization and Development), Chapter 12 (Co-operation in Investment and Industrial Development), Chapter 13 (Co-operation in Standardization on Quality Assurance, Metrology and Testing), Chapter 14 (Monetary and Financial Co-operation), Chapter 15 (Co-operation in Infrastructure and Services), Chapter 16 (Co-operation in the Development of Human Resources, Science and Technology), Chapter 17 (Free Movement of Persons, Labour, Services, Right of Establishment and Residence), Chapter 18 (Agriculture and Food Security), Chapter 19 (Co-operation in Environment and Natural Resources Management), Chapter 20 (Co-operation in Tourism and Wildlife Management), Chapter 21 (Health, Social and Cultural Activities), Chapter 22 (Enhancing the Role of Women in Socio-Economic Development), Chapter 23 (Co-operation in Political Matters), Chapter 24 (Legal and Judicial Affairs), Chapter 25 (The Private Sector and the Civil Society), Chapter 26 (Relations With Other Regional and International Organizations and Development Partners) and Chapter 27 (Co-operation in Other Fields)); see also Ravenhill, 'Future of Regionalism', at 212.

'compensate for the inevitable erosion of their autonomy in policy-making'.[70] Such flexibility is also important given the diversity not only of the economies of individual members of the RTAs, but of differences based on their culture, geography, ethnicity, religion and political allegiances as well. This multiplicity of identities and loyalties could present insurmountable barriers to integration if African RTAs were constructed as unitary and inflexible frameworks. Such rigidity would make cooperation difficult along any axis as steps are taken towards increasing legitimacy for broader forms of cooperation within the heterogeneous nature of African societies. Inflexibility can only contribute to entrenching resistance to the legitimacy of cooperative frameworks along any of these lines of difference and asymmetry. Flexibility, by contrast, enmeshes very well within this context of heterogeneity and diversity.

Enmeshment within the African context is also manifested by the fact that African RTAs bring to the foreground issues of equity and balance in the relations among their members, while commitments to the promotion of free trade as a source of economic growth are relegated to the background.[71] This is informed in large part by the fact that the prospects of regional integration have often been severely limited by the legacy of unequal gains from integration,[72] not merely because it is market based,

70 *Ibid.*, at 214; see also Maphanyane, 'SADCC-Future Challenges', at 176. Maphanyane also argues that SADCC eschewed the conventional market integrationist path to regional integration. A gradualist approach was instead adopted which aimed at consensus and avoidance of anything that would infringe on national sovereignty that had just been acquired often through the long and bitter and bloody struggle. It was the most sensible way to proceed in Southern Africa under the circumstances. Regional integration had to be a maturing process.
Ibid.

71 See C.B. Thompson, 'African Initiatives for Development: The Practice of Regional Economic Cooperation in Southern Africa', *Journal of International Affairs* 46 (1992) 125, 133. In its 1992 summit meeting, SADCC adopted a development integration model which:

> stresse[d] the need for close political cooperation at an early stage of the integration process, not at the end. Second, it call[ed] for equity and balance in relations among Member States, including compensatory measures for the weaker members in any transactions that might adversely affect them, such as trade or monetary liberation. Third, it [saw] a need for increased trade to be predicated on regional industrial planning, involving regional resource mobilization.

Ibid.

72 See L. Mytelka, 'The Salience of Gains in Third-World Integrative Systems', *World Politics* 25 (1973) 236.

but because it often pits economically richer countries against economically poorer countries.[73] That is why there has been a long-standing argument in favour of compensatory schemes for poorer African countries in the initial stages of economic integration with richer countries, so that integration commitments do not impose high administrative costs without immediate advantages.[74]

3 *African RTAs as forums of integrated development and functionally specific projects*

In addition, African RTAs often serve as forums for integrated development of common resources with their secretariats or various arms serving as inter-governmental agencies for such purposes.[75] For example, the East African Community nestles within it the Lake Victoria Basin Commission, which coordinates the management and utilization of the basin among three of the five community states which share the Lake Victoria Basin.[76] There is a long history of integrated

73 See N. Poku, *Regionalization and Security in Southern Africa* (London: Palgrave Macmillan, 2001), 15–38. In the South African context, for example, South Africa was the imperial power both within SACU and SADC in the colonial and apartheid eras when it played a destabilizing role against the frontline states that were opposed to apartheid. *Ibid.* Poku further notes that 'SACU is unlikely to provide the framework for greater regionalism for the simple reason that the ending of apartheid has not eradicated a general suspicion among countries of southern Africa of South Africa's imperial project.' *Ibid.* at 89.

74 See P. Robson, *Economic Integration in Africa* (Evanston, IL: Northwestern University Press, 1968), 285 (arguing that Gambia's integration within UMOA would deprive it of its monetary autonomy unless a mechanism for the equitable distribution of benefits and costs between the countries involved was devised). Chapter II addresses the various types of compensatory arrangements devised in African RTAs to close the gap in opportunities between poor and richer members of an RTA.

75 See e.g., S.K.B. Asante *et al.*, *Towards An African Economic Community* (Africa Institute of South Africa, 2001), 15 (arguing in favour of increased efforts to harmonize and promote the implementation of joint projects given 'the small size of most African economies').

76 See East African Community, 'The Lake Victoria Basin Commission', 1, available at www.eac.int/lvdc.pdf. Among the goals of this autonomous body within the EAC are: 'harmonizing policies and laws of the Lake's environment and catchment area; the management and conservation of aquatic resources including fisheries; promotion of investments and development in the basin and the revamping of the transport system on and around the Lake'. *Ibid.* Also nestled within the EAC as an institution of the Community is the Lake Victoria Fisheries Organization, established by the Member States in 1994 by treaty to manage the lake's fisheries resources. See generally, 'Lake Victorian Fisheries Organization: An Institution of East African Communities', available at www.lvfo.org.

development of river basins among African countries, some within economic integration arrangements[77] and others that were developed by long-standing treaties entered into during the colonial period.[78] Some have called this approach 'development integration'.[79] Moreover, these integrated development arrangements have sometimes been designed with re-distributional considerations.[80]

In short, African RTAs do not merely centre integration around a vision of market-led integration.[81] They are also designed as forums for a variety of initiatives, such as facilitating cooperation around common resources like international rivers and basins among riparian states,[82]

77 See U. Ezenwe, *ECOWAS and the Economic Integration of West Africa* (London: Palgrave Macmillan, 1983), 114–16. For example, Gambia and Senegal have long sought to cooperate on the exploitation of the Gambia River Basin within UMOA. *Ibid.* See also P. Robson, 'Problems of Integration Between Senegal and Gambia', in A. Hazlewood (ed.), *African Integration and Disintegration* (Oxford University Press, 1967), 115, 126–8 (noting Gambia's economic weakness relative to Senegal and the challenge of ensuring opportunities available to equalize gains between the two countries). The author also notes that the two countries entered into a defence agreement under which cooperation on mutual assistance from external threat was agreed. *Ibid.*

78 See F. Amdetsion, 'Scrutinizing the Scorpion Problematique: Arguments in Favor of the Continued Relevance of International Law and a Multidisciplinary Approach to Resolving the Nile Dispute', *Texas International Law Journal* 44 (2008) 1, 19–27 (providing analysis of the best example of a long-standing treaty entered into during the colonial period, the Nile River basin that is in part governed by a treaty entered into by Egypt and Anglo-Egyptian Sudan on 7 May 1929).

79 See W.A. Axline, 'Underdevelopment, Dependence and Integration: The Politics of Regionalism in the Third World', in P. Ghosh (ed.), *Economic Integration in the Third World* (Gamani Corea, 1994), 25.

80 See O.S. Saasa, 'Background to Regional Integration in Africa', in O.S. Saasa (ed.), *Joining the Future: Economic Integration and Co-operation in Africa* (Nairobi: African Centre for Technology Studies Press, 1991), 1, 14.

81 See *ibid.* at 21. According to Oliver Saasa, the

> emphasis on non-market components of regional integration in developing countries . . . in no way implies that production efficiency and considerations of costs are irrelevant. To the contrary, it is fully acknowledged here that since such vehicles for integration involve astronomical sums of money and demand joint programming and execution, market integration that demands cost considerations and rational responses to price signals is important. Instead it is suggested that integration derived advantages usually result from areas of cooperation in which the market alone is not the principal variable accounting for such economic benefits.

Ibid.

82 See K.L. Powers, 'Why Do States Pursue Water Cooperation through Regional Trade Agreements? Trade, Environment and Security Linkages in International River Basins' (1 Sept. 2005) (unpublished manuscript, on file with the American Political Science Association).

and cross-border challenges that include trade,[83] security[84] and health.[85] Rather than simply using the expansion of intra-regional trade as a framework for industrial growth, product diversification and the improvement of the global competitiveness of these products as ways of overcoming small domestic markets, African RTAs were and continue to be seen as frameworks for development cooperation as well.[86] As Oliver Saasa put it, this approach 'is fundamentally dependent upon increased industrial production through specialization, exploitation of economies of scale, external economies, coordinated programming and development of infrastructure'.[87] Here, regional cooperation is at the level of production in the arenas of capital and labour, rather than merely in trade.[88] This amounted to industrial planning in many regions complete with licensing legislation designed to 'encourage investment in industry serving the regional market'.[89] For this reason, regional integration in Africa has been

83 See E.D. Mansfield and R. Bronson, 'Alliances, Preferential Trading Arrangements, International Trade', *American Political Science Review* 91 (1997) 94.

84 See K.L. Powers, 'International Institutions, Trade and Conflict: African Regional Trade Agreements From 1950–1992', Ph.D Dissertation, Ohio State University (2001); D. Bearce, 'Grasping the Commercial Institutional Peace', *International Studies Quarterly* 47 (2003) 347.

85 See V. Agu, A.N. Correia and K. Behbehani, 'Strengthening International Health Co-Operation in Africa Through the Regional Economic Communities', *African Journal of Health Science* 14(3–4) (2007) 104, 105 (noting in part that 'One of the important lessons arising . . . is that effective integration requires more than reducing tariffs and quotas. Wide ranging policy measures (which go beyond traditional trade policies) are needed to remove barriers which have the effect of segmenting markets and impeding the free flow of goods, services, investments, and ideas').

86 See Ezenwe, *Economic Integration of West Africa*, at 45.

87 O.S. Saasa, 'Economic Cooperation and Integration Among Developing Countries', in Saasa (ed.), *Joining the Future*, 20. Saasa further argues that:

> contrary to the neo-classical theory of integration, increased, planned and co-ordinated industrial infrastructural development that recognizes the efficiency and developmental roles of industrial complementarity, specialization, external economies and economies of scale should be primary goals of Third World regional integration efforts. Thus trade expansion in these countries should be perceived as a tool for expanded industrial production, and not the other way around.

Ibid. at 25.

88 See A. Hazlewood, *Economic Integration: The East African Experience* (New York: St. Martin's Press, 1975), 14.

89 *Ibid.* at 121. Hazlewood also notes that the

> Raisman Commission had been unsympathetic to the use of the licensing system as an instrument of industrial development planning, and it did not fit easily into the market-oriented regulatory scheme of the Treaty [of the East African Community].

and continues to be based on such planning, 'rather than laissez faire forces'.[90]

A major impetus to approaching integration with emphasis on co-operation at the level of production, and not simply in trade, is its dual emphasis on distributional equity amongst its members,[91] rather than merely on market efficiency and competition between firms, and on providing a forum for cooperation on agreed projects that have tangible benefits for regional development.[92] This has led advocates of regional integration in Africa to suggest that the initial stages of trade integration should be 'production-oriented and task directed approaches to economic integration which necessarily imply coordinated industrial production at the regional level'.[93] This explains why the objectives of many African RTAs have a huge number of specific sector cooperative goals. In turn, such objectives play a significant role in setting the stage for trade among

> Under the Treaty, industrial licensing was to continue, but only until 1973, when the existing licenses expired, and no new industries were to be scheduled.

Ibid. at 121–2. Instead of depending on regulation through a licensing scheme, the treaty has 'established a market regulator, the transfer tax being the main device for influencing market forces in the desired direction'. *Ibid.* at 168. Note also, that under the treaty, trade and development were to take place under market conditions rather than state planning or industrial licensing 'as influenced by a common system of fiscal incentives and by the activities of the East African Development Bank'. *Ibid.* at 127.

90 Ravenhill, 'Future of Regionalism', at 210.

91 This desire for compensatory and corrective measures to accompany African RTAs takes into account the reality of highly unequal trading partners within one regional group. In East Africa, for example, Kenya is the dominant economy relative to the other members. This was one of the major reasons for the dissolution of the original EAC in 1977. See A. Mugomba, 'Regional Organizations and African Underdevelopment: The Collapse of the East African Community', *Journal of Modern African Studies* 16 (1978) 261–3. The new EAC carefully balances the goals of trade integration with those of distributional equity and variable geometry (defined as the principle of flexibility which allows for progression in cooperation among a sub-group of members in a larger integration scheme in a variety of areas and at different speeds), the principle of asymmetry (which the treaty defines as a principle which addresses variances in the implementation of measures in an economic integration process for purposes of achieving a common objective) and distributional equity as fundamental principles of the community. See Treaty Establishing the East African Community, at Art. 6(e) and (h).

92 See O.S. Saasa, 'SADCC Industrial Co-Operation and Donor Support', in Saasa (ed.), *Joining the Future*, 59.

93 *Ibid.* One problem with such an approach is that where competing industries in different countries in a region are operating at below full capacity, the incentive for engaging in coordinated regional planning and investment is not very high. See Ezenwe, *ECOWAS and the Economic Integration of West Africa*, 33.

cooperating countries, which, after all, is a prerequisite for undertaking regional trade liberalization.[94]

In this sense, integration is regarded as a diplomatic strategy of co-operation on a range of issues including infrastructural, industrial, political and economic concerns,[95] as well as for balancing forces between the RTA members on the one hand, and the global economic system on the other.[96] Some have argued that this approach of integration by projects,

94 Ravenhill, 'Future of Regionalism', at 210 (arguing that it cannot be assumed that there already exists a basis for integration where there are 'low levels of development and . . . limited possibilities for profitable inter-regional exchange'). This kind of sectoral integration has been referred to as neo-functional integration in so far as it seeks to promote transnational activities around a set of functional needs. See E. Haas, *The Uniting of Europe* (Stanford University Press, 1958), 313; Haas, 'The Study of Regional Integration'. Notably, the limits identified by all of these theorists about the absence of interest groups and 'modern associational groups' supportive of regional integration decades ago is no longer accurate. In the East African Community, for example, there is a very active East African Business Council as well as the East African Law Society to name but a few. Theorists who have postulated that absence of such groups was not consistent with achieving regional integration include Ernest Haas (arguing that 'absence of pluralism makes the formation of voluntary groups on a regional basis very difficult', *ibid.* at 14–15); J. Nye, 'Comparing Common Markets: A Revised Neo-Functionalist Model', in Lindberg and Scheingold (eds), *Regional Integration* (arguing that the absence or weakness of such groups and political parties deprives regional bureaucrats of necessary allies); Ravenhill, 'Theory and Practice of Regional Integration', at 48–50 (arguing that low levels of economic development preclude the emergence of such groups).

95 See Saasa, 'Economic Cooperation and Integration'. Arthur Hazlewood also argues that 'the operation and development of services, such as transport, communications, electric power, and research, in common is a further measure of integration between states. Integration of this kind can operate even where there are no other forms of integration between the states': Hazlewood, 'Problems of Integration', at 4–5.

96 See T.M. Shaw, 'Towards a Political Economy of Regionalism in Africa', in Onwuka and Sesay (eds), *The Future of Regionalism in Africa*, at 14. See generally G. Myrdal, *Economic Theory and Underdeveloped Regions* (New York: Harper & Row, 1957) (warning that adopting market-based integration ideals among members with huge differences in the levels of economic development among countries would result in benefiting more developed member countries at the expense of poorer ones). According to Myrdal, '[t]he freeing and widening of markets will often confer such competitive advantages on the industries in the already established centers of expansion, which usually work under conditions of increasing returns, that even the handicrafts and industries existing earlier in the other regions are thwarted'. *Ibid.* at 28. See also P. Robson, *Integration, Development, and Equity: Economic Integration in West Africa* (London: Unwin Hyman, 1968), 33 (arguing that a linear approach to integration which merely focused on reallocating resources based on the theory of comparative advantage without more would not necessarily be beneficial for developing countries). Constantine Vaitsos has suggested that the content and social legitimacy of integration arrangements in a developing context should take account of their social, economic and political structures, the need for development and

rather than through integration of markets, has accentuated underdevelopment rather than solved development problems.[97] This issue of distributional equity and its merits and demerits is addressed at further length in Chapter II.

4 Multiplicity of objectives: The merits and de-merits of nestling non-trade objectives in African RTAs

As we saw above, African integration often forewent development cooperation without wholly abandoning trade integration.[98] Thus, critics of African integration have missed the mark by failing to appreciate the importance of African RTAs as frameworks for developing political consensus among their members around regional challenges, including those involving development, politics, or security. In short, while RTAs are established through treaty frameworks, operationally they are forums for nestling regional challenges and developing political consensus on how to cooperate.[99] There is indeed evidence showing that there are gains in non-trade areas, such as security, arising from economic integration arrangements associated with commercial institutions like regional trade agreements.[100] There are a variety of ways in which economic integration arrangements provide a framework for resolving security and other regional problems. For example, countries that belong to a regional integration framework like an RTA may regard the increased expectations of benefits from regional trade and investment as raising the opportunity costs of war. In addition, RTAs provide a forum for negotiating peaceful outcomes.[101] Paul Collier has recently shown that although many African countries are small and poor, their military spending is high and often wasteful.[102] Collier suggests that cooperation is the solution to curtailing the arms race in Africa.[103] However, cooperation in the absence of

the new conditions such as internal dynamics and integration effects: Vaitsos, 'Crisis in Regional Economic Cooperation', at 736. Such an approach serves as an alternative to a linear market-led process imported from elsewhere.

97 See *ibid.* at 720.

98 See Maphanyane, *SADCC-Future Challenges*, at 175 (noting that it is often erroneously argued that SADCC 'does not have a programme of market integration through trade').

99 For similar arguments in the context of linking non-trade issues like human rights within the WTO, see Alvarez, 'How Not to Link', at 15.

100 Bearce, 'Commercial Institutional Peace', at 347.

101 See P. Collier, *Wars, Guns and Votes: Democracy in Dangerous Places* (New York: HarperCollins, 2009), 191–6.

102 *Ibid.* at 117.

103 *Ibid.*

enforcement would only encourage a country's 'neighbors to coordinate reduction in their military spending while not doing so itself'.[104]

In addition, regional institutions established under the auspices of an integration arrangement may provide information about the military capabilities of Member States to each other so that each is able to assess the probable results of a war compared to or contrasted with peaceful bargaining. Consequently, even where disparities are apparent, such institutions may help to cement trust so that power asymmetries will not be exploited in future.[105] These institutions bring together their executive and military leaders periodically, thereby providing a forum within which they can interact and hopefully develop some trust amongst themselves in order to achieve peaceful bargaining and resolution of conflicts.[106] Thus, the nesting or nestling of security and development matters within trade integration agreements is a significant but overlooked phenomenon since it does not fit in especially well with standard integration models such as the European Community.[107]

As a Nigerian Minister for External Affairs once noted:

> While focusing on certain economic development issues to be solved by sub-regional integration, the integrations in the ECOWAS have not failed to recognize the import of security. Integration and development are only likely to be guaranteed in the context of peaceful political and

104 *Ibid.* (suggesting designating a 'policeman' to oversee military spending in addition to implementing restrictions on arms exports).

105 Bearce, 'Commercial Institutional Peace', at 358.

106 *Ibid.* See also T. Ohlson and S.J. Stedman, 'Towards Enhanced Regional Security in Southern Africa?', in Oden (ed.), *Southern Africa After Apartheid*, at 106. Ohlson and Stedman argue that security cooperation:

> would be an excellent instrument for confidence-building and increased transparency with respect to armed forces, the quality and quantity of military arsenals, actual and perceived threats and threat projections, etc. Second, it could provide a useful framework for regional conflict management and resolution. Third, it could provide the framework for an orderly planned, coordinated and mutually agreed regional disarmament process, involving reduced military spending, force level and hardware reductions, and conversion projects. Fourth, it could, with time, contribute to institutionalization that could further a process of equity based regional cooperation and integration over a wide range of issues, including but not only, economic issues. Conversely, dealing with economic and security aspects of cooperation and integration in the same framework could – if progress is made in the economic arena – contribute to reduced threat perceptions and, thus lead to quicker assessments and redefinitions of national security needs.

Ibid.

107 Bearce, 'Commercial Institutional Peace', at 363.

> socio-economic environment, both at the national and sub-regional levels. Hence, the first decade had also been characterized by certain forms of defence cooperation and initiatives.[108]

Indeed, in the context of the Economic Community of West African States (ECOWAS), trade integration was very early recognized as incapable of being pursued while ignoring economic development and regional security issues.[109] After all, trade integration was not possible within a context of insecurity both among and within the Member States.[110] Thus, soon after ECOWAS was established, a non-aggression pact was entered into in 1979 which also called on the Member States to recognize the current borders.[111] In 1981, the states entered into a mutual defence pact to repulse external aggression or armed internal conflict.[112] Security coordination and cooperation was institutionalized with the establishment of permanent structures of conflict management, prevention and resolution.[113]

It is in this sense that Thomas Ohlson and Stephen J. Stedman's argument that 'conflict, insecurity and underdevelopment are inextricably interlinked in Southern Africa', is true of most of sub-Saharan Africa.[114] The types of conflicts include those involving control over territory and governments, inclusion and exclusion in governance based on race and identity, inequitable resource distribution and insecurities created by war and reconciliation in light of vast imbalances in the distribution of military power.[115] Conflicts have had a decisive impact on regional integration efforts in Africa, particularly given that those regions with the most conflict have witnessed the slowest growth in regional integration.[116] In the horn of Africa, the Inter-Governmental Authority on Development

108 I. Nwachukwu, *Nigeria and the ECOWAS Since 1985: Towards a Dynamic Regional Integration* (Nigeria: Fourth Dimension Publishing Co., 1991), 21, as cited in Bearce, 'Commercial Institutional Peace', at 364.

109 *Ibid.* at 357. 110 *Ibid.* 111 *Ibid.* 112 *Ibid.*

113 *Ibid.* It is therefore surprising that some commentators suggested that the idea of having an Assembly of the Heads of State and Government of the African Economic Community was unwise because the cost would be prohibitive and 'the achievements of the deliberations not always of probative value'. See Professor O. Akanle, 'The Legal and Institutional Framework of the African Economic Community', in M.A. Ajomo and O. Adewale (eds), *African Economic Community Treaty: Issues, Problems and Prospects* (Nigerian Institute of Advanced Legal Studies, 1993), 31. This view does not take into account the potential such forums offer for resolution of challenges such as security.

114 Ohlson and Stedman, 'Enhanced Regional Security', at 87. 115 *Ibid.* at 88.

116 *Assessing Regional Integration in Africa II* (Addis Ababa: United Nations Economic Commission for Africa, 2004), 17, available at www.uneca.org/aria2 (follow 'Chapter 1: The Drivers of Regional Integration of Africa's Development' hyperlink).

(IGAD), one of the African Union's designated regional economic communities, which I discuss at greater length in Chapter IV, has a primary focus on rebuilding security in the region.[117] In South Africa, insecurity surrounding inmigration of African workers resulted in riots and violence in 2008, indicating, yet again, the potentially conflicting nature of migration across borders.[118] Today, the importance of economic development as a remedy to violence is increasingly being recognized and emphasized.[119]

5 *African RTAs as bulwarks of self-reliance and economic independence*

Another aspect of regional integration in Africa that is often understated is that second-generation integration efforts of the post-colonial order were often designed as frameworks within which African countries could eliminate dependence on their former colonizers with a view to attaining self-reliance.[120] This is reflected in the seventh preambular paragraph to the Treaty Establishing the African Economic Community.[121] Some of the treaties establishing regional economic communities share a common preambular paragraph.[122] Article 3(b) of the Treaty Establishing the Economic Community of Central African States (ECCAS) makes 'solidarity and collective self reliance' a principle to be adhered to by the members.[123] Article 4(1)(a) provides that the integration of African economies is aimed at increasing 'economic self-reliance' and to promote 'endogenous and self-sustained development'.[124] Similarly, Article 4(b) of the ECOWAS Treaty provides 'solidarity and collective self-reliance' as a

117 See C. Mwaura and S. Schmeidl (eds), *Early Warning and Conflict Management in the Horn of Africa* (Lawrenceville, NJ: The Red Sea Press, Inc., 2002).

118 See Ohlson and Stedman, 'Enhanced Regional Security', at 92; see also Isaken, 'Prospects for SACU', at 199 (predicting that a future South African government would face as a main problem 'the de-escalation of labour migration from neighboring countries [which is] likely to be considerable').

119 Collier, 'Democracy in Dangerous Places'; A. Gat, *War in Human Civilization* (Oxford University Press, 2006), 658.

120 See e.g., Monrovia Declaration of Commitment on the Guidelines and Measures for National and Collective Self-Reliance in Economic and Social Development for the Establishment of a New International Economic Order, 17–20 July 1979, available at www.africa-union.org/root/au/Documents/Decisions/hog/pHoGAssembly1979.pdf.

121 Treaty Establishing the African Economic Community, at Preamble para. 7.

122 See Treaty Establishing the Economic Community of Central African States, para. 3, 19 Oct. 1983, 23 ILM 945 (1984).

123 *Ibid.* at Art. 3(b).

124 *Ibid.* at Art. 4(1)(a).

fundamental principle,[125] as does Article 6(b) of the COMESA Treaty.[126] Article 5(1)(d) of the SADC Treaty makes it an objective to 'promote self-sustaining development on the basis of collective self-reliance, and interdependence of member states'.[127]

These provisions demonstrate that regional economic integration in Africa has been justified as a necessary step for realizing self-sustaining economic development.[128] On this view, Africa's external economic dependence and its lop-sided participation in the international trading system are key factors accounting for the dismal economic performance on the continent that are regarded as addressable through economic self-reliance on a continental level.[129]

Economic self-determination is a theme strongly associated with the first generation of regional integration efforts in the post-colonial era.[130] For example, Kwame Nkurumah envisioned Africa's economic unity as a necessary precondition for its economic self-determination.[131] Many have since argued that Africa risks being further marginalized if it does not fulfil the dream of early pan-Africanists like Kwame Nkurumah and Julius Nyerere.[132] These early pan-Africanists dreamed of a single African

125 See Treaty Establishing the Economic Community of Western African States, Art. 4(b), signed 28 May 1975, available at www.comm.ecowas.int/sec/index.php?id=treaty&lang=en.

126 Treaty for the Establishment of the Common Market for East and Southern Africa, at Art. 6(b).

127 Treaty of the Southern African Development Community (SADC), Art. 5(1)(d), signed 17 Aug. 1992.

128 See J. Gathii, 'Third World Approaches to International Economic Governance', in R. Falk, B. Rajagopal and J. Stevens (eds), *International Law and the Third World: Reshaping Justice* (Abingdon: Routledge-Cavendish, 2008), 255.

129 *Ibid.*

130 See K. Nkurumah, *Africa Must Unite* (London: Panaf Books, 1963), 101.

131 *Ibid.* at 163. Nkurumah said:

> I can see no security for African States unless leaders like ourselves have realized beyond all doubts that salvation for Africa lies in unity. If we are to remain free, if we are to enjoy the benefits of Africa's enormous wealth, we must unite to plan the exploitation of our human and material resources in the interest of all our people.

See also Organization for African Unity (OAU), *Lagos Plan of Action for Economic Development of Africa 1980–2000* (Addis Ababa: OAU, 1980) (affirming the commitment by African leaders to ensure the economic, social and cultural integration of the continent under the African Economic Community by the year 2000).

132 See J.K. Nyerere, *Ujamaa-Essays on Socialism* (Oxford University Press, 1968). Nkurumah is said to have told a meeting in Addis Ababa that 'we shall be haggling and wrangling among ourselves until we are colonized again and become the tools of a far greater colonialism than we suffered hitherto'. T.M. Franck, *East African Unity Through Law*

political system within which Africa could address the challenges of its development and confront the control that its former colonizers exercised upon it.[133] Today, Muammar Gaddafi continues to subscribe to this model of immediate African political unity.[134]

By contrast, another group of pan-Africanists – who would today be referred to as the gradualists or incrementalists[135] – subscribed to having a consociational design, or loose federation, beginning with 'the regions of Africa which have developed a historical affinity [beginning] to lay the foundations for a wider unity'.[136] Today the incrementalists have the upper hand. They subscribe to economic and eventually political unity over time, although there is no consensus yet on the time frame or on the precise modalities for proceeding towards such a goal.[137]

(Yale University Press, 1964), 3, citing D. Apter, *The Political Kingdom of Uganda* (Princeton University Press, 1961), 7.

133 This model was referred to as the mobilization model. See *ibid.* at 4–7 (using the mobilization metaphor). See also Franck, *East African Unity*, at 3, citing B. Boutros-Ghali, 'The Addis Ababa Charter', *International Conciliation* 546 (1964) 19.

134 Gaddafi's proposal for a United States of Africa resulted in a Committee of Heads of State and Government on the Proposals of the Great Socialist Peoples' Libyan Arab Jamahiriya chaired by President Yoweri Museveni of Uganda. The Committee issued a report entitled 'Report of the Committee of Heads of State and Government on the Proposals of the Great Socialist Peoples' Libyan Arab Jamahiriya' dated 13 June 2005, available at www.africa-union.org/Doc/Report_of_the_Committee_of_Heads_of_State_and_Government_on_the_Proposals_of_Libya.doc. The African Union's 50th anniversary meeting in 2007 held in Accra, Ghana, was devoted to discussing the report of the Committee.

135 In their final decision, the Heads of State at the African Union Meeting in Ghana on the discussion on the 'Grand Debate on the Union Government', only agreed to accelerate Africa's economic and political unity and to further study the proposals of the Union Government Proposal. See Accra Declaration of the African Union Summit Meeting (3 July 2007), available at http://ausummit-accra.org.gh/index1.php?linkid=242&page=2&sectionid=303.

136 Franck, *East African Unity*, at 3. The Report of the Committee of Heads of State and Government on the Proposals of the Great Socialist Peoples' Libyan Arab Jamahiriya did not embrace the idea of an immediate political union, but instead reiterated the 'need to work towards the *ultimate* formation of Union Government in Africa [and] encouraged those parts of Africa that are able to form political federations to do so'. African Union, 'Report of the Committee of Heads of State and Government on the Proposals of the Great Socialist Peoples' Libyan Arab Jamahiriya', at para. 12 (presented at the AU-CSO Pre-Summit Meeting in Accra, Ghana).

137 See Nigerian President, Olusegun Obasanjo, 'Study on An African Union Government: Towards the United States of Africa', Presented to the Seventh Session of the Assembly of the Heads of States of the African Union in Banjul (July 2006), available at www.africa-union.org/Doc/study_on_AUGovernment_june2006.pdf.

This looser idea of a federation with regional building blocks is the one adopted in the Treaty for the Establishment of an African Economic Community.[138] Both the loose federation and political union ideas share a commitment to self-sufficiency as embodied in initiatives such as the New International Economic Order of the 1970s.[139] This theme was also reflected in the Lagos Plan of Action, which linked self-sufficiency to Africa's economic integration.[140] As Thomas Biersteker has explained, economic self-reliance or disengagement:

> is not a call for complete autarky or absolute national self-sufficiency. Rather, disengagement is a call for a partial reduction in the magnitude of international economic transactions with industrial countries and for the attainment of self-sufficiency only in particular sectors of activities.[141]

This means reducing dependence on foreign investment and economic assistance, as well as combining extremely limited individual markets and their scarce resources with a view to being better able to bargain for foreign capital and technology.[142] Most recently, this theme of economic self-reliance has been embraced by African leaders like Muammar Gaddafi, who has asked African leaders not to beg for aid from the West.[143] Another proponent of African self-sufficiency is Robert Mugabe of Zimbabwe, who has recently urged COMESA members to pay into its development fund as a way of cutting dependence on foreign assistance.[144] Notably,

138 See Treaty for the Establishment of an African Economic Community.

139 Asante *et al.*, *African Economic Community*, at 1–2; see also Gathii, *War, Commerce and International Law*, Ch. 5.

140 Organization of African Unity, 'Lagos Plan of Action for the Economic Development of Africa 1980–2000'. This plan was adopted at the OAU Meeting in its Second Extraordinary Session, Preamble, para. 3(iii), 28–9 April 1980 (stating 'We commit ourselves individually and collectively, on behalf of our governments and peoples, to establish national, sub-regional and regional institutions which will facilitate the attainment of objectives of self-reliance and self-sustainment'); see also K. Mengisteab, *Globalization and Autocentricity in Africa's Development in the 21st Century* (Trenton, NJ: Africa World Press, 1996), 172.

141 T.J. Biersteker, 'Self-Reliance in Theory and Practice in Tanzanian Trade Relations', *International Organizations* 34 (1980) 229, 231.

142 Green and Seidman, *Unity of Poverty*, at 80–1 (also arguing that 'the continental market is broad enough to absorb the products of planned industrial and agricultural growth. But as long as the individual states of Africa attempt to "go it alone," few if any, will achieve the real economic independence and higher living standards to which all Africans aspire').

143 P. de Bendern, 'Gaddafi Urges Self-Reliance at Africa Summit', Reuters, 4 July 2005, available at www.int.iol.co.za/index.php?set_id=1&click_id=68&art_id=qw1120478401298B261.

144 See M. Dzirutwe, 'Mugabe Calls For Self-Reliance, End to Conflicts', Reuters, 7 June 2009, available at http://in.reuters.com/article/businessNews/idINIndia-40138720090607.

these supporters of economic integration were all influenced by Africa's struggles against colonialism, imperialism and apartheid.[145]

While the theme of economic self-determination still has its cache of support, the African Union's New Partnership for Africa's Development (NEPAD) shows a commitment towards market-friendly development approaches, particularly with the goal of obtaining foreign funding to finance Africa's development needs.[146] Thabo Mbeki, the former South African president, has represented this dual theme of self-sufficiency and the necessity of foreign funding in his own call for an African renaissance and his support of NEPAD.[147] NEPAD aims to generate both internal and external resources for development. According to Mbeki, Africa's regeneration depends on its ability 'to generate internal resources' for its development.[148] From the resources generated from within Africa, a Pan-African Infrastructure Development Fund (PAIDF) has been set up to 'finance large-scale infrastructural projects'.[149] A fund manager has been appointed and by October 2007 had raised $625 million to finance energy, technology, transport and water projects in Africa.[150]

NEPAD's capital flows initiative is slated to be primarily funded by western donors who condition access to their funds to the adoption of market-based policies.[151] Alongside this commitment to market-based policies within NEPAD, the African Group at the 2003 Cancun World Trade Organization (WTO) Ministerial Meeting played a crucial role in the formation of the 'Group of Twenty'.[152] The group lobbied heavily in

145 Z. Cervenka, *The Unfinished Quest for Unity: Africa and the OAU* (London: Julian Friedmann, 1977) (noting the similarity in goals among various groups of African states 'in the fundamental aims . . . particularly those concerning decolonization, racial discrimination, maintenance of world peace, and the urgent need for economic cooperation between African States', at 1).

146 See J. Gathii, 'A Critical Appraisal of the NEPAD Agenda in Light of Africa's Place in the World Trade Regime in an Era of Market Centered Development', *Transnational Law and Contemporary Problems* 13 (2003) 179 (providing information on NEPAD's origins, background and analysis).

147 President Thabo Mbeki, 'Address of the President of South Africa to the Joint Session of the Parliament of Nambia' (30 October 2007), available at www.polity.org.za/article/sa-mbeki-parliament-of-namibia-joint-session-30102007–2007–10–30.

148 *Ibid.* 149 *Ibid.*

150 For more information, see the PAIDF fund manager website at www.harith.co.za/investors/ index.html.

151 African Union, 'The New Partnership for African Development', para. 147 (October 2001), available at www.nepad.org/home/lang/en (follow the NEPAD Framework link).

152 F. Jawara and A. Kwa, *Behind the Scenes at the WTO: The Real World of Trade Negotiations: The Lessons of Cancun XV* (London: Zed Books, 2004); see also J. Gathii, 'The High Stakes of WTO Reform', *Michigan Law Review* 104 (2006) 1361, 1366.

favour of ensuring that development remained at the centre of the latest round of the WTO's trade negotiations.[153]

While the theme of self-sufficiency has been a strong one, political differences between neighbouring countries, as well as the unwillingness of better off countries to sacrifice national economic gains for the sake of regional cooperation, have hindered the success of the movement towards self-sufficiency.[154] The move towards self-sufficiency has also been delayed because many African countries are competing with each other as potential locations for industrialized country firms, or as suppliers of raw materials to developed economies or to the quickly growing economies of India and China.[155] Often the competition for industrialized country firms may be regarded as outweighing regional integration, particularly if the choice is presented as one that might involve giving up the prospects, real or perceived, of foreign investors who will manufacture for export.[156] Such a choice would certainly look brighter than regional cooperation, especially if such cooperation would involve the sharing of benefits with weaker Member States.[157] A large number of African countries have passed legislation giving foreign investors very attractive incentives in this race for their capital, skills and technology.[158]

Thus, within the African Union, and particularly in so far as regional economic integration is concerned, one sees a commitment to a number of varied approaches. There is the continuing theme of economic self-reliance, but there is also the recognition of the importance of foreign funding embraced within NEPAD, as well as the continuing efforts to realize more favourable trading relationships with the rest of the world within the WTO.[159] This multifaceted approach was best captured in the

153 Jawara and Kwa, *Behind the Scenes*, at xix.

154 Ravenhill, 'Theory and Practice of Regional Integration', at 37.

155 *Ibid.* See also Jian-Ye Wang, 'What Drives China's Growing Role in Africa?' (IMF Working Paper No. 07/211, 2007), 23.

156 *Ibid.*, at 5.

157 Ravenhill, 'Theory and Practice of Regional Integration', at 49.

158 For example, the 1991 Investment Code in Uganda set up the Uganda Investment Authority, whose primary purpose is to promote foreign investment in Uganda, see e.g., www.ugandainvest.com/uia.php?uhpl=mission&&uhpl1=Mission,Vision,Role; in Rwanda, Law No. 14/98 of 18/12/1998 established the Rwanda Investment Promotion Agency with the mandate of promoting foreign investment in the country, see e.g., www.gov.rw/economy/rwanda_investment_promotion_agency.htm.

159 See J. O. Adésínà, Y. Graham and A. Olukoshi (eds), *Africa and Development Challenges in the New Millennium: the NEPAD Debate* (London: Zed Books, 2006).

first Africa Forum for Dialogue organized by the African Union in Geneva by the Director General of the United Nations Industrial Development Organization, who declared that the challenges facing Africa had to be met by Africans and that while Africa 'can blame colonialism for the past 350 years' it cannot do so for the next fifty.[160] Echoing the same view, Jean Ping, the African Commission's chairperson, noted that, while Africa has unequal economic relations with the rest of the world, this did not mean that Africa did not need the rest of the world or that it could dispense with the need to open up.[161]

A common theme that cuts across the range of responses to Africa's economic challenges is the consensus on strengthening regional economic cooperation. As a result, the Accra Declaration, arising from the African Union's 50th Anniversary Meeting in 2007,[162] resolved to review and shorten the time frame towards the establishment of an African economic community and to use the regional economic communities to achieve these objectives.[163]

In the next chapter, I will examine another feature of flexibility in African RTAs, the commitment to variable geometry.

160 A. Sander, Africa: 'Africa Should Seize Control of Its Development', 29 May 2009, available at http://allafrica.com/stories/200905290267.html.

161 *Ibid.*

162 The meeting was timed to coincide with Ghana's 50th anniversary of independence. Ghana was the first African country to be freed from colonial rule. See Opening Statement by Nana Akufo-Addo, Minister for Foreign Affairs of the Republic of Ghana and Chairperson of the Executive Council of the African Union, at the 11th Ordinary Session of the Executive Council on 28–9 June 2007, available at www.africa-union.org/root/au/conferences/2007/june/summit/9thAUSummit.htm.

163 See Accra Declaration of the African Union Summit Meeting (3 July 2007), available at http://ausummit-accra.org.gh/index1.php?linkid=242&page=2&sectionid=303. The Declaration memorialized the intent of the parties 'to accelerate the economic and political integration of the African continent'. *Ibid.* para. 1. The parties also agreed:

> to rationalize and strengthen the Regional Economic Communities, and harmonize their activities, in conformity with our earlier decision, so as to lead to the creation of an African common market, through the stages set in the Treaty Establishing the African Economic Community (Abuja Treaty), with a reviewed and shorter timeframe to be agreed upon in order to accelerate the economic and where possible, political integration.

Ibid. para. 2(a).

II

Variable geometry: A defining aspect of African RTAs

> The strategy of promoting trade liberalization . . . without concomitantly phased positive policies promises to be a recipe for stagnation.[1]

> If the economic characteristics of the countries of Africa are examined in the light of these various criteria for a beneficial customs union, it would appear that the formation of customs unions in Africa was irrelevant, if not positively harmful.[2]

> [N]on-trade equilibrating mechanisms . . . must be built into multinational economic cooperation schemes; if the regional development process is left to liberalization and to market forces alone, these schemes are bound to fail.[3]

A Introduction

This chapter discusses the principle of variable geometry as adopted in African Regional Trade Agreements (RTAs). The aim of this section of the chapter is to show how variable geometry is a central feature of

1 P. Robson, *Integration, Development, and Equity: Economic Integration in West Africa* (London: Unwin Hyman, 1968), 123.

2 A. Hazlewood, 'Problems of Integration Among African States', in A. Hazlewood (ed.), *African Integration and Disintegration* (Oxford University Press, 1967), 6.

3 M.S. Wionczek, 'Introduction – Present Status and Prospects of Economic Integration Movements in Developing Countries: Political Atomization and Economic Backwardness of the Southern Hemisphere', in M.S. Wionczek, *Economic Cooperation in Latin America, Africa and Asia* (Cambridge, MA: MIT Press, 1969), 15. Wionczek notes that arrangements to ensure equitable sharing of regionalization benefits include:

> a regional development bank; a regional mechanism for financial settlements and for monetary policy coordination; a regime harmonizing incentives for regional and external private investment; an instrument for the promotion of industrial specialization by agreement; and a formula for the equitable distribution of customs revenues and other taxes, with due account being taken of the development needs of the most backward participants.

Ibid. at 16.

African RTAs as flexible regimes. The chapter begins by outlining the origins of this principle and giving examples of how various African RTAs incorporate and use it. The last section then discusses the April 2009 Advisory Opinion of the East African Court of Justice (EACJ) on the appropriate relationship between the principle of variable geometry and the rule of consensus decision making in the Treaty for the Establishment of the East African Community.

Although variable geometry is a central feature of African RTAs, this has largely been overlooked, particularly in the legal literature on RTAs. In the African context, variable geometry refers to rules, principles and policies adopted in trade integration treaties that give Member States, particularly the poorest members: (i) policy flexibility and autonomy to pursue at slower paces timetabled trade commitments and harmonization objectives; (ii) mechanisms to minimize distributional losses by creating opportunities such as compensation for losses arising from implementation of region-wide liberalization commitments and policies aimed at the equitable distribution of the institutions and organizations of regional integration to avoid concentration in any one member; and (iii) preferences in industrial allocation among members in an RTA and preferences in the allocation of credit and investments from regional banks.

Variable geometry therefore limits more ambitious trade liberalization goals, since it is designed to accommodate less well-off or unwilling members of an RTA that are concerned about the economic and political costs of liberalization for themselves in the short run. From this perspective, it is arguable that African RTAs undercut the more stringent multilateral (GATT/WTO) liberalization commitments that their members have assumed. In fact, African RTAs do not systematically adopt the unconditional most favoured nation treatment.[4] Where this principle or other non-discrimination principles are adopted, they have rarely, if ever, been used to challenge adoption of discriminatory trade measures.[5] This is most acutely demonstrated in the East African Court of Justice's recent

4 See Y. Yang, 'Africa in the Doha Round: Dealing with Preference Erosion and Beyond' (IMF Policy Discussion Paper No. 05/8, 2005).

5 For example, Art. 43 of the Treaty for the Establishment of ECOWAS provides for the most-favoured-nation treatment in the following terms:

> (1) Member States shall accord to one another in relation to trade between them the most favored nation treatment. In no case shall tariff concessions granted to a third country by a Member State be more favourable than those applicable under this Treaty.

decision on variable geometry.[6] In this advisory opinion that the Council of Ministers of the East African Community sought from the Court, the Council framed the issue not as one of squaring the principle of variable geometry with that of non-discrimination under the Treaty for the Establishment of the East African Community (EAC), but as a question of reconciling the principle of variable geometry and that of consensus decision making.[7]

B Reasons for the adoption of variable geometry

One of the greatest impediments to regional integration schemes in Africa has been the question of unequal benefits that accrue from integration

(2) Any Agreement between a Member State and a third country under which tariff concessions are granted, shall not derogate from the obligation of that Member State under this Treaty.
(3) Copies of such agreements referred to in paragraph 2 of this Article shall be transmitted by the Member States which are parties to them, to the Executive of the Secretariat of the Community.

Treaty of ECOWAS (signed 28 May 1975), available at www.comm.ecowas.int/sec/index.php?id=treaty&lang=en. This provision not only establishes the classic most favoured nation (MFN) treatment within ECOWAS, but it also prohibits member countries from giving third countries more favourable treatment than that made available to the Economic Community of West African States (ECOWAS) member countries. It further obliges Member States to report any agreements in which tariff concessions are made to third countries to the Executive of the Community Secretariat. Notably, the provision 'in no case shall tariff concessions granted to a third country by a Member State be more favourable than those applicable under this Treaty' of Art. 43(1) of the ECOWAS Treaty does not definitively establish the type of unconditional MFN obligation in Art. 1 of the GATT 1948. This Article obliges members of the WTO to extend on an unconditional and immediate basis 'any advantage, favor, privilege or immunity . . . to any product originating in or destined for any other country . . . to the like product originating in or destined for the territories of all other contracting parties'. See General Agreement on Tariffs and Trade (GATT) 1948, 30 Oct. 1947, Art. 1, available at www.wto.org/english/docs_e/legal_e/gatt47_e.pdf. Article 35 of the Treaty Establishing the Economic Community of Central African States (ECCAS) establishes the MFN norm in exactly the same terms as Art. 43 of the Treaty for the Establishment of ECOWAS. See Treaty Establishing the Economic Community of Central African States (adopted 18 Oct. 1983, entered into force 1985), available at www.chr.up.ac.za/undp/subregional/docs/eccas1.pdf. However, the ECCAS Treaty has a fourth sub-paragraph not present in the ECOWAS Treaty. Article 35(4) of the ECCAS Treaty provides: 'No member shall conclude with any third country an agreement whereby the latter would grant such Member State tariff concessions not granted to the other Member States.'

6 See *In the Matter of a Request by the Council of Ministers of the East African Community for an Advisory Opinion, App. No. 1 of 2008, Opinion* (E. Afr. Ct. of Justice at Arusha, 1st inst. Div. 24 April 2008).

7 See *infra* Chapter III.

that is primarily focused on trade liberalization.[8] Distributional equity in African RTAs is not only a question of the asymmetrical economic benefits of trade integration, but also a function of unequal 'networks of power, information and knowledge'[9] between African economies. Compensating countries that suffer losses from liberalization commitments has long been identified as one of the 'most serious difficulties' encountered in the integration process.[10] This is reflected in the technological and economic dominance of countries like Kenya in East Africa, Nigeria in West Africa and South Africa in the Southern African region.[11]

8 O.S. Saasa, 'Economic Cooperation and Integration Among Developing Countries', in O. Saasa (ed.), *Joining the Future: Economic Integration and Co-operation in Africa* (Nairobi: African Centre for Technology Studies Press, 1991), 14. Saasa notes that the 'management of distributional questions has . . . remained a difficult task in most, if not all, integration schemes in developing countries'. *Ibid.* at 15. See also U. Ezenwe, *ECOWAS and the Economic Integration of West Africa* (London: Palgrave Macmillan, 1983), 58–65, 151 (declaring 'ECOWAS represents another glaring case of a partnership of unequal partners'); UN Conference on Trade and Development, 'Current Problems of Economic Integration: The Distribution of Benefits and Costs of Integration Among Countries', UN Doc. No. TD/B/394 (New York: UN, 1973). For the case of Latin America, see M. Edel, 'Regional Integration and Income Distribution: Complements or Substitutes?', in R. Hilton (ed.), *The Movement Toward Latin American Unity* (New York: F.A. Praeger, 1969), 185. Edel notes that:

> It is felt, for example, that capital, which is normally mobile across borders, will be drawn to the region in which wages are lowest, thus helping to reduce the difference [between rich and poor countries]. However, these effects are no more certain . . . There seem, over long periods in a country or region's development, to be strong tendencies for industry to concentrate in the already most industrialized locations. These effects, often described in terms of 'polarization', 'dominance', or 'backwash' effects, have not been fully explored in theory, but they seem to have a basis in economies of scale in infrastructure, external economies in the labor market and elsewhere, and mutual support of market demand created in advanced sub-regions, when trade throughout the region even free of tariffs is subject to transport costs.

Ibid. at 189.

9 Saasa, 'Economic Cooperation and Integration', at 2.

10 A. Philip, 'Preface' to F. Kahnert *et al.*, *Economic Integration Among Developing Countries* (Paris: OECD Development Centre, 1969), 9. Philip notes that:

> the aim of preventing a widening gap between participating countries . . . [make it] essential that financial compensation should be given to the weaker members. But in any association of poor countries, this compensation cannot be provided without external help. In a situation where international aid is stagnating, if not declining every country considering participating in an attempt at regional integration will be convinced that the aid granted to the integrated group will turn out to be less than the sum of the aid previously granted to the same countries individually.

Ibid. at 10.

11 S. Rugumamu, 'Africa's Search for Regional Cooperation and Integration in the Twenty-First Century', African Foundation for Capacity Building Paper No. 3 of 2004,

Differences in the benefits of cooperation in Africa date back to the colonial period.[12] The EAC, whose origins date back to 1917,[13] had a long history of disputes about Kenya's disproportionate benefits relative to (then) Tanganyika and Uganda.[14] Kenya not only had a bigger

at 12, available at www.acbf-pact.org/knowledge/documents/ACBF%20WORKING%20PAPER%20NO.%203.pdf.

12 See T.M. Franck, *East African Unity Through Law* (Yale University Press, 1964), 28–54 (explaining how white settlers pursued the East Africa Federation during the colonial period with opposition from Africans, culminating in a Hilton Young Commission and hearings in London in 1931 before a Joint Parliamentary Committee at which African representatives protested against federation in East Africa). See also, A. Hazlewood, 'The Economics of Federation and Dissolution in Central Africa', in A. Hazlewood (ed.), *African Integration and Disintegration* (Oxford University Press, 1967), 248, 249 (noting that the removal of all trade restrictions between Northern Rhodesia, Southern Rhodesia and Nyasaland, together with the development of a common tariff, resulted in disadvantaging Nyasaland and Northern Rhodesia and for Nyasaland's case, 'fiscal transfers failed to compensate for the adverse effects of the customs union'). This problem has arisen in a variety of developing country regional arrangements as well. For example, Art. 39 (Promotion of Industrial Development in Less Developed Territories) of the 1965 Caribbean Free Trade Association Agreement (Text Consolidating the Provisions of the Principal Agreement and the Supplementary Agreement) allowed the less developed territory upon application to suspend area tariff treatment of imports 'in order to promote the development of an industry in any of those Territories'. See Wionczek, 'Economic Integration Movements', at 150.

13 A. Hazlewood, *Economic Integration: The East African Experience* (New York: St. Martin's Press, 1975), 22–3. Hazlewood notes that the features of the East African Customs Union completed in 1927 included:

> an external tariff common to the three territories, but enacted separately in each territory; a single collection of import duty at the point of entry into East Africa and subsequent free movement of imported goods within East Africa; the allocation of customs revenue between the territories on the basis of 'derivation', that is according to the territory of ultimate destination, the allocation being based on information from the Transfer forms which were returned to the customs administration when goods were moved between the territories; free trade between the territories in products of East African origin and from 1949 a common customs administration. In addition, there was free movement of capital and substantially free movement of labour. The economic unity of the area was supported, and transactions with the area fostered by a common currency and the common administration of transport and communications and other 'infra-structure'.

14 *Ibid.* at 21. Hazlewood also notes that, for example, 'in 1922, the East African customs union consciously embarked on the protective policy it continued to pursue, and which according to persistent claims by Tanganyika and Uganda has been primarily protective of Kenyan interests'; that 'from 1957 . . . it came to be felt more and more strongly in Tanganyika and Uganda that the customs union was designed for the benefit of Kenya'; and that 'by the 1950s it was widely appreciated that if the integration arrangements were to survive, their benefits would have to be spread more evenly'. *Ibid.* at 25–6. For a

share of the employees of the various institutions of the community, most of which were located in Kenya, but also the largest share of customs revenue.[15] Mechanisms to redistribute the gains were put in place from time to time.[16] For example, in 1961 the Raisman Commission proposed fiscal distributions to compensate for losses suffered particularly by Tanganyika, but also for the purpose of keeping the customs union together.[17] Article 87 of the 1967 Treaty for East African Co-operation sought to end the unequal distribution of the organs of the Community which were concentrated in Kenya. Article 87 provided that Arusha would become the headquarters of the Community and its Tribunal; the East African Community Bank as well as the East African Posts and Telecommunications Corporation would be headquartered in Kampala, Uganda; and that Dar-es-Salaam, Tanzania would be the headquarters of the East African Harbours Corporation, while Nairobi would be the headquarters of the East African Railways Corporation and the East African Airways Corporation.[18] In the Union Douanière et Economique de l'Afrique Centrale (UDEAC) established in 1964 among Cameroon, Central African Republic, Chad, Congo Brazzaville and Gabon, a Solidarity Fund to apportion revenue among the members as a method of compensating for the differences in revenue accrued from UDEAC integration.[19]

In addition, distributional questions may arise because regional co-operation pursued 'solely on the basis of commercial integration' often results in an increase in the 'bargaining power of transnational corporations', which then bargain with each government for the best conditions

commentary on Hazlewood's assessment of protective tariffs, see R.N. Wood, 'The East African Common Market: A Reassessment', *Oxford University Bulletin of Economics and Statistics*, 28(3) (Nov. 1966); see also A.J. Brown, 'Economic Separation Versus a Common Market in Developing Countries', *Yorkshire Bulletin of Economics and Social Research* (May 1961, 33–40; and Nov. 1961, 80–96).

15 Hazlewood, *Economic Integration*, at 21–6, 38–45 (pointing out that 'The staffing of the Organization was, in fact, a cause of contention between the countries. There were complaints that an inordinate proportion of EACSO officials were Kenyans. One reason was that the headquarters of the Organization were in Kenya, as were most of the other departments and institutions. It was said to be easier to recruit Kenyans for this reason, and also because the supply of suitable candidates for the appointments at that time was much greater from Kenya than from the other two countries', *ibid.* at 38).

16 *Ibid.* at 39–45. 17 *Ibid.* at 43.

18 Treaty for East African Co-operation, Art. 87, Kenya–Uganda–Tanzania, 6 June 1967, 6 ILM 932.

19 See P. Robson, 'Economic Integration in Equatorial Africa', in Hazlewood (ed.), *African Integration and Disintegration*, 36–41.

they can obtain.[20] Regional integration in developing countries results in the merger of locally controlled firms. For example, in the European Union, competition policy has encouraged mergers of such firms.[21] By contrast, African regional integration has not encouraged such mergers and this often results in local subsidiaries of foreign firms enjoying the protection of both regional and national tariff walls.[22] From this view, unequal gains in trade integration schemes arise where integration is solely based on a classical free market/comparative advantage model.[23] Besides unequal national gains, integration based on a classical free trade/comparative advantage model does not necessarily create new opportunities that induce a greater number of people to enjoy the benefits of growth in poor economies that largely share the same characteristics.[24] The adoption of such a model without adapting it to the African context of huge disparities in the export and economic power among the countries is one of the reasons for the failure and ultimate disbandment of the original EAC in 1977.[25] At the time, Kenya's unequal gains, relative to both Uganda and Tanzania, accentuated the conflicts among the three countries. Notably, in 1964, Kenya declined to formally ratify the Kampala Agreement that embodied 'corrective measures' that would have arrested the 'growing inequalities' among EAC members.[26]

Often distributional questions are exacerbated by regional insecurity, including civil and other wars as well as a time horizon problem – gains from integration arise from gains in dynamic efficiency that take time to materialize. Politicians, by contrast, focus on short-term gains and losses, yet trade integration schemes take time for demonstrable benefits to be visible.[27] This makes the utilization of methods of compensating countries that may lose revenues and other benefits from trade liberalization

20 C.V. Vaitsos, 'Crisis in Regional Economic Cooperation (Integration) Among Developing Countries: A Survey', *World Development* 6 (1978) 729–36 and generally C.V. Vaitsos, 'The Role of Transnational Enterprises in Latin American Economic Integration Efforts: Who Integrates With Whom, How and for Whose Benefit?', UNCTAD/ST/ECDC/19 (New York: UN, 1978) (analysing transnational enterprises and their effects on economic integration).

21 Vaitsos, 'Crisis in Regional Economic Cooperation', at 730.

22 *Ibid.* at 730–6. 23 *Ibid.* at 739. 24 *Ibid.*

25 Saasa, 'Economic Cooperation and Integration', at 14.

26 *Ibid.* See also Hazlewood, *Economic Integration*, at 57–68 (discussing Kenya's decision not to ratify the Kampala Agreement, even though the Kenyan President signed it in a meeting with the other Heads of State in January 1965). Kenya had signed the agreement subject to there being a common currency board in East Africa which Tanzania later reneged on, and as a result decided not to ratify the Kampala Agreement. *Ibid.* at 67.

27 Saasa, 'Economic Cooperation and Integration', at 14.

attractive to assuage groups that lose out. There is a rough analogy here with developed economies, like the United States, that establish trade adjustment assistance programmes for industries and workers that suffer from production or sale losses pursuant to international trade liberalization commitments.[28]

C Variable geometry as a solution of adjusting the costs and benefits of integration

To address this problem, African RTAs have come up with mechanisms to adjust the benefits and burdens of trade adjustment among themselves.[29] Some of these mechanisms of moderating and containing unequal benefits have been borrowed from other developing country RTAs.[30] Over time they have included non-financial and financial redistributive policies. The discussion below illustrates the example of how the Southern African Customs Union (SACU) engages in financial redistribution through its development account. Non-financial redistributive policies have included the allocation of key industries to disadvantaged countries as a way of countering the tendency of investors to 'gravitate towards the already developed member countries'.[31] In the Andean Pact, the following mechanisms were used:

(1) a relatively longer period to adjust to import competition;
(2) longer time given to them to harmonize their national tariffs with the common external tariff;

28 The Trade Act of 1974, as amended, establishes Trade Adjustment Assistance which authorizes the president to provide relief to workers, farmers, communities and fishermen seriously injured or threatened with serious injury due to surges of imports: 19 USC s. 2251 *et seq.* (2006). See also 19 USC s. 2102 (2006) (stating the purpose of the Act); the Trade Act of 2002, 19 USC s. 3802(c)(5) (2006) (requiring that the president report to Congress the impact of future trade agreements on US employment, including labour markets, and that the report be made public). The Trade Act of 1974, in establishing Trade Adjustment Assistance, also authorizes the president to provide relief to workers adversely affected by the reduction in production or sales which results from international competition arising from a free trade agreement. See 19 USC s. 2272 (2006) (listing group eligibility requirements).

29 This is somewhat analogous to the Trade Adjustment Assistance Program in the United States except that the assistance is targeted to industries and individuals who lose out because of trade liberalization, while in the African context the assistance is to the countries that lose out. See 19 USC s. 2101 *et seq.* (2006).

30 African RTAs have borrowed from the Andean Community, formerly the Andean Pact, many of the variable geometry ideas such as those listed in *infra* nn. 32–72.

31 Saasa, 'Economic Cooperation and Integration', at 17.

(3) preference for foreign direct investment in the least developed economies under Decision 24; and
(4) preferential treatment for the least developed states from the Andean Development Corporation in terms of loans disbursements.[32]

Other mechanisms include having harmonized industrial and investment policies to make sure that members of an RTA get 'a fair share in the distribution of integration-induced projects and their benefits',[33] advancing generous access to development funding and credit to less developed countries, as well as designing tax concessions for them.[34]

In the original EAC, five arrangements were agreed upon in 1965 to address the imbalances in inter-territorial trade:

- shifting the 'territorial administration of production by a number of firms which operated in two or more of the countries';
- instituting 'quotas on inter-territorial trade';
- allocating 'certain major industries between the countries';
- increasing 'sales from a country in deficit in inter-territorial trade'; and
- making 'allocations of industry to secure an equitable distribution of industrial development between the three countries'.[35]

The creation of these mechanisms to equalize the benefits of customs cooperation in terms of development and revenue in the mid-1960s indicates beyond any doubt how central the equal sharing of benefits of development (in terms of the location of factories, industries etc) and trade imbalances were considered crucial in relations between more and less developed integrating members. The introduction of measures such as quotas and the equitable allocation of industries, while important in rebalancing the inequities, undermined the primary purpose of integration under a market-based model of free competition among the most efficient producers. The EAC Treaty of 1967 continued a variety

32 *Ibid.* at 26 n. 9. In addition, such countries can receive 'complementary support . . . , market studies, technical and managerial assistance etc.' *Ibid.* at 17. For more on similar proposals, see Ezenwe, *ECOWAS and the Economic Integration*, at 20–8 (discussing the following instruments of achieving equity: fiscal compensation; fiscal incentives to influence the emergent location of industry; regional industrial policy and planned industrial specialization and planning models). Other similar positive measures designed to help poorer countries in a regional integration scheme might include permitting them to 'operate less restrictive rules of origin . . . [and] to enter into transitional bilateral agreements involving balanced trade expansion'. See P. Robson, *Integration, Development, and Equity: Economic Integration in West Africa* (London: Unwin Hyman, 1968), 121–2.

33 Ezenwe, *ECOWAS and the Economic Integration*, at 56.

34 *Ibid.* at 55–6.

35 Hazlewood, *Economic Integration*, at 57.

of these arrangements, though it primarily adopted market mechanisms for achieving integration.[36] For example, it established an East African Bank with a view to investing 'more of its funds in each of the two less-developed partner states than in Kenya', although each state contributed the same amount to its equity.[37] Here, the financing of development projects through a bank, rather than through the previous system of industrial planning and licensing in East Africa, eventually collapsed in 1973.[38] The preference of a bank as opposed to industrial planning and licensing indicated some movement towards market-based integration initiatives even in this area of equalizing the benefits of integration among the members.

Even though the 1967 Treaty Establishing the EAC did away with some of Kenya's dissatisfaction with bearing an unequal burden within the Community, it nevertheless failed to effectively deal with the issue, and this was a primary factor leading to its dissolution in 1977.[39] This pointed to the double-edged sword of efforts to equalize opportunities for countries at different levels of development. As pointed out more than three decades ago:

> Fiscal transfers from more fortunate to less prosperous members of a regional scheme are in themselves an insufficient solution to the distribution problem. Such transfers may amount to little more than the customs revenue foregone as a result of the exclusion of extra-regional imports,

36 *Ibid.* at 168 (noting that the 1967 Treaty of the EAC 'established a market regulator, the transfer tax being the main device for influencing market forces in the desired direction', instead of the industrial licensing that pre-existed it). In addition, under the Treaty, trade and development were to take place under market conditions rather than state planning or industrial licensing 'as influenced by a common system of fiscal incentives and by the activities of the East African Development Bank'. *Ibid.* at 129. But see J. Ravenhill, 'The Theory and Practice of Regional Integration in East Africa', in C. Potholm and R. Fredland (eds), *Integration and Disintegration in East Africa* (Lanham: University Press of America, 1980), 44 (noting that '[t]he principal regulatory device introduced by the Treaty – the transfer tax system – would seem a somewhat perverse method of attempting to equalize the benefits from regional co-operation for, in promoting this objective, the principle of the free movement of goods within the region was breached by the imposition of intra-community tariffs').

37 Hazlewood, *Economic Integration*, at 104. Kenya also contributed 'about half of the total revenue of the General Fund . . . and this fact has led to some feeling that Kenya subsidizes the other partner states through the General Fund Services'. *Ibid.* at 92–3.

38 *Ibid.* at 119–23.

39 Ravenhill, 'Theory and Practice', at 42. Ravenhill also notes that even 'if the Treaty had provided an effective long-term answer to the distribution problem, it would still have to be judged a failure since its inability to furnish means for an immediate amelioration of the problem was the cause of its inconsequential impact on partner states' perceptions.' *Ibid.* at 43.

> and are an inadequate substitute for the employment opportunities and such spinoffs as improved local skills, technology and infrastructure – not to forget prestige – which is brought by industrial development. Manipulation of rates of taxation to encourage substitution of local production for imports from more developed states within a region has the effect – regardless of whether this was the intention – of encouraging the duplication of inefficient plants within a region. Frequently the primary beneficiary of such policies are multinational corporations, able to establish an uneconomic plant which is protected from competition from within the region by the tax system, and from extra-regional rivals by the external tariff. One of the principal justifications for the creation of customs unions – the realization of the economies of scale in producing for a larger market – is also undermined.[40]

Notwithstanding the questionable efficacy of efforts to equalize gains, today, almost without exception the treaties establishing these regional trade agreements provide for ways of dealing with unequal gains. For example, Article 21 of the ECOWAS Treaty establishes a 'Fund for Co-operation, Compensation and Development of the Community', while Article 48 provides for a mechanism to compensate a Member State for loss of import duties suffered as a result of the liberalization of trade commitments contained in Chapter VII of the ECOWAS treaty.[41] This is anticipated by Article 4 of the Treaty, which specifies ECOWAS's fundamental principles.[42] These include the 'equitable and just distribution of the costs and benefits of economic cooperation and integration'.[43] Peter Robson argued that the Fund is of 'potentially great importance for promoting positive integration, development and balance'.[44]

40 *Ibid.* at 47–8. See also Hazlewood, 'Problems of Integration', at 6. Hazlewood also argues that the trouble with compensatory mechanisms is 'that they deprive the country offering them of revenue. The less-developed members of the union could ill afford this loss of revenue, particularly as their concessions might have to be very great if their disadvantages for industry were to be significantly reduced'. *Ibid.* at 18.

41 Revised Treaty of the Economic Community of West African States (ECOWAS) (24 July 1993), 35 ILM 660, Arts. 21, 48. Ch. 7 is entitled 'Co-Operation in Trade, Customs, Taxation, Statistics, Money and Payments'.

42 *Ibid.* at Art. 4.

43 *Ibid.* In addition, Art. 4(b) makes solidarity and collective self-reliance fundamental principles.

44 Robson, *Integration, Development and Equity*, at 119. Robson, however, notes that though the fund provides compensation for revenue losses, it does not:

> compensate for the contingent losses from trade creation, which – in the absence of an effective Community regional policy – could be significant, or for the important constraints on development policy that the acceptance of the programme would necessarily impose upon them. In these circumstances, the less advanced countries

Notably, by embracing distributional equity, African RTAs do not abandon formal equality. Thus the ECOWAS Treaty, like all African RTAs, recognizes equality among the Member States as a fundamental principle.[45] In this sense, therefore, one sees in African RTAs an interesting recognition of both equality between states, and of substantive equality in terms of sharing of the benefits of cooperation.

ECOWAS has set up a Protocol Relating to the Fund for Cooperation, Compensation and Development of the Economic Community of West African States.[46] This Protocol sets out the purposes of the Fund to include:

- providing 'compensation and other forms of assistance to Member States which have suffered losses as a result of the application' of the ECOWAS Treaty;[47]
- providing 'compensation to Member States which have suffered losses as a result of the location of Community enterprises';[48]
- providing grants for financing development activities[49] or feasibility studies of such activities;[50]
- guaranteeing foreign investments undertaken pursuant to ECOWAS Treaty commitments;[51]
- providing the 'means to facilitate the sustained mobilization of internal and external financial resources for the Member States and the Community';[52] and
- promoting 'development projects in the less developed Member States of the Community'.[53]

The procedure for compensation is set out in the Protocol Relating to the Application of Compensation Procedures for Loss of Revenue Incurred by ECOWAS Member States as a Result of the Trade

may justifiably be tempted to hang back from implementing formal commitments to trade liberalizations until they are assured, either through the ECOWAS Fund or in other ways, that their interest will be fully safeguarded.

Ibid. at 121.

45 Revised Treaty of the Economic Community of West African States, at Art. 4(a). This Article recognizes equality and inter-dependence of Member States as fundamental principles.

46 Protocol Relating to the Fund for Co-operation, Compensation and Development of the Economic Community of West African States, 5 Nov. 1976, available at www.comm.ecowas.int/sec/index.php?id=ap051176fund&lang=en.

47 *Ibid.* at Art. 2(a). 48 *Ibid.* at Art. 2(b). 49 *Ibid.* at Art. 2(c).

50 *Ibid.* at Art. 2(d). 51 *Ibid.* at Art. 2(e). 52 *Ibid.* at Art. 2(f).

53 *Ibid.* at Art. 2(g).

Liberalization Scheme.[54] There is also a Protocol on Assessment of Loss of Revenue by Member States.[55] In 2002, for example, Benin received over 373 million CFA francs as compensation for customs revenue lost for the years 1998–2000.[56]

Furthermore, Article 34 of the SACU Agreement of 2002 makes provision for a revenue-sharing formula among SACU members. It provides that:

> Member States agree that in determining their respective shares of the total customs, excise and additional duties collected in the Common Customs Area during any financial year, the share accruing to each Member State will be calculated from three distinct components as set out in the paragraphs below.[57]

With regard to financing the costs of the Secretariat, Tariff Board and Tribunal, the treaty provides that it will come from proportionate deductions from the 'gross amounts of customs, excise and additional duties collected, before distribution' from customs, excise and development of SACU components.[58] For the customs component, a member's share is determined based on 'the value of goods imported from all other Member States in a specific year as a percentage of total intra-SACU imports'.[59] The excise component is determined as a percentage of the total SACU gross domestic product in any specific year.[60] To achieve some equitable balance among the SACU members, the distribution of the development component of SACU, which is funded from fixed percentages of the excise component,[61] is 'weighted in favour of the less developed Member

54 Protocol Relating to the Application of Compensation for Loss of Revenue Incurred by ECOWAS Member States as a Result of the Trade Liberalisation Scheme, May 2002, available at www.ehu.es/ceinik/tratados/11TRATADOSSOBREINTEGRACIONYCOOPERACIONENAFRICA/111ECOWAS/IC11121.pdf.

55 Protocol Relating to the Assessment of Loss of Revenue by Member States, 5 Nov. 1976 available at www.ehu.es/ceinik/tratados/11TRATADOSSOBREINTEGRACIONYCOOPERACIONENAFRICA/111ECOWAS/IC1113.pdf.

56 Annual Report of the Executive Secretary of ECOWAS, Fostering Regional Integration through NEPAD Implementation, ECW/CM/XLIX/2, para. 204 (2002), available at www.sec.ecowas.int/sitecedeao/english/rapport/es_annual_ report_2002.pdf.

57 Southern African Customs Union (SACU) Agreement 2002 (21 Oct. 2002), Art. 34, available at www.sacu.int/main.php?include=docs/legislation/2002-agreement/part7.html.

58 *Ibid.* at Art. 34(2).

59 *Ibid.* at Art. 34(3)(b).

60 *Ibid.* at Art. 34(4)(b). The Treaty's Annex A provides for the exact methods and procedure of calculating each state's share of their customs, excise and development components. See *ibid.* at Arts. 34(3)(c), 34(4)(c) and 34(5)(c).

61 *Ibid.* at Art. 34(5)(a).

States'.[62] The equitable distribution of SACU's development fund as well as the 'generous' system of compensatory payments that South Africa gives to participant states has been regarded as an important part of SACU's success.[63] In addition, SACU has exempted its poorest members, Swaziland and Lesotho, from the tariff reduction commitments made by the other members.[64]

Provisions like this show how small, economically weak states have sought or demanded accountability from bigger, more economically advanced states in making decisions on how to proceed with economic liberalization through RTAs. For example, Article 5(2) of the Treaty for the Establishment of the EAC provides that the gains of cooperation 'shall be equitably shared' and that development in the community shall be 'harmonious and balanced'.[65] Article 6(e) makes the 'equitable distribution of benefits' a fundamental principle of the community, while Article 7(1)(f) makes the 'equitable distribution of benefits accruing or to be derived from the operations of the Community and measures to address economic imbalances that may arise from such operations', an operational principle of the Community.[66] The Treaty defines 'equitable distribution of benefits' as the 'fair and proportionate distribution of benefits'.[67]

Moreover, the EAC Treaty provides for the principles of variable geometry according to which some members are allowed to progress in the integration 'in various fields and at different speeds'.[68] The Treaty for the Establishment of the EAC also recognizes the principle of asymmetry which allows 'variances in implementation of measures in an economic integration process for purposes of achieving a common objective',[69] thus

62 *Ibid.* at Art. 34(5)(b).

63 N. Poku, *Regionalization and Security in Southern Africa* (London: Palgrave Macmillan, 2001), 89 (also noting that it has been in South Africa's interest to improve trust among its neighbours since it also creates a market for its producers); but see U. Kumar, 'Economic Dominance and Dependence: The Case of the Southern African Customs Union', in Saasa (ed.), *Joining the Future*, 101 (quoting from a report conceding that the 'existing SACU provisions failed to fuel economic development' in Botswana, Lesotho and Swaziland).

64 Poku, *Regionalization and Security*, at 95.

65 Treaty Establishing the East African Community (adopted 30 Nov. 1999, entered into force 7 July 2000), 2144 UNTS 255 at Art. 5(2). Article 5(3)(a) of the Treaty further provides that in pursuance of the Community's objectives, the members shall ensure 'the attainment of sustainable growth and development of the Partner States by the Promotion of a more balanced and harmonious development of the Partner States'.

66 *Ibid.* at Arts. 6(e), 7(1)(f).

67 *Ibid.* at Art. 1 (interpreting the Treaty).

68 *Ibid.* at Art. 7(f).

69 This definition of the principle of asymmetry is contained in Art. 1(1) of the Treaty for the Establishment of the East African Community.

illustrating that flexibility is built into the framework of RTAs.[70] As we shall see in more detail in the next section, the East African Court of Justice has recently interpreted the principle of variable geometry as providing flexibility in making progress towards integration by allowing activities, projects and programmes to proceed at different speeds.[71] The purpose of this approach is 'for the avoidance of internal conflict and a possible emergence of mistrust among the Partner States', so that decisions are not 'forced upon an unready Partner just as refusal or delay of implementation thereof need not be used to block a ready Partner or Partners'.[72]

These types of provisions show the responsiveness of the integration arrangements to these concerns of inequity. Invariably, these provisions and decisions influence the degree and patterns of trade integration – integration therefore ought not to be regarded as being effortlessly pursued through binding non-reversible commitments or as being spurred effortlessly by technology. Instead, the RTA treaties embed within themselves accommodations on integration that show sensitivity to how the gains and losses are shared.

One way of viewing these clauses addressing distributional equity is as mechanisms of addressing collective action problems among respective RTA members. They are initiatives aimed at creating regional coordination and cooperative mechanisms to overcome collective action problems and prevent free riding and domestic political constraints, such as those involving Tanzania's opposition to joining the East African Common Market, which is addressed in more detail below.[73] Of course, they could also easily be regarded as brakes on trade integration initiatives, but this would miss the larger point about the importance of these clauses in rebalancing the unequal costs and benefits that arise from trade integration opening.

Are redistributive mechanisms a recipe for unequal gains, and what is their effect on integration initiatives? Arthur Hazlewood, in reflecting on the break-up of the common market arrangements in East Africa at the end of the 1960s, answered this question pessimistically when he noted:

> ['The relative backwardness' of the Ugandan and Tanzanian economies] would not have neutralized the disadvantages under which they labored. The dissolution of the common market, given the small size of the economies of Tanzania and Uganda, would not have diverted much

70 *Ibid.* at Art. 7(h). 71 See *infra* Chapter III.

72 Council of Ministers of the East African Community Advisory Opinion Report, EACJ at 35.

73 See *infra* Chapter III.

> industrial development to them from Kenya, though it would have been likely significantly to reduce the future rate of industrial growth in East Africa as a whole.[74]

This is the dilemma that economic integration schemes between countries with highly disparate economic structures face when they integrate. In East Africa, this problem is now compounded by the fact that the even smaller and landlocked economies of Rwanda and Burundi have joined the EAC, further exacerbating the relative differences between poorer and richer countries. The expanded market size resulting from Rwanda and Burundi becoming members of the EAC increases the scope for economies of scale for efficient industries, but may not entirely negate the disparities in the economies in the EAC.[75] One of the EAC's recent initiatives is an EAC Development Fund,[76] which will mobilize resources from domestic sources and partner states to finance productive sectors including energy, transportation and infrastructure.[77] President Kibaki of Kenya suggested, upon Rwanda and Burundi joining the EAC, that the Fund, as well as the enhanced contributions of the partner states approved in November 2006, would help defray the additional cost of running the affairs of the Community.[78] Such an approach in a large measure departs from the early efforts of attaining a balance of benefits using redistributive schemes. Instead, it relies on the development of projects that will promote regional trade.

D The East African Court of Justice's Variable Geometry Advisory Opinion

While in the past doubts were expressed about the significance of trade integration based on market-led integration,[79] today there are clearly

74 Hazlewood, *Economic Integration*, at 67.

75 In joining the East African Community in 2005, Rwanda and Burundi increased the market size to 120 million people, see 'Rwanda and Burundi Join EAC Customs Union', in e-EAC Newsletter Issue No. 30, 15 July 2009.

76 The decision to establish the fund was made by the EAC Council of Ministers on 8 August 2005. See D.S.O. Nalo, Permanent Secretary, Ministry of East African Community on Kenya National Consultation Workshop for the Study on the Establishment of the East African Community Development Fund, Statement at the Grand Regency Hotel (6–7 Oct. 2008), at 2, available at www.meac.go.ke (follow 'Permanent Secretary's Speeches' hyperlink).

77 *Ibid.* at 3.

78 B. Kikechi, 'Rwanda and Burundi Join the East African Community', 19 June 2007, available at http://allafrica.com/stories/200706181801.html.

79 See Ravenhill, 'Theory and Practice', at 48. See also T. Ostergaard, 'Classical Models of Regional Integration – What Relevance for Southern Africa?', in B. Oden (ed.), *Southern*

efforts and commitments that show that regional development cooperation is understood as capable of being undertaken alongside market-led integration, rather than as an extreme alternative to market-based integration. In the EAC, for example, the Treaty carefully balances the liberalization commitments, on the one hand, with those relating to equity and distribution among the members, on the other.[80] The East African Court of Justice recently confirmed this in its Advisory Opinion on whether the rule on consensus decision making was inconsistent with the principle of variable geometry that allows Member States flexibility to assume commitments in a variety of areas at different speeds.[81]

This case before the EACJ arose against the background of the then ongoing common market negotiations in the EAC.[82] These negotiations made it increasingly clear that the five members of the EAC were not in agreement on what common market commitments they were willing to make, both as a Community and as individual members of the Community.[83] Tanzania, for example, objected to opening up land ownership to other East Africans, fearing that it would upset its policy against landlessness by allowing residents of other countries to buy land there.[84] Tanzania also proposed that each member country in the common market

Africa After Apartheid: Regional Integration and External Resources (Uppsala: Nordiska Afrikainstitutet, 1993), 27.

80 Similarly, the sixth preambular paragraph to the South African Customs Union Agreement 2002 notes that the members are mindful of 'the different levels of economic development of the Member States'.

81 Council of Ministers of the East African Community Advisory Opinion Request, EACJ at 10 (finding that there is no conflict between the principle of variable geometry – which allows for phased implementation of community commitments – and that of consensus in decision making within the organs of the East African Community).

82 See the Treaty for the Establishment of the EAC, which provides the common market as the second stage of integration after the establishment of a customs union. See EAC, Art. 76. An East African Community Protocol was signed on 20 November 2009, available at http://eabc.info/node/410.

83 Council of Ministers of the East African Community Advisory Opinion Request, EACJ at 38. According to the Court, the context for the Council seeking the Advisory Opinion emerged because:

> as integration deepens, different Partner States continue to have differing attachments to certain policies and their citizens continue to have differing passions toward such policies. In that environment, understandably, choices become tougher, decisions become harder and the perceived unanimity enjoyed in decision making over the years begins to be less forthcoming. This in our view explains the emergence of this debate at this particular time.

Ibid.

84 See EAC Common Market Protocol, at Art. 15.

retain its own labour laws, further limiting the adoption of the right of residence, which confers automatic rights to work anywhere in the EAC.[85]

The lack of agreement on the details of the common market negotiations meant that the Council of Ministers and the Summit could delay the negotiations until consensus was reached or they could agree to proceed in a manner that accommodated the differences. Consequently, the Council of Ministers asked the EAC Secretariat to seek an Advisory Opinion on the application of the principle of variable geometry because, according to the Council, interpreting variable geometry as permitting progression of the different activities, projects and programmes at different speeds, was 'contestable on the basis of the fundamental requirement under the Treaty and relevant annexes for consensus as a basis for decision-making by the Heads of State and the Council of Ministers'.[86]

Under the Treaty for the Establishment of the EAC, the Summit[87] and Council[88] are required to make decisions by consensus. The Council's request for an Advisory Opinion, therefore, posited a conflict between the rule of consensus decision making, on the one hand, and the principle of variable geometry, on the other. It sought a ruling from the EACJ, which is the principal judicial body of the Community with jurisdiction to 'ensure the adherence to law in the interpretation and application of and compliance with [the] Treaty'.[89] In addition to the Court having 'initial jurisdiction over the interpretation and application of [the] Treaty',[90] it also has jurisdiction to issue advisory opinions on request from the Summit, a partner state or the Council of Ministers.[91]

The Community asked the Court to decide if the Treaty's rule of consensus decision making implied unanimity of all the Member States[92] and 'whether the principle of variable geometry can apply to guide the integration process, the requirement on consensus in decision-making notwithstanding'.[93]

85 *Ibid.*, Annex II at 3.

86 Council of Ministers, 'Proposal for Requesting Advisory Opinion of the East African Court of Justice' (13 Sept. 2008), reproduced in Council of Ministers for the East African Community Advisory Opinion Request, EACJ at 3.

87 EAC Treaty, at Art. 12(3).

88 *Ibid.* at Art. 15(4). Article 2(1) of the Protocol states which decisions are to be made by consensus and Art. 2(2) specifies which are to be made by majority rule.

89 *Ibid.* at Art. 23.

90 *Ibid.* at Art. 27.

91 *Ibid.* at Art. 36(1). For further discussion on the EACJ, see Chapter VII.

92 Council of Ministers of the East African Community Advisory Opinion Request, EACJ at 6.

93 *Ibid.*

1 *The arguments of the partner states and the East African Law Society as* amici

The Community argued that the outcome would help guide its process of decision making, which was critical for its 'institutional development' and would 'contribute to the development of regional jurisprudence as envisioned under Articles 6, 7 and 126 of the Treaty'.[94]

According to the Community, variable geometry, an innovation of European law, allowed 'Member States to negotiate exemptions from certain Treaty provisions and to individually apply a greater speed on some integration processes than others, using the institutions and procedures laid down in the Treaty'.[95] In the Community's view, 'variable geometry principles could considerably ease some of the tensions among sub-regional integration arrangements in the Community and enhance the prospect of closer and more regional co-operation'.[96]

For this reason, the Community supported decisions to be made by majority rather than by consensus because this would allow for agreement among 'smaller sub-groups to move faster than the whole group'.[97] In the Community's view, there had been movement away from consensus decision making toward majority decision making within the United Nations and the European Union. The Community, therefore, argued that the EACJ should construe the EAC Treaty consistently with this trend.[98]

The Community argued that consensus decision making resulted in delays, was time consuming, and came with the dangers of 'intransigence' and the possibility of vetoes, which would allow 'individuals or small minorities to block agreement'.[99] Rwanda argued that consensus decision making and variable geometry did not conflict with each other since each

94 *Ibid.*

95 *Ibid.* The Community's counsel also offered the examples of Denmark, Ireland and the United Kingdom as countries that opted out of the European Community's provisions of free movement of persons, asylum and immigration, respectively. *Ibid.* at 7.

96 *Ibid.* 97 *Ibid.* 98 *Ibid.*

99 *Ibid.* at 8. In addition, the Community argued that the increase of members from three to five increased the susceptibility to disruption, with small groups obstructing the others. In this manner the Community argued consensus decision making could 'reward the least accommodating group members while punishing the most accommodating'. *Ibid.* at 9. According to the Community, consensus decision making can result in the Abilene Paradox, where a group unanimously agrees on a course of action no single member wants, 'because no one individual is willing to go against the perceived will of the decision-making body'. *Ibid.*

was designed for different circumstances.[100] For Rwanda, 'the Treaty gives no flexibility to some groups' since it required all the partner states to 'agree on each and every activity'.[101] Additionally, Rwanda remarked that the Community was founded on the 'principles of mutual trust, political will and sovereign equality', as set forth in Article 6(a) of the Treaty, without which the Community was in danger of collapsing very much like the original EAC.[102] As such, according to Rwanda, the principle of variable geometry allowed groups of members to engage in activities outside the Community, rather than within it.[103]

By contrast, Burundi argued that the rule of consensus decision making and the principle of variable geometry were not in harmony based on the practice of the Community.[104] For Burundi, consensus decision making 'requires complete agreement by all Partner States', while variable geometry requires flexibility in the integration process.[105]

Kenya argued that the term 'consensus' did not necessarily equate to unanimity as Burundi had contended.[106] Kenya argued that the practice in the European Community was to permit members 'to opt out of unwanted policies rather than being obliged to choose between vetoing them or accepting a majority verdict'.[107] Consensus decision making and variable geometry, Kenya argued, could co-exist as long as the sphere and scope of the operation of each could be clearly defined.[108] According to Kenya:

> [V]ariable geometry . . . permits Member States in a regional integration arrangement to pursue integration at different levels in different fields/policy areas, so long as the enhanced integration contributes to enhancing integration in the regional integration arrangements, and does not create a barrier to trade or discriminate among Member States.[109]

Thus, while Kenya supported variable geometry, it argued that if the policy allowed countries to cherry-pick their favourite policies and create smaller groups of similarly minded countries, there was a danger that 'some fundamental policies will not be addressed by some Member States'.[110] The question of multiple and overlapping memberships in African RTAs will be discussed in Chapter III.

100 *Ibid.* at 10. 101 *Ibid.* 102 *Ibid.* 103 *Ibid.* at 11.
104 *Ibid.* 105 *Ibid.* at 12.
106 Council of Ministers of the East African Community Advisory Opinion Request, EACJ at 12–13.
107 *Ibid.* at 14. 108 *Ibid.* at 15. 109 *Ibid.* 110 *Ibid.* at 16.

For Kenya, therefore, the role of the Court in issuing the Advisory Opinion was to clarify what the Treaty refers to as consensus decision making because such uncertainty was slowing down the integration process.[111] According to Kenya:

> [E]ach country has a different rate of economic growth, different socio-economic factors and varying national policies that it takes into consideration when deciding whether or not to vote in favour of a specific proposal . . . . [V]ariable geometry is an important principle that operates side by side with consensus decision making as it accommodates each country's unique features and that as such it should be embraced by the Community and not ignored by forcing States to adopt blanket proposals which may not be best suited to their interests.[112]

Thus, Kenya sought guidance from the Court as to whether consensus decision making required unanimity, a two-thirds majority, or a simple majority, because this would 'eliminate confusion and uncertainty in the future'.[113]

Tanzania, like Rwanda and Burundi, argued that consensus decision making under the Treaty meant unanimity.[114] It believed that such an interpretation was supported by provisions in the Treaty on consensus decision making because of 'the stark reality' recognized in the Treaty 'that each Partner is a Sovereign State and that in the Partner States' peaceful co-existence, mutual trust is of the essence'.[115] For Tanzania, the partner states had designed the Treaty (as recognized in the operational principles in Article 7 and the fundamental principles in Article 6), in order to have a 'single voice, notwithstanding their variations in terms of sizes or stages of development'.[116] Tanzania also argued that such an interpretation was consistent with 'the dual mandate of the leaderships of the Partner States to the people they represent, on the one hand, and to the Community, on the other [which in Tanzania's view] demands that the leaderships and their people be heard and their positions respected'.[117] Tanzania also objected to the request for an Advisory Opinion, since a Treaty amendment had been initiated through the political process by the Sectoral Committee on Legal and Judicial Affairs to clarify how variable geometry and consensus decision making were related.[118] Seeking an Advisory Opinion from the Court, Tanzania argued, removed the question from the political process, 'where the matter belongs', and as such the request for an Advisory Opinion

111 *Ibid.* 112 *Ibid.* at 16–17. 113 *Ibid.* at 16. 114 *Ibid.* at 20.
115 *Ibid.* at 19. 116 *Ibid.* 117 *Ibid.* 118 *Ibid.* at 20.

was 'an abuse of the process of the court'.[119] The Court rejected this argument.[120]

Uganda also shared the view that the question of the proper relationship between consensus decision making and variable geometry belonged to the political process through Treaty amendment.[121] Uganda argued that the question before the Court was whether the organs of the Community could make decisions using variable geometry.[122] For Uganda, variable geometry 'would allow each country to pace changes brought about in the Treaty at a speed and course that meets and fits unique local conditions of each specific Partner State'.[123] The two principles could not, according to Uganda, be put alongside each other because one had to first 'decide on a policy or objective before arriving at variable geometry which has to take account of practical realities in the different Partner States on the mode and speed of implementation of the policy'.[124] In essence, Uganda was suggesting that the question before the Court was a non-justiciable political matter within the sovereign prerogatives of the partner states.[125]

The East African Law Society argued that variable geometry permitted 'flexibility in the integration process and . . . progression in the East African Community activities by some Partner States and not all'.[126] It contended that there was not much merit to the claim that decisions not in accordance with consensus decision making as required by the Treaty could be challengeable if made by applying the principle of variable geometry.[127] The Society maintained that in the European Union, differentiation in the integration structure was permissible to accommodate irreconcilable differences, permitting 'a permanent separation between a group of Partner States and a number of less developed integration units'.[128] The Society reasoned that variable geometry was a 'flexible and pragmatic approach to integration' that allowed countries to proceed on

119 *Ibid.*

120 *Ibid.* at 41. According to the Court:

> the process of amending the Treaty reported to be underway in the Executive Organs of the Community, as well as this Application for an Advisory Opinion are perfectly compatible. The application was brought to this court on a directive of the Council, the very organ reported to be overseeing the said amendment. It was properly brought and the Court has jurisdiction.

Ibid.

121 *Ibid.* at 23. 122 *Ibid.* 123 *Ibid.* at 22. 124 *Ibid.*

125 According to Uganda, the question was one for 'the governing bodies and administrators of the East African Community', but not for the Court. *Ibid.* at 23.

126 *Ibid.* at 24. 127 *Ibid.* 128 *Ibid.*

the integration agenda based on the extent of their interest.[129] As such, variable geometry applied because of differences in sizes, priorities and levels of political and economic development, as well as in culture and language, 'which make it difficult for members to meet the criteria for membership at the same speeds and depths'.[130] The Society argued that the principle of variable geometry and the rule of consensus decision making were not necessarily inconsistent with each other, and therefore, the Court could advise the partner states to amend the Treaty and related protocols 'to provide for application of the principle of variable geometry in specific areas of activity'.[131]

Based on these submissions, it is clear that Kenya favoured a rapid progression of the Community into a common market much more readily than Tanzania, Rwanda and Burundi, which interpreted the consensus decision making as requiring unanimity.

2 *The decision of the Court*

The Court began by noting that the two issues it had to decide were, first, whether the principle of variable geometry was in harmony with the rule of consensus decision making, and second, whether the principle of variable geometry could be applied to guide the process of integration, notwithstanding the requirement of consensus decision making.[132] The Court noted that the Treaty defined the principle of variable geometry, but provided no definition of consensus. It therefore proceeded to develop a definition from extraneous sources.[133] Surprisingly, the Court first resorted to Wikipedia, The Free Encyclopedia.[134] This online source is hardly recommendable for an authoritative dictionary meaning of any word.

According to the Court: '[c]onsensus as applied in the Treaty and Protocols . . . is purely and simply a decision-making mechanism in Summit, Council and in the other executive organs of the Community while variable geometry as used therein is a strategy for implementation'.[135] The Court then distinguished between decisions consistent with the objectives of the Treaty, where 'the basis for making the decision is consensus', with the implementation of the decision.[136] It is in the implementation of decisions that 'the practical realities such as the vital national interests, the

129 *Ibid.* at 25. 130 *Ibid.* 131 *Ibid.* at 27. 132 *Ibid.* at 28. 133 *Ibid.*

134 *Ibid.* at 29; see also Wikipedia, available at www.wikipedia.org.

135 Council of Ministers for the East African Community Advisory Opinion Request, EACJ at 30.

136 *Ibid.*

negotiations, the give and take of consultations that each Partner State will inevitably have to take care of for the good of the Partner State and ultimately that of the Community'.[137] Notably, the Court did not give any basis at all in the Treaty or the EAC's protocols for this distinction between decision and implementation.[138] This is not to suggest there could be no such basis, but the Court did not try to establish any at all.

Based on this distinction between decision and implementation, the Court found consistency between the principle of variable geometry and the rule of consensus decision making.[139] This consistency was established by noting that consensus in decision making is a 'suitable operational principle, which may well be variable geometry . . . to govern the practical implementation of that particular decision'.[140] Thus, establishing the distinction between decision and implementation from the onset, the Court proceeded to find that both are different stages in a single process, except that variable geometry is not always the implementation choice if there are no considerations such as those necessitating differentiated implementation of a decision.[141]

As had been argued by the partner states and the *amicus* East African Law Society, the court noted that the considerations relevant to identifying how variable geometry squares with consensus decision making are tailored as ways to accommodate countries intent on proceeding with integration decisions that may not be uniformly shared. From this perspective, variable geometry was therefore a strategy for accommodating countries that are unable to proceed with certain integration decisions.[142] This definition of variable geometry adopted by the Court and used by the partner states is consistent with accommodating laggard partner states. In essence, variable geometry gets a very positive spin – it is a policy of allowing forward movement without compelling unwilling countries to do so. One alternative that the Court did not accept, and in fact explicitly rejected, is consensus decision making as requiring unanimity.[143] By excluding this possibility of the meaning of consensus it became possible to reconcile variable geometry with the rule of consensus decision making.[144] As a result, the Court neatly integrated variable geometry and consensus decision making into a single process:

137 *Ibid.* 138 *Ibid.* 139 *Ibid.* 140 *Ibid.* 141 *Ibid.* 142 *Ibid.*

143 *Ibid.* at 37. The Court held: '[i]mplying that consensus decision-making as used in the Treaty means unanimity of Partner States is mere perception . . . . Such perception is, in our view, neither supported by the Treaty nor the definitions surveyed.' *Ibid.* at 38.

144 *Ibid.*

> Partner States may agree on implementation at different speeds due to different readiness levels or different priorities, some may choose or opt out of implementation altogether due to national realities, yet others may decide to 'opt out' and at a future time they will 'opt in'. All these will be agreed by the Partner States, by consensus.[145]

In addition, the Court also held 'that the principle of variable geometry . . . is a strategy of implementation of Community decisions and not a decision making tool in itself'.[146] This is consistent with Article 7 of the Treaty, which provides that its operational principles 'shall govern the practical achievement of the objectives of the Community . . . '.[147] The Court found that 'the principle of variable geometry has been internationally applied to deepen integration',[148] and gave the examples of SADC, the European Union[149] and the 'Provisions of Enhanced Cooperation' of the Treaty of the European Union.[150] The Court recommended that the EAC 'study, and possibly emulate some of the examples of application of these concepts to deepen integration'.[151]

Of course, if the only meaning of variable geometry available was that of allowing countries willing to proceed with integration to move forward rather than be held back, the Court is right. Yet, it is not entirely clear that variable geometry is necessarily a win–win for deeper integration if laggard states can avoid proceeding with implementation of deeper integration measures. Variable geometry is as much a framework for allowing a group of like-minded states to proceed with certain integration initiatives as it is for objecting states opting out of timetabled integration commitments when the decision to assume the commitments and begin implementation arrives.

That is why the Court advised the Community to consider using variable geometry 'as an exception, not as the rule, as indeed institutionalized

145 *Ibid.* at 30. 146 *Ibid.* at 34. 147 *Ibid.* 148 *Ibid.* at 31.

149 The Court referenced the 1985 European Union (EU) Schengen Agreement and the 1990 Schengen Convention which Ireland and the United Kingdom opted out of and retained their 'national border controls on the movement of persons from other EU Member States'. *Ibid.* Another example is EU Economic and Monetary Union, from which Ireland and the United Kingdom have opted out, and the EU Social Policy Agreement from which the United Kingdom has opted out. See *ibid.* at 31–2.

150 *Ibid.* at 33–4. The 'Provisions of Enhanced Cooperation' in the Treaty of the European Union are contained in Arts 43 and 43(b), Treaty of Lisbon Amending the Treaty on European Union and the Treaty Establishing the European Community, 13 Dec. 2007, 2007 OJ (C 306) 1.

151 Council of Ministers for the East African Community Advisory Opinion Request, E. Afr. Ct. of Justice, at 34.

flexibility might lead to break-up of the Community or its transformation into "a mere free trade area"', as contemplated by the provisions of Article 43(b) of the Treaty of the European Union.[152] The Court also recommended that the EAC borrow from the European Union the idea of a set of 'core and periphery' obligations which would require members to determine areas over which variable geometry could and could not apply.[153]

In conclusion, the Court held:

> [F]or avoidance of internal conflict and a possible emergence of mistrust among the Partner States, and in accordance with the Treaty provisions above discussed, decisions should be taken with the above two aspects in mind [variable geometry and consensus decision making] and simultaneous implementation thereof need not be forced upon an unready Partner just as refusal or delay of implementation thereof need not be used to block a ready Partner or Partners.[154]

In so doing, the Court avoided giving states sceptical of progressing into the common market stage of East African cooperation a reason to derail the commitment of those states that support this transition to a common market.[155] The Court then expressed the view, which it also noted was shared in the submissions before it, 'that the problems associated with obtaining consensus' arose from the hesitation to make certain decisions, rather than a rejection of such decisions.[156] Indeed, according to the Court, a rejection of a decision consistent with the Treaty was not possible since it 'would be tantamount to a rejection of a particular treaty provision'.[157] The hesitation seemed to arise from the requirement that decisions needed simultaneous implementation by all partner states.[158] Yet, according to the Court:

> Simultaneous implementation is impracticable in some circumstances and Partner States cannot be expected to operate within such strait jacket or one size fits all situations. Variable geometry is, therefore, intended, and

152 *Ibid.* Article 43(b) of the EU Treaty provides: 'Enhanced cooperation may be undertaken only as a last resort, when it has been established within the Council that the objectives of such cooperation cannot be attained within a reasonable period by applying relevant provisions of the Treaty.'

153 Council of Ministers for the East African Community Advisory Opinion Request, EACJ at 34.

154 *Ibid.* at 35.

155 For further discussion on the common market, see Chapter V.

156 Council of Ministers for the East African Community Advisory Opinion Request, EACJ at 35.

157 *Ibid.*

158 See *ibid.*

> actually allows, those Partner States who cannot implement a particular decision simultaneously or immediately to implement it at a suitable certain future time or simply at a different speed while at the same time allowing those who are able to implement immediately to do so.[159]

The Court cited Judge Tanaka in the 1966 ICJ Reports to the effect that 'to treat unequal matters differently according to their inequality is not only permitted but required'.[160] In this manner, the Court found that consensus was required under the Treaty for arriving at Community decisions, but that variable geometry played a role 'in deciding the implementation of the programme'.[161] It also found that the term consensus decision making was not defined in the Treaty for the Establishment of the EAC or in Community Protocols.[162] Thus, rather than equate the term with unanimity, the Court recommended amending the Community's instruments.[163]

Notably, the Court and those who appeared before it did not address the related principle of asymmetry under the Treaty for the Establishment of the EAC.[164] This principle allows Member States to vary 'the implementation of measures in an economic integration process for purposes of achieving a common objective'.[165] It would seem that there is a close relationship between the principles of variable geometry and that of asymmetry, to the extent that both allow variation in implementation timetables, yet the Court did not allude to it. In fact, the Court did not necessarily have to refer to examples from the European Union; it could have looked at the East African Customs Union Protocol, which already incorporates the principles of variable geometry and asymmetry by virtue of the variation in the tariff reduction schedule.[166] While the Customs Union Protocol urges Member States to eliminate all internal tariffs and similar charges on trade among the partner states upon the entry into force of the Protocol,[167] it nevertheless gives Uganda and Tanzania more favourable tariff removal commitments than those given

159 *Ibid.* 160 *Ibid.* at 36. 161 *Ibid.*

162 In particular, the Court rejected the argument that Art. 148 of the Treaty for the Establishment of the EAC could be construed as implying 'that consensus is synonymous with unanimity'. *Ibid.* at 40.

163 *Ibid.* at 38. 164 *Ibid.*; see *supra* n. 65 and accompanying text.

165 This definition is provided in Art. 1(1) of the Treaty for the Establishment of the EAC. The principle is provided as an operational principle of the treaty in Art. 7(h).

166 See Protocol on the Establishment of the East African Customs Union, 30 Nov. 1999, available at www.eac.int/customs/index.php?option=com_content&view=article&id=2:customs-union-protocol&catid=3:key-documents&Itemid=141.

167 *Ibid.* at Art. 10(1).

to the more economically developed Kenya under other provisions. For example, Article 11(2) provides that as between Uganda and Tanzania, goods are duty free,[168] and goods from Uganda and Tanzania into Kenya are duty free.[169] However, Kenyan goods do not enjoy such duty-free treatment in Uganda and Tanzania.[170] Article 11(3) provides for the categorization of goods from Kenya into Uganda and Tanzania.[171] This section sets out two categories of goods – Category A goods, which are 'eligible for immediate duty free treatment', and Category B goods, which are 'eligible for gradual tariff reduction'.[172] Further, Category B goods from Kenya into Uganda will have a five-year phase-out tariff reduction period for all products.[173] This phase-out tariff reduction period begins by 10% during the first year, 8% during the second, 6% during the third, 4% during the fourth and 2% during the fifth.[174] Additionally, Category B goods from Kenya into Tanzania have a similar phase-out tariff reduction period.[175] The underlying requirement is that no internal tariff can exceed the common external tariff with respect to any of the specified products.[176] The differentiation in the tariff schedules benefit Uganda and Tanzania pursuant to the principle of variable geometry.

In any event, the Court's variable geometry decision is a highly significant one, because it provides an existing route within the Treaty framework for states like Tanzania, which are deeply suspicious that they will be economically disadvantaged by relatively more economically powerful states like Kenya.[177] The principle of variable geometry has given states like Tanzania a legal foothold within the EAC not to make commitments that they believe will unfairly distribute rewards. For those states willing to continue in the common market stage of the integration process, the decision also provides a legal basis for their continued cooperation, since objecting states will not be regarded as wielding a veto under the rule of consensus decision making, but rather as exercising their right to opt out of commitments under the principle of variable geometry. This flexibility, as noted before, is a central feature of second generation African RTAs.[178]

168 *Ibid.* at Art. 11(2)(a). 169 *Ibid.* at Art. 11(2)(b).

170 *Ibid.* at Art. 11(3)(b) (Category B goods include agricultural products, building materials, plastics, wood, paper, textiles, iron and steel and other manufactured goods).

171 *Ibid.* at Art. 11(3). 172 *Ibid.* at Art. 11(3)(a) and (b). 173 *Ibid.* at Art. 11(4).

174 *Ibid.* 175 *Ibid.* at Art. 11(5). 176 *Ibid.* at Art. 11(6).

177 J. Gathii, 'Spat With Dar Over Trade Unnecessary', *Business Daily Africa*, 8 Feb. 2008, available at http://allafrica.com/stories/200802070871.html.

178 See discussion *infra.*

E Conclusion

Having seen how African RTAs have adopted various versions of variable geometry and discussed the EACJ's variable geometry decision, it is now time to briefly and preliminarily evaluate the effectiveness of these measures. To do so, a variety of baselines could be used. One obvious point of departure is whether these measures promote or undermine trade liberalization, a question that is addressed at greater length in the discussion of multiple memberships in RTAs in Chapter III. Another is whether these measures nudge countries that would otherwise not adopt even minimal liberalization commitments to do so. Finally, one may ask whether variable geometry plays a non-economic role in encouraging integration. This section addresses each of these in turn.

Variable geometry, especially as phased implementation that allows some countries to remain behind while others proceed to higher levels of trade integration, slows down trade liberalization. Therefore, the question is whether the increased levels of integration with minimal variable geometry are better than no liberalization at all. The answer to this question is complicated by the fact that variable geometry also involves paying off countries that lose from gains made by other Member States as well as the preferential access to capital in regional development banks.[179] From this perspective, variable geometry can only confidently be argued to primarily serve goals other than encouraging deeper trade integration.

Clearly, some measures of variable geometry are indispensable in encouraging countries to participate in integration schemes, but they may not necessarily encourage deeper liberalization than a beneficiary country is likely to undertake in the absence of such measures of accommodation. This is clearly the case of Tanzania in the EAC. From this perspective, variable geometry helps to build trust and confidence among members whose benefits from integration are likely to be rather

179 See e.g., L. Castro, C. Kraus and M. de la Rocha, 'Regional Trade Integration in East Africa: Trade and Revenue Impacts of the Planned East African Community Customs Union', World Bank Africa Region Working Paper Series No. 72, 29 Aug. 2004 (Washington, DC: World Bank) (arguing that there is a possible need for a compensation fund to address the cost/benefit imbalances among EAC members that 'Kenyan exporters got the lion share of the benefit from economic linkages', under the East African Customs Union).

lop-sided, rather than necessarily to nudge liberalization otherwise not possible.

Variable geometry stands in sharp contrast to the premise of the global trading regime, which punishes defections from the rules under a sanctions regime backed up by a compulsory and binding dispute settlement system. African RTAs have yet to threaten sanctions against one another where there has been non-compliance with liberalization commitments.[180]

So what are the benefits of collaboration and cooperation under RTAs that are characterized by variable geometry measures in the absence of coercive mechanisms? African RTAs are only beginning to provide avenues of increased transparency and openness in regional trade in ways that are particularly useful in breaking down the especially high tariff and non-tariff barriers to regional trade in Africa. They are also beginning to provide regional checks on domestic interest groups and industries that are opposed to trade liberalization.[181] However, these benefits are still in their infancy in terms of becoming a reality on the ground. In the meantime, variable geometry remains one of the most visible features of

180 For example, while COMESA has granted Kenya safeguards for its sugar and wheat produce, COMESA member countries have not threatened retaliatory sanctions against Kenya for imposing an auction for sugar import licences that caused COMESA members like Egypt and Swaziland to lose market share in the Kenyan sugar market. Instead, in September 2009 COMESA sent a Sugar Sector Safeguard Assessment Mission to Kenya which recommended removal of the auctioning of import licences for sugar. Following this recommendation, Kenya removed this auction system for sugar licence imports. See Reuters, 'Kenya Cancels Auction of Sugar Import Rights' (10 Mar. 2010), available at http://af.reuters.com/article/investingNews/idAFJOE6270CP20100308. See also J. Okuye, 'COMESA Likely to Petition Kenya Over Safeguards on Sugar', *The East African Standard* (1 Dec. 2009), available at www.standardmedia.co.ke/mag/InsidePage.php?id=1144029312&cid=457&.

181 *Ibid.* Following COMESA's decision recommending that Kenya remove the auction of import licences for sugar, the sugar industry in Kenya declared it was going to be ready to compete with duty-free sugar from the COMESA region in 2012 when the COMESA safeguards end. W. Menya, 'Sugar Industry in Bitter Wars Ahead of COMESA Date', *Business Daily* (Apr. 2009), 12 available at http://multimedia.marsgroupkenya.org/?StoryID=253746&page=4 (citing the Chairman of Kenya Sugarcane Millers Association, Dr. Evans Kidero, about the readiness of Kenyan sugarmillers to compete after the end of the safeguards). For an analysis of the variety of roles interest groups have played in the EAC from a liberal inter-governmentalism perspective, see M. Chacha, 'The New Community: Liberal Intergovernmentalism and East Africa Integration', Paper prepared for presentation at the Annual Meeting of the American Political Science Association, Toronto, Canada (3–6 Sept. 2009), available at http://papers.ssrn.com/sol3/papers.cfm?abstract_id=1449277.

African RTAs today. As argued throughout this chapter, variable geometry is one of the most important features that demonstrates the flexibility of African RTAs.

The next chapter discusses multiple memberships in African RTAs. As noted in Chapter I, multiple memberships are a defining feature of African RTAs understood as flexible regimes.

III

Multiple memberships in African RTAs

A Introduction

This chapter will examine another important feature of the flexibility of African RTAs – multiple memberships. Of the fifty-one countries in Africa, only six belong to a single RTA.[1] The other forty-five belong to at least two or more RTAs.[2] Swaziland belongs to three RTAs – COMESA, SADC and SACU.[3] Of all five countries in the EAC, four are also members of COMESA, while Tanzania is a member of SADC.[4] Of the fifteen countries in SADC, eight are also members of COMESA.[5] Figures 3.1 to 3.4 illustrate the prominence of multiple memberships in African RTAs.

Overlapping memberships in several RTAs is a reflection of the large number of bilateral and RTAs in Africa, an occurrence that Jagdish Bhagwati has referred to as the 'spaghetti bowl'.[6] Next, I will examine how multiplicity of memberships and the variety of RTAs is a further illustration of the thesis of this chapter – that African RTAs are flexible regimes. This chapter also examines the extent to which this multiplicity of memberships and trade agreements has contributed to the 'spaghetti bowl', which is addressed in further detail below.

Multiple memberships in RTAs is a reflection of the character of African RTAs as flexible regimes. This does not understate or underestimate the criticisms of multiple memberships. These criticisms can be divided into two main categories. The first relates to the fact that multiplicity of memberships in RTAs is a reflection of the undesirable proliferation of RTAs

1 Assessing Regional Integration in Africa (Economic Commission for Africa, 2004), 40.

2 See Figures 3.1–3.4, *infra*. 3 See Figure 3.1, *infra*. 4 *Ibid.* 5 *Ibid.*

6 J. Bhagwati, 'U.S. Trade Policy: The Infatuation With Free Trade Areas', in J. Bhagwati and A.O. Krueger (eds), *The Dangerous Drift to Preferential Trade Agreements* (Washington, DC: AEI Press, 1995), 2 (according to Bhagwati, the 'spaghetti bowl' phenomenon results when countries and intergovernmental organizations enter into multiple criss-crossing, instead of participating in multilateral trade). See also, S. Cho, 'Defragmenting World Trade', *Northwestern Journal of International Law and Business* 27 (2006) 39.

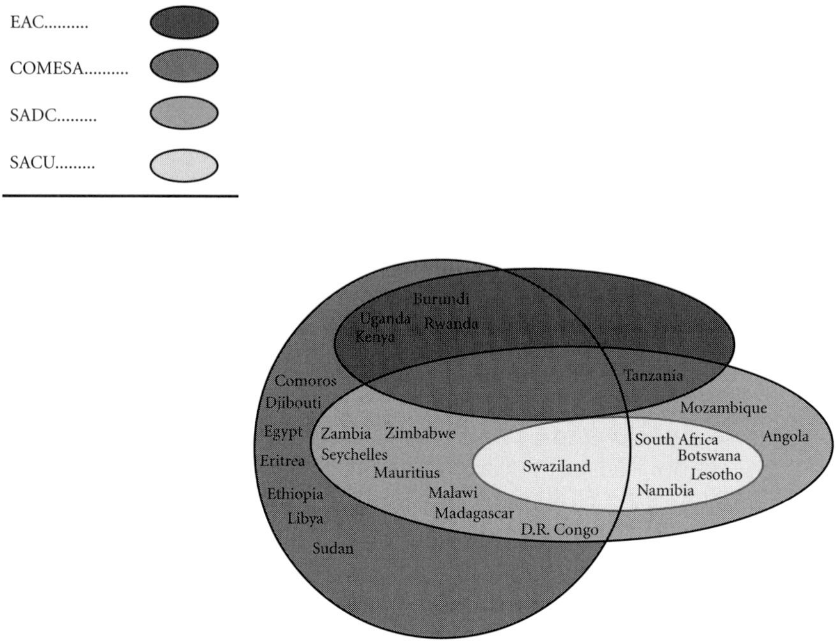

Figure 3.1 Multiple memberships in COMESA/EAC/SADC/SADU

in creating a spaghetti bowl. A second category of criticisms relates to the high transaction costs and administrative difficulties of complying with multiple Rules of Origin (RoOs).[7] Multiple memberships also prevent African governments from focusing on a single regional economic bloc, diminishing the little trade capacity and budgets of these countries. In addition, jurisdictional uncertainty arises as a result of overlapping legal regimes.

The chapter also examines the reasons accounting for multiple memberships in African RTAs and how multiple memberships are a reflection of Africa's diversity. It then examines criticisms of the multiplicity of memberships in African RTAs. The final part addresses the spaghetti bowl critique of the multiplicity of RTAs.

7 RoOs specify when a product will qualify for duty-free movement within the RTA, and what proportion of value must be added if it originates within the trade bloc, or whether it is required that a product undergo a substantial transformation in a country before being allowed to cross the border duty free. For more on RoOs see *infra* nn. 99–113 and accompanying text.

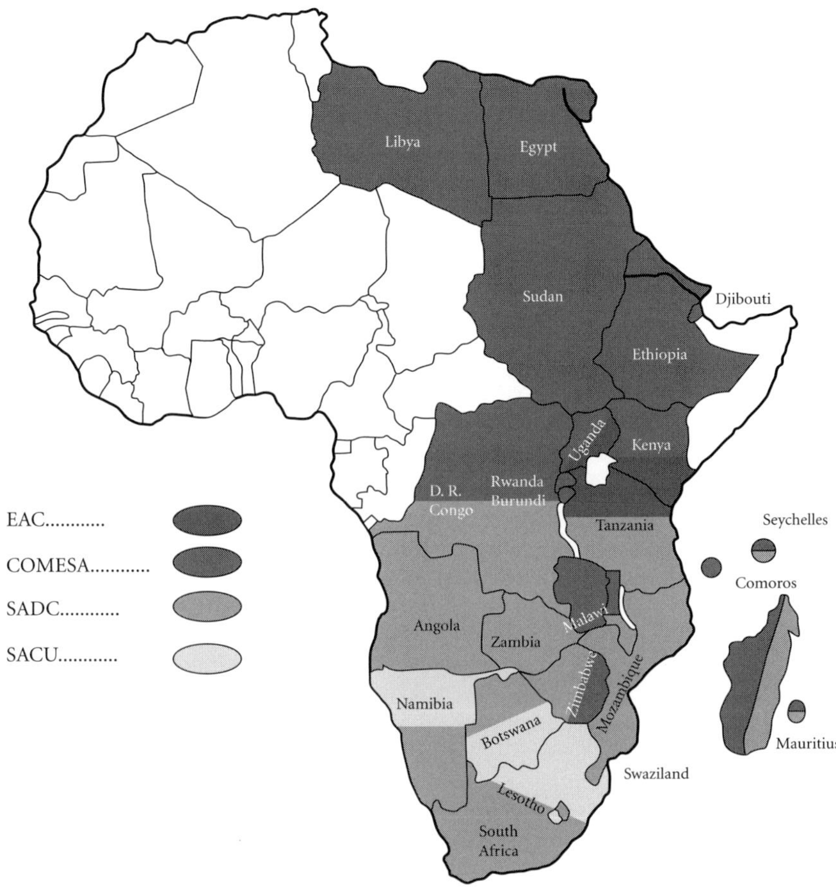

Figure 3.2 Multiple memberships in COMESA/EAC/SADC/SADU

B Why countries have multiple memberships in RTAs

Multiple memberships reflect the desire of countries to pick and choose various options offered by competing RTAs.[8] Different RTAs offer benefits to members beyond providing the reduction or removal of tariff barriers

8 A. Panagariya, 'The Regionalism Debate: An Overview', Columbia University Policy Papers (1998), available at www.columbia.edu/~ap2231/Policy%20Papers/overview-we(1).pdf, p 36 ('Even in the absence of any increase in trade barriers against nonmembers, the proliferation of crisscrossing FTAs leads to a replacement of the nondiscriminatory MFN tariff by a spaghetti bowl whereby tariffs vary according to the ostensible origin of the product').

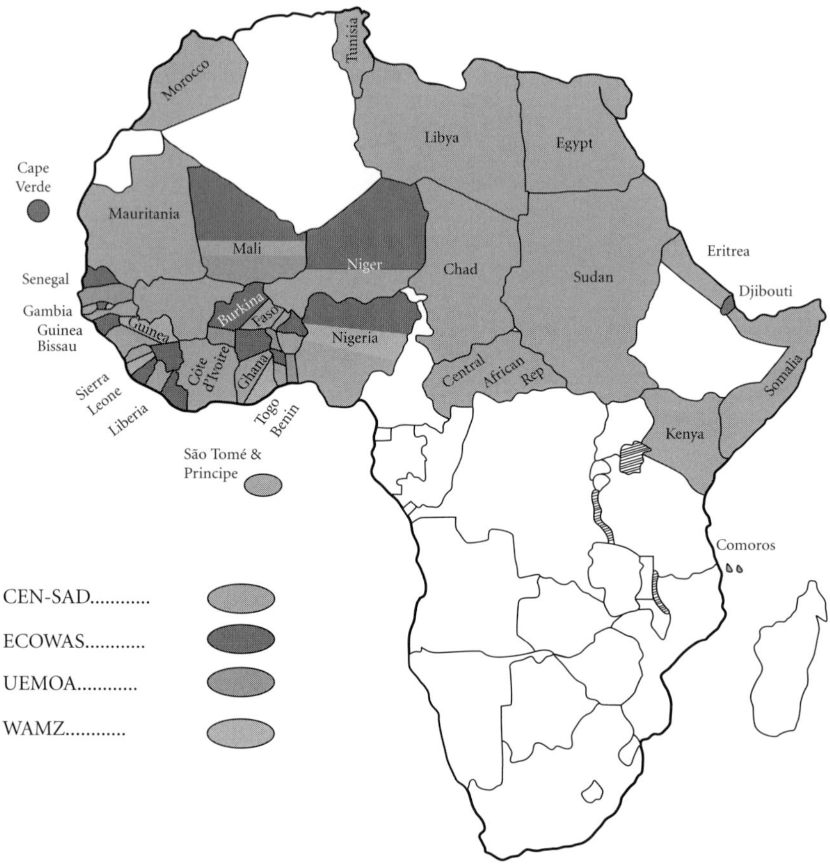

Figure 3.3 Overlapping memberships in ECOWAS/CENSAD/UEMOA/WAMZ

and the harmonization of trade policies like customs policies.[9] For example, the international transportation of commodities through waterways in Africa developed because the continent has the largest river basin coverage in the world.[10] Since waterways do not divert or conform to the signing and changing climate of trade agreements, the use and rights of these waterways that span through multiple free trade areas (FTAs) requires

9 See K.L. Powers, 'Why Do States Pursue Water Cooperation through Regional Trade Agreements? Trade, Environment and Security Linkages in International River Basins' (1 Sept. 2005) (unpublished manuscript, on file with the American Political Science Association), 3–4.

10 *Ibid.* at 16.

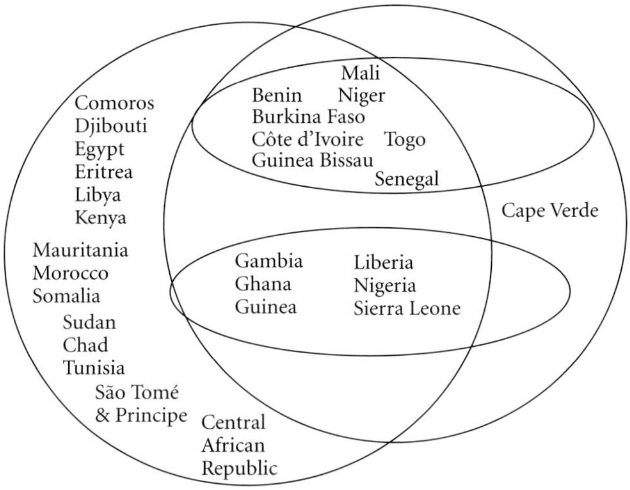

Figure 3.4 Overlapping memberships in ECOWAS/CENSAD/UEMOA/WAMZ

cooperation between RTAs, and offers an important reason for multiple trade bloc membership. Such multiple trade bloc membership gives member countries access to aquatic trade routes that would otherwise be unavailable to them. This contributes to the diversification of agreements by landlocked countries, since transport costs limit competitiveness.[11] As a result, Africa's landlocked countries and the coastal nations they border are members of the same RTAs, sharing ports and trade routes.[12] Water basin states, in fact, often share membership in more than one RTA, and some RTAs overlap in the basins that they manage.[13]

African RTAs, therefore, serve as institutions of basin management demonstrating 'the entwined relationships among trade, environment, and security aspects of international river basins'.[14] From this perspective RTAs are trade-plus institutions to the extent to which trade is linked to environment issues as well as to security issues.[15] In short, natural resource management and water cooperation, on the one hand, are interwoven with trade and security, on the other.[16] Indeed, Chapter I examined how

11 N. Charalambides, 'The Private Sector's Perspective, Priorities and Role in Regional Integration and Implications for Regional Trade Arrangements', ECDPM Discussion Paper No. 66 (ECDPM, 2005), 10.

12 Y. Yang and S. Gupta, 'Regional Trade Arrangements in Africa: Past Performance and the Way Forward' (IMF Working Paper 05/36, 2005), 9.

13 Powers, 'Water Cooperation', at 18. 14 *Ibid.* at 11. 15 *Ibid.* at 25. 16 *Ibid.*

African RTAs nestle within them a variety of non-trade objectives and institutions.

Another major benefit of multiple memberships in RTAs is the ability to shift lawmaking initiatives from one international venue to another that offers different advantages. This is referred to as regime-shifting.[17] According to Laurence Helfer, 'the existence of multiple, discrete regimes, any one of which may plausibly serve as a site for future policy development, leaves considerable room for maneuvering by different clusters of states (or states and NGOs) seeking to maximize their respective interests'.[18] On this argument, countries enter into regimes to reduce the transaction costs and information problems that plague uncoordinated state relations.[19] A few examples are necessary to illustrate this point more fully in the African RTA context.

At present, Kenya is a member of COMESA and the EAC.[20] There are benefits that Kenya accrues under COMESA, currently unavailable under the EAC.[21] COMESA gives Kenya the opportunity to protect its economy against dumping, as it has done in the case of sugar and wheat exports, which Kenya has sought and obtained.[22] Although the EAC has a trade remedy regime, as Chapter VIII shows, it does not currently offer Kenya that important possibility.[23] In addition, COMESA offers a broader group of countries from which Kenya can defend itself against unfair trade practices than does the EAC.[24] The EAC also has advantages that COMESA does not give Kenya.[25] For example, the EAC provides a closer regional proximity with Kenya's immediate and near neighbours than does the expansive COMESA region that spans to Egypt in North Africa.[26] In short, there are things Kenya can better achieve in one regional bloc than in another.

During the latter stages of South Africa's apartheid era, SACU was comprised of Botswana, Lesotho, Namibia (which became a member

17 See L.R. Helfer, 'Regime Shifting: The TRIPs Agreement and New Dynamics of International Intellectual Property Lawmaking', *Yale Journal of International Law* 29 (2004) 5, n. 17 (explaining that the term international 'regime' refers to the principles, norms and rules governing a particular issue area of international relations and the institutional structures and decision-making procedures through which they are developed). Helfer also explains that regimes are formed when the interests of states converge around certain shared objectives that can best be achieved through interstate cooperation. *Ibid.*

18 *Ibid.* at 8. 19 *Ibid.* at 7.

20 EAC, 'East African Community – Kenya, Uganda, Tanzania, Rwanda, Burundi', available at www.eac.int.

21 J. Gathii, 'Spat With Dar Over Trade Unnecessary', *Business Daily Africa*, 8 Feb. 2008, available at http://allafrica.com/stories/200802070871.html.

22 *Ibid.* 23 *Ibid.* 24 *Ibid.* 25 *Ibid.* 26 *Ibid.*

upon its independence in 1990) and Swaziland (BLNS), as well as South Africa.[27] As part of a customs union, these countries enjoyed a higher level of economic integration than would be found in either a preferential trade area (PTA) or an FTA.[28] However, rather than being an organization based on interdependence and mutual cooperation, SACU was a direct reflection of the high level of dependence of the BLNS countries on South Africa.[29] Geographic and economic factors such as shared boundaries, interlinked transportation and employment exemplified this dependent relationship.[30] This dependency was the root of much conflict due to South Africa's maintenance of a white-minority government.[31] Geographic proximity and integration economically prevented BLNS from breaking off ties fully with South Africa, even though the BLNS countries repeatedly denounced South Africa's apartheid system.[32] While the BLNS countries were strongly opposed to the South African form of government and the dominant role South Africa played in their economies, it was not in their best interests to take an extreme position against South Africa, as it might have crippled them economically.[33] The other problem the BLNS countries faced was that South Africa's apartheid government not only alienated itself from a number of international organizations, but also resulted in the rejection of SACU as a whole.[34] The result of this was an increasing effort on the part of the BLNS countries to lessen their dependency on South Africa gradually by exploring other economic options.[35] This was referred to as 'gradual disengagement', and led to the BLNS contingency joining other economic affiliations such as SADCC.[36] The resulting multiple memberships of the BLNS countries was not

27 R.D.A. Henderson, 'The Southern African Customs Union: Politics of Dependence', in R.I. Onwuka and A. Sesay (eds), *The Future of Regionalism in Africa* (London: Macmillan Education, 1985), 225.

28 *Ibid.* at 226. 29 *Ibid.* at 239. 30 *Ibid.* 31 *Ibid.* at 241.

32 See *ibid.* at 238 (explaining that the BLNS countries are open to South African economic pressure for being dependent on South Africa for a large portion of their government revenue in the form of shares from the common customs pool, for their manufactured goods and food and for wage employment).

33 *Ibid.* at 241 (stating that any attempt to impose economic sanctions against South Africa would certainly result in serious economic disruption within the BLNS countries as well as certain neighbouring countries).

34 The best example of the BLNS countries joining others in the region in rejecting South Africa's dominance of SACU is the Lusaka Declaration. See Southern Africa Development Coordination Conference (SADCC), 'Southern Africa: Towards Economic Liberalization: A Declaration by the Governments of Independent Africa Made at Lusaka on the 1st of April 1980', in *Record of the Southern African Development Coordination Summit Conference* (Lusaka, 1980), 35.

35 Henderson, 'South African Customs Union', at 243–4. 36 *Ibid.*

intended to directly compete with South Africa or BLNS's obligations with SACU, but rather to complement the goal of making these countries more economically independent, and less dependent on a country denounced by the world for its racist policies.[37]

The Communauté Economique de l'Afrique de l'Ouest (CEAO) and ECOWAS offer another example from West Africa that has historical reasons accounting for multiple memberships.[38] CEAO was an economic grouping that carried over from the colonial period, while ECOWAS was created in an effort to cut across cultural and linguistic barriers.[39] Instead of abandoning one in favour of the other because they both were based on the same principles, the members of CEAO agreed to join ECOWAS while being able to retain their membership in CEAO.[40] The economic dominance of Nigeria is very similar to South Africa's dominance in the previous example.[41] However, Nigeria's dominance had the opposite effect, of drawing members into ECOWAS instead of pushing them away as South Africa had done.[42]

These examples show that in some cases, multiple memberships were anticipated from the beginning. In such cases, changing political, social and economic environments play a major role in multiple memberships. These examples add to one of the central claims pursued in this chapter as well as the preceding two chapters, that African RTAs are trade-plus regimes that reflect a broad set of goals and are not simply trade treaties. Seeing African RTAs as flexible regimes adds to the argument that countries that are members of more than one RTA may well regard treaties establishing RTAs as providing a framework for cooperation, but not necessarily as treaties creating binding obligations.[43] For these countries, multiple memberships in RTAs offers them flexibility and adaptability, since they can retain their sovereignty and accrue benefits from multiple regimes otherwise not available through sole memberships.

37 *Ibid.* at 244 and n. 44.

38 S.K.B. Asante, 'ECOWAS/CEAO: Conflict and Cooperation in West Africa', in Onwuka and Sesay (eds), *Future of Regionalism*, at 74, 78.

39 *Ibid.* at 75–6. 40 *Ibid.* at 78.

41 S. Rugumamu, 'Africa's Search for Regional Cooperation and Integration in the Twenty-First Century', African Foundation for Capacity Building Paper No. 3 of 2004, at 12, available at www.acbf-pact.org/knowledge/documents/ACBF%20WORKING%20PAPER%20NO.%203.pdf.

42 See *ibid.* at 82 and n. 13 (citing John Ravenhill, who observed that Nigeria's presence in ECOWAS allows it to sustain existing integrative arrangements and to extend into new areas of cooperation).

43 See Helfer, 'Regime Shifting', at 10 and n. 20.

1 *Multiple memberships reflect Africa's diversity*

As noted in Chapter II, regionalism in Africa is often regarded as necessary to aggregate bargaining power to negotiate with powerful trading partners like the European Union (EU).[44] While this argument has much merit and ought not to be downplayed, it presumes that unity in regionalism can overcome the variety of ways in which African countries are divided. Indeed, presuming that African unity through regionalism is easily achievable is based upon 'certain sociological, cultural and psychological affinities already identified' and 'conceives of Africa's foreign policy as being singular and consensual'.[45] Further, such a view presumes that for Africa's voice to be heard in the world trade arena, it must be 'unified through "externalization" for continental integration as well as extra continental effectiveness'.[46] Yet while the hope of unity for these purposes would ideally serve Africa well, the search for African unity and regional integration has proven very daunting. Multiple memberships reflect the reality of diversity among African countries and the complexity of their conflicting, overlapping and sometimes congruent interests.[47] In fact, as William Zartman, a leading Africanist, has argued:

> The recognition of overlapping systems in interpreting foreign policy alternatives and possibilities for states with dual membership is both a more helpful and more realistic way of looking at foreign policies than is the attempt to force such states exclusively into one area or the other.[48]

Zartman's support for overlapping systems for African countries, espoused several decades ago, continues to have relevance today. Consider, for example, how some African states have recently defected from signing Economic Partnership Agreements (EPAs) with the EU in their

44 See C.V. Vaitsos, 'The Role of Transnational Enterprises in Latin American Economic Integration Efforts: Who Integrates With Whom, How and For Whose Benefit?', UNCTAD/ST/ECDC/19 (New York: UN, 1982) (referencing C.V. Vaitsos, 'Crisis in Regional Economic Cooperation (Integration) Among Developing Countries: A Survey', *World Development* 6 (1978) 719, 729–36).

45 T.M. Shaw, 'Towards a Political Economy of Regionalism in Africa', in Onwuka and Sesay (eds.), *Future of Regionalism*, at 13.

46 *Ibid.* 47 See *infra* Chapter IV, section A.

48 I.W. Zartman, 'Africa as a Subordinate State in International Relations', *International Organization* 21(3) (Summer 1967) 549. See also, W. Lyakurwa, A. Mckay, N. Ng'eno and W. Kennes, 'Regional Integration in Southern Africa: A Review of Experiences and Issues', in A. Oyejide, I. Elbadawi and P. Collier (eds), *Regional Integration and Trade Liberalization in Subsaharan Africa: Framework Issues and Methodological Perspectives* (London: Palgrave Macmillan, 1997), 196.

designated regional groupings.[49] This is only an abbreviated discussion to illustrate how overlapping regimes arise. Chapter X discusses EPAs more fully. One major reason for emergence of overlapping RTAs in the context of EPAs is exemplified by non-least developed countries (LDCs)[50] in ECOWAS, which decided to go it alone and signed their own EPA with the EU.[51] In addition, Ghana and Côte D'Ivoire, two of the three non-LDCs, signed interim EPAs under pressure from the EU, thus further widening the wedge among ECOWAS Member States.[52] ECOWAS LDCs were concerned that signing an EPA with the EU would allow Nigeria to become a conduit for channelling goods originating from Europe into their economies.[53] Thus, differing interests among ECOWAS members resulted in multiplying the number of EPAs the EU was signing with ECOWAS members, further exacerbating multiplicity of trade and related agreements in Africa.

Another example is Tanzania's decision to stay away from the Eastern and Southern Africa (ESA) group of countries (essentially the members of the EAC), in the negotiations over an EPA. Tanzania decided to negotiate its EPA under the SADC group, with which it is more ideologically aligned, rather than with the ESA group.[54] In so doing, Tanzania's choice of SADC, made to protect its strategic interests, is a reflection of the argument advanced here – that African RTAs offer alternative choices of how best to advance the interests of the member countries. Indeed, Tanzania's interests as an LDC are not necessarily consistent with those of countries like Kenya, which is not an LDC under the classifications used by the United Nations.[55]

49 K. Akaoha, 'ECOWAS EPA – The Facts and the Fallacies' (21 Jan. 2008), available at www.bilaterals.org/article.php3?id_article=10985.

50 'Least developed country' is a term of art used by the United Nations to describe countries which exhibit the lowest levels of socio-economic development. See Office of the High Representative for the Least Developed Countries, Landlocked Developing Countries and the Small Island Developing States, 'Least Developed Countries: Criteria for Identification of LDCs', available at www.unohrlls.org/en/ldc/related/59/ (explaining the criteria by which countries are evaluated to determine their LDC status).

51 *Ibid.* 52 *Ibid.*

53 It is, of course, not clear once Nigeria signs an EPA with the EU that this will necessarily protect these LDCs from EU exports destined for Nigeria reaching them. See *ibid.*

54 Gathii, 'Spat with Dar'.

55 See United Nations, 'World Population Prospects Population Database', available at http://esa.un.org/unpp/definition.html (defining 'least developed countries' and listing which countries are included in the group of least developed countries).

In SACU, Angola and Botswana are signing different EPA agreements than those being signed by the rest of SADC's members.[56] In all, fifteen SADC members are negotiating EPAs under four different configurations.[57] Under the EPAs, African, Caribbean and Pacific Group of States (ACP)[58] duty-free and full quota access to the EU will end and they will be required to open their own borders to European products and services.[59] EPA negotiations in the SACU region present a potential conflict between SACU's Common External Tariffs (CET) structure, on the one hand, with the free trade commitments among SADC Member States who are negotiating their own EPA with the EU, on the other. The overlap between the SACU CET and the free trade commitments under SADC are likely to result in transshipment. This is because importers enjoying a CET within SACU can export such imports to non-SACU members who are members of SADC.[60] I illustrate this with the example of Swaziland a little further below.

The Cotonou Agreement, which is the basis of the EU's negotiations with ACP countries over EPAs does not also address the question of who the proper parties to the EPAs should be.[61] Are the proper parties the regions or countries themselves? Ultimately, it is the countries that ought to sign the agreements under their own constitutional rules. Yet, they have to negotiate as groups – groups with differing interests. As we have seen above, this has resulted in the formation of de facto coalitions within the context of EPA negotiations.

56 'Southern Africa Region Makes Progress on EPA', *Bridges* 13(1) (Feb.–Mar., 2009) 15, available at http://ictsd.org/downloads/bridges/bridges13–1.pdf.

57 *Ibid.* For a fuller discussion see *infra* Chapters IV and XI.

58 The African, Caribbean and Pacific Group States (ACP) is a group of countries created by the Georgetown Agreement in 1975. The group's main objectives are sustainable development and poverty reduction within its Member States, as well as their greater integration into the world's economy. All of the Member States, except Cuba, are signatories of the Cotonou Agreement with the European Union. See generally 'ACP Member States', The Secretariat of the African, Caribbean and Pacific Group States, available at www.acpsec.org/en/acp_states.htm (listing the ACP Member States).

59 See Bridges, 'Southern Africa Region Makes Progress on EPA'.

60 S. Woolfrey, 'South Africa's Concerns over the Interim Economic Partnership Agreement' (7 Oct. 2009), available at www.tralac.org/cgi-bin/giga.cgi?cmd=cause_dir_news_item&cause_id=1694&news_id=75268&cat_id=1058.

61 See generally European Commission, 'The Cotonou Agreement', available at http://ec.europa.eu/development/geographical/cotonouintro_en.cfm (providing an overview of the Agreement).

C Criticisms of multiple memberships

As noted at the beginning of this chapter, there are two categories of criticisms regarding the multiplicity of memberships in Africa. Each of these is addressed in turn.

1 *Spaghetti bowl: Are RTAs building or stumbling blocks?*

The path towards the establishment of an African Economic Community is preceded by the establishment of six RTAs. These six trade agreements, referred to as the pillars of the yet to be formed African Economic Community, are: The East African Community; the Economic Community of West African States; the Inter-Governmental Authority on Development; the Southern African Development Community; the Common Market for Eastern and Central Africa; and ECCAS and the Arab Maghreb Union.[62] In this sense, the Treaty for the Establishment of the African Economic Community regards these RTAs as building blocks towards an eventual continent-wide trade bloc.

The economist Jagdish Bhagwati has argued that multiple regional and bilateral trade agreements are a stumbling rather than a building block for the multilateral trade regime.[63] Bhagwati has referred to this increase in the number of bilateral and RTAs as the spaghetti bowl.[64] Since the goal of each of these agreements is to liberalize trade within the group, Bhagwati argued that these agreements had discriminatory consequences for trade creation.[65] For example, the same product gets different tariff treatment depending on its origin, since members of a preferential trade arrangement treat their members better than they would non-members, even if the same product from the non-member was produced at a lower cost.[66] In effect, multiple bilateral and RTAs undermine the goal of non-discriminatory international trade under the umbrella of the GATT/WTO framework since they create RoOs that discriminate across products and countries.[67] The ten-year assessment of the WTO, referred to as the Sutherland Report, regretted the lack of harmonization produced by the complex web of inconsistent RoOs in multiple RTAs

62 For an extended discussion of each of these RTAs, see Chapter V.

63 J. Bhagwati, *The World Trading System at Risk* (Princeton University Press, 1991); see also J. Bhagwati *et al.*, 'Trading Preferentially: Theory and Policy', *The Economic Journal* 108 (1998) 1128, 1138.

64 Bhagwati, 'U.S. Trade Policy', at 1138. 65 *Ibid.* 66 *Ibid.*

67 A. Panagariya, 'Preferential Trade Liberalization: The Traditional Theory and New Developments', *Journal of Economic Literature* 38(2) (2000) 287, 328.

which in turn increased transaction costs for business and hampered trade flows.[68] These complex webs of RoOs also counteract trade creation, as the ability of a partner country to undermine an inefficient domestic industry is reduced, since they have the effect of requiring a country bound by them to purchase inputs from less efficient sources.[69] In effect, the trade preferences which are extended under bilaterals and RTAs undermine the GATT/WTO rule that requires members to unconditionally extend any trade concessions made to one WTO member to all WTO member countries.[70]

One of the primary justifications for the formation of RTAs is geographic proximity among a group of countries.[71] However, Bhagwati and Panagariya argue, geographic proximity does not provide benefits between natural trading partners, as presumed by its proponents, for a number of reasons.[72] First, they contend that arguments about natural trading partners are based on static theories that say little about trade diversion as a primary reason for the establishment of RTAs.[73] Another justification in support of the natural trading partners thesis is that geographic proximity favours the formation of trading unions between neighbours since this would eliminate large transport costs in addition to promoting specialization in production.[74] But according to Bhagwati and Panagariya, eliminating tariffs between member countries in a regional grouping leaves each country worse off, as the resulting welfare gain will be less than the revenue lost by the elimination of tariffs.[75] In addition to lost revenue, RTAs also result in trade diversion.[76] Trade diversion occurs where the creation of an RTA in one country leads to the production of a similar product in a different country that is less efficient than the first country, but is less expensive to the other country because preferential tariffs reduce the final cost of the good.[77]

68 P. Sutherland *et al.*, 'The Future of the WTO: Addressing Institutional Challenges in the New Millennium', Report by the Consultative Board to the Director-General, Supachai Panitchpakdi (WTO, 2005), 22, available at www.wto.org/english/thewto_e/10anniv_e/future_wto_e.pdf.

69 Panagariya, 'Regionalism Debate', at 18.

70 This is the Most Favoured Nation (MFN) rule found in Art. 1 of the General Agreement on Tariffs and Trade (GATT) 1948, 30 Oct. 1947, available at www.wto.org/english/docs_e/legal_e/gatt47_e.pdf.

71 Panagariya, 'Preferential Trade Liberalization', at 311.

72 Bhagwati, *World Trading System*, at 1134. 73 *Ibid.* at 1129. 74 *Ibid.* at 1130.

75 *Ibid.* 76 *Ibid.* at 1129.

77 For a full, and quite useful explanation of trade diversion, see Panagariya, 'Preferential Trade Liberalization', at 290.

Bhagwati and Panagariya also dispute the claim that RTAs reduce tariffs among members. Their argument is based on the fact that the Uruguay Round of GATT talks, which ended in the mid-1990s, left a number of tariffs in place, particularly in agriculture.[78] As such, preferential trade agreements among these countries would be particularly harmful, because their exposure to high external tariffs encouraged other countries to diversify from the products that are protected by high tariff walls.[79]

Finally, Bhagwati and Panagariya refute two other arguments often made in favour of RTAs – that reduced transportation costs are a basis for formation of RTAs (which are alluded to in a different context above),[80] and that a high volume of trade resulting from an RTA is good for both trading partners.[81] They argue that it is unlikely that a high initial volume of trade will offset any form of trade diversion caused by two states entering into an RTA.[82] This is unlikely because elasticity of production is the primary determinant of the amount of trade diversion, not the volume of trade.[83] They point out that in countries with imperfect substitutes, a gradual reduction in tariffs leads to an eventual loss of welfare by each of the states even though each state is specialized in the form of production for each good.[84]

For transport costs, the common wisdom is that lower transport costs will allow countries to capture more of the marginal cost of production because of fewer costs of production and sale.[85] Bhagwati and Panagariya argue that this is not necessarily true, since a specialized producer can act as a monopolist and the increased cost of transport makes a distant country have a higher elasticity.[86] As a result, it is not always the best course of action to sell only to countries with lower costs of transport.[87] Bhagwati and Panagariya also argue that lower transport costs for a neighbouring partner may also be outweighed by cost advantages in a distant one, as is currently demonstrated by China's ability to compete with other producers in the textile market of many countries around the world.[88] Bhagwati and Panagariya therefore argue that these theories for the formation of RTAs are 'static' to the extent that they assume all welfare gains and losses are created at the same time and are therefore instantaneous.[89] For this reason, Bhagwati and Panagariya recommend a dynamic model of free trade.[90] To them, such dynamic theory of free trade is more consistent with a WTO-type system than with the proliferation of RTAs.[91]

78 Bhagwati, *World Trading System*, at 1130. 79 *Ibid.*
80 See *ibid.* at 1134 and accompanying text. 81 See *ibid.* at 1132.
82 *Ibid.* 83 *Ibid.* 84 *Ibid.* 85 *Ibid.* 86 *Ibid.* at 1134.
87 *Ibid.* 88 *Ibid.* at 1142. 89 *Ibid.* 90 *Ibid.* 91 *Ibid.*

For these reasons, free trade economists argue that the best solution to the problems posed by proliferation of RTAs is to speed up multilateral, unconditional, MFN non-discriminatory trade liberalization, since tariff preferences would disappear once external tariffs drop to zero.[92]

2 High transaction and administrative costs

A second category of criticisms relates to the high transaction costs and administrative difficulties of complying with multiple RoOs.[93] Multiple memberships sap the little trade capacity and budgets of African governments from focusing on a single regional economic bloc. In addition, jurisdictional uncertainty arises as a result of overlapping legal regimes. This criticism has much in common with the 'spaghetti bowl' argument we saw above and may, in fact, be regarded as a subset of it.[94]

One of the most important features of a customs union is that all the member countries adopt one CET.[95] This raises a major concern with regard to loss of revenue for countries that enjoy monies from tariffs through their various trade interests. In joining a customs union (CU), these countries would be subject to one CET which could significantly diminish the funds they previously collected through their own agreements.[96] There is also a fear that once a country joins a CU, its trading policy cannot be altered without the consent of the other union members.[97] Further, exporters who have benefited from regional preferential market access will want to keep their unique markets, and local producers who have benefited from favourable RoOs will resist reductions in external trade barriers and efforts to make rules less restrictive.[98]

Difficulties may also arise from countries participating in various RTAs, including the human and financial costs associated with membership, lack

92 Panagariya, 'Preferential Trade Liberalization', at 328.

93 W.M. Choi, 'Defragmenting Fragmented Rules of Origin of RTAs: A Building Block to Global Free Trade', *Journal of International Economic Law* 13 (2010) 111, 115 (arguing that RoOs tend to discriminate, especially against small poor developing countries, and that they act like tariffs on intermediate products levied by the country importing the final good).

94 See *infra* section C1.

95 Article XXIV8(a)(i) of the GATT defines a customs union as 'the substitution of a single customs territory for two or more territories, so that duties and other restrictive regulations of commerce... are eliminated with respect to substantially all the trade between the constituent territories of the union, or at least with respect to substantially all the trade in products originating in such territories.'

96 Yang and Gupta, 'Regional Trade Arrangements', at 14. 97 *Ibid.* at 6. 98 *Ibid.*

of harmonization of policies in the areas of RoOs, customs procedures and the changing political climate of RTAs or the countries themselves.[99] Legal uncertainties may also arise in cases where more than one trade arrangement applies to trade between two countries.[100] Controversies regarding which RTA has proper jurisdiction in cases where there is more than one dispute settler may hinder trade, by increasing transaction costs as well as uncertainty among the member countries.[101]

When a country has membership in multiple RTAs, multiple RoOs need to be applied. RoOs specify when a product will qualify for duty-free movement within the RTA, and what proportion of value must be added if it originates within the trade bloc, or whether it is required that a product undergo a substantial transformation in a country before being allowed to cross the border duty free.[102] Knowing which RoOs to follow depends on where commodities originate, and for states involved in various RTAs, this undoubtedly makes the customs clearance process more complex and delays transactions.[103] The more RTAs a country is involved in, the higher the likelihood that the cost of shipping goods would climb higher in order to offset the need for increases in administrative supervision necessary to keep track of proper origin documentation and procedures.[104] This may in turn have the effect of producers turning to other countries not involved in multiple RTAs, or to those requiring less complex procedures.

Since Free Trade Agreements (FTAgs) allow each of their Member States to implement its own tariff structure, RoOs need to be included in

99 A. Geda and H. Kebret, 'Regional Economic Integration in Africa: A Review of Problems and Prospects with a Case Study of COMESA', *Journal of African Economics* 17 (June 2008) 357, 371–2.

100 C. Jakobeit *et al.*, 'Overlapping Membership in COMESA, EAC, SACU and SADC: Trade Policy Options for the Region and for EPA Negotiations' (*Deutsche Gesellschaft für Technische Zusammenarbeit* (GTZ), 2005), 22, available at www.gtz.de/de/dokumente/en-epa-overlapping-memberships-2005.pdf.

101 See e.g., W.J. Davey and A. Separ, 'The Soft Drinks Case: The WTO and Regional Agreements', *World Trade Review* 8 (2009) 5, 15 (arguing that '[i]t would obviously be desirable from the perspective of avoiding duplication of proceedings and conservation of resources if there were agreements negotiated as to how to allocate jurisdiction over disputes in respect of international agreements covering subjects in a way that multiple dispute-settlement procedures might be expected to be invocable' at 17.

102 Panagariya, 'Regionalism Debate', at 17.

103 See A.O. Krueger, 'Problems with Overlapping Free Trade Areas', in O. Takatoshi and A.O. Krueger (eds), *Regionalism Versus Multilateral Trade Arrangements* (University of Chicago Press, 1997), 9, 18.

104 *Ibid.* at 16.

agreements involving FTAs in order to prevent transshipment.[105] Because FTAs do not have a CET, which is typical of a Customs Union (CU), RoOs are important in order to ensure that a product destined for a high-tariff member country is not first imported through a lower-tariff member country.[106] CETs already in place make this type of trade deflection less of a problem in CUs.[107] These are real and complex issues regarding the transportation of goods among Member States and non-Member States, and states belonging to multiple RTAs that would need to be addressed before CUs are established. However, according to Yang and Gupta, 'given the small share of intraregional trade in Africa's total trade, the direct contribution of any trade deflection to overall trade performance is likely to be limited'.[108] Further, an elimination of RoOs altogether may be a solution to this problem as well. Transshipment would be inevitable, as products would no doubt find their way into high-tariff countries through low-tariff members; however, it could be argued that this would force the high-tariff members to lower their external tariffs in order to be competitive.[109] This would, in effect, minimize trade diversion and have the secondary effect of creating a CU in which the members of the FTA would be forced to agree on a set CET.[110]

Multiple memberships in RTAs open up the possibility that a country is at once a CU as well as a member of an FTA. Such a country would be able to enjoy preferential tariffs from the FTA, but would not be able to reciprocate the preferential favour to the FTA, since it has to uphold its CET in the CU. If the commodities are valuable enough, those in the FTA may deem these transactions to supersede the benefits of special tariffs that they are unable to enjoy. This situation is currently exemplified by Swaziland and its multiple memberships. Swaziland is currently a member of SACU, COMESA, (both CUs) as well as SADC, which is currently an FTA.[111] Swaziland is therefore a member of two CUs and an FTA. As a COMESA member, Swaziland enjoys free market access within COMESA, which has a fully developed FTA, but its duty-free importing beyond COMESA and SACU is limited due to their CETs.[112] Membership in SACU's and COMESA's CETs limits Swaziland's ability to extend

105 Jakobeit *et al.*, 'Overlapping Membership', at 46.
106 Panagariya, 'Regionalism Debate', at 12.
107 Krueger, 'Overlapping Free Trade Areas', at 15.
108 Yang and Gupta, 'Regional Trade Arrangements', at 19.
109 Panagariya, 'Regionalism Debate', at 17–18.
110 *Ibid.* 111 See *supra* Figure 3.1.
112 Jakobeit *et al.*, 'Overlapping Membership', at 60.

more generous unilateral concessions to non-SACU and non-COMESA members, since this would undermine Swaziland's CET commitments. If Swaziland was to extend such unilateral concessions, say to SADC member countries who are neither SACU nor COMESA members, it would undermine these CUs and effectively downgrade them into FTAs. In such a situation the respective RoOs would apply, thereby effectively making Swaziland a transit country.[113]

3. *Implications for African RTAs*

If the goal of trade liberalization is to increase efficient production and therefore to lower costs, African RTAs seem to have strayed far from this goal. Reducing costs on each unit of trade created by entering into the next RTA does not appear to be the primary motivation for African countries belonging to more than one RTA. Instead, multiple memberships in RTAs have been driven by historical circumstances, political and ideological considerations, as well as strategic considerations such as access to riparian waterways.[114] In this sense, trade diversion may very well have increased the magnitude of costs of production, further exacerbating the problems of trade liberalization within Africa.

Indeed, African RTAs are not regarded by their members as exclusively trade regimes.[115] Rather, they serve multiple goals, including as frameworks for coordination of development projects as alluded to more fully in Chapter I. Further, to the extent to which African RTAs are regarded as trade regimes, African countries have been most concerned with balancing gains and losses and ensuring that the poorest members are compensated for any losses they suffer as a result of liberalization commitments, as was demonstrated at length in the discussion on variable geometry in Chapter II.

Large external tariffs still remain in place in a variety of African countries, while other countries have lower tariffs on the same product.[116] This results in product diversion between countries and effectively reduces the

113 *Ibid.* 114 See *supra* Chapter II.

115 Notably, Pravin Krishna and Jagdish Bhagwati have argued that it is possible to pursue non-economic benefits within CUs and for the members to come out better off. See generally P. Krishna and J. Bhagwati, 'Necessarily Welfare Enhancing Customs Unions With Industrialization Constraints: The Cooper-Massell-Johnson-Bhagwati Conjecture', *Japan and the World Economy* 9 (1997) 441.

116 See Yang and Gupta, 'Regional Trade Arrangements', at 13.

effectiveness of RTAs as liberalizing trade regimes in Africa.[117] Much of the current available data supports the notion that RTAs are either ineffective at stimulating inter-regional trade, or are at best, non-factors.[118] If RTAs are to work optimally in promoting liberalizing trade, more regional trade should be occurring and external trade increasing due to specialization. However, between 2004 and 2006, many African countries did not get involved with a great amount of inter-regional trade.[119] In this period, three countries, Swaziland, Togo and Zimbabwe, exported more than half of all exports to countries inside their regional grouping – SADC.[120] Only five countries exported more than half of their exports to Africa generally, including Djibouti and Mali in addition to the countries listed above.[121] Many countries contributed ten per cent or less of total exports to Africa and even less to their regional trade group.[122] Based on this data, ECCAS had three of the ten bottom countries for inter-regional trade, while COMESA had two.[123] Out of all of the RTAs, ECCAS had the lowest volume of intra-regional trade, with only $320m of exports traded between the countries.[124]

In COMESA, Kenya leads with a third of all exports, the main export link being Kenya to Uganda.[125] While many of these countries do not contribute significantly to regional trade, many have an obvious link to external markets. Gambia, for instance, contributes twenty-three per cent of its exports to intra-regional trade among ECOWAS countries.[126] While this is higher than many African countries, seventy-one per cent of Gambian exports go to developed European countries.[127] The same trend holds for Botswana and Burundi. Both contribute around thirteen per cent of exports to inter-regional trade but eighty-three and sixty-five per cent of exports, respectively, to Europe.[128] This data again supports the idea that transport costs are not the only factor, if even a large factor in inter-regional trade success. A better example might be Chad, a landlocked, unstable country that contributes only 0.01 per cent of exports to the ECCAS, but 99.8 per cent of exports to Europe, the United States and Asia.[129] If transport costs are the large barrier they are assumed to be, then

117 *Ibid.* 118 *Ibid.*

119 N. Lebale *et al.*, 'Economic Development in Africa: Report 2009: Strengthening Regional Economic Integration for Africa's Development', United Nations Conference on Trade and Development (New York: UN, 2009), 34.

120 *Ibid.* 121 *Ibid.* 122 *Ibid.* 123 *Ibid.* 124 *Ibid.* at 35.

125 *Ibid.* 126 *Ibid.* 127 *Ibid.* 128 *Ibid.* 129 *Ibid.*

Chad would probably be doing a much larger amount of inter-regional trade due to trade diversion created by increased costs.

More recent data suggests the impact of the global recession on African exports to the United States. Total African exports to the United States for the year 2008 to 2009 were down from four per cent to ninety-nine per cent for some countries. However, some countries have increased their share of trade with the United States.[130] Chad's share dropped fifty-nine per cent while South Africa's dropped fifty-two per cent.[131] The question here becomes whether this is a permanent drop or just a demand-generated price shock that will resolve itself in the short and medium term.

D Conclusions

The first three chapters of this book have demonstrated that African RTAs are flexible legal regimes. These agreements are not designed to commit their members to scrupulous and rigorous adherence; rather, they have been designed as flexible regimes of cooperation. These regimes provide a forum for cooperation on a whole range of objectives, including trade liberalization. They nestle or nest within these regimes an entire range of other objectives, including those relating to security and the sharing of common river ways.

In so far as trade liberalization is concerned, African RTAs have modified the neo-classical/comparative advantage classical free-trade model in two significant ways. First, they have embraced the principle of variable geometry according to which timetabled liberalization commitments are undertaken at different speeds depending on the economic ability and interest of members. Second, these regimes have made distributional equity amongst themselves a central feature. This means that they have designed compensatory mechanisms to ensure losses arising from liberalization commitments are given to the losers. By foregrounding variable geometry and distributional equity concerns, African RTAs have correspondingly distanced themselves from non-discriminatory free trade.

In addition, the multiplicity of memberships in African RTAs, while further confirming their nature as flexible regimes, also illustrates how they are a classic case of the 'spaghetti bowl'. Thus, while flexibility has enmeshed well with the preferences of African governments not to build

130 AGOA, 'Resource on the African Growth and Opportunities Act', available at www.agoa.info.

131 *Ibid.*

strong supranational bureaucracies, it has undermined the achievement of more thorough intra-regional trade. Since African governments understand these RTAs as flexible regimes, they regard them less from the efficiency gains that non-discriminatory free trade may offer, but rather from the short-term benefits that these regimes offer, particularly as forums for integrated development of common resources such as river basins, and in terms of any gains arising from functionally specific objectives that may be nestled within these regimes that do not have to await the long-term horizon which non-discriminatory free trade is likely to offer.

IV

African RTAs in the context of Article XXIV of the GATT

A Introduction

This chapter examines the requirements of Article XXIV of the General Agreement on Tariffs and Trade (GATT) for the formation of free trade areas (FTAs) and customs unions (CUs). First, I examine the requirements for the formation of RTAs under Article XXIV and the various debates surrounding the interpretation of this GATT Article. I then examine the GATT/WTO framework as a trade constitution before proceeding to examine the problems encountered in the examination process of RTAs at the WTO, particularly in relation to defining 'substantially all the trade' under Article XXIV (8), 'interim agreements' under Article XXIV 5(c); 'other regulations of commerce' as well as 'other restrictive regulations of commerce' under those Articles. The chapter then examines liberalization of restrictive rules of origin before proceeding to examine the enabling clause as it relates to the formation of RTAs. The chapter then discusses the EC-GSP case and, briefly, the EU-ACP EPA agreements to conclude the chapter. The EPAs are further discussed in Chapter XI.

The GATT was initially established in 1947 to address concerns of economic nationalism and economic isolationism.[1] It laid the 'groundwork for the re-establishment of the multilateral most-favoured nation principle', replacing the existing patterns of preference with 'a set of rules to lend support for [the principle's] coherent application over time'.[2] Before the creation of the GATT, customs unions were traditionally treated as receiving an exemption from the most-favoured-nation (MFN) principle in bilateral arrangements, and this practice was preserved through the Havana Conference and in the final International Trade Organization (ITO) Charter.[3] A similar exemption was created for free trade areas, which were an unknown concept before the GATT, in order to allow less

1 J.H. Mathis and J. Bhagwati, *Regional Trade Agreements in the GATT/WTO: Article XXIV and the Internal Trade Requirement* (The Netherlands: T.M.C. Asser Press, 2002), 18.
2 *Ibid.* at 13. 3 *Ibid.* at 31.

formal preferential arrangements that arguably would not 'cause the dislocation which Article 16 was designed to prevent'.[4] With the failure to ratify the ITO Charter, the GATT became the vehicle for international economic cooperation.

The requirements for the formation of CUs and FTAs are found in Article XXIV of the GATT. Article XXIV allows for the formation of such RTAs notwithstanding other provisions of the GATT, namely Article I which contains the MFN principle. The formation of these 'complete' agreements is allowed because they have been recognized to promote trade liberalization through the removal of barriers to substantially all of the trade between members to such agreements.[5] Additionally, these two types of RTAs are regarded by some as capable of helping developing economies 'implement domestic reforms and open up to competitive market pressures at a sustainable pace, thus facilitating their integration in the world economy'.[6] Other less 'complete' types of preferential trade agreements are not recognized under the GATT because of the concern over the protectionism that may result from the granting of such preferences, which may undermine the multilateral trading system if allowed. RTAs created under Article XXIV of the GATT must comply with the WTO rules for their formation, but the Committee on Regional Trade Agreements (CRTA) has had difficulty in verifying such compliance due in part to controversies over the interpretation of the GATT provisions against which their compliance is assessed.[7] The proliferation of RTAs in recent years has made it clear that the controversy over such provisions must be resolved in order to ensure that such agreements being formed will not frustrate the goal of the GATT and the WTO.

B Article XXIV of the GATT: Requirements for the formation of RTAs

Article XXIV of the GATT recognizes the positive effects of free trade that can be attained by closer integration between parties to RTAs. The purpose

4 *Ibid.* at 38, citing a comment by the representative of Iraq, E/CONF.2/C.3/SR.4.

5 L. Grimett, 'Protectionism and Compliance with the GATT Article XXIV in Selected Regional Trade Agreements' (thesis submitted to Rhodes University, 1999), i, available at http://eprints.ru.ac.za/208/01/grimett-thesis.pdf.

6 J. Crawford and R. Firoentino, 'The Changing Landscape of Regional Trade Agreements', Discussion Paper No. 8 (WTO, 2005), 1, available at www.wto.int/english/res_e/booksp_e/discussion_papers8_e.pdf.

7 Mathis and Bhagwati, *Regional Trade Agreements in the GATT/WTO*, at 227.

of such agreements 'should be to facilitate trade between the constituent territories and not to raise barriers to the trade of other contracting parties with such territories'.[8] This purpose is reflected in the requirements for the formation of customs unions and free trade areas listed in paragraphs (5)–(8) of Article XXIV of the GATT.

Article XXIV (5) of the GATT lays out the external requirements for the formation of CUs and FTAs. Paragraph (5)(a) allows for the formation of a CU if the duties and other regulations of commerce imposed upon its formation are not, on the whole, higher or more restrictive than the general incidence of those applicable in the constituent territories before the CU was formed. Paragraph (5)(b) allows for the formation of an FTA if the duties and other regulations of commerce maintained in each of the constituent territories and applicable at the formation of the FTA to the trade of WTO members not included in such area are not higher or more restrictive than those existing before the FTA was formed. Paragraphs (5)(a) and (b) are aimed at avoiding trade diversion by allowing the formation of RTAs that have a neutral impact on non-member countries. Article XXIV of the GATT also allows for these conditions to be met gradually through interim agreements that lead to the formation of either a CU or FTA. Paragraph (5)(c) requires any such interim agreement to 'include a plan and schedule for the formation of such a customs union or of such a free-trade area within a reasonable length of time'.[9]

Article XXIV (6) of the GATT applies when a contracting party under paragraph (5)(a) 'proposes to increase any rate of duty inconsistently with the provisions of Article II'.[10] If this occurs, the procedure set forth in Article XXVIII, regarding the modification of schedules, should apply. Additionally, Article XXIV (6) of the GATT provides that, in 'providing for compensatory adjustment, due account shall be taken of the compensation already afforded by the reduction brought about in the corresponding duty of the other constituents of the union'.[11]

As the formation of a regional integration scheme is an exception to the MFN principle, the formation of an RTA must be notified to the WTO. Article XXIV (7)(a) of the GATT sets out the requirements for any contracting party that decides to enter into a CU, FTA, or an interim agreement leading to the formation of such an agreement. A party so deciding must notify the contracting parties and must make available to them any

8 The General Agreement on Tariffs and Trade 1948, 30 Oct. 1947, Art. XXIV para. 4, available at www.wto.org/english/docs_e/legal_e/gatt47_e.pdf.

9 *Ibid.* at para. 5(c). 10 *Ibid.* at para. 6. 11 *Ibid.*

'information regarding the proposed union or area as will enable them to make such reports and recommendations to contracting parties as they may deem appropriate'.[12] Paragraph (7)(b) applies when the contracting parties find that an interim agreement (containing a plan and schedule per paragraph (5)) is not likely to result in the formation of a CU or FTA within the anticipated period, or the period contemplated by the parties is not a reasonable one. If this happens, the parties must not maintain, or put into force the agreement, unless they are prepared to modify it in accordance with the recommendations made by the contracting parties. Paragraph (7)(c) deals with any substantial change in the plan or schedule contained in an interim agreement referred to in paragraph (5)(c). Any such change must be 'communicated to the contracting parties, who may then request the contracting parties concerned to consult with them if the change seems likely to jeopardize or delay unduly the formation of the customs union or of the free-trade area'.[13]

Article XXIV (8) defines a CU and an FTA for the purposes of the GATT. Paragraph (8) lays out the internal requirements for the formation of a CU or an FTA with the goal of maximizing trade creation between the parties to the RTA through the elimination of trade barriers. A CU is defined as:

> the substitution of a single customs territory for two or more territories, so that duties and other restrictive regulations of commerce . . . are eliminated with respect to substantially all the trade between the constituent territories of the union, or at least with respect to substantially all the trade in products originating in such territories.[14]

There is also an external requirement for the formation of a CU – the application of 'substantially the same duties and other regulations of commerce . . . by each of the members of the union to the trade of territories not included in the union'.[15] An FTA is defined as a 'group of two or more customs territories in which the duties and other restrictive regulations of commerce . . . are eliminated on substantially all the trade between the constituent territories in products originating in such territories'.[16] In both paragraphs (8)(a)(i) and (b) of Article XXIV of the GATT there are exceptions where, out of necessity, a member is allowed to impose duties or other restrictive regulations of commerce. The duties and regulations that may be imposed are confined to those found in Articles XI–XV and

12 *Ibid.* at para. 7(a). 13 *Ibid.* at para. 7(c). 14 *Ibid.* at para. 8(a)(i).
15 *Ibid.* at para. 8(a)(ii). 16 *Ibid.* at para. 8(b).

Article XX of the GATT. The Appellate Body in *Turkey – Textiles* stated that 'it may not always be possible to determine whether not applying a measure would prevent the formation of a customs union without first determining whether there *is* a customs union'.[17] Since Article XXIV (8) is definitional in nature, an examination of WTO compatibility must begin there before the other provisions conditioning the exception to the MFN principle may be examined.

C Economic rationales of Article XXIV of the GATT

The economic justifications underlining Article XXIV of the GATT were first made by Jacob Viner in his 1950 treatise *The Customs Union Issue.*[18] Viner distinguished between the trade-creating effects of preferential trade agreements and the trade-diverting effects of such agreements, noting for the first time that CUs may be capable of diverting more trade than they create and, thus, are economically irrational.[19] Previously it had been assumed that all CUs were economically beneficial and that Article XXIV of the GATT reflected this in its requirement that complete agreements are to be formed. In his treatise, Viner noted that 'if the distinction is made to rest, as often seems to be the case, on some supposed virtue in a 100 per cent preference, which suddenly turns to maximum evil at 99 per cent, the degree of evil tapering off as the degree of preference shrinks, it is a distinction as illogical . . . as this way of putting it makes it sound'.[20] Viner pointed out that 100 per cent preferential treatment can be more trade diverting than lesser degrees of preferences in the formation of preferential trade agreements, and thus it is illogical to promote 100 per cent preferences over partial preferences.

Kenneth Dam followed up on Viner's theory in his economic analysis of Article XXIV of the GATT.[21] Dam noted that the tariff reductions included in preferential agreements move towards free trade and such preferential arrangements often involve less discrimination against non-members.[22]

17 WTO Appellate Body Report, *Turkey – Restrictions on Imports of Textile and Clothing Products*, WT/DS34/AB/R, adopted 19 Nov. 1999, para. 59.

18 J. Viner, *The Customs Union Issue* (New York: Carnegie Endowment for International Peace, 1950).

19 *Ibid.* at 49–50.

20 *Ibid.*, as cited in Mathis and Bhagwati, *Regional Trade Agreements in the GATT/WTO*, at 104.

21 See K. Dam, 'Regional Economic Arrangements and the GATT: The Legacy of a Misconception', *University of Chicago Law Review* 30 (1963) 615–65.

22 *Ibid.* at 633.

Like Viner, Dam found that Article XXIV of the GATT was illogical in its preference for fully formed CUs and FTAs and its proscription of incomplete preferential trade agreements.[23] He urged a revision of Article XXIV, specifically the requirement in paragraph 4 – that parties not raise barriers to the trade of other contracting parties – to the position of an independent legal requirement.[24] Thus, the 'substantially all the trade' requirement in paragraph 8 would, on this proposal, be superseded by the requirement that members refrain from raising barriers to the trade of non-members.[25] The focus instead would be on external barriers and the conditions in paragraph 5. An RTA would be GATT compatible if it served the purpose of being trade creating rather than trade-diverting.[26]

The theory behind Article XXIV of the GATT as developed by Viner and explored by Dam has been adapted to adopt a balancing approach that favours regional formations which would, in the end, create rather than diminish global economic welfare.[27] The most ideal result of a preferential arrangement under this approach to Article XXIV, is the expansion of production by each relatively efficient producer or source of supply, both internal and external to the agreement.[28] To reach this goal, it is argued that the only preferences that should be permitted in such an arrangement are those which reward efficient regional, rather than external, producers.[29] This creates a conflict with the legal requirements, 'as any such arrangement, while maximizing welfare, is also likely to be incomplete in regard to its regional trade coverage'.[30] It also conflicts with the internal trade requirement of Article XXIV (8), which imposes the requirement that 'substantially all of the trade' between the parties to the agreement is to be covered by the RTA. From this perspective, many economists have concluded that Article XXIV of the GATT is economically irrational.[31] This is mainly because an agreement that covers all the trade between the parties, shifting production from efficient external producers to less efficient internal producers, may result in a higher degree of trade diversion and welfare reduction. An incomplete formation, one that covers only part of the trade between the parties and, thus, does not qualify as a CU or FTA under the definitional requirement of Article XXIV (8) of the GATT, may be more economically rational than a complete formation.

The economic approach to interpreting Article XXIV of the GATT explored by modern economists focuses on the welfare of non-members

23 *Ibid.* 24 *Ibid.* at 635. 25 *Ibid.* at 663. 26 *Ibid.*

27 Mathis and Bhagwati, *Regional Trade Agreements in the GATT/WTO*, at 103.

28 *Ibid.* 29 *Ibid.* 30 *Ibid.* 31 *Ibid.* at 104.

to the preferential agreement and the global trading system as a whole. John McMillan proposed that an RTA should be assessed for GATT compatibility by examining the preservation of trade flows of non-members.[32] The test he proposes asks whether the agreement has resulted in diminished trade flows between member countries and outside countries.[33] More specifically, an agreement is compatible if, for each item traded, the volume of imports into the region is at least as high as the net volume imported from non-members by the member countries before the formation of the agreement.[34] This approach is advantageous to non-members as their trade volumes are guaranteed not to be hurt by the formation of an RTA. It also allows member countries to restrict intra-regional trade because it focuses on the external impact of such a formation. For this reason it is inconsistent with Article XXIV of the GATT and raises the questions of whether 'any economic characterization should frame the test for Article XXIV compatibility in the future, and particularly if it results in lower paragraph 8 requirements permitting more agreements to be formed . . .' and whether 'there is a possibility of placing a welfare analysis, if necessary at all, into some aspect of assessing compatibility outside the domain of paragraph 8'.[35]

From the perspective of non-member welfare and in the interests of the multilateral system as a whole, FTAs and looser preferential agreements are preferred over CUs and other high-level regional integration schemes. From this perspective, Article XXIV of the GATT could be reworked to remove or loosen the internal requirements for the formation of an FTA or a CU. 'This would permit the parties to freely engage a sector by sector examination and then permit all preferences between members for those sectors that do not interfere with the existing trade of non-members.'[36] However, there are several justifications for the internal trade requirement. First, it prevents member countries from selecting only trade-diverting preferences by requiring them to remove barriers to substantially all the trade between member countries without discrimination in selecting which barriers to remove.[37] Second, the stringent

32 J. McMillan, 'Does Regional Integration Foster Open Trade?', in K. Anderson and R. Blackhurst (eds), *Regional Integration and the Global Trading System* (New York: Harvester Wheatsheaf, 1993), 292–310.

33 *Ibid.* 34 *Ibid.*

35 Mathis and Bhagwati, *Regional Trade Agreements in the GATT/WTO*, at 110.

36 *Ibid.* at 113.

37 F. Roessler, 'The Relationship between Regional Integration Agreements and the Multilateral Trade Order', in Anderson and Blackhurst (eds), *Regional Integration and the Global Trading System*, 292–310, 314.

requirement may prevent the proliferation of RTAs and can be seen to help 'differentiate between politically unavoidable and containable deviations from the most-favoured-nation principle'.[38] As the MFN principle is important because it compels equal treatment, the internal trade requirement is important because it sets restrictive conditions for the exception to the MFN principle. With the proliferation of RTAs, whether or not an economic approach should be incorporated into the compatibility examination process is a hotly debated issue. As we saw in Chapter III, Jagdish Bhagwati and Arvind Panagariya have accumulated a large body of evidence showing the trade-distorting effects of regional and preferential trade agreements.

D The GATT and WTO as a constitution

The GATT and the WTO have traditionally been regarded as solely concerned with the promotion of free trade norms concentrating on the reduction of tariff and non-tariff barriers to trade and, as such, are largely removed from the greater international legal system of the United Nations (UN). Although no text of the GATT/WTO framework contends they are a constitution, scholars have argued that they constitute a trade constitution 'having the capacity to provide a legal framework for the universalization of binding norms of substantive law, which have a significant impact on private individuals at the domestic level'.[39]

The GATT was originally intended to be an interim agreement until the ITO was established, but due to the failure to ratify the Havana Charter, the GATT became the vehicle for international economic cooperation. Although it did not establish a formal institution, it acquired institutional structures that included a secretariat and a dispute settlement mechanism. With the growing complexity of the system, contracting parties met in Uruguay to come up with a single set of agreements. The final agreements were signed in 1994 to establish a formal organization, introduce dispute settlement and extend disciplines to new areas. The WTO Charter adopted during the Uruguay Round 'gives the world a trade constitution that has a defined organizational structure and a

38 *Ibid.* at 314.

39 G. Evans, 'Lawmaking under the Trade Constitution: A Study in Legislating by the WTO', *Studies in Transnational Economic Law* 14 (The Netherlands: Kluwer Law International, 2000). For a contrary and perhaps a more accurate view, see J. Dunoff, 'Constitutional Conceits: The WTO's "Constitution" and the Discipline of International Law', *European Journal of International Law* 17 (2006) 647.

distinct legal personality'.[40] After the Uruguay Round, it was structurally possible to discern in the WTO the inklings of a system which, at its base, appeared to have constitutional aspirations. There was a loose assembly, a basic administration and a forum for settling disputes. Constitutional aspirations were present substantively as well, because in its jurisdiction the WTO purported to include a multitude of new issues which had previously been entirely within the national legal domain. Thus, after the Uruguay Round, the idea that the WTO might be constitutionalizing began to take hold, along with concerns about what implications such constitutionalization might have. Some 'who harboured the fantasy of building a system of binding international law above the particularism of the nation state' saw the constitutionalization as promising improved economic order.[41] Others saw it as a threat to national sovereignty, as the WTO interfering with national policy choices, or a threat to the democratic community of the state. The idea faced opposition on the part of the trade law establishment, developing countries and non-governmental organizations (NGOs), and generated international protests because of the perception of the constitutionalized WTO as 'an elite, non-national, unelected, and unrepresentative body, extending its power beyond its pure trade mandate and illegitimately influencing the democratic decisions of national governments'.[42]

The term 'constitution' is traditionally used with regard to a document that explains how an international organization is structured as an independent entity. This definition is consistent with the classical international legal system, which is designed as a way of regulating relationships between sovereign states. In light of the development of new transnational mechanisms of governance, however, it is suggested that the concept of a constitution may be given a broader meaning. One scholar defines the term as encompassing the constituting documents of the governing institution as well as 'the means of ordering relationships within a multi-level governance structure'.[43] In this sense a constitution is concerned with the manner in which political power is organized and applied institutionally, the relationship between the institutions that exercise public power and the relationship between such institutions and private individuals in society.

40 Evans, 'Lawmaking under the Trade Constitution', at 10.

41 D. Cass, *The Constitutionalization of the World Trade Organization* (Oxford University Press, 2005), 16.

42 *Ibid.* 43 Evans, 'Lawmaking Under the Trade Constitution', at 23.

John Jackson first described the domestic and international law relating to trade as embodying a 'trade constitution' which serves to 'impose different levels of restraint on the policy options available to public or private leaders'.[44] Restraint is seen as necessary to avoid the mutual engagement by states in destructive trade wars that occurred during the inter-war period in the form of high tariffs, which led to sharp declines in imports and exports. Evans contends that Jackson's definition of trade constitution should be expanded in light of the inclusion of substantive laws, which means that the WTO Charter is able to impose restraints on the options available to private individuals as well.[45]

One account identifies three essential components of any constitutional instrument. These essential components include: the existence of a body having the power to enact provisions binding on private individuals, constitutional principles about how laws are to be made, and effective enforcement of the law by an executive or judicial agency.[46] The original GATT of 1947 contained none of these elements, as it was seen as an interim agreement designed to fill the gap until the Havana Charter came into force. 'With the demise of the ITO, the GATT was subject to a process of constitutional growth and transformation', in that the GATT members 'exercised their authoritative power to provide an institutional framework for decision-making and to allocate indispensible functions'.[47] Its constitutionalization was marked by increased lawmaking activity through the GATT Council, meetings between contracting parties and trade and tariff negotiating rounds. The emergence of the GATT trade constitution was also due to the work of the dispute settlement panels and the Member States' decisions to follow panel recommendations.[48]

On this view, the WTO is regarded as constitutional in three main respects. First, its laws are binding on Member States.[49] The legal framework of the WTO directs members regarding the substantive content of their laws and how those laws are to be made. Second, it has a coercive mechanism for judicial review and law enforcement.[50] This is manifested by the creation of a trade super-court in a compulsory, binding system of dispute settlement. Third, its laws impact the legal options that are available to private entities and persons.[51] Take the example of the trade mark provisions of the Trade-Related Intellectual Property Rights

44 *Ibid.* at 24, citing J. Jackson, *The World Trading System: Law and Policy of International Economic Relations* (Cambridge, MA: MIT Press, 1989), 299–308.

45 Evans, 'Lawmaking Under the Trade Constitution', at 25.

46 *Ibid.* at 26.

47 *Ibid.* at 28.

48 *Ibid.*

49 *Ibid.* at 240.

50 *Ibid.* at 242.

51 *Ibid.*

(TRIPS) Agreement and their implementation in Australian law. There, 'trade mark owners stood to benefit from an extension of their exclusive right to use the mark in connection with certain goods and services, while would-be competitors were comparatively disadvantaged, to the extent that the scope of the trade mark monopoly was increased'.[52]

WTO lawmaking may also be characterized as constitutional. The features of its lawmaking process can be distinguished from the contractarian mode of treaty making in that they include a potentially open legislative agenda; its potential breadth of subject matter for legislation facilitated by linkage to the trade constitution; the participation of private actors such as NGOs; legislating in respect of private rights and obligations such as the TRIPS Agreement, linking subject matter concerning private rights to the trade constitution; and detailed substantive provisions of the kind that previously came within the competence of national legislatures.[53] These features may be argued to illustrate the effectiveness of the trade constitution as a vehicle for constructing and universalizing substantive norms of law. The linkage phenomenon, or the expansion of legislative competence, shows that legislative power exists at the transnational level and indicates that the WTO is moving from a legislative forum having a narrow competence ('trade' narrowly defined to include only import and export measures) to a generalized competence in 'trade-related' areas, including private law. The participation of private actors, even though without legal standing, foreshadows changes in the composition of the lawmaking body with the erosion of the old dichotomy between private and public entities, state and individual, 'which represented the established order within the classical international legal system'.[54]

From this view, the MFN principle has evolved into a constitutional principle requiring Member States' compliance with an extensive body of substantive commercial law. From the grant of unconditional MFN treatment flows several otherwise unrecognized rights – such as the right of every state to equality, the right of non-discrimination and the right of freedom of commerce – that apply to free trade in order to restrict the exercise of national sovereignty in law and policymaking. The MFN principle is also constitutional in that it impacts both the sovereignty of states and the relationship between states and their nationals. The extension of the MFN principle to new subject matters during the Uruguay Round and the manner of mandatory adoption marked its prominence in the universalization of WTO law and the constitutionalization of the GATT.

52 *Ibid.* at 244. 53 *Ibid.* at 245. 54 *Ibid.*

The national treatment principle also plays a role in the implementation of international substantive law and operates as a restraint on national legislative power in so far as national legislatures are required to refrain from imposing internal measures that would discriminate against imported goods and services. Evans argues, however, that international standards of legal protection are secured by the extent and mandatory nature of the substantive provisions of the WTO Agreements, and that the scope and operation of the principle of national treatment has thus been diminished: 'The diminished importance of national treatment reflects the assignment of sovereignty to the transnational level under the trade constitution. The principle of national treatment has relatively little scope to operate in conjunction with what is, in effect, a form of material reciprocity, embodied in the obligation to implement a comprehensive set of substantive provisions for the worldwide protection' in areas such as intellectual property.[55] In contrast, the significance of the MFN principle has increased in proportion to the need to globalize law, assuming the status of an absolute principle under the trade constitution that is capable of providing a structure for the univeralization of commercial law.

The WTO trade constitution has the capacity to construct, implement and enforce substantive law on a global basis. This lawmaking mechanism, however, lacks legitimacy. The trade constitution 'experienced an initial period of unquestioning approbation', but increasingly, 'scholars, and citizens at large, will challenge the use of law as an instrument of global economic integration without a commensurate growth in legitimacy and political accountability to accompany the process'.[56] In this regard, the challenges facing the trade constitution include a lack of democratic representation and participation in the lawmaking process by private entities, difficulties in its implementation and issues of due process regarding the adequacy of legal representation and open hearings.[57] A shift of power from Member States to the WTO has resulted from the creation of the WTO and the expansion of the scope of its lawmaking, in the Member States' recognition of the necessity for greater economic cooperation and their subsequent agreement to limit the scope of their national sovereignty in favour of a collective sovereignty. The question is whether there are sufficient constitutional safeguards to protect the rights of individual citizens. Thus, a just distribution of power must be agreed upon 'concerning the scope given to law and decision-making at the transnational level at the expense of the autonomy of national legislatures'.[58] Unless there is sufficient accountability in the lawmaking process, there is a democratic

55 *Ibid.* at 246. 56 *Ibid.* at 63. 57 *Ibid.* 58 *Ibid.* at 204.

deficit when substantive lawmaking takes place at the global level. Thus, opportunities for greater accountability must be built into the lawmaking process. To achieve this, the trade governance structures must become more representative and participatory at all levels – global, national and local.[59]

In the area of dispute resolution, the 'principle of the state as the sole actor dominates international litigation . . . The prohibition on the participation of individuals in international dispute resolution can no longer be justified on the basis that states are the primary subjects of international law'.[60] Since individuals have become the subjects of international law, because international law affects their rights, individuals should, where their interests are affected, have a right to participate in enforcement proceedings.[61] In this regard, procedures must be built into the dispute settlement mechanism that would allow private entities and individuals to defend directly, or contest their rights, without prejudice to the greater public interest in equal access to justice. Additionally, the international legal system traditionally lacks any coherent system for law enforcement, or a global rule of law. The rule of law may serve as an integral part of a liberal democratic order and may play a role in the maintenance of a balance between the contrary notions of individual state sovereignty and international public order. To meet these challenges, the existing intergovernmental institutions will have to be reformed and strengthened and the means of private representation and participation will have to be improved.

To remedy the current lack of effectiveness of the WTO's surveillance of RTAs, Cottier and Foltea have suggested reinforcement of the principle of primacy of WTO law by the adoption of 'an explicit constitutional approach of regulating preferential agreements by and through the disciplines of WTO law'.[62] By clearly establishing the supremacy of WTO law over RTA rules, regional agreements that are inconsistent with WTO law will be declared null and void, or unlawful under international law. Treating inconsistent RTAs as unlawful would, in turn, trigger state responsibility. However, the unlawful agreements could be amended so that they conform to the requirements of Article XXIV. Such proposals have been criticized as being a constitutional overstretch and as

59 See *ibid.* 60 *Ibid.* at 208. 61 See *ibid.*

62 T. Cottier and M. Foltea, 'Constitutional Functions of the WTO and Regional Trade Agreements', in L. Bartels and F. Ortino (eds), *Regional Trade Agreements and the WTO Legal System* (Oxford University Press, 2006), 43–76, 67.

threatening to widen the constitutional credibility gap between the WTO's actual capabilities and its constitutional expectations.

E Problems encountered in the examination process

The CRTA was formed in 1996 following the Singapore Ministerial Meeting. The formation of the CRTA ended the ad hoc Working Party Review system of the GATT practice. The CRTA is a standing review committee for RTAs and was designed to streamline the examination process. Its purpose is to examine individual RTAs notified under Article XXIV of the GATT, Article V of the General Agreement on Trade in Services (GATS), and the Enabling Clause, and to 'consider the systematic implications of the agreements for the multilateral trading system and the relationship between them'.[63] The examination process serves two purposes: it ensures the transparency of RTAs, and 'allows members to evaluate an agreement's consistency with WTO rules'.[64] However, no examination report has been completed since 1995 because of a lack of consensus.[65] The problems encountered by the CRTA include the relationship between reports on the examination, or the CRTA consistency judgment, and the dispute settlement process, as well as controversies over the interpretation of the WTO rules governing RTAs. In addition, the different positions taken on the interpretation of the relevant WTO rules by countries entering into RTAs has made it difficult to determine a feasible standard. Other attempts to clarify the substantive rules of Article XXIV of the GATT include the 1994 Understanding on the Interpretation of GATT Article XXIV, and the 2006 WTO General Council Decision on the Transparency Mechanism for Regional Trade Agreements. Clarifying the substantive rules contained in Article XXIV of the GATT, explored below, would significantly improve the effectiveness of the CRTA.

F The 'substantially all the trade' issue in Article XXIV (8) of the GATT

Article XXIV (8) of the GATT provides the extent to which trade in goods may be excluded from a country's internal trade liberalization programme within a regional trade arrangement. This is the first provision

63 WTO, 'Work of the CRTA', available at www.wto.org/english/tratop_e/region_e/regcom_e.htm.

64 *Ibid.* 65 *Ibid.*

to consider in an evaluation of WTO compliance, as it is definitional and identifies characteristics which must be present for the RTA to qualify for an exception to the MFN principle. If a regional arrangement fails to eliminate the designated barriers on the appropriate amount of trade, such a formation is not understood to constitute an FTA or a CU and is therefore not eligible for exemption from the fundamental principles of the GATT. Most economists, beginning with Viner in his 1950 treatise, consider the internal requirement to be trade-diverting because it would divert trade away from efficient external sources to duty-free internal sources.[66] The framers, however, intended it to restrict trade diversion by requiring the across the board removal of substantially all barriers to trade, instead of the selective removal of only those barriers that would benefit the members' economies.

The requirement that duties and other regulations of commerce must be eliminated with respect to substantially all trade is very important and has been a sticking point in assessing the compliance of RTAs with WTO rules. What constitutes 'substantially all the trade' is vague and undefined. The term 'substantially' suggests that some trade may be left out of a liberalization scheme, or in other words, that a member country may keep in place some, but not all, duties and other restrictive regulations of commerce. The issue is to what extent member countries must remove barriers to trade in their internal trade liberalization programmes.

The Understanding on the Interpretation of Article XXIV of the GATT was adopted in 1994 in an attempt to clarify some of the ambiguities in the Article. The only provision that is relevant to the 'substantially all the trade' issue, however, is a brief reference in the Preamble. The relevant portion provides that 'Recognizing the contribution to the expansion of world trade that may be made by closer integration between the economies of the parties to such agreements . . . also that such contribution is increased if the elimination between the constituent territories of duties and other restrictive regulations of commerce extends to all trade, and diminished if any major sector of trade is excluded'.[67] This portion of the Preamble suggests that if any major sector of trade is excluded from the internal trade liberalization scheme, the duties and other restrictive regulations of commerce have not been eliminated with respect to substantially all the

66 Viner, *The Customs Union Issue*, at 49.

67 Understanding on the Interpretation of Article XXIV of the GATT 1994, Preamble, available at www.wto.org/english/docs_e/legal_e/10–24_e.htm.

trade between the constituent territories. This, however, does not clarify the provision in any meaningful manner.

The only other place that the term 'substantially' appears in Article XXIV of the GATT is in paragraph (8)(a)(ii).[68] This provision was interpreted by the WTO Panel and Appellate Body in the *Turkey – Textiles* case. The Panel in that case ruled that 'comparable' duties and regulations could qualify for the requirement.[69] The Appellate Body corrected the Panel, however, by requiring 'something closely approximating "sameness"'.[70] The Appellate Body rejected the lower standard in favour of a higher standard, and defined the term 'substantially' as requiring a higher degree of sameness because it qualified the word 'same'. If this logic is to be applied to the similar requirement of paragraph (8)(a)(i), it would suggest a higher, rather than lower, threshold of trade to be covered.

There are two main approaches, and several suggested approaches, to the interpretation of 'substantially all the trade'. The first is a quantitative approach. This view focuses on a certain percentage, typically between 80 and 90 per cent of trade between member countries, regardless of which sectors of trade or products are included or excluded. Thus, an entire field of trade can be excluded from the liberalization scheme, such as agriculture, as long as the minimum threshold is met. The European Union's (EU) interpretation of the 'substantially all the trade' requirement has been that 90 per cent of trade should be liberalized between the members of an RTA.[71] The 90 per cent can, however, be split between the parties so that the average amount of trade liberalized adds up to 90 per cent. For example, in its free trade agreement with South Africa, the EU liberalized 98% of its trade while South Africa liberalized 82 per cent, so that the EU's liberalized 98% covered the difference between the threshold of 90 per cent and South Africa's coverage of 82%.[72]

68 GATT Art. XXIV(8)(a)(ii) reads: 'A customs union shall be understood to mean the substitution of a single customs territory for two or more customs territories, so that . . . substantially the same duties and other regulations of commerce are applied by each of the members of the union to the trade of territories not included in the union.'

69 WTO Panel Report, *Turkey – Restrictions on Imports of Textile and Clothing Products*, WT/DS34/R, 31 May 1999, at para. 9.151.

70 WTO Appellate Body Report, *Turkey – Textiles*, at paras 48–50.

71 R. Lang, 'Renegotiating GATT Article XXIV: a Priority for African Countries Engaged in North-South Trade Agreements', Working Paper No. 33 (African Trade Policy Centre, Feb. 2006), 12, available at http://uneca.org/atpc/Work%20in%20progress/33.pdf.

72 *Ibid.*

The second approach is qualitative. This view suggests that 'no sector (or at least no major sector) is to be kept out of intra-RTA trade liberalization'.[73] A qualitative benchmark measures the quality of internal elimination of duties and other restrictive regulations of commerce between members to an RTA. It prevents the exclusion of any sector from an internal liberalization scheme where the restrictive barriers that were in place before the formation of the agreement hindered trade. This approach is alluded to in the Preamble to the Understanding on the Interpretation of Article XXIV of the GATT 1994 as quoted above, with the goal of world trade expansion to be attained by maximizing the benefits resulting from RTAs. In looking at the qualitative approach, it might be helpful to examine the parallel requirement in the GATS. There, members agreed that 'regional agreements should not provide for the *a priori* exclusion of any mode of supply'.[74] If a similar principle is applied to Article XXIV (8)(a)(i) of the GATT, it is not likely that the exclusion of an entire sector of trade in an internal liberalization scheme would be considered GATT compatible. One potential problem with this approach, however, is the definition of the term 'sector' of trade for the purpose of compatibility evaluation.

A third approach is a mixture of both quantitative and qualitative views. This approach was taken by the Appellate Body in the *Turkey – Textiles* case regarding the requirement contained in Article XXIV (8)(a)(ii) of the GATT that in a CU, 'substantially the same duties and other regulations of commerce' must be applied to the external trade with third countries. It ruled that 'the ordinary meaning of the term "substantially" in the context of subparagraph 8(a) appears to provide for both qualitative and quantitative components'.[75] If this is to be applied to the 'substantially all the trade' requirement, it suggests that an exclusive approach, either quantitative or qualitative, should be abandoned in favour of combined treatment of the issue.

73 R. Scollay, '"Substantially All Trade": Which Definitions are Fulfilled in Practice?', Report for the Commonwealth Secretariat (15 Aug. 2005), 8, available at www.thecommonwealth.org/shared_asp_files/uploadedfiles/54198A83–736D-4D36-B484–27400E267BCE_SATPaperforComsecCompleteJano6.pdf.

74 GATS Art. V (1)(a) n. 1, available at www.wto.org/english/docs_e/legal_e/26-gats_01_e.htm#fnt1; see also G. Marceau and C. Reiman, 'When and How is an RTA Compatible with the WTO?', *Legal Issues of Economic Integration* 28(3) (2001) 297–336, 316.

75 WTO Appellate Body Report, *Turkey – Textiles*, at para. 49 (quoting the WTO Panel Report, *Turkey – Restrictions*, at para. 9.148).

One suggested approach is to supplement the coverage of trade benchmark, a quantitative approach, with an assessment of trade coverage measured by the number of tariff lines. 'A combined average threshold would ensure that RTAs cover existing as well as potential future bilateral trade between parties, while partly accommodating the traditional differences in Members' emphasis on the two forms of possible benchmarks.'[76] Another suggested approach is to refine the quantitative approach by calculating the percentage of trade between the parties carried out under the RTA's rules of origin. Hence, 'the more liberal the preferential Rules of Origin of a PTA, the higher the percentage of intra-PTA trade should be covered by the PTA to meet the substantially all trade threshold of Article XXIV'.[77] Md. Rizwanul Islam and Shawkat Alam write that while this could put an end to the tendency to use preferential rules of origin as a trade-diverting device, no consensus has been reached on how to measure 'substantially all the trade'.[78]

Negotiations in the Uruguay Round and in the CRTA have proved inconclusive in resolving which benchmarks should be used in the determination of how much intra-regional trade should be included in the members' trade liberalization schemes. Concerning this issue, a report by the Secretariat in 2002 provided that the 'percentage of trade method has been traditionally favored as an indication of RTA coverage in the GATT/WTO context'.[79] This method may reveal the amount of actual trade between members that is duty free or subject to concessions, or in other words, it 'might be helpful to consider the percentage-of-trade method as offering insights into parties' *traded*, as opposed to their *tradable*, goods'.[80] However, the shortcoming of this method is that trade statistics, which distinguish import flows according to their tariff treatment, do not exist in the public domain. The alternative method for calculating the percentage, totalling the members' imports from other members for the tariff lines containing concessions, may give biased results as

76 European Commission, 'Clarification and Improvement to GATT Art. XXIV Provisions', Second Submission on Regional Trade Agreements by the European Communities (26 Apr. 2005), 3, available at http://trade.ec.europa.eu/doclib/docs/2005/may/tradoc_123424.pdf.

77 Md. Rizwanul Islam and S. Alam, 'Preferential Trade Agreements and the Scope of GATT Article XXIV', *Netherlands International Law Review* 56 (May 2009) 1, 19.

78 *Ibid.* at 20.

79 European Commission, 'Clarification and Improvement to GATT Art. XXIV Provisions', at 2.

80 Secretariat's Report, 'Coverage, Liberalization Process and Transition Periods in Regional Trade Agreements', WTO Doc. No. WT/REG/W/46 (5 Apr. 2002), 5.

there 'is no guarantee that all imported goods under a preferential tariff line actually benefitted from the preferential treatment outlined in an agreement'.[81]

Even without a defined standard, the issue of partial preferences may arise in a situation in which trade in a sector is only partially liberalized between members while the rest of the trade in that sector is left uncovered, or at an MFN level. In that situation, the question arises of whether the partial-preference sectors can be included under the concept of 'elimination of duties' and be counted towards the portion of trade dedicated to meet the 'substantially all the trade' test. Such partial preferences usually apply in the transitional stage, and an intermediate interpretation is that the elimination requirement would apply at the end of the transition period, and that, until then, such non-zero preferential tariffs should be allowed because they contribute to the elimination process.[82]

Angela Estrella and Gary Horlick offer an interpretation of the 'substantially all the trade' issue and partial preferences in light of the Appellate Body's decision in *Turkey – Textiles*.[83] They conclude that Article XXIV (8) of the GATT should be construed as mandating the abolition of duties and other restrictive regulations of commerce as to the part of the trade within RTAs counting towards the fulfilment of the 'substantially all trade' requirement.[84] In other words, partial preferences should not be considered as having been 'eliminated' and, thus, should not count towards the fulfilment of the 'substantially all the trade' requirement.

The Appellate Body in the *Turkey – Textiles* case made it clear that Article XXIV (8) of the GATT lays down the standard that must be met for the formation of a CU or FTA in the internal trade between members. It noted that the terms of paragraph (8) offer some flexibility to members in their internal trade liberalization schemes, which can either be in the form of liberalizing less than all the trade or maintaining the restrictions in the exceptions list within the regional trade arrangement.[85] The Appellate Body further cautioned 'that the degree of "flexibility" that sub-paragraph 8(a)(i) *allows* is *limited* by the requirement that "duties and

81 *Ibid.*

82 Negotiating Group on Rules, 'Compendium of Issues Related to Regional Trade Agreements', Doc. No. TN/RL/W/8/Rev.1 (1 Aug. 2002), para. 83.

83 A.T. Gobbi Estrella and G.N. Horlick, 'Mandatory Abolition of Anti-Dumping, Countervailing Duties and Safeguards in Customs Unions and Free Trade Areas Constituted between WTO Members', in Bartels and Ortino (eds), *Regional Trade Agreements and the WTO Legal System*, 136.

84 *Ibid.*

85 WTO Appellate Body Report, *Turkey – Textiles*, at para. 48.

other restrictive regulations of commerce" be "eliminated with respect to substantially all" internal trade'.[86] Estrella and Horlick go on to examine the 'substantially all the trade' issue in light of the Appellate Body's findings.

They start with the ordinary meaning of the expression 'are eliminated'. The ordinary definition of the verb 'to eliminate' is 'to expel', 'to exclude', 'to remove' and 'to get rid of'.[87] In light of this definition, duties and other restrictive regulations of commerce must be abolished for the internal trade requirement of Article XXIV (8) of the GATT to be satisfied. Additionally, the authors conclude that the intra-regional trade to which any duty and other restrictive regulation of commerce remains applicable cannot be counted towards the fulfilment of the 'substantially all the trade' threshold. This remains true even where no duty or other regulation is effectively imposed. This is because a duty or regulation that is still applicable cannot be said to be expelled, excluded, removed, or eliminated. Thus, an interpretation that elimination of duties and other restrictive regulations of commerce may be assessed using a volume of trade threshold is inconsistent with the text of Article XXIV (8) of the GATT.

There is also textual support for the argument that Article XXIV (8) of the GATT requires the complete elimination of the possibility that duties and other restrictive regulations of commerce apply to the part of the regional trade that is meant to count towards the 'substantially all the trade' threshold. As initially drafted, the provision read 'all tariffs and other restrictive regulations of members of the union are substantially eliminated . . .'[88] There, the term 'substantially' modifies 'eliminated', whereas in the revised version, 'substantially' modifies the phrase 'all the trade'. Thus, the drafters' intent can be inferred to be that complete elimination, or abolition, is required and the flexibility remains in the amount of trade to be included in the liberalization scheme. In *Turkey – Textiles*, the Appellate Body interpreted the 'substantially the same regulations of commerce' requirement of Article XXIV (8)(a)(ii) of the GATT.[89] It ruled that CU members may be deemed to have fulfilled the requirement even when some regulations are different, as long as most regulations of commerce are the same.[90] The same logic cannot, however, be extended

86 *Ibid.* (emphasis added).

87 Estrella and Horlick, 'Mandatory Abolition', at 137 (citing *The Compact Edition of the Oxford English Dictionary* (Oxford: Clarendon, 1971), 845).

88 Mathis and Bhagwati, *Regional Trade Agreements in the GATT/WTO*, at 46.

89 For the text of GATT Art. XXIV (8)(a)(ii), see *supra* n. 68.

90 WTO Appellate Body Report, *Turkey – Textiles*, at para. 50.

to the 'substantially all the trade' requirement of Article XXIV (8)(a)(i) and (b) of the GATT. Since 'substantially' no longer modifies 'eliminated' by the design of the drafters at the Havana Conference, Article XXIV (8) of the GATT cannot be interpreted to allow parties to an RTA to eliminate less than all of the duties and other restrictive regulations of commerce that are applicable to the part of the intra-regional trade covered by the internal trade liberalization programme. Therefore, regarding the internal trade requirement, 'it is in the amount of trade to be liberalized that, as noted by the Appellate Body in *Turkey – Textiles*, resides the "flexibility" offered by the terms of Article XXIV:8 of the GATT, not in the rule on elimination of duties and ORRC [other restrictive restrictions of commerce]'.[91] Thus, there is no textual support for the proposal that Article XXIV (8)(a)(i) and (b) of the GATT allows for grades in the elimination of duties and other restrictive regulations of commerce.

Estrella and Horlick conclude that duties and regulations must be completely eliminated (expelled, excluded, removed or got rid of) in the part of the trade included in the trade liberalization scheme, and 'that no trade restrictions can remain applicable for any part of the intra-RTA trade which is intended to comprise part of the SAT threshold'.[92] In other words, partial trade preferences such as reduced duties or less restrictive regulations of commerce, or the non-application of duties and other regulations that are still in the books, should not be regarded as duties and regulations that have been 'eliminated' in Article XXIV (8) of the GATT.

G Interim agreements under Article XXIV (5)(c) of the GATT

Article XXIV of the GATT only makes an exception to the GATT principles of MFN and national treatment for the formation of CUs and FTAs. Article XXIV recognizes that such formations take time due to the necessity of adjusting policies and regulations that govern trade, and thus allows for interim agreements that lead to the formation of CUs or FTAs only if the agreement fulfils the conditions of the Article. Transition periods are important to allow industries to adapt to increased competition within the region and to introduce compensatory measures for tariff losses resulting from regional integration. Setting a time limit, however, ensures that progress is made and that the integration process does not remain stagnant. Because interim agreements can potentially last for an

91 Estrella and Horlick, 'Mandatory Abolition', at 139. 92 *Ibid.* at 141.

indefinite period of time, Article XXIV (5)(c) of the GATT sets some time guidance within which they must evolve into either a CU or FTA. Article XXIV (5)(c) provides that any interim agreement leading to the formation of such a union or area mentioned in Article (5)(a) or (b) 'shall include a plan and schedule for the formation of such a customs union or of such a free trade area within a reasonable length of time'.[93] This provision aims to encourage the evolution of CUs and FTAs from less complete preferential trade agreements, because such 'full' agreements are more trade liberalizing and more conducive to trade expansion.[94]

Like the 'substantially all trade' requirement, the 'reasonable length of time' requirement is unclear. The Understanding on the Interpretation of Article XXIV of the GATT 1994 provides that a reasonable length of time should not exceed 10 years, save in exceptional cases.[95] Where a country party to an interim agreement believes that 10 years is insufficient to form a CU or FTA, they should provide to the Council for Trade in Goods a full explanation of the need for a longer period of time.[96] This clarification, however, is only marginally helpful, as what constitutes an 'exceptional case' or a 'full explanation' is not defined. Clarification of this requirement is important because while it remains unclear the legal security of interim agreements is jeopardized. For example, in the 'case of EPAs, a large difference in development levels between parties could probably constitute an exceptional case, as would the structural weakness of members, for example LDCs or Small islands'.[97]

In 2002, the Secretariat carried out a survey of the coverage, liberalization process and transitional provisions in RTAs.[98] The purpose of the survey was to examine the progress of the liberalization process and of product coverage in RTAs to compare all the regional agreements in light of the relevant WTO provisions. It is noted in the report that 'only in rare cases' do transition periods in notified RTAs exceed 10 years.[99] However, the European Communities (EC) submitted a paper on RTAs to the WTO in which it was noted that, in the recent surge of RTAs, transition periods

93 GATT Art. XXIV, at para. 5(c).

94 See P. Hilpold, 'Regional Integration According to Article XXIV GATT – Between Law and Politics', in *Max Planck Yearbook of United Nations Law* 7 (2003) 219–60, 226, available at www.mpil.de/shared/data/pdf/pdfmpunyb/hilpold_7.pdf.

95 Understanding on the Interpretation of Article XXIV of the GATT 1994, at para. 3.

96 *Ibid.* 97 Lang, 'Renegotiating GATT', at 18.

98 See Secretariat's Report, 'Coverage, Liberalization Process and Transition Periods in Regional Trade Agreements'.

99 *Ibid.* at 18.

have been known to last for longer than ten years and that such cases 'are becoming the rule rather than the exception'.[100] The EC paper suggests that 'the lack of authoritative guidance of the concept of "exceptional cases"' might be the cause of the present situation.[101] Bartels notes that it is 'relatively common for the implementation period to stretch up to 12 years, and in some cases further', and also notes that the obligation to 'provide a full explanation of the need for a longer period' has not been taken seriously by WTO members.[102]

Since 1995, none of the RTAs notified to the CRTA have been notified as an interim agreement,[103] 'despite the fact that virtually none of these agreements formally meets the requirements of a full customs union or free trade area'.[104] Bartels notes that, in practice, conditions that are *de jure* only applicable to interim agreements are being applied *de facto* to notified 'full' agreements, largely for the purpose of circumventing binding recommendations by the WTO Council of Trade in Goods.[105] Looking at the formal requirements for interim agreements, WTO members must be satisfied that a notified interim agreement will lead to the formation of an FTA or CU within a reasonable length of time, 'otherwise, they may make binding recommendations to ensure that this will happen'.[106] By notifying what are, in actuality, interim agreements as 'full' RTAs with an implementation period, the conditions controlling interim agreements are bypassed, such binding recommendations are circumvented and any dispute settlement proceedings are avoided.[107] Bartels argues that this practice is sanctioned by the Transparency Decision, which speaks solely of CUs and FTAs, providing that parties to such agreements must submit information that includes, '*when the agreement is to be implemented by*

100 European Commission, 'Clarification and Improvement to GATT Art. XXIV Provisions', at 3.

101 *Ibid.* at 4.

102 L. Bartels, '"Interim Agreements" under Article XXIV GATT', *World Trade Review* 8(2) (2009) 339–50, 346. Bartels cites Jordan's response to a question on the matter of providing a full explanation in the examination of the EC–Jordan FTAg that 'both Parties had agreed that Jordan would need twelve years in order to provide the needed time to improve the competitiveness of Jordan's economic sectors and allow national exporters to adjust to the new requirements'. CRTA, 'Examination of the EC–Jordan Euro-Mediterranean Agreement – Note on the Meeting of 29 March 2004', WT/REG141/M/1 (28 Apr. 2004), para. 8.

103 See WTO, 'Regional Trade Agreements Notified to the GATT/WTO and in Force', available at www.wto.org/english/tratop_e/region_e/type_e/xls.

104 Bartels, 'Interim Agreements', at 344. 105 *Ibid.* at 344–5. 106 *Ibid.* at 349.

107 This is because dispute settlement proceedings can only take place once a 'full' RTA is established. *Ibid.* at 350.

stages, a full listing of each party's preferential duties to be applied over the transition period'.[108] Bartels argues that this codifies the practice of WTO members of notifying what are, in fact, interim agreements as 'full' RTAs with transitional periods in order to circumvent the regulations of interim agreements prior to their completion. This practice 'may have practical implications for the regulation of regional trade agreements in the WTO' and leaves the question of whether this practice is *ultra vires* open.[109]

Md. Rizwanul Islam and Shawkat Alam express the belief that the exception for interim agreements leading to the formation of an FTA is unnecessary because of the practical differences between the formation of FTAs and the formation of CUs.[110] The formation of an FTA merely involves the elimination of border barriers while the formation of a CU can sometimes involve the amendment of a country's constitution and the development of new institutions. However, this belief is not reflected in Article XXIV (5)(c), and therefore the formation of both a CU and FTA from an interim agreement must be within a reasonable period of time.

As we will see in the next chapter, African RTAs set unrealistic realization time frames. These time frames are, therefore, rarely met, and extensions are the norm rather than the exception. To the extent any of the FTAs or CUs are notified to the WTO, none of the interim agreements have been notified. In addition, the complexity built into these agreements through principles such as variable geometry and asymmetry, further distances the African experience from the prerequisites of Article XXIV, particularly if read in isolation of the Enabling Clause, which is discussed below.

H 'Other regulations of commerce' and 'other restrictive regulations of commerce' in Article XXIV of the GATT

There is an extensive discussion in the CRTA over the terms 'other regulations of commerce' as contained in the external requirements of Article XXIV (5) and (8)(a)(ii), and 'other restrictive regulations of commerce' as contained in the internal requirements of Article XXIV (8)(a)(i) and (b) of the GATT. Examples of the issues include whether

108 General Council, 'Decision on a Transparency Mechanism for Regional Trade Agreements of 16 Dec. 2006', WT/L/671, adopted 18 Dec. 2006, para. 2(a)(ii) (emphasis added).

109 Bartels, 'Interim Agreements', at 339.

110 Islam and Alam, 'Preferential Trade Agreements', at 19.

these phrases are synonymous and what types of measures are included in either phrase.

In the context of Article XXIV (5) of the GATT, the Panel in *Turkey – Textiles* wrote that the terms 'other regulations of commerce' included any regulation that has an impact on trade.[111] It gives examples of regulations having an impact on trade as being measures in the fields covered by WTO rules, such as anti-dumping, technical barriers to trade, sanitary and phytosanitary and any other trade-related domestic regulation.[112] This is a broad definition, but would most likely be sustained if reviewed, because the analysis of Article XXIV (5) of the GATT relates to the impact of undertaken measures upon non-members.[113] The WTO Secretariat produced a list of regulations that may affect trade between third parties and members of an RTA.[114] The list includes, but is not limited to, quantitative restrictions and other measures of similar effect, rules of origin, standards (technical barriers to trade and sanitary and phytosanitary measures), safeguards, anti-dumping and countervailing measures, subsidies and state aid, sector-specific provisions and other measures such as measures associated with customs administration, import licensing and customs valuation.[115]

The phrase 'other restrictive regulations of commerce' is contained in the internal requirements of Article XXIV (8)(a)(i) and (b) of the GATT. One of the preliminary issues is the definition of the phrase. To begin with, the Articles listed as exceptions that may be allowed suggest that trade measures taken in accordance with those Articles constitute 'other restrictive regulations of commerce'. These are Articles XI (quantitative restrictions), XII (restrictions to safeguard the Balance of Payment), XIII (non-discriminatory administration of quantitative restrictions), XIV (exemptions to the rule of non-discrimination), XV (exchange agreements) and XX (general exceptions). The Understanding on the Interpretation of Article XXIV of the GATT 1994 does not clarify the term in any significant way. The only relevant phrase is contained in the Preamble and states that contribution of RTAs to the expansion of world trade 'is increased if the elimination between the constituent territories of duties and other restrictive regulations of commerce extends to all trade, and

111 WTO Panel Report, *Turkey – Textiles*, at para. 9.120. 112 *Ibid.*

113 Mathis and Bhagwati, *Regional Trade Agreements in the GATT/WTO*, at 251.

114 WTO Secretariat, 'Standard Format for Information on Regional Trade Agreements', WTO Doc. No. WT/REG/W/6 (Aug. 1996).

115 Lang, 'Renegotiating GATT', at 9.

diminished if any major sector of trade is excluded'.[116] This suggests that greater levels of regional trade should be covered in internal trade liberalization schemes rather than lesser, so the term should be construed in favour of a broad interpretation, including a larger amount of restrictive regulations.

Prior to the Havana Conference, there was only a provision in Article XXIV (8) for the formation of a CU. Because of this, the drafters may have considered the phrase 'other restrictive regulations of commerce' to be clear regarding the formation of a CU as including those measures that the drafters would have thought to be necessary for such formation. The subject matter of the external policies being changed at the formation of a CU would include states' protectionist trade measures. In a completed CU, the elimination of such policies between members would also be required. Thus, following this reasoning, 'other restrictive regulations of commerce' would refer to 'those trade measures other than tariff duties that would be necessary to "eliminate" in order to give effect to a normally functioning customs territory operating in the form of a customs union, and probably not more'.[117] With the addition of the exception for the formation of an FTA, there was nothing to suggest that the same phrase found in that requirement was intended to be less inclusive or different in any respect. In support of this argument, Viner drew the conclusion that the meaning of this newly introduced term 'for the purposes of the Charter must . . . be sought wholly within the text of the Charter'.[118] This implies that the GATT Articles must themselves 'form the primary source as to what would constitute the nature of the requirements' and, 'to the extent that the free-trade area provisions mimic those for customs unions, any previous practice developed to customs unions does have an informative role in determining the meaning of terms applied to free-trade area requirements when ambiguity occurs'.[119]

James Mathis suggests an approach using the two-part test of *Turkey – Textiles*. To pass the first test, the fulfilment of the requirements of Article XXIV (8) and (5), there must be a commitment to the elimination of the duty or other restrictive regulation of commerce that is made evident by the RTA in its plan and schedule.[120] For an MFN challenge that is based on

116 Understanding on the Interpretation of Article XXIV of the GATT 1994, Preamble.

117 J. Mathis, 'Regional Trade Agreements and Domestic Regulation', in Bartels and Ortino (eds.), *Regional Trade Agreements and the WTO Legal System*, 79, 87.

118 Viner, *The Customs Union Issue*, at 124.

119 Mathis and Bhagwati, *Regional Trade Agreements in the GATT/WTO*, at 43.

120 Mathis, 'Trade Agreements and Domestic Regulation', at 83.

a non-accorded preference, it is reasonable to assume that the elimination of a duty or other restrictive regulation of commerce would be found as necessary to complete the regional formation. Except for whatever flexibility is allowed for 'substantially' all the trade, 'RTA enactments that fall within the scope of ORRC should be understood to fall within the exception' from the MFN principle.[121] In the same light, measures that do not fall within the scope of 'other restrictive regulations of commerce' should not be considered as 'necessary' for the formation of an RTA under Article XXIV of the GATT. This point was articulated by the Panel in *US – Line Pipe*, where it was stated that if the 'alleged violation of GATT 1994 forms part of the elimination of "duties and other restrictive regulations of commerce", there can be no question of whether it is necessary for the elimination of "duties and other restrictive regulations of commerce"'.[122]

One of the issues regarding the term 'other restrictive regulations of commerce' is whether it includes safeguards and other trade remedies. Trade remedies are typically retained as protectionist measures against the impact of the formation of the RTA. The argument that the term does encompass safeguards and trade remedies such as anti-dumping and countervailing duties centres around the fact that the Articles relating to such measures are not included in the listed exceptions to the duties and regulations that must be eliminated with regard to substantially all the trade. In this line of reasoning, an RTA that has not eliminated such measures would be inconsistent with Article XXIV of the GATT. From one economic perspective, the elimination of trade remedies in intra-regional trade would be trade-creating within the region but also trade diverting and welfare-reducing because it might reduce the amount of trade between third countries and members. From the drafters' point of view, however, the elimination of other restrictive regulations of commerce, including trade remedies, with respect to substantially all the trade between members, would restrict trade diversion as it would not allow members to pick and choose the measures to eliminate or retain.

I Rules of origin

As intra-regional trade expands because of the trade liberalization process eliminating tariff and non-tariff barriers to trade, administered protection

121 *Ibid.* at 84.
122 WTO Panel Report, *US – Line Pipe*, WT/DS202/R, 8 March 2002.

becomes directed towards the imports of non-members. Such protectionist measures take the form of preferential rules of origin (RoOs) and trade remedies. These measures have become increasingly prominent with the proliferation of RTAs and the intra-regional elimination of tariffs. There are two types of RoOs – preferential and non-preferential. Preferential rules are used to determine the country of origin of certain products for the purpose of receiving preferential tariff treatment. Non-preferential rules are used to distinguish between foreign and non-foreign goods for the purposes of applying anti-dumping and countervailing duties, safeguard measures and other product- or country-specific trade regulations that restrict entry.

Preferential RoOs are very important aspects of the formation of an FTA. In a CU there is a common external tariff and, therefore, RoOs determine solely whether a good is eligible for preferential treatment between members. In the absence of a common external tariff, however, RoOs serve an additional function: preventing re-exportation and trade deflection. Without a common external tariff, goods may enter the region via the country with the lowest external tariff and then circulate duty free within the region. Thus, the country with the lowest external tariff in a certain good would receive all the tariff revenue from that product. Preferential RoOs require a product to originate, to a certain degree, within the region covered by the FTA or CU in order to qualify for preferential treatment and, thus, deter re-exportation and trade deflection.

RoOs can define 'the minimum percentage of the value of a good that must be added within the FTA, or certain manufacturing processes that must take place within the FTA', or an RoO could require a change in tariff heading, a certain amount of domestic content, or that the good be 'substantially transformed' in order for a good to be classified as of FTA origin.[123] If a good satisfies the RoO, preferential treatment is accorded to it within the region. If a good does not satisfy the RoO, the MFN tariff rate would be applied. RoOs should be neutral and not overly restrictive. Neutral rules simply identify the goods that qualify for preferential tariff treatment. Restrictive rules, however, extend further protection to goods originating in member countries in addition to the protection offered by reducing or eliminating tariffs between members. If the preferential origin rules require a greater transformation of the product than is reasonable

123 J.A. Rivas, 'Do Rules of Origin in Free Trade Agreements Comply with Article XXIV GATT?', in Bartels and Ortino (eds.), *Regional Trade Agreements and the WTO Legal System*, 150.

or necessary under the circumstances, they may be restricting trade and thereby labelled discriminatory. Thus, the issue regarding RoOs is whether or not they are abusively designed and implemented.

The purpose of preferences is to shift sources of production in an effort to promote regional development. RoOs may provide an incentive for regional producers to buy goods from regional sources in order to make their product 'originate' within the FTA, even if the prices of the regional sources are higher than those for the same product from external sources. Preferential RoOs shift production from external to regional producers, benefiting the members of the FTA. The more restrictive the RoOs are, the more incentive producers have to shift their sources of production to regional sources. As such, origin rules are designed to increase the amount of investment in production and assembly of intermediate goods as well as to enhance the position of existing intermediate producers.[124] RoOs have risen to prominence largely because of the globalization of the means of production, which has made designating the origin of products dispute-prone and complex.

RoOs were originally designed as uncontroversial and neutral devices for authentication and statistical purposes.[125] However, they have increasingly become tools for the implementation of discriminatory trade policies. Since origin rules are negotiated industry by industry, there is a lot of room for well-organized industries to devise suitable rules to essentially insulate themselves from the effects of the FTA. RoOs can be complex and controversial, which suggests that they might be strategically used to protect members to the agreement, as we saw in Chapter III. The complexity of origin rules can themselves operate as barriers to trade, thus becoming an obstacle to free trade. Their complexity and technical nature also makes it difficult to realize when origin rules are being used for restrictive purposes. The growing restrictions placed on tariff and non-tariff trade barriers by the GATT has led to an increased use of preferential origin rules as tools for discrimination, since they are not effectively regulated by the GATT.[126] Since the liberalization of tariff barriers, narrow RoOs have been used by member countries as the second-best means of protecting domestic industries from foreign competition.

Preferential RoOs may also encourage inefficiency. Because their purpose is to shift production, member countries may alter production

124 'Free Trade Agreements and Rules of Origin', International Center for Economic Growth Brief No. 0012, 2.

125 *Ibid.* at 3. 126 *Ibid.*

patterns for the sole purpose of fulfilling the rules for market access. Members may choose an inefficient and more expensive supplier to fulfil the RoOs and not to reduce costs and improve efficiency. This has a trade-diverting effect, as producers are induced to shift their imports to member sources in order to be eligible for preferential tariff treatment. Additionally, overlapping and inconsistent RoOs have proved to be obstacles to trade facilitation, as various origin regimes impose different requirements on importers and exporters, a theme also covered in further detail in the discussion of overlapping RTAs in Chapter III.[127]

RoOs had not been addressed in the WTO as a potential non-tariff barrier to trade until the Uruguay Round in 1994. The Agreement on Rules of Origin, finalized after negotiations in the Uruguay Round, aims to ensure that non-preferential rules do not create obstacles to trade.[128] Additionally, the Agreement aims toward the long-term goal of harmonizing non-preferential RoOs among all WTO members.[129] The Common Declaration contained in Annex II of the Agreement sets forth principles to be applied to preferential RoOs. Until the completion of the harmonization programme, members are to 'ensure that their rules of origin are transparent; that they do not have restricting, distorting or disruptive effects on international trade; that they are administered in a consistent, uniform, impartial and reasonable manner; and that they are based on a positive standard (in other words, they should state what *does confer origin rather than what does not*)'.[130] The prohibition of the use of non-preferential origin rules to pursue trade objectives is contained in the Agreement, but neither the Agreement nor the Common Declaration contains a prohibition of the use of preferential RoOs.

The Agreement on Rules of Origin and the Common Declaration included in Annex II of the Agreement do not prohibit RoOs for imports from third countries from being more restrictive than the previously applicable rules. Whether or not RoOs should be considered 'other regulations of commerce' is a contested issue. The United States has argued that, because of the Agreement's exclusion of preferential RoOs, such rules in an RTA deal only with intra-regional trade to determine the

127 *Ibid.*

128 Agreement on Rules of Origin, Preamble, available at www.wto.org/english/docs_e/legal_e/22-roo_e.htm.

129 *Ibid.*

130 WTO, 'Non-Tariff Barriers: Red Tape, etc.', available at www.wto.org/english/thewto_e/whatis_e/tif_e/agrm9_e.htm#origin.

preferences granted.[131] From this view, they do not affect the trade of third countries, which is how the WTO Panel in *Turkey – Textiles* broadly defined 'other regulations of commerce'. The United States has further argued that preferential RoOs do not fall within the category of 'other regulations of commerce', as contained in Article XXIV (5), because they are not regulations that affect trade with third countries. Therefore, according to the United States, preferential RoOs do not have to satisfy the conditions in Article XXIV (5) of the GATT regarding external trade in order to be WTO compatible.[132]

José Rivas contends, however, that Article XXIV, particularly paragraph 5(b), read in light of paragraph 4, governs such RoOs. Rivas argues that RoOs qualify as 'other regulations of commerce' as provided in Article XXIV (5) and, thus, must satisfy the conditions for such regulations in order to be compatible with Article XXIV of the GATT.[133] Preferential RoOs are defined in paragraph 2 of the Common Declaration with regard to Preferential Rules of Origin as 'those laws, regulations and administrative determinations of general application applied by any member to determine whether goods qualify for preferential treatment under contractual or autonomous trade regimes leading to the granting of tariff preferences'.[134] In addition to being defined as regulations in the Common Declaration, the Negotiating Group on Rules gives three interpretations of this issue. First, such origin rules constitute an 'other regulation of commerce'.[135] Second, such origin rules do not constitute an 'other regulation of commerce' because they do not affect trade with third parties.[136] Third, such origin rules should be examined on a case-by-case basis to see if these rules have had restrictive effects on trade with third parties.[137] Rivas argues that 'it has long been contended and demonstrated in various trade and economic studies that FTA rules of origin may divert trade' by shifting sources of production to local sources.[138] Additionally, the Panel in *Turkey – Textiles* stated that 'the ordinary meaning of the terms "other regulations of commerce" could be understood to include any regulation having an impact on trade'.[139] As defined in the Common Declaration, RoOs can be regulations and, as noted by Rivas, they may have the effect of diverting trade. Thus, Rivas concludes that RoOs in

131 Rivas, *Rules of Origin*, at 151. 132 *Ibid.* at 152. 133 *Ibid.*

134 Common Declaration with regard to Preferential Rules of Origin, Annex II of the Agreement on Rules of Origin, para. 2, available at www.wto.org/english/docs_e/legal_e/22-roo_e.htm.

135 'Compendium of Issues Related to RTAs', Negotiating Group on Rules, at para. 78.

136 *Ibid.* 137 *Ibid.* 138 Rivas, *Rules of Origin*, at 153.

139 WTO Panel Report, *Turkey – Textiles*, at paras 9.105, 9.120.

FTAs are 'other regulations of commerce' as set out in Article XXIV (5) and are, therefore, governed by the disciplines set forth in Article XXIV.[140] In this line of reasoning, the restrictiveness of FTA RoOs is limited only by the restrictions in Article XXIV which state that, upon the formation of an FTA, its 'other regulations of commerce' should not be more restrictive than before.

Rivas goes on to interpret Article XXIV (5)(b) regarding preferential RoOs as 'other regulations of commerce'. The Appellate Body in *Turkey – Textiles* gave two conditions that must be fulfilled for restrictions imposed on imports from non-member countries to be allowed under Article XXIV of the GATT. First, the measure must meet the requirements of Article XXIV (5)(a) or (b) and (8)(a) or (b).[141] Second, the measure must be necessary for the formation of the CU or FTA at issue, or in other words, such formation would be prevented if the party was not allowed to introduce the measure.[142] The first part of the test requires determining whether the measure falls within the meaning of 'duties or other regulations of commerce'. According to Rivas, since RoOs are 'other regulations of commerce', it must be proven that such rules imposed at the formation of an RTA are not more restrictive than those applied before such formation. If the origin rule survives that test, it must then be proven that its imposition is necessary for the formation of the CU or FTA in question. If it is found to be necessary for the formation of the CU or FTA, then the preferential rule or RoOs will be allowed under the Appellate Body's test.

In the current situation of the globalization of means of production, there is no single correct way to designate RoOs. The WTO has made efforts towards the long-term harmonization of RoOs in order to promote trade facilitation, by ensuring that unnecessary obstacles to trade are not created by the implementation of origin rules.[143] Origin rules must be easy to understand and conform to in order to reduce costs of compliance. Rules that maximize trade creation and minimize trade diversion should be adopted. RoOs should be transparent, consistent and predictable and should not be disguised non-tariff barriers to trade.

J Additional issues in Article XXIV of the GATT

One primary issue that has been raised is the relation between RTAs and the multilateral system. One argument is that Article XXIV of the GATT

140 Rivas, *Rules of Origin*, at 153.

141 WTO Appellate Body Report, *Turkey – Textiles*, at para. 58.

142 *Ibid.*

143 WTO, 'Legal Texts: the WTO Agreements', available at www.wto.org/english/docs_e/legal_e/ursum_e.htm#iAgreement.

only derogates from Article I of the GATT, which sets forth the MFN principle. The opposing view is that Article XXIV of the GATT is an exception to other GATT provisions in addition to Article I. In *Turkey – Textiles*, it was articulated that the first view limiting the exception to Article I of the GATT has not been sustained.[144] That decision was in light of the proviso of Article XXIV (5), which states that 'the provisions of this Agreement shall not prevent' the formation of a CU or FTA, or the adoption of an interim agreement leading to either. Because the phrase is 'provisions of this Agreement' and not 'provisions of Article I', the Appellate Body suggested that a measure may be permitted, even if it violates some other provision of the GATT, as long as it satisfies paragraphs 5 and 8 of Article XXIV, and the measure is necessary to the formation of the CU or FTA.[145]

Another controversy is whether Article XXIV (4) of the GATT imposes a distinct legal obligation separate from those contained in paragraphs 5–8. More specifically, the question is whether 'qualified formations should be made to show evidence of external trade creation, or at least be able to indicate that trade diversion will not occur as a result of the elimination of trade barriers between members'.[146] Imposing such an economic test would undermine the requirements of paragraph 8, as an RTA could be formed without satisfying its 'substantially all the trade' requirement. Paragraph 5 would become more prominent, as the formulation would focus on external effects and not internal requirements. The Appellate Body in *Turkey – Textiles* resolved this issue in favour of a non-obligatory construction of paragraph 4. There it noted that paragraph 4 'does not set forth a separate obligation itself, but, rather, sets forth the overriding and pervasive purpose for Article XXIV which is manifested in operative language in the specific obligations that are found elsewhere in Article XXIV'.[147] Similarly, Marceau and Reiman write that it is 'not unreasonable to assume that paragraphs 5 and 8 of Article XXIV were drafted with a view to suggesting criteria that would ensure the respect of the parameters of paragraph 4, i.e. some balancing between . . . the desirability of facilitating trade between the constituent territories and . . . the undesirability of raising barriers to the trade of other WTO Members'.[148]

144 WTO Appellate Body Report, *Turkey – Textiles*, at paras 42–5.

145 *Ibid.* para. 58.

146 Mathis and Bhagwati, *Regional Trade Agreements in the GATT/WTO*, at 231.

147 WTO Appellate Body Report, *Turkey – Textiles*, at para. 57.

148 Marceau and Reiman, *RTA Compatible with the WTO*, at 315.

Thus, the legal requirements of paragraphs 8 and 5 control and give effect to the expressed purpose in paragraph 4.[149]

This leads to an evaluation of RTA compatibility with GATT. As previously mentioned, Article XXIV (8) of the GATT is definitional and must be considered first in a compatibility examination. The external effects of a CU or FTA cannot be measured without first establishing that a CU or FTA has actually been formed or will be formed under the agreement. In this line of reasoning, the question of whether a trade-liberalizing measure taken in accordance with Article XXIV (8) of the GATT has a negative external effect is divisible. First, a CU or FTA must have been formed before the external effect can be evaluated. 'In short, paragraph 8 would be viewed as listing requirements and criteria that are expected to be undertaken by regional parties, and not as a list of requirements that may be undertaken by regional parties as long as they do not hurt non-members'.[150] This process avoids 'an external-effects examination for otherwise non-qualified agreements',[151] or, in other words, avoids unnecessary examination processes on RTAs that do not in the first place fit into the definitional requirements of Article XXIV (8) of the GATT.

Another substantive provision of Article XXIV of the GATT with which the CRTA has had difficulty, and which has been a subject of some discussion, is the timing of notification of RTAs to the GATT, contained in paragraph 7(a) of Article XXIV.[152] Article XXIV (7)(a) provides that parties are to notify the WTO upon their decision to enter into either a CU or FTA. The language used suggests that what is to be notified is prospective, not retrospective, action. Mavroidis posits that the CRTA 'was probably intended to serve a function similar to that of an antitrust authority when examining a merger: the merger cannot be consumed absent a "green light"'.[153] In practice, however, RTAs have been notified *ex post facto*, or after their establishment, contrary to the language of Article XXIV (7)(a) of the GATT. Thus, 'what was originally supposed to be an *ex ante* review

149 Mathis and Bhagwati, *Regional Trade Agreements in the GATT/WTO*, at 232.

150 *Ibid.* at 233. 151 *Ibid.*

152 GATT Art. XXIV para. 7(a) reads: 'Any contracting party deciding to enter into a customs union or free-trade area, or an interim agreement leading to the formation of such a union or area, shall promptly notify the CONTRACTING PARTIES and shall make available to them such information regarding the proposed union or area as will enable them to make such reports and recommendations to contracting parties as they may deem appropriate.'

153 P. Mavroidis, 'If I Don't Do it, Somebody Else Will (or Won't): Testing the Compliance of PTAs with the Multilateral Rules', 27, available at www.ycsg.yale.edu/focus/gta/if_i_dont.pdf.

became slowly an *ex post* review with all the problems that such a shift in the timing of notification might entail'.[154] This has led to a domino effect of problems, such as what should be done, other than dissolution, if an RTA is found to be inconsistent with the relevant WTO rules, and whether RTA members ought to be required to compensate their trading partners for any trade diversion caused by the agreement. The problems suffered by the CRTA have been a contributory factor towards increasing tolerance of potentially non-compatible RTAs.

K The Enabling Clause

1 Events leading to the adoption of the Enabling Clause

The principle of non-discrimination was built into the GATT, in the form of the MFN principle contained in Article I, in order to avoid the discriminatory trade practices and preferential arrangements that were prevalent during the period between World War I and World War II.[155] The MFN principle was designed to apply to all tariffs, rules and formalities applying to imports and exports.[156] However, in order to gain the widespread acceptance necessary for ratification there had to be a compromise, which was achieved in the form of two exceptions to the principle – Article XXIV of the GATT and the preferential arrangements grandfathered into Article I of the GATT.[157] However, one area in which consensus was not reached was the proper path to economic development. The United States believed that developing countries could best develop by participating fully in the multilateral trading system with the lowest possible tariffs and no quantitative restrictions.[158] Developing countries, on the other hand, believed that economic development required the creation of import substitution industries and the use of high tariffs and quotas.[159] Within a decade after its ratification, it became clear that developing countries were not benefiting from the system, and concerns over the fairness of the rules arose.[160] Developing countries began to raise concerns over special challenges faced by their developing economies. The starting point of these concerns was that sustainable increases in income

154 *Ibid.* at 28.

155 Mathis and Bhagwati, *Regional Trade Agreements in the GATT/WTO*, at 13.

156 H. Mutai, 'The Regulation of Regional Trade Agreements: Harnessing the Energy of Regionalism to Power a New Era in Multilateral Trade' (PhD thesis, School of Graduate Studies (Law), University of Melbourne, July 2005) 90–1.

157 *Ibid.* at 91. 158 *Ibid.* at 93. 159 *Ibid.* 160 *Ibid.*

and output could only be achieved through increased industrialization, and there was the concern that 'liberal trade policies would not promote industrialization and development because of the then prevailing patterns of international specialization'.[161] In the meantime, the first generation of African RTAs, as we saw in Chapters I and II, varied greatly the principle of comparative advantage to trade liberalization through devices such as variable geometry.

Developing countries began to push for the relaxation of the stringency of the GATT rules in their favour.[162] They needed a legal means to gain access to larger markets while protecting their domestic market.[163] Because developing countries did not feel that their needs were being addressed through the GATT provisions, they urged and eventually were rewarded with the formation of the United Nations Conference on Trade and Development (UNCTAD). UNCTAD was a separate organization created to deal explicitly with problems of trade and development and through which developing countries could pursue their trade agendas during this period. UNCTAD 'derided the GATT rules and called for new multilateral trade rules that took account of the special position of developing countries', arguing that the status quo was imbalanced and primarily served the interests of developed countries.[164] To respond to these demands, Articles XXXVI, XXXVII and XXXVIII were added in 1965 to make up Part IV of the GATT on Trade and Development. These Articles stressed the need for efforts to enable developing countries to share in the growth in international trade and to further their economic development.[165] Part IV of the GATT on Trade and Development articulated the principle of non-reciprocity, or special and differential treatment, and exhorted developed members to implement measures that would increase the trading opportunities of developing countries.[166]

In 1968, a Generalized System of Preferences (GSP) was established on a voluntary basis by the developed countries.[167] The GSP would allow developed countries to grant tariff preferences without reciprocity to

161 C. Michalopoulos, 'The Role of Special and Differential Treatment for Developing Countries in the GATT and the WTO', World Bank Policy Research Working Paper No. 2388 (July 2000), 3, available at http://papers.ssrn.com/sol3/papers.cfm?abstract_id=630760.

162 See Mutai, 'Regulation of Regional Trade Agreements', at 93. 163 *Ibid.* at 94.

164 E. Kessie, 'The Legal Status of Special and Differential Treatment', in G. Bermann and P. Mavroidis (eds), *WTO Law and Developing Countries* (Cambridge University Press, 2007), 12–35, 17.

165 GATT Part IV on Trade and Development, available at www.wto.org/english/docs_e/legal_e/gatt47_02_e.htm#articleXXXVI.

166 *Ibid.* 167 Mutai, 'Regulation of Regional Trade Agreements', at 94.

almost all developing countries on a wide range of products.[168] The Agreed Conclusions of the UNCTAD Special Committee on Preferences recognized that preferential tariff treatment accorded under a generalized scheme was necessary for developing countries to increase export earnings, promote industrialization and accelerate rates of economic growth.[169] The GSP was not implemented in the GATT until 1971, when the Decision on Generalized System of Preferences was adopted.[170] The 1971 Decision did not impose any new obligations on the part of developed countries, and they were allowed to choose the products to include in their preference schemes, thereby allowing developed countries to safeguard their interests in key areas such as industry and agriculture.[171] In addition, in 1971 a decision was adopted to allow the Protocol Relating to Trade Negotiations among Developing Countries to be implemented.[172] This waived the MFN principle of Article I of the GATT and gave developing countries greater legal freedom to use protectionist measures and discrimination in their own markets. This waiver was to last for a period of 10 years.

The Tokyo Round of negotiations in 1979 sought to consolidate the 1971 waiver, which was shortly due to expire. The outcome of the Tokyo Round was the adoption of the Enabling Clause, which made the authorization to grant preferential tariff treatment to developing countries by developed countries permanent.[173] The Enabling Clause also expanded the authorization to cover additional preferential measures.[174] It provided for the preferential market access of developing countries to developed country markets on a non-reciprocal, non-discriminatory basis; 'more favourable' treatment for developing countries in other GATT rules dealing with non-tariff barriers; the introduction of preferential trade regimes between developing countries; and the special treatment of least-developed countries in the context of specific measures for developing countries.[175] The Enabling Clause gave a stronger legal basis for the

168 *Ibid.*

169 Agreed Conclusions on Preferences in UNCTAD (24 Apr. 1985), available at www.chasque.net/frontpage/suns/trade/areas/develope/unctad/04240085.htm.

170 Mutai, 'Regulation of Regional Trade Agreements', at 94.

171 *Ibid.* at 95.

172 *Ibid.*

173 'Differential and More Favourable Treatment, Reciprocity and Fuller Participation of Developing Countries', Decision of 28 Nov. 1979, GATT Doc. L/493, available at www.wto.org/english/docs_e/legal_e/enabling1979_e.htm.

174 *Ibid.*

175 Michalopoulos, 'Differential Treatment of Developing Countries', at 7.

special and differential treatment of developing countries, although still in discretionary and permissive, not legally binding, terms.

2 The 1979 decision

The 1979 decision, entitled 'Differential and More Favourable Treatment, Reciprocity and Fuller Participation of Developing Countries' allows for derogation from Article I of the GATT by allowing contracting parties to grant preferential treatment to developing countries without granting the same preferences to other contracting parties. The exception applies to:

> (a) Preferential tariff treatment accorded by developed contracting parties to products originating in developing countries in accordance with the Generalized System of Preferences;
> (b) Differential and more favourable treatment with respect to the provisions of the General Agreement concerning non-tariff measures governed by the provisions of instruments multilaterally negotiated under the auspices of the GATT;
> (c) Regional or global arrangements entered into amongst less-developed contracting parties for the mutual reduction or elimination of tariffs and, in accordance with criteria or conditions which may be prescribed by the CONTRACTING PARTIES, for the mutual reduction or elimination of non-tariff measures, on products imported from one another;
> (d) Special treatment on the least developed among the developing countries in the context of any general or specific measures in favour of developing countries.[176]

Paragraph 3(a) of the Enabling Clause provides that any preferential treatment should be designed to facilitate and promote trade and not 'to raise barriers to or create undue difficulties for the trade of any other contracting parties'.[177] Paragraph 3(b) provides that any preferential treatment should not 'constitute an impediment to the reduction or elimination of tariffs and other restrictions to trade on a most-favoured nation basis'.[178] Additionally, with respect to preferences granted by developed countries to developing countries, such preferential treatment should be designed or modified, if necessary, to 'respond positively to the development, financial and trade needs of the developing countries'.[179]

176 Differential and More Favourable Treatment, Enabling Clause, at s. 2.
177 *Ibid.* at s. 3(a). 178 *Ibid.* at s. 3(b). 179 *Ibid.* at s. 3(c).

Paragraph 4 provides that any contracting party taking action pursuant to paragraphs 1, 2 or 3, or 'subsequently taking action to introduce modification or withdrawal of the differential and more favourable treatment' should notify the contracting parties and furnish them with any appropriate and relevant material.[180] Such contracting party should additionally afford an opportunity for consultations, if so requested, by any interested contracting party regarding any difficulty or matter that may arise. If such a request is made, the contracting party should consult with all contracting parties concerned regarding the matter with a view to reach a solution satisfactory to all.

Paragraph 5 of the Enabling Clause sets forth the concept of non-reciprocity. Developed countries should not expect reciprocity for commitments made by them to reduce or eliminate tariffs and other barriers to the trade of developing countries. Developed countries should not expect developing countries 'to make contributions which are inconsistent with their individual development, financial and trade needs'.[181] Thus, developed countries should not seek, and less-developed countries should not be required to make, concessions that are contrary to their development, financial and trade needs. When seeking concessions or contributions for commitments made by them, developed countries should 'exercise the utmost restraint' and the less-developed countries should not be expected to 'make concessions or contributions that are inconsistent with the recognition of their particular situation and problems'.[182]

Paragraph 7 of the Enabling Clause provides that any obligations assumed 'under the provisions of the General Agreement should promote the basic objectives of the Agreement, including those embodied in the Preamble and in Article XXXVI'.[183] Paragraph 7 goes on to express the concept of graduation, agreed upon as a counterweight to the provisions for special and differential treatment in the Enabling Clause. Graduation means that the capacity of developing countries to 'make contributions or negotiated concessions or take other mutually agreed action under the provisions and procedures of the General Agreement' will improve with the progressive development of their economies and trade situations, and, thus, fuller participation by such countries in the framework of rights and obligations of the multilateral trading system.[184] This provides the basis for developed contracting parties to phase-out non-reciprocal market access measures to contracting

180 *Ibid.* at s. 4(a). 181 *Ibid.* at s. 5. 182 *Ibid.* at s. 6.
183 *Ibid.* at s. 7. 184 *Ibid.*

parties which, over time, are deemed to have achieved a sufficient level of progress. Because preferences granted under the Enabling Clause are permissive and non-binding, and because of this 'fuller participation' clause, 'developing countries could have no legal recourse in the GATT against such action'.[185]

Paragraph 8 provides for particular account to be taken of the difficulties faced by the least-developed countries in making concessions and contributions in view of their economic situation and their development, financial and trade needs.

Paragraph 9 provides collaboration in the arrangements for review of the operation of the Enabling Clause provisions, 'bearing in mind the need for individual and joint efforts by contracting parties to meet the development needs of developing countries and the objectives of the General Agreement'.[186]

3 Discussion

It has been argued that the Enabling Clause, by exempting developing countries from the application of Article XXIV of the GATT, has weakened the capacity of the WTO to effectively regulate RTAs.[187] The Enabling Clause does not contain any reference to Article XXIV of the GATT, leaving open the question of whether it created a new framework for developing countries. Henry Mutai argues that the Enabling Clause was directed towards extending to the Protocol Relating to Trade Negotiations among Developing Countries the same permanent waiver that was extended to the GSP, and not towards creating an alternative procedure for the creation of RTAs by developing countries.[188] In practice, however, the Enabling Clause has been used as a cover for RTAs between developing countries.[189] Mutai argues that the Enabling Clause has, thus, weakened the exception contained in Article XXIV of the GATT, changed the legal nature of developing countries' obligations and has weakened the normative force of the MFN principle.[190]

One of the policy goals of the GATT was to make discrimination predictable, in the sense that an RTA under Article XXIV of the GATT would be considerably less distortive and disruptive than an RTA consisting

185 Michalopoulos, 'Differential Treatment of Developing Countries', at 3.
186 Differential and More Favourable Treatment, Enabling Clause, at s. 9.
187 Mutai, 'Regulation of Regional Trade Agreements'. 188 *Ibid.* at 97.
189 *Ibid.* 190 *Ibid.*

of selective partial preferences capable of expanding or deepening each year.[191] Thus, the exemption of developing countries from the obligations of Article XXIV of the GATT can be considered to have been counterproductive because developing countries could no longer be constrained to adopt optimal trade policies.[192]

The Enabling Clause does not refer specifically to either CUs or FTAs. It provides only that the discretion to grant differential and more favourable treatment applies to regional or global arrangements amongst developing countries for the mutual reduction or elimination of tariffs, and the mutual reduction or elimination of non-tariff measures, in accordance with criteria or conditions prescribed by the contracting parties.[193] According to the Enabling Clause, then, developing countries have a choice as to whether to reduce or eliminate tariffs on imports from one another. In comparison, Article XXIV of the GATT requires members to commit to the elimination of duties and other restrictive regulations of commerce.[194] The lack of such requirements in the Enabling Clause suggests that it does not cover preferential arrangements that fall short of FTAs or CUs. An opposing argument is that Article XXIV (5) of the GATT authorizes interim agreements that have not yet reached the stage of FTA or CU. Further, Paragraph 3 of the Enabling Clause contains similar requirements in its condition that the preferences granted do not raise barriers to the trade of third countries. These two points illustrate the debate over whether the Enabling Clause can be used to notify CUs and FTAs.

In addition, Mutai argues that the exclusion of any external requirements regarding the formation of a CU in the Enabling Clause, especially regarding setting up a common external tariff, suggests that CUs among developing countries were not intended to be eligible to be notified to the WTO under the Enabling Clause.[195] Before the adoption of the Enabling Clause, 'developing countries had been notifying customs unions under Article XXIV of the GATT'.[196] Further, 'among contracting parties, views differ as to whether the Enabling Clause covers regional integration agreements (customs unions and free trade areas) for which provision is also made in Article XXIV of the GATT'.[197] This furthers

191 *Ibid.* at 100. 192 *Ibid.*

193 Differential and More Favourable Treatment, Enabling Clause, at s. 2(c).

194 GATT Art. XXIV, at s. 8.

195 Mutai, 'Regulation of Regional Trade Agreements', at 103. 196 *Ibid.*

197 S. Healy, R. Pearce and M. Stockbridge, 'The Implications of the Uruguay Round Agreement on Agriculture for Developing Countries' (FAO, 1998), Ch. 7, available at www.fao.org/docrep/004/w7814e/W7814E11.htm.

Mutai's argument that the Enabling Clause was not aimed at creating an alternative procedure for the creation of RTAs between developing countries.

The view that the Enabling Clause is not merely an alternative procedure for the formation of RTAs between developing countries is also articulated by Jacques Berthelot.[198] Berthelot argues that interpreting Paragraph 2(c) of the Enabling Clause as creating an alternative procedure for the formation of CUs and FTAs would be redundant with Article XXIV of the GATT, which already allows for the formation of such arrangements.[199] Further, the WTO Appellate Body in *US – Gasoline* stated that 'one of the corollaries of the "general rule of interpretation" in the Vienna Convention is that interpretation must give meaning and effect to all the terms of a treaty. An interpreter is not free to adopt a reading that would result in reducing whole clauses or paragraphs of a treaty to redundancy or inutility'.[200] Instead, Berthelot suggests reading paragraphs 1 and 2 of the Enabling Clause together. Berthelot contends that paragraph 1 implies that 'contracting parties' are developed, not developing countries, because it allows 'contracting parties' to grant preferences to developing countries.[201] The Enabling Clause provides that the provisions of paragraph 1 are to apply to the provisions in paragraph 2. Subsection (c) of paragraph 2 authorizes preferential agreements between developing countries. Following this logic, 'contracting parties', or developed countries, would be allowed to grant preferential treatment to developing countries within regional trade arrangements. This would avoid redundancy with Article XXIV of the GATT. The current state of GATT law, however, does not follow this line of reasoning.

Mutai concludes that the reversal of GATT policy in the 1960s with respect to constraints on preferential treatment was an error based on mistaken economic assumptions.[202] The creation of a 'parallel' GATT system of preferences among developing countries resulted in trade diversion and the establishment of inefficient local industries. Additionally, the

198 J. Berthelot, 'David and Goliath: Argument Against the EPAs between the European Union and African, Caribbean and Pacific Countries' (19 Dec. 2006), available at www.acp-eu-trade.org/library/files/Berthelot_EN_191206_Solidarite_David-Goliath-argument-against-the-EPAs.pdf.

199 *Ibid.* at 13.

200 WTO Appellate Body Report, *United States – Standards for Reformulated and Conventional Gasoline*, WT/DS2/AB/R, 29 Apr. 1996, paras 1596–7.

201 Berthelot, 'David and Goliath', at 13.

202 Mutai, 'Regulating Regional Trade Agreements', at 134.

fact that the substantive provisions of Article XXIV of the GATT are so ambiguous renders the flexibility for developing countries offered by the Enabling Clause unnecessary, as such ambiguity leaves sufficient leeway for governments to structure their trade liberalization schemes to suit their unique economic needs.[203] The Enabling Clause and its lax application diminished the ability of the WTO to regulate RTAs by removing any substantive constraints on the creation of such agreements amongst developing countries. This gave free range to developing countries to pursue regional integration based on partial preferences instead of the formation of FTAs and CUs based on the elimination of trade barriers. Mutai suggests that a legal regime in which developing countries accept greater legal discipline, and in which all RTAs were subject to the scrutiny of Article XXIV of the GATT, would be to the benefit of the multilateral trading system and developing countries alike.[204]

L European Communities: Conditions for the granting of tariff preferences to developing countries

India's original complaint challenged aspects of the European GSP scheme. The scheme afforded more generous preferences to the least-developed countries, to developing countries that undertook particular measures to protect the environment and labour rights and to 12 countries that were involved in efforts to combat drug trafficking. India originally challenged all three preferences, but later limited its complaint to only the drug-related preferences.[205] The complaint focused on the requirement of non-discriminatory preferences as provided in footnote 3 of the Enabling Clause, citing the system contemplated in the 1971 waiver. India argued that when a country grants a preference on a particular product, that preference must be extended to all developing countries, the only permitted difference being the proviso that least-developed countries can receive greater preferences.[206] The complaint alleged that the preferences did not meet the requirement of non-discrimination under the Enabling Clause and, thus, violated the EC's MFN obligation under Article I of the GATT.[207]

203 *Ibid.* 204 *Ibid.* at 136.

205 G. Grossman and A. Sykes, 'A Preference for Development: The Law and Economics of GSP', in Bermann and Mavroidis (eds), *WTO Law and Developing Countries*, 255–82, 260.

206 *Ibid.* at 262. 207 *Ibid.*

The EC's first response was that the Enabling Clause removed GSP schemes from the coverage of Article I of the GATT altogether, and thus the Clause did not create an exception to Article I, and that India's complaint therefore inaccurately alleged a violation of Article I but not of the Enabling Clause.[208] The Panel read the Enabling Clause as an exception to Article I of the GATT in the sense that, but for the exception, the granting of preferences would violate Article I, and therefore held that India's complaint raised the proper issue.[209] Also, the Panel held that the burden of demonstrating that its programme was covered by the exception contained in the Enabling Clause fell on the EC.[210] After the Panel held that GSP preferences fall under an exception to Article I of the GATT, it concluded that India had made out a prima facie violation and turned to the question of whether the EC could invoke the Enabling Clause to establish its affirmative defence.[211] The EC alleged, using paragraph 3(c) of the Enabling Clause, that different developing countries have different 'development, financial and trade needs' and thus preferences must be modified in order to respond to those differing needs, which inevitably would produce differences in the preferences granted to different beneficiaries.[212] Second, the EC claimed that 'discrimination' entailed arbitrary differences in the treatment of similarly situated countries, and that as long as differences could be justified by a legitimate objective and were reasonable in pursuit of that objective, no discrimination should be found.[213] Third, the EC argued, using paragraph 2(a) of the Enabling Clause, that if the drafters had intended to require that preferences be extended to all developing countries, they would have inserted the term 'all' into the text.[214] The fact that they did not indicated, according to the EC, that they did not so intend.

The Panel found that the cited portions of the Enabling Clause were ambiguous and so 'it turned to the context of the treaty text, its object and purpose, and other aids to interpretation', following the Vienna Convention.[215] It noted that the Enabling Clause referred back to the 1971 waiver, which referenced 'mutually acceptable' preferences which were apparently those negotiated under UNCTAD and embodied in the Agreed Conclusions. After reviewing the Agreed Conclusions, the Panel

208 *Ibid.* 209 *Ibid.*

210 WTO Panel Report, *European Communities – Conditions for the Granting of Tariff Preferences to Developing Countries*, WT/DS246/R, 1 Dec. 2003, paras 7.31–7.54.

211 *Ibid.* at paras 7.55–7.60.

212 Grossman and Sykes, 'Preference for Development', at 263.

213 *Ibid.* 214 *Ibid.* 215 *Ibid.*

found that some limitations on product coverage were anticipated, but did not find anything that seemed to consider discrimination among developed countries on the basis of their development or other 'needs'.[216] Thus, the Panel found that the phrase 'developing countries' in paragraph 2(a) of the Enabling Clause means all developing countries, that paragraph 3(c) does not permit differences in preferences other than those contemplated by the UNCTAD negotiators, and that footnote 3 requires identical preferences under GSP schemes to be provided to all developing countries, without differentiation, except for the differential treatment contemplated in the Agreed Conclusions.[217]

The Appellate Body affirmed the Panel's decision that the Enabling Clause is an exception to Article I of the GATT, and held that the Clause does not exclude the applicability of Article I.[218] Procedurally, the Enabling Clause is to be read together with Article I of the GATT. In other words, when the Enabling Clause is implicated, consistency with Article I should be examined first, and if it is found not to be consistent, the dispute settlement body should then examine whether the challenged measure is covered under the Enabling Clause. The Appellate Body noted the vital role held by the Enabling Clause in the promotion of trade as a means of stimulating economic growth and development, and found that the Clause was not a typical exception or defence that could be found in the GATT.[219] Under the ordinary practice involving typical exceptions, the exception is invoked by the responding party. Under the Enabling Clause, however, the Appellate Body held that the complainant, in this case India, must raise the Enabling Clause in making its claim of inconsistency with Article I of the GATT and must identify the specific provisions which it believes were violated by the challenged measure.[220] The Appellate Body also affirmed the Panel's decision that the respondent, the EC, had the burden of justifying the challenged measure under the Enabling Clause provisions.[221]

The only issue on appeal was the question of whether the EC's GSP scheme was consistent with paragraph 2(a) of the Enabling Clause and with footnote 3, which requires 'non-discriminatory' preferences.[222]

216 *Ibid.* at 264.

217 WTO Panel Report, *EC – Tariff Preferences*, at paras 7.174, 7.116, 7.161.

218 Grossman and Sykes, 'Preference for Development', at 264–5.

219 WTO Appellate Body Report, *European Communities – Conditions for the Granting of Tariff Preferences to Developing Countries*, WT/DS246/AB/R, 7 Apr. 2004, para. 106.

220 *Ibid.* at paras 113–14, 125.

221 *Ibid.* at para. 11 5.

222 *Ibid.* at para. 142; see also Grossman and Sykes, 'Preference for Development', at 265.

The Appellate Body held that discrimination entailed disparate treatment of those similarly situated, but did not define the phrase 'similarly situated'.[223] It overruled the Panel's decision and held that 'the absence of the word "all" before the phrase "developing countries"' in paragraph 3(c) of the Enabling Clause 'implies that there is no obligation imposed by the text to treat all developing countries alike'.[224] The Appellate Body was 'of the view that, by requiring developed countries to "respond positively" to the "needs of developing countries", which are varied and not homogeneous, paragraph 3(c) indicates that a GSP scheme may be "non-discriminatory" even if "identical" tariff treatment is not accorded to "all" GSP beneficiaries'.[225] It held that the countries granting preferences are permitted to treat the beneficiary countries differently, when such differences 'respond positively' to varying 'development, financial and trade needs'.[226] However, 'identical tariff treatment must be available to all GSP beneficiaries with the "development, financial [or] trade need" to which the differential treatment is intended to respond'.[227] It subsequently upheld the Panel's decision that the EC failed to prove that its measure was non-discriminatory, that the closed list of beneficiary countries which contained 12 total countries could not ensure that the preferences would be available to all similarly situated beneficiaries, or those that suffered from illicit drug production and trafficking, and that the criterion was not objective in its distinction between beneficiary countries.[228]

The Appellate Body in this case established two important principles. The first is that footnote 3 of the Enabling Clause is a binding legal obligation that requires 'generalized, non-reciprocal and non-discriminatory preferences'; the second is that preference-granting countries may afford differential treatment to beneficiary countries if it is based on differences in their 'development, financial and trade needs'.[229] Additionally, the Appellate Body confirmed the legal effect of the Enabling Clause in its acknowledgement that the Clause has become part of the GATT 1994.[230] Yet these principles give rise to many issues that have not yet been addressed. Such issues include: what constitutes a development, financial

223 WTO Appellate Body Report, *EC – Tariff Preferences*, at para. 154.

224 Grossman and Sykes, 'Preference for Development', at 265.

225 WTO Appellate Body Report, *EC – Tariff Preferences*, at paras 160, 175–6.

226 *Ibid.* at paras 175–6.

227 *Ibid.* at paras 165, 180.

228 Grossman and Sykes, 'Preference for Development', at 265–6.

229 *Ibid.* at 269.

230 WTO Appellate Body Report, *EC – Tariff Preferences*, at para. 143.

or trade need; the magnitude of the permissible differential treatment to address heterogeneous development, financial and trade needs; how much discretion donor countries have in selecting the 'needs' that they will address through differential treatment; whether a system that completely excludes enumerated import-sensitive manufactured products can be aligned with the obligation to provide 'generalized' preferences; and the issue regarding the 'non-reciprocal' preferences requirement and the conditionality of modern GSP schemes.[231]

M EU–ACP Economic Partnership Agreement

The EU-ACP Economic Partnership Agreement (EPA), a comprehensive aid and trade agreement concluded between 77 ACP (African, Caribbean and Pacific) countries and the EU, was signed in 2000 in Cotonou, from which it is commonly known as the Cotonou Agreement.[232] The Cotonou Agreement builds on 25 years of cooperation between the EU and ACP countries under the Lomé Conventions, which provided a model of development cooperation.[233] The Agreement is to last for 20 years, with provisions for revision every five years and a financial protocol that indicates the financial resources available to the ACP through the European Development Fund (EDF) covering each five-year period.[234]

ACP-EU cooperation is based on three complementary pillars: economic and trade cooperation, development cooperation and aid. The trade regime would 'undergo a profound transformation' from the previous Lomé Conventions with the 'current all-ACP non-reciprocal tariff preferences'[235] to be maintained until the end of 2007, when they would be replaced at the start of 2008 with EPAs that would be compatible with WTO rules.[236] The Cotonou Agreement provides that the '[e]conomic and trade cooperation shall take account of the different needs and levels of development of the ACP countries and regions' and reaffirms the parties' attachment to 'ensuring special and differential treatment for all ACP countries and to maintaining special treatment for ACP LDCs'.[237]

231 See Grossman and Sykes, 'Preference for Development', at 269–71.

232 'Cotonou Infokit 2: The Cotonou Agreement at a Glance' (ECDPM, 2002), available at www.ecdpm.org/Web_ECDPM/Web/Content/Navigation.nsf/index2?readform&http://www.ecdpm.org/Web_ECDPM/Web/Content/Content.nsf/vwDocID/A68AE1325FBA33DCC1256C7500580251?OpenDocument.

233 *Ibid.* 234 *Ibid.* 235 *Ibid.*

236 Cotonou Agreement, Pt. 3, Title II, Ch. 2, Art. 37(1), available at www.acpsec.org/en/conventions/cotonou/accord1.htm.

237 *Ibid.* at Ch. 1, Art. 35(3).

The least-developed countries will be 'entitled to maintain non-reciprocal preferences' and ACP countries are invited to sign as groups or individually, 'building on their own regional integration schemes'.[238] The EPAs introduced in 2008 are aimed to 'progressively liberalise trade in a reciprocal way', and this gradual removal of trade barriers is 'expected to result in the establishment of Free Trade Areas between the EU and ACP regional groups in accordance with the relevant WTO rules and help further existing regional integration efforts among the ACP'.[239] The development strategies of the Cotonou Agreement include the areas of gender, environment and natural resources and institutional development and capacity building.[240] The third pillar is aid, or financial and technical cooperation, through which the largest share of the financial resources is grants to financial development programmes in ACP countries or in the ACP regions.[241] These grants are to support long-term development through the ACP countries' National Indicative Programmes or the ACP regions' Regional Indicative Programmes.

N Compatibility with the WTO

Among the challenges facing the EPAs is compatibility with WTO rules. Ruth Kelly sets forth and examines three different options for rendering EPAs compatible with WTO law: the waiver process, the Enabling Clause and justification as an RTA.[242] The least restrictive option, she posits, is the waiver process under Article IX paragraphs 3–4 of the WTO Agreement.[243] The waiver process allows the EU extensive policy space in the drafting of EPAs because it removes the obligation to tailor the EPAs to fall within any of the other exceptions of WTO law. Since the former Lomé Conventions and the current provisions on trade in the Cotonou Agreement are based on preferential treatment in favour of ACP countries, the EU and the ACP countries had to seek a waiver from

238 'Cotonou Infokit 2: The Cotonou Agreement at a Glance'.

239 A. Keck and R. Piermartini, 'The Economic Impact of EPAs in SADC Countries', WTO Economic Research and Statistics Division Staff Working Paper No. 2005–04 (Aug. 2005), 2.

240 Cotonou Agreement, Title I, Ch. 2, s. 4.

241 'Cotonou Infokit 2: The Cotonou Agreement at a Glance'.

242 R. Kelly, 'WTO Compatibility and the Legal Form of EPAs: A Case Study of Eastern and Southern Africa', Working Paper No. 48–08, Inaugural Conference, Geneva (Society of International Economic Law, 15–17 July 2008), 2, available at www.ssrn.com/link/SIEL-Inaugural-Conference.html.

243 *Ibid.* at 3.

the WTO in order to implement such preferential treatment. The EU has gradually become reluctant to use this approach, however, and has stressed the importance of EPA compatibility with WTO rules.[244] In fact, the EU pledged that the waiver requested under the Cotonou Agreement would be the last covering EU-ACP relations.[245] The decision to make the future trade arrangements WTO compatible could have been motivated in part by concerns over renewal of the waiver. Obtaining a waiver requires extensive negotiations in the WTO, and possibly having to grant compensations to third parties for their agreements, due to the consensus decision-making process prevalent in the WTO system. Further, once a waiver is granted it is subject to legal challenge, as well as modification and termination during annual review. For these reasons, waivers are often unstable in their function as the basis of trade arrangements.[246]

1 The Enabling Clause to justify EU–ACP preferences

The GSP Scheme under the Enabling Clause is another option to justify EU-ACP preferences. The current EU GSP scheme has three elements: 'the general GSP arrangement, open to all developing countries; the GSP+ arrangement, open to countries who ratify and implement various international treaties; and the Everything but Arms (EBA) arrangement, granting duty-free and quota-free access for all products except arms and munitions originating in least-developed countries'.[247] The general EU GSP arrangement does not put ACP countries at an advantage over other developing countries, and as from 2007, none of the ACP countries is covered under the GSP+ arrangement, even though its selectiveness would better protect their privileged position.[248] For the preferences to be justified under the GSP+ arrangement, the EU would have to 'open GSP+ to ACP countries' or 'create a new GSP+ style scheme restricted to ACP countries'.[249] Further, not all ACP countries are least-developed countries, and thus the EBA arrangement cannot be used as a justification.

Kelly finds that the current EU GSP scheme is WTO compatible because it satisfies the three-step test articulated by the Appellate Body in *EC – Tariff Preferences*.[250] The first step is that the existence of a 'development, financial [or] trade need must be assessed according to an *objective* standard'.[251] The Appellate Body noted that '[b]road-based recognition

244 *Ibid.* 245 *Ibid.* at 4. 246 *Ibid.* 247 *Ibid.* at 5. 248 *Ibid.*
249 *Ibid.* at 6. 250 *Ibid.*
251 WTO Appellate Body Report, *EC – Tariff Preferences*, at para. 163.

of a particular need, set out in the *WTO Agreement* or in multilateral instruments adopted by international organizations, could serve as such a standard'.[252] The EU GSP scheme satisfies this requirement as regional integration is the basis for EU-ACP relations and is recognized as a development need in Article XXIV paragraph 4 of the GATT as well as in the Preamble to the Understanding on the Interpretation of Article XXIV of the GATT 1994. Kelly suggests that the scheme could be confined to Eastern and Southern Africa by reference to the Millennium Development Declaration, which is a multilateral instrument with broad recognition adopted by the UN, an international organization.[253] The second step, that any scheme must be open to all GSP beneficiaries with that particular need, is satisfied because negotiations are taking place regarding EPAs with Central, East, Southern and West African regions.[254] However, Kelly contends that this could be further confined to Eastern and Southern Africa, due to the complexity of integration in that particular region.[255] The third step of the test is that there must be a sufficient nexus between the preferential treatment and the development need in question.[256] This step is derived from paragraph 3(c) of the Enabling Clause. The Appellate Body in *EC-Tariff Preferences* concluded that the 'positive response' of paragraph 3(c) of the Enabling Clause 'must be taken with a view to *improving* the development, financial and trade situation of a beneficiary country, based on the particular need at issue' and qualified this subjective test by providing that a 'sufficient nexus should exist between . . . the preferential treatment . . . and . . . the likelihood of alleviating the . . . need'.[257] Thus, to satisfy this third step, the EU's reasonable intention in concluding the EPAs must have been to address the failure of regional integration efforts and other development needs of Eastern and Southern Africa. Kelly concludes that the EAC EPA is the only EPA that fully responds to existing regional integration efforts, although it can be argued that 'the EC's response was necessary to rationalize increasingly fragmented and overlapping arrangements'.[258] The fulfilment of the three-step test illustrates that a GSP scheme could be created for Eastern and Southern African ACP countries that is WTO compatible.

However, one of the difficulties of creating a special GSP scheme for ACP countries, and the principle of non-reciprocity in general, is the unilateral and uncertain nature of such a scheme.[259] Preferential treatment is

252 *Ibid.* 253 Kelly, 'WTO Compatibility', at 10. 254 *Ibid.* 255 *Ibid.*
256 WTO Appellate Body Report, *EC – Tariff Preferences*, at para. 164.
257 *Ibid.* 258 Kelly, 'WTO Compatibility', at 13. 259 *Ibid.* at 14.

imposed unilaterally and can be withdrawn unilaterally. The uncertainty makes developing countries dependent on developed countries' goodwill and also makes developing countries more vulnerable to non-trade conditionalities.[260] Reciprocity may also benefit the EU because the EPAs will allow them to have preferential access to ACP countries' markets, especially beneficial since ACP products are increasing in importance as vital resources, such as minerals, are becoming scarce.[261]

2 GATT Article XXIV to justify EU–ACP preferences

Lastly, EPAs could be justified under Article XXIV of the GATT and Article V of the GATS. The RTA exception waives WTO provisions and allows for the formation of FTAs and CUs, and interim agreements leading to either, that would otherwise be prevented by WTO provisions. The formation of RTAs is conditioned upon certain procedural requirements (GATT Art. XXIV (7)) as well as both internal and external substantive requirements (GATT Art. XXIV (5), (8)). Paragraph 7 of Article XXIV of the GATT sets forth that RTAs must be notified before the agreement enters into force and thus, Kelly concludes, since Eastern and Southern African EPAs have yet to be notified, they are inconsistent with this provision.[262] This implies that the political benefits of reciprocal RTAs, rather than the requirements of WTO law, were more important in choosing the legal form of EPAs.[263]

3 Internal requirement of GATT Article XXIV (8)(b)

Further, the Panel in *Bananas II* found that the plural use of the word 'territory' under paragraph 8(b) of Article XXIV of the GATT[264] establishes a reciprocity requirement for FTAs and excludes all completely non-reciprocal agreements from the scope of the exception.[265] However, the Panel left room for a different approach to the interpretation of agreements with limited reciprocity in its emphasis on the lack of any obligation for reciprocal liberalization in the Bananas Protocol, making the

260 *Ibid.* 261 *Ibid.* at 15. 262 *Ibid.* at 17. 263 *Ibid.*

264 GATT Art. XXIV para. 8(b) reads: a 'free-trade area shall be understood to mean a group of two or more customs *territories* in which the duties and other restrictive regulations of commerce . . . are eliminated on substantially all the trade between the constituent *territories* in products originating in such *territories*' (emphasis added).

265 WTO Panel Report, *EEC – Import Regime for Bananas*, WT/DS38/R, 11 Feb. 1994, para. 159.

Protocol 'substantially different' from FTAs as defined in paragraph 8(b) of Article XXIV of the GATT.[266] However, the extent of the reciprocity requirement is ambiguous, permitting an asymmetric approach to the Article XXIV requirements for RTAs concluded between developed and developing countries. This is demonstrated by the heavy liberalization burden placed on the EU as compared to that on the ACP countries. An interpretation of the reciprocity requirement must take into consideration the development objective in the WTO-covered agreements, as paragraph 3 of Article XXXVI of the GATT and the Preamble to the WTO Agreement both recognize the need for 'positive efforts' to guarantee that developing countries 'secure a share in the growth of international trade commensurate with the needs of their economic development'.[267] Thus, the reciprocity requirement should be interpreted in light of the development level of the countries involved, and this compilation of the reciprocity requirement and development objective legitimates an asymmetric approach under Article XXIV of the GATT.[268]

The term 'substantially all the trade' is 'sufficiently flexible to allow for limits on intra-FTA liberalisation without legitimising non-reciprocal preferences'.[269] The term was, to some extent, clarified in the Preamble to the Understanding on the Interpretation of Article XXIV of the GATT 1994, which recognizes that RTAs' contribution to the expansion of world trade is 'diminished if any major sector of trade is excluded'.[270] However, the flexibility or ambiguity of the term 'substantially all the trade' makes a legal analysis of the internal requirement difficult. The 'substantially all the trade' requirement contains a list of exceptions for contingency measures or other exceptions, and any such measures or exceptions[271] that are not listed under paragraph 8 of Article XXIV of the GATT 'are relevant for the calculation of the SAT requirement'.[272] The EU-ACP EPAs contain both listed and unlisted contingency measures and exceptions,[273] but the internal requirement of paragraph 8 of Article XXIV of the

266 *Ibid.*

267 Agreement Establishing the WTO, Preamble para. 2, available at www.wto.org/english/docs_e/legal_e/04-wto.pdf; see also GATT Part IV, at Art. XXXVI s. 3.

268 See Kelly, 'WTO Compatibility', at 22.

269 *Ibid.* at 25.

270 Understanding on the Interpretation of Article XXIV of the GATT 1994, Preamble.

271 Non-discriminatory and necessary tariff barriers and Sanitary and Phytosanitary Standards measures should also be excluded from the calculation of the science and technology requirement in so far as they clarify Art. XX of the GATT, which is one of the listed exceptions. Kelly, 'WTO Compatibility', at 26.

272 *Ibid.* at 28.

273 EC-EAC EPA, Arts 15.2, 17.2, 19, 20; EC-ESA EPA Arts 19, 20, 56–7; EC-SADC EPA, Arts 24, 32–4, 65–6, 90–2, Chs. V and VI.

GATT does not apply to those interim agreements.[274] This is because if the internal requirement was to apply to interim agreements and the threshold was applied immediately, it would render transition periods useless. In support of this point, paragraph 8 of Article XXIV of the GATT does not mention interim agreements, while there are references in paragraph 5(a), (b) and (c).

Paragraph 3 of Article V of the GATS allows flexibility for RTAs involving developing countries 'in accordance with the level of development of the countries concerned, both overall and in individual sectors and subsectors'.[275] Kelly suggests that similar flexibility should be read into the text of the internal requirement of paragraph 8(b) of Article XXIV of the GATT, 'i.e. lower thresholds should be set for developing countries than for developed countries under both quantitative and qualitative approaches'.[276] This would allow developing countries to maintain those barriers to trade that are linked to development needs, such as the protection of infant industries and revenue losses due to the removal of such barriers, without violating the internal requirement.

The potential compatibility of the completed EPAs can be assessed based on the end targets of the liberalization schedule under paragraph 8(b) of Article XXIV of the GATT. Kelly assesses the potential compatibility of Eastern and Southern African EPAs at the basis of individual customs territories and interprets the 'substantially all the trade' requirement in light of the development objective which allows for the variation of the requirement depending on the level of development in each country.[277] If the proposed 70 per cent of tariff lines is used to examine the qualitative element, the EU-EAC EPA, liberalizing 74 per cent of tariff lines, and the SACU states that are signatories to the EU-SADC EPA, liberalizing 86 per cent of tariff lines and an additional 47 tariff lines, will have met that threshold.[278] No information is available on the percentage of tariff lines liberalized under the EU-ESA EPA.[279] The EU has suggested that 80 per cent of trade coverage should be used to assess the quantitative element of the 'substantially all the trade' requirement.[280] Each Eastern and Southern African EPA will meet this if the liberalization targets are met by the end of the transition period.[281] If the 95 per cent threshold is used, as suggested by Australia, only Seychelles and Mauritius will meet the requirement as signatories to the EU-ESA EPA.

274 Kelly, 'WTO Compatibility', at 28. 275 GATS Art. V, at para. 3(a).
276 Kelly, 'WTO Compatibility', at 32. 277 *Ibid.* 278 *Ibid.* at 34.
279 *Ibid.* 280 *Ibid.* 281 *Ibid.* at 35.

The EU also gives some information on the products excluded from the liberalization scheme, and if the proposed distinction between major and more specific sectors of trade is used, problems could arise with each of the Eastern and Southern African EPAs.[282] The EU-SADC EPA 'excludes agriculture and some processed agricultural products from liberalization', and even if some agricultural products are included in the liberalization scheme, the exclusion of a large portion could be interpreted as *de facto* exclusion of a major sector.[283] The EU-EAC EPA excludes seemingly major sectors such as agricultural products, glassware, chemicals, plastics, wines and spirits, textiles and clothing and footwear.[284] Each of the five signatories of the EU-ESA EPA excludes a different range of products; examples of broad categories include fish and products of animal origin, vehicles and beverages.[285] However, all three EPAs in the region exclude these products for the purpose of protecting infant industries in response to development needs, so it can be argued that the internal requirement read in light of the development objective could allow for the exclusion of these major sectors for developing countries.

4 *Rules of origin*

The internal requirement in paragraph 8(b) of Article XXIV of the GATT limits 'substantially all the trade' to products originating within the region that are covered by the RTA. To determine whether a product is 'originating', RoOs are used. RoOs have a protective function and are also necessary to prevent trade deflection, but it is difficult to determine when they cross the line from being necessary to become protectionist. It is also difficult to excise the protectionist portion while leaving the necessary function intact. Protocols on Rules of Origin for Eastern and Southern African EPAs have not yet been concluded, so their protective function cannot yet be analysed.[286]

If EPAs with Cotonou-type rules of origin had been adopted in 2008, the values of preferences could have increased to 4.5 per cent of exports, but if EPAs were concluded with simple origin rules, preferences could be much higher, because several export products could become more competitive in the EU market.[287]

282 *Ibid.* at 34. 283 *Ibid.* 284 *Ibid.* 285 *Ibid.* 286 *Ibid.* at 29.

287 M. Hoppe, 'Economic Partnership Agreements: Does Preferential Access of Non-LDC African Countries Increase?', World Bank Group, Trade Note No. 32 (12 July 2007), 2.

5 *Transition periods*

The Eastern and Southern African EPAs are interim agreements leading to the formation of an FTA, as shown by the plan and schedule of liberalization attached as required under paragraph 5(c) of Article XXIV of the GATT. The transition period must not exceed a 'reasonable length of time', which, as clarified by the Understanding on the Interpretation of Article XXIV of the GATT 1994, means that it must not exceed ten years, except under 'exceptional circumstances' where a 'full explanation' is given.[288] However, there are several cases in which the transition period has been extended up to 20 years, the majority of extensions applying to the developing party only.[289] Existing transition periods have been adopted by the parties unilaterally and have not been approved by the Committee on Regional Trade Agreements or the Dispute Settlement Body, which might make them examples of state practice but not as giving legal guarantees.[290] Within the EU-ACP EPAs, the EU has agreed to liberalize trade within 10 years, while the 2004 submission by ACP countries proposes a transition period of not less than 18 years for developing countries.[291] Article 1(f) of the EU-SADC interim agreement provides that liberalization will be 'progressive and asymmetric'.[292] The only transition period to exceed the proposed 18 years is that of the EU-EAC EPA, which allows for a period of 25 years, even though the threshold amount of liberalization to comply with the internal requirement will likely be met within 15 years.[293] The transition period in the EU-ESA EPA is 14 years, ending in 2022, and under the EU-SADC EPA the transition period will be two years for SACU members, while Mozambique will liberalize most of its trade as soon as the EPA enters into force.[294]

It is difficult to discern what justifies an exception to the ten-year 'reasonable length of time' requirement, since paragraph 5(c) of Article XXIV of the GATT is open to all 'exceptional cases'. The EU proposes that such cases be limited to developing countries to allow for institutional capacity building or infant industry protection.[295] These

288 Understanding on the Interpretation of Article XXIV of the GATT 1994, at para. 2.

289 An exception to this is the US FTAgs with Chile and Argentina which set transition periods of 15 and 18 years, respectively, for the USA. See Kelly, 'WTO Compatibility', at 25.

290 *Ibid.*

291 ACP's WTO submission, Doc. No. TN/RL/W/155, 26 Apr. 2004, s. 11(ii).

292 EU-SADC EPA, Art. 1(f), available at www.bilaterals.org/article.php3?id_article=9719.

293 Kelly, 'WTO Compatibility', at 26.

294 *Ibid.*

295 'Communication from the EC', Doc. No. TN/TF/W/37, 29 Apr. 2005, paras 12, 18.

factors may fulfil the requirement for a 'full explanation' without illuminating possible minimum grounds for exception. In accordance with the development objective mentioned above, the duration of transition periods could be related to the level of development of the country involved. However, the length of transition periods in the Eastern and Southern African EPAs do not seem to relate to the level of development of those countries, and Kelly concludes that the EPAs are open to legal challenge on this ground.[296]

6 *Developing countries and EPAs*

While LDCs will continue to benefit from quota- and duty-free access to the EU market under the EBA initiative, it is unclear what alternatives could be available to non-least developed developing countries.[297] The Cotonou Agreement provides that countries opting against signing an EPA should end up no worse than under the current preference scheme.[298] In his Trade Note, Hoppe sets forth that the 'alternative to an EPA will lie between the two extremes of an EPA with 100% product coverage and (presumably) liberal rules of origin, and preferences being granted under' the GSP.[299] A preferential trade agreement is WTO compatible if, among various other conditions, it fulfils the 'substantially all the trade' requirement of paragraph 8 of Article XXIV of the GATT. This requirement is usually understood as requiring coverage of at least 90 per cent of the total current trade flows.[300] The EU offered to grant quota- and duty-free market access for 97 per cent of products to least-developed ACP countries during the Doha Round of trade negotiations, but it is unclear if an EPA would cover all imports into the EU.[301] Research suggests that the EU's suggestion of 'substantially all the trade' could 'be applied in such a way that in many ACP states the revenue effect is delayed (giving time to put in place alternative taxes) and the adjustment effect muted'.[302]

If EPA negotiations were to be successful and duty-free market access were to become available to developing countries, EPAs would provide only a marginal increase in preferences from the preferences granted under the Cotonou Agreement. This is because few products are omitted from

296 Kelly, 'WTO Compatibility', at 26.

297 See Hoppe, 'Economic Partnership Agreements', at 1.

298 *Ibid.* 299 *Ibid.* 300 *Ibid.* 301 *Ibid.*

302 C. Stevens, 'Economic Partnership Agreements (EPAs): Where We Are', ODI Briefing Paper (June 2006), 2.

the generous access offered by the Cotonou Agreement.[303] The actual value of preferences under an EPA is dependent on the rules of origin that are to be implemented, as non-restrictive and simple rules may increase the value of preferences. If no EPAs are formed at the expiration of the Cotonou Agreement, the value of preferences will fall for developing countries.

303 See Hoppe, 'Economic Partnership Agreements', at 3.

V

Trade liberalization commitments and realization time frames

A Introduction

This chapter comprehensively introduces all eight African Regional Trade Agreements (RTAs), that are slated eventually to combine to form the African Economic Community (AEC) as we saw in Chapter IV and the Southern African Customs Union and its Trade Liberalization Scheme. For each RTA, the relevant section of the chapter begins with an overview that includes its founding date, purposes and members, as well as the sequence contemplated to be followed in the integration plan. Each of these integration schemes, free market, customs market, common market, monetary union and where there is planned political union, is examined in turn. For each RTA, a section evaluating progress made in the integration agenda concludes the discussion.

Since I could not find any prior work that put together the trade liberalization commitments and realization time frames, this effort is necessarily long and detailed. Having such details opened an opportunity to have the plans contemplated by African countries in their regional integration schemes speak for themselves, even where, as in most cases, the actual realization of these plans is still a work in progress.

As argued in Chapter I, this chapter shows the trade liberalization objectives are one of a variety of other non-trade objectives. In addition, the problems arising from overlapping memberships in more than one RTA, as well as the resulting obligations and conflicting liberalization time frames, become very clear in this chapter. In addition, the detailed examination of each RTA shows how flexibility is built into each of them, particularly in giving poorer African countries more time to meet the agreed liberalization obligations.

Ultimately, this chapter shows that African countries have not been in short supply of detailed integration plans and schemes in addition to particularly well-thought-out policy statements, as well as the periodic statements of their highest policy-making organs declaring the leadership's commitment to attaining the goals set out in integration treaties and associated documents. The fact that many of the plans discussed in this chapter have not come to fruition ought not to be a reason to dismiss what may be regarded merely as paper commitments. As I noted in Chapter I, African RTAs must be understood in their own context rather than through the prism that the treaties underlying have necessarily lost any legal efficacy, since they are observed more in the breach than otherwise. African RTAs have the best laid plans, and this chapter captures those plans.

B The Economic Community of West African States

1 Overview

The Economic Community of West African States (ECOWAS) was founded in 1975 when the treaty, also known as the Treaty of Lagos, was signed. The Protocols launching ECOWAS were signed on 5 November 1976.[1] ECOWAS currently consists of fifteen West African states: Benin, Burkina Faso, Cape Verde, Côte d'Ivoire, Gambia, Ghana, Guinea, Guinea-Bissau, Liberia, Mali, Niger, Nigeria, Senegal, Sierra Leone and Togo. The objectives of ECOWAS are to 'promote cooperation and integration leading to the establishment of an economic union in West Africa in order to raise the living standards of its peoples, and to maintain and enhance economic stability, foster relations among Member States and contribute to the progress and development of the African Continent'.[2] The ultimate goal of ECOWAS is to establish an economic and monetary union to stimulate economic growth and development in the region. ECOWAS is one of the five regional pillars of the AEC.

The ECOWAS Treaty aims to achieve the goal of economic integration through the harmonization and coordination of national policies and the promotion of integration programmes. A common market is to be established through the elimination of customs duties on imports and exports, the elimination of non-tariff barriers to establish an FTA, the adoption of a common external tariff and a common trade policy towards third countries and the removal of obstacles to the free movement of persons, goods, services and capital between Member States, along with

1 African Union, 'Profile: Economic Community of West African States', 2, available at www.africa-union.org/root/au/recs/ECOWASProfile.pdf.

2 Treaty Establishing the Economic Community of Western African States, Chapter 2, Art. 3(1), p. 5, available at www.worldtradelaw.net/fta/agreements/ecowasfta.pdf.

the right of residence and establishment.[3] An economic union is to be established through the 'adoption of common policies in the economic, financial, social and cultural sectors, and the creation of a monetary union'.[4] A Revised Treaty, signed in July 1993, was designed to accelerate the process of economic integration and to increase political cooperation.[5]

Along with COMESA, SADC, ECCAS and IGAD, ECOWAS signed the Protocol on Relations between the AEC and the Regional Economic Communities (RECs) in February 1998.[6]

2 *Sequencing*

The sequencing envisioned by the ECOWAS Treaty toward achieving its goals is as follows:

Step	Common market (1)	Customs union (2)	Monetary union (3)	Economic and Monetary union (4)
ECOWAS action	No date had been set as of August 2010 for the establishment of a common market	A customs union was supposed to be completed by 2000. It has not yet been achieved	The goal of the revised treaty was to have monetary union by 2004. Additionally, the formation of an economic and monetary union was to occur no later than 5 years after the formation of a customs union. A new date for completion has not been set	The goal of the revised treaty was to have an economic union by 2005. Additionally, the formation of an economic and monetary union was to occur no later than 5 years after the formation of a customs union. A new date for completion has not been set

3 *Ibid.* Art. 3(2)(d), p. 6. 4 *Ibid.* Art. 3(2)(e), p. 6.

5 African Union, 'Profile: ECOWAS', at 2.

6 *Ibid.* See *infra* Chapter IX on intra-African RTA cooperation.

3 *Common market*

In order to achieve the goals of the Community, the ECOWAS Treaty sets forth that Member States should strive to create a common market.[7] The ECOWAS Treaty requires Member States to implement several steps in order to achieve that. It requires, in order to liberalize trade between Member States, that imports, exports and non-tariff trade barriers should be eliminated to create an FTA.[8] Further, efforts to remove barriers to the free movement of 'persons, goods, services and capital, and to the right of residence and establishment' should be undertaken.[9] Additionally, Member States are to create a common external tariff and trade policy.[10]

Progress in liberalizing trade has been slow for ECOWAS. Progress is being made, however, to create a common external tariff. A proposed common external tariff that would enact a '10% tax on social goods and basic necessities; 5% for raw materials and capital goods; 10% for intermediate goods and 20% for finished products' is currently being implemented.[11] Additionally, a fifth band to the common external tariff, which levies a 35 per cent duty on 'certain goods imported into the region' was approved by the ECOWAS Heads of State and Government in June 2009.[12] Further, at the 26th meeting of the Heads of State and Government, the conference welcomed the additional progress made towards achieving an FTA by praising the adoption of rules of origin, a new ECOWAS certificate of origin, new approval procedures and compensation procedures for customs revenue losses.[13]

It should also be noted that with respect to the right of free movement of people, enumerated in Article 2 of the ECOWAS Treaty, the 26th meeting of the Heads of State and Government took exception to some Member States' failure to implement this portion of the Treaty. The Heads of State and Government found that some Member States had placed checkpoints

7 ECOWAS Treaty, at Art. 2(d). 8 *Ibid.* at Art. 2(d)(I). 9 *Ibid.* at Art. 2(d)(III).
10 *Ibid.* at Art. 2(d)(II).
11 F. Alli, 'Nigeria: Common External Tariff Ready Jan. 2009', AllAfrica.com, available at http://allafrica.com/stories/200810130451.html.
12 'Ecowas Leaders Approve New Common External Tariff Regime', Afrique en Ligne, available at www.afriquejet.com/news/africa-news/ecowas-leaders-approve-new-common-external-tariff-regime-2009062330285.html. Please note that these are not official numbers from ECOWAS. I was unable to find any official documentation on the Common External Tariff.
13 Final Communiqué of the 26th Meeting of the ECOWAS Heads of State and Government, Art. 19 (31 Jan. 2003).

and barriers to entry along their roads to prevent the free movement of people into their territories. The Heads of State and Government called for the immediate removal of such barriers and again on all Member States to implement all provisions of the Treaty.[14]

On 1 January 2004, the ECOWAS Bank for Investment and Development (EBID) was created. The vision for EBID was to create a regional investment and development bank that will serve to promote private sector development in order to create wealth, job promotion and help to alleviate poverty.[15] In addition to funding private sector endeavours within the region, EBID also strives to support the objectives of ECOWAS by 'supporting projects that are aimed at creating regional infrastructure or any other public or private sector development projects [as well as] the financing of special programs'.[16] It has strategically positioned itself to finance infrastructure programmes with a more specific focus on the areas of 'telecommunications, energy, industry, transport, the environment and natural resources'.[17] Through the financing of public sector infrastructure programmes, EBID aims to create the 'bedrock for production' which in turn will aid the private sector to become more cost-effective and competitive. With regard to the private sector, it will focus on funding projects that increase production, quality and competitiveness, as well as projects that will add diversity to the industrial and services sectors of the community.[18]

Since EBID's inception in 2004, the bank has loaned in excess of \$702.45m in aid to Member States,[19] paired with 1.5%–4% interest rates for public sector projects and 6.5%–12% interest rates for private sector projects.[20] By 2013, EBID hopes to have funded roughly \$1.5 billion to fund projects.[21] It will continue to spend more than half of its resources on funding private sector projects which will further the goals of the community, as well as 40 per cent of its anticipated resources on improving intra-regional trade. The remainder of its funding will be spent on sponsoring special projects such as a regional airline, a telecommunications fund and investment in biofuels and renewable energy.[22]

As noted more fully in Chapter IV, ECOWAS Member States have been negotiating Economic Partnership Agreements (EPAs) with the European Union (EU). In respect of trade, ECOWAS and the EU have emphasized

14 *Ibid.*

15 'EBID in Brief', ECOWAS Bank for Investment and Development, 2, available at www.bidc-ebid.org/en/documentation.php.

16 *Ibid.* 17 *Ibid.* at 4. 18 *Ibid.* 19 *Ibid.* at 5. 20 *Ibid.*

21 *Ibid.* 22 *Ibid.* at 10.

the 'importance of regional economic integration in fighting poverty, furthering sustainable development and longer-term conflict prevention'.[23] In mid-July 2009, the EU was pushing for 80 per cent liberalization of the ECOWAS market for its goods, while ECOWAS leaders were pushing for 60 per cent liberalization.[24] This EPA is discussed further in Chapter IX.

4 Customs union

The ECOWAS Treaty calls for the progressive establishment of a customs union during a period of ten years beginning on 1 January 1990. Within the customs union, customs duties and other similar charges on the importation of goods originating within the region will be eliminated.[25] Specifically, 'Member States shall reduce and ultimately eliminate customs duties and any other charges with equivalent effect . . . imposed on or in connection with the importation of goods which are eligible for Community tariff treatment.'[26] Article 36 of the ECOWAS Treaty provides for the treatment of specific types of goods: 'Community-originating unprocessed goods and traditional handicraft products shall circulate within the region free of all import duties and quantitative restrictions' and there is no compensation for any loss of revenue that may result from the importation of these products.[27] Additionally, import duties on industrial goods that are eligible for Community tariff treatment will be eliminated in accordance with the decisions of the Authority and Council.

In order to implement this duty reduction scheme, the ECOWAS Member States have released several decisions regarding the time frames in which duties should be reduced with regard to various goods under a trade liberalization scheme.[28] For example, the Authority of the Heads of State and Government released a decision regarding the time frame and manner in which industrial products originating from Member States should have duties reduced. The decision breaks the Member States into 3 groups of countries with different time requirements for the reduction

23 Seventh EU–ECOWAS Ministerial Troika Meeting, Luxembourg, 18 May 2005, available at www.europa-eu-un.org/articles/en/article_4706_en.htm.

24 F. Kokutse, 'Trade: ECOWAS Delay on EPA Allows Ghana to Rethink', *Global Issues* (29 June 2009) available at www.globalissues.org/news/2009/06/29/1970.

25 ECOWAS Treaty, at Chapter 8, Art. 35(1), p. 22.

26 *Ibid.* Art. 36(1), p. 22.

27 *Ibid.* Art. 36(2), p. 22.

28 Documentation on the ECOWAS trade liberalization scheme is unavailable through the internet with the exception of a scheme for the liberalization of industrial materials.

of duties on priority and non-priority industrial goods.[29] For example, Group 3, which is composed of Côte d'Ivoire, Ghana, Nigeria and Senegal, must reduce its duties on priority industrial products by 25% each year over a period of 4 years, and its duties on non-priority industrial products by 16.66% each year over a period of 6 years, until duties on all goods are reduced to 0%.[30]

Article 36(4) of the ECOWAS Treaty sets forth that the Authority may decide, at any time, that any import duties should be reduced more rapidly or eliminated earlier than laid out in any previous instrument or decision, on the recommendation of the Council. However, the Council shall 'examine whether such reductions or eliminations shall apply to some or all goods and in respect of some or all the Member States' not later than one year before the reductions or eliminations come into effect.[31] Once this is done, the Council must report the result for the decision of the Authority.

In addition, the ECOWAS Treaty requires that 'quota, quantitative or like restrictions or prohibitions and administrative obstacles to trade among the Member States shall also be removed'.[32]

A 'common external tariff in respect of all goods imported into the Member States from third countries shall be established and maintained.'[33] The common external tariff will be established gradually in accordance with a schedule that is to be recommended by the Trade, Customs, Taxation, Statistics, Money and Payments Commission. In accordance with such schedule, the Member States must abolish existing differences in their external customs tariffs.[34]

Fiscal charges in excess of those charges applied to domestic goods shall not be applied directly or indirectly by Member States to imported goods from any Member State. No such charges shall be imposed for the effective protection of domestic goods.[35] Further, Member States 'shall eliminate all effective internal taxes or other internal charges that are made for the protection of domestic goods not later than four (4) years after the commencement of the trade liberalization scheme referred to

29 The document describing priority and non-priority industrial goods, Decision C/DEC.3/5/8, is not available online.

30 Decision A/Dec.1/5/83 relating to the adoption and the implementation of a single trade liberalization scheme for industrial products originating from Member States, Art. 5 (30 May 1983), available at www.sec.ecowas.int/sitecedeao/english/adec010583.htm.

31 ECOWAS Treaty, at Chapter 8, Art. 36(4), p. 22.

32 *Ibid.* Art. 35, p. 22.

33 *Ibid.* Art. 35(2), p. 22.

34 *Ibid.* Art. 37(1) and (2), pp. 22–3.

35 *Ibid.* Art. 40(1), p. 24.

in Article 54'.[36] If a Member State has an existing contract that makes it unable to comply with the provisions of Article 40 of the ECOWAS Treaty, that Member State must notify the Council and must not renew or extend the contract when it expires. Article 40(3) of the Treaty further provides that Member States must progressively eliminate all revenue duties that are designed to protect domestic goods by the end of the period for the application of the trade liberalization scheme.

Over a period of four years from the launching of the trade liberalization scheme, Member States are obliged to relax and remove all then existing quota, quantitative or like restrictions or prohibitions that apply to imported goods originating in the other Member States.[37] The Member States must also refrain from imposing any further restrictions or prohibitions. If a Member State has an existing contract that makes it unable to comply with the provisions of Article 41 of the Treaty, it must notify the Council and must not extend or renew the contract at its expiration. The Authority may decide that any quota, quantitative or like restriction or prohibition shall be reduced or eliminated sooner than the four-year period set out in Article 41(1) of the ECOWAS Treaty. Article 41(3) lists several exceptions to the elimination of quota, quantitative or like restrictions or prohibitions. However, Member States cannot exercise the right to introduce or continue to execute the restrictions listed in Article 41(3) of the Treaty to impede the free movement of goods.

5 *ECOWAS Trade Liberalization Scheme*

The ECOWAS Trade Liberalization Scheme (TLS) aims to establish an economic and monetary union in West Africa. The ECOWAS TLS for Industrial Products originating from Member States classifies the Member States into three groups for its implementation: Group 1 consists of Cape Verde, Gambia, Guinea Bissau, Mali, Mauritania, Niger and Upper Volta. These are the weakest economies in the region; Group 2 consists of Benin, Guinea, Liberia, Sierra Leone and Togo; Group 3 consists of Ghana, Côte d'Ivoire, Nigeria and Senegal. These are the strongest economies in the region. All Member States are required to implement the ECOWAS TLS for Industrial Products in respect of originating industrial products. Details of the ECOWAS TLS for Industrial Products originating from Member States is set out in tabular form below. As they and the amended TLS details that follow show, the poorer economies in ECOWAS are permitted more time to liberalize and they are required to liberalize at

36 *Ibid.* Art. 40(2), p. 24. 37 *Ibid.* Art. 41(1), p. 24.

much lower rates. Thus, ECOWAS adopts phased implementation of its obligation in accordance with the economic ability of its members. As we saw in Chapter II, this is referred to as variable geometry.

Country groups (G)	Priority industrial products (P1)	Non-priority industrial products (P2)
G1: Cape Verde, Gambia, Guinea-Bissau, Mali, Mauritania, Niger, Upper Volta	8 years on the basis of 12.5% reduction each year	10 years on the basis of 10% reduction each year
G2: Benin, Guinea, Liberia, Sierra Leone, Togo	6 years on the basis of 16.66% reduction each year	8 years on the basis of 12.5% reduction each year
G3: Ghana, Côte d'Ivoire, Nigeria, Senegal	4 years on the basis of 25% reduction each year	6 years on the basis of 16.66% reduction each year[38]

The Community decided that priority industrial products were industrial products originating from Member States, which had to be manufactured by industries established in the sub-region, and they had to be priority products belonging to the industrial sectors approved by the Council of Ministers: 'These included food, agrochemicals, telecommunication, wood, steel, and pharmaceutical industries.'[39] The ECOWAS TLS for Industrial Products was to enter into force on 28 May 1983 as an amendment to the Decision of the Authority dated 28 May 1980. The date of implementation was pushed back to 1 January 1990 by an amendment to the 1983 decision.[40] The implementation of the TLS was hindered by difficulties in fulfilling the rules of origin, the minimum national participation in the equity capital or production enterprises and the structure of the TLS involving the categorization of industrial products as priority and non-priority goods.[41] Part of the reason for its lack of success was members' dependence on trade taxes for government revenue. Members were thus reluctant to implement any scheme which would threaten their

38 See Decision No. A/DEC.1/5/83 of the Authority of Heads of State and Government, Art. 5, available at www.comm.ecowas.int/sec/index.php?id=adec010583&lang=en.

39 K. Kufuor, *The Institutional Transformation of the Economic Community of West African States* (Aldershot: Ashgate Publishing Ltd., 2006), 26.

40 Decision No. A/DEC.6/6/89 of the Authority of Heads of State and Government, Art. 1, available at www.comm.ecowas.int/sec/index.php?id=adec060689&lang=en.

41 Decision No. A/DEC.6/7/92 of the Authority of Heads of State and Government, Preamble, available at www.comm.ecowas.int/sec/index.php?id=adec060792&lang=en.

interests. The ECOWAS fund, designed to compensate members for any reduction in revenue from the TLS, was not successful because of a lack of regular contributions by members and the lack of authority of the Secretariat to sanction those who did not contribute. Additionally, there was concern over who would reap the benefits from adopting the scheme. The concern was that foreign firms with production bases located in some of the countries, specifically Côte d'Ivoire and Senegal, would benefit more than would the ECOWAS members. This led to stringent rules of origin being adopted that only 17 manufacturing firms fulfilled. The 1983 TLS for Industrial Products was thus amended in 1992 for simplification, to speed up effective implementation. The amended TLS proposed timetable is shown below:

Country groups	Period within which tariffs are to be eliminated	Rate of reduction of customs duties and taxes
Group 1: Burkina Faso, Cape Verde, Gambia, Guinea Bissau, Mali, Mauritania, Niger	10 years	10% reduction per year
Group 2: Benin, Guinea, Liberia, Sierra Leone, Togo	8 years	12.5% reduction per year
Group 3: Côte d'Ivoire, Ghana, Nigeria, Senegal	6 years	16.6% reduction per year[42]

The amended TLS for Industrial Products originating from Member States was signed and entered into force on 19 July 1992.

The ECOWAS TLS for Traditional Handicrafts includes total exemption from import duties and taxes; free movement without any quantitative restriction; and no compensation for losses of revenue resulting from their importation.[43] To benefit from this TLS, a certificate of origin must be obtained in respect of the products.

42 *Ibid.*, New Art. 5, available at www.comm.ecowas.int/sec/index.php?id=adec060792&lang=en.

43 Decision No. A/DEC.1/5/81 of the Authority of Heads of State and Government, Art. 1, available at www.comm.ecowas.int/sec/index.php?id=adec010581&lang=en.

6 *Economic and monetary union*

The ultimate goal of ECOWAS is to establish an economic and monetary union. Article 54(1) of the ECOWAS Treaty provides that the status of an economic union shall be achieved within a maximum period of fifteen years after the implementation of the regional trade liberalization scheme, which was adopted by the Authority in 1983 and launched on 1 January 1990.

Article 55 of the ECOWAS Treaty sets forth the goals for the completion of economic and monetary union. It is to be established within five years following the creation of a customs union. This is to be accomplished through the 'adoption of a common policy in all fields of socioeconomic activity'; the 'total elimination of all obstacles to the free movement of people, goods, capital and services and the right of entry, residence and establishment'; and the 'harmonisation of monetary, financial and fiscal policies, the setting up of West African monetary union, the establishment of a single regional Central Bank and the creation of a single West African currency'.[44] The Authority may decide, on the recommendation of the Council, at any time, 'that any stage of the integration process should be implemented more rapidly than otherwise provided for' in the ECOWAS Treaty.[45]

Under Article 51 of the Treaty, some of the steps that Member States have agreed to undertake are: to harmonize their economic policies, facilitate intra-regional transactions, promote a greater role for commercial banks and establish a community central bank and a common currency.[46] In order to ensure that these goals are achieved, the ECOWAS Treaty provides for the establishment of institutions that will aid in the creation of a monetary union. First, the treaty provides for a Committee of West African Central Banks. The Committee will be composed of the governors of the central banks of member nations and its main focus will be to make recommendations to the community with respect to the operation of a payment clearing system and other monetary issues.[47] In addition to the Central Banks Committee, the treaty provides for the creation of a Capital Issues Committee. The focus of the Capital Issues Committee is to aid in ensuring the unimpeded flow of capital throughout the community, as well as to aid Member States in establishing and regulating national as well as regional stock exchanges.[48] Notably, members of ECOWAS like

44 ECOWAS Treaty, at Chapter 9, Art. 55(1), p. 30. 45 *Ibid.* Art. 55(2), p. 30.
46 *Ibid.* at Art. 51(1). 47 *Ibid.* at Art. 52. 48 *Ibid.* at Art. 52.

Niger, Benin, Senegal and Côte d'Ivoire are also members of the West African Economic and Monetary Union (WAEMU). As such, the institutions WAEMU has set up, such as the West African Central Bank, would duplicate the structures established by ECOWAS and vice versa.

At the 26th Meeting of the ECOWAS Heads of State and Government in 2003, there was an evaluation of the progress towards the creation of ECOWAS monetary union, and in particular the process of integrating all Member States to use a single currency. The Heads of State and Government determined that the launch of a monetary union and creation of a single currency would not be possible by 2004 as planned because of the unstable macroeconomic and political situations of some of the Member States.[49]

7 Progress

Regional integration has not been at the centre of the national development agenda and 'the potential of regionalism has not been properly explored and utilized'.[50] Although West Africa was declared an FTA in 2000, ECOWAS member countries have failed to remove tariff and non-tariff barriers to intra-regional trade.[51] One of the problems facing ECOWAS is that most of the countries are classified as least-developed countries (LDCs) by the UN. ECOWAS 'accounts for 35% of the African LDC's – making West Africa the foremost LDC region in Africa and, indeed the world as a whole'.[52] Additionally, the West African region covered by ECOWAS has one of the highest levels of poverty in the world, which has led to dependence on foreign aid and loans, as well as national debt. Many countries have reduced the amount of their debt, but indebtedness remains a substantial burden for most countries. Because of these burdens, eradicating poverty, and peace and security in the region, have been the major focuses of the national development agenda, taking attention away from regional integration. In addition to poverty, regional challenges to integration include human insecurity, a high cost of doing business in the region giving other countries a comparative advantage, an over-dependence on commodity exports, vulnerable population groups, inadequate physical infrastructures, population growth-related

49 Final Communiqué of the 26th Meeting of the ECOWAS Heads of State and Government, Art. 14 (31 Jan. 2003).

50 ECOWAS Vision 2020 Document. 51 *Ibid.* at 2. 52 *Ibid.* at 3.

challenges and inadequate provision of social services, including utilities such as water and waste management.

There have been recent socio-economic and political reforms in the member countries, along with structural and procedural transformations of key ECOWAS institutions. These reforms and transformations are positive developments and 'hold considerable promise for enhanced regional economic development, particularly concerning efficiency, transparency and effectiveness in the administration of the Community's affairs'.[53] However, these challenges pose substantial obstacles to the achievement of long-term development. One of the institutional changes has been the transformation of the Secretariat into the ECOWAS Commission. This transformation will, ideally, help to speed up the process of integration. Before the transformation, the obligations of the Member States were contained mostly in protocols and conventions, which are subject to prolonged parliamentary ratification processes. This delayed their entry into force and thus slowed the integration process. Under this new legal regime, the adoption of protocols and conventions will be de-emphasized in an attempt to make the integration process less reliant on domestic ratification processes. It is not certain that such a shift will mean that ECOWAS members will take their responsibilities any more seriously.

The elimination of tariffs on approved industrial products was to be accompanied by the full elimination of non-tariff barriers and other administrative obstacles to trade. However, through certain norms and requirements administrative barriers to the entry of approved industrial products within the region seem to persist in practice. There also seems to be a lack of clear national guidelines in some ECOWAS countries regarding the implementation of the trade liberalization scheme by the customs administrations. This constitutes an obstacle to intra-regional trade. ECOWAS achieved the status of an FTA and targeted the launch of the ECOWAS customs union by 2009, the launch having been originally planned to be in 2008. As of August 2010, the customs union had still not been launched.

Within ECOWAS there is a bloc of 8 countries belonging to the West African Economic and Monetary Union (UEMOA). UEMOA was formed in 1994 by Benin, Burkina Faso, Côte d'Ivoire, Guinea Bissau, Mali, Niger, Senegal and Togo. UEMOA has a common currency, the CFA franc, and 'enjoys undeniable political recognition from Member States and notable support from Nigeria, which has made considerable effort in the

53 *Ibid.* at 8.

resolution of many regional conflicts'.[54] UEMOA is discussed in further detail in Chapter VIII.

Due to the slow progress in implementing the fast-track approach to realizing the ECOWAS common currency, the ECOWAS Authority, at its Summit in June 2007, 'mandated the ECOWAS Commission to collaborate with other regional institutions to review the current strategy with a view to recommending a single and accelerated approach to achieving the regional common currency'.[55] The ECOWAS Convergence Council established an Inter-Institutional Working Group in 2008 to develop a term of reference for a revised strategy to achieve the single currency initiative. A new strategy for achieving the regional common currency was expected to have been adopted sometime after March 2009. By August 2010, ECOWAS had still not launched a common currency.

The West African Monetary Zone (WAMZ) is a group of five ECOWAS member countries that plan to introduce a common currency amongst those countries. The WAMZ members are Gambia, Ghana, Guinea, Nigeria and Sierra Leone.[56] Liberia has expressed an interest in joining the WAMZ and has been granted observer status. Cape Verde has also expressed an interest in joining. The Second West African Monetary Zone was created when the Accra Declaration was signed in 2000. The member countries agreed to reform their economies to meet specific convergence targets prior to the introduction of the common currency, the Eco. The Eco is planned to circulate simultaneously with the CFA franc in an effort to eventually create a single monetary zone for the entire Community. The Eco was initially expected to be launched by December 2009, but as a result of the global economic downturn, the December 2009 deadline was pushed back to 2020.[57]

C Intergovernmental Authority on Development (IGAD)

1 Overview

The Intergovernmental Authority on Development (IGAD) was created in 1996 to supersede the Intergovernmental Authority on Drought and

54 African Union, 'Status of Integration in Africa', 14, para. 24, available at www.africa-union.org/root/ua/conferences/2009/mai/ea/07–08mai/status%20of%20integration%20in%20africa%2027–04–09.pdf.

55 *Ibid.* at 17, para. 39.

56 *Ibid.* at 19, para. 44.

57 R. Jaidev, 'Governors Gloomy on Outlook for Pan-African Currency', Risk.net (7 July 2010), available at www.risk.net/risk-magazine/news/1721130/governors-gloomy-outlook-pan-african-currency.

Development (IGADD), which had been in existence since 1986.[58] After the severe drought and recurring natural disasters that occurred between 1974 and 1984, IGADD was created to coordinate the efforts of the Member States in combating desertification and promoting efforts to mitigate the effects of drought.[59] As such, the objectives of IGADD were mainly food security and environmental protection. The founding members of IGADD were Djibouti, Ethiopia, Kenya, Somalia, Sudan and Uganda, with Eritrea joining in 1993 after attaining independence. IGADD came to be used as a forum not just for dealing with drought and environmental issues, but also for leaders of the countries to tackle emerging socio-economic and political issues in a regional context.[60] Realizing this potential, the Heads of State and Government met in 1995 to revitalize IGADD. The Letter of Instrument to Amend the IGADD Charter/Agreement was signed in early 1996 and IGAD was launched on 26 November 1996.[61] IGAD expanded the areas of regional cooperation to include economic and political issues and put in place a new organizational structure. The three most important areas of cooperation were stressed as being: food security and environmental protection; conflict prevention, management and resolution; and economic cooperation and integration.[62] The mission of IGAD is to assist and complement the Member States' efforts to achieve economic integration through increased cooperation in these three areas.

The IGAD Strategy was elaborated in 2003 and adopted by the 10th Summit of Heads of State and Government. It highlights some of the strengths and weaknesses of IGAD. Among the strengths is the political commitment to IGAD as an institution among the large and diverse population, the creation of platforms and fora for technical experts from the Member States for discussing issues in the programmes, and activities on capacity building such as organizing, conducting or facilitating workshops covering a range of IGAD activities.[63] Among the challenges facing IGAD is that its programmes should be derived directly from national programmes, as the two are to be synergistic, not parallel or competitive.[64] Also, the goal is to reach sustainable results, which is not always the case with the traditional project approach to solving development problems. Further, both inter- and intra-regional conflicts sometimes create a political environment that is not conducive to the harmonization of policies

58 IGAD, 'About Us', available at http://igad.int/index.php?option=com_content&view=article&id=93&Itemid=124. The Eco is also discussed briefly in Chapter VIII.

59 *Ibid.* 60 *Ibid.* 61 *Ibid.* 62 *Ibid.* at 2.

63 See the IGAD Strategy, s. 1.3.1, p. 3, available at http://igad.org/about/igad_strategy.pdf.

64 *Ibid.* at s. 1.3.2, p. 3.

among the Member States. Similarly, IGAD is challenged to keep up with the ever-increasing demands of the region due to emerging problems such as international terrorism and the HIV/AIDS pandemic. Member States are not always committed and dedicated to the regional cooperation which is required to resolve such problems.

IGAD has been one of the pillars of the AEC since it signed the Protocol on Relations between the African Economic Community and the Regional Economic Communities in 1998.[65] It has worked with COMESA and the EAC to divide projects amongst themselves to avoid duplication and to avoid approaching the same donors with the same projects.[66] This collaboration accords with IGAD's treaty, because the IGAD Treaty lists as one of its objectives the realization and promotion of the objectives of COMESA and the AEC.[67]

2 Sequencing

Details of the proposed timetable for implementation of the Treaty provisions is as follows:

	Customs union	Common market	Monetary union	Political federation
IGAD	Implementation of a customs union is discussed in the IGAD Strategy report, but no time frame is given	The implementation of a common market had not been discussed as of 1 July 2009	The implementation of a monetary union had not been discussed as of 1 July 2009	The implementation of a political federation had not been discussed as of 1 July 2009
Timetable	No time frame had been established as of 31 Aug. 2010	No time frame had been established as of 31 Aug. 2010	No time frame had been established as of 31 Aug. 2010	No time frame had been established as of 31 Aug. 2010

65 'IGAD Profile', African Union, 2, available at www.africa-union.org/Recs/IGAD_Profile.pdf.

66 *Ibid.*

67 Agreement Establishing IGAD, Art. 7(i), 8, available at http://igad.org/about/agreement_establishing_igad.pdf.

3 *The IGAD Treaty and strategy*

The objectives of the IGAD Treaty include the harmonization of trade policies, the promotion of free movement of goods, services and people and the creation of an enabling environment for foreign, cross-border and domestic trade and investment.[68] The IGAD Treaty provides for the use of protocols to achieve these aims and objectives.

Since 1986, IGADD had adopted several strategies to respond to its mandate. After IGAD was revitalized in 1996, a new IGAD Strategy was adopted that articulated the objectives and procedures for achieving IGAD mandate.[69] This IGAD Strategy did not meet the expectations of some of the stakeholders and thus a revised strategy was called for that would have a more focused vision, missions and programmes, articulate the general direction and focus for IGAD and make it mean the same thing to all stakeholders. In 2003, a revised IGAD Strategy was adopted that focused on the promotion of 'regional cooperation in order to achieve sustainable development, peace and security in the Region'.[70] The strategic objectives emanate from the three priority areas of food security and environmental protection, peace and stability in the region and the promotion of regional economic integration and cooperation. The various programmes, projects and sectors of the IGAD Strategy support each other, enabling IGAD to address its obligations in a holistic and integrated approach, to achieve the overall objective of the Authority.

Two of the most important characteristics of the IGAD Strategy are flexibility and dynamism. The Strategy's flexibility allows it to 'accommodate the changing interests and development needs of the Member States and its beneficiaries' and its dynamism allows it to 'respond proactively and to address new emerging issues that may occur'.[71] The IGAD Strategy will, accordingly, be revisited periodically to be adjusted to the changing environment in the region. IGAD's work is mostly carried out in a process approach that involves intensive background studies followed by workshops and meetings in order to come up with common regional positions on the issues.[72]

The IGAD trade programme also faces the challenge of having as its members several low-income economies. All of its member countries, with the exception of Kenya, are categorized as LDCs. They mostly produce primary raw materials which attract low prices in the international

68 *Ibid.* at Art. 7, p. 7.
69 IGAD Strategy, at s. 2.1, p. 5.
70 *Ibid.* at s. 2.3, p. 5.
71 *Ibid.* at s. 2.10, p. 9.
72 *Ibid.* at s. 2.6, p. 7.

market and are vulnerable to externally influenced price fluctuations. The IGAD trade programme under the Economic Cooperation Sector focuses on the harmonization of trade practices and policies of the Member States and the elimination of tariff and non-tariff barriers to trade. The long-term goal of IGAD is to create an economic and customs union. This is to be accomplished in stages in which IGAD will focus on changing and harmonizing the policies, procedures and standards necessary to encourage increased trade among Member States in two areas – grain and livestock.[73] These two agricultural products are the most critical in terms of moving towards the achievement of food security in the region. For this purpose, efforts during the first years of the IGAD Strategy will be focused on the development of mutually accepted policies and procedures to facilitate a substantial increase in trade in the two critical agricultural areas. Such policies and procedures will include 'quality standards, phyto-sanitary standards, customs procedures and paperwork to ensure timely transactions and movement of commodities'.[74]

The trade and infrastructure development programmes are closely inter-linked. Policy harmonization between the two areas is projected to promote trade development between Member States. The plan is that such intra-trade development will lead to the increased transportation of goods and services which requires an adequate infrastructure system. Thus, 'the development of infrastructure and the removal of physical and non-physical barriers to interstate transport and communications are essential to regional co-operation and integration'.[75] At a sectoral level, the economic cooperation sector will collaborate with the agriculture and environment sectors to improve policy harmonization in livestock and grain marketing. The objective of the facilitation of movement of goods and services in the economic cooperation sector is intended to benefit the objectives of the agriculture sector. Such strategic inter-linkages are regarded as essential to the achievement of the IGAD mandate of food security and the fostering of regional economic integration and cooperation. Like most other regions, therefore, IGAD has well laid out plans. It will be another thing for them to come to fruition.

4 The importance of livestock to the IGAD Community

The IGAD region has one of the largest concentrations of livestock in the world, but this has not translated into any meaningful prosperity

73 *Ibid.* at s. 4.1.3(a), p. 16. 74 *Ibid.*, p. 17. 75 *Ibid.* at s. 4.1.3(b), p. 17.

for IGAD Member States individually or as a collective body. The IGAD Livestock Policy Initiative (issued by the IGAD Livestock Policy Initiative) cites the spread of disease among livestock, the inability of IGAD to influence international sanitary standards for livestock and the inability of IGAD to form a single cohesive policy with regard to exporting livestock, as the major reasons for the community's failures.

The Policy Initiative argued that 'the animal disease situation of the IGAD region is perhaps the single most important reason why the livestock wealth of the region has not been translated into meaningful export revenues for those countries'.[76] Contagious livestock diseases such as Rinderpest, foot-and-mouth disease and Rift Valley are prevalent in the region.[77] In many cases, an outbreak of any one of these diseases in a country can often result in the denial of access to foreign markets, including the markets of the most developed countries.[78] For example, the World Organization for Animal Health (OIE) will recognize a country as foot-and-mouth disease free without vaccination, or foot-and-mouth disease free with vaccination upon the meeting of certain criteria. Generally, to show that a country is foot-and-mouth disease free, they will have to send a declaration, as well as proof of animal disease reporting, which shows that there have been no outbreaks, evidence of infection or vaccination against the disease within the last 12 months; any state that cannot meet this burden will be labelled a foot-and-mouth disease infected area.[79] The problem for IGAD is that, according to the World Animal Health Information Database (WAHID), the information regarding IGAD Member States is not up to date and nations such as Sudan reported as little as two outbreaks of foot-and-mouth disease in 2004.[80] The inaccurate reporting mechanisms in the IGAD Member States, in combination with very real disease conditions, have caused many of the IGAD nations to be labelled as infected countries for one or more forms of disease. The inability of IGAD nations to combat disease, to report disease statistics accurately and to meet international standards has been a major factor in the Member States' inability to export their goods.

When dealing with animal health in the IGAD region, the organization that sets standards for animal health is the OIE.[81] The OIE lists as its three main objectives: to promote and coordinate international disease research when appropriate; promote awareness to governments about the spread

76 IGAD Livestock Policy Initiative, 'The Regulatory Framework for Trade in IGAD Livestock Products', IGAD LPI Working Paper No. 07–08, 31.

77 *Ibid.* at 30. 78 *Ibid.* 79 *Ibid.* at 33. 80 *Ibid.* at 34. 81 *Ibid.* at 28.

of epizootic diseases and methods of preventing them; and to provide a means of helping governments enforce sanitary standards for animals.[82] The OIE implements what is known as the Terrestrial Animal Health Code, which is established to ensure the sanitary safety of terrestrial animals and their by-products. The OIE enforces this health code and by establishing guidelines for veterinarians and import and export authorities for the safe import and export of animals and their by-products. Once the standards of the Terrestrial Animal Health Code are met, the OIE can then designate a nation as a disease-free zone. The designation as a disease-free zone is a necessity for any country that wishes to export livestock internationally and can be 'the single most important factor in an otherwise resource rich country's ability to export its animals and animal products'.[83]

When dealing with food and safety standards the Codex Alimentarious Commission has been established in order to 'protect consumers against food borne diseases and encouraging international trade in safe food through the harmonization of food standards'.[84] Since the inception of the Codex almost 40 years ago, the Commission has created general standards, as well as over 300 product-specific guidelines for food and safety standards.[85] Although the majority of food that IGAD nations are looking to export is livestock and not processed foods, IGAD member nations have a vested interest in the application of Codex standards because the sale of processed foods made from IGAD livestock will add value to their exports as well as mitigate some of the damages caused by having a disease animal status under OIE regulations.[86]

The export of livestock is influenced by a variety of sources including OIE, Codex and sometimes even more stringent standards being set by some developing countries and manufacturers.[87] The result of the myriad of regulations on IGAD Member States is that they are struggling to implement these standards, in part because they have little capacity. As a result, the trading interest of IGAD Member States continues to suffer. By contrast Botswana, which has managed to keep its livestock disease free, has been able to keep its market share of beef exports to the EU. The failure of IGAD states to attain the type of standards that Botswana has successfully been able to implement and the fact that IGAD and other developing countries have almost no input into the standards that they are required to comply with to gain access to external markets like Europe, severely limits the export of IGAD beef. The IGAD Livestock Report noted that

82 *Ibid.* at 29. 83 *Ibid.* at 30. 84 *Ibid.* at 37.
85 *Ibid.* at 38. 86 *Ibid.* 87 *Ibid.* at 48.

the influence of poorer countries in determining standards has remained weak because they have a poor level of attendance at the meetings of governing bodies; inadequate representation in committee leadership; and an inability to implement technically complex international standards at a national level.[88]

In addition to the inability of IGAD Member States to influence standards, the Livestock Report takes note of another crucial factor it has deemed relevant in the inability of IGAD Member States to make their livestock exports profitable: the inability of IGAD to form a cohesive policy with regard to the export of livestock. IGAD Member States face challenges in implementing a region-wide policy on livestock partly because of:

> Uncertainties signifying a weak and inefficient judiciary, disregard for the law in day to day decision making, lack of effective coordination among different levels of government in the enforcement of laws, absence of established communication channels between livestock business operators and government institutions and an overall lack of capacity to use law as an instrument in implementing policy decisions.[89]

The Livestock Report concludes by underscoring the problems that the 'human, financial and technical constraints' faced by IGAD members in trying to adhere to international sanitary standards for livestock is too large to be faced by a single IGAD member alone.[90] For example, currently the EU has a host of benefits and privileges for developing countries, including IGAD, in which access is granted to their markets.[91] The problem lies with the fact that while the EU can treat nations favourably with respect to market access, it cannot lower its own food safety standards to admit food from developing countries, because the EU's primary duty is to protect its citizens. The EU offers access to developing nations, but that access is often limited by stringent sanitary and phytosanitary requirements that prevent even legitimate exports from regions like IGAD.

5 *Progress*

When IGAD was first revitalized in 1996, its efforts were focused mainly on the more vital issues of peace and security in the region. Additionally, IGAD created a number of programmes that concerned food security

88 *Ibid.* 89 *Ibid.* at 78. 90 *Ibid.* at 92. 91 *Ibid.*

and the environment, as well as sustainable development, health and other issues. Economic integration was not a priority issue. At the 12th Ordinary Summit of the Heads of State and Government in 2008, the Secretariat was directed to undertake an inventory of what had been achieved so far in the way of integration and cooperation. The Secretariat was also directed to 'make recommendations on the way forward as well as develop and implement regional integration programs' designed to make IGAD relevant as a building block of the African Union.[92] A Minimum Integration Plan has been submitted to the senior officials of the Member States and the final study was due to be submitted by mid-March 2009. Approval of the roadmap to integration will set a time frame for the establishment of the IGAD FTA. This will provide for IGAD's transformation from a politically focused organization to an economic organization and will allow IGAD to join the ranks of the other RECs.

The 3rd Ministerial Troika Meeting between IGAD and the EU was held in Brussels on 31 March 2009. There, the parties noted that IGAD was in a stage of reform and revitalization, 'focusing its activities on priority areas of regional cooperation and strengthening the effectiveness of the IGAD Secretariat and Member States' commitments'.[93] The EU stated its readiness to support these efforts at revitalization and welcomed the Minimum Integration Plan as a means to deepen regional integration and cooperation: 'It should create synergies with the overall economic integration effort within the continent as a whole and in concert with other regional organisations'.[94]

A Joint Africa–EU Strategy is to enhance economic development and promote sustainable development through economic cooperation of the EU and African countries, identifies strategic priorities in the areas of trade and regional integration, peace and security and democratic governance and human rights. To avoid duplication of efforts and resources, IGAD has promoted the COMESA trade programme which includes the FTA, WTO negotiations and EPAs. IGAD and COMESA have a Memorandum

92 Communiqué of the 12th Ordinary Summit of the Heads of State and Government of IGAD, available at www.igad.int/index.php?option=com_content&view=article&id=107:communique-of-the-12th-summit-of-heads-of-state-and-government-of-igad-&catid=47:communique&Itemid=149.

93 Communiqué, IGAD–EU Ministerial Troika Meeting, available at www.igad.int/index.php?option=com_content&view=article&id=141:communique-igad-eu-ministerial-troika-meeting&catid=47:communique&Itemid=149.

94 *Ibid.*

of Understanding with reciprocal commitments on trade issues. Furthermore, IGAD is involved in the process of rationalization with other RECs within the AU/AEC/REC framework.[95] Communications infrastructure must be improved and national macroeconomic policies must first be coordinated in order to realize the goal of harmonizing policies and programmes with COMESA and the other RECs.

However, as with a few of the other African RECs, it has become apparent that the organization was created as an institutional framework open to all willing countries, a supply-driven response, rather than having membership based on economic readiness and compatibility.[96] At a technical meeting in March 2009, IGAD Executive Secretary, Eng. Mahboub Maalim, stated that 'in order to maximize our efforts, resources and time in our endeavor to build a beneficial regional economic community, we need to move beyond talking and planning and focus on implementing what we envisage.'[97] Despite the creation of programmes and initiatives, progress towards regional integration and trade and economic development has been slow due to insufficient transport and communications infrastructure; unreliable power; widespread disease such as HIV/AIDS and malaria; and inter- and intra-regional conflict. Transport infrastructure, in particular road transport, must be improved in order to promote national growth by reducing transport costs and to realize the ultimate goal of regional integration.[98]

D The Common Market for Eastern and Southern Africa

1 Overview

The Common Market for Eastern and Southern Africa (COMESA) was formed in December 1994. COMESA replaced the former Preferential Trade Area (PTA) which had been in existence since 1981, with the objective of ultimately creating a larger market for greater social and economic

95 African Union, 'Status of Integration in Africa', at 81.

96 'Assessing Regional Integration in Africa II' (African Union and the Economic Commission for Africa, May 2006), 38.

97 IGAD, 'Roadmap for Regional Integration' (19 Mar. 2009), available at http://igad.int/index.php?option=com_content&view=article&id=161:roadmap-for-regional-integration-plan&catid=44:economic-cooperation&Itemid=127.

98 Short Term Consultancy on the Status of Implementation of Overload Control and other Trade Facilitation Instruments in the IGAD Region, IGAD (June 2010), 2, available at http://igad.int/attachments/221_TOR_FOR_A_SHORT_CONSULTANCY_OF_the_WB%5B1%5D%5B1%5D.pdf.

cooperation between members and eventually resulting in a common market.[99] The COMESA Treaty was signed on 5 November 1993 in Kampala, Uganda and later ratified on 8 December 1994 in Lilongwe, Malawi. Its current members are Burundi, Comoros, the Democratic Republic of the Congo, Djibouti, Egypt, Eritrea, Ethiopia, Kenya, Libya, Madagascar, Malawi, Mauritius, Rwanda, Seychelles, Sudan, Swaziland, Uganda, Zambia and Zimbabwe.

The central objective of COMESA is to form 'a large economic and trading unit that is capable of overcoming some of the barriers that are faced by individual states'.[100] Eventually COMESA aims to achieve a 'fully integrated, competitive regional economic community'.[101] The strategy chosen to attain full integration is trade development through the removal of trade and investment barriers. For the achievement of its goals, a three-stage path has been laid out. The first stage to be completed is the establishment of an FTA in which all tariffs on trade in goods between COMESA members will be eliminated.[102] Additionally, in the first stage, non-tariff barriers to trade between COMESA members will be eliminated.[103] The second stage is the formation of a customs union with a common external tariff, which would allow Member States to become competitive regionally 'through the process of restructuring, mergers, acquisition and privatization'[104] and eventually become internationally competitive through the application of a common tariff on imports from non-COMESA nations. The third and final step would be the formation of a monetary union[105] with a 'common currency issued by a common central bank by 2025'.[106] The specific undertakings set forth in the COMESA Treaty are to be adhered to by all Member States with the exceptions of Lesotho, Namibia and Swaziland in trade liberalization and customs cooperation,[107] as well as the fields of finance and monetary affairs,[108] in recognition of the special circumstances faced by these nations. The FTA was to be established by 2000, the

99 COMESA, 'History of COMESA', available at http://about.comesa.int/lang-en/overview/history-of-comesa.

100 COMESA, 'Overview', available at http://about.comesa.int/lang-en/overview.

101 COMESA, 'COMESA Strategy', available at http://about.comesa.int/lang-en/overview/comesa-strategy.

102 Treaty Establishing the Common Market for Eastern and Southern Africa, Chapter 6, Art. 45, p. 26, available at http://about.comesa.int/attachments/comesa_treaty_en.pdf.

103 *Ibid.* at Art. 49(1), p. 27.

104 COMESA, 'COMESA Strategy'.

105 COMESA Treaty, at Chapter 3, Art. 4(4)(a), p. 10.

106 COMESA, 'COMESA Strategy'.

107 COMESA Treaty, at Chapter 3, Art. 4(1)(f), p. 9.

108 *Ibid.* at Art. 4(4)(d), p. 10.

customs union and common external tariff by 2004 and monetary union by 2025.

2 Sequencing

The sequencing envisioned by the COMESA Treaty toward achieving the goal of a monetary union is as follows:

	Common market	Free trade area	Customs union	Political union (monetary union)
COMESA	1. A common market is established with the formation of COMESA	2. On 31 October 2000, COMESA announced the formation of a free trade area[109]	3. On 8 June 2009, COMESA announced the formation of a customs union[110]	4. COMESA hopes to establish monetary union[111] with a single currency issued by a central bank[112]
Timetable	8 December 1994	8 December 1994–31 October 2000	8 December 1994–8 June 2009	2025

3 Free trade area

The first step is the reduction and ultimate elimination of customs duties and other similar charges on or in connection with the importation of goods, intended to have been completed by the year 2000.[113] The COMESA Treaty prohibits Member States with existing contracts which render them unable to comply with the provisions of Article 46 from renewing or extending such a contract at its expiration, and they must notify the Council of inability to comply. No Member State may impose any new duties and taxes, or increase existing ones, during the time period in which the reduction and elimination of customs duties is to take place.

109 COMESA, 'COMESA Strategy'.

110 Final Communiqué of the 13th Summit of the COMESA Authority of Heads of State and Government (8 June 2009), 6.

111 COMESA Treaty, at Chapter 3, Art. 4(4)(a), p. 10.

112 COMESA, 'COMESA Strategy'.

113 COMESA Treaty, at Chapter 6, Art. 46, p. 26.

In addition, the Authority may reduce any import duty more rapidly or eliminate it earlier than is scheduled.

The proposed schedule for the establishment of an FTA by 2000 was supposed to be a gradual reduction in tariff and non-tariff trade barriers to intra-COMESA trade. The tariff reduction, ending in the elimination of tariffs, begins with a 60% reduction intended to have been eliminated by 31 October 1993.[114] There was to be a 70% reduction by 31 October 1994, an 80% reduction by 31 October 1996, a 90% reduction by 31 October 1998 and a full 100% reduction by 31 October 2000.[115] The removal of these tariffs was planned to result in an FTA which, as we shall see below, was launched in October 2000.

In addition to the tariff reduction schedule, the Treaty calls for the removal of all non-tariff barriers that existed at the formation of the Community to the importation of goods into Member States that originated in other Member States.[116] After the removal of these barriers, the Member States are not permitted to impose any further restrictions or prohibitions. The process of removing non-tariff barriers to trade includes the harmonization of information systems, documents and procedures in order to facilitate trade.[117] The reduction of intra-COMESA tariffs and non-tariff barriers is still incomplete. COMESA Member States have devised many programmes in an effort to remove non-tariff barriers between them. For example, the creation and continuing improvement of the COMESA Customs Document (COMESA-CD) has facilitated and improved trade between COMESA nations.[118] By implementing the COMESA-CD and having a standardized form for import, export, transport and warehousing for use by all Member States, the paperwork, costs and delays that have operated as non-tariff barriers to trade in the past are targeted to be greatly reduced.[119] In some instances, the importation of goods required the use of up to 32 different forms. The use of the COMESA-CD has reduced that number to one and has simplified the movement of goods between Member States.[120] Additionally, COMESA has implemented the Automated System of Customs and Data Management (ASYCUDA) in order to computerize customs and trade statistics.[121] The ASYCUDA system has helped COMESA make their customs process more efficient

114 COMESA, 'COMESA Strategy'. 115 *Ibid.*

116 COMESA Treaty, at Chapter 6, Art. 49, p. 27. 117 *Ibid.*

118 COMESA Programmes, 'Trade Facilitation', available at http://programmes.comesa.int:80/index.php?option=com_content&view=article&id=55&Itemid=63&lang=en.

119 *Ibid.* 120 *Ibid.* 121 *Ibid.*

by allowing revenue from customs transactions to be recorded and collected more accurately, as well as improving the ability to perform risk analysis, monitor the movement of goods and reduce the time it would normally take goods to clear customs. An example of how the ASYCUDA system has improved customs efficiency is that prior to the systems implementation, it used to take between 24 and 48 hours for goods to clear customs at an airport in Mauritius, whereas after the implementation of the system it now takes roughly 30 minutes.[122]

4 *Customs union*

The COMESA Treaty proposes the formation of a customs union within ten years from the effective date of the Treaty.[123] Article 47 provides: 'the Member States agree to the gradual establishment of a common external tariff in respect of all goods imported into the Member States from third countries within a period of ten years from the entry into force of this Treaty and in accordance with a schedule to be adopted by the Council.'[124] By December 2004, according to the provisions of the Treaty, a customs union with a common external tariff was supposed to have been established. The establishment of a common external tariff was intended to make Member States regionally competitive 'through the process of restructuring, mergers, acquisitions and privatization',[125] with the ultimate goal of becoming internationally competitive.

At the 11th Meeting of the COMESA Council of Ministers, held in Cairo in May 2001, a roadmap was created for the establishment of a customs union by December 2004.[126] The four main objectives that the Council of Ministers set out were the creation of a common external tariff: increasing intra-COMESA trade, the further simplification of customs procedures and the finalization of structures to implement the common external tariff as well as the customs union itself.[127] However, the customs union was not officially launched until 8 June 2009. The first of several steps taken toward the creation of the customs union was the formation of a common external tariff as authorized by Article 47 of the COMESA Treaty.[128] A four-band common external tariff was established at the 12th Summit of

122 *Ibid.* 123 COMESA Treaty, at Chapter 6, Art. 45, p. 26.

124 *Ibid.* at Art. 47, p. 26. 125 COMESA, 'COMESA Strategy'.

126 Final Communiqué of the 13th Summit of the COMESA Authority of Heads of State and Government (8 June 2009), 6.

127 Eleventh Meeting of the COMESA Council of Ministers, 20–1 May 2001, Art. 68.

128 COMESA Treaty, at Chapter 6, Art. 47, p. 26.

the COMESA Heads of State and Government held in Nairobi in May 2007. The four-band tariff structure imposes a 10% tariff on intermediate products, a 25% tariff on finished goods and a 0% tariff on capital goods and raw materials imported from non-COMESA nations.[129]

5 *Monetary union*

The ultimate goal of COMESA is to form a monetary union with a single currency. The short-term goal leading to the achievement of this long-term goal is to establish monetary stability within the region with an efficient exchange and payments system. An efficient system of exchange and payments is aimed at facilitating economic integration efforts and the attainment of sustainable economic development.[130] In 1992, the Authority of Heads of State and Government approved a programme toward the establishment of a monetary union by 2025.[131] The programme consisted of four stages. The first was to take place from 1992 to 1996. This stage involved the consolidation of existing instruments of cooperation in monetary and financial matters and the implementation of policy measures geared toward achieving macroeconomic convergence. As to this stage, the COMESA Treaty provides that Member States were supposed to 'undertake to coordinate their macro-economic policies and economic reform programmes with a view to promoting the economic and social balance of the Common Market and to develop a framework for macro-economic planning and programming'.[132] The second stage was to take place from 1997 to 2000 and was to introduce some degree of currency convertibility and informal exchange rate union. The COMESA Treaty provides that Member States shall 'undertake to establish . . . currency convertibility which shall make their currencies convertible into one another'.[133] Towards this end, all restrictions on current transactions shall be abolished by the Member States. Additionally, the Treaty provides that the Member States shall 'undertake to establish . . . an Exchange Rate Union' and 'agree to the immutable fixing of the exchange rates of their currencies within a band to be prescribed by the Council'.[134] The third stage is to take place from 2000 to 2024. In this stage, a formal exchange rate union is to be created and economic policies are to be coordinated by a

129 Communiqué of the 12th Summit of the COMESA Heads of State and Government, 22–3 May 2007, 7.

130 COMESA Treaty, at Chapter 10, Art. 72, p. 39.

131 COMESA, 'COMESA Strategy'.

132 COMESA Treaty, at Chapter 10, Art. 79, p. 41.

133 *Ibid.* at Art. 77, p. 40.

134 *Ibid.* at Art. 78, p. 40.

common monetary institution. After the first three stages are completed, the fourth and final stage is the creation of a full monetary union with a single common currency. This is intended to be achieved by the year 2025 and is the ultimate goal of COMESA.

6 *Rules of origin*

The COMESA rules of origin serve to protect the interests of COMESA Member States by ensuring that the common market tariff treatment implemented by the FTA, which imposes zero tariff on goods traded between COMESA Member States, is applied solely to those Member States,[135] and that all foreign importers are subject to the common external tariff that was adopted as a part of the customs union. Article 48 of the COMESA Treaty provides that goods qualify as eligible for common market tariff treatment if they are deemed to have originated in a COMESA Member State.[136] In order to help determine which goods qualify as originating in a COMESA Member State, the Rules of Origin Protocol sets forth a five-part test, requiring that goods meet at least one of the enumerated criteria in order to obtain status as originating from a Member State.

The first of the criteria in determining if a good qualifies for common market tariff is to determine if the goods have been wholly produced in a Member State.[137] Rule 3 of the Rules of Origin Protocol provides a list of goods that are to be considered as produced in a Member State. Examples of these include: vegetable products harvested within the borders of a Member State, products obtained from the sea, rivers and lakes of Member States and livestock born or raised within Member States.[138] The next criterion states that goods that are produced in Member States should not have the cost, insurance and freight value of foreign materials exceed 60 per cent of the total cost of materials used in the production of the good.[139] Alternatively, a good produced in a Member State may obtain common market tariff treatment if it obtains at least 35 per cent value

135 Procedures Manual on the Implementation of the Protocol on the Rules of Origin for Products to be traded between the Member States of the Common Market for Eastern and Southern Africa, Chapter 1.1 (Nov. 2002) available at http://about.comesa.int/attachments/059_Revised_Procedures_Manual.pdf.

136 COMESA Treaty, at Chapter 6, Art. 48(1), p. 26.

137 COMESA Rules of Origin Protocol, Rule 2(1)(a), available at http://about.comesa.int/attachments/059_Protocol_on_the_Rules_of_Origin.pdf.

138 *Ibid.* at Rule 3.

139 *Ibid.* at Rule 2(1)(b)(i).

added to the ex-factory cost of the goods,[140] or if non-originating goods are used in the production of a good in a Member State, they may obtain common market tariff treatment if they have changed so substantially that they can no longer be classified under the same tariff heading as the original product.[141] Lastly, goods produced in Member States that have been designated to be 'goods of particular importance to the economic development of Member States'[142] must contain a minimum value added of at least 25 per cent, in spite of Rule 2(1)(b)(ii).

7 *Areas of cooperation*

COMESA sets forth specific areas for cooperation between Member States in order to further the goals of the common market. The areas of co-operation in the COMESA Treaty include the fields of trade liberalization, industry, energy, transport, finance, agriculture, economic development and social development.[143] COMESA recognizes that in order to have long-term economic growth and prosperity in these fields, it must focus heavily on the areas of science and technology, infrastructure development and investment development.[144]

The focus of the investment development initiative will be to enhance productivity as well as the quality of goods coming from COMESA Member States.[145] Investment development will be focused in the areas of 'industry, agriculture, livestock, fisheries, and irrigation'[146] as well as service-based sectors. The strategy envisaged for these sectors is to identify investment opportunities, promote higher productivity through training and collaboration, fostering a favourable investment environment, the implementation of market development programmes and the formation of programmes to mainstream gender.[147] For example, at the 12th Summit of the COMESA Heads of State and Government in 2007, the Agreement for the COMESA Common Investment Area (CCIA) was adopted.[148] The CCIA will serve as a tool by which foreign and domestic investment will be promoted by guaranteeing investment against nationalization and expropriation, offering arbitration mechanisms for resolving disputes,

140 *Ibid.* at Rule 2(1)(b)(ii). Ex-factory costs refers to 'the value of total inputs required to produce a given product'. *Ibid.* at Rule 1.

141 *Ibid.* at Rule 2(1)(b)(iii).

142 *Ibid.* at Rule 2(1)(c).

143 COMESA Treaty, at Chapter 3, Art. 4, p. 10.

144 COMESA, 'COMESA Strategy'.

145 *Ibid.*

146 *Ibid.*

147 *Ibid.*

148 Communiqué of the 12th Summit of the COMESA Heads of State and Government, 22–3 May 2007, 11.

improving the transparency of investment rules and regulations of Member States as well as allowing for national treatment to be granted to investors by 2010, which will allow foreign investors to enjoy the same treatment as domestic investors.[149]

In order for COMESA to achieve its goals of having free movement of goods, people and services, there must be a strong infrastructure to support those goals. The current transportation and communication sectors of Member States, in COMESA and other RTAs, are not strong enough to support the organization's goal of having a fully integrated economic zone, as more fully discussed in Chapter X.[150] The infrastructure development initiative will focus its efforts on facilitating transit programmes, identifying investments in the transport, communication and energy sectors as well as instituting reform in the areas of transport, telecom, postal, environmental and energy sectors.[151] For example, in order to ensure the more efficient movement of people and goods and to maximize the use of existing infrastructure, some of the measures COMESA has implemented are the harmonization of road traffic charges and axle load limits, the creation of a COMESA carrier licence and transit plates, the implementation of new transit declaration documents and more advanced cargo information systems.[152] In addition to the maximization of current infrastructure assets such as roadways and air space, COMESA has embarked on a mission to invest in the improvement of other infrastructure assets such as energy. An example of this is the creation of initiatives such as the Eastern Africa Power Pool (EAPP) whose mission is to stabilize growth and development in the region by decreasing the cost of energy production while simultaneously increasing energy output for the region.[153]

Lastly, COMESA strives to increase cooperation and productivity in the areas of science and technology. In the past, the areas of science and technology have been neglected because investment in the research and development of new technologies has been so small among COMESA Member States.[154] The United Nations Economic and Social Council (UNESCO) has noted that nations in Sub-Saharan Africa over the past 30 years have invested an average of only 0.3% of their gross national

149 COMESA Programmes, 'Investment Promotion and Private Sector Development', available at http://programmes.comesa.int/index.php?option=com_content&view=article&id=82&Itemid=66&lang=en.

150 COMESA, 'COMESA Strategy'. 151 *Ibid.* 152 *Ibid.*

153 COMESA Programmes, 'Infrastructure', available at http://programmes.comesa.int/index.php?option=com_content&view=article&id=110&Itemid=50&lang=en.

154 COMESA, 'COMESA Strategy'.

product, as compared with 2.2% investment made by developed countries over the same time.[155] COMESA is striving to increase investment in science and technology through policy initiatives in order for the technology that is developed to serve as an engine of growth and change for the member nations.[156] For example, the Electronic Transaction Act of 2000 was enacted with the objectives of creating a legal infrastructure for implementing secure electronic transactions, increasing the electronic filing of documents and encouraging the use of electronic signatures for online forms, as well as to foster confidence in the use of electronic transactions.[157] COMESA hopes that initiatives like the Electronic Transaction Act will foster confidence, as well as investment, from the private and the public sector in research and development of technologies to be used in furthering the integration of the COMESA marketplace.[158]

8 *Progress*

COMESA Member States began tariff reduction in 1984 and were expected to have eliminated all tariffs by 2000, the anticipated date for the launching of the COMESA FTA. Eleven COMESA Member States committed themselves to reducing tariffs regarding intra-regional trade to zero by 31 October 2000 at the COMESA policy organs meetings of May 2000. These eleven members were Djibouti, Eritrea, Egypt, Kenya, Madagascar, Malawi, Mauritius, Sudan, Uganda, Zambia and Zimbabwe.

The COMESA FTA was launched on 31 October 2000 when nine Member States eliminated tariffs on COMESA-originating products according to the schedule adopted at the 1992 Summit. The initial nine Members were Djibouti, Egypt, Kenya, Madagascar, Malawi, Mauritius, Sudan, Zambia and Zimbabwe. Burundi and Rwanda joined the FTA on 1 January 2004, and Comoros and Libya in 2006. Two of the remaining 6 countries to join the FTA, Uganda and Eritrea, have reduced tariffs by 80 per cent;[159] Ethiopia has reduced its tariffs by 10 per cent.[160] Namibia

155 *Ibid.* 156 *Ibid.*

157 Electronic Transactions Act of 2000, Act No 23 of 2000, Art. 3 (1 Aug. 2001), available at http://programmes.comesa.int/attachments/128_Electronic%20Transaction%20Act.pdf.

158 COMESA, 'COMESA Strategy'.

159 'Non-Tariff Barriers Monitoring Mechanism', Regional Trade Facilitation Programme, available at http://ntb.africonnect.com.

160 International Trade Agreements Leaflet No. 10, p. 2, available at www.zra.org.zm/publications/TradeAgreement.pdf.

and Swaziland were granted special exemptions from the provisions of the COMESA Treaty due to their membership in other RECs. At the 11th Summit of the COMESA Heads of State and Government in 2006, Swaziland's derogation from reciprocating tariff preferences until the end of 2008 was in order to enable Swaziland to complete consultations with SACU partners. This was done to allow Swaziland to join the COMESA FTA.[161] The Member States that have joined the COMESA FTA 'have removed all barriers to intra-regional trade, granted trade preferences to COMESA members that are not yet part of FTA, and retain tariffs on imports from outside COMESA'.[162] Disagreement over the Common External Tariff has contributed to the remaining COMESA members' reluctance to join the FTA as well as to the delay in launching the COMESA customs union by the long-past target date of 2004.[163]

The Report and Decisions of the 10th Meeting of the COMESA Council of Ministers on 7 and 8 December 2000 published the following tabled details of tariff rate reductions for members of the FTA, as well as for those COMESA Member States not yet participating in the FTA:

FTA countries	Non-FTA countries	
No duties or charges of equivalent effect from 31 Oct. 2000		Rate of reduction (%)
Djibouti	Angola	Nil
Egypt	Burundi	60
Kenya	Comoros	80
Madagascar	Congo D.R.	70
Malawi	Eritrea	80
Mauritius	Ethiopia	Nil
Sudan	Namibia	Under derogation
Zambia	Rwanda	60
Zimbabwe	Seychelles	To join FTA on 6 Jan. 2001
	Swaziland	
	Uganda	80

161 Final Communiqué of the 11th Summit of the COMESA Heads of State and Government (1 Dec. 2006), 4.

162 High Commission of India, 'Brief on COMESA' (Aug. 2010), available at http://meaindia.nic.in/foreignrelation/23fr01.pdf.

163 *Ibid.*

This shows the rate of reduction of tariffs and customs duties in countries that were not participating in the FTA at the time of the meeting. Further discussion led to the decision that trade between two non-FTA Member States would be on a reciprocal basis at the lower customs reduction rate between the two of them. For example, if Burundi were to trade with Comoros, the tariff rate would be at a 60% reduction. Additionally, trade with a non-free trade area Member State that has not reduced tariffs will be at full import duty rates, such as those applicable with third countries. Additionally it was decided that all Member States would become members of the FTA by 31 October 2001. Those that have not joined by that date will trade with the FTA Member States at full national MFN rates.

After the successful elimination of tariffs on originating goods, the focus turns to the elimination of restrictions and non-tariff barriers to trade. Non-tariff barriers restrict intra-regional trade and impair the ability of members to optimize on gains from preferences granted by RTAs. They are seen by COMESA as a major challenge to the realization of the region's growth[164] and are an important step in the direction of launching the COMESA customs union. Potential sources of non-tariff barriers include customs clearance procedures, import regulations, sanitary and phytosanitary measures, non-tariff charges, technical regulations and transit fees. The breakdown of such barriers in COMESA is as follows: 44% are customs clearance procedures, 8% are import regulations, 16% are excise duties, 12% are sanitary and phytosanitary measures, 12% are administrative obstacles and 8% are technical barriers to trade.[165] Some progress has been made in the elimination of non-tariff barriers, such as import licensing requirements, foreign exchange restrictions, the removal of import and export quotas, the easing of customs formalities and improved functioning of border posts.[166] However, a number of non-tariff barriers continue to impede the flow of trade between COMESA Member States.

In 2001, COMESA adopted a roadmap for the elimination of non-tariff barriers, but following a period of inactivity it was decided in May 2006 to put in place a permanent mechanism for the resolution of disputes

164 Regional Trade Facilitation Programme, 'Non-Tariff Barriers Monitoring Mechanism', m.a., m.d., available at http://mtb.afficonnect.com.

165 G. Osoro, 'An Overview of the Elimination of Non-Tariff Barriers' (23 Apr. 2009), available at www.mcci.org/photos/ntbs.ppt.

166 High Commission of India, 'Brief on COMESA' (Aug. 2010), available at http://meaindia.nic.in/foreignrelation/23fr01.pdf.

arising from non-tariff barriers. It was also decided that advance notification of non-tariff barriers should be made by Member States and that a regional policy should be developed and all Member States should adhere to the common standards.[167] The Non-Tariff Barrier Monitoring and Reporting System also covers SADC and EAC. The implementation of the strategy regarding non-tariff barriers was designed not to be detrimental to legitimate demands for better protection of health, safety and the environment, and should not put national market regulatory regimes in jeopardy.[168] The application of the monitoring and elimination instrument has, however, been constrained by a 'lack of consensus over national trade laws, regulations, practices and procedures that are to be categorized as NTBs'.[169]

In an effort to eliminate non-tariff barriers to trade and facilitate intra-regional, cross-border trade, COMESA has finalized the implementation of its Simplified Trade Regime.[170] The programme came into effect on 31 May 2010 and functions to reduce the cost and time of clearing goods at borders by using simplified trade instruments. The simplified instruments include the COMESA Simplified Certificate of Origin, the COMESA Simplified Customs Document and the list of products which qualify under the programme. The value threshold for eligible goods is pegged at US $500, meaning that any trade carrying goods on the eligible list that are valued at $500 or less, and which also has the COMESA Simplified Certificate of Origin, qualifies automatically for duty- and quota-free entry.[171] Goods must still have the requisite permits in compliance with the regular food safety, plant and animal health regulations.[172] The list of eligible products include tea and coffee; maize, wheat and sorghum; cotton; sisal; fish and fish products; raw milk; livestock and livestock products; fruits; nuts; oils; seeds; poultry and poultry products; vegetables; root crops; and sugar cane.[173]

COMESA has achieved the status of an FTA and had plans to launch the customs union by 2009. The customs union was initially to be launched in 2004, but was delayed until 2008 and again until 2009. A

167 Regional Trade Facilitation Programme, 'Non-Tariff Barriers Monitoring Mechanism'.

168 Imani Development, 'Inventory of Regional Non-Tariff Barriers: Synthesis Report' (July 2007), 11, available at http://ntb.africonnect.com/media/ntb_synthesis_2007_final.pdf.

169 *Ibid.*

170 *The Herald*, Harare, 'COMESA Finalises New Trade Regime', Trade Law Centre for Southern Africa (29 July 2010), available at www.tralac.org/cgi-bin/giga.cgi?cmd=cause_dir_news_item&cause_id=1694&news_id=90513&cat_id=1026.

171 *Ibid.* 172 *Ibid.* 173 *Ibid.*

common external tariff was to be adopted in 2004 in accordance with the terms of Article 47 of the COMESA Treaty. By 2005, the COMESA Member States had negotiated a provisional common external tariff in which capital goods would be assessed at 0%, raw materials at 5%, intermediate goods at 15% and finished goods at 30%.[174] The COMESA customs union was officially launched on 8 June 2009 at the 13th Summit of the COMESA Heads of State and Government held in Victoria Falls, Zimbabwe. The common external tariff that was officially adopted is structured as follows: raw materials, 0%; capital goods, 0%; intermediate goods, 10%; and finished goods, 25%.[175] The common external tariff will be reviewed periodically, taking into account the specific situations of Member States, in order to provide for flexibility in the customs union and to provide for evaluation and adjustment if necessary.[176] The formation of a customs union is a process, beginning with short-term measures which include adopting and implementing the COMESA Tariff Nomenclature and matching national tariff structures with the COMESA common external tariff in order to produce tariff alignment schedules.[177] Long-term measures in the process of establishing a customs union include ensuring that all Member States adopt and implement the common external tariff, fully implementing the COMESA Regional Trade Policy, and minimizing or eliminating sensitive products from the COMESA Tariff Nomenclature and the common external tariff.[178]

At the 27th meeting of the COMESA Council of Ministers held in December 2009, the Council approved a formula to be used by Member States to adjust their national tariffs to the COMESA common external tariff. Where alignment of the national and COMESA tariffs requires

174 M. Abdoulahi, 'Progress Report on Regional Integration Efforts in Africa towards the Promotion of Intra-African Trade' (African Trade Policy Centre, Dec. 2005), 8, available at www.uneca.org/eca_programmes/trade_and_regional_integration/atpc/Work%20in%20progress/30.pdf.

175 Official Gazette of the Common Market for Eastern and Southern Africa (COMESA), vol. 15, no. 1, Part III, Art. 7, p. 11 (9 June 2009), available at http://about.comesa.int/attachments/062_2009%20Gazette%20Vol.%2015%20No1.pdf.

176 COMESA Programmes, 'COMESA Customs Union', available at http://programmes.comesa.int/index.php?option=com_content&view=article&id=119&Itemid=73&lang=en.

177 COMESA Programmes, 'The COMESA Customs Union: Status on Sensitive Products and Implementation of the Transition Period', 5, available at http://programmes.comesa.int/attachments/119_comesa_customs_union_status_03%2006%202010.pdf.

178 *Ibid.*

a reduction in the national tariff, the national tariff should be reduced by 25% in the first year, 25% in the second year and 50% in the third year.[179] Where alignment requires an increase in the national tariff, it should be increased by 50% in the first year, 25% in the second year and 25% in the third year.[180] COMESA Secretary General, Sindiso Ngwenya, announced recently that the group may fail to reach the goal of achieving a duty-free trade area by 2012 because some countries have delayed in submitting their tariff alignments proposals.[181] The reluctance of some of the Member States may be due to the perceived loss of sovereignty over setting and administering the country's tariff structure. In order to complete the requisite steps in the three-year transitional period set at the launch of the customs union, a comprehensive timetable and programme must be established so that outstanding issues and concerns are resolved and the progress made towards implementing the customs union road map can be monitored and evaluated.[182]

Steps have been taken by COMESA towards enhancing cooperation in areas other than trade. For example, COMESA Member States were recently encouraged to implement the Comprehensive Africa Agriculture Development Programme (CAADP), an AU/NEPAD initiative designed to address food security and agricultural production issues.[183] The programme's objective is to develop the agriculture sector in order to achieve regional food security, sustainable agricultural growth, sector competitiveness and ultimately to reduce poverty levels in the region. At the COMESA Third Joint Meeting of Ministers of Agriculture, Environment and Natural Resources, Member States were urged to implement policies that prevent additional environmental degradation and ecosystems losses in order to ensure long-term growth and development.[184] Additionally, the United States Agency for International Development (USAID)/East Africa recently made a contribution to provide capacity building and technical assistance to the EAPP,

179 *Ibid.* at 8. 180 *Ibid.*

181 'COMESA May Miss Deadline for Duty-Free Trade', Trade Law Centre for Southern Africa (24 June 2010), available at www.tralac.org/cgi-bin/giga.cgi?cmd=cause_dir_news_item&cause_id=1694&news_id=88882&cat_id=1026.

182 *Ibid.*

183 W. Masinga, 'COMESA Members to Implement Agriculture Policies', Trade Law Centre for Southern Africa (21 July 2010), available at www.tralac.org/cgi-bin/giga.cgi?cmd=cause_dir_news_item&cause_id=1694&news_id=90109&cat_id=1026.

184 *Ibid.*

a specialized COMESA institution whose objective is to improve access to affordable, clean energy through regional electricity trade exchange.[185] The Eastern Africa regional electricity market will be developed further by the Powering Progress project, which will assist the EAPP to promote reliability, to address shortages, to lower access costs and to expand regional power capacity within the region.[186] High energy costs have been a long-standing impediment to the area's competitiveness and poverty-reducing economic growth, and the programme is expected to increase regional electricity trade exchanges which will reduce power shortages in the region. The programme will also encourage the harmonization of regional policies and regulations for enhanced cross-border trade, address specific policy and regulatory barriers to increase investment by the private sector in electricity and improve the performance of EAPP member utilities.[187]

A Memorandum of Understanding has been signed between COMESA, EAC, IGAD and the Indian Ocean Commission (IOC), under which these organizations have agreed to adopt and implement the COMESA trade liberalization and facilitation programme. Additionally, COMESA and SADC have formed a joint task force to harmonize their economic integration programmes. This partnership was joined by the EAC and the first Tripartite Summit was held in Kampala, Uganda in 2008. It is important to the progress of these three organizations that the Summit decisions regarding the harmonization of projects and programmes be implemented. It is expected that COMESA, SADC and EAC will work towards the formation of a unified FTA and ultimately the convergence of the COMESA customs union encompassing all 26 countries. However, the tripartite FTA has ambitious goals. For example: to promote customs co-operation and trade facilitation, to combat unfair trade practices and import surges, to simplify trade structures among its large membership and to try to relax restrictions on the movement of business people.[188] The wide range of ambitious goals, potential conflicts over controversial issues such as rules of origin and the movement of people and capital flows,

185 D. Muwanga, 'COMESA to Address Power Shortage', Trade Law Centre for Southern Africa (22 July 2010), available at www.tralac.org/cgi-bin/giga.cgi?cmd=cause_dir_news_item&cause_id=1694&news_id=90181&cat_id=1026.

186 *Ibid.* 187 *Ibid.*

188 'African Free Trade', Trade Law Centre for Southern Africa (5 July 2010), available at www.tralac.org/cgi-bin/giga.cgi?cmd=cause_dir_news_item&cause_id=1694&news_id=89373&cat_id=1026.

overlapping membership and existing arrangements such as EPAs with the EU, have hindered any progress towards forming the tripartite FTA.[189] But pressure is on African countries to participate in such an arrangement in order to keep up with the movement towards global free trade and to protect their markets. In order to make sure that the smaller African countries are not negatively affected by such an arrangement, the concentration should be on encouraging diversification away from primary commodities and towards industrialization, value-added manufacturing and sectoral industrial policy rather than focusing significantly on the reduction of tariffs.[190] One suggestion is that because the economic inequalities within the region require some kind of protection for certain industries, the free trade agreement should provide for some leeway for sensitive products in its tariff reduction schedule and also possibly a compensation mechanism to reimburse smaller countries that do not reap the benefits of the agreement.[191]

E East African Community

1 Overview

The Treaty establishing the East African Community (EAC) was signed on 30 November 1999 and entered into force 7 July 2000. Its original members were Kenya, Tanzania and Uganda. Burundi and Rwanda became members in 2007. The goal of the EAC is to 'widen and deepen economic, political, social and cultural integration in order to improve the quality of life of the people of East Africa through increased competitiveness, value added production, trade and investment'.[192] The EAC Treaty aims to establish an export-oriented economy that will enable the 'free movement of goods, persons, labor, services, capital [and] information technology', as an important objective.[193] Through a series of transitional stages consisting of the establishment of a customs union, a common market and a monetary union, the Treaty Establishing the EAC ultimately is aimed towards the establishment of a political federation.

189 *Ibid.* 190 *Ibid.* 191 *Ibid.*

192 EAC Development Strategy 2006–10, Executive Summary, 7, available at www.eac.int/home.html.

193 Treaty Establishing the East African Community, Art. 7(c), available at www.eac.int.

2 Sequencing

The sequencing envisioned by the EAC Treaty toward achieving its goals is as follows:

	Customs union	Common market	Monetary union	Political federation
EAC	1. The protocol on the establishment of the EAC customs union comes into force	2. The protocol on the establishment of the EAC common market was being negotiated as of 18 June 2009	3.	4.
Timetable	1 Jan. 2005	Anticipated 1 Jan. 2010	No time frame has been set as of the present	No time frame has been set as of the present

3 Customs union

The Treaty Establishing the EAC calls for the establishment of a customs union, the details of such establishment to be contained in a protocol.[194] The Treaty requires the conclusion of the Protocol by the Partner States within four years from the effective date of the Treaty.[195] The Protocol for the Establishment of the East African Customs Union was signed on 2 March 2004 after several delays and entered into force on 1 January 2005. The Protocol sets out the requirements for the formation of the East African Community Customs Union within five years after the entry into force of the Protocol.[196] The objectives of the customs union are to 'further liberalise intra-regional trade in goods on the basis of mutually beneficial trade arrangements among the Partner States; promote efficiency in production within the Community; enhance domestic,

194 *Ibid.* at Chapter 11, Art. 75(1), p. 57.

195 *Ibid.* at Art. 75(7), p. 58.

196 Protocol on the Establishment of the East African Customs Union, Part B, Art. 11(1), p. 14, available at www.eac.int/customs.

cross border and foreign investment in the Community; and promote economic development and diversification in industrialisation in the Community'.[197] The customs union is to be established progressively over this five-year transitional period in order to fulfil these objectives.

The Protocol provides a number of requirements to achieve the goals of trade liberalization and the establishment of a customs union. First, Partner States must eliminate all internal tariffs and similar charges on trade among the Partner States upon the entry into force of the Protocol.[198] Tariff rates can be eliminated more quickly than set out in the Protocol if so decided by the Council. Second, to make the transition to a customs union easier, the Protocol sets out specific requirements for internal tariffs and categorization of goods going into and out of the Partner States. Article 11(2) provides that goods to and from Uganda and Tanzania and goods from Uganda and Tanzania into Kenya are duty free. Article 11(3) provides for the categorization of goods from Kenya into Uganda and Tanzania. This section sets out two categories of goods – Category A goods, which are eligible for immediate duty-free treatment, and Category B goods, which are eligible for gradual tariff reduction. Further, Category B goods from Kenya into Uganda will have a five-year phase-out tariff reduction period for all products. This phase-out tariff reduction period begins by 10% during the first year, 8% during the second, 6% during the third, 4% during the fourth and 2% during the fifth. Additionally, Category B goods from Kenya into Tanzania have a similar phase-out tariff reduction period. The underlying requirement is that no internal tariff can exceed the common external tariff with respect to any of the specified products.[199]

The categorization of goods and varied tariff reduction schedules recognizes the principles of variable geometry and asymmetry. The principle of asymmetry is defined by the EAC Treaty as a 'principle which addresses variances for the implementation of measures in an economic integration process'.[200] It allows EAC Member States to address possible negative effects that the implementation of customs union policies might have on Member States through the application of variable geometry, as we saw in Chapter II. The EAC Treaty defines variable geometry as a principle that allows Member States to cooperate in the greater goals of the community while retaining the flexibility to work towards those goals at speeds that differ from other members.[201] The use of variable

197 *Ibid.* at Art. 3, p. 9. 198 *Ibid.* at Art. 10(1), p. 14.
199 *Ibid.* at Art. 11, pp. 14–15. 200 EAC Treaty, at Art. 1, p. 8. 201 *Ibid.*

geometry as a tool for the progression of cooperation and the integration of larger schemes in various fields at varying speeds is a practical principle to the achievement of the objectives of the EAC.[202] In September 2008, the East African Court of Justice issued an Advisory Opinion regarding the application of variable geometry. It noted that 'simultaneous implementation [of policy] is impracticable in some circumstance and Partner States cannot be expected to operate within such strait jacket or one size fits all situations'.[203] The Court held that variable geometry allows Member States that cannot implement a decision at the same time as other Member States to implement that decision at a later date or at a slower speed than other Member States.[204]

The establishment of a harmonized external tariff, or a common external tariff, in trade between Partner States and third countries is essential to the formation of a customs union. Within a customs union, Partner States must act as a single trading bloc and customs territory. The Protocol establishes a three-band common external tariff: a minimum rate of 0%, a middle rate of 10% and a maximum rate of 25% in respect of all products imported into the region.[205] After five years, the maximum rate of the common external tariff will be reviewed by the Partner States, and the Council can review the structure of the common external tariff and approve measures to remedy any adverse effects experienced by any of the Partner States as a result of the implementation of this Article. In exceptional circumstances, the Council may approve measures designed to safeguard community interests.[206] These provisions of the Protocol are in accordance with the EAC Treaty, which reads 'the Partner States shall, within the framework of the Protocols . . . take measures to address imbalances that may arise from the application of the provisions of this Treaty'.[207] Article 78(1) of the EAC Treaty defines the exceptional circumstances in which safeguard measures may be approved by the Council as causing serious injury to the economy of a Partner State after the application of the provisions of Chapter 11.[208]

Further, Article 13 of the Protocol requires Partner States to immediately remove any non-tariff barriers to the importation of goods originating in other Partner States and thereafter not to impose any new barriers. This provision is directly mirrored by Article 75(5) of the EAC Treaty. The

202 *Ibid.* at Art. 7(1)(e), p. 14.

203 In East African Court of Justice at Arusha First Instance Division, Application No. 1 of 2008, Advisory Opinion (13 Sept. 2008), 35.

204 *Ibid.*

205 East African Customs Union Protocol, Part B, Art. 12(1), p. 15.

206 *Ibid.* at Art. 12(2), (3), p. 15.

207 EAC Treaty, at Chapter 11, Art. 77, p. 59.

208 *Ibid.* at Art. 78(1), p. 59.

elimination of non-tariff barriers, as well as customs duties and tariffs, is essential to the attainment of the goal of a single market and investment area because such barriers can hinder trade between the Partner States.

In order to address and efficiently manage trade- and customs-related matters, the EAC Customs Management Act was assented to on 31 December 2004 and took effect on 1 January 2005. The Act created the Directorate of Customs,[209] whose duty is to coordinate and monitor the administration of the common external tariff; the enforcement of the customs laws; trade facilitation as provided for in the Protocol; the administration of the Rules of Origin; the compilation and dissemination of trade statistics; the application of information technology in customs administration; the training in customs-related matters; the quality control in customs operations and the customs negotiations.[210] In addition to creating the Directorate of Customs, the Customs Management Act also detailed standards and procedures for the implementation of trade and duties in areas such as the import, export and warehousing of goods; the departure of and clearing of vessels and aircraft; duties; inward and outward processing; and penalties for violating customs laws such as forfeitures and seizures of property.

The EAC Customs Management Act enumerates a number of goods which it considers either prohibited for importation or restricted for import.[211] For example, soaps containing mercury, hazardous waste, pornographic materials, narcotics and used car and light truck tyres are all prohibited from being imported.[212] Additionally, precious metals and stones, ivory, specific types of firearms and ammunition and historical artefacts are considered restricted imports.[213] The Customs Management Act also enumerates several goods to be either prohibited or restricted for export.[214] The Act provides that prohibited goods for export are all 'goods the exportation of which is prohibited under this Act or by any written law for the time being in force in the Partner States'.[215] The Customs Management Act also provides a more specific list of goods which are considered restricted for export. For example, waste and scrap ferrous cast iron; timber from wood grown in Partner States; fresh unprocessed fish; and wood charcoal are all goods that are restricted for export.[216] Additionally, warehoused goods, goods under duty drawback and

209 East African Community Customs Management Act of 2004, Art. 3, available at www.usig.org/countryinfo/laws/Uganda/East%20African%20Community%20Customs%20Management%20Act%202004.pdf.

210 *Ibid.* at Art. 4.

211 *Ibid.* at Art. 18.

212 *Ibid.* at Second Schedule, Part A.

213 *Ibid.* at Second Schedule, Part B.

214 *Ibid.* at Art. 70.

215 *Ibid.* at Third Schedule, Part A.

216 *Ibid.* at Third Schedule, Part B(1).

transshipped goods are prohibited from being exported unless they are on vessels with registers greater than 250 tonnes.[217] In addition to providing for which items may or may not be exported or imported from Member States, the Act provides procedures for unloading imports from various vessels, such as aeroplanes,[218] overland routes[219] and goods in transit.[220]

In addition to regulating the types of goods that may cross borders within the community, the Customs Management Act also enumerates guidelines for the administration of duties on those goods. The Act specifies the duty rate for certain types of goods, as well as what goods will be exempt from certain duties. For example, the Act provides that goods 'originating from Member States will be accorded community tariff treatment in accordance with the rules of the protocol'.[221] However, the Act also provides for exceptions to tariff duties, such as the exception of goods that have entered into a Member State from another Member State from duty liability if the goods are to be exported out of that Member State.[222]

In computing the duty to be paid on goods, the Customs Management Act provides different standards for a variety of goods. For example, the duty to be paid on goods for home consumption will be the rate that is in force at the time the goods enter the country.[223] However, if the goods are imported overland, the duty rate will be that of when the duty is actually paid.[224] Further, when goods are liable to an import duty that is *ad valarem*, or taxed according to value, the import duty will be paid according to the Fourth Schedule of the Customs Management Act.[225] Additionally, if there is an export duty to be paid, the rate at which the duty will be paid is the rate which is current at the time the goods are to be exported.[226]

Until the EAC agreed upon its own rules of origin, its Member States applied the COMESA rules of origin in their intra-community trade relations. The EAC envisaged anti-dumping, compensatory measures and safeguards to cover material damage to the industry and economy of the importing country.[227] Trade remedy rules are discussed more fully in Chapter VIII. Before the full implementation of a compensation mechanism, EAC members were allowed to invoke loss of revenue and to either wholly or partially restore the tariff and non-tariff measures that

217 *Ibid.* at Third Schedule, Part B(2). 218 *Ibid.* at Arts. 73–82.
219 *Ibid.* at Arts. 83, 84. 220 *Ibid.* at Arts. 85–7. 221 *Ibid.* at Art. 111(1).
222 *Ibid.* at Art. 115. 223 *Ibid.* at Art. 120. 224 *Ibid.* 225 *Ibid.* at Art. 122(1).
226 *Ibid.* at Art. 120(2).
227 Abdoulahi, 'Progress Report on Regional Integration Efforts', at 12.

were in force before the trade liberalization programme.[228] Article 14 of the EAC Customs Union Protocol states that the EAC customs union shall have rules of origin for the purpose of determining whether goods originate in Member States in order for those goods to receive community tariff treatment from other Member States.[229] A good that receives community tariff treatment is a good that will be able to avail itself to the more favourable tariff rates presently available to EAC members as opposed to paying the common external tariff rate. The Rules of Origin specify criteria that will allow origin to be conferred on a good. The first criterion will allow a good to have origin conferred upon it if the good is wholly produced in a Member State.[230] Examples of products that the Rules of Origin would consider as being wholly produced in a Member State include: vegetable products harvested within a Member State, products obtained from bodies of water or vessels within a state and livestock that were born and raised within a Member State.[231] The second criterion will confer origin if goods have been wholly or partially produced by goods that do not originate in a Member State but are transformed such that their CIF (cost, insurance and freight) value does not exceed 60 per cent of the total cost of the materials used in production, the value added from production is at least 35 per cent of the ex-factory cost as detailed in the First Schedule of the Rules of Origin[232] and the goods have changed in character such that they are no longer able to be classified under the tariff heading in which they were originally imported.[233]

4 *Common market*

The formation of a common market is provided for in Article 76 of the EAC Treaty Article 76 provides that a common market shall be established in order to provide 'free movement of labor, goods, services, capital and the right of establishment'.[234] Additionally, it provides that the implementation of the common market will be done progressively in accordance with schedules set out by the Council of Ministers[235] and provides that EAC Member States will create a protocol on a common market.[236]

228 *Ibid.* at 9. 229 East African Customs Union Protocol, Part E, Art. 14(1), p. 17.

230 East African Community Customs Union (Rules of Origin) Rules, Art. 4(1)(a), p. 4, available at www.tralac.org/unique/tralac/pdf/20060629_Rules_of_Origin.pdf.

231 *Ibid.* at Art. 5(1), p. 6. 232 *Ibid.* at First Schedule.

233 *Ibid.* at Art. 4(1)(b), p. 4. 234 EAC Treaty, at Art. 76(1).

235 *Ibid.* at Art. 76(2). 236 *Ibid.* at Art. 76(4).

That protocol and its several annexes and schedules came into force on 1 July 2010. That makes the EAC the most advanced RTA in the continent, since no other RTA has moved from a customs to a common market.

The plans for a common market had begun long before 1 July 2010. For example, on 8 June 2009, the EAC had put out a press release regarding the progress of a high-level task force charged with negotiating the annexes to the EAC Common Market Protocol. The EAC press release announced that it anticipated the signing of the EAC Common Market Protocol by November 2009 and for the launch of the EAC common market to take effect in January 2010.[237] At the 11th Ordinary Summit of the EAC Heads of State held on 20 November 2009, the Protocol Establishing the EAC Common Market was signed and approved.[238] That the EAC Common Market Protocol was signed by Member States in November 2009 and that it came into force in July 2010, only six months after its planned entry into force, makes it one of the most quickly negotiated RTA treaties that also came into force within a very short period of time.

The overall objective of the common market is to 'widen and deepen cooperation among the Partner States in the economic and social fields'[239] through accelerated economic growth and the strengthening, coordinating and regulating of economic and trade relations among the Partner States, maintaining the expansion and integration of economic activities within the EAC.[240] The EAC Common Market Protocol aims to achieve its goals by eliminating tariff and non-tariff barriers to trade, removing restrictions on the movements of labour, services, capital and people[241] as well as the coordination of economic, and financial and monetary policies.[242] The common market is to be guided by the fundamental and operational principles of the EAC as provided in Articles 6 and 7 of the EAC Treaty.[243] Furthermore, by ratifying the Common Market Protocol the Partner States undertake to observe the principles of non-discrimination of nationals of other Partner States on the basis

237 Press Release: 'Negotiations on the Annexes to the EAC Common Market Protocol Ongoing in Kigali, Rwanda' (8 June 2009).

238 T. Thorp, 'Challenges of Incorporating the Economic Acquis Communautaire of the East African Community in a New Common Market', Working Paper No. 2010/14 (Society of International Economic Law, 29 June 2010), 1, available at http://papers.ssrn.com/sol3/papers.cfm?abstract_id=1632439.

239 Protocol on the Establishment of the East African Community Common Market, Art. 3(1), p. 6.

240 *Ibid.* at Art. 3(2)(a) and (b), p. 6.

241 *Ibid.* at Art. 4(2), p. 6.

242 *Ibid.* at Art. 4(3)(a), p. 7.

243 *Ibid.* at Art. 3(1), p. 6.

of nationality, to accord equal treatment to nationals of other Partner States, to ensure transparency in matters concerning the other Partner States and to share information for the implementation of the Common Market Protocol.[244]

The EAC Common Market Protocol provides that the common market is to allow for the free movement of goods, persons, services and capital, labour, the right of establishment and the right of residence between Member States.[245] Under the Common Market Protocol, the free movement of goods is to be implemented in accordance with Article 39 of the EAC Customs Union Protocol.[246] Article 39 of the Protocol provides that the laws of the Community shall consist of the relevant protocols of the treaty, the protocol and annexes of the Customs Union Protocol, decisions and directives made by the court and Council, Acts of the Assembly or legislature and applicable principles of international law.[247]

Under the EAC Common Market Protocol, the Member States agreed to guarantee the free movement of citizens of other Member States within their borders.[248] They also agreed to ensure the non-discrimination of citizens from other Member States by allowing them entry into their territory without a visa, allowing citizens of other Member States to remain in their territory and to leave their territories without restrictions.[249] The Member States further agreed to guarantee the protection of other members' citizens while in their territories in accordance with their national laws, although travelling citizens are not exempt from prosecution for crimes committed and Member States may impose limitations for public policy, security, or public health purposes.[250] In order to facilitate the free movement of people between Member States, the Member States should also establish a standardized identification and documentation scheme.[251] The principle of non-discrimination, which encompasses the national treatment and MFN principles, is especially important to the EAC because the organization aims not only to create a single economic bloc, but rather, a single political group. The importance of the non-discrimination principle is evidenced in the fact that the Common

244 *Ibid.* at Art. 3(2), p. 6.
245 *Ibid.* at Art. 2, pp. 5–6.
246 *Ibid.* at Part C, Art. 6(1), p. 10.
247 East African Community Customs Union Protocol, at Art. 39, p. 33.
248 East African Community Common Market Protocol, at Art. 7(1), p. 10.
249 *Ibid.* at Art. 7(2), p. 11.
250 *Ibid.* at Art. 7(3), p. 11; see also Thorp, 'Incorporating the Economic Acquis Communautaire', at 18.
251 East African Community Common Market Protocol, at Art. 8, p. 12.

Market Protocol contains a general statement of the principle in addition to several national treatment obligations pertaining to specific provisions, rights and freedoms.

Under the EAC Common Market Protocol, the Member States agreed to guarantee the free movement of labour, which allows workers who are citizens of other states into their territory.[252] Under the Common Market Protocol, workers are entitled to apply for employment and accept job offers in other Member States; move freely between Member States for the purposes of employment; remain within a Partner State for the purposes of employment; enjoy the benefits of the Member State's national labour laws; conclude contracts without discrimination; and enjoy the social security benefits that are awarded to nationals of that Member State.[253] In addition to the rights that would be afforded to a worker in a foreign Member State, a worker would be allowed to bring a spouse and a child who will also be afforded the same privileges available to the worker.[254] Additionally, workers are entitled to receive the same employment assistance and social security benefits as are accorded to workers of the host country.[255] The provisions regarding movement of labour are limited to employment in the private sector unless the national laws and regulations of a host Member State provide for employment in the public service.[256] Discrimination is prohibited on the basis of nationality, remuneration or other conditions of work and employment,[257] although a host Partner State is permitted to impose limitations on the free movement of workers for purposes of public policy, public security or public health.[258]

EAC citizens seeking to enter, travel within, or exit another EAC Member State for the purpose of employment must present a valid common standard travel document or national identity card, as well as a contract of employment, to immigration officials, and must declare all information relevant to entry and exit.[259] The worker will then be issued a pass which entitles the worker to enter into the host Partner State's territory and stay for a period of up to six months for the purpose of completing the formalities required to obtain a work permit.[260] The worker's spouse, children and dependants will also be provided with a six-month pass, pending the

252 *Ibid.* at Art. 9(1), p. 12. 253 *Ibid.* at Art. 7(3), p. 11.

254 *Ibid.* at Art. 7(4), p. 11; see also at Art. 10(5), pp. 13–14.

255 *Ibid.* at Art. 10(7), p. 14. 256 *Ibid.* at Art. 10(10), p. 14.

257 *Ibid.* at Art. 10(2), p. 13. 258 *Ibid.* at Art. 10(11), p. 14.

259 East African Community Common Market (Free Movement of Workers) Regulations, Annex II to the East African Community Common Market Protocol, Reg. 5(2).

260 *Ibid.* at Reg. 5(4).

completion of formalities necessary to obtain a dependant pass.[261] The passes issued under these regulations are to be issued without a fee.[262] The procedure for acquiring a work permit is detailed in Regulation 6 of the EAC Common Market (Free Movement of Workers) Regulations.[263]

In the effort to ensure the free movement of labour, under the EAC Common Market Protocol, Partner States undertake to harmonize and mutually recognize academic and professional qualifications in order to aid the movement of more highly educated and skilled workers across borders.[264] Annex VII specifically deals with the mutual recognition of academic and professional qualifications. Annex VII specifically requires Member States to recognize university awards from universities in other Member States,[265] as well as to create a database of regulated professions and sanctions authorities for those professions in order to establish standards and criteria for acceptance between Member States.[266] Additionally, Member States agreed to seek to harmonize their labour policies and national laws and programmes to facilitate the free movement of labour within the region.[267] EAC Partner States also undertake to review and harmonize their national social security policies and systems in order to cover self-employed workers who are citizens of other Member States.[268] The implementation of these provisions is to be in accordance with directives and regulations issued by the Council.[269] However, it is important to note that there have been some issues regarding the integration of particular workers. For example, Kenyan companies wishing to bring their legal representatives into countries like Tanzania are not permitted to do so, while Tanzanian and Ugandan lawyers are allowed to practise in Kenya.[270] This example underscores some of the difficulties in integrating the community. For example, in the case of lawyers, problems arise because Member States, like Rwanda and Burundi, use a francophone legal system while other Member States, particularly Kenya and Tanzania, use the British system of law.[271]

261 *Ibid.* at Reg. 5(5). 262 *Ibid.* at Reg. 5(6). 263 *Ibid.* at Reg. 6.

264 EAC Common Market Protocol, at Art. 11, p. 15.

265 East African Community Common Market (Free Movement of Workers) Regulations, Annex VII to the East African Community Common Market Protocol.

266 *Ibid.* at Annex VII, p. 11.

267 East African Community Common Market Protocol, at Art. 12, p. 15.

268 *Ibid.* at Art. 12(2), p. 15. 269 *Ibid.* at Art. 12(3), p. 15.

270 'EAC Regional Integration: Can't Take Your Lawyer?', *Ratio Magazine* (27 Jan. 2009), available at www.ratio-magazine.com/20090127392/EAC-Regional/EAC-Regional-Integration-Can-t-Take-Your-Lawyer.html.

271 *Ibid.*

Additionally, there is an underlying cultural mistrust of Kenyan lawyers, whom Tanzanians view as 'pushy'.[272] Further, after the break-up of the EAC in 1977, countries like Kenya and Tanzania took divergent paths, with Kenya pursuing a capitalist economy where Tanzania pursued a socialist one.[273] These are themes that are likely to play out again over time over a variety of integration issues.

Though Member States are committed to allowing the free movement of workers under the Common Market Protocol, there have been some differences as to how it should be implemented. For example, with respect to issuing work permits, Tanzania has proposed a regulation that would require Partner States to work within their national laws in issuing work permits, and furthermore that these work permits would state the holder's nationality and the type of work he performs.[274] However, Rwanda, Uganda, Kenya and Burundi require the same specifics as the Tanzanian proposal, but in addition require that the worker request a work permit within three months of entering the host country.[275] The subcommittee report on Annex II to the Common Market Protocol suggests that in order to give effect to the free movement of labour more efficiently, Partner States shall create an East African Employment Services Agency whose duties would include the facilitation of cooperation between employment services and workers as well as the keeping of statistics and employment data.[276]

Under the EAC Common Market Protocol, Member States agree to the right of establishment of nationals of other Member States in their territory.[277] Under the Common Market Protocol, the right of establishment entitles nationals of other Member States to pursue self-employment; manage and set up economic undertakings; and allows a self-employed citizen of another Member State to partake in the social security system of the Member State in which he is residing.[278] Member States under the Common Market Protocol are also required to recognize the right of residence of workers and self-employed individuals who are nationals of other Member States working within their territory under provisions 9 and 12 of the Protocol.[279] Additionally, the Common Market Protocol provides that a national of any Member State and their

272 *Ibid.* 273 *Ibid.*

274 Sub-Committee Report on Annex II of the Protocol on the Establishment of the East African Common Market, 2.

275 *Ibid.* 276 *Ibid.* at Art. 5.

277 East African Common Market Protocol, at Art. 22(1), p. 26.

278 *Ibid.* at Art. 12(3), p. 15. 279 *Ibid.* at Art. 13, p. 16.

accompanying spouse and child who reside in another Member State for a period of five years may be granted permanent resident status pursuant to any conditions that the Member State may have.[280]

The rights of establishment and residence are incorporated into the EAC Common Market Protocol, with the goal of creating parity between the nationals of a Member State and nationals of other Member States in gaining access to certain economic activities. The rights of establishment and residence seek to give foreign nationals of Member States access to areas of investment, which include 'real estate, the practice of professions, employment in certain spheres and entry into business'.[281] The rights of residence and establishment which the Common Market Protocol seeks to address, raise a variety of questions that have the potential to cause conflict in the future. For example, in allowing for the right of establishment, there is a lack of any standard in international law that would dictate whether or not a host country has the right to discriminate between nationals and foreigners in an investment context. To answer that question, one must consider who would qualify as an East African foreign investor. Defining an East African investor based on that particular investor's nationality alone might prove to be insufficient for the purposes of the common market.[282] Additionally, a situation in which an East African company enters into a borrowing arrangement with a foreign creditor, such that the East African company would be completely or partially acquired by the foreign creditor, is a potential back door for non-East African companies to take advantage of the benefits of the common market.[283] Additionally, the Common Market Protocol might in future seek to address the issue as to whether or not companies in Member States would be allowed to show preference to their own citizens when selecting executives for branches or subsidiaries located within their countries.[284]

Member States under the Common Market Protocol would guarantee the free movement of services supplied by nationals and service suppliers of Member States.[285] Under the Protocol, service consumers and service providers will be able to access each other freely even if they are in

280 East African Common Market Protocol (this is an unnumbered article in the draft which immediately precedes Art. 1, but is not labelled).

281 M. Sonarajah, *The International Law on Foreign Investment* (2004), 154.

282 *Ibid.* at p. 8. 283 *Ibid.* 284 *Ibid.*

285 East African Common Market Protocol, at Art. 14(1), p. 18.

separate Member States.[286] Additionally, Member States would agree to treat services provided by those in Member States at least as well as services provided by non-member nations.[287] The free movement of services under the Common Market Protocol would 'enable capital investments and services to realize higher returns'. The free movement of services will return greater profits and economic success for Member States because it will allow firms in Member States to have access to improved facilities, labour and other factors of production that were previously unavailable to them.[288]

The EAC Common Market Protocol calls for the elimination of restrictions to the free movement of capital as a part of the Community's overarching plan to progressively move to an integrated financial system and eventually to an economic and monetary union.[289] The provisions and regulations regarding the free movement of capital provide for the progressive liberalization of capital movements, save in exceptional circumstances. Member States agreed to eliminate the restrictions on the free movement of capital by removing restrictions within the region; removing restrictions based on nationality discrimination; refusing to introduce new restrictions to the movement of capital; and removing restrictions with regard to current payments on goods, persons, services or capital between EAC Member States.[290] Member States, however, reserve the right to restrict the free movement of capital for reasons of prudential supervision; public policy consideration; money laundering; and the application of financial sanctions by other Member States.[291] Partner States must notify the Secretariat and the other EAC Members and must furnish proof that the action taken was 'appropriate, reasonable and justified'.[292]

To date, there has been no time frame set for the removal of obstacles to the free movement of capital. However, Annex VIII to the Common Market Protocol has focused on key areas in which the efforts to remove restrictions will be targeted, as well as how these efforts will be applied in each Member State. Annex VII concerns itself with the removal of barriers to the movement of capital in the areas of direct investments; investment in real estate; the operation of securities dealt on the capital and money markets; collective investment undertakings; loans and financial credit; sureties; insurance contracts; movement of personal capital;

286 *Ibid.* at Art. 14(2), p. 18. 287 *Ibid.* at Art. 16, p. 20. 288 *Ibid.* at p. 8.
289 East African Common Market Protocol, at Art. 22, p. 26.
290 *Ibid.* at Art. 22(1), p. 26. 291 *Ibid.* at Art. 23(1), p. 26.
292 *Ibid.* at Art. 25(2), p. 28.

physical import and export of financial assets; and other miscellaneous movement of capital such as royalties, refunds having to do with contract cancellations and death duties.[293]

5 *Monetary union*

Article 5 of the EAC Treaty lists the establishment of a monetary union as one of the steps to achieving the goals of the EAC community. As part of the strategy for achieving its goals, Article 82 of the EAC Treaty requires that Member States harmonize their macroeconomic policies,[294] cooperate with each other in financial matters and ensure that their currencies are convertible so as to serve as a basis for the establishment of a monetary union.[295] With the establishment of the common market in July 2010, monetary union is now slated to be established by 2012 and there is in fact a draft Monetary Union Protocol.[296]

6 *Political federation*

The final step in the process to achieving the goals set forth in the EAC Treaty is the formation of a political federation.[297] The EAC Treaty provides that the formation of a political federation requires Member States to establish common foreign and security policies.[298] However, before Member States begin to establish such policies, the Council of Ministers shall determine how and when the provisions of Article 123 will be implemented and the Summit of the Heads of State must direct the Council of Ministers to begin the process of forming a political federation. In 2005, the Council of Ministers was ordered to begin the process of collecting the views of the peoples of East Africa with regard to the formation of a political union.[299] The consultations initiated in May 2005 were concluded and submitted to the Extraordinary Summit for consideration in June 2007.[300] The Summit of the Heads of State subsequently directed Rwanda and Burundi to begin the consultation process with their citizens in order to stimulate greater political interest, information and resolve regarding

293 *Ibid.* at Annex VIII, pp. 12–15. 294 EAC Treaty, at Art. 82(1)(b).

295 *Ibid.* at Art. 82(1)(a).

296 D. Mushi, 'Why EAC Monetary Union Talks Should Be Landed', *Daily News*, 25 Jan. 2011, available at www.dailynews.co.tz/feature/?n=166648cat=feature.

297 *Ibid.* at Art. 5(2). 298 *Ibid.* at Art. 123(1).

299 The Third Extraordinary Summit of the Heads of State of the EAC, Joint Communiqué, Art. 9 (29–30 May 2005).

300 EAC, 'Towards the EAC Political Federation', available at www.eac.int/summit/201-towards-the-eac-political-federation.html.

the formation of a political union.[301] A report was received at the 10th Ordinary Summit of the EAC Heads of State in April 2009 that detailed the results of the national consultative process conducted by Rwanda and Burundi with respect to the fast-tracking of a political federation.[302] The Summit noted that the citizens of Rwanda and Burundi showed support for a political federation and subsequently ordered the Council of Ministers to review the report in greater detail and to submit recommendations to the Summit at its next meeting in November 2009.[303] Despite the findings of the Summit and the anticipated recommendations of the Council of Ministers, there are some civil society organizations within Member States which are apprehensive about moving towards a political federation too quickly. For example, in a draft memorandum between the Federal Republic of Germany and the EAC regarding the integration of member nations into the EAC, there were mixed responses among civil society organizations of the Member States with respect to moving towards a political federation. In particular, Tanzanian civil society organizations expressed concerns about entering into a political federation for fear that they would be overrun by Kenyan civil society organizations and business people.[304] The possible discrepancy between the findings of EAC reports and public sentiment may become an issue in future debates regarding the integration of Member States into a political federation.

7 Progress

According to the EAC Treaty, a customs union was to be formed by 2004, followed by a common market, a monetary union and finally a political federation. For the formation of the customs union, EAC Member States were to eliminate customs duties and other taxes of equivalent effect, reduce and eliminate tariff and non-tariff barriers to intra-regional trade and establish a common external tariff regarding trade with third countries. Initially, the Member States had undertaken a gradual tariff reduction with 90 per cent tariff reduction for Kenya and 80 per cent for

301 *Ibid.*

302 Communiqué of the 10th Extraordinary Summit of the Heads of State of the East African Community, Art. 3(ii) (29 Apr. 2009).

303 *Ibid.*

304 Supporting Regional Integration in East Africa through Strengthening CSO's Regional Approaches and Capacities', EAC/GTZ Programme 'Support to the Integration Process', available at www.eacgermany.org/index.php/eac-gtz-programme.

Tanzania and Uganda. The EAC members had coordinated and harmonized their trade policies and programmes. In March 2004, the protocol establishing the customs union was signed.[305] The EAC Customs Union Protocol came into effect on 1 January 2005 with the three original EAC members – Kenya, Uganda and Tanzania. Burundi and Rwanda became full members of the EAC in July 2007. The EAC members were working towards the establishment of a common market in 2010, a monetary union by 2012 and ultimately a political federation.

The main objective of the EAC is to improve the standard of living in the region through increased competitiveness, value-added production, trade and investment. Ultimately, the desired sustainable development will lead to a prosperous, internationally competitive, secure and politically united region. By pooling together each of the five Member States' potential and resources, EAC members are in a better position to realize their development goals. The formation of the EAC customs union has had a positive impact on intra-regional trade and has increased revenues in all of the EAC countries.[306] However, the EAC still suffers from the effects of unfavourable terms of trade. The region imports twice as much as it exports, or it consumes twice as much as it produces, and exports mainly primary, unprocessed products and imports mainly finished, consumer and capital goods.[307] The skewed trade and production pattern reflects an underdeveloped industrial base and has led to high levels of dependency and debt.[308] To reverse this trend, the EAC must address the poverty issue and boost the productive base by promoting and attracting investment, as well as promoting manufacturing industries.[309] Realizing this, the third EAC Development Strategy focuses on promoting a regional industrialization strategy. In order to continue to be effective, the EAC needs sustained political will and commitment to its regional programmes.

Effective integration calls for the mobilization of large amounts of resources. The EAC cannot generate the amount necessary and is, to an extent, dependent upon outside sources of funding for its regional programmes.[310] Dependency on outside sources of funding is not sustainable and the EAC is exploring solutions to this problem. The EAC Development Fund is to be created as the financial vehicle that can be used to mobilize the resources necessary for regional projects and programmes. To avoid marginalization that may be caused by globalization,

305 EAC Customs Union Protocol.

306 African Union, 'Status of Integration in Africa', at 101.

307 *Ibid.* at 104. 308 *Ibid.* 309 *Ibid.* at 105. 310 *Ibid.* at 108.

the EAC is forging partnerships with global partners such as the EU and regional partners such as COMESA and SADC. Such partnerships will strengthen and enlarge the EAC market, enabling it to be competitive in the global economy, giving it access to those markets, and attracting local and international investment.

The EAC has implemented programmes and established institutions and organs towards the goal of forming a political federation. Such institutions include the East African Legislative Assembly, the East African Court of Justice, the Defense Liaison Office, the coordination of foreign policy and of monetary and fiscal policies.[311] During the Special Summit held in 2004, the Heads of State decided to fast-track the formation of the political federation of East Africa. The report submitted by the Committee on Fast Tracking East African Federation (the Wako Committee) recommended the establishment of the East African Federation by 2013.[312] At the Extraordinary Summit in 2007, the Heads of State directed that steps be taken to expedite the establishment of the common market by 2010 and monetary union by 2012 as a phased and systemic build-up to achieve a political federation by 2013. The full implementation of the EAC customs union was planned to come into effect between 2005 and 2010, with the first round of reduction on products from Kenya to Tanzania and Uganda implemented in January 2006 and the second round in January 2007. The programme for the elimination of tariffs was to be completed as planned on 1 January 2010 with all tariffs on intra-regional trade to be eliminated. The provisions of the customs union were to be phased into operation in Burundi and Rwanda by July 2009. A fully fledged customs union entered into force on 1 January 2010, five years after the Customs Union Protocol became effective.[313] With the establishment of the EAC customs union came the implementation of a three-band common external tariff, the structure of which is as follows: raw materials and capital goods, 0%; intermediate goods, 10%; and finished goods, 25%.[314] Overall, the level of intra- and extra-EAC trade has benefited from the implementation of the common external tariff and it has led to increased imports under the three-tiered structure, has greatly liberalized the region in that average applied tariffs have decreased in the Partner States, and it has enhanced predictability for exporters and investors.[315] However, Kenyan traders

311 *Ibid.* at 114. 312 *Ibid.*

313 Thorp, 'Incorporating the Economic Acquis Communautaire', at 1. 314 *Ibid.* at 13.

315 *Ibid.*; see also E. Mugisa, 'An Evaluation of the Implementation and Impact of the East African Community Customs Union', Final Report, EAC Secretariat (Mar. 2009).

recently raised objections over the way the common external tariff has been administered by EAC Member States, claiming that other members have ignored or flouted the common external tariff covering sectors in which Kenya has a comparative advantage.[316] An implementation and monitoring mechanism must be adopted in order to ensure that all members are applying the common external tariff uniformly.

By 30 April 2010, all five EAC Partner States had ratified the Common Market Protocol, and the EAC common market was launched on 1 July 2010. Juma Mwapachu, the EAC Secretary General, stated that what has been created so far is 'only the basic legal framework that outlines what needs to be done', and that national laws must be harmonized with the provisions of the Protocol.[317] In particular, national policies regarding trade facilitation must be adjusted so as to eliminate security measures such as immigration laws and road blocks that have acted as non-tariff barriers to trade.[318] These national security measures have frustrated trade by hindering the free flow of goods between member countries and have had an adverse effect on the region's competitiveness.[319] The administration of the EAC rules of origin by Partner States has also acted as a burden to the trade facilitation process in the region, and Partner States must provide a more harmonized approach to the interpretation, application and enforcement of the rules of origin in order to overcome this hurdle.[320] These obstacles must be removed in order fully to implement the Common Market Protocol and reap the benefits of the free movement of persons, labour, goods, services and capital. These challenges are especially relevant within the framework of the COMESA–SADC–EAC tripartite and must be overcome in order to realize the objectives of such regional cooperation and to avoid trade deflection that may arise out of the use of such procedures as protectionist measures.[321] In

316 G. Omondi, 'EAC Traders Take Tariffs War to Minister', Trade Law Centre for Southern Africa (16 July 2010), available at www.tralac.org/cgi-bin/giga.cgi?cmd=cause_dir_news_item&cause_id=1694&news_id=89910&cat_id=1026.

317 J. Kron, 'East African Countries Form a Common Market', *New York Times* (1 July 2010), available at www.nytimes.com/2010/07/02/business/global/02africa.html?src=busln. Article 47 of the Common Market Protocol provides that the 'Partner States undertake to approximate their national laws and to harmonise their policies and systems, for purposes of implementing this Protocol', at Art. 47(1), p. 49.

318 E. Njoroge, 'East African States Urged to Ease Trade Barriers', Trade Law Centre for Southern Africa (9 July 2010), available at www.tralac.org/cgi-bin/giga.cgi?cmd=cause_dir_news_item&cause_id=1694&news_id=89604&cat_id=1026.

319 *Ibid.*

320 Thorp, 'Incorporating the Economic Acquis Communautaire', at 13.

321 *Ibid.*

addition to cumbersome procedures, inadequate transport and communications infrastructure has acted as an obstacle to the full realization of the region's development and growth potential. To achieve a strong, regionally integrated economy under the common market, cooperation should be intensified in key areas such as infrastructure development, regional industrialization, agricultural development and food security and harmonization of educational curricula.[322] The transition to a common market with the free movement of labour, goods, services and capital will not be instantaneous, however, but rather will be a process to be undertaken over several years because it will require many amendments to the national laws of the Member States.[323] Since the launching of the common market, the EAC has focused on improving deficient transport and communication infrastructure to improve transportation networks, minimize border post delays and attract investment in infrastructure development.[324]

For the purpose of implementing the Common Market Protocol, the EAC Council's duty is to issue directives for the Partner States to implement their undertaking to approximate their national laws and harmonize their policies and systems.[325] The Council and the EAC Summit directed that Partner States enact enabling legislation to integrate the provisions of the Common Market Protocol into domestic law by 21 August 2010, and to review their domestic law to ensure that it is consistent with the EAC Treaty.[326] This is an ambitious goal, as the scope and number of laws to be harmonized is extensive and no roadmap for legal approximation is provided in the EAC Common Market Protocol.[327] Rwanda and Kenya have established national task forces which are charged with the duty to audit their national laws and to ascertain any conflicts with the Common Market Protocol, and other Partner States have initiated similar

322 Press release, 'Secretary General, Japanese Delegation Discuss Common Market' (5 July 2010), available at www.eac.int/component/content/461.html?task=view.

323 J. Oyuke, 'Dawn of an Era for East Africans', *The Standard* (1 July 2010), available at www.standardmedia.co.ke/InsidePage.php?id=2000012871&cid=4.

324 J. Oyuke, 'EAC Intensify Co-operation in Infrastructure Development', *The Standard* (9 July 2010), available at www.standardmedia.co.ke/InsidePage.php?id=2000013439&cid=464&story=EAC%20intensify%20co-operation%20in%20infrastructure%20development.

325 EAC Common Market Protocol, at Art. 45, p. 49.

326 Press release, 'Council Chairperson Assures Community on Ratification of Common Market Protocol' (26 Apr. 2010), available at www.eac.int/news/index.php?option=com_content&view=article&id=226:ratification-of-common-market-protocol&catid=48:eac-latest&Itemid=69.

327 Thorp, 'Incorporating the Economic Acquis Communautaire', at 25.

measures.[328] To facilitate the harmonization and approximation of laws, the EAC Secretariat has commissioned a project to identify and inventory commercial laws that relate to the implementation of the common market.[329] This project was due to be finalized by the end of June 2010 and is interrelated with the work of the Committee on the Approximation of Laws, which has also launched a study on the harmonization of commercial laws.[330] As of April 2010, '45 pieces of legislation on trading, business registrations, investment, insurance and banking had been identified'.[331] In addition to commercial laws and other matters such as intellectual property and competition policy, the four freedoms and two rights contained in the Common Market Protocol require immediate work to audit and approximate national laws relating to these cornerstone areas. Schedules to progressively implement the Common Market Protocol must be developed and approved by the Council. Partner States are expected to act in good faith to incorporate the Common Market Protocol and its regulations into their municipal laws, and directives may be issued when members have not performed their obligations.[332]

At different speeds, not simultaneously, all of the EAC's members appear to be taking some action to approximate, reform or revise their laws in conformity with the Common Market Protocol and the EAC Treaty.[333] The principle of variable geometry is recognized in the EAC Treaty as an implementation strategy that allows for flexibility in the progression of integration activities and programmes and differentiation in terms of the speed at which members incorporate EAC policies and programmes.[334] Schedules and roadmaps must be developed and approved by the Council in order to allow for approximation of domestic laws with the Common Market Protocol, taking into account the varied stages of development among Partner States. Currently, the EAC is attempting to find a way to align the long-term development plans of its members and create a regional vision to allow the organization to reach its ultimate goal of deeper regional integration.[335] While the members'

328 *Ibid.*

329 Press release, 'Council Chairperson Assures Community on Ratification of Common Market Protocol'.

330 Thorp, 'Incorporating the Economic Acquis Communautaire', at 25.

331 Press release, 'Council Chairperson Assures Community on Ratification of Common Market Protocol'.

332 Thorp, 'Incorporating the Economic Acquis Communautaire', at 27.

333 *Ibid.* 334 EAC Treaty, at Chapter 1, Art. 1, p. 8.

335 E. Njoroge, 'East African States to Harmonize Blueprints', Trade Law Centre for Southern Africa (16 Aug. 2010), available at www.tralac.org/cgi-bin/giga.cgi?cmd=cause_dir_news_item&cause_id=1694&news_id=91259&cat_id=1026.

development strategies are in different stages of implementation, the EAC Permanent Secretary believes that they all have similarities in major areas which should be aligned in order to inform the EAC's fourth development strategy, which is to come into effect in 2011.[336]

Cooperation among Member States across a wide range of issues is an important focus of the EAC, as coordination of trade policies will create a larger and more competitive market as well as foster relationships between the members. Towards this end, the EAC is cooperating with SADC and COMESA to form a single free trade area in order to alleviate the issues caused by overlapping membership in the three groups. The three African regional trade arrangements formed a task force whose duties include streamlining trade and transport instruments and other trade facilitation measures, and creating compatible rules of origin, customs documents, a common tariff nomenclature and tariff elimination schedules. These groups must work together to harmonize and simplify customs procedures and rules and regulations in order to benefit from enhanced cooperation and integration. The combined free trade area would link African countries across the continent and would lead to the improvement of the infrastructural system and the removal of trade barriers between the regions, and would also create a larger market which would potentially lead to increased regional trade and attract investment.

A monetary union with a common currency is expected to be established by 2012 and a political federation is envisaged for the year 2015. Since the launch of the EAC common market, the region has attracted a flurry of attention from international investors, who view the common market as a chance to form partnerships which would enable them to tap into new opportunities in the enlarged market and as a gateway to the region.[337]

F Arab Maghreb Union

1 Overview

The Arab Maghreb Union (AMU) Treaty was signed on 17 February 1989 at Marrakesh, Morocco by the five Maghrebi countries – Algeria, Libya,

336 *Ibid.*

337 A. Odhiambo, 'Global Economies Rush to Strengthen Ties in EAC Market', Trade Law Centre for Southern Africa (13 Aug. 2010), available at www.tralac.org/cgi-bin/giga.cgi?cmd=cause_dir_news_item&cause_id=1694&news_id=91084&cat_id=1026.

Mauritania, Morocco and Tunisia – its current members.[338] These five countries have had close ties for centuries, with the idea of a unified northern Africa becoming stronger since the formation of the League of Arab States after World War II and the independence of many of its countries during the 1950s and 1960s.[339] The first Conference of Maghreb Economic Ministers that took place in Tunis in 1964 launched the Conseil Permanent Consultatif du Maghreb (CPCM) between Algeria, Libya, Morocco and Tunisia to coordinate and harmonize those countries' development plans and intra-regional trade and relations with the EU.[340] These plans were not carried out for a number of reasons, but mostly because of political rivalries and the dispute between Algeria and Morocco over the question of Western Sahara's sovereignty.[341] Following reconciliation between the member countries in the late 1980s, the first Maghreb Summit of the five heads of state was held in June 1988 at Zeralda, Algeria, and resulted in the establishment of the Maghreb High Commission and five specialized sub-committees to draft a treaty to bring together the northern African countries.[342] A year later, the AMU Treaty was formally signed and ratified.

The objectives and aims of the AMU, as identified in the treaty establishing the AMU, include: reinforcing the fraternal links binding together the Member States and their peoples; realizing progress and prosperity for the Member States and defending their rights; contributing to the preservation of peace based on justice and equality; the pursuit of a common policy in different domains; and working towards the progressive realization of the free movement of persons, services, goods and capital.[343] The main objectives of the AMU are to strengthen all forms of ties among its Member States in order to maintain regional stability and enhance policy coordination and to gradually introduce the free movement and circulation of goods, services and factors of production. The AMU's economic goals include realizing the industrial, agricultural, commercial and social development of its Member States through the commitment of the necessary means to achieve this end, particularly by launching joint projects and expanding global and sectoral economic cooperation programmes.[344]

338 Arab Maghreb Union, 'History', available at www.maghrebarabe.org/en/uma.cfm; see also Department of International Relations and Cooperation of the Republic of South Africa, 'Arab Maghreb Union', available at www.dfa.gov.za/foreign/Multilateral/africa/amu.htm.

339 *Ibid.* 340 *Ibid.*

341 M. Finaish and E. Bell, 'The Arab Maghreb Union', IMF Working Paper WP/94/55, at 1.

342 *Ibid.* at 2. 343 AMU Treaty, Art. 2. 344 *Ibid.* at Art. 3.

At the third meeting of the Council of Heads of State in Libya in March 1991, guidelines were adopted for a strategy of joint Maghreb development specifying four stages of economic integration – a free trade area was to be formed by the end of 1992, a customs union by the end of 1995, a common market by the end of 2000 and a monetary union at some point in time thereafter.[345] No clear and detailed strategy has been developed for the fulfilment of these economic goals, although technical discussions between officials of the Member States have clarified the most important:

FTA	Customs union	Common market	Monetary union
End of 1992	End of 1995	End of 2000	No deadline

However, despite these plans and guidelines, little progress has been made to meet these deadlines. Political instability caused a cessation in the AMU's activities in 1995, disrupting the decision-making process of the organization and preventing the countries from forming mutually beneficial economic arrangements. A lack of adequate infrastructure facilities for intra-market access, of marketing institutions and incentive systems among the countries, high production costs preventing the Maghreb countries from producing internationally competitive products and the undiversified character of the countries' productive activities have all resulted in little intra-regional trade and a stagnation in the regional integration process. However, the Member States have accrued some benefits from the creation of the AMU and subsequent negotiations, such as increased dialogue between the countries and strengthened ties among them. Despite the lack of progress, the regular meetings of the political heads of state have reinforced the members' resolve to address their economic problems together using an integrated strategy.[346]

2 *Organizational structure*

The highest institutional organ of the AMU is the Presidential Council, which is comprised of the heads of state of all of the Member States.[347] Only the Presidential Council has the power to make decisions, which must be made unanimously.[348] The presidency of the Council rotates among the five members, with each country's head of state holding the

345 Finaish and Bell, 'The Arab Maghreb Union', at 7.

346 *Ibid.* at 10.

347 AMU Treaty, at Art. 4.

348 *Ibid.* at Art. 6.

position for a period of one year.[349] The Presidential Council meets regularly twice a year, or extraordinarily if the circumstances so dictate.[350] A Council of Foreign Affairs Ministers also meets regularly to prepare the sessions of the Presidential Council and to examine the questions or proposals submitted to it by the Follow-Up Committee and the Specialized Ministerial Committees.[351] The Follow-Up Committee is comprised of representatives from each Member State who are in charge of the Union's affairs or follow the implementation of Presidential Council resolutions, and which submits the results of its work to the Council of Foreign Affairs Ministers.[352] A Consultative Council, which is comprised of thirty representatives from each Member State, delivers opinions on draft decisions submitted to it by the Presidential Council and makes recommendations on reinforcing the AMU's action and realizing its objectives.[353] The AMU Treaty calls for a Permanent Secretariat General to be defined and a Secretary General designated by the Presidential Council.[354] Several specialized committees have been formed, including committees on the interior, human resources, infrastructure, economy and finances and food security.[355]

The AMU Treaty also establishes a judicial authority comprised of two judges from each Member State, for six-year terms, to 'rule on disputes related to the interpretation and application of the Treaty and agreements concluded within the framework of the Union, submitted to it by the Presidential Council or one of the States parties to the dispute'.[356] The judgments of the judicial authority are enforceable and final.[357] It may also deliver advisory opinions submitted to it by the Presidential Council.[358]

3 *Economic achievements*

During the 1990s, around 25 multilateral agreements have been signed by the five countries that cover a range of subjects such as taxation, customs and central banking, but only five agreements have been ratified by all five Member States.[359] One of the five multilateral treaties that has been signed by all five members is an agreement on trade and tariffs

349 *Ibid.* at Art. 4. 350 *Ibid.* at Art. 5. 351 *Ibid.* at Art. 7. 352 *Ibid.* at Art. 8.
353 *Ibid.* at Art. 12. 354 *Ibid.* at Art. 11.
355 Article 10 of the AMU Treaty provides for the creation of specialized ministerial committees set up by the Presidential Council, which shall define its attributions.
356 AMU Treaty, at Art. 13. 357 *Ibid.* 358 *Ibid.*
359 'Arab Maghreb Union', *Encyclopedia of Business* (2nd edn), available at www.referenceforbusiness.com/encyclopedia/A-Ar/Arab-Maghreb-Union.html.

covering all industrial products.[360] This agreement is aimed at establishing free trade among the members through the elimination of tariffs as well as the elimination of non-tariff barriers.[361] Various projects have been accomplished and initial steps toward a common market have been taken, such as a freer flow of goods and persons among the member countries.[362] Visas are no longer required for member nationals to travel, and there are plans for a common identity card.[363] Resolutions on the integration of transportation have been reached and infrastructural improvements are underway on a railway connecting Tunis, Tunisia and Marrakesh, Morocco and a pipeline to transport gas to Europe from Algeria through Morocco.[364]

Little has been done to implement the agreements or the objectives of the treaty, and despite the creation of many working groups and the initiation of several projects, little tangible progress has been made towards economic integration. Political rivalry has consistently been an issue for cooperation in the region, particularly with respect to the Western Sahara conflict between Morocco and Algeria, the AMU's largest members. Other political issues dividing the North African countries include the international sanctions imposed against Libya, and Libya's dissatisfaction with the other members for their lack of support in opposing the sanctions, civil war in Algeria and border disputes that have interrupted or stalled the free movement of goods and persons within the region.[365] Because of these and other political disputes, the heads of state met only six times before Morocco called for a suspension of the Union's activities in 1995.[366] Furthermore, an increase in terrorist activity has led the AMU member countries to focus attention on anti-terrorism efforts, putting economic and financial reform on the back burner.[367]

360 Finaish and Bell, 'The Arab Maghreb Union', at 8. The other four are agreements in respect of trade in agricultural products, investment guarantees, avoidance of double taxation and phyto-sanitary standards.

361 *Ibid.*; see also 'Arab Maghreb Union – Request for Observer Status: Communication from the Arab Maghreb Union', L/7548 (2 Nov. 1994), 3, available at www.wto.org/gatt_docs/English/SULPDF/91820125.pdf.

362 L. Martinez, 'Algeria, the Arab Maghreb Union and Regional Integration' (Oct. 2006), 6, available at www.euromesco.net/images/59_eng.pdf.

363 'Arab Maghreb Union', *Encyclopedia of Business.* 364 *Ibid.*

365 R.A. Mortimer, 'The Arab Maghreb Union: Myth and Reality', in Y. H. Zoubir (ed.), *North Africa in Transition: State, Society, and Economic Transformation in the 1990s* (1999); see also 'Arab Maghreb Union', *Encyclopedia of Business.*

366 Mortimer, 'The Arab Maghreb Union'.

367 G.C. Hufbauer and C. Brunel, *Maghreb Regional and Global Integration: A Dream to be Fulfilled* (Edward Brothers, Inc., 2008), 10.

The lack of progress can also be attributed to economic obstacles. Intra-regional trade has stagnated at around 3%, a weak trade rate compared to the EU's 60%, 22% for ASEAN and almost 20% for the Southern Common Market (MERCOSUR) countries.[368] AMU's weak intra-regional trade rate can be attributed to the numerous non-tariff and regulatory trade barriers as well as the lack of complementary economic structures between the countries.[369] Morocco and Tunisia, the AMU countries at the most advanced stage of economic development, have relatively open economies and diversified exports, while the economies of Libya and Algeria are more centrally controlled, with exports heavily concentrated in energy products.[370] Furthermore, the EU is the primary importer of products produced in the Maghreb countries and the AMU countries are heavily dependent upon European imports, resulting in less efficient AMU producers because of the proximity, diverse production structures and size of the European markets.[371] This reliance on European and other foreign suppliers is in part because of the strict border restrictions on the flow of people and goods that result in reduced commerce and less inter-regional economic activity.[372]

It has been suggested that bilateral agreements between Maghreb and European countries have the potential to create economic growth.[373] Tunisia has signed several bilateral treaties with other Maghreb and with European countries in recent years, and trade exchanges between Tunisia and the AMU member countries more than doubled between 2005 and 2008.[374] Individual association agreements have also been signed between the EU and Algeria, Morocco and Tunisia and a free trade agreement (FTAg) has been entered into between Morocco and the United States. A direct trade agreement between the AMU and the EU will allow the northern African region to double its exports to the EU and increase per

368 Martinez, 'Algeria, the Arab Maghreb Union', at 6. 369 *Ibid.*

370 Finaish and Bell, 'The Arab Maghreb Union', at 15.

371 *Ibid.* at 14; see also Lahcen ACHY, 'Trade in North Africa: Assessing Regional Integration Potential in North Africa', UN Economic Commission for Africa, ECA-NA/RABAT/ICE/XXI/3/I (April 2006), 5, available at www.uneca.org/sros/na/documents/Trade.pdf.

372 Hufbauer and Brunel, 'Maghreb Regional and Global Integration', at 1.

373 M. Yahia, 'Tunis forum targets Maghreb unity as solution to economic crisis', Magharberia (14 May 2009).

374 *Ibid.* Trade exchanges between Tunisia and the other Maghreb countries went from 1.9 billion dinars in 2005 to 4.2 billion dinars in 2008. Tunisian exports to Maghreb countries increased from 1 billion dinars in 2005 to 1.9 billion dinars in 2008 and imports increased from 900 million dinars in 2005 to 2.3 billion dinars in 2008. *Ibid.*

capita income in the region.[375] It will take an estimated twenty years for Algeria, Morocco, and Tunisia to 'reach the levels of per capita income of those countries, which are at the tail-end in the development list of the Organization for Economic Co-operation and Development'.[376] The World Bank claims that if the AMU pursues commercial and economic integration with the EU through bilateral treaties signed individually, the AMU can achieve a fifteen per cent increase of per capita income.[377] However, most observers using gravity models to estimate trade potentials between member countries based on geographical distance, economic size and other characteristics have consistently found that the level of integration in the northern African region is below that which was expected.[378] These bilateral agreements adopted as the initial approach of the Union aiming at a broad-based liberalization of most products proved unrealistic because of the differences in the Member States' economic, trade and social policies.[379] Attempts to extend these bilateral agreements on a multilateral basis have been unsuccessful, as the countries have found it difficult to agree on a common list of products to circulate freely within the region.[380] There must be macroeconomic and structural reforms to harmonize the economic policies of the AMU members as well as the harmonization of standards such as licensing requirements.[381]

The Maghreb Bank for Investment and External Trade was established in 2002 to engage the private sector and promote trade and investment in the region.[382] The bank provides finance to facilitate trade and undertake agricultural and industrial projects at a national and regional level.[383] The formation of the Maghreb Bank is argued to have the potential to lead to deeper financial integration and to allow for the freer movement of capital within the region through stabilizing exchange rates and making currency fully convertible among the member countries. Progress in reducing tariffs through bilateral preferential trade agreements with the EU and other countries has been made, although the average tariff protection is still

375 C.D. Felice, 'According to the World Bank, Maghreb is Key to EU Development', Medibtikar (13 Apr. 2007).

376 *Ibid.* 377 *Ibid.*

378 World Bank, 'Regional Integration for Global Competitiveness', 36, available at http://siteresources.worldbank.org/INTMENA/Resources/EDP2008_Chap_2.pdf.

379 Finaish and Bell, 'The Arab Maghreb Union', at 23. 380 *Ibid.* at 24. 381 *Ibid.*

382 'Assessing Regional Integration in Africa III', Economic Commission for Africa, African Union (2008), 16, available at www.iss.co.za/uploads/ARIA3NOV08.PDF.

383 *Ibid.*

higher than the world average.[384] Regional integration will create a large regional market, which in turn will bring efficiency gains and attract foreign investment.[385] However, regulatory and other non-tariff barriers to trade must be removed before the AMU can achieve its first goal of attaining the status of a free trade area.

Recent integration initiatives focusing on trade facilitation between Algeria, Morocco and Tunisia began in 2005 at a conference in Algiers, and Libya and Mauritania have been invited to participate in the follow-up work and subsequent conferences.[386] A work programme was formulated at the conference that focuses on seven areas:

(1) harmonizing trade regulations linked to the implementation of FTAs, particularly with respect to non-tariff barriers and preferential treatment of goods from the Maghreb region, as well as rules and associated procedures of origin;
(2) eliminating trade distortions in order to reduce informal trade flows;
(3) continuing tariff reforms aimed at simplifying and reducing customs tariffs;
(4) moving forward with customs reforms;
(5) streamlining document processing;
(6) improving payment systems; and
(7) improving the logistical chain, including transport infrastructure and services related to trade.[387]

An action plan was drawn up by technical working groups that includes: activating the intra-Maghreb Customs Committee to reduce trade distortions and informal trade caused by tariffs and non-tariff barriers; developing a one-stop document processing system; and creating a private sector-led unit to monitor the region's foreign trade.[388] Subsequent regional conferences were scheduled to deal with financial sector reform and financial integration in the region and to address private sector development.[389]

Towards the goal of greater integration in Northern Africa, the Social and Economic Council of the Arab League concluded the Agreement on

384 L. Allain and B. Loko, 'Fresh Impetus Toward Maghreb Integration', IMF Middle East and Central Asia Department (12 Sept. 2007), available at www.imf.org/external/pubs/ft/survey/so/2007/car0912b.htm.

385 Martinez, 'Algeria, the Arab Maghreb Union', at 6.

386 IMF, 'Regional Economic Outlook: Middle East and Central Asia' (Sept. 2006), 24, available at www.imf.org/external/pubs/ft/reo/2006/ENG/02/mreo0906.pdf.

387 *Ibid.* 388 *Ibid.* 389 *Ibid.*

the Greater Arab Free Trade Area (GAFTA) in 1997 to establish GAFTA within ten years, beginning 1 January 2008.[390] GAFTA has seventeen members, including Bahrain, Egypt, Iraq, Jordan, Kuwait, Lebanon, Libya, Morocco, Oman, Palestine, Qatar, Saudi Arabia, Sudan, Syria, Tunisia, United Arab Emirates and Yemen.[391] The Agreement called for the gradual reduction of tariffs and non-tariff barriers on intra-regional trade within a period of ten years by an average rate of ten per cent each year to reach full elimination by 2007.[392] However, the Social and Economic Council decided to accelerate the transition period so that it would end in 2005 instead of 2007, thus increasing the rate of tariff and non-tariff barrier reductions to 20 per cent for the years 2004 and 2005.[393] The Agreement is the most far-reaching trade liberalization agreement in the region, partly because it includes the removal of not only tariffs but also administrative, monetary and quantitative non-tariff barriers to trade such as quotas and provides for trade liberalization in agriculture.[394] It also provides for individual countries to agree to accelerate the liberalization process through bilateral or sub-regional agreements.[395] By liberalizing trade among the Arab countries, the Agreement aims to increase the trade volume within the region, to distribute production among member countries according to their comparative advantages and enhance production efficiency, create competitive domestic markets by providing greater product variety for consumers, attract more foreign direct investments by creating a larger market and to increase economic interdependence between the Arab countries to enhance the stability and security in the region.[396]

In 2005, the tariff removal schedule was completed, although the schedule for the removal of non-tariff barriers was only partially completed.[397] The benefits of GAFTA are disputed. Although intra-regional trade has increased, it is highly concentrated in a few more developed countries, as are imports and exports.[398] Concerns regarding the implementation of

390 'Implementation of the Great Arab Free Trade Agreement: The Case of Syria', Working Paper No. 8, National Agriculture Policy Center of the Ministry of Agricultural and Agrarian Reform, 4, available at www.napcsyr.org/dwnld-files/working_papers/en/08_gafta_en.pdf.

391 *Ibid.* 392 *Ibid.* 393 *Ibid.*

394 J. Abedini and N. Péridy, 'The Greater Arab Free Trade Area (GAFTA): An Estimation of the Trade Effects' (Canadian Economics Association, 2007), 3, available at http://economics.ca/2007/papers/0300.pdf.

395 *Ibid.*

396 *Ibid.*; see also National Agriculture Policy Center, 'Implementation of the Great Arab Free Trade Agreement', at 5.

397 Abedini and Péridy, 'GAFTA', at 1. 398 *Ibid.* at 4.

GAFTA include many issues beyond those affecting the general implementation of African regional integration agreements such as the AMU, like inadequate transport infrastructure and incompatible currencies. One of the major concerns is with the number of exemptions provided for in the Agreement, generally regarding agricultural commodities[399] and the potential for the numerous exemptions to hinder the trade liberalization process and the growth of inter-regional trade. Furthermore, non-tariff barriers remain a constant hindrance to intra-regional trade, although a few forms are addressed by the Agreement.[400] Despite progress with respect to tariff elimination, the integration process in the Arab countries remains behind the AMU's schedule.

G The Southern African Development Community

1 Overview

The Southern African Development Community (SADC) was formed in 1980 with 9 Member States, as the Southern African Development Coordination Conference (SADCC). The SADCC was formed after the adoption of the Lusaka Declaration – Southern Africa: Towards Economic Liberation – in 1980.[401] The founding Member States were Angola, Botswana, Lesotho, Malawi, Mozambique, Swaziland, Tanzania, Zambia and Zimbabwe.[402] The primary aim of the SADCC was to coordinate development programmes to lessen economic dependence on South Africa, which at that time still had an apartheid regime. The Coordination Conference transformed into the Development Community in 1992 when the Declaration and Treaty was signed. SADC's current members include, in addition to the founding members, the Democratic Republic of the Congo, Madagascar, Mauritius, Namibia, Seychelles and South

399 J. Gendrano, 'League of Arab States: The Greater Arab Free Trade Agreement' (2007), 13. With the 'agricultural calendar' provision, each GAFTA state was allowed to use protectionist measures for at most ten agricultural products for seven months out of twelve months a year, with a maximum of 45 months in total for a specific commodity. The reasoning behind the exemptions was to protect certain commodities from facing competition from other states in the region, particularly states participating in GAFTA. States are abusing the exemption list by adding products potentially subject to non-Arab competition to their exception list, fearing strong competition from outside the region.

400 *Ibid.* at 15.

401 SADC, 'Profile', available at www.sadc.int/index/browse/page/52.

402 SADC currently has fifteen members – Angola, Botswana, the Democratic Republic of Congo, Lesotho, Madagascar, Malawi, Mauritius, Mozambique, Namibia, Seychelles, South Africa, Swaziland, Tanzania, Zambia and Zimbabwe. *Ibid.*

Africa: 'The signatories of the SADC Treaty agree that underdevelopment, exploitation, deprivation and backwardness in Southern Africa will only be overcome through economic cooperation and integration.'[403] The objectives of the SADC include the promotion of 'sustainable and equitable economic growth and socio-economic development that will ensure poverty alleviation with the ultimate objective of its eradication', the enhancement of the 'standard and quality of life of the people of Southern Africa' and the support of the 'socially disadvantaged through regional integration'.[404] Additionally, the SADC aims to 'promote self-sustaining development on the basis of collective self-reliance, and the interdependence of Member States'.[405] To achieve this goal, the SADC aims to eliminate barriers to the free movement of goods and services, and capital and labour. The SADC has adopted milestones to facilitate the integration. An FTA was to be formed by 2008, a customs union by 2010, a common market by 2015, a monetary union by 2016 and a single currency by 2018.[406] The SADC successfully launched the SADC FTA on 17 August 2008 during the 28th Summit of SADC Heads of State and Government.

2 *Sequencing*

The sequencing envisioned by the SADC Treaty toward achieving its goals is as follows:

FTA	Customs union	Common market	Monetary union	Economic union with a single currency
To be launched by 2008	To be launched by 2010	To be launched by 2015	To be launched by 2016	To be launched by 2018

3 *The SADC Treaty*

The Treaty Establishing the SADC aims to promote integration and cooperation. In this direction, Article 22 calls for the conclusion of protocols that spell out the objectives and scope of cooperation and integration as

403 *Ibid.*

404 Treaty Establishing the SADC, Chapter 3, Art. 5(1)(a), p. 8, available at www.sadc.int/index/browse/page/52.

405 *Ibid.* at Art. 5(1)(d), p. 8.

406 SADC, available at www.sadc.int.

necessary.[407] These protocols enter into force 30 days after ratification, and Member States can become a party to a protocol by accession. A protocol is only binding on the Member States that are party to the protocol in question.

The Protocol on Trade was created in 1996 with the objectives of furthering the liberalization of intra-regional trade in goods, furthering economic development, diversification and industrialization and forming an FTA in the SADC region. Twelve members of the SADC have ratified the Protocol on Trade, and Angola and the Democratic Republic of Congo will join the SADC FTA at a later stage. Implementation of the SADC Protocol on Trade began in September 2000.

The Protocol on Trade sets out the guidelines for the attainment of the goal of trade liberalization. The process for the phased elimination of tariffs and non-tariff barriers is to be determined by the Committee of Ministers responsible for trade matters, who should have regard for preferential trade agreements between Member States and that the elimination of barriers to trade should be eliminated 'within 8 years from the entry into force of this Protocol'.[408] In determining the process for the elimination of tariffs and non-tariff barriers, the Committee is required to bear in mind that countries which may be or have been adversely affected by the removal of such barriers can apply for more time to eliminate the trade barriers, and that different tariff lines may be applied to different products during the process of eliminating tariffs and non-tariff barriers.

Under the SADC Protocol on Trade, 85 per cent of all intra-regional trade was to be duty free by 2008, and the remaining 15 per cent, consisting of sensitive products, to be liberalized by 2012.[409] Countries were able to choose the products on which to reduce duties so long as the overall goal was achieved. Mauritius agreed to allow 65% of imports to enter its markets duty free in 2000, although Tanzania could only offer 9% that year with the removal of its tariffs to be staggered, 88% by 2008 and 100% lifted by 2012.[410] SADC members that are also members of SACU are required to reduce tariffs on intra-SADC trade faster than other members. SACU provides duty-free entry for 77% of non-SACU imports from SADC members by 2000, and 97% by 2008. South Africa is to eliminate all tariffs by 2012.[411]

407 SADC Treaty, at Chapter 7, Art. 22(1), p. 17.

408 SADC Protocol on Trade, Part 2, Art. 3(1), available at www.sadc.int.

409 Abdoulahi, 'Progress Report on Regional Integration', at 7.

410 *Ibid.* 411 *Ibid.*

The Protocol on Trade calls for the elimination through a phased reduction of import duties on goods originating in Member States.[412] Article 4 further provides that fees and other charges that are commensurate with the costs of any services rendered are to be excluded from the provisions of that Article. [413] Article 7 of the Protocol provides that Member States shall not apply any new quantitative restrictions, and phase out existing quantitative restrictions on the import of goods originating in Member States, but Member States may apply a quota system if the tariff rate under such a system is more favourable than the rate applied under the protocol.[414]

Article 5(1) provides that Member States may not impose any export duties on goods for export into other Member States. Article 5(2), however, allows any Member State to apply export duties that are necessary to prevent erosion of any prohibitions or restrictions which may apply to exports outside of the SADC if no less favourable treatment is granted to Member States than to third countries.[415] The Protocol on Trade Article 8(1) additionally provides that no Member State shall apply any quantitative restrictions on exports to any other Member State. Like Article 5(2), Article 8(2) allows any Member State to take necessary measures 'to prevent erosion of any prohibitions or restrictions which apply to exports outside the Community provided that no less favourable treatment is granted to Member States than to third countries'.[416]

The Trade Protocol requires the Member States to phase out existing quantitative restrictions on imports and exports, and refrain from imposing any new quantitative restrictions, except where otherwise provided in the Protocol. Article 9 lists general exceptions to the phase-out requirement, provided that the measures do not arbitrarily or unjustifiably discriminate between Member States or are not disguised restrictions on intra-SADC trade. Leticia Anthea Grimett argues, with sleight of hand in my view, that 'although the general exceptions clause contains a proviso which aims to prevent protectionism between contracting Member States,

412 SADC Protocol on Trade, at Part B, Art. 4(1).

413 L.A. Grimett, 'Protectionism and Compliance with GATT Article XXIV in Selected Regional Trade Arrangements', 223, available at http://eprints.ru.ac.za/208/01/grimett-thesis.pdf (arguing Art. 4 is inconsistent with the provisions of Art. XXIV (8)(b) of the GATT, since it authorizes the maintenance of quantitative restrictions. That argument, however, ignores the fact that the Enabling Clause creates independent justification for intra-LDC regional cooperation outside of Art. XXIV of the GATT as we saw in Chapter IV).

414 SADC Protocol on Trade, at Part B, Art. 7.

415 *Ibid.* Art. 5(2).

416 *Ibid.* Art. 8(2).

the fact that it provides for the application of these quantitative restrictions between Member States at all, could be interpreted as an infringement of Article XXIV (8)(b)'.[417] GATT aims to eliminate quantitative restrictions in Article XI: General Elimination of Quantitative Restrictions. Article XI (1) reads:

> no prohibitions or restrictions other than duties, taxes or other charges, whether made effective through quotas, import or export licences or other measures, shall be instituted or maintained by any contracting party on the importation of any product of the territory of any other contracting party or on the exportation or sale for export of any product destined for the territory of any other contracting party.[418] Article XI(2) lists specific exceptions when quantitative restrictions may be allowed, and Article XX lists general exceptions in similar language to that found in Article 9 of the SADC Trade Protocol. Quantitative restrictions are discouraged because they 'reduce imports, so that domestic demand pushes up domestic prices until the gap between domestic demand and supply is equal to the quota'.[419] Tariffs are preferred because a tariff 'adds to the import price, reducing domestic demand and increasing domestic supply, so that imports are less'.[420] Tariffs also yield government revenue, can be used to reduce monopolies on domestic industries, and allow for increased imports in certain circumstances which would be to the benefit of the domestic economy.

However, the claim that the SADC Protocol on Trade somehow violates the provisions of Article XXIV of GATT is not well founded. Such a claim is based on textual comparisons; no conduct pursuant to the protocol that is in violation of any GATT provision is available. Second, the enabling clause, as we saw in Chapter IV, provides independent justification for LDC RTAs well outside of Article XXIV, and that argument has not been persuasively dismissed except by reference to GATT as a constitution. Even if GATT was to be regarded as a trade constitution, and I have no problems with that, the interpretations of Article XXIV are so contested that they provide no benchmark at all for assessing whether particular provisions of a regional trade treaty are consistent with the Article or not.

417 Grimett, 'Protectionism and Compliance', at 221–2.

418 GATT Art. XI (1), available at www.wto.org/english/docs_e/legal_e/gatt47_01_e.htm#articleXI.

419 'Quantitative Restrictions on Trade', a Revised Paper presented at the Seventh Trade Policy Coordinating Meeting of CAREC on 6 Sept. 2007, p. 2, available at www.adb.org/Documents/Carec/QRStudy.pdf.

420 *Ibid.*

The Protocol on Trade calls for the gradual reduction of tariffs through a phase-down period. All goods are broken down into four categories of tariffs: A, B, C and E. In Category A, all tariff lines are immediately eliminated from the date of implementation. For Category B goods, the principle of asymmetry applies. In this category, the SACU countries (South Africa, Botswana, Lesotho, Namibia, and Swaziland) reduce their tariff lines by equal instalments from year 1 to year 8, Mauritius and Zimbabwe reduce their tariff lines by equal instalments from year 4 to year 8, and the MMTZ countries (Malawi, Mozambique, Tanzania and Zambia) reduce their tariff lines by equal instalments from year 6 to year 8. Category C applies to sensitive goods, which are goods of economic importance to the Member States. Tariff reduction on these goods starts after the 8-year period. Sensitive goods represent 15 per cent or less of tariff lines. Category E consists of very few goods that are excluded from the tariff reduction scheme, such as firearms.[421] The Protocol on Trade provides that Member States should implement policies and measures to eliminate all forms of existing non-tariff barriers, and refrain from imposing new non-tariff barriers, in relation to intra-SADC trade.[422]

With regard to GATT Article XXIV (5)(b), Grimett argues that the SADC Trade Protocol is compliant.[423] Article XXIV (5)(b) requires an agreement leading to the formation of an FTA not to raise or increase the restrictiveness of duties or regulations on trade with third countries that existed in the territories before the agreement or formation of the FTA. Member States have agreed not to raise import duties beyond those that were in existence before the Trade Protocol and have also agreed not to grant less favourable treatment to third countries than they give to Member States where export duties and quantitative export restrictions are applied. These undertakings ensure that protectionism in trade with third countries will be minimal.

The Trade Protocol allows for Member States to apply for an extension to eliminate tariffs and non-tariff barriers to trade if they may be or have been adversely affected by the removal of tariffs and non-tariff barriers to trade.[424] As most of the countries, excluding South Africa, that are members of SADC are classified as developing or least-developed economies, it is not unpredictable that most will need an extension to eliminate

421 See the SADC FTA Brochure, 7, available at www.sadc.int/fta.
422 SADC Protocol on Trade, at Part B, Art. 6.
423 Grimett, 'Protectionism and Compliance', at 222.
424 SADC Protocol on Trade, at Part B, Art. 3(1)(c).

substantially all trade barriers. However, the time period for the removal of tariffs and non-tariff barriers, according to the Trade Protocol, is eight years. Thus an extension of two years can be granted and still conform to the provisions of GATT Article XXIV (5)(c). The Understanding on the Interpretation of Article XXIV of GATT 1994 provides that a reasonable period of time is ten years, except in exceptional cases. In such circumstances, the country may apply for an extension to the Council for Trade in Goods. Because this provision is similar to that found in Article 3(1)(c) of the SADC Trade Protocol, and because an extension longer than two years is likely to be necessary only in exceptional cases, the 'extension of the period for eliminating tariffs and non-tariff barriers is not an infringement of Article XXIV'.[425]

4 Progress

The Protocol on Trade was signed in 1996 and the implementation of the SADC FTA began in 2000. The liberalization of tariffs has taken place at different rates, the developed countries generally reducing tariffs at a faster rate. Three countries (South Africa, Botswana and Namibia), removed most tariffs in 2000. Middle-income countries, such as Mauritius, gradually reduced their tariffs each year between 2000 and 2008. For LDCs, such as Mozambique and Zambia, tariff reductions were generally introduced during 2007–2008.[426]

SADC attained the status of an FTA in January 2008. Since then, producers and consumers have paid no import tariffs on an estimated 85 per cent of all trade in community goods in the initial 12 countries.[427] The remaining tariff lines will be eliminated by 2012.[428] The Member States have agreed to remove all non-tariff barriers and not to impose any new restrictions, but removal of import and export restrictions has proved difficult and little progress has been made.[429] The reason is that non-tariff barriers often arise from policies that are not intended to restrict imports. For example, an outbreak of foot-and-mouth disease may result in restrictions on the exportation of animals, meat and meat products originating in the affected area. Such a restriction, however, may fall within the general exceptions listed in Article 9 of the Protocol

425 Grimett, 'Protectionism and Compliance', at 222.
426 SADC FTA, available at www.sadc.int/fta.
427 *Ibid.* 428 SADC FTA Brochure, at 7.
429 See the SADC FTA leaflet, available at www.sadc.int/fta.

on Trade. Article 9 allows measures to be taken, as long as they are 'not applied in a manner which would constitute a means of arbitrary or unjustifiable discrimination between Member States, or a disguised restriction on intra-SADC trade', if they are:

(a) Necessary to protect public morals or to maintain public order;
(b) Necessary to protect human, animal or plant life or health;
(c) Necessary to secure compliance with laws and regulations which are consistent with the provisions of the WTO;
(d) Necessary to protect intellectual property rights, or to prevent deceptive trade practices;
(e) Relating to transfer of gold, silver, precious and semi-precious stones, including precious and strategic metals;
(f) Imposed for the protection of national treasures of artistic, historical or archaeological value;
(g) Necessary to prevent or relieve critical shortages of foodstuffs in any exporting Member State;
(h) Relating to the conservation of exhaustible natural resources and the environment; or
(i) Necessary to ensure compliance with existing obligations under international agreements.[430]

To solve the problem of eliminating non-tariff barriers, SADC is establishing a Trade Monitoring and Compliance Mechanism (TMCM) for monitoring the implementation of the FTA with a specific mechanism for identifying and eliminating non-tariff barriers: 'This mechanism has the potential to facilitate the movement of goods and will lead to increased trade'.[431] Another concern is that the rules of origin have become increasingly restrictive and product-specific, resulting in increased administrative costs and making it more difficult for exporters to take advantage of SADC preferences.[432]

The next goal to be achieved is the establishment of a customs union which was expected to be established by 2010, and which includes a common external tariff and the harmonization of behind-the-border policies. The main challenges facing the transition from an FTA are effective implementation, full participation by members and full engagement of the region's business community, and the public in general.[433] The

430 SADC Protocol on Trade, at Art. 9.

431 SADC FTA leaflet.

432 P. Khandelwal, 'COMESA and SADC: Prospects and Challenges for Regional Trade Integration', IMF Working Paper WP/04/227 (Dec. 2004), 12, available at www.imf.org/external/pubs/ft/wp/2004/wp04227.pdf.

433 African Union, 'Status of Integration in Africa', at 58.

Secretariat has concentrated on conducting studies leading to preparations for negotiations on the formation of the customs union, the first two focusing on the model of the customs union and the compatibility of trade policies. The SADC Council of Ministers has approved the establishment of technical working groups which are to initiate work in key areas leading to the formation of the customs union, including a common external tariff, revenue collection and the harmonization of agricultural, industrial, infrastructure, competition and other sectoral policies.[434]

The membership of some SADC countries in the South African Customs Union (SACU), which as a customs union is at a more advanced stage of integration than SADC, makes it necessary for all SADC Member States to reach its level before the SADC customs union can be launched.[435] The membership of several SADC member countries in COMESA, which established a customs union in June 2009, poses additional challenges, because several SADC countries now concurrently belong to two customs unions, with two different common external tariffs and different tariff schedules. Furthermore, overlapping membership has other negative consequences such as duplication of efforts, conflicting duties and obligations and spreading scarce human and financial resources too thinly, resulting in less than full participation and compliance.[436] Thus, there is a need for all of the RECs in the region to collaborate and possibly merge in order to move the integration process forward. To this end, SADC formed a Joint Task Force with COMESA in 2001 in order to harmonize their trade liberalization policies. The Joint Task Force was expanded in 2007 with the inclusion of the EAC, which had adopted a common external tariff and became a customs union in 2005. The first Tripartite Summit was held in Kampala, Uganda in 2008 and efforts to form an EAC, SADC and COMESA FTA are well under way, as we saw earlier in the chapter. Such an FTA would be a step towards resolving the issue of overlapping membership and advancing integration in the region. Along with the issue of overlapping membership, challenges to the process of deepening regional integration that face the region 'include differentiated levels of economic integration within the region, the varied pace of implementation, inadequate infrastructure and capacity constraints at both the Member State and the regional/Secretariat level'.[437]

434 'Assessing Regional Integration in Africa IV', UN Economic Commission on Africa, 14–15, available at www.uneca.org/eca_resources/Publications/books/aria4/ARIA4Full.pdf.

435 African Union, 'Status of Integration in Africa', at 64.

436 Khandelwal, 'COMESA and SADC', at 14.

437 African Union, 'Status of Integration in Africa', at 65.

The Regional Indicative Strategic Development Plan (RISDP), launched in August 2004, was designed to provide strategic direction for the SADC programmes and projects by aligning the objectives and priorities with the policies and strategies that are to be pursued in order to achieve these objectives over a fifteen-year period.[438] Most of the SADC policies and programmes were designed by independent sectoral committees and thus lacked coordination and had weak inter-sectoral linkages.[439] The RISDP identifies and strengthens linkages between the programmes and policies of the various sectors in order to improve efficiency and the effective implementation of the SADC Program of Action.[440] Indicative in nature, the RISDP outlines the necessary conditions to be attained towards the goal of regional integration and development, setting four targets to be reached within a reasonable and feasible time frame that takes into account constraints particular to the region.[441] The RISDP recognizes the need for a flexible approach to the implementation of policy reforms and deepening regional integration due to the differences existing between member countries.[442] Such flexibility is certainly a primary feature of African RTAs, as I argued more fully in Chapters I, II and III.

The objectives of the Strategic Plan include enhancing economic competitiveness and the diversification of production structures and exports through the promotion of intra-regional trade, productive investment and technology cooperation.[443] The ultimate goal to be achieved through the stages of economic integration is the formation of an economic union. Towards this end, SADC drafted a Competition Policy Model and finalized the harmonization framework expected to have been put in place by 2009 for implementation by 2010.[444] The Model, by removing barriers to competition, is to create conditions which will enable markets to function competitively to the benefit of consumers and businesses alike.[445]

SADC is working towards the establishment of a customs union. The formation of a customs union poses difficulties because the varying levels and complexity of tariff structures of individual member countries will make it difficult to formulate a common external tariff.[446] Another

438 SADC Regional Indicative Strategic Development Plan, Chapter 1, s. 6, available at www.sadc.int/index/browse/page/319.

439 *Ibid.* 440 *Ibid.* 441 *Ibid.* 442 *Ibid.*

443 *Ibid.* at Annex Table 4.10, Trade and Economic Liberalization and Development.

444 African Union, 'Status of Integration in Africa', at 66. 445 *Ibid.*

446 P. Elago and P. Kalenga, 'Whither the SADC Customs Union?', in *Monitoring Regional Integration Yearbook 2007* (Tralac, 2008), 8, available at www.garnet.sciencespobordeaux.fr/Garnet%20papers%20PDF/ELAGO%20Paulina%20&%20KALENGA%20Paul.pdf.

difficulty facing the establishment of a common external tariff regime is harmonizing the different rationales behind individual countries' use of tariffs, as some are heavily dependent on customs duties for government revenue, while others primarily use tariffs as protectionist measures with respect to sensitive sectors or as a part of their industrial policy goals.[447] A customs revenue collection, disbursal and sharing mechanism needs to be created in order to mitigate the effects of the adoption of a common external tariff policy.[448] Progress towards establishing a customs union is also hampered by overlapping membership in multiple RECs. To resolve these issues, the three RECs in the region, COMESA, SADC and EAC, met in October 2008 and agreed to form a larger FTA, encompassing the three organizations, leading eventually to the formation of a single customs union.[449] At the 2008 meeting, the Heads of State and Government of the three RECs also agreed to develop a roadmap towards the goal of establishing the enlarged FTA and directed the three groups to accelerate the development of joint programmes to enhance cooperation and coordination in industrial and competition policies.[450] With overlapping membership and its consequences in mind, SADC made a decision in 2009 to delay the establishment of a customs union.[451] However, it has failed to reach the revised deadline for adopting a customs union and it is reported that the ministerial task force on regional integration will discuss the protocol in December 2011.[452] It has been agreed that there is a need to first continue with the consolidation of the SADC FTA, with particular emphasis on coordinating and furthering the development of the SADC-EAC-COMESA Tripartite FTA.[453] Another issue that has delayed the implementation of the SADC customs union is the membership of five SADC members in SACU and the ensuing complications over the adoption of a common external tariff. Since SACU is already at the level of a customs union, the two trade blocs must work closely with one another

447 *Ibid.* at 8–9. 448 *Ibid.* at 12.

449 UN Economic Commission on Africa, 'Assessing Regional Integration in Africa IV', at 16.

450 *Ibid.*

451 E. Bursvik *et al.*, 'Supporting Regional Integration in East and Southern Africa – Review of Select Issues' Preface (28 Apr. 2010), available at www.tralac.org/cgi-bin/giga.cgi?cmd=cause_dir_news_item&cause_id=1694&news_id=86141&cat_id=1033.

452 Botswana Press Agency, Gaborone, 'SADC Fails to Meet Deadline', Trade Law Centre for Southern Africa (19 Aug. 2010), available at www.tralac.org/cgi-bin/giga.cgi?cmd=cause_dir_news_item&cause_id=1694&news_id=91465&cat_id=1026.

453 *Ibid.*

to create complementary policies and to advance all SADC members to the level of the SACU members.

The SADC has also made little progress towards the implementation of its Protocol on the Facilitation of Movement of Persons – of the nineteen SADC members, only nine have signed it, and a mere four have ratified it.[454] The 2010 FIFA World Cup, held in South Africa, provided an impetus towards the implementation of the Protocol and the conclusion of bilateral agreements on establishing visa exemptions in order to facilitate travel during the World Cup.[455] Since the 2009 Meeting of the SADC Ministers of Foreign Affairs Council, the organization has taken significant steps towards facilitating the free movement of goods and services as well; for example, harmonizing customs procedures and instruments such as the electronic exchange of customs data, adopting a single customs administrative document, the SADC CD, to streamline customs declarations within the region, creating a nomenclature of common tariffs, reviewing the rules of origin and coordinating trade liberalization through the tripartite task force between COMESA, EAC and SADC.[456] Trade policies must be harmonized and infrastructure must be improved to enhance market access and promote intra-regional trade in order to achieve deeper regional integration and sustainable development.

SADC now aims for the establishment of a customs union in 2012, when all of its Member States' tariff regimes are expected to be liberalized.[457] SADC reportedly has liberalized 85 per cent of trade and is now in the process of phasing out tariffs for trade in sensitive goods.[458] Slowing down the process of becoming a full FTA is the fact that not all SADC Member States are members of the FTA, and three unnamed SADC members that are members of the FTA have requested extensions or deferrals of the phase-out schedule for sensitive products.[459] The organization's pattern of delaying and extending deadlines could develop into a serious problem, because members may begin to think that they are not being held fully accountable and can renege on commitments without serious consequences. In order to prevent this mindset within the region, SADC must establish an effective implementation and monitoring mechanism through which members are held accountable for commitments and progress is monitored to ensure accomplishment of set goals.

454 Bursvik, 'Supporting Regional Integration', at 21. 455 *Ibid.* at 22. 456 *Ibid.*

457 F. Njini, 'SADC Limps Towards a Common Market', Trade Law Centre for Southern Africa (13 Aug. 2010), available at www.tralac.org/cgi-bin/giga.cgi?cmd=cause_dir_news_item&cause_id=1694&news_id=91207&cat_id=1026.

458 *Ibid.* 459 *Ibid.*

H Southern African Customs Union

1 Overview

The Southern African Customs Union (SACU), the world's oldest customs union, was initially formed as a result of the 1889 Customs Union Convention between the British Colony of Cape of Good Hope and the Orange Free State Boer Republic.[460] A new agreement, signed on 29 June 1910, was in effect until 1969. The primary goal of the customs territory was to promote economic development through the regional coordination of trade.[461] The 1910 Agreement created a common external tariff on goods imported into the region from third countries, the free movement within the region of SACU-manufactured products without any duties or quantitative restrictions and a revenue-sharing formula for the distribution of customs and excise revenues collected by the SACU.[462] During the period in which the 1910 Agreement was in force, South Africa administered the common SACU revenue pool, set SACU import duties and excise policy.[463] After issues arose from the inequitable revenue-sharing and structural issues of management and decision-making processes came into play, the British High Commission Territories called for a revision of the 1910 Agreement, and negotiations began after the British High Commission Territories gained their independence in the 1960s.[464] The new agreement was signed on 11 December 1969 by Botswana, Lesotho, Swaziland and South Africa. Two major changes provided in the 1969 agreement were the inclusion of excise duties in the revenue pool and a multiplier in the revenue-sharing formula that enhanced Botswana, Lesotho and Swaziland revenues each year by 42 per cent.[465] However, problems similar to those under the 1910 Agreement arose, particularly regarding South Africa's sole decision-making power over customs and excise policies.[466] Concerns over the fairness of the revenue-sharing formula still existed, and negotiations to reform the 1969 Agreement began after the democratic transition in South Africa in November 1994, culminating in the creation of a new agreement, which was signed on 21 October 2002.[467]

The 2002 Agreement, which entered into force on 16 July 2004, addressed several issues that had plagued the customs territory since its

460 SACU, 'History of SACU', available at www.sacu.int/about.php?include=about/history.html.

461 *Ibid.* 462 *Ibid.* 463 *Ibid.* 464 *Ibid.*

465 *Ibid.* 466 *Ibid.* 467 *Ibid.*

inception. First, the 2002 Agreement established an independent Administrative Secretariat, with headquarters in Windhoek, Namibia, which was designed to oversee SACU.[468] Several other independent institutions were also created under the 2002 Agreement in order to establish a system of joint decision-making processes in which each member country participated equally.[469] Additionally, policy coordination in several areas, including agriculture, industry, competition, unfair trade practices and protection of infant industries, was provided for in the 2002 Agreement.[470] Second, the revenue-sharing formula was revised to include a customs excise and development component.[471] Under the 2002 agreement, South Africa was to manage the Common Revenue Pool for a transitional period of two years, after which a Member State or a SACU institution is to be appointed by the Council to manage the Pool.[472] Finally, the question of external trade was addressed, such as the need to develop strategies that enhance the region's political, social, economic and cultural integration – while simultaneously taking into consideration the protection of the economies of the smaller Member States.[473]

In addition to addressing several outstanding issues, the 2002 Agreement also states the objectives of SACU. Among the objectives listed in Article 2 are: the facilitation of cross-border movement of goods between Member States; the promotion of conditions of fair competition in the customs territory; to increase substantially the economic development, diversification, industrialization and competitiveness of its members; the promotion of Member States' integration into the global economic system through enhanced trade and investment; and the facilitation of the development of common policies and strategies.[474] The SACU vision is to establish an 'economic community with equitable and sustainable development' that is 'dedicated to the welfare of its people for a common future'.[475]

2 *Trade Liberalization Scheme*

Part 5 of the 2002 SACU Agreement sets forth the trade liberalization scheme to be followed by SACU Member States. Goods imported into one

468 Southern African Customs Union Agreement 2002, Arts 3, 10, available at www.sacu.int/main.php?include=docs/legislation/2002-agreement/part3.html.

469 SACU, 'History of SACU'. 470 *Ibid.* 471 *Ibid.*

472 SACU Agreement 2002, at Pt. 6, Art. 33(1), (3). 473 SACU, 'History of SACU'.

474 SACU Agreement 2002, at Pt. 1, Art. 2.

475 SACU, 'About SACU: Vision and Mission', available at www.sacu.int/about.php?include=about/mission.html.

Member State from another Member State which are grown, produced or manufactured in the region are to be free of customs duties and quantitative restrictions, although member countries retain the right to impose restrictions on imports or exports for the protection of certain enumerated areas in accordance with national legislation and regulations.[476] Additionally, members are not allowed to impose any duties on goods originally imported to a member from outside the region upon the importation of such goods into a Member State.[477] On the recommendation of the Tariff Board, the Council is to approve customs duties that are to be applied to goods imported into the region from outside the area.[478] Further, members are to apply identical rebates, refunds or drawbacks of customs duties on imported goods.[479]

In SACU, the trade facilitation programme is a comprehensive and integrated approach aimed towards developing a predictable, transparent and consistent system in which international trade transactions are completed. It covers all of the steps necessary to facilitate the free movement of goods across borders. Trade facilitation in SACU is based on 'internationally accepted norms and practices resulting from the simplification of formalities and procedures; the standardization and improvement of physical infrastructure and facilities and the harmonization of applicable laws and regulations'.[480] Ultimately, trade facilitation aims to reduce transaction costs and the complexity of international trade as well as to improve the region's trading environment while optimizing efficient, effective levels of governmental control and revenue collection.[481] One of SACU's primary objectives is to facilitate the cross-border movement of goods between Member States, and accordingly, the 2002 Agreement provides for freedom of transit across members' territories and the non-discrimination of transport operators from within the region.[482] The 2002 SACU Agreement requires the application of similar legislation regarding customs and excise duties, customs cooperation, use of common customs documentation and common procedures and practices.[483]

Under the 2002 Agreement, SACU Member States are obliged to take appropriate measures to ensure that the provisions of the agreement are effectively and harmoniously applied, including arrangements regarding customs cooperation, and members must also take such measures as

476 SACU Agreement 2002, at Pt. 5, Art. 18. 477 *Ibid.* at Art. 19.

478 *Ibid.* at Art. 20(1). 479 *Ibid.* at Art. 20(2).

480 SACU, 'Trade Facilitation: An Overview', available at www.sacu.int/tradef.php?include=about/tradef/overview.html.

481 *Ibid.* 482 SACU Agreement 2002, at Arts 2, 24, 27.

483 SACU, 'Trade Facilitation: An Overview'.

are necessary to facilitate the simplification and harmonization of trade procedures and documentation.[484] SACU countries must apply similar legislation with regard to customs and excise duties.[485]

The 2002 SACU Agreement provides for the freedom of transit of goods consigned to and from the territories of other Member States, without discrimination. However, a member may impose conditions upon such transit as are deemed necessary to protect its legitimate interests respecting goods whose importation into the member country is prohibited on certain grounds, such as public morals, health or security, or in pursuance of a multilateral international agreement to which the member is a party.[486] Further, under the 2002 Agreement, SACU Member States 'recognize the right of each Member State to prohibit or restrict the importation into or exportation from its area of any goods for economic, social, cultural or other reasons as may be agreed upon by the Council'.[487] This provision does not permit the prohibition or restriction on imports of goods grown, produced or manufactured in other member countries for the purpose of protecting the member's own industries producing such goods.[488] The SACU members commit to refrain from subjecting the transit of goods through their territory to transport rate discrimination by public authorities, and undertake to ensure that applicable tariffs within each member's territory to the conveyance of goods by publicly-owned transport to and from other members' countries are equally favourable as the tariffs applicable to the carriage of similar goods within such member's area.[489]

Under the 2002 Agreement, Member States are permitted to maintain preferential trade and other similar arrangements that are in existence at the time the agreement enters into force, although members are not allowed to negotiate or enter into new preferential trade arrangements with third parties or to amend existing arrangements without the other members' consent.[490] For the purpose of undertaking negotiations with third parties, a common negotiating mechanism is to be established by the Member States.[491]

The 2002 SACU Agreement permits the governments of Botswana, Lesotho, Namibia or Swaziland to temporarily levy additional duties on imported goods in order to enable infant industries within their territory to meet competition from other producers and manufacturers in the

484 SACU Agreement 2002, at Art. 23. 485 *Ibid.* at Art. 22. 486 *Ibid.* at Art. 24.
487 *Ibid.* at Art. 25(1). 488 *Ibid.* at Art. 25(3). 489 *Ibid.* at Art. 27.
490 *Ibid.* at Art. 31(1), (3). 491 *Ibid.* at Art. 31(2).

SACU region if such duties are levied equally on goods grown, produced or manufactured in the region and similar products originating externally.[492] This provision applies irrespective of whether externally-produced goods are imported directly or from another Member State. The term 'infant industry' as used in the agreement refers to an industry which has been established in a Member State's territory for no longer than eight years, and the protection of such infant industries is to last for a period of eight years.[493]

In an effort to promote trade facilitation and modernize customs administrations, a consultation process was initiated in 2007 between SACU Member States and the World Customs Organization (WCO).[494] The focus of the consultation was on the identification of priority areas of intervention to be regionally implemented, which culminated in the formation of a comprehensive Customs Development Programme for SACU. This programme was adopted by the SACU Council of Ministers in December 2008. The Customs Development Programme builds on the progress achieved under the five customs initiatives pursued by SACU since 2004. The programme's ultimate objective is to contribute to the development of a sustainable and improved economy with respect to trade, security and social protection. This is to be accomplished through: the development of customs authorities, which are to be fair and effective trade management partners; the development of revenue collection services and modern social protection; assisting SACU members in complying with international customs instruments; and modernizing the Member States' respective customs administrations.[495] Specifically, the programme aims to assist the customs authorities in designing and implementing a comprehensive regional reform programme, focusing on various areas, including regional customs policy, customs legislation, risk management, trade partnerships, standard operating procedures in the region and information technology connectivity.[496] It is envisaged that once the programme is successfully completed and incorporated, SACU as a whole and individual member countries will realize benefits such as: reduced costs to governments and traders; predictability and transparency

492 *Ibid.* at Art. 26(1).

493 *Ibid.* at Art. 26(2), (3). The protection accorded to infant industries under the SACU Agreement 2002 is to last for an eight-year period unless 'otherwise determined by the Council'. *Ibid.* at Art. 26(3).

494 SACU, 'Trade Facilitation: SACU-WCO Customs Development Programme', available at www.sacu.int/tradef.php?include=about/tradef/customs.html.

495 *Ibid.* 496 *Ibid.*

in procedures and legislative requirements; increased competitiveness of regional firms; improved cooperation and collaboration with various stakeholders; and sustainable customs reform and modernization efforts in the region.[497]

3 Progress

One of the problems consistently plaguing SACU is the high degree of inequality in the levels of economic development between the Member States. South Africa has traditionally dominated the region and such dominance has been reflected in SACU's history, particularly South Africa's sole decision-making power over trade and industrial policies and its control and management of the revenue-sharing formula and the Common Revenue Pool. South Africa's dominance in the region is reflected in SACU's statistics. For example, during the period studied in the 2009 WTO Trade Policy Review, South Africa accounted for over 90 per cent of the area's GDP.[498] As of November 2009, the only trade policy instruments that had been harmonized were: the applied customs tariff; excise duties; duty rebates, refunds and drawbacks; customs valuation; non-preferential rules of origin; and contingency trade remedies.[499] While the common external tariff has been somewhat simplified since 2003, internal taxes such as the value-added tax, as well as customs procedures, must also be harmonized in order to foster economic integration.[500] The 2009 WTO Trade Policy Review suggests that the complete implementation of the 2002 Agreement would result in the further harmonization of policies, deeper economic integration and more balanced development.[501] In an effort to further harmonize trade policy, SACU members have agreed to negotiate new preferential trade arrangements with third parties as a group.[502]

SACU has made little progress on regional integration since the signing of the 2002 Agreement. The Agreement called for the establishment of several institutions to form a more democratic organization, yet institutions such as the SACU Tariff Board, the Common Negotiating Mechanism and

497 *Ibid.*

498 'WTO Trade Policy Review: Report by the Secretariat', Southern African Customs Union Doc. No. WT/TPR/S/222 (30 Sept. 2009), at 1, para. 1, available at www.wto.org/english/tratop_e/tpr_e/tp322_e.htm.

499 *Ibid.* at vii, para. 4. 500 *Ibid.* at 16, para. 73. 501 *Ibid.* at vii, para. 4.

502 *Ibid.* at vii–viii, para. 8; see also 2002 SACU Agreement, at Art. 31(3).

the Ad Hoc Tribunal have yet to become operational.[503] Furthermore, the 2002 Agreement calls for the adoption of joint policies, but no common SACU policies are currently in place.[504] At the July 2010 Summit of the SACU Heads of State, it was agreed that SACU will work on strengthening internal matters, such as ensuring that all agreements on industrial, agricultural and competition policies, unfair trade practices and other priority commitments in the 2002 Agreement are being implemented.[505] The Heads of State decided that policies and procedures must be developed which will lead to the establishment of competent institutions. It was further agreed that a SACU trade and tariff policy should be developed, along with a trade strategy that supports industrialization within the region and initiatives to promote intra-regional trade.[506]

A step has been taken by one SACU member towards the goal of establishing the SACU Tariff Board which, under the 2002 Agreement, is to make recommendations to be approved or denied by the Council as to the level and changes of customs, anti-dumping, countervailing and safeguard duties on goods imported from outside the region.[507] Each Member State is to establish a national body, whose function is to conduct preliminary investigations and to make recommendations to the Tariff Board regarding any tariff changes.[508] These national bodies are to be established by April 2011. Botswana is expected to become the first SACU member to establish such a national body.[509] Botswana's national body will be responsible for various trade issues, such as investigating and evaluating applications for alleged dumping or subsidized exports into the country, instituting safeguard measures, amending customs duties, determining eligibility for infant industry protection, regulating the import and export of restricted goods and making recommendations to the SACU Tariff Board.[510] The Tariff Board was to have been established by March 2009, but is not currently operational. Other issues, such as

503 G. Erasmus, 'Will SACU Have a Permanent Summit?', Trade Law Centre for Southern Africa (11 May 2010), available at www.tralac.org/cgi-bin/giga.cgi?cmd=cause_dir_news_item&cause_id=1694&news_id=86783&cat_id=1058.

504 *Ibid.*

505 D. Heita, 'SACU Advocates Win-Win Solution on EPA Negotiations', Trade Law Centre for Southern Africa (10 July 2010), available at www.tralac.org/cgi-bin/giga.cgi?cmd=cause_dir_news_item&cause_id=1694&news_id=90029&cat_id=1026.

506 *Ibid.*

507 SACU Agreement 2002, at Art. 8(2).

508 *Ibid.* at Art. 14(1).

509 M. Mguni, 'Botswana Pioneers SACU Tariff Body', Trade Law Centre for Southern Africa (28 July 2010), available at www.tralac.org/cgi-bin/giga.cgi?cmd=cause_dir_news_item&cause_id=1694&news_id=90444&cat_id=1026.

510 *Ibid.*

EPA negotiations with the EU and dealing with the global recession, have taken the stage and pushed the implementation of the 2002 Agreement to the back burner.[511] The organization's centenary celebration in 2010 brought renewed vigour to the issue of regional integration and efforts will hopefully be made towards implementing the 2002 Agreement, especially regarding the establishment of effectively functioning institutions.

Differences between the SACU Member States' policies have been exacerbated by the recent EPA negotiations with the EU and the signing of an interim EPA by three of the SACU members – Botswana, Lesotho and Swaziland. The signing of the interim EPA by only a few of the Member States calls into question their commitment to the customs union, as under the 2002 Agreement members are bound to negotiate collectively with third parties.[512] However, Botswana and Namibia were faced with a difficult decision regarding their beef exports to the EU, since outside of the EPA the two countries would have to rely on a general system of preferences which does not include beef.[513] Without the EPAs, Botswana, Swaziland and Lesotho would lose their preferential access to key European markets and aid.[514] After the summit held on 15 and 16 July 2010, the Department of Trade and Industry Chief Director for Multilateral Relations, Xololwa Mlumbi-Peter, said that the Heads of State agreed that the organization should take a unified approach and should continue to engage collectively in negotiations regarding the EPAs.[515] SACU Executive Secretary, Tswelopele Moremi, stated that although following the principle of unified engagement in trade negotiations with third parties, the different levels of development between Member States and individual states' capacities must be taken into account. Moremi stated that 'current calendars and strategic opportunities require that we do things in a different way to the benefit of all members of SACU'.[516] A compromise must be reached between the SACU countries that have signed the EPA and South Africa and Namibia, who maintain that the EPAs undermine regional integration efforts and that the EU's increased access to the SACU markets will have a negative effect on the African countries' economies.[517]

511 *Ibid.*

512 D. Pressly, '"Disappointing" SACU Talks Fail to Resolve Disunity over EU Deals', Trade Law Centre for Southern Africa (20 July 2010), available at www.tralac.org/cgi-bin/giga.cgi?cmd=cause_dir_news_item&cause_id=1694&news_id=90030&cat_id=1026.

513 *Ibid.* Beef is a key export item for both of the countries.

514 *Ibid.* 515 *Ibid.* 516 Heita, 'SACU Advocates Win-Win'.

517 M. Cohen, 'Southern African Leaders Hold Summit to Rescue 100-Year-Old Customs Union', Trade Law Centre for Southern Africa (15 July 2010), available

The global recession has also created tensions within the group, as pressure on the budget mounts. The financial crisis has spurred South Africa to voice complaints regarding the revenue-sharing formula that is currently in place and the perception in South Africa that its customs receipts are bankrolling the smaller SACU nations.[518] Officially devised as a method of compensating the smaller SACU economies for their long-standing cessation of trade and industrial policy autonomy to South Africa, revenue sharing has been an outstanding issue within SACU for years.[519] At the July 2010 Summit, the SACU Heads of State agreed to reconsider the revenue-sharing formula.[520] South Africa wants to revise the formula so that it would retain some of the income generated by the tariffs on goods imported into its territory, although a move that would decrease the amount of revenue received by the other SACU members under the formula would have drastic consequences for the smaller economies.[521] The four smaller SACU nations, in particular Swaziland and Lesotho, who derive over half of their budget revenue from SACU's income, are dependent upon the revenue received from the Common Revenue Pool and have already suffered from the decreased revenues due to the downturned economy.[522]

In order to rebound from its current unstable position, SACU must implement many changes. Most importantly, strong institutions in which all Member States participate equally must be established and become operational to speak on behalf of SACU. These institutions must work to formulate joint policies and to harmonize existing policies in order to present a united front when dealing with third parties. The harmonization of SACU policies with those of the other African RTAs is also important as plans for deeper integration are set in motion by the other organizations. An agreement must be reached with regard to the EPAs being negotiated with the EU that takes into account the divergent levels of economic development within the region, while complying with the 2002 Agreement's requirement of unified engagement with third parties in trade negotiations.

It has been mentioned that the 2002 SACU Agreement may be renewed in a direction that would include areas that have previously been ignored,

at www.tralac.org/cgi-bin/giga.cgi?cmd=cause_dir_news_item&cause_id=1694&news_id=89865&cat_id=1026.

518 E. Cropley, 'Southern Africa Grasps Trade Subsidy Nettle', Trade Law Centre for Southern Africa (19 July 2010), available at www.tralac.org/cgi-bin/giga.cgi?cmd=cause_dir_news_item&cause_id=1694&news_id=89969&cat_id=1026.

519 *Ibid.* 520 *Ibid.* 521 Erasmus, 'Permanent Summit?'.

522 *Ibid.*; see also Cropley, 'Southern Africa Grasps Trade'.

such as market and monetary integrations, trade in services, finance and investment, government procurement and the environment.[523] Expanding the areas of cooperation and policy harmonization will only serve to facilitate regional economic integration in the future. But first the organization must establish operational institutions that are capable of administering the trade arrangement and developing unified policies across the various areas of cooperation.

I Community of Sahel-Saharan States

1 Overview

The Community of Sahel-Saharan States (CEN-SAD) was established on 4 February 1998 in Tripoli.[524] Its six founding members are Burkina Faso, Chad, Libya, Mali, Niger and Sudan, but since its creation twenty-two other countries have joined its ranks.[525] CEN-SAD was established as a framework for integration and was designed to work together with the other RECs and the African Union to strengthen peace, security and stability in the region and to achieve global economic and social development.[526] CEN-SAD was recognized as a regional economic community during the 36th Ordinary Session of the Conference of Leaders and Heads of State and Government of the Organization of African Unity in July 2000.[527] The overall objective of CEN-SAD is to satisfy the wish for economic, political, social and cultural integration in accordance with the United Nations Charter, the OAU Charter, the Abuja Treaty and the constitutive documents of the other RECs.[528]

523 W. Masinga, '2002 SACU Deal to be Renewed', Trade Law Centre for Southern Africa (14 July 2010), available at www.tralac.org/cgi-bin/giga.cgi?cmd=cause_dir_news_item&cause_id=1694&news_id=89788&cat_id=1026.

524 CEN-SAD, 'About CEN-SAD', available at www.cen-sad.org/new/index.php?option=com_content&task=view&id=33&Itemid=76.

525 *Ibid.* The other members include Benin, Central African Republic, Comoros, Côte d'Ivoire, Djibouti, Egypt, Eritrea, Gambia, Ghana, Guinea, Guinea–Bissau, Kenya, Liberia, Mauritania, Morocco, Nigeria, São Tomé and Príncipe, Senegal, Sierra Leone, Somalia, Togo and Tunisia.

526 See African Union, 'Regional Economic Communities, Community of Sahel-Saharan States', available at www.africa-union.org/root/au/recs/cen_sad.htm.

527 *Ibid.*

528 Observer Status for the Community of Sahel-Saharan States in the General Assembly, 'Explanatory Memorandum: Annex 1 to the Letter dated 24 July 2001 from Permanent Representative of Sudan to the United Nations addressed to the Secretary-General', A/56/191, 2, available at www.un.org/documents/ga/docs/56/a56191.pdf.

2 *Treaty establishing the Community*

Article I of the Treaty establishing CEN-SAD lists as the overriding objective of the organization to establish a comprehensive economic union by implementing a strategy based on a development plan to be integrated into the national development policies of its Member States.[529] The development plan is to include investment in the agricultural, industrial, energy, social and cultural fields.[530] All restrictions hampering the integration of the member countries are to be removed by facilitating free movement of persons and capital and promoting the interests of the citizens of Member States, ensuring freedom of residence, employment, ownership and economic activity, and ensuring the free movement of services, goods and commodities of regional origin.[531] External trade is to be promoted through the formulation and implementation of an investment policy for Member States and increased provision is to be made for improvement to infrastructural links between Member States such as land, air and maritime transport and communications through the implementation of joint projects.[532] An agreement is to be reached giving citizens of the signatory countries equal rights, privileges and duties as provided in the member countries' individual constitutions, and all levels of educational and pedagogical systems – in the technical, scientific and cultural fields – are to be harmonized and coordinated.[533]

The trade liberalization programme was launched in 1991 in accordance with the Abuja Treaty and with the technical assistance and guidance of the UN Economic Commission for Africa and the African Development Bank.[534] It also launched the process of facilitating the free movement of persons, goods and services, which is an important issue to CEN-SAD's major objectives and identified in the treaty establishing the Community.[535] A protocol on free movement is planned and transitional measures that exempt holders of diplomatic and service passports and special envoys from visas are in place.[536]

CEN-SAD has concluded several partnership and cooperation agreements with the UN Economic Commission for Africa and the Permanent Inter-State Committee on Drought Control in the Sahel.[537] Since its establishment, CEN-SAD has been working towards the goal of creating a common market. To this end, the organization has implemented a variety

529 *Ibid.* 530 *Ibid.* 531 *Ibid.* 532 *Ibid.* at 3. 533 *Ibid.*
534 UN Economic Commission on Africa, 'Assessing Regional Integration in Africa IV', at 17.
535 *Ibid.* 536 *Ibid.* at 18. 537 *Ibid.* at 3–4.

of sectoral programmes and policies with emphasis on some priority sectors such as infrastructure, food security, desertification control and the promotion and facilitation of intra-regional trade.[538] At the 6th Ordinary Session of the Executive Council in 2001, the Council exchanged views on the economic integration process and considered that the steps taken by CEN-SAD should be based on a long-term global strategic plan.[539] This integration plan, it was determined, should take into consideration the needs of member countries and the possibilities of integration of projects of goods and services production, as well as the financial resources.[540]

The second meeting of ministers in charge of trade, held in Tunis in March 2003, recommended the creation of a free trade zone after analysing the intra-community trade.[541] Subsequently, at the 5th Session of the Conference of Leaders and Heads of State of CEN-SAD held in Niamey in March 2003, a recommendation was made to the General Secretariat to continue the discussions both between Member States and the international organizations with a view to meet the requirements for the creation of a free trade zone.[542] A study was conducted in 2006 by the General Secretariat in collaboration with the African Development Bank to evaluate the trade situation of Member States by identifying tariff and non-tariff obstacles and to propose a trade liberalization programme with an implementation plan to intensify intra-regional trade.[543] The findings of the study were structured around three proposed scenarios for tariff elimination. The first takes into account the differences in development levels between the members and proposes a specific tariff elimination schedule – for LDCs there is an annual tariff reduction of 12.5% over a period of eight years, and for the rest of the countries a four-year period in which to eliminate tariffs, with the annual rate of 20% for the first two years and 30% for the last two years.[544] The second scenario provides for an identical tariff elimination scheme for all countries alike over a six-year period, with an annual reduction rate of 20% for the first two years and 20% for the remaining four years.[545] Under the third scenario,

538 Report of the 6th Ordinary Meeting of the Executive Council, 22–3 August 2001, available at www.uneca.org/CEN-SAD/reportofthe6thordinarysessionoftheEC.htm.

539 *Ibid.* 540 *Ibid.*

541 CEN-SAD, 'Trade Sector', available at www.cen-sad.org/new/index.php?option=com_content&task=view&lang=en&id=150.

542 *Ibid.* 543 *Ibid.*

544 African Union, 'Status of Integration in Africa', at 94. 545 *Ibid.* at 95.

each Member State presents a tariff elimination scheme over an eight-year period, beginning 1 January 2007 and ending 31 December 2014.[546] The findings of the study were examined at a meeting of experts held in Tunis in April 2006, who concluded that the first and second scenarios were the most feasible.[547] A hybrid alternative, combining the first and second scenarios is expected.[548] The 11th Session of the Ordinary Session of the Conference of Leaders and Heads of State of CEN-SAD held in May 2009 reasserted the pressing need to turn the African Union into a political and institutional reality and reasserted the leaders' commitment to accelerate the African integration process through the gradual harmonization of the members' development policies in conformity with the Abuja Treaty.[549]

Little actual progress has been made in the way of concrete steps towards integration, despite broad statements of the organization's resolution to take action towards forming an FTA. This is most likely a result of overlapping membership in multiple RTAs – many CEN-SAD members are also members of ECOWAS, ECCAS, COMESA and other regional trade blocs that are at a more advanced stage in their integration process. This makes it difficult to coordinate trade and economic policies between members of the groups, which in turn leads to a decreased level of intra-regional trade because of trade barriers and a lack of harmonized market integration programmes.[550] Overlapping membership also results in a duplication of efforts which unnecessarily consumes scarce human and financial resources.[551] As a result, more than half of CEN-SAD member countries do not pay their required contributions.[552] Overlapping membership, therefore, serves as an obstacle to the achievement of regional integration and trade liberalization. Consequently, the CEN-SAD free trade zone has not been implemented and likely will never be practically implemented because of its members' overlapping membership in other African RECs. To achieve the objective of establishing an FTA, CEN-SAD should establish trade policies that are compatible with the other African RECs in order to further the goal of creating an enlarged FTA and eventually a customs union encompassing all of the regional trading blocs. To

546 *Ibid.* 547 *Ibid.* 548 *Ibid.*

549 CEN-SAD, 11th Ordinary Session of the Conference of Leaders and Heads of State, available at www.cen-sad.org/new/index.php?option=com_content&task=view&id=282&Itemid=236.

550 UN Economic Commission on Africa, 'Assessing Regional Integration in Africa II', at 55.

551 *Ibid.* 552 *Ibid.* at 59.

accomplish this and increase intra-regional trade, there must be a coordinated regional and continent-wide approach to infrastructure financing, institutional harmonization and policy coordination as well as improved transportation infrastructure.[553]

Food security remains an obstacle to integration, as the food crisis cripples the economies and populations of the CEN-SAD Member States.[554] The first phase Regional Food Security Programme began in January 2004 in five CEN-SAD Member States and was satisfactorily completed in June 2007.[555] The final programme evaluation mission conducted in January 2009, concluded that the Regional Food Security Programme had achieved its objectives at an appreciable rate.[556] The second phase of the programme is to be implemented over a five-year period and is designed to reinforce the gains of the first phase in twelve Member States at the national level and to build technical partnership at the community level.[557] In order to deal with the current food crisis, CEN-SAD members must commit themselves to the successful implementation of the Regional Food Security Programme. Furthermore, transportation infrastructure must be improved in order to ameliorate the existing weak infrastructure which makes it difficult to link agricultural production areas to urban consumption and export markets.[558] Recognizing that infrastructure and services development plays a crucial role in promoting sustainable development in the region, the CEN-SAD Community Plan aims to increase the incomes of its population to reduce or eliminate poverty.[559] Because the CEN-SAD region includes countries that belong to several other RECs, the Plan is oriented to promote their global integration through programmes of action in the transport, energy, mining and telecommunications fields that will constitute linkages between the various RECs to address the constraints that limit integration within the region.[560] The Plan will primarily involve: improving the planning and coordination of actions and investments at the regional level; creating new transit routes and corridors; maintaining and improving the quality of infrastructure services; integrating and coordinating policies; harmonizing laws, standards, regulations and procedures; and involving the private sector in financing joint projects.[561] In the transport sector, the main objective is to implement sufficient, efficient and integrated infrastructure in order

553 *Ibid.* 554 African Union, 'Status of Integration in Africa', at 88.

555 *Ibid.* at 87. The five countries involved in the first phase were Burkina Faso, Chad, Mali, Niger and Sudan.

556 *Ibid.* 557 *Ibid.* at 88. 558 *Ibid.* at 93. 559 *Ibid.* at 89.

560 *Ibid.* 561 *Ibid.* at 90.

to facilitate regional integration with the goal of eradicating poverty.[562] To this end, the specific objectives include: ensuring the extension and maintenance of the transit routes and corridors network; improving the operational efficiency of the services; deregulating the regional transport market; promoting the safe and secure use of integrated systems; and improving accessibility to rural areas.[563] However, only three countries have repaved more than 50 per cent of their road network and only eight have railway lines.[564]

J Economic Community of Central African States

1 Overview

In December 1991, the leaders of the Central African Customs and Economic Union (UDEAC) agreed in principle to form a wider community of Central African states.[565] The UDEAC members and the members of the Economic Community of the Great Lakes States established the Economic Community of Central African States (ECCAS) on 18 October 1983.[566] Its members include Angola, Burundi, Cameroon, Central African Republic, Chad, Congo, Democratic Republic of Congo, Equatorial Guinea, Gabon, Rwanda and São Tomé and Príncipe.[567] The objectives of ECCAS include the promotion and strengthening of harmonious cooperation and self-sustained development in all fields of social and economic activity in order to 'achieve collective self-reliance, raise the standard of living of its peoples, increase and maintain economic stability, foster close and peaceful relations between Member States and contribute to the progress and development of the African continent'.[568] To achieve this goal the Community aims to eliminate customs duties and similar charges levied on exports and imports as between Member States, to abolish quantitative restrictions and other non-tariff trade barriers between Member States, to establish an external common customs tariff and trade policy vis-à-vis third states, and to progressively abolish obstacles to the free movement of

562 *Ibid.* 563 *Ibid.* 564 *Ibid.* at 94.

565 African Union, 'Economic Community of Central African States: Profile', 2, available at www.africa-union.org/Recs/ECCASoverview.pdf. See also Chapter III for more on UDEAC.

566 *Ibid.*

567 *Ibid.* at 1. Rwanda withdrew its membership in June 2007. N. Alusala, 'Is There Hope for ECCAS?' (Institute for Security Studies, 19 Oct. 2007), available at www.iss.co.za/pgcontent.php?UID=27157.

568 Treaty Establishing ECCAS, Chapter II, Art. 4, para. 1, p. 9.

persons, goods, services and capital and to the right of establishment.[569] The ECCAS Treaty also calls for the harmonization of national policies to promote Community activities.[570] The ultimate goal of ECCAS is to establish a Central African common market.

ECCAS began functioning in 1985 but was inactive for a period of several years because of financial difficulties due to the non-payment of membership contributions and the conflict in the Great Lakes area.[571] Another significant factor in the non-functioning of the organization is the conflict in the Democratic Republic of Congo, as Angola and Rwanda fought on opposing sides.[572] ECCAS is a designated pillar of the AEC, but formal contact between the two organizations was only established in 1999 when ECCAS signed the Protocol on Relations between the AEC and the RECs due to ECCAS's inactivity since 1992.[573]

2 *Treaty establishing the Community*

The ECCAS Treaty calls for the gradual establishment of the Community over a period of twelve years, broken down into three subdivisions of four-year stages.[574] The stages are as follows:

Stage 1	Stage 2	Stage 3
• Stability of the fiscal and customs regime existing at the date of entry into force of the treaty • Carrying out of studies to determine the timetable for the progressive removal of tariff and non-tariff barriers to intra-Community trade • Setting a timetable for increases or decreases in the customs tariffs of Member States with a view to the adoption of a common external tariff	• Creation of an FTA (application of the timetable for the progressive elimination of tariff and non-tariff barriers to intra-Community trade)	• Establishment of the customs union (adoption of the common external tariff)[575]

569 *Ibid.* at para. 2(a)–(e), pp. 9–10. 570 *Ibid.* at para. 2(f), p. 10.
571 African Union, 'ECCAS: Profile', at 2. 572 *Ibid.* 573 *Ibid.*
574 Treaty Establishing ECCAS, at Chapter II, Art. 6, para. 1, p. 10.
575 *Ibid.* at para. 2, p. 11.

The total duration of the stages may be increased or reduced only by a decision adopted by consensus and the transition period may not be reduced to ten years or under, or increased to more than twenty years from its initiation.[576]

During the first stage, the Member States may not establish new or increase existing customs duties between them.[577] At the end of the first stage and during the second stage, members are to progressively reduce and ultimately eliminate customs duties between them.[578] Additionally during this time period, members shall 'eliminate differences between customs duties in their respective customs tariffs',[579] with a view to the progressive establishment of a common external tariff that is applicable to goods imported into Member States from third countries.[580] At the end of the second stage, 'no Member State shall levy customs duties on goods originating in one Member State and transferred to another Member State' or on 'goods coming from third countries which are in free circulation in Member States and are transferred from one Member State to another'.[581] Quota restrictions and other non-tariff barriers to intra-Community trade are to be gradually relaxed and ultimately removed by the end of the second stage at the latest, and Member States are to refrain from imposing any further restrictions or prohibitions.[582] At the end of the second stage and during the third stage, the Council of Ministers shall propose to the Conference of Heads of State and Government the adoption of a common customs and statistical nomenclature for all Member States.[583]

The ECCAS Preferential Tariff was created as a plan to gradually eliminate tariffs on intra-regional trade. For traditional handicraft and local products, there was to be a 100% reduction from 1 July 2004.[584] For mineral and manufactured products there was to be a 50% reduction from 1 July 2004; a 70% reduction from January 2005; a 90% reduction from January 2006; and a 100% reduction by January 2007.[585] ECCAS undertook to harmonize commercial policies such as rules of origin and means of identifying the origin of a product with CEMAC. However, a WTO Trade Policy Review on the Central African Republic reported that as of March 2007, the tariff reduction process had not yet begun.[586]

576 *Ibid.* 577 *Ibid.* at Chapter IV, Art. 28, para. 1, at p. 21.
578 *Ibid.* at para. 2, at p. 21. 579 *Ibid.* at para. 2, at p. 22.
580 *Ibid.* at para. 1, at p. 21. 581 *Ibid.* at Art. 31, para. 1, at p. 22.
582 *Ibid.* at Art. 33, para. 1, at p. 23. 583 *Ibid.* at Art. 29, para. 3, at p. 22.
584 UN Economic Commission on Africa, 'Assessing Regional Integration in Africa IV', at 14.
585 *Ibid.* 586 *Ibid.*

At the 1999 Conference of the Heads of State and Government, four priority fields were identified: to develop capacities to maintain peace, security and stability, all of which are essential prerequisites for economic and social development; to develop physical, economic and monetary integration; to develop a culture of human integration; and to establish an autonomous financing mechanism for ECCAS.[587]

Due to conflicts within the region, little progress has been made with respect to these economic goals. It was during the period of inactivity that it became apparent that if the organization was to be functional again it would need to go beyond economic issues and incorporate peace and security in the region into its wider operations efforts.[588] ECCAS Member States created the Council for Peace and Security in Central Africa (COPAX) in February 1999 in order to promote, maintain and consolidate peace and security in Central Africa.[589] COPAX established two mechanisms, the Multinational Peace Keeping Force in Central Africa (FOMAC), and the Early Warning Observation and Monitoring System for Central Africa (MARAC), both of which have proved largely ineffective.[590] Conflicts among Member States continue, and non-payment of member fees is still an issue, leaving ECCAS disempowered as members continue to withdraw or join other RECs. In the face of continuing challenges, ECCAS remains committed to pursuing new projects, such as the recent joint project with the EU aimed at supporting and aiding the ECCAS Department of Human Integration, Peace, Stability and Security in fulfilling its role to detect, prevent and manage conflict within the Central African region.[591] The joint project plans to equip MARAC with an early warning mechanism that will enable it to examine, analyse and react to crises in the region in a timely manner.[592] Other objectives of the joint project are to enable ECCAS to mediate conflicts between members and to equip ECCAS to work closely with its members in the fight against various factors promoting conflict in the region, like the illicit proliferation of small arms, cross-border crime and the illegal exploitation of the region's natural resources.[593] Financed by the European Development Fund, the EU–ECCAS project began in February 2007 and was to be implemented over a period of three-and-a-half years.[594]

587 African Union, 'ECCAS: Profile', at 3.
588 Alusala, 'Is there Hope?'.
589 *Ibid.* However, COPAX did not enter into force until 2004.
590 *Ibid.*
591 African Union, 'Status of Integration in Africa', at 47.
592 *Ibid.*
593 *Ibid.*
594 *Ibid.*

The ECCAS re-launching process was initiated in 1998 with technical assistance from the UN Economic Commission on Africa to help establish an autonomous financing mechanism and an FTA.[595] The strategy was aimed to improve the interests of the other institutions in the region, such as CEMAC and COMESA, while avoiding conflict with the existing institutions, in order to establish a single regional market for Central Africa.[596] To this end, the strategy enabled the formation of an FTA over a period of four years, from 2004 to 2007, as opposed to the twelve years initially planned.[597] After the four-year period, during which the strategy will only apply to non-CEMAC members, ECCAS is expected to be at the same level as CEMAC, which has reached the customs union stage, and will then apply uniform and residual standards and norms will be harmonized.[598] On 24 January 2003, the EU signed a financial agreement with ECCAS and CEMAC conditional on the two African groups merging into one organization for the purpose of ultimately concluding an Economic Partnership Agreement with Central Africa.[599]

ECCAS achieved the status of an FTA in July 2004 and was expected to launch the ECCAS customs union in 2010. The customs union was initially to be launched in 2008, four years after the formation of the FTA,[600] but its launch was delayed by a lack of political will and financial support within the region.[601] In order to form a customs union, ECCAS must speed up the harmonization of the common external tariff and continue to work on the removal of non-tariff barriers as well as harmonizing national policies so as to facilitate the free movement of persons and goods across borders.

The implementation of protocols aimed at facilitating the movement of goods and services has been hindered by lack of stability in the region and inadequate infrastructure linking the member countries. For ECCAS, transport infrastructure is particularly important for increased intra-regional trade because 80 per cent of its trade is provided by ground transportation.[602] In January 2004, a plan to develop the transportation infrastructure in the region, referred to as the Blueprint Consensus on

595 African Union and Economic Commission for Africa, 'Assessing Regional Integration in Africa II', at 50.

596 *Ibid.* 597 *Ibid.* 598 *Ibid.*

599 WTO Trade Policy Review, 'Central African Republic', WT/TPR/S/183 (7 May 2007), 15.

600 *Ibid.* 601 *Ibid.*

602 A.M. Pibasso, 'ECCAS: 8000 Billion FCFA for Roads', BusinessinCameroon.com (25 Nov. 2009), available at www.businessincameroon.com/real-estate-and-constructions-news/eccas-8000-billion-fcfa-for-roads.

Transport in Central Africa (PDCT-AC), was launched with the objective of providing Central Africa with secure, reliable and efficient transport infrastructure and to offer services at affordable costs.[603] The PDCT-AC, as a short-term goal, aimed to make it possible to travel on paved roads from one capital in the region to another by 2010.[604] As a medium-term goal, the PDCT-AC aims to have a consensus framework for negotiations in order to mobilize investments in the transportation infrastructure field and, in the long term, to ensure that the region has a transport system that encompasses all modes of transportation and whose infrastructure and services encourage the free movement of persons and goods.[605] However, the short-term goal to have paved roads connecting the region's capitals by 2010 has not been reached, as only two capitals are currently connected by road – Yaounde and Libreville.[606] In addition to the weak transport infrastructure and political instability, development programmes focusing on food security, the free movement of persons, health issues such as HIV/AIDS, gender issues and the environment should be created and implemented as these issues are key aspects of economic integration.

603 R. Mvogo, '6.41 Billion USD to Mobilize for the Tarring of Roads International Capitals', Emploi Service (20 March 2010).
604 African Union, 'Status of Integration in Africa', at 54.
605 *Ibid.* 606 Pibasso, '8000 Billion FCFA for Roads'.

VI

Financing African RTAs

A Introduction

This chapter addresses the legal framework for financing African RTAs as well as the legal, policy and practical challenges that arise in the context of their financing. In my research, I did not come across any similar effort. I confronted challenges of getting reliable and up-to-date data to show where African RTAs were raising their revenue – whether through member contributions, donors or other sources. As this chapter shows, financing African RTAs has been a huge challenge.

Where I was able to locate RTA budgets, there were significant discrepancies between the approved budget by the responsible RTA institution, and the actual budget. This is caused, in large part, by the fact that many Member States within RTAs are unable to, or simply do not, meet their assessed contributions, and by the uncertainty involved in how much external funding from donors like the European Union (EU) will be available from year to year. And, as with any large organization, often there are significant differences between what the budget estimates for revenue and expenditures and the actual budget at the end of the year.

The challenges facing African international institutions in terms of raising funding were well stated by Ambassador Brownson N. Dede, Organization of African Unity (OAU) Secretary General for Economic Development and Cooperation, in 1993:

> In the continent as a whole, there exists nearly 100 inter-governmental organizations devoted to the pursuit of the noble but seemingly elusive objective of economic integration. Many of them are in a state of financial coma, starved of funds and the resources, human and material, necessary for the achievement of their objectives.[1]

1 Keynote Address by His Excellency Ambassador Brownson N. Dede, OAU Secretary General for Economic Development and Cooperation, 'The Legal and Institutional Framework of the African Economic Community', in Prof. M.A. Ajomo and O. Adewale, *African Economic Community Treaty: Issues, Problems and Prospects* (Nigerian Institute of Advanced Legal Studies, 1993), at xxxiv.

There are two major problems facing African RTAs. First, it is often financially difficult for African states, especially the small and poorer ones, to make their contributions to the two, three, or more international organizations that they are members of. This is because, as we saw in Chapter III, multiple membership in African RTAs is the norm rather than the exception. Such multiple memberships by countries that can hardly afford to pay their membership contribution has led to a shortage of funds and personnel for all organizations. Second, overlapping economic organizations bring with them overlapping economic policies, which can result in the kind of challenges we saw in Chapter III.

The African Economic Community (AEC), as we saw in Chapter I, will come to fruition after the dissolution of all the eight regional economic communities in Africa to form the AEC as a continental-wide integration institution. The Abuja Treaty which establishes the AEC was passed on 3 June 1991 by the Assembly of Heads of State and Government of the OAU, and was ratified by the requisite two-thirds of Member States in 1994. The OAU, now the African Union (AU), and the AEC operate as a single entity, with the institutions of the AU performing dual functions. This chapter outlines the financing of the AEC and the AU as a single entity before proceeding to examine the funding frameworks of the RTAs.

Before examining the financing of the AEC, it is important to note that the AEC today exists as part of the AU. That is because the Treaty establishing the AEC contemplated no separate existence of the Community outside the then OAU, now the AU. The Treaty did so both in the Preamble and in Article 1(c), as well as Article 98(i). These provisions clearly show that the AEC was contemplated as an integral part of the AU. In addition, the AEC's definition of its organs in defining the terms Assembly,[2] Council,[3] Commission,[4] Secretariat,[5] and Secretary General[6] equated them with similar organs in the OAU Treaty.[7]

As such, it is not surprising that the AU Secretariat doubles as the Secretariat of the AEC. The AEC

> has no such thing as a Secretary General of its own with the requisite qualifications, expertise and experience to carry out independently the functions prescribed for it under Article 22 of the Treaty. Similarly, unlike

2 Treaty Establishing the African Economic Community, 27th Assembly of Heads of State and Government (adopted 3 June 1991, into force 12 May 1994), at Art. 19(h).

3 *Ibid.* at Art. 1(i). 4 *Ibid.* at Art. 1(k). 5 *Ibid.* at Art. 1(n). 6 *Ibid.* at Art. 1(o).

7 Ambassador A.O. Oshodi, 'The Legal Framework of the A.E.C.', in Ajomo and Adewale, *African Economic Community Treaty*, at 38.

> the RECs ... the AEC has no special or independent secretariat or even a letterhead of its own. It has no identity, and its functions are completely dominated by... the politically oriented OAU Secretariat, as is evident in the deliberations of the annual summits of the OAU.[8]

However, while there is institutional overlap in the AU's and AEC's organs, the constitutive treaties of the OAU and AEC are different in some respects. Thus, while the OAU Treaty was strong in advocating for the sovereign equality of its members,[9] the AEC Treaty spoke in the language of interdependence of the members;[10] while the OAU Treaty spoke of the non-interference with the internal affairs of the members,[11] the AEC Treaty spoke in the language of solidarity and collective self-reliance;[12] while the OAU Treaty spoke in the language of sovereignty and territorial integrity of each state and its inalienable right to independent existence,[13] the AEC Treaty spoke of inter-state cooperation, harmonization of policies and integration of programmes.[14] Indeed, while the OAU Treaty was critical of political assassinations and subversive plots from neighbouring countries,[15] the AEC Charter embraced peaceful settlement of disputes among Member States as a prerequisite to their economic development.[16] One challenge that regional integration faces, as we saw in Chapter III, is the overlapping nature of membership in African RTAs.

B Financing the AEC

At the outset it is important to note that while, as we have seen above, the AU and the AEC are one and the same entity, the OAU and AEC treaties are worded differently with respect to the financial obligations of the members. The Treaty Establishing the African Economic Community (Abuja Treaty) provides that the budget of the AEC is to be an 'integral part' of the OAU's budget, and that the budget is to be funded by contributions made

8 S.K.B. Asante, F.O.C. Nwonwu and V.N. Mizvidziwa, 'Towards An African Economic Community', Paper presented at the 40th Anniversary Conference of the Africa Institute of South Africa (AISA, 2001), 7–8.

9 Organization for African Unity Charter, 1st Assembly of Heads of State and Government (25 May 1963), at Art. III(1).

10 AEC Treaty, at Art. 3(a).

11 OAU Charter, at Art. III(2).

12 AEC Treaty, at Art. 3(b).

13 OAU Charter, at Art. III(3).

14 AEC Treaty, at Art. 3(c).

15 OAU Charter, at Art. III(5).

16 AEC Treaty, at Art. 3(f). I am grateful for the foregoing contrasts to C.A. Ogan, 'The International Personality of the African Economic Community', in Ajomo and Adewale, *African Economic Community Treaty*, 52–3.

by Member States in accordance with the OAU's scale of assessment.[17] The OAU Charter states that the Organization may accept 'gifts, bequests and other donations made to the Organization'.[18] The Abuja Treaty similarly provides that the Organization may 'accept donations, bequests and gifts'.[19] Neither the OAU nor the AU, which succeeded the OAU in 2002, specifically included contributions by third parties in its budget until 2006.[20] This notwithstanding, the OAU/AU regularly accepted donations to its general budget and to specific programmes and institutions from external sources like the United Nations (UN) and EU. Indeed, from time to time, the OAU/AU and the AEC have specifically asked parties external to the Organization for donations and financial contributions.[21]

The OAU Charter provided that the budget of the OAU was to be prepared by the Secretary-General of the Organization, subject to approval by the Council of Ministers.[22] The budget was to be funded by Member States in accordance with the scale of assessment.[23] Article XXIII, the budget provision, contains no mention of funding from external sources. However, Article XXX states that the Secretary-General may accept gifts and donations to the Organization, subject to approval by the Council of Ministers.[24] The Abuja Treaty, which entered into force on 12 May 1994, has very similar wording to that of the OAU Charter. The Secretary-General was charged with preparing the budget.[25] The Council of Ministers was given the responsibility of submitting the Secretary-General's proposed budget to the Assembly of Heads of State and Government for approval.[26] The Assembly then had the ability to approve the budget, and also was responsible for determining the annual contributions due from each Member State.[27] This budget, like that of the OAU, was to be funded by the Member States, and there was no mention of external funding.[28] The Secretary-General could, however, accept gifts and donations, as

17 AEC Treaty, at Art. 82. 18 OAU Charter, at Art. XXX. 19 AEC Treaty, at Art. 98.

20 Decisions, 8th Extra Ordinary Session of the Executive Council, Ext/EX.CL/Dec.1 (VIII) (19 Jan. 2006).

21 For example, Declarations and Resolutions as Adopted by the 21st Ordinary Session of the Assembly of Heads of State and Government, AHG/Decl.1 (XXI) (20 July 1985) (noting the drastic economic situation of the African Continent and appealing to the World Bank and the international community for assistance with the famine, drought and financial crisis in Africa); see also Decisions, 13th Executive Council, EX.CL/Dec.423(5) (XIII) (28 June 2008) (asking third-party humanitarian organizations and donors to assist with displaced persons in Africa).

22 OAU Charter, at Art. XXIII. 23 *Ibid.* 24 OAU Charter, at Art. XXX.

25 AEC Treaty, at Art. 22(2)(c). 26 *Ibid.* at Art. 11(3)(c). 27 *Ibid.* at Art. 8(3)(i).

28 *Ibid.* at Art. 82(2).

long as they were approved by the Council.[29] These gift provisions had the effect of allowing the Secretary-General, the Council of Ministers and the Assembly of Heads of State and Government to use external contributions in the budget without specifically relying on them. As a matter of practice, it was assumed that since Member States may from time to time be unable to make their assessed contributions, the gift provisions would help make up shortfalls.

The contributions owed by each Member State to the AEC were a percentage determined using the scale of assessment.[30] Given that as a factual matter the AEC and the AU are indeed the same entity, the scale of assessment that is used for the AEC is that of the OAU/AU.[31] When the AEC Treaty first entered into effect in 1994, the OAU's scale had been in effect since 1 June 1988.[32] On 1 June 1995 a new scale entered into effect.[33] This scale lasted until 1 June 2004, when another new scale entered into effect.[34] On 1 January 2006 yet another new scale of assessment entered into effect. This is the current scale.[35] The 2006 scale was approved by the Assembly of the AU in Decision 88 on 5 July 2005. This scale is based on what the Executive Council called the principle of 'Capacity to Pay of Member States'. It established a ceiling of 15 per cent, no floor and decided that the scale should be reviewed every three years. In the Decision, the Assembly noted that five Member States, namely Algeria, Egypt, Libya, Nigeria and South Africa, had volunteered to each contribute the maximum of 15 per cent.[36] It is also important to note that more than three years have passed since the July 2005 Decision, but no Assembly

29 *Ibid.* at Art. 98(3)(c). 30 *Ibid.* at Art. 82(2). 31 *Ibid.*

32 Resolutions adopted by the 47th Ordinary Session of the Council of Ministers, CM/Res. 1130 (XLVII) (27 Feb. 1988) (deciding to implement Table 6 of Document CM/1465 as the new scale beginning 1 June 1988). See also Resolutions adopted by the 61st Ordinary Session of the Council of Ministers, CM/Res. 1555 (LXI) ANNEX (27 Jan. 1995) (listing the 1988, adopted 1995 and proposed 1995 scales of assessment for the OAU).

33 *Ibid.* and CM/Res. 1555 (LXI) ANNEX.

34 Decisions and Declarations, 2nd Assembly of the African Union, AHG/Dec.31(II) (12 July 2003) (endorsing the recommendation in EX/CL/Dec.35 and establishing the scale of assessment located in Table 16 of Doc. EX/CL/40, which places the ceiling at 8.25% and places two floors of 0.25% and 0.75%). The Annex to this Decision, and Doc.EX/CL/40 have been, thus far, unavailable.

35 Decisions, Declarations and Resolution, 5th Assembly of the African Union, Assembly/AU/Dec. 88 (V) (5 July 2005) (noting the recommendations in EX.CL/Dec. 223; approving the scale of assessment based on the principle of 'Capacity to Pay of Member States', with a ceiling of 15% and no floor, located in Document EX.CL/192 (VII); and deciding that the scale should be reviewed every three years). The Annex to this Decision, and Doc.EX.CL/192 have been, thus far, unavailable.

36 *Ibid.*

or Executive Council documents that are available have mentioned the scale.[37]

The Abuja Treaty mandated that the AEC budget would be approved by the Assembly, but from its entrance into force in 1994 until the end of 2002 (the year the AU displaced the OAU) the AEC budget was approved by the Council. This was because there was a discrepancy between the OAU Charter and the Abuja Treaty, as the OAU Charter stated that the budget would be approved by the Council. Since the OAU was the larger organization, and the Abuja Treaty stated that the AEC budget was to come from the OAU anyway, the treaty provision requiring budgetary approval by the Assembly was all but thrown out.[38] This discrepancy was eliminated by the Constitutive Act of the AU, which specifically stated:

> The provisions of this Act shall take precedence over and supersede any inconsistent or contrary provisions of the Treaty establishing the African Economic Community.[39]

The Constitutive Act did not mention the budget other than to state that the budget would be adopted by the Assembly.[40] This seemed to cut the OAU General Secretariat (now the AU Commission) and the OAU Council of Ministers (now the AU Executive Council), out of the budgetary process. However, the Act also allowed the Assembly to determine the functions of the Commission,[41] and Article 9(2) allowed the Assembly to delegate any of its express powers to any organ of the Union.[42] As early as one year after the entrance into force of the Constitutive Act, the Assembly gave the Commission the responsibility of adjusting the budget.[43] Since then, the Assembly has all but assumed that the Commission would be responsible for drafting the budget, though no decision specifically authorizes this. Another impact of Article 9(2) of the Constitutive Act is that the Assembly itself has only approved the budgets for

37 The Decisions of the 7th Assembly from mid-2006, 9th Council from mid-2006, and 14th Council from the beginning of 2009 have all been unavailable so far.

38 See OAU Charter, at Art. XXIII; see also AEC Treaty, at Art. 82(1).

39 Constitutive Act of the African Union, 36th Assembly of Heads of State and Government (adopted 11 July 2000, into force 9 July 2002), at Art. 33(2).

40 *Ibid.* at Art. 9(1)(f). 41 *Ibid.* at Art. 20(3). 42 *Ibid.* at Art. 9(2).

43 Decisions and Declarations, 2nd Assembly of the African Union, AHG/Dec. 8 (II) (12 July 2003).

2003,[44] 2004,[45] 2007,[46] 2009[47] and 2010.[48] The Assembly gave the Executive Council the authority to re-examine the 2004 budget in March 2004 in order to make any necessary changes.[49] The Executive Council seems to have omitted any mention of this duty.[50] The Assembly mandated the Executive Council to adopt the 2005 budget, which it did[51] in July 2004. In 2005, the Assembly mandated that the Council hold an extra session in January 2006 to approve the 2006 budget, which it did.[52] Finally, the Assembly seems to have omitted any mention of the 2008 budget from its 2007 and 2008 Decisions, leaving the Executive Council to approve the 2008 budget without specifically being granted this authority.[53]

1 AEC's budgetary process

As noted above, the OAU Charter provided that the budget of the AEC was first to be proposed by the Secretary-General,[54] and then approved by the Council of Ministers.[55] Once the AU replaced the OAU this changed. Instead, the budget was proposed by the Commission and approved by

44 *Ibid.*, AHG/Dec. 7 (II) (12 July 2003) (setting the 2003 budget).

45 *Ibid.*, AHG/ Dec. 8 (II) (setting the budget for 2004).

46 Decisions and Declarations, 8th Assembly of the African Union, Assembly/AU/Dec. 154 (VIII) (30 Jan. 2007) (adopting the budget for 2007).

47 Decisions, Declarations, Message of Congratulations and Motion, 12th Assembly of the African Union, Assembly/AU/Dec. 208 (XII) (3 Feb. 2009) (adopting the budget for 2009).

48 Decisions, Declarations, Message of Congratulations and Motion, 14th Assembly of the African Union, Assembly/AU/Dec.287 (XIV) (3 Feb. 2010) (adopting the budget for 2010).

49 Decisions and Declarations, 2nd Assembly of the African Union, AHG/Dec. 8(4) (II) (12 July 2003).

50 See Decisions of the 4th Ordinary Session of the Executive Council (16 March 2004).

51 Decisions, 3rd Assembly of the African Union, Dec. 47 (III) (8 July 2004) (mandating that the Executive Council approve the 2005 budget during its Extraordinary Session scheduled for November 2004). The 2004 Decisions of the Executive Council have been unavailable so far, but the Council indicates that it had set the budget for 2005, in Decisions, 7th Executive Council, EX.CL/Dec. 217 (VII) (2 July 2005).

52 Decisions, Declarations and Resolution, 5th Assembly of the African Union, Assembly/AU/Dec. 89 (V) (5 July 2005) (mandating the Executive Council to convene in an Extraordinary Session to adopt the 2006 budget). Decisions, 8th Extraordinary Session of the Executive Council, Ext/EX.CL/Dec.1 (VIII) (19 Jan. 2006) (approving the 2006 budget).

53 Decisions and Declaration, 12th Executive Council, EX.CL/Dec. 378 (XII) (29 Jan. 2008) (setting the 2008 budget).

54 AEC Treaty, at Art. 22(2)(c).

55 OAU Charter, at Art. XXIII.

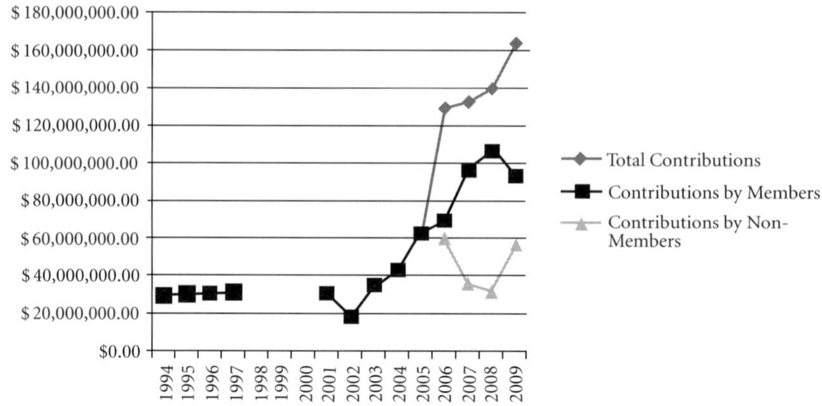

Figure 6.1 AU Budget (as passed) 1994–2009

the Assembly.[56] Nevertheless, the Assembly has mandated the Executive Council to approve the budget in lieu of the Assembly on several occasions.[57] Due to problems in the collection of mandatory Member State contributions, the actual budget has traditionally been very different from the approved budget, as indicated in Figure 6.1.

The revenue collected through contributions, donations and gifts is much harder to track down than the budgets as passed. The information on which my analysis is based are the reports of the Board of External Auditors,[58] the Economic, Social and Cultural Council (ECOSOCC),[59] budgetary reports of the Commission, reports of the Committee on Contributions and reports of the Permanent Committee on the Scale of Assessment.

56 Constitutive Act of the African Union, 36th Assembly, at Art. 33(2) (stating that the Constitutive Act would take precedence over all inconsistent provisions in the Abuja Treaty); see also *ibid.* at Art. 9(1)(f) (stating that the budget would be approved by the Assembly).

57 Decisions, 3rd Assembly of the African Union, Dec. 47 (III) (8 July 2004) (mandating that the Executive Council approve the 2005 budget during its Extraordinary Session scheduled for November 2004); and Decisions, Declarations and Resolution, 5th Assembly of the African Union, Assembly/AU/Dec. 89 (V) (5 July 2005) (mandating the Executive Council to convene in an Extraordinary Session to adopt the 2006 budget).

58 Mandated by AEC Treaty, at Art. 86; also mentioned in various Assembly documents, which show that the Board exists within the Organization: for example, Decisions, 11th Executive Council, EX.CL/Dec. 371 (XI) (29 June 2007) (deciding on a report of the Board of External Auditors).

59 Constitutive Act of the African Union, 36th Assembly, at Art. 22 (establishing ECOSOCC).

2 *Problems encountered in raising revenue*

The main problem facing the AEC is that there is no process of guaranteeing that Member States will make their 'mandatory' contributions. The relevant provision in this regard is Article 84 of the Treaty Establishing the AEC which states:

> Upon the decision of the Assembly, any Member State of the Community having arrears in the payment of its contribution to the budget of the Community, shall not have the right to vote or participate in taking decisions of the Community if the amount of its arrears is equal to, or is in excess of the contribution payable by such State for the last preceding two financial years. Such Member State shall cease to enjoy other benefits arising by virtue of this Treaty as well as the right to address meetings. In addition, it shall lose the right to present candidates for vacant posts within the Community and shall not be eligible for office in the deliberative organs of the Community. The Assembly may, where necessary, impose other sanctions on a Member State for non-payment of contributions.[60]

Notwithstanding this provision, the AEC/AU has infrequently imposed sanctions. This practice is consistent with other international organizations such as the UN, which has almost never denied the right to vote to a Member for non-payment of dues for two consecutive years, even though this is the penalty prescribed by Article 19 of the Charter of the UN.[61] This has resulted in a series of exemptions from sanctions, unenforced and delayed sanctions or imposition of sanctions that have only had a minimal impact on a Member State's willingness to make its contributions.

The AEC also cannot continue to consistently rely on donations and contributions from external entities, particularly if a major reason for the formation of the RECs is attaining self-reliance an economic self-determination, as we saw in Chapter I. Indeed, African leaders have long acknowledged that it is not in their interest to become dependent on the financial contributions of external donors.[62] This, of course, has not stopped the African countries from accepting contributions of external

60 AEC Treaty, at Art. 84(1).

61 This power was affirmed by the ICJ in the *Certain Expenses* case: *Certain Expenses of the United Nations* (Article 17, paragraph 2, of the Charter), Advisory Opinion of 20 July 1962, ICJ Reports 1962. For further discussion, see J. Alvarez, *International Organizations as Law Makers* (Oxford University Press, 2005).

62 Declarations and Resolutions as adopted by the 21st Ordinary Session of the Assembly of Heads of State and Government, AHG/Decl. 1(10) (XXI) (20 July 1985) (noting that it is important for Africa to gain the capability to cope with disasters without outside aid).

entities, such as the US$15 billion over five years that the United States pledged in 2003 to combat the spread of HIV/AIDS in Africa.[63]

AU sanctions against Member States for non-payment of mandatory contributions, which of course carry over to the AEC, have been few in number and relatively ineffective for coercing Member States to meet their payment obligations. The OAU did not impose sanctions on any Member State until 1995.[64] This followed passage of Resolution 1279 in 1990, which provided that in addition to the sanction imposed by the Financial Rules and Regulations,[65] further sanctions would be imposed on any Member State that owed an amount equal to or greater than its total contribution due for two years.[66] The sanctions in the Financial Rules and Regulations limited the punishment to a removal of the right to vote and to participate in decisions until payment was made.[67] Resolution 1279 added removal of: the right to speak at OAU meetings, the right to present candidates for OAU posts and the right to present candidates for OAU decision-making bodies.[68]

By mid-1994, only 14 of 52 Member States were up to date on their contributions.[69] South Africa, the 53rd member, had just joined that year and so could not be considered behind or caught up. The fact that a large majority of Member States were behind in their contributions prompted the Assembly to reaffirm its decision to begin imposing sanctions on Member States that were far behind in their contribution requirements.[70] The Assembly had created a Credentials Committee in early 1994[71] to examine and monitor arrears. Its name was changed to the Committee on Contributions in mid-1994.[72] The Committee was responsible for

63 Decisions and Declarations, 2nd Assembly of the African Union, Assembly/AU/Decl. 6 (II) (12 July 2003).

64 Declarations and Resolutions adopted by the 31st Ordinary Session of the Assembly of Heads of State and Government, CM/Res.1580 (LXII) (23 June 1995) (announcing that sanctions against Member States that owe will begin on 29 June 1995 and granting an exemption to Somalia and Liberia).

65 The original Financial Rules and Regulations have been amended since their inception, but neither version has been available thus far.

66 Resolutions adopted by the 52nd Ordinary Session of the Council of Ministers, CM/Res. 1279 (LII) (8 July 1990).

67 *Ibid.* at CM/Res. 1279(2)(d).

68 *Ibid.*

69 Resolutions adopted by the 60th Ordinary Session of the Council of Ministers, CM/Res. 1514 (LX) (11 June 1994) (noting that sanctions for non-payment of contributions will begin on 1 June 1995).

70 *Ibid.* at CM/Res. 1514(3).

71 Resolutions adopted by the 59th Ordinary Session of the Council of Ministers, CM/Res. 1480 (LIX) (4 Feb. 1994) (establishing the Credentials Committee).

72 CM/Res. 1514 (LX) (changing the name of the Credentials Committee to the Committee on Contributions).

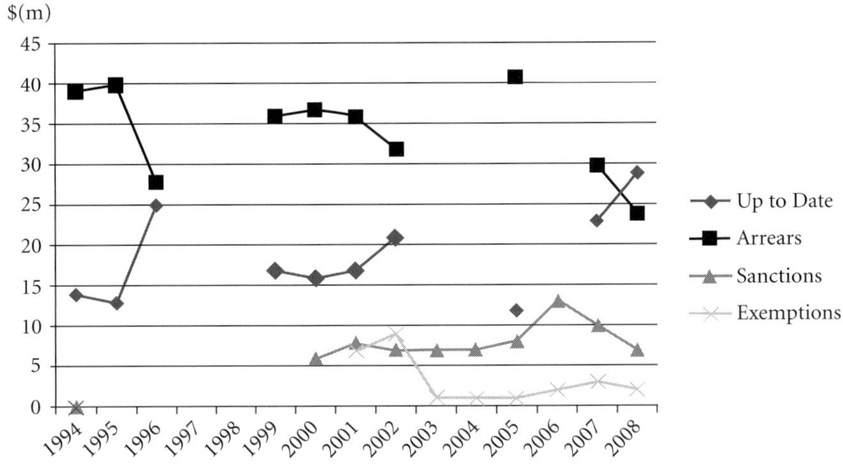

Figure 6.2 Member State contributions

recommending to the Council of Ministers steps that should be taken against defaulting Member States, as well as those that should be granted a temporary exemption from sanctions.

The OAU began imposing sanctions on Member States in 1995, and immediately began granting exemptions to these sanctions. The specific Member States against which sanctions were imposed were unknown until 2001, when the Council of Ministers finally began listing them.[73] The exemptions that were known publicly at the time included that Liberia, Somalia and any other member that managed to pay 25 per cent of its arrears before the exemption period expired would receive an exemption, beginning 29 June 1995.[74] That year only 13 members were up to date in their contributions.[75]

By 1996 it appeared that the sanctions were doing their job, as 25 members were suddenly up to date with their contributions, as shown in Figure 6.2.[76] In 1999, the Council decided that it would grant an exemption to any Member State which proposed a payment rescheduling plan,

73 A listing of which Member States had sanctions imposed on them between 1995 and 2000 would be contained in the Reports of the Committee on Contributions, currently unavailable to me.

74 Resolutions adopted by the 61st Ordinary Session of the Council of Ministers, CM/Res. 1556 and 1580 (LXI) (27 Jan. 1995).

75 *Ibid.*

76 Resolutions adopted by the 63rd Ordinary Session of the Council of Ministers, CM/Res. 1617 (LXIII) (28 Feb. 1996) (commending those Member States who were up to date with contributions).

got it approved and then followed through with payments as promised.[77] The Council has reiterated this Decision in many subsequent Decisions.[78] Since 1995, it has really appeared that sanctions are not the factor that is driving Member States to meet their contribution requirements. For example, a cursory examination of the number of Member States who were up to date with their payments and the number of Member States with sanctions for non-payment shows little, if any, correlation or causality. The highest number of sanctions in any one year was 13 in 2006,[79] and the most Member States up to date with contributions in any one year was 29 in 2008.[80]

3 *Financing the AMU*

The Treaty Establishing the AMU came into force on 1 June 1989.[81] The Treaty Establishing the Arab Maghreb Union (AMU) makes no mention whatsoever of the budget or financing.[82] Information about the AMU is very difficult to obtain, especially since its institutions have rarely met since the late 1990s. Since the inception of the AMU there have been only about a dozen summits involving the Presidential Council, the highest organ of the Community.[83] It appears that the budget of the AMU is funded by equal contributions totalling US$1.7m since 1992.[84]

4 *Financing CEN-SAD*

CEN-SAD is by far the hardest African RTA to collect information on. It is even difficult to find the Treaty Establishing CEN-SAD in English. So

77 Decisions and Regulations of the 69th Ordinary Session of the Council of Ministers, CM/Dec. 437 (LXIX) (23 March 1999) (endorsing the recommendations in Document CM/2092 (LXIX)).

78 For example, Decisions of the 76th Ordinary Session OAU Council of Ministers and 11th Ordinary Session of the AEC, CM/Dec. 652 (LXXVI).

79 Decisions, 8th Extraordinary Session of the Executive Council Ext/EX.CL/Dec. 2 (VIII) (19 Jan. 2006).

80 Decisions and Declaration, 12th Executive Council, EX.CL/Dec. 379 (XII) (29 Jan. 2008).

81 Treaty Establishing the Arab Maghreb Union (adopted 17 Feb. 1989, into force 1 July 1989), at Art. 4.

82 *Ibid.* (creating a regional economic community between Morocco, Tunisia, Algeria, Libya, and Mauritania).

83 A. Bensouiah, 'Stunted Growth of the Arab Maghreb Union', PANA Press (21 June 2002), available at www.panapress.com/newslatf.asp?code=eng008203&dte=21/06/2002.

84 AEC, 'Profile: Arab Maghreb Union', available at www.africa-union.org/Recs/AMUOverview.pdf.

far the only information that has been discovered is that the 2008/2009 budget was set at US$10,340,000.[85]

5 *Financing COMESA*

The Treaty Establishing the Common Market for Eastern and Southern Africa (COMESA) provides that the Council of Ministers, the second most powerful organ of COMESA, has the responsibility of considering and approving the budgets as proposed by the Secretariat and the Court.[86] The Secretariat is charged with creating the budget of the common market and then submitting it to the Intergovernmental Committee, another organ of COMESA, for recommendation to the Council of Ministers.[87]

The Treaty Establishing COMESA also provides that it is to be financed primarily through contributions by Member States.[88] It anticipates that extra-budgetary resources like 'grants, donations, funds for projects and programmes and technical assistance', as well as income from COMESA programmes, can be used to finance the budget.[89]

Under the Treaty Establishing COMESA, the Secretary-General has the responsibility of creating a draft budget for COMESA.[90] COMESA's Court of Justice drafts its own budget, but all of the policies that are applicable to the Secretariat's general budget also applies to the Court's budget.[91] Once drafted, the budget is approved by the Council.[92] It is empowered to determine the contribution rates for each Member State according to a formula that it creates, and it is authorized to make this determination whenever the Council deems prudent.[93] The Treaty also states that 50 per cent of contributions must be made within one month of the end of the financial year, and the balance within six months of the end of the financial year.[94] Furthermore, the Treaty instituted a COMESA levy to generate revenue,[95] in addition to member contributions and donations from external sources.

85 'Le Budget 2008 de la CEN-SAD Estimé à Plus de 10 Millions de Dollars', *African Manager* (15 June 2008), available at www.africanmanager.com/articles/117232.html.

86 Treaty Establishing the Common Market of Eastern and Southern Africa (adopted 21 Dec. 1981, into force 30 Sept. 1982), at Art. 9(2)(f).

87 *Ibid.* at Art. 17(8)(d). 88 *Ibid.* at Art. 166(4). 89 *Ibid.* at Art. 168(3).

90 *Ibid.* at Art. 166(2). 91 *Ibid.* at Art. 42. 92 *Ibid.* at Art. 166(3).

93 *Ibid.* at Art. 166(5). 94 *Ibid.* at Art. 166(6).

95 Treaty Establishing COMESA, at Art. 168(1).

Table 6.1 *EAC Annual Budget as passed (US$)*

Financial Year	2004/2005	2005/2006	2006/2007	2007/2008	2008/2009	2009/2010
Total Budget	12,300,000	18,930,000	20,609,962	28,313,559	40,499,096	54,257,291
Secretariat			13,423,112		23,400,000	25,655,155
Defense Liaison Unit			379,265		Unknown	1,939,113
Directorate of Customs and Trade			1,171,941		3,371,886	2,982,096
Legislative Assembly			2,924,128		7,348,643	8,573,761
Court of Justice			724,576		2,601,540	2,868,613
Lake Victoria Basin Commission			1,986,941		2,440,826	12,238,553
Financed						
Partner States (members)		10,447,692	4,054,973	22,184,399	24,377,675	27,966,699
Development Partners (external)		8,459,835	7,753,300	6,129,220	16,121,421	26,223,665
Revenue float			662,180			
Miscellaneous income		28,565	29,563			66,927

6 *Financing the EAC budget*

The Treaty Establishing COMESA provides that the budget of the EAC is to be funded by:

> equal contributions by the Partner States and receipts from regional and international donations and any other sources as shall be determined by the Assembly on the recommendation of the Council.[96]

Grants and donations are expressly allowed,[97] the financial year starts on 1 July and ends on 30 June.[98] There is an Audit Commission made up of the Auditors General of the Partner States.[99]

Based on the financial information available and summarized in Table 6.1 above, it would seem that the EAC has become increasingly dependent on external contributors (Development Partners). The total budget has increased at a fairly steady rate: 54% for 2005/2006, 9% increase for 2006/2007, 37% for 2007/2008, 43% for 2008/2009 and 34% for 2009/2010. But the percentage that was expected to come from external sources went from 22% in 2007/2008 to 40% in 2008/2009 and 48% in 2009/2010. This would indicate that the rate of increase of the budget as passed is fairly steady, but the proportion that is to come from external sources is growing as well. Germany contributed €8 million in 2004 and €6 million in 2008 to the construction of the EAC headquarters in Arusha,[100] while France contributed US$550,000 to the Lake Victoria Basin Commission to help develop shipping inspection, search and rescue, oil spill prevention and navigation aid.[101] The increasing reliance on external revenue streams puts the EAC into financial straits for at least two reasons. First, funding from partner states is low at the beginning of the fiscal year; and second, 'funding for most EAC programmes and projects com[es] from Regional Integration Support Program (RISP) and the [European] Partnership Fund'. The Secretary General of the EAC has argued this had to change, noting that the 'EAC must become more financially robust and self sustaining [since] [d]onor dependency for this

96 Treaty Establishing the East African Community (adopted 30 Nov. 1999, into force 7 July 2000), at Art. 132(4).

97 *Ibid.* at Art. 133. 98 *Ibid.* at Art. 132(7). 99 *Ibid.* at Art. 134(1).

100 Staff reporter, 'Germany Tops Up EAC Commitment with Euro 6m', *Arusha Times* (1 Aug. 2008), available at www.arushatimes.co.tz/2008/29/local_news_4.htm.

101 S. Chhatbar, 'France and EAC Sign Lake Victoria Agreement', *Arusha Times* (22 Mar. 2002), available at www.arushatimes.co.tz/2002/12/features_1.htm.

type of organization implies serious consequences when resources do not flow in.'[102]

The EAC Treaty provides that the Secretariat drafts the budget[103] and then submits it to the Council for consideration.[104] After consideration, the Council, which is the policy organ of the EAC, submits it to the East African Legislative Assembly, the legislative organ of the EAC, for approval.[105] Since acts of the Assembly must be assented to by the Summit in order to gain force,[106] the budget order of the Assembly must then be approved by the Summit.

7 Financing ECCAS

The Treaty Establishing ECCAS says that it is to be financed by contributions as assessed by the Conference of the Heads of State and Government (hereinafter 'the Conference'), and of 'all the other sources determined by the Conference'.[107] The Conference, therefore, decides what portion of the budget should be paid by which Member States. The Conference is the highest institution in ECCAS.[108] The treaty also allows ECCAS to accept gifts and donations from external sources.[109]

It provides that if a Member State is in arrears for longer than a year, and does not have a legitimate reason, the Conference may decide to deprive the member from participating in, and benefiting from, the Community.[110] Furthermore, a board of three auditors are to be appointed and removed by the Conference with the Council of Minister's recommendation.[111]

The Treaty Establishing ECCAS states that the General Secretariat prepares the draft budget,[112] which is then presented to the Council of Ministers, which then submits the draft budget and a proposal of annual contributions to the Conference.[113] The Conference then decides what to do with these two proposals: approve them, or send them back down for alterations and improvements.[114] A board of three auditors is appointed and removed by the Conference with the Council's recommendation.[115]

102 East African Community, 'Council Commends Secretariat and Organs for Receiving Unqualified Accounts', Press Release, 22 Oct. 2010.

103 EAC Treaty, at Art. 71(1)(j). 104 *Ibid.* at Art. 14(3)(e). 105 *Ibid.* at Art. 4(2)(b).

106 *Ibid.* at Art. 62(1).

107 Treaty Establishing the Economic Community of Central African States (adopted 18 Oct. 1983, into force 1985), at Art. 79(4).

108 *Ibid.* at Art. 8(2). 109 *Ibid.* at Art. 87(e). 110 *Ibid.* at Art. 80(2).

111 *Ibid.* at Art. 82. 112 Treaty Establishing ECCAS, at Art. 20(c).

113 *Ibid.* at Art. 13(c). 114 *Ibid.* at Art. 9(i). 115 *Ibid.* at Art. 82.

The Treaty Establishing ECCAS states that if a Member State is in arrears for longer than a year, and does not have a legitimate reason, the Conference may decide to deprive the member from participating and from benefiting from the Community.[116]

8 *Financing ECOWAS*

The Treaty of ECOWAS says that it is to be financed by a Community levy and 'such other sources as may be determined by the Council'.[117] The Council of Ministers is the second-highest institution within ECOWAS.[118] These 'other sources' likely include gifts and donations, as in most of the other RTAs' treaties. The levy is 'a percentage of the total value of import duty derivable from goods imported into the Community from third countries'.[119] The Council determines the levy's percentage.[120] A Board of Auditors is appointed by the highest organ of ECOWAS, the Authority of Heads of State and Government.[121]

In mid-2003 the ECOWAS Ministers of Trade and Finance met with representatives of the EU in Accra, Ghana and asked that the EU contribute more funds to ECOWAS.[122] This indicates that ECOWAS had trouble funding its programmes and that external entities were requested to assist in closing the financing gap.

The Treaty of ECOWAS states that the Executive Secretariat is to prepare draft budgets and programmes for the Council, and to supervise their execution once approved.[123] The Administration and Finance Commission (AFC), a Specialized Technical Commission, also recommends draft budgets to the Council, and this is generally done by the Finance Department of the AFC.[124] Individual institutions within ECOWAS can bypass the Executive Secretariat and submit draft budgets to the Council for approval.[125] The Council, therefore, is responsible for approving work programmes and budgets for ECOWAS.[126]

116 *Ibid.* at Art. 80(2).

117 Treaty Establishing the Economic Community of West African States ECOWAS Authority of Heads of State and Government (adopted and enacted 24 July 1993), at Art. 70(1) (replacing the 1975 Treaty of Lagos as the Treaty Establishing ECOWAS).

118 Treaty of ECOWAS, at Art. 10. 119 *Ibid.* at Art. 72(2). 120 *Ibid.* at Art. 72(3).

121 *Ibid.* at Art. 7(3)(e); 7(1).

122 'ECOWAS Seeks Increased EU Funding', *African Business* (1 June 2003), available at www.thefreelibrary.com/ECOWAS+seeks+increased+EU+funding.+(Business+Briefs:+Funding)-a0102660558.

123 Treaty of ECOWAS, at Art. 19(3)(d). 124 *Ibid.* at Art. 69(4).

125 *Ibid.* at Art. 69(3). 126 *Ibid.* at Art. 10(3)(g).

The only information that is currently available on the actual budget of ECOWAS is that the 2001 Operational Budget was set at UA4,161,400 in income, and UA4,090,000 in expenditure:[127] 'UA' stands for 'Units of Account' and it is currently unknown how this translates into US dollars. The 2001 Capital Expenditure Budget was set at UA270,000.[128]

9 *Financing IGAD*

The Agreement Establishing IGAD states that it is to be financed by Member State contributions and 'other sources'.[129] These other sources are donations and grants from external sources.[130] The amount of contributions by Member States are determined based on a scale of assessment that is created by the Assembly of Heads of State and Government,[131] the highest institution within IGAD.[132] The Agreement states that if a Member State falls into arrears for two years or longer, then that Member State is to be barred from speaking and voting at meetings and cannot present candidates for managerial positions at the Secretariat.[133]

IGAD has had extreme difficulty raising revenue from its members. As a result, it readily admits that it is reliant on donor funding. In January 1997 the IGAD Assembly established the IGAD Partners Forum (IPF).[134] The IPF is a body made up of external states and entities that donate funds to IGAD, naturally encouraging it to become economically dependent on the members of IPF. The current members are: Austria, Belgium, Canada, Denmark, France, Germany, Greece, Ireland, Italy, Japan, Netherlands, Norway, Sweden, Switzerland, UK, USA, the European Commission, the International Organization for Migration, the UN Development Programme and the World Bank.[135]

127 Resolution No. 5/11/2000 Relating to the Operational Budget of the ECOWAS Fund for the 2001 Financial Year, ECOWAS Council of Ministers, Resolution No. 5/11/2000 (14 Nov. 2000).

128 Resolution No. 6/11/2000 Relating to the Capital Expenditure Budget of the ECOWAS Fund for the 2001 Financial Year, ECOWAS Council of Ministers, Resolution No. 6/11/2000 (14 Nov. 2000).

129 Agreement Establishing the Inter-Governmental Authority on Development, Intergovernmental Authority on Drought and Development Assembly of Heads of State and Government (adopted 21 March 1996, into force 25 Nov. 1996), at Art. 14(a).

130 *Ibid.* at Art. 15. 131 *Ibid.* at Art. 14(b). 132 *Ibid.* at Art. 9(1).

133 *Ibid.* at Art. 14(c)(i–ii).

134 IGAD, 'About IGAD – IGAD Partners Forum (IPF)', available at http://igad.int/index.php?option=com_content&view=article&id=93&Itemid=124&limitstart=5.

135 *Ibid.*

The Agreement Establishing IGAD states that the Executive Secretary, the chief of the Secretariat, prepares the draft budget for submission to the Council of Ministers,[136] the second-highest institution within IGAD. The Council then approves the draft budget and sends it up to the Assembly for approval.[137]

10 Financing SADC

The Treaty of SADC states that it is to be financed by member contributions, income from enterprises, and from external donations, loans, grants and gifts.[138] Contributions by Member States are made according to a contribution formula to be created by the Summit of Heads of State or Government,[139] the highest policy-making organ of SADC.[140] The Treaty states that any Member State which is in arrears without good cause may have sanctions imposed against it.[141] The Treaty also provides that the Council of Ministers, represented by one minister of each Member State,[142] is to appoint external auditors and, in addition, that the Executive Secretary is to audit its own accounts.[143]

Like other African RTAs, SADC traditionally has trouble with financing its own institutions and programmes. Oliver Saasa pointed this out in 1991, one year before SADC replaced SADCC on 17 August 1992:

> The level of foreign finance in SADCC, constituting 86.26 per cent of the total SADCC requirements as of August 1987, raises issues regarding the extent to which SADCC's objectives of reduction of economic dependence particularly, but not only, on the RSA [Republic of South Africa], is being realized. Hence although there is a lot of enthusiasm within SADCC at the level of project identification, those regional projects which fail to attract foreign blessing usually lag behind, if they are not completely abandoned. As a result, since SADCC was created in 1980, the pace and pattern of project implementation has been critically influenced by the availability of foreign finance.[144]

136 Agreement Establishing IGAD, Intergovernmental Authority on Drought and Development, at Art. 13(j).

137 *Ibid.* at Arts. 10(2)(b); 9(2)(e).

138 Treaty of the Southern African Development Community (adopted and into force 17 Aug. 1992, amended 14 Aug. 2001), at Arts 26 and 25(3).

139 *Ibid.* at Art. 28(2). 140 *Ibid.* at Art. 10(1). 141 *Ibid.* at Art. 33(1)(c).

142 Treaty of SADC, at Art. 11(1). 143 *Ibid.* at Art. 29.

144 O.S. Saasa, 'SADCC Industrial Co-Operation and Donor Support', in O. Saasa (ed.), *Joining the Future: Economic Integration and Co-Operation in Africa* (Nairobi: ACTS Press, 1991), 78–9.

Table 6.2 *SADC Annual Budget as passed (US$)*

Financial Year	2004/2005	2005/2006	2006/2007	2007/2008	2008/2009	2009/2010
Total Budget	16,399,423	37,543,966	39,000,000	45,300,000	49,200,000	50,734,279
Members			14,769,800		24,770,000	24,771,000
Cooperating Partners (external)			23,763,439		24,430,000	28,187,000
Revenue			466,761			

SADC, then, is failing in its goal to bring economic independence to the region of southern Africa.

The Treaty of SADC provides that the Secretary, who heads the Secretariat, is responsible for preparing the budget and auditing the accounts of SADC, and that the Council is responsible for approving these measures.[145] See Table 6.2 for details of the Annual Budget passed 2004/05–2009/10.

Based on the foregoing budget summary, SADC's budget has only increased by a total of 35 per cent since the 2005/2006 financial year, and the amount expected from members has only increased by US$10m. The amount expected from external sources only increased by about half of that. The available figures indicate that SADC may be becoming increasingly self-reliant. In the 2006/2007 financial year, about two-thirds of the budget was expected to come from external sources, while in the 2009/2010 financial year just over half of the budget was expected to come from external sources.

C Conclusion

A major challenge in establishing the true status of the budgetary situations of African RTAs is that these organizations do not consistently make the financial information public. This notwithstanding, the information in this chapter shows that African RTAs and the AU have traditionally had a good deal of trouble in collecting mandatory contributions from Member States. In fact, as early as 1985 late payment of obligations was expected, as pointed out by Peter Robson when he wrote, 'promptness

145 Treaty of SADC, at Art. 15(1)(i).

in meeting financial obligations towards the community cannot yet be invariably relied upon'.[146]

The following additional observations can be made of the financing of African RTAs; (1) RTA overlap has made it very difficult for members to make their contributions or institute policies; (2) sanctions have an unreliable, coercive effect on members of the AEC and, in fact, of any of the RTAs; (3) as far as the budgets as passed go, some RTAs seem to be on the way to self-reliance, while others have dug themselves a hole of debt that only contributions by external entities can dig them out of; (4) some RTAs, like IGAD and the EAC, are openly dependent on external entities and their financial problems do not appear as if they will be resolved any time soon; (5) most of the RTAs seem to be creating more and more institutions with overlapping responsibilities, leading to increased operational costs and less efficiency; and (6) budgets are steadily increasing, while the percentage of up-to-date contributions wavers up and down according to international incidents, internal economic policies and current events.

146 P. Robson, 'Regional Integration and the Crisis in Sub-Saharan Africa', 23 *Journal of Modern African Studies* 609 (1985).

VII

African RTA Judiciaries

A Introduction

This chapter focuses on African Regional Trade Agreement (RTA) judiciaries. African RTAs entertain a broad range of disputes from an extremely broad category of litigants. They are not simply custodians of the trading arrangements – in fact, they do much less dispute settlement around trade issues compared to the broad range of cases they have assumed jurisdiction over. Many of these judiciaries, as we shall see, have also often entertained cases that are well beyond their treaty-defined jurisdictional bases.

Another feature of African RTA judiciaries that comes out clearly is the boldness of their decisions in relation to the fact they are relatively new institutions operating in a context in which adherence to notions of national sovereignty is very strong. The East African Court of Justice (EACJ) has, for example, decided cases relating to human rights, even though there is no explicit treaty basis for the court to assume jurisdiction over human rights cases that challenge the conduct of Member State governments. For taking such bold steps, the leaders of the East African Community (EAC) amended the Treaty Establishing the EAC as a statement of the disapproval of the EACJ's decision in the *Nyong'o* case. Another example is the ECOWAS Court of Justice, whose jurisdiction was expanded in 2005 to allow cases challenging the conduct of Member States with respect to human rights, a jurisdiction it has since not spared in its use. In short, this chapter shows that African RTA judiciaries are not sleeping sentinels of the treaties under which they are established, and it is therefore a call for more attention to be focused on these judiciaries. Of the eight RTAs that are regarded as pillars to the African Economic Community, the Arab Maghreb Union (AMU) and the Intergovernmental Organization on Development (IGAD) do not have judiciaries that, so far as I could find, are operational.

B The COMESA Court of Justice

The Treaty Establishing the Common Market for Eastern and Southern Africa (hereinafter 'Treaty') established the COMESA Court of Justice (hereinafter 'CoJ').[1] The Treaty mandates that the CoJ 'shall ensure the adherence to law in the interpretation and application of this Treaty'.[2] Judgments of the CoJ are 'final and conclusive and not open to appeal'.[3] 'Any dispute concerning the interpretation or application of th[e] Treaty or any of the matters referred to the [CoJ] . . . shall not be subjected to any method of settlement other than those provided for in th[e] Treaty.'[4]

The CoJ is composed of seven judges, appointed by the Authority, and chosen based on their qualifications as impartial and independent judges in their own countries.[5] No two judges may be nationals of the same Member State.[6] The judges on the CoJ serve a five-year term and may be re-appointed to an additional five-year term.[7] The judges on the CoJ were first appointed by the Authority on 30 June 1998.[8] In March 2003 the Authority decided that the seat of the CoJ would be Khartoum, Sudan.[9]

Decisions of the CoJ on the interpretation of the Treaty have precedence over the decisions of the Member States' national courts.[10] However, '[e]xcept where the jurisdiction is conferred on the [CoJ] by or under [the] Treaty, disputes to which the Common Market is a party shall not on that ground alone, be excluded from the jurisdiction of national courts'.[11] As discussed below, Member States' national courts may request a preliminary ruling from the CoJ where a question is raised before such national court concerning the application or interpretation of the Treaty or the validity of an action by COMESA.[12] Where any such question is raised in a Member State's national court and the laws of that Member State do not provide for a judicial remedy for such violation of the Treaty, the national court shall refer the entire matter to the CoJ.[13]

1 Treaty Establishing the Common Market of Eastern and Southern Africa (adopted 21 Dec. 1981, into force 30 Sept. 1982), at Art. 7(1)(c).
2 *Ibid.* at Art. 19. 3 *Ibid.* at Art. 31(1). 4 *Ibid.* at Art. 34(1).
5 *Ibid.* at Art. 20. 6 *Ibid.* at Art. 20(2). 7 *Ibid.* at Art. 21(1).
8 COMESA, 'COMESA Court of Justice', available at http://about.comesa.int/lang-en/institutions/court-of-justice.
9 *Ibid.* 10 Treaty Establishing COMESA, at Art. 29(2).
11 *Ibid.* at Art. 29(1). 12 *Ibid.* at Art. 30(1). 13 *Ibid.* at Art. 30(2).

1 *Jurisdiction*

The Treaty provides that the CoJ has 'jurisdiction to adjudicate upon all matters which may be referred to it pursuant to this Treaty'.[14] 'The Authority, the Council or a Member State may request the Court to give an advisory opinion regarding questions of law arising from the provisions of this Treaty affecting [COMESA].'[15] Where a Member State considers that another Member State or the Council has acted or omitted to act in violation of the Treaty, such Member State may refer the matter to the CoJ.[16] Member States may also refer matters involving 'the legality of any act, regulation, directive or decision of the Council on the grounds that such act, regulation, directive or decision is ultra vires or unlawful or an infringement of the provisions of this Treaty or any rule of law relating to its application or amounts to a misuse or abuse of power'.[17]

Where the Secretary-General considers that a Member State has violated the Treaty, s/he submits his/her findings to the Member State concerned so that the Member State may submit its findings on the matter.[18] Where such Member State does not submit its findings, or such findings are unsatisfactory, the Secretary-General then presents the issue to the Council for consideration.[19] If 'the Council fails to resolve the matter, the Council shall direct the Secretary-General to refer the matter to the [CoJ]'.[20]

Natural and legal persons may refer matters to the CoJ which involve actions or omissions of the Council or a Member State which violate the Treaty.[21] '[W]here the matter for determination relates to any act, regulation, directive or decision by a Member State, such person shall not refer the matter for determination under this Article unless s/he has first exhausted local remedies in the national courts or tribunals of the Member State.'[22] This grant of standing to natural and legal persons illustrates the broadness of jurisdiction of not only the COMESA CoJ, but indeed, all other African RTA judiciaries discussed in this chapter.[23]

The CoJ also has 'jurisdiction to hear disputes between [COMESA] and its employees that arise out of the application and interpretation of

14 *Ibid.* at Art. 23. 15 *Ibid.* at Art. 32(1). 16 *Ibid.* at Art. 24(1).
17 *Ibid.* at Art. 24(2). 18 *Ibid.* at Art. 25(1). 19 *Ibid.* at Art. 25(2).
20 *Ibid.* at Art. 25(3). 21 *Ibid.* at Art. 26. 22 *Ibid.*
23 *Ibid.*; see J. Alvarez, *International Organizations as Lawmakers* (Oxford University Press, 2005), 116 (arguing that 'African institutions anticipate international organizations charged with discharging the kind of plenary executive, legislative, and even judicial powers once associated exclusively with national governments').

the Staff Rules and Regulations of the Secretariat or the terms and conditions of employment of the employees of [COMESA]'.[24] The CoJ may also hear claims by third parties against COMESA or any of its institutions for acts of COMESA employees in the performance of their official duties.[25]

Where COMESA, or any of its institutions, is a party to an agreement, and such agreement allows the CoJ to arbitrate, then the CoJ has jurisdiction to hear the dispute.[26] Where there is a dispute between Member States and they make a special agreement to allow the CoJ to hear the case, the CoJ has jurisdiction to hear such dispute.[27] Member States' national courts may also request a preliminary ruling from the CoJ where a question is raised before such national court concerning the application or interpretation of the Treaty or the validity of an action by COMESA.[28] Where any such question is raised in a Member State's national court and the laws of that Member State do not provide for a judicial remedy for such violation of the Treaty, the national court shall refer the entire matter to the CoJ.[29]

The COMESA Council of Ministers is explicitly given the power and responsibility to 'give directions to all other subordinate organs of the Common Market *other than the [CoJ] in the exercise of its jurisdiction*'.[30] This clause gives the CoJ freedom from intervention by the executive and legislative institutions of COMESA. Perhaps more important is Article 34 of the Treaty, which provides that: the CoJ shall be the sole interpreter of the Treaty;[31] where a dispute has been referred to the CoJ, 'Member States shall refrain from any action which might be detrimental to the resolution of the dispute or might aggravate the dispute';[32] both Member States and the Council must 'take, without delay, the measures required to implement a judgment of the [CoJ]';[33] and the CoJ 'may prescribe such sanctions as it shall consider necessary to be imposed against a party who defaults in implementing the decisions of the Court'.[34]

Former Lord President of the Court of Justice of COMESA, Honourable Mr. Justice A. M. Akiwumi, has opined that the CoJ has 'brought together persons of differing legal traditions to produce a smooth-functioning

24 Treaty Establishing COMESA, Art. 27(1). 25 *Ibid.* at Art. 27(2).
26 *Ibid.* at Art. 28(a). 27 *Ibid.* at Art. 28(b). 28 *Ibid.* at Art. 30(1).
29 *Ibid.* at Art. 30(2). 30 *Ibid.* at Art. 9(2)(c) (emphasis added).
31 *Ibid.* at Art. 34(1). 32 *Ibid.* at Art. 34(2). 33 *Ibid.* at Art. 34(3).
34 *Ibid.* at Art. 34(4).

and authoritative institution', an impressive feat given the varying legal traditions of the COMESA Member States.[35]

C The East African Court of Justice

The EACJ was established under the Treaty Establishing the East African Community.[36] It is tasked with 'ensur[ing] the adherence to law in the interpretation and application of and compliance with [the EAC] Treaty'.[37] The EAC Treaty gives the EACJ 'jurisdiction over the interpretation and application of [the EAC] Treaty . . . [as well as] such other original, appellate, human rights and other jurisdiction as . . . determined by the Council . . . [in] a protocol . . . '.[38] Decisions of the EACJ are 'final, binding and conclusive and not open to appeal'[39] and '[a]ny dispute concerning the interpretation or application of [the EAC] Treaty . . . shall not be subjected to any method of settlement other than those provided for in [the EAC] Treaty'.[40] The EACJ became operational on 30 November 2001, but has since remained in a transitional period, meaning that it only convenes when the need to do so arises, because the Summit has not yet determined that there is enough business to make it fully operational.[41]

The EAC Treaty provides that the judges on the EACJ are to be appointed to the Summit on recommendation by the Partner States.[42] Before the 2006 amendments, the EAC Treaty provided that the EACJ would consist of no more than six judges, with no more than two from

35 A.M. Akiwumi, 'Towards an Independent and Effective Judiciary in Africa', speech given at the African Development Forum Conference, 'Governance for a Progressing Africa', held in Addis Ababa (11–15 Oct. 2004), available at www.uneca.org/adfiv/documents/speeches_and_presentations/speech_akiwumi.htm. Notably, in May 2010, the COMESA CoJ announced that it had contracted with a company to develop a website which 'will provide information on the establishment of the Court, how to access the Court, judgements [*sic*], advisory opinions, arbitration awards, pending cases and news updates from the Court. Once operational, the public will be able to file cases and even conduct searches on cases and rulings online', see 'COMESA Court of Justice to Improve its Visibility' (30 May 2010), available at www.comesa.int/lang-en/component/content/article/34-general-news/382-comesa-court-of-justice-to-improve-its-visibility.

36 Treaty Establishing the East African Community (adopted 30 Nov. 1999, into force 7 July 2000, amended 14 Dec. 2006 and 20 Aug. 2007) (establishing a regional economic community between Burundi, Kenya, Rwanda, Tanzania and Uganda).

37 *Ibid.* at Art. 23(1).

38 *Ibid.* at Art. 27.

39 *Ibid.* at Art. 35(1).

40 *Ibid.* at Art. 38(1).

41 East African Community, 'East African Court of Justice – Role of the Court', Corporate Communications and Public Affairs Department, available at www.eac.int/organs/eacj.html?start=2.

42 EAC Treaty, at Art. 24(1).

each of the original three Partner States.[43] The EAC Treaty as amended split the EACJ into a First Instance Division and an Appellate Division and provides that the Court shall be composed of a maximum of fifteen judges with a maximum of ten for the First Instance Division and five for the Appellate Division.[44] No more than two judges from each of the now five Partner States can be appointed to the First Instance Division and no more than one from each Partner State to the Appellate Division.[45] The seat of the EACJ is to be determined by the Summit.[46] It has not yet determined the permanent seat of the Court, but the temporary seat is in Arusha, Tanzania.[47] In August 2010, the EACJ Court of Appeals held a sitting in Nairobi, Kenya as part of its programme to familiarize East African citizens with its role, while announcing the appellate decision in the *Nyong'o* case.[48] It has also had similar temporary sittings in other East African cities such as Mombasa, Dar es Salaam and Kampala.

The EAC Treaty states that the decisions of the EACJ on the interpretation and application of the EAC Treaty have precedence over the decisions of the national courts.[49] Where jurisdiction is conferred upon the EACJ the national courts have no jurisdiction.[50] However, simply because the Community is a party to a dispute does not mean that the dispute is excluded from the jurisdiction of national courts.[51]

The EACJ expanded the scope of its jurisdiction in 2007 with its decision in *Prof. Peter Anyang' Nyong'o and Others* v. *Attorney General of Kenya and Others*.[52] The Court had been petitioned under Article 30[53] to enjoin the swearing-in of Kenya's nine members of the East African Legislative Assembly.[54] The claimants contended that Kenya had violated Article 50 of the EAC Treaty when selecting its nine members and that the elections were therefore void.[55] Article 50 provides that 'the elected members shall,

43 *Ibid.* at Art. 24 (adopted 30 Nov. 1999).

44 *Ibid.* at Art. 24(2) (adopted 30 Nov. 1999, amended 14 Dec. 2006 and 20 Aug. 2007).

45 *Ibid.* at Art. 24(1). 46 *Ibid.* at Art. 47.

47 East African Community, 'East African Court of Justice', available at www.eac.int/organs/eacj.html?start=5.

48 Press Release, 'East African Court Takes Justice Closer to the People' (13 Aug. 2010), available at http://news.eac.int/index.php?option=com_content&view=article&id=276:eacj-closer-to-the-people&catid=48:eac-latest&Itemid=69.

49 EAC Treaty, at Art. 33(2). 50 *Ibid.* at Art. 33(1). 51 *Ibid.*

52 *Prof. Peter Anyang' Nyong'o and Others* v. *Attorney General of Kenya and Others*, EACJ, Ref. No. 1 of 2006 (30 Mar. 2007).

53 EAC Treaty, *supra* n. 36, at Art. 30.

54 *Nyong'o and Others* v. *Attorney General of Kenya and Others*, at 2. 55 *Ibid.* at 3.

as much as feasible, be representative of specified groups', and sets out the qualifications for election.[56] The Attorney General of Kenya, in a petition for the respondents, argued that Article 52(1) specifically reserved jurisdiction to the High Court of Kenya, and so the EACJ did not have jurisdiction to hear the case.[57] That Article provides, in relevant part: 'Any question that may arise whether any person is an elected member of the Assembly . . . shall be determined by the institution of the Partner State that determines questions of the election of members of the National Assembly.'[58] The EACJ, however, disagreed, finding that since an Article 50 election had not taken place, application of Article 52(1) in the first instance was precluded.[59]

Senior officials within the EAC Partner States and justices of the highest national courts have supported a movement that would allow appeals from the highest national courts to the EACJ.[60] This would also give the Court greater authority to punish corruption, strengthen the judiciaries within the region and harmonize the judicial branches of the Partner States and the EAC itself.[61]

There is also a proposal to amend the EAC Treaty to give the EACJ the authority to try human rights violators.[62] As the Honourable Justice Harold Reginald Nsekela, President of the EACJ, has argued:

> If East Africans are serious about meaningful regional integration, they must be willing and prepared to invest in it, particularly in institutions that will make people develop with dignity. A fully-fledged East African Court of Justice with all its attendant jurisdictional roles is one such institution. East African leaders cannot expect a strong East African Community unless they invest in institutions that will guarantee its existence. We should not expect to reap where we have not sown.[63]

56 *Ibid.* 57 *Ibid.* at 13. 58 EAC Treaty, at Art. 52(1).

59 *Nyong'o and Others* v. *Attorney General of Kenya and Others*, at 14–22.

60 J. Karuhanga, 'EAC Judges Call for Stronger Judicial Systems', *The New Times* (10 Dec. 2009), available at http://allafrica.com/stories/200912100297.html.

61 J. Oyuke, 'EAC Judges Call for a Harmonized Judiciary', *The Standard* (3 Jan. 2010), available at www.standardmedia.co.ke/InsidePage.php?id=2000000137&cid=14&j=&m=&d.

62 F. Oluoch, 'Bid to Let Regional Court of Justice Try Genocide and Human Rights Suspects', *East African* (12 Oct. 2009), available at http://allafrica.com/stories/200910120115.html.

63 President of the East African Court of Justice, H.R. Nsekela, 'The Role of the East African Court of Justice in the Integration Process', presentation during the 3rd East African Community Media Summit (22 Aug. 2009).

The EAC National Human Rights Commission has reviewed the draft EAC Bill of Rights:[64] 'The EAC draft Bill attempts to harmonise the rights and freedoms obtaining in the Partner States. It examines the various national constitutions and other international and regional instruments with a view to standardize and adopt international best practices.'[65] The bill, which contains the right to a fair hearing,[66] would require Partner States to guarantee a large number of rights or be in violation of the EAC Treaty, which in turn would grant the EACJ greater jurisdiction.

Partner States may request advisory opinions from the EACJ.[67] Additionally, Partner States can refer a matter to the EACJ for adjudication where that state 'considers that another Partner State or an organ or institution of the Community has failed to fulfill an obligation under [the EAC] Treaty or has infringed a provision of [the EAC] Treaty'.[68] The EAC Treaty also provides:

> A Partner State may refer for determination by the Court, the legality of any Act, regulation, directive, decision or action on the ground that it is *ultra vires* or unlawful or an infringement of the provisions of this Treaty or any rule of law relating to its application or amounts to a misuse or abuse of power.[69]

Where a question is raised before a national court regarding the validity of some act by the Community the court may request the EACJ to give a preliminary ruling.[70] In such a case, the national court is merely asking the EACJ for an opinion on the matter and is still responsible for issuing the ultimate decision. The national court does not have to request such a ruling and can interpret the EAC Treaty on its own.[71] However, this

64 Press release, 'Heads of Human Rights' Commissions Review EAC Draft Bill of Rights' (EAC Department of Corporate Communications and Public Affairs, 1 June 2010), available at www.news.eac.int/index.php?option=com_content&view=article&id=250:heads-of-human-rights-commissions-review-eac-draft-bill-of-rights&catid=48:eac-latest&Itemid=69; press release, 'Heads of Human Rights Commissions Recommend Draft EAC Bill of Rights to Council of Ministers' (EAC Department of Corporate Communications and Public Affairs, June 4, 2010), available at: www.news.eac.int/index.php?option=com_content&view=article&id=253:nhrcs-recommend-bill-of-rights&catid=48:eac-latest&Itemid=69. (The National Human Rights Commission has recommended the Bill of Rights to the EAC Council of Ministers and it was due to be discussed at EAC Conference on Good Governance in August 2010.)

65 *Ibid.* 66 *Ibid.* 67 EAC Treaty, at Art. 36. 68 *Ibid.* at Art. 28(1).

69 *Ibid.* at Art. 28(2). 70 *Ibid.* at Art. 34. 71 *Ibid.* at Art. 33(1).

is subject to the caveat that any decisions made by the EACJ on 'similar matter[s]' have precedence.[72]

Any natural or legal person who is a resident of a Partner State may refer any matter regarding 'the legality of any Act, regulation, directive, decision or action of a Partner State or an institution of the Community on the grounds that such Act, regulation, directive, decision or action is unlawful or is an infringement of the [EAC] Treaty'.[73] In *Nyong'o*, the Attorney General of Kenya argued that the claimants did not have *locus standi* and therefore no cause of action existed for the claimants.[74] The Court recognized that in order for an adverse litigant to possess *locus standi* he must: (1) have sufficient interest in the subject matter of the adjudication; and (2) 'be seeking a remedy in respect of a legal right, which has been infringed or violated'.[75] However, the Court determined that these requirements apply more to 'actions in tort and suits for breach of statutory duty or breach of contract .... [A] cause of action created by statute or other legislation ... [has i]ts parameters ... defined by the statute or legislation which creates it'.[76] Therefore, since Article 30 imposes no *locus standi* requirement, no such requirement exists for suits brought under Article 30.[77] The same rule applies for Articles 28 (Partner States) and 29 (EAC Secretary General). As such, the EACJ, like the COMESA CoJ, can entertain suits from an extremely broad range of litigants. This is hardly the practice in the European Court of Justice, or even the International Court of Justice, which only entertain suits between states.

Where the EAC Secretary General considers that a Partner State has violated the EAC Treaty, its findings are submitted to that Partner State to submit its observations on the findings.[78] Where such state fails to submit observations within four months, or where the observations are not satisfactory, the Secretary General then refers the matter to the Council, which must then decide to either immediately resolve the issue or order the Secretary General to submit the matter to the EACJ.[79]

The Summit, the highest organ in the Community, can request advisory opinions.[80] The EAC Council, the second-highest organ in the Community, may also request advisory opinions.[81] On 29 April 2009, the EACJ released an Advisory Opinion on the conflicting principles of variable

72 *Ibid.* at Art. 33(2). 73 *Ibid.* at Art. 30.
74 *Nyong'o and Others* v. *Attorney General of Kenya and Others*, at 12. 75 *Ibid.*
76 *Ibid.* at 15. 77 *Ibid.* at 16. 78 EAC Treaty, at Art. 29(1).
79 *Ibid.* at Art. 29(2)–(3). 80 *Ibid.* at Art. 36. 81 *Ibid.* at Arts 14(4) and 36.

geometry and consensus in the EAC's decision-making process, which I have discussed at length elsewhere, as well as in Chaptger II.[82]

The EACJ has jurisdiction to hear and determine disputes between the EAC and its employees where the dispute arises out of 'terms and conditions of employment ... or the application and interpretation of the staff rules and regulations and terms and conditions of service of the [EAC]'.[83] The EACJ can also hear disputes arising from:

> [A]n arbitration clause contained in a contract or agreement which confers such jurisdiction to which the Community or any of its institutions is a party; or a dispute between the Partner States regarding this Treaty if the dispute is submitted to it under a special agreement between the Partner States concerned; or an arbitration clause contained in a commercial contract or agreement in which the parties have conferred jurisdiction on the Court.[84]

On 20 November 2009 the EAC Summit ratified a protocol establishing the EAC Common Market.[85] The protocol states '[a]ny dispute between the Partner States arising from the interpretation or application of this Protocol shall be settled in accordance with the provisions of the Treaty'.[86] Furthermore, the Partner States guaranteed:

> [A]ny person whose rights and liberties as recognised by this Protocol have been infringed upon, shall have the right to redress, even where this infringement has been committed by persons acting in their official capacities; and ... the competent judicial, administrative or legislative authority or any other competent authority, shall rule on the rights of the person who is seeking redress.[87]

Judges on the EACJ may hold office for a maximum of seven years.[88] A judge is to hold office for his or her full term unless: (1) s/he resigns; (2) s/he attains the age of 70; (3) s/he dies; or (4) s/he is removed from office in accordance with the EAC Treaty.[89] Under Article 26(1), a judge may only be removed from office by the Summit:

82 *In the Matter of a Request by the Council of Ministers of the East African Community for an Advisory Opinion*, EACJ Advisory Opinion, App. No. 1 of 2008 (Apr. 2009). See J. Gathii, 'African Regional Trade Agreements as Flexible Legal Regimes', *North Carolina Journal of International Law and Commercial Regulation* 35 (2010) 571.

83 EAC Treaty, at Art. 31. 84 *Ibid.* at Art. 32.

85 Protocol on the Establishment of the East African Community Common Market, East African Community (adopted 20 Nov. 2009).

86 *Ibid.* at Art. 54(1). 87 *Ibid.* at Art. 54(2). 88 EAC Treaty, at Art. 25(1).

89 *Ibid.* at Art. 25(2).

(a) for misconduct or for inability to perform the functions of his or her office due to infirmity of mind or body;
(b) in the case of a judge who also holds judicial office or other public office in a Partner State –
   (i) is removed from that office for misconduct or due to inability to perform the functions of the office for any reason; or
   (ii) resigns from that office following allegation of misconduct or of inability to perform the functions of the office for any reason;
(c) if the judge is adjudged bankrupt under any law in force in a Partner State; or
(d) if the judge is convicted of an offence involving dishonesty or fraud or moral turpitude under any law in force in a Partner State.[90]

The Summit may also suspend a judge when an investigation as to misconduct is pending or where the judge is charged with an offence under Article 26(1)(d).[91]

1 The EACJ's jurisprudence

Based on the EACJ's decisions in *Nyong'o*, discussed above, *East African Law Society* and *Katabazi*, discussed below, and the events surrounding those decisions, it would seem that the EACJ has a greater amount of independence than intended by the drafters of the EAC Treaty. As will be seen in the following analysis of *East African Law Society*, the Court has asserted itself as the supreme authority over the EAC Treaty.

In November 2006 the EACJ issued an interim order to prevent Kenya's appointment of representatives to the EALS and, in March 2007, the Court decided in *Nyong'o* that citizens of Kenya, despite having no *locus standi*, could challenge Kenya's appointments under Article 30 of the EAC Treaty.[92] The EAC Council criticized this exercise of jurisdiction and recommended to the Summit that certain amendments be passed to curtail the Court's power, ultimately resulting in the EAC Treaty's amendment on 14 December 2006.[93] These amendments included:

90 *Ibid.* at Art. 26(1). 91 *Ibid.* at Art. 26(2).

92 *East African Law Society and Others* v. *Attorney General of the Republic of Kenya and Others*, EACJ Judgment Ref. No. 3 of 2007 (Sept. 2008), 2–3. For more on this see *supra.*

93 *Ibid.* at 4. While the final decision in *Nyong'o* was not released until four months after the amendments, the Court had announced that it was granting the claimants jurisdiction in November 2006. *Ibid.* at 3.

(1) restructuring the Court into two divisions: a First Instance Division and an Appellate Division; (2) adding additional grounds for removing a judge from office: 'to limit the Court's jurisdiction so as not to apply to "jurisdiction conferred by the Treaty on organs of Partner States"'; (3) adding a two-month time limit for cases brought by legal and natural persons; and (4) providing grounds for appeal to the Appellate Division of the EACJ.[94]

The amendments allow the removal from office of an EACJ judge who also holds judicial office in a Partner State where that judge is removed from office for misconduct in that position.[95] At the time this amendment was passed, the two Kenyan judges were in the middle of just such a suspension following allegations of corruption against them that had been made in 2003.[96] The Kenyan government attempted to get these two justices, Justices Moijo ole Keiwua and Kasanga Mulwa, removed from the EACJ bench pursuant to the amendments, but their efforts were stopped dead in their tracks.[97]

Several East African national law societies, using Article 30, then challenged the legality under Article 150 (amendment of the Treaty) of the EAC Treaty of the ratification procedures that were employed for these amendments.[98] The four respondents, as in *Nyong'o*, challenged the capacity of the claimant law societies to bring the issue before the Court. The Attorney General of Tanzania and the Secretary General of the EAC argued 'that under international law, the applicants were not competent to challenge the sovereign right of the Partner States to amend the Treaty to which they were parties'.[99] The EACJ concluded that the claimants were not challenging the Partner States' sovereign right to amend; rather, they were contesting the failure to abide by the amendment procedures prescribed by the EAC Treaty.[100]

94 *Ibid.* at 4–5; see also EAC Treaty, at Arts 23(2) (Role of the Court), 26(1)–(2) (Removal from Office and Temporary Membership of the Court), 27(1) (Jurisdiction of the Court), 30 (Legal and Natural Persons) and 35(a) (Appeals).

95 EAC Treaty, at Art. 26(1)(b).

96 Staff writer, 'Kibaki Rails at EAC Court as Rwanda, Burundi Join Up', *The East African* (4 Dec. 2006), available at www.theeastafrican.co.ke/news/-/2558/252342/-/t6awg5z/-/index.html.

97 M. Mati, 'Kenya is Guilty of Judicial Interference', *The East African* (26 Feb. 2007), available at www.theeastafrican.co.ke/opOrEd/-/434748/253402/-/rbk891z/-/index.html.

98 *East African Law Society and Others* v. *Attorney General of the Republic of Kenya and Others*, at 2.

99 *Ibid.* at 9.

100 *Ibid.* at 13.

The Attorney General of Uganda argued that the claim was 'incompetent and misconceived because there was no dispute amongst the parties to the [EAC] Treaty'.[101] Since Article 30 gives legal persons the right to petition the court when there is an infringement of the Treaty this argument was deemed irrelevant.[102]

The Attorney General of Kenya argued that the amendments were actually decisions of the Summit and, thus, not reviewable under Article 30.[103] The Court decided that even though Article 30 makes no mention of an organ of the Community, restricting the Article so that it could not be used where an organ violated the Treaty would defeat its purpose.[104] Further, the Court held that:

> The alleged infringement is the totality of the process of the Treaty amendment, which amendment was, and can only be made by the parties to the Treaty, namely the Partner States, acting together through the organs of the Community. It follows that if in the amendment process the Treaty was infringed, it was infringed by the Partner States. The reference therefore cannot be barred on the ground that its subject matter are decisions and actions of organs of the Community.[105]

Therefore, the Court had jurisdiction.

The EACJ went on to conclude the ratification process that was used in making the amendments constituted an infringement of Articles 150, 5(3)(g) and 7(1)(a) of the EAC Treaty because the Partner States had not allowed the participation of the private sector and civil society in the drafting of the amendments.[106] However, the Court decided not to invalidate the amendments because:

> [T]he infringement was not a conscious one[;] . . . after this clarification of the law on the matter the infringement is not likely to recur[; and] . . . not all the resultant amendments are incompatible with Treaty objectives . . .[107]

In the case of *James Katabazi and 21 Others* v. *Secretary General of the East African Community and Another*, the EACJ was petitioned to determine the lawfulness of the detention of Ugandan prisoners.[108] Sixteen

101 *Ibid.* at 9. 102 *Ibid.* at 13–14. 103 *Ibid.* at 9. 104 *Ibid.* at 15.

105 *Ibid.* at 16. 106 *Ibid.* at 31. 107 *Ibid.* at 43–4.

108 *James Katabazi and 21 Others* v. *Secretary General of the East African Community and Another*, EACJ Judgment Ref. No. 1 of 2007 (1 Nov. 2007).

people had been brought before the Ugandan High Court and charged with treason.[109] The Court granted bail to fourteen of them and it was immediately surrounded by security personnel who re-arrested the men, interfered with the preparation of the bail documents, and took the men back to jail.[110] They were taken before a military general court martial and charged with unlawful possession of firearms and terrorism, stemming from the same facts as the previous charges.[111] The issues of interference with court process and conducting simultaneous civil and military prosecutions was brought before the Constitutional Court of Uganda, which ruled that the interference was unconstitutional and that bail had to be granted to the men.[112] They were not released, and the issue was brought before the EACJ.[113]

The respondents, the Secretary General of the East African Community and the Attorney General of Uganda, challenged the EACJ's jurisdiction to deal with matters of human rights considering that no such jurisdiction had been granted by the EAC Treaty or by the Council under Article 27(2).[114] The Court stated that '[t]he quick answer is: No [this court] does not have [jurisdiction]'.[115] The Court went on to say:

> It very [*sic*] clear that jurisdiction with respect to human rights requires a determination of the Council and a conclusion of a protocol to that effect. Both of those steps have not been taken. It follows, therefore, that this Court may not adjudicate on disputes concerning violation of human rights *per se*.[116]

Despite this, the Court determined that '[w]hile the Court will not assume jurisdiction to adjudicate on human rights disputes, it will not abdicate from exercising its jurisdiction of interpretation under Article 27(1) merely because the reference includes allegation of human rights violation'.[117] In other words, as long as a dispute gives the EACJ jurisdiction under Article 27, the fact that the dispute involves human rights is merely incidental.

The EACJ then discussed whether it had Article 27 jurisdiction. It determined that Article 23 provides that the EACJ 'shall ensure the adherence to law', which meant that where the law has not been adhered to the EACJ would have Article 27(1) jurisdiction to compel adherence.[118] The

109 *Ibid.* at 1. 110 *Ibid.* at 2. 111 *Ibid.* 112 *Ibid.* 113 *Ibid.*
114 *Ibid.* at 12. 115 *Ibid.* at 14. 116 *Ibid.* at 15. 117 *Ibid.* at 16.
118 *Ibid.* at 23.

Court then determined that Articles 5(1),[119] 6,[120] 7(2)[121] and 8(1)(c)[122] require Partner States to abide by the decisions of their courts.[123] It held:

> [T]he intervention by the armed security agents of Uganda to prevent the execution of a lawful Court order violated the principle of the rule of law and consequently contravened the Treaty. Abiding by the court decision is the corner stone of the independence of the judiciary which is one of the principles of the observation of the rule of law.[124]

Therefore, since the issue in the case was whether Articles 5 to 8 had been adhered to, Article 23 gave the EACJ Article 27(1) jurisdiction, making the issue of human rights incidental and giving the Court jurisdiction to hear the case.[125]

The EACJ based its decision in *Katabazi* on the objectives and purposes clauses of the Treaty, which are regarded as preambles that do not create binding obligations. Objectives and purposes clauses are therefore not thought of as creating independent or substantive grounds for granting relief. Rather, they are meant to give the Treaty context. In 2000, the Iran-United States Claims Tribunal put it this way:

> [W]hen one is dealing with the object and purpose of a treaty, which is the most important part of the treaty's context, the object and purpose does not constitute an element independent of that context. The object and purpose is not to be considered in isolation from the terms of the treaty;

119 *Ibid.* at 15 ('The objectives of the Community shall be to develop policies and programmes aimed at widening and deepening co-operation among the Partner States in political, economic, social and cultural fields, research and technology, defence, security and legal and judicial affairs, for their mutual benefit') (quoting the EAC Treaty, at Art. 5(1)).

120 *Ibid.* 'Article 6 sets out the fundamental principles of the Community which governs the achievement of the objectives of the Community, of course as provided in Article 5 (1). Of particular interest here is paragraph (d) which talks of the rule of law and the promotion and the protection of human and peoples rights in accordance with the provisions of the African Charter on Human and Peoples' Rights.'

121 *Ibid.* at 16. 'The Partner States undertake to abide by the principles of good governance, including adherence to the principles of democracy, the rule of law, social justice and the maintenance of universally accepted standards of human rights' (quoting the EAC Treaty, *supra* n. 36, at Art. 7(2)).

122 *Ibid.* '[T]he Partner States undertake, among other things, to: Abstain from any measures likely to jeopardize the achievement of those objectives or the implementation of the provisions of this Treaty' (quoting the EAC Treaty, at Art. 8(1)(c)).

123 *James Katabazi and 21 Others* v. *Secretary General of the East African Community and Another*, at 15–23.

124 *Ibid.* 125 *Ibid.* at 23.

> it is intrinsic to its text. It follows that, under Article 31 of the Vienna Convention,[126] a treaty's object and purpose is to be used only to clarify the text, not to provide independent sources of meaning that contradict the clear text.[127]

Notwithstanding this, the EACJ determined that Article 5(1), which spells out one of the objectives of the Community, requires Partner States to abide by the decisions of their courts. The *Katabazi* decision illustrates the interpretive boldness of the EACJ, not only in seizing jurisdiction over cases that raise sovereignty questions for the Member States as well as in creatively using preambular provisions of the Treaty Establishing the EACJ to determine cases brought before it when such cases involve human rights which are not an enumerated base for the exercise of jurisdiction by the ground.

D The ECOWAS Community Court of Justice

The Treaty of ECOWAS (hereinafter 'Treaty') establishes the Community Court of Justice (hereinafter 'CCJ').[128] The Treaty limits the CCJ's

126 Vienna Convention on the Law of Treaties (signed 23 May 1969, into force 27 Jan. 1980), at Art. 31.

1. A treaty shall be interpreted in good faith in accordance with the ordinary meaning to be given to the terms of the treaty in their context and in the light of its object and purpose.
2. The context for the purpose of the interpretation of a treaty shall comprise, in addition to the text, including its preamble and annexes:
   (a) any agreement relating to the treaty which was made between all the parties in connection with the conclusion of the treaty;
   (b) any instrument which was made by one or more parties in connection with the conclusion of the treaty and accepted by the other parties as an instrument related to the treaty.
3. There shall be taken into account, together with the context:
   (a) any subsequent agreement between the parties regarding the interpretation of the treaty or the application of its provisions;
   (b) any subsequent practice in the application of the treaty which establishes the agreement of the parties regarding its interpretation;
   (c) any relevant rules of international law applicable in the relations between the parties.
4. A special meaning shall be given to a term if it is established that the parties so intended.

127 *United States* v. *Iran* (Iran-U.S. Cl. Trib. Rep. 2000) No. 130-A28-FT, para. 58.

128 Revised Treaty Establishing the Economic Community of West African States, ECOWAS Authority of Heads of State and Government (adopted and enacted 24 July 1993) (replacing the 1975 Treaty of Lagos as the Treaty Establishing ECOWAS), at Arts. 7(1)(e), 15(1).

authority to 'perform[ing its] functions and act[ing] within the limits of the powers conferred on [it] by this Treaty and by the Protocols relating thereto'.[129] However, '[j]udgments of the Court of Justice [are] binding on the Member States, the institutions of the Community and on individuals and corporate bodies'.[130] The CCJ's judges were appointed on 30 January 2001.[131]

The Community Court Protocol (hereinafter 'Protocol') came into force on 5 November 1996[132] and was amended in 2005.[133] The Protocol expanded the CCJ's authority by mandating:

> The Court has competence to adjudicate on any dispute relating to the following:
>
> (a) the interpretation and application of the Treaty, Conventions and Protocols of the Community;
> (b) the interpretation and application of the regulations, directives, decisions and other subsidiary legal instruments adopted by ECOWAS;
> (c) the legality of regulations, directives, decisions and other subsidiary legal instruments adopted by ECOWAS;
> (d) the failure by Member States to honour their obligations under the Treaty, Conventions and Protocols, regulations, directives, or decisions of ECOWAS;
> (e) the provisions of the Treaty, Conventions and Protocols, regulations, directives, or decisions of ECOWAS Member States;
> (f) the Community and its officials; and
> (g) the action for damages against a Community institution or an official of the Community for any action or omission in the exercise of official functions.[134]

The Treaty also mandated the creation of an Arbitration Tribunal of the Community.[135] The Arbitration Tribunal has yet to be set up, but until

129 *Ibid.* at Art. 7(2). 130 *Ibid.* at Art. 15(4).

131 African International Courts and Tribunals, 'ECOWAS CCJ', available at www.aict-ctia.org/courts_subreg/ecowas/ecowas_home.html.

132 A.O. Enabulele, 'Reflections on the ECOWAS Community Court Protocol and the Constitutions of the Member States', *International Community Law Review* 12 (Mar. 2010) 111, 115.

133 *Ibid.* at 117; see also 'Supplementary Protocol, A/SP.1/01/05 Amending the Preamble and Articles 1, 2, 9, 22 and 30 of Protocol A/P.1/7/91 Relating to the Community Court of Justice and Article 4 Paragraph 1 of the English Version of Said Protocol', 28th Session of the Authority of Heads of State and Government (19 Jan. 2004).

134 ECOWAS Community Court of Justice, Protocol A/P.1/7/91 (adopted 6 July 1991, into force 5 Nov. 1996, amended by Supplementary Protocol A/SP.1/01/05 in 2005), at Art. 9(1).

135 Treaty of ECOWAS, at Art. 16(1).

then the Protocol allows the CCJ to act in that capacity.[136] The Treaty mandates that '[t]he status, composition, powers, procedure and other issues concerning the Court of Justice shall be as set out in a Protocol relating thereto'.[137] The Protocol mandates that the CCJ shall consist of seven judges, appointed by the Authority of Heads of States and Government from a pool of nominees, two from each state.[138] Members of the CCJ are appointed for a five-year term and may be re-appointed only once.

The Treaty states '[t]he Court of Justice shall carry out the functions assigned to it independently of the Member States and the institutions of the Community'.[139] Furthermore, the Member States agreed to 'undertake to co-operate in judicial and legal matters with a view to harmonizing their judicial and legal systems'.[140] The Protocol allows national courts to present certified questions on issues of interpretation and application of the Treaty and other ECOWAS texts.[141]

Article 10 of the Protocol allows the CCJ to give advisory opinions to any Member State, the President of the ECOWAS Commission and any ECOWAS institution, upon request.[142] The Treaty also provides that '[a]ny dispute regarding the interpretation or the application of the provisions of this Treaty shall he [*sic*] amicably settled through direct agreement without prejudice to the provisions of this Treaty and relevant Protocols'.[143] In the event such agreement cannot be reached, 'either party or any other Member States or the Authority may refer the matter to the Court of the Community whose decision shall be final and shall not be subject to appeal'.[144] The Protocol authorizes Member States and the Executive Secretary to bring an action before the CCJ for the alleged failure of a Member State to perform an obligation.[145] Furthermore, Member States, the Council of Ministers and the Executive Secretary may bring a proceeding before the CCJ to determine the legality of an action in relation to any ECOWAS text.[146]

The Authority of Heads of States and Government also has the 'power to grant the Court the power to adjudicate on any specific dispute that

136 Community Court Protocol A/P.1/7/91, at Art. 9(5).
137 Treaty of ECOWAS, at Art. 15(2).
138 Community Court Protocol A/P.1/7/91, at Art. 2.
139 Treaty of ECOWAS, at Art. 15(3). 140 *Ibid.* at Art. 57(1).
141 Community Court Protocol A/P.1/7/91, at Art. 10(f).
142 *Ibid.* at Art. 10. 143 Treaty of ECOWAS, at Art. 76(1).
144 *Ibid.* at Art. 76(2).
145 Community Court Protocol A/P.1/7/91, at Art. 10(a).
146 *Ibid.* at Art. 10(b).

it may refer to the Court other than those specified in [the Protocol]'.[147] Individuals and corporate bodies may also bring a proceeding before the CCJ 'for the determination of an act or inaction of a Community official which violates the rights of the individuals or corporate bodies'.[148] Individuals are also explicitly granted the right to bring cases of violations of human rights before the CCJ.[149]

Where an agreement gives the CCJ jurisdiction over dispute settlement, the CCJ has such jurisdiction.[150] The staff of any ECOWAS institution can also bring an action before the CCJ once it has 'exhausted all appeal processes available . . . under the ECOWAS Staff Rules and Regulations'.[151] Where an issue of interpretation as to the COMESA Treaty, COMESA protocols, or COMESA regulations arises within a Member State's national court, such national court may, of its own volition, or at the request of a party to the action, refer the issue to the CCJ for interpretation.[152]

Prior to the 2005 amendment of the Protocol by the Supplemental Protocol,[153] individuals were not allowed to bring suit in the CCJ.[154] This was a heavy restriction on the power of the CCJ to enforce the Treaty upon ECOWAS Member States and ECOWAS stood apart from other RTA judiciaries which, as we have seen so far, allow such cases.[155] The 2003 case of *Olajide Afolabi* v. *Federal Republic of Nigeria*[156] and the 2004 case of *Frank Ukor* v. *Rachard Lalaye,*[157] discussed below, emphasized this fact.[158]

In 2003, Nigeria closed its common border with Benin, which hurt many of the businesses along the border.[159] A Nigerian citizen applied to the CCJ to have his suit heard on the ground that the border closure had caused loss to his business in violation of the Treaty.[160] Nigeria objected to the CCJ's jurisdiction to hear the case under the Treaty and the Protocol.[161] The CCJ agreed, and dismissed the case. In 2004, Benin seized a national's truck and goods.[162] The citizen applied to the CCJ to quash the order that his truck and goods be seized as violative of the Treaty.[163] Benin objected to jurisdiction and, again, the CCJ dismissed the case.[164] These cases are,

147 *Ibid.* at Art. 9(8). 148 *Ibid.* at Art. 10(c). 149 *Ibid.* at Art. 10(d).
150 *Ibid.* at Art. 9(6). 151 *Ibid.* at Art. 10(e). 152 *Ibid.* at Art. 10(f).
153 Supplementary Protocol A/SP.1/01/05, *supra* n. 134.
154 Enabulele, 'Reflections on the ECOWAS Community Court Protocol', at 116–19.
155 *Ibid.*
156 *Olajide Afolabi* v. *Federal Republic of Nigeria*, ECW/CCJ/APP/01/03 (2003).
157 *Frank Ukor* v. *Rachard Lalaye*, ECW/CCJ/APP/01/04 (2004).
158 Enabulele, 'Reflections on the ECOWAS Community Court Protocol', at 116.
159 *Ibid.* 160 *Ibid.* 161 *Ibid.* 162 *Ibid.* at 117. 163 *Ibid.* 164 *Ibid.*

in large part, the reason why the Supplemental Protocol was established in 2005.[165]

Since the 2005 amendments to the Protocol, many citizens of Member States have brought cases before the CCJ, and many have won. In 2008, a citizen of Niger brought suit in the CCJ against Niger for failing to protect her human rights, as she had been a slave for almost her entire life.[166] The citizen won the case and was awarded about $17,000.[167]

A more controversial decision of the CCJ came in 2009, in the case of *Socio-Economic Rights and Accountability Project (SERAP)* v. *Federal Republic of Nigeria and Universal Basic Education Commission*.[168] In this case, SERAP, a human rights non-governmental organization (NGO), brought suit in the CCJ as a legal person against Nigeria for human rights violations on the ground that Nigeria had not adequately implemented its Basic Education Act and Child's Rights Act of 2004, and had thus violated both the African Charter and the ECOWAS Treaty.[169] Nigeria alleged that the CCJ did not have jurisdiction, notwithstanding the express provision of the Protocol.[170] The CCJ noted that Article 9(4) of the Protocol states '[t]he [CCJ] has jurisdiction to determine cases of violation of human rights that occur in any Member State'; that Article 4(g) of the ECOWAS Treaty affirms that the Member States must adhere to the 'recognition, promotion and protection of human and peoples' rights in accordance with the provisions of the African Charter on Human and Peoples' Rights'; and that Article 17 of the African Charter states that '[e]very individual shall have the right to education'.[171] Thus, the CCJ determined that it had jurisdiction, but there is yet to be a decision on the substantive issues of the case, namely whether Nigeria had actually violated its citizens' right to an education.[172]

Some commentators believe a severe conflict between the CCJ and the constitutions of the various Member States is inevitable, and that the only reason this conflict has yet to come to light is due to the relative youth

165 *Ibid.* at 116–19.

166 P. Walker, 'Niger Guilty in Landmark Slavery Case', *The Guardian* (27 Oct. 2008), available at www.guardian.co.uk/world/2008/oct/27/niger-slave-court; see also *Hadijatou Mani Koraou* v. *Republic of Niger*, Judgment No. ECW/CCJ/APP/08/08 (unofficial translation of Judgment No. ECW/CCJ/JUD/06/08 (27 Oct. 2008)).

167 *Ibid.*

168 Judgment No. ECW/CCJ/APP/08/08.

169 ESCR-Net, *Socio-Economic Rights and Accountability Project (SERAP)* v. *Federal Republic of Nigeria and Universal Basic Education Commission*, Judgment No. ECW/CCJ/APP/0808 (International Network for Economic, Social and Cultural Rights, 2009), available at www.escr-net.org/caselaw/caselaw_show.htm?doc_id=1143047.

170 *Ibid.*

171 *Ibid.*

172 *Ibid.*

of the CCJ.[173] The 2005 Protocol does not give citizens of Member States the right to bring cases involving the interpretation and application of the Treaty. Instead, it authorizes citizens to bring suits before the CCJ that involve, generally, alleged violations of human rights.[174] As pointed out by A.O. Enabulele:

> Article 3 of the Constitution of the Republic of Benin, 1990; Article 4 of the Constitution of the Gambia, 1997; Article 1(2) of the Constitution of the Republic of Ghana, 1992; Article 2 of the Constitution of Liberia, 1984; [and] Section 1(3) of the Constitution of The Federal Republic of Nigeria, 1999; [make] the various constitutions supreme and binding on all persons and authorities within their respective spheres of influence. Any law that is inconsistent with the provisions of any of the constitutions, within its sway is null and void to the extent of its inconsistency.[175]

Therefore, if the CCJ were to hear a human rights case and find that some action by a Member State violates the Treaty, yet one of that Member State's national courts also determined the action was authorized under the national constitution, then there would be an irreconcilable conflict between national and international law.[176] However, as I have observed elsewhere, the supremacy of national constitutions over international law, particularly in commonwealth African countries, is slowly ebbing away.[177]

E The SADC Tribunal

The Treaty of the Southern African Development Community (hereinafter 'Treaty') establishes the Tribunal 'to ensure adherence to and the proper interpretation of the provisions of this Treaty and subsidiary instruments and to adjudicate upon such disputes as may be referred to it'.[178] Further emphasis is given to this objective in Article 32: 'Any dispute arising from the interpretation or application of this Treaty, the interpretation, application or validity of Protocols or other subsidiary instruments made under this Treaty, which cannot be settled amicably,

173 Enabulele, 'Reflections on the ECOWAS Community Court Protocol', at 111.
174 Community Court Protocol A/P.1/7/91, at Art. 10(d).
175 Enabulele, 'Reflections on the ECOWAS Community Court Protocol', at 121.
176 *Ibid.* at 121–34.
177 J. Gathii, 'Kenya's Piracy Prosecutions', *American Journal of International Law* 104 (2010).
178 Treaty Establishing the Southern African Development Community (adopted and into force 17 Aug. 1992, amended 14 Aug. 2001), at Arts 1(g) and 16(1).

shall be referred to the Tribunal.'[179] The Treaty mandates '[t]he decisions of the Tribunal shall be final and binding'.[180] Furthermore, subsection 2 of Article 16 of the Treaty states, '[t]he composition, powers, functions, procedures and other related matters governing the Tribunal shall be prescribed in a Protocol, which shall, notwithstanding the provisions of Article 22 of this Treaty, form an integral part of this Treaty, adopted by the Summit'.[181] Article 22 is the Article which addresses the requirements of the ratification process for protocols to the Treaty.[182]

The Protocol on Tribunal and the Rules of Procedure Thereof was passed by the Summit in August 2000 in accordance with Article 16 of the Treaty.[183] While the tribunal has begun operating, the Protocol on Tribunal has not yet been ratified by two-thirds of Member States as required by Article 22.[184] There is much dispute over whether this protocol in particular can be given effect without such ratification. I will return to this topic below. The Protocol on Tribunal mandated the Council to determine where the seat of the tribunal would be located.[185] The Council eventually chose Windhoek, Namibia.[186]

The Treaty for the Establishment of SADC states: 'Members of the Tribunal shall be appointed for a specified period.'[187] The Protocol mandates: 'The Tribunal shall consist of not less than ten (10) Members, appointed from nationals of States who possess the qualifications required for appointment to the highest judicial offices in their respective States or who are jurists of recognised [*sic*] competence.'[188] The Summit, on recommendation of the Council, is to appoint the ten members,[189] five of which it is to designate as 'regular Members', those who 'shall sit regularly on the Tribunal'.[190] The other five 'constitute a pool from which the President [of the Tribunal] may invite a Member to sit on the Tribunal whenever a regular Member is temporarily absent or is otherwise unable to carry out his or her functions'.[191] The Protocol states that the Tribunal

179 *Ibid.* at Art. 32. 180 *Ibid.* at Art. 16(5).

181 *Ibid.* at Art. 16(2). 182 *Ibid.* at Art. 22.

183 Southern African Development Community, Protocol on Tribunal and the Rules of Procedure Thereof (adopted 7 Aug. 2000).

184 Zimbabwe Human Rights NGO Forum, 'Status and Meaning of Ratification of SADC Treaty and Tribunal Protocol', press release (6 Sept. 2009), available at www.zimbabwedemocracynow.com/2009/09/06/status-and-meaning-of-ratification-of-sadc-treaty-and-tribunal-protocol.

185 SADC Protocol on Tribunal, at Art. 13.

186 SADC, 'SADC Tribunal', available at www.sadc.int/tribunal.

187 SADC Treaty, at Art. 16(3). 188 SADC Protocol on Tribunal, at Art. 3(1).

189 *Ibid.* at Art. 4(4). 190 *Ibid.* at Art. 3(2). 191 *Ibid.*

is constituted by three members, but it may decide to constitute all five for any case.[192] The Tribunal only sits when there is a case submitted to it[193] and the President of the Tribunal decides who shall sit for any case.[194] The Council may increase the number of members on a proposal from the Tribunal.[195]

At any time, none of the members may be nationals of the same state.[196] To this end, each Member State nominates one candidate and the Council chooses amongst these candidates, with due consideration given to gender representation.[197] The members of the Tribunal serve a five-year term and may only be re-appointed for an additional five-year term.[198] The Tribunal only sits when there is a case, although the Council may decide to make it a full-time position and, if it does, members would no longer be allowed to hold any other office or employment.[199] Regardless of this, members are not allowed to exercise any political or administrative function or engage in any trade that would interfere with their duties, impartiality, or independence as a member of the Tribunal.[200] The President of the Tribunal is elected by the members and holds this position for 3 years.[201] Members and the President may resign at any time, and may only be dismissed in accordance with the Tribunal Rules.[202]

With regard to the relationship between the tribunal and Member States, the Treaty for the Establishment of SADC provides that 'the members of the Tribunal . . . shall be committed to the international character of SADC, and shall not seek or receive instructions from any Member States, or from any authority external to SADC'.[203] The Tribunal 'may rule on a question of interpretation, application or validity of the provisions in issue if the question is referred to it by a court or tribunal of a State'.[204]

The Tribunal also has original jurisdiction over all disputes and all applications referred to it in accordance with the Treaty and this Protocol which relate to:

(a) the interpretation and application of the Treaty;
(b) the interpretation, application or validity of the Protocols, all subsidiary instruments adopted within the framework of the community, and acts of the institutions of the community; and

192 *Ibid.* at Art. 3(3). 193 *Ibid.* at Art. 6(2). 194 *Ibid.* at Art. 3(4).
195 *Ibid.* at Art. 3(5). 196 *Ibid.* at Art. 3(6). 197 *Ibid.* at Art. 4(1), (2) and (3).
198 *Ibid.* at Art. 6(1). 199 *Ibid.* at Art. 6(2) and (3). 200 *Ibid.* at Art. 9(1).
201 *Ibid.* at Art. 7(1). 202 *Ibid.* at Art. 8. 203 SADC Treaty, at Art. 17(2).
204 SADC Protocol on Tribunal, at Art. 16.

(c) all matters specifically provided for in any other agreements that states may conclude among themselves or within the community and which confer jurisdiction on the Tribunal.[205]

The Tribunal is directed to develop its own case law, 'having regard to applicable treaties, general principles and rules of public international law and any rules and principles of the law of States'.[206] The Protocol provides: 'Where a dispute is referred to the Tribunal by any party the consent of other parties to the dispute [is] not . . . required.'[207] The Tribunal does not have original jurisdiction, but it may give preliminary rulings in certain cases.[208]

According to the Treaty for the Establishment of the SADC, 'The Tribunal shall give advisory opinions on such matters as the Summit or the Council may refer to it.'[209] The SADC Summit and Council are the only entities that the Treaty and the Protocol allow to request advisory opinions. The Tribunal has 'exclusive jurisdiction over all disputes between the States and the Community. Such disputes may be referred to the Tribunal . . . by the competent institution or organ of the Community'.[210] It also has 'exclusive jurisdiction over all disputes between natural or legal persons and the Community. Such disputes may be referred to the Tribunal . . . by the competent institution or organ of the Community.'[211]

The Tribunal has 'jurisdiction over disputes between States'.[212] Where there is a dispute between the community and a state, the state may refer the issue to the Tribunal.[213] The Tribunal 'may [also] rule on a question of interpretation, application or validity of the provisions in issue if the question is referred to it by a court or tribunal of a State for a preliminary ruling in accordance with this Protocol'.[214] As such, the Tribunal has 'jurisdiction to give preliminary rulings in proceedings of any kind and between any parties before the courts or tribunals of States'.[215] In addition, as is typical of other African RTA judiciaries, the Tribunal has exclusive jurisdiction over all disputes between natural and legal persons and the SADC, and the person may bring the suit.[216] A natural or legal

205 *Ibid.* at Art. 14. 206 *Ibid.* at Art. 21. 207 *Ibid.* at Art. 15(3).

208 *Ibid.* at Art. 16. For an explanation of these instances, see *supra* this section.

209 SADC Treaty, at Art. 16(4); SADC Protocol on Tribunal, at Art. 20 ('The Tribunal shall have jurisdiction to give advisory opinions, which may be requested by the Summit or by the Council').

210 *Ibid.* at Art. 17. 211 *Ibid.* at Art. 18. 212 *Ibid.* at Art. 15(1).

213 *Ibid.* at Art. 17. 214 *Ibid.* at Art. 16(2). 215 *Ibid.* at Art. 16(1).

216 *Ibid.* at Art. 18.

person may not bring suit against a Member State 'unless he or she has exhausted all available remedies or is unable to proceed under the domestic jurisdiction'.[217] Finally, the Tribunal has 'exclusive jurisdiction over all disputes between the Community and its staff relating to their conditions of employment'.[218]

The Tribunal's legitimacy has been brought into sharp focus as a result of its decision on Zimbabwe's land reform programme. Following that decision, many officials within Zimbabwe's government argued that the Tribunal does not currently exist, for reasons we shall see below. The Tribunal has reported its findings to the Summit and is awaiting action to determine if the Tribunal's decision should be recorded by the Member States. The next section of this chapter examines the Tribunal's jurisprudence.

1 The SADC Tribunal's jurisprudence

The case that started the controversy over the SADC Tribunal's legitimacy is *Mike Campbell (Pvt) Ltd. and 78 Others* v. *The Republic of Zimbabwe*.[219] The applicants (natural and legal persons), in that case were land-owners challenging Zimbabwe's land reform programme which essentially permitted taking the applicants' land from them and redistributing it.[220] The Tribunal determined that it only had jurisdiction if: (1) the applicants had standing in that they had 'exhaust[ed] all available remedies or . . . [were] unable to proceed under the domestic jurisdiction of [Zimbabwe]'; and (2) the dispute related to interpretation and application of the Treaty.[221]

The Tribunal first determined if the dispute was within its scope of jurisdiction.[222] The applicants began their case at the Tribunal on 11 October 2007 with an application for an interim measure under Article 28 of the Protocol on Tribunal to restrain the government of Zimbabwe from removing the applicants from their land.[223] However, the respondent argued that the applicants had not exhausted all of their local remedies, as they had begun a case before the Supreme Court of Zimbabwe.[224] The Tribunal, however, determined:

217 *Ibid.* at Art. 15(2). 218 *Ibid.* at Art. 19.

219 *Mike Campbell (Pvt) Ltd. and 78 Others* v. *The Republic of Zimbabwe*, SADC (T) Case No. 2/2007 [2008] SADCT 2 (28 Nov. 2008).

220 *Ibid.* at 4–7. 221 *Ibid.* at 17–18. 222 *Ibid.* at 17–23.

223 *Ibid.* at 4. 224 *Ibid.* at 19–21.

> The rationale for exhaustion of local remedies is to enable local courts to first deal with the matter because they are well placed to deal with the legal issues involving national law before them. It also ensures that the international tribunal does not deal with cases which could easily have been disposed of by national courts.[225]

Therefore, the Tribunal reasoned:

> [W]here the municipal law does not offer any remedy or the remedy that is offered is ineffective, the individual is not required to exhaust local remedies. Further, where . . . the procedure of achieving the remedies would have been unduly prolonged, the individual is not expected to exhaust local remedies.[226]

The Tribunal thus determined that if an applicant's local remedies suffered from *de facto* exhaustion, the Tribunal would have jurisdiction. In fact, the Supreme Court of Zimbabwe had already rendered a decision in the applicants' case,[227] as discussed below.

The applicants in the Tribunal's case were challenging Section 16B of Amendment 17 of the Constitution of Zimbabwe.[228] Subsection (3)(b) of that section states: 'a person having any right or interest in the [reorganized] land . . . shall not apply to a court to challenge the acquisition of the land by the State, and no court shall entertain any such challenge'.[229] Therefore, the Tribunal determined, the amendment had 'ousted the jurisdiction of the courts of law in Zimbabwe from any case related to acquisition of agricultural land and that, as such, the first and second Applicants were unable to institute proceedings under the domestic jurisdiction'.[230] The Tribunal noted that this position was confirmed by the Supreme Court of Zimbabwe on 22 January 2008 in the applicants' case.[231]

The Tribunal next had to determine if there was a proper basis of jurisdiction such that it could hear the dispute; that is, whether the dispute related to interpretation and application of the Treaty.[232] On this issue, the respondent argued there was no such base, as the Treaty only mentions human rights as a principle of the SADC and there is no protocol that governs human rights standards or agrarian reform.[233] The respondent went on to argue that, in the absence of such protocols, the Tribunal

225 *Ibid.* at 20. 226 *Ibid.* at 21 (internal quotations omitted).

227 *Mike Campbell (Pty) Ltd.* v. *Minister of National Security Responsible for Land, Land Reform and Resettlement* (124/06) [2008] ZWSC 1 (22 Jan. 2008).

228 *Ibid.* at 8. 229 *Ibid.* at 11. 230 *Ibid.* at 21. 231 *Ibid.*

232 *Mike Campbell (Pvt) Ltd. and 78 Others* v. *The Republic of Zimbabwe*, at 23–6.

233 *Ibid.* at 23.

cannot adopt '[human rights] standards from other Treaties as this would amount to legislating on behalf of SADC Member States'.[234] The Tribunal, however, noted that Article 21(b) of the Treaty mandates the Tribunal to develop its own jurisprudence and to do so having regard for general principles and rules of public international law.[235] Article 4(c) requires Member States to act in accordance with 'human rights, democracy and the rule of law'.[236] Therefore, as long as one of these interconnected principles had been violated by Zimbabwe, the Tribunal had jurisdiction to hear the dispute under Article 15(2) of the Treaty. The Tribunal noted that Amendment 17 of the Constitution of Zimbabwe denied the respondents access to the courts and the right to a fair hearing and so determined that their human rights, democracy and the rule of law had been violated, and that the Tribunal had jurisdiction.[237]

After granting jurisdiction, the Tribunal went on to discuss the substantive questions raised in the case. In its ruling, it held that the applicants had been discriminated against on the ground of race, the respondent owed the applicants fair compensation for the lands that had been taken from them, and both the respondent and Amendment 17 itself were in breach of Articles 4(c)[238] and 6(2)[239] of the Treaty.[240]

Zimbabwe did not comply with the Tribunal's ruling.[241] Instead, it argued it had not ratified the Protocol on Tribunal and therefore it did not have to abide by the decision of the Tribunal. Second, Zimbabwe argued that as the Summit had not formally made the SADC Tribunal operational, it was not yet established and as such it did not in fact exist.[242] The first of these two arguments is certainly the weaker. Even though Article 22 of the Treaty states, 'Each Protocol shall be binding only on the Member States that are party to the Protocol in question', the Article which sets up the Tribunal, Article 16, states, 'The composition, powers, functions, procedures and other related matters governing the

234 *Ibid.* 235 *Ibid.* at 24. 236 *Ibid.* at 25. 237 *Ibid.* at 26–41.

238 'SADC and its Member States shall act in accordance with the following principles: human rights, democracy and the rule of law', SADC Treaty, at Art. 4(c).

239 'SADC and Member States shall not discriminate against any person on grounds of gender, religion, political views, race, ethnic origin, culture, ill health, disability, or such other ground as may be determined by the Summit', SADC Treaty, at Art. 6(2).

240 *Mike Campbell (Pvt) Ltd. and 78 Others* v. *The Republic of Zimbabwe*, at 57–9.

241 N. Nkomo, 'South African High Court Approves Legal Action Against Harare in Land Case', *Voice of America News* (13 Jan. 2010), available at www1.voanews.com/zimbabwe/news/human-rights/Zimbabwe-South-African-Group-Granted-Right-to-Sue-Zimbabwe-13Jan10–81347412.html.

242 Press release, 'Status and Meaning of Ratification of SADC Treaty and Tribunal Protocol'.

Tribunal shall be prescribed in a Protocol, which shall, notwithstanding the provisions of Article 22 of this Treaty, form an integral part of this Treaty, adopted by the Summit.'[243] In other words, once the Protocol has been officially adopted it becomes binding on all Member States, as is the Treaty itself, regardless of individual ratification.

The second argument is a bit stronger. SADC protocols only come into force once they have been approved by the Summit on recommendation by the Council[244] and are ratified by two-thirds of the Member States.[245] As of September 2009, only five of the SADC's 15 Member States had ratified it.[246] However, going back to Article 16, the two-thirds ratification requirement specifically does not apply to the Protocol on Tribunal. Notably, the Article 22 two-thirds ratification requirement, and the Article 16 exemption from that requirement, were added in 2001, when the Treaty was amended.[247] So even though some Zimbabwean officials have argued that the 2001 amendment itself is invalid and therefore the exemption does not apply,[248] this offers no support to Zimbabwe's position because, if the amendment is invalid, so is the two-thirds ratification requirement itself.

Perhaps the simplest and best argument for the enforcement of Tribunal decisions is that the ratification of the Protocol on Tribunal is irrelevant to the Tribunal's existence and authority. Article 9(1)(g) of the Treaty which establishes the Tribunal and Article 16(1) thereof spells out its jurisdiction. It is important to note that Zimbabwe nominated a current Tribunal Member, Justice Antonia Guvava, to the Tribunal in 2005,[249] which contradicts its claim that it does not believe the Tribunal to be in existence. Justice Guvava was, in fact, appointed to the Tribunal and is one of the five alternate members of the court.[250] In September 2009, Justice Minister Patrick Chinamasa of Zimbabwe announced that they

243 SADC Treaty, at Arts 22(9) and 16(2).

244 *Ibid.* at Art. 22(2). 245 *Ibid.* at Art. 22(4).

246 Press release, 'Status and Meaning of Ratification of SADC Treaty and Tribunal Protocol'. The five Member States are Botswana, Lesotho, Malawi, Mauritius and Namibia. M. Sasa, 'SADC Tribunal Does Not Exist', *The Herald – Zimbabwe* (10 Aug. 2009), available at http://allafrica.com/stories/200908100127.html.

247 S. Jarvis, 'Chinamasa Wrong on SADC Tribunal Pull Out', *The Standard – Zimbabwe* (3 Oct. 2009), available at www.thestandard.co.zw/opinion/21583-chinamasa-wrong-on-sadc-tribunal-pull-out.html.

248 Press release, 'Status and Meaning of Ratification of SADC Treaty and Tribunal Protocol'.

249 C. Manyukwe, 'Gov't to Withdraw Judge from Tribunal', *Financial Gazette* (17 Sept. 2009), available at http://allafrica.com/stories/200909220904.html.

250 *Ibid.*

would be withdrawing Guvava from the Tribunal.[251] It is noteworthy that no official action was ever taken on the part of Zimbabwe's government to withdraw Guvava or to pull out of Tribunal participation.[252]

On 29 July 2008 the High Court of South Africa decided in *Von Abo* v. *Government of the Republic of South Africa and Others* that citizens of South Africa whose property had been taken by the Zimbabwean government would be owed damages from the government of South Africa, where the government had failed to protect their interests through diplomatic intervention.[253] The Court made the following orders: South African citizens have a right to 'diplomatic protection' from violations of their rights by the government of Zimbabwe to be given to them by the government of South Africa; the government of South Africa has a constitutional obligation to provide this protection; the government of South Africa had to remedy the violations of the applicant's rights; and an award of damages to the applicant was postponed pending South Africa's compliance with the order of the High Court and subsequent judicial proceedings.[254]

On 7 May 2009, William Michael Campbell, the second applicant in the Tribunal's *Mike Campbell* case, discussed above, and Richard Thomas Etheredge, petitioned the Tribunal for a declaration that Zimbabwe was in breach and contempt of the decision in *Mike Campbell*.[255] The Tribunal made such a declaration in June 2009 and reported its finding to the Summit for appropriate action under Article 32(5)[256] of the Protocol on Tribunal.[257]

The *Von Abo* applicant then went before the Constitutional Court of South Africa, whose decision was made on 5 June 2009.[258] Section 172(2)(a) of the Constitution of South Africa states: 'a High Court . . . may

251 *Ibid.*

252 D.F. Eagle, 'SA: Zimbabwe Tribunal Court Ruling Stands', *Metro Zimbabwe* (6 Feb. 2010), available at www.zimbabwemetro.com/current-affairs/sazimbabwe-tribunal-court-ruling-stands/?utm_medium=newzimsituation&utm_source=newzimsituation.com.

253 *Von Abo* v. *Government of the Republic of South Africa and Others* (3106/07) [2008] ZAGPHC 226 (29 July 2008).

254 *Ibid.* at para. 161.

255 *Campbell and Another* v. *Republic of Zimbabwe* (SADC (T) 03/2009) [2009] SADCT 1 (5 June 2009).

256 SADC Protocol on Tribunal, at Art. 32(5) ('If the Tribunal establishes the existence of [a failure to comply with a decision of the Tribunal], it shall report its finding to the Summit for the latter to take appropriate action').

257 *Campbell and Another* v. *Republic of Zimbabwe* at 2 (pdf version).

258 *Von Abo* v. *President of the Republic of South Africa* (CCT 67/08) [2009] ZACC 15 (5 June 2009).

make an order concerning the constitutional validity of . . . any conduct of the President, but an order of constitutional invalidity has no force unless it is confirmed by the Constitutional Court'. On 5 June 2009, the Constitutional Court of South Africa held that the order of the High Court did not need to be affirmed by the Constitutional Court in this instance, because the High Court declared the conduct of the South African government to be invalid, rather than the conduct of the president individually, within the meaning of section 172(2)(a).[259]

2 South Africa–Zimbabwe Bilateral Investment Promotion and Protection Agreement and Fick

In late November 2009, the governments of South Africa and Zimbabwe were on their way towards signing the Bilateral Investment Promotion and Protection Agreement (BIPPA).[260] The BIPPA was aimed at providing security for South African investments in Zimbabwe, but it expressly excluded past claims arising from Zimbabwe's land reform programme,[261] the very programme at issue in *Mike Campbell.* In November 2009, South African legal consultants, Jeremy Gauntlett and F.B. Pelser, advised the South African government that if it were to sign BIPPA as it was, South Africa would be in violation of international law, as it would compromise the Tribunal's order and unlawfully terminate all remedies for past human rights violations, including the uncompensated taking of land.[262]

On 27 November 2009, AfriForum, a farmers' rights organization, petitioned the High Court of South Africa to enjoin the South African government from signing BIPPA.[263] The parties settled out of court that day in *Fick and Three Others* v. *Government of the Republic of South Africa and Two Others.*[264] The South African North Gauteng High Court in Pretoria announced the agreement in its entirety as follows:

259 *Ibid.* at para. 49.

260 Staff writer, 'BIPPA Goes Against SA Law – Legal Consultants', *Zimbabwe Independent* (26 Nov. 2009), available at www.theindependent.co.zw/local/24475-bippa-goes-against-sa-law–legal-consultants.html.

261 *Ibid.* 262 *Ibid.*

263 V. Sifile and J. Dube, 'Farm Invasions Illegal – SA', *The Standard – Zimbabwe* (28 Nov. 2009), available at www.thestandard.co.zw/local/22423-farm-invasions-illegal–sa.html.

264 *Fick and Three Others* v. *Government of the Republic of South Africa and Two Others* (72068/09) [2009] ZAGPPHC (27 Nov. 2009).

1. The proposed Bilateral Agreement for the Promotion and Reciprocal Protection of Investments (BIPPA) between the government of Zimbabwe and that of South Africa, to be concluded on 27 November 2009 in Harare, aims to create legal and other remedies for South African citizens over and above existing remedies in terms of international law.
2. The First and Second Respondent hereby give the Applicants (and other South African Citizens in the Applicants' position) the assurance that BIPPA does not affect existing rights or remedies in terms of other sources of international law, in particular those in terms of the Treaty of the Southern African Development Community (SADC).
3. Thus the efficacy of the rulings and orders by the SADC Tribunal in *Mike Campbell (Pvt) Ltd and Others v Republic of Zimbabwe* [2008] SADC (T) 02/2007 (28 November 2008) and *William Michael Campbell and Another v The Republic of Zimbabwe* [2009] SADC (T) 03/2009 (05 June 2009) is not affected by entering into the proposed BIPPA, which rulings and orders the Government of the Republic of South Africa respects and undertakes to honour [sic] in terms of its own obligations in terms of the SADC Treaty.
4. The matter is removed from the roll, with no order as to costs.[265]

That same day, the governments of Zimbabwe and South Africa signed BIPPA.[266]

On 5 February 2010, the North Gauteng High Court of South Africa in Pretoria continued where it had left off in 2008.[267] In the continued proceedings, the Court ruled that the government of South Africa was bound by the decision of the Tribunal in *Mike Campbell*.[268] The Court decided that the South African government was at fault for not protecting the applicant's property rights in Zimbabwe through the use of diplomatic intervention, that the government had not complied with the High Court's 2008 ruling and, as such, determined that the South African government was 'liable to pay to the applicant such damages as he may prove that he has suffered as a result of the violation of his rights by the Government of Zimbabwe'.[269] AfriForum announced its intention to the Supreme Court of South Africa to fully enforce the Tribunal's ruling in South Africa, on 23 February 2010.[270]

265 *Ibid.*

266 Staff writer, 'Commitment Now Needed', *The Financial Gazette* (4 Dec. 2009), available at www.financialgazette.co.zw/index.php?option=com_content&view=article&id=2165:commitment-now-needed&catid=30:comment&Itemid=13.

267 *Von Abo* v. *Government of the Republic of South Africa and Others* at para. 3.

268 *Ibid.* at para. 59.

269 *Ibid.* at paras 65–8.

270 Nkomo, 'South African High Court Approves Legal Action Against Harare in Land Case', *Voice of America News* (13 Jan. 2010), available at www1.voanews.com/

When the *Fick* settlement above is read in conjunction with the High Court's rulings in the *Von Abo* case, it seems that South Africa has found a way to successfully protect its citizens while simultaneously abiding by the Tribunal's decision in *Mike Campbell* and allowing Zimbabwe to continue seizing land. As long as South Africa is willing to pay damages to its citizens who suffered injury as a result of Zimbabwe's land reform programme, it is abiding by *Von Abo*, *Mike Campbell* and the BIPPA. However, this ignores the fact that Zimbabwe continues to decline to abide by the Tribunal's ruling, discussed below. South Africa would only be made whole if Zimbabwe abides by the BIPPA.[271] The Commercial Farmers' Union of Zimbabwe has reported that three farmers whose land was seized in December 2009 and January 2010 were covered by the BIPPA.[272]

On 26 January 2010, the High Court of Zimbabwe in Harare dismissed a suit by Gramara Ltd, one of the 'other' applicants in *Mike Campbell*, which sought a declaration that the Tribunal's decision in *Mike Campbell* should be enforced in Zimbabwe.[273] The Court found that Amendment 17, Section 16B(3)(b)'s domestic constitutionality was affirmed by the Supreme Court of Zimbabwe in *Mike Campbell (Pty) Ltd.* v. *Minister of National Security Responsible for Land, Land Reform and Resettlement*.[274] That section states that 'a person having any right or interest in the [reorganized] land . . . shall not apply to a court to challenge the acquisition of the land by the State, and no court shall entertain any such challenge'.[275] The Court explained that since 'the indirect consequence of the Tribunal's judgment is to impugn the legality of the programme sanctioned by the Supreme Court . . . [and] challenge[s] the decision of the Supreme Court within its jurisdictional domain and thereby undermine[s] the authority of th[e Supreme] Court in Zimbabwe', the Tribunal's decision must be

zimbabwe/news/human-rights/Zimbabwe-South-African-Group-Granted-Right-to-Sue-Zimbabwe-13Jan10-81347412.html.

271 Staff writer, 'AfriForum gets Green Light to Sue Zim', *Farmers' Weekly* (29 Jan. 2010), available at www.farmersweekly.co.za/index.php?p[IGcms_nodes][IGcms_nodesUID]=8e3a0284a973f3576d1560e65712a69f.

272 *Ibid.*

273 *Gramara (Pvt) Ltd. and One Other* v. *The Government of the Republic of Zimbabwe and Two Others* (HC 33/09) [2010] ZWHHC 1 (26 January 2010); A. Bell, 'Outrage as High Court Dismisses SADC Land Ruling', SW Radio Africa News (27 Jan. 2010), available at www.swradioafrica.com/news270110/outrage270110.htm.

274 *Mike Campbell (Pty) Ltd.* v. *Minister of National Security Responsible for Land, Land Reform and Resettlement*. This was the case the Tribunal cited as affirming that Amendment 17 had effectively denied the applicants access to the courts, violating their human rights and giving the Tribunal jurisdiction in the first place.

275 *Ibid.* at 11.

ignored.[276] Furthermore, the Court maintained, section 3 of the Constitution of Zimbabwe proclaims: 'This Constitution is the supreme law of Zimbabwe and if any other law is inconsistent with this Constitution that other law shall, to the extent of the inconsistency, be void.'[277] This is in clear conflict with Article 27 of the Vienna Convention on the Law of Treaties, which provides that, 'A party may not invoke the provisions of its internal law as justification for its failure to perform a treaty.' Since the Tribunal was 'constituted to ensure adherence to and the proper interpretation of the provisions of [the SADC] Treaty and subsidiary instruments and to adjudicate upon such disputes as may be referred to it'[278] and '[t]he decisions of the Tribunal [are] final and binding',[279] any violation of an order of the Tribunal is a violation of the SADC Treaty itself, regardless of domestic law.

The High Court of Zimbabwe, however, determined that:

> [E]nforcement of the [*Mike Campbell (Pvt) Ltd.*] decision . . . would ultimately necessitate the Government having to reverse all the land acquisitions that have taken place since 2000. Apart from the political enormity of any such exercise, it would entail the eviction, upheaval and eventual relocation of many if not most of the beneficiaries of the land reform programme. This programme, despite its administrative and practical shortcomings, is quintessentially a matter of public policy in Zimbabwe, conceived well before the country attained its sovereign independence.
>
> As for the doctrine of legitimate expectation, the applicants before the Tribunal and others in their position are absolutely correct in expecting the Government of Zimbabwe to comply with its obligations under the SADC Treaty and to implement the decisions of the Tribunal. However, I take it that there is an incomparably greater number of Zimbabweans who share the legitimate expectation that the Government will effectively implement the land reform programme and fulfil their aspirations thereunder. Given these countervailing expectations, public policy as informed by basic utilitarian precept would dictate that the greater public good must prevail.[280]

Therefore, the Tribunal's decision in *Mike Campbell* was found to be contrary to Zimbabwean law, both judicially and constitutionally, and Zimbabwean public policy.[281]

276 *Gramara*, at 14.

277 *Mike Campbell (Pty) Ltd.* v. *Minister of National Security Responsible for Land, Land Reform and Resettlement*, at 15.

278 SADC Treaty, at Art. 16(1).

279 *Ibid.* at Art. 16(5).

280 *Ibid.* at Arts 15–16.

281 *Ibid.* at Art. 16.

It would seem that the SADC Tribunal as well as South African and Zimbabwean courts have zeroed in quite a bit on Zimbabwe's land seizure. SADC Tribunal Registrar Mkandawire has said, 'The Zimbabwe issue is no longer in the hands of the Tribunal. We have done what we are mandated to do but cannot enforce the decisions. We have reported the farm violations to the SADC summit. It is the SADC summit which now has to enforce the decisions made by the Tribunal.'[282] Therefore, the legitimacy of the Tribunal rests in the hands of the Summit.

F Conclusions

This chapter's discussion of African regional trade judiciaries indicates that their relative invisibility in academic and policy discussions is unwarranted. These judiciaries have exercised their jurisdiction over a burgeoning number of cases, particularly in the area of human rights and increasingly over economic and trade disputes. The EACJ, as well as the SADC tribunals, have been exemplary in making bold decisions, which were not well received by Member States. The ECOWAS Tribunal had its jurisdiction expanded to include human rights cases. These trends show that even while African governments are not fully committed to fully funding these regional judiciaries, the judiciaries have nevertheless begun to actively build an emerging regional jurisprudence that only a few short years ago did not exist. That these judiciaries have been able to do so much with relatively little support from respective member governments is testimony to the emerging cadre and high calibre of judges who staff these regional courts.

What is needed now is continuing to expand the number of legal practitioners who can advise their clients on how these African RTA regimes offer them opportunities to use the remedies the RTA judiciaries are empowered to give. Such remedies, of course, include the trade remedy regimes of anti-dumping and countervailing duty law which have been borrowed from the WTO. They, of course, also include the possibility of challenging the broad range of non-tariff barriers measures that exist in trade between African countries. The potential for using these African RTA judiciaries is, therefore, quite broad, and this potential awaits future exploitation to the hilt.

282 S. Chirinda, 'Land Seizures now SADC Issue – Tribunal', ReliefWeb (8 Feb. 2010), available at http://reliefweb.int/rw/rwb.nsf/db900SID/KHII-82G4S4?OpenDocument.

VIII

Trade remedy regimes

A Introduction

This chapter examines the trade remedies available under the Common Market for Eastern and Southern Africa (COMESA). It proceeds as follows. The first part will provide a brief explanation of what COMESA is and what its main objectives are. Section B will examine COMESA's internal mechanisms, specifically those that function to oversee and review the use of trade remedies. Section C will describe the three trade remedies available to COMESA members, namely, safeguards, anti-dumping measures and subsidies, as well as detailing the pre-conditions for use of each, as well as explore some of the procedural rules which govern those three remedy areas. Section C4 will examine how the implementation of COMESA safeguard measures on Kenya's sugar and wheat industries has impacted on them.

B COMESA's institutional mechanisms for overseeing and reviewing trade remedies

COMESA's Trade Remedies Committee and a Group of Experts on Trade Remedies are responsible for overseeing the application of COMESA trade remedies.[1] In 2001, at the 12th meeting of the COMESA Council of Ministers, Regulations on Trade Remedy Measures were adopted to 'ensure there was uniformity among Members of COMESA in the conduct of trade remedy investigations'.[2] The Regulations were adopted primarily to ensure that trade remedy investigations conducted by COMESA and

1 See Regulations on Trade Remedy Measures, Part VI: General, Reg. 49: Surveillance.

2 Applications of Anti-dumping Measures and Safeguard Provisions under the COMESA Treaty, Paper presented during the Workshop on Sugar Importers Forum held at the Holiday Inn Hotel, Westlands, 3–4 April 2002, available at www.kenyalink.org/sucam/documents/safeguards1.html; see also Uganda Export Promotion Board, COMESA, COMESA Trade Remedies, www.ugandaexportsonline.com/comesa.htm (noting 'The Twelfth Meeting of the Council of Ministers in Lusaka, Zambia, on 30 November 2001, adopted Trade Remedy

its members fell within the Framework of the World Trade Organization (WTO) Agreements on Safeguards, Anti-dumping and Subsidies.[3] The 2001 adoption of these Regulations was an important unifying step for COMESA, because at that time sixteen members of COMESA were also members of the WTO, three were observers (two of which were seeking accession) and two were completely uninvolved in the WTO.[4] This meant that some COMESA members were subject to and could invoke the WTO Agreements on Safeguards, Anti-dumping and Subsidies and Countervailing Measures, while other members could not. This created inconsistency among COMESA members. As a result, COMESA adopted Regulations on Trade Remedies borrowed directly from WTO agreements, with a view to harmonizing trade remedy regimes in COMESA.[5] As a result, a uniform set of trade remedy rules applies within COMESA whether they are members of the WTO or not.[6]

An important part of COMESA's institutional framework regarding trade remedies is the COMESA Group of Experts on Trade Remedies. The Group was established in 2001 by COMESA's Regulations on Trade Remedy Measures, and is composed of representatives of each of the Member States.[7] The Group's functions are to report annually to the Trade and Customs Committee on the implementation and operation of the Regulations and to make recommendations for improvement of the regulations.[8] The Group will also find, upon the request of an affected member, whether or not the procedural requirements of the Regulations have been complied with, and report on those findings to the Committee

Regulations for invocation of safeguard, anti-dumping, subsidies and countervailing measures'); Regulations on Trade Remedy Measures, Part VI: General, Reg. 49: Surveillance, sub. 49.1.

3 See *The Results of The Uruguay Round of Multilateral Trade Negotiations* (Cambridge University Press, 2007) (containing the text of the following agreements: Implementation of Article VI (Anti-dumping), Agreement on Subsidies and Countervailing Measures and Agreement on Safeguards).

4 See About COMESA, 'History of COMESABU', about.comesa.int/lang-en/component/content/article/1-general/14-history-of-comesa.

5 The text of COMESA's Regulations on Trade Remedies follows nearly word-for-word the WTO Agreements on Safeguards, Anti-dumping, and Subsidies and Countervailing Measures.

6 See World Trade Organization, Agreement on Safeguards, Agreement on Implementation of Article VI of the General Agreement on Tariffs and Trade, and Agreements on Subsidies and Countervailing Measures, available at www.wto.org/english/docs&e/legal&e/final&e.htm. See also COMESA Regulations on Trade Remedy Measures.

7 Regulations on Trade Remedy Measures, P. VI: General, Reg. 49: Surveillance, subs. 49.1.

8 *Ibid.*, at subs. 49.2(a).

on Trade Remedies.[9] The Group can also assist members in their consultations with other members, review the requests of members taking safeguard measures, and examine existing measures, as well as monitoring the phasing-out of measures where appropriate.[10] The Group also receives and reviews all notifications provided for in the Regulations and reports to the Trade and Custom Committee.

The responsibilities of the COMESA Committee on Trade Remedies is to examine notifications submitted at special sessions to be held every three years, as well as examining reports submitted at each meeting of the Committee.[11] The Regulations also provide that the Committee shall review annually the implementation and operation of the Regulations and inform the COMESA Secretary General of developments.[12]

C Trade remedies provided for by COMESA

At a meeting of the COMESA Council of Ministers in 2001, Trade Remedy Regulations for the invocation of safeguard, anti-dumping, subsidies and countervailing measures were adopted.[13] The Regulations provide states with remedies for three specific instances: safeguards, '[e]mergency measures to limit imports temporarily', so as to 'safeguard' domestic industries;[14] anti-dumping measures, '[a]ctions taken against dumping (selling at an unfairly low price)';[15] and '[s]ubsidies and "countervailing" duties to offset export subsidies'.[16] Because these Regulations were adopted to harmonize trade practices within the region and ensure that COMESA regulations fall within the framework of the WTO Agreements, much of COMESA's Regulations on Trade Remedy Measures appears identical to the WTO Agreements.[17]

When it comes to implementing the remedies, it is generally the sector of a domestic industry that produces a product which initiates the process

9 *Ibid.*, at subs. 49.2(b). 10 *Ibid.*, at subs. 49.2(c), (d), (e).

11 *Ibid.*, at subs. 49.4, 49.5. 12 *Ibid.*, Reg. 52: Other Final Provisions, subs. 52.6.

13 COMESA Programmes, Trade Remedies and Safeguards, programmes.comesa.int//index.php?option=com_content&view=article&id=54.

14 *Ibid.* (quoting from Regulations on Trade Remedy Measures, P. II: Safeguards, Reg. 9: Serious Injury or Threat Thereof, subs. (1)).

15 *Ibid.* (quoting from subs. (2)).

16 *Ibid.* (quoting from subs. (3)).

17 World Trade Organization, Agreement on Safeguards, www.wto.org/english/tratop&e/safeg&e/safeint.htm.

for safeguard, anti-dumping or countervailing actions:[18] 'The domestic industry keeps a watch on the flow of imports and on its own situation. When it considers that it needs protection and the pre-conditions mentioned above are satisfied, it moves government to start appropriate action.'[19] Once an industry has made a request for trade remedy action, there are procedures for carrying out investigations provided for in the Regulations on Trade Remedy Measures to establish whether or not trade remedies may be used in that particular situation.[20] Each has its own procedures for taking action, and has 'a competent authority to carry out investigations into the existence of the pre-conditions for safeguard, countervailing or anti-dumping action'.[21] That authority will then conduct an investigation into: 'the increase in import, the existence of serious injury or threat thereof; and the causal link between the increased import and the injury'.[22] In each and every investigation, public notice is given to all possible interested parties, and '[a]n opportunity is given to importers, exporters and other interested parties to present their views and evidence'.[23] All parties are also given an opportunity to respond to each others' evidence and to give their opinion on whether such measure would be in the best interest of the public.[24] The Investigating Authority of the state then prepares and publishes a report of its findings and conclusions on the matter.

Once the report has been received by the state it must make a decision on whether or not to apply the trade remedy measures. If the state decides to undertake trade remedy measures, it must then hold consultations with other interested parties.[25] Thereafter, a state may take measures

18 COMESA Programmes, 'Trade Remedies and Safeguards, Initiation of Safeguard Measures or Actions Against Subsidy and Dumping', programmes.comesa.int//index.php?option=com_content&view=article&id=54%20.

19 *Ibid.*

20 See Regulations on Trade Remedy Measures, P. II: Safeguard Measures, Reg. 8: Investigation; P. III Anti-dumping, Reg. 18: Initiation and Subsequent Investigation; P. IV Subsidies and Countervailing Measures, Reg. 29: Initiation and Subsequent Investigation.

21 COMESA Programmes, 'Trade Remedies and Safeguards, Investigation'.

22 *Ibid.* 23 *Ibid.* 24 *Ibid.*

25 See Regulations on Trade Remedy Measures, Reg. 5: Interpretation: ('Interested Parties shall include: (i) an exporter producer in the exporting country, or the importer of a product subject to investigation, or a trade or business association a majority of which are producers, exporters, or importers of such a product; (ii) the government of the exporting member; (iii) a producer of the like product in the territory of the importing COMESA Member. The Investigating Authority shall allow, upon request, domestic or foreign parties other than those included as interested parties in the investigation').

by: increasing tariffs, imposing quantitative restrictions, imposing anti-dumping duties, or imposing countervailing duties.[26] However, a Member State may only take such measures to the degree which they are necessary to prevent or remedy injury or facilitate an adjustment within the domestic industry.[27]

There are also procedural rules which govern a state defending itself against a trade remedy measure.[28] When a state receives a notice from another Member State that it is initiating an investigation, the government of that state should 'examine the facts regarding serious injury as alleged in the notice. It may contest the matter before the competent authority of the investigating country, mainly on grounds of non-existence of serious injury, its threat or lack of linkage between increased import and injury'.[29] There is even an additional measure of protection for states defending themselves against trade remedy measures: '[i]f a member State whose exports have been subject of investigation is dissatisfied with the actions of the member State investigating the matter, the former may refer the matter to a dispute settlement panel established by COMESA'.[30]

Below, I outline in further detail the three specific trade remedies provided for by the COMESA Regulations, the preconditions which must be met before they are invoked, as well as remedy-specific procedural rules which govern their application and review.

1 Safeguards

The first remedy made available to states under the Trade Remedy Regulations allows a state to take safeguard measures.[31] The state may take these safeguard measures by temporarily restricting the importation of a product when its own domestic industry is injured or threatened by a surge in imports.[32] There are, however, specific conditions that must be present in the market in order for a state to invoke this exception and take safeguard measures.[33]

26 COMESA Programmes, 'Imposition of Safeguard, Countervailing or Anti-dumping Measures'.

27 *Ibid.*

28 COMESA Programmes, 'What a Government Must Do to Defend Itself Against a Trade Remedy Measure'.

29 *Ibid.* 30 *Ibid.*

31 See Regulations on Trade Remedy Measures, P. II Safeguard Measures.

32 *Ibid.* Reg 7: Conditions. 33 *Ibid.*

There are three pre-conditions listed in the Trade Remedy Regulations which must be proved before a state can take safeguard actions.[34] There must be an '[i]ncrease in import, either absolute over past imports or relative to domestic production', and a '[c]ause of serious injury or threat of serious injury'[35] to the state's own domestic industry as well as a '[c]ausal link between the increase in imports and injury or threat of injury'.[36] If an investigation by the Investigating Authority of that state, pursuant to the Trade Remedy Regulations, establishes that the increased importation of a certain product has caused or will cause serious injury to its domestic market, the state may then use the safeguard remedy provided for by COMESA.[37] They may do so by taking 'important restraint measures in the form of tariff-type measures (e.g. import surcharge, levy, and increased traffic) or [placing] quantitative restrictions on the import of that product'.[38]

There is a specific regulation which governs the finding of a 'serious injury of threat thereof'.[39] It provides that when investigating to determine whether an increase in imports has caused or is threatening to cause 'serious injury', the Investigating Authority should evaluate all factors which are relevant, 'of an objective and quantifiable nature' and which have a bearing on that industry's level of development, particularly 'the rate and amount of the increase in imports of the product concerned in absolute and relative terms'.[40] A determination that the increased imports have caused or threaten to cause serious injury should be made on an examination of all relevant evidence, but cannot be made unless the Investigating Authority has obtained objective evidence of the causal link between the increase in imports and the injury or threat thereof.[41] Thus, the Investigating Authority should examine all factors relevant to the injury, and must differentiate between factors that can be attributed to an increase in imports and those which cannot.[42] The Investigating Authority must then immediately publish a detailed analysis of the case under investigation, as well as evidence of the relevant factors that it has examined in making its determination.[43]

For situations in which the delay associated with an investigation would clearly cause further injury that would be hard to repair, there are provisional trade remedy measures. These measures are normally in the form

34 *Ibid.* 35 See *ibid.* Reg. 9: Serious Injury or Threat Thereof. 36 *Ibid.*
37 *Ibid.* Reg. 8: Investigation, subs. (1). 38 *Ibid.*
39 *Ibid.* Reg. 9: Serious Injury or Threat Thereof. 40 *Ibid.* at subs. 1.
41 *Ibid.*, at subss. 2, 3. 42 *Ibid.*, at subs. 3. 43 *Ibid.*, at subs. 4.

of a tariff increase and promptly refunded if subsequent, detailed investigations do not prove existence of injury or threat of serious injury.[44] The duration of such a measure cannot, however, exceed 200 days.[45]

There are also regulations in place to limit the application of safeguard measures once it has been established that they may be applied by a state.[46] The main limitation on the use of safeguard measures is the duration of their use. This limitation provides that 'a safeguard action should apply only for such a period necessary to remedy serious injury or prevent serious injury; and to facilitate adjustment of the injury'.[47] The duration of a safeguard action is limited to four years.[48] However, this 'may be extended if the Investigative Authority of the State has determined . . . that the safeguard measure continues to be necessary to prevent or remedy serious injury and there is evidence that the [domestic] industry is adjusting.'[49]

A member proposing to apply safeguard measures or seeking to extend a safeguard measure, must endeavour to maintain a substantially equivalent level of concession and other obligations to that existing between it and the exporting members which will be or are affected by such a measure.[50] To achieve this, members concerned may agree on any adequate means of trade compensation for the adverse effects of the measure on their trade.[51] Therefore, a Member State must enter into consultations with Member States that have a substantial export interest in the product to which the state will apply safeguard measures.[52] If the states do not reach an agreement in the consultations within 30 days, then 'the affected Member States may suspend the application of substantially equivalent concessions 90 days after application of the measure in respect of trade of the member State applying the safeguard measure'.[53] Suspension, however, cannot be exercised within the first three years that the safeguard measure is in effect if the measure is being taken as a result of an absolute increase in imports.[54]

There is also a regulation which deals specifically with notifications a Member State must make, as well as consultations they must have

44 *Ibid.* Reg. 11: Provisional Safeguard Measures. 45 *Ibid.*
46 *Ibid.* Reg. 10: Application of Safeguard Measures. 47 See *ibid.*, at subs. 1.
48 *Ibid.* Reg. 12: Duration and Review of Safeguard Measures, subs. 1.
49 See *ibid.*, at subs. 2.
50 See *Ibid.* Reg. 13: Level of Concession and Other Obligations (1) and Reg. 15: Notification and Consultation (3).
51 *Ibid.* Reg. 13: Level of Concession and Other Obligations. 52 See *ibid.*
53 *Ibid.* 54 *Ibid.*

with other interested parties.[55] All notifications on safeguards are made through the Committee on Trade Remedies.[56] Regulation 15 provides that a Member State must immediately notify the Committee when initiating an investigation or making a finding of a serious threat of injury or threat thereof, and when making a decision to apply or extend a safeguard.[57] The Member State must also provide the Committee on Trade Remedies with evidence that the increase in imports has in fact caused the serious injury or threat thereof.[58] Member States must always notify the Committee before taking provisional safeguard measures.[59] Additionally members must notify the Committee of their laws and regulations relating to safeguard measures, as well as any modifications made to them.[60] Any Member States may notify the Committee of another state's laws and regulations if that state has not made such required notifications.[61]

Quantitative restrictions, in particular, have procedural rules restrictions.[62] For example, the restriction must not reduce the import level of the product below the average level of the last three years, or the member must provide a justification for seeking to restrict the import to a lower level.[63] The state must also seek agreement with other Member States who have a substantial interest in exporting the product.[64]

2 *Anti-dumping actions*

A product is considered to have been 'dumped' when it is introduced into the market of an importing country at less than its normal value.[65] The problem with dumping is that companies sometimes use it in a predatory fashion in order to eliminate competition from the market.[66] Thus, in determining whether a product has been dumped, the export price and normal value must both be determined and compared. If a disparity is found between the normal value and the export value, Member States are

55 *Ibid.* Reg. 15: Notification and Consultation. 56 *Ibid.*, at subs. 9.

57 *Ibid.*, at subs. 1.

58 *Ibid.*, at subs. 2 (this includes: 'a precise description of the product involved and the proposed measure, proposed date of introduction, expected duration and timetable for progressive liberalization. In case of an extension of a measure, evidence that the industry concerned is adjusting shall also be provided').

59 *Ibid.*, at subs. 4. 60 *Ibid.*, at subs. 6. 61 *Ibid.*, at subs. 7.

62 COMESA Programmes, 'Quantitative Restrictions'. 63 *Ibid.* 64 *Ibid.*

65 Regulations on Trade Remedy Measures, P. III: Anti-Dumping, Reg. 16: Determination of Dumping, subs. 16.1.

66 COMESA Programmes, 'Trade Remedies and Safeguards, Dumping'.

entitled to take action in order to protect their own domestic industries from being injured by the dumping.[67]

There are pre-conditions that must be met before a state may take actions against dumping.[68] It must be determined by the Investigating Authority that dumping is indeed taking place.[69] Next, it must be determined that the domestic market of the importing state has sustained an injury or faces a threat of injury.[70] Finally, it must be determined that the injury or threat of injury to the domestic market has been caused by the dumping of the goods.[71] Only when an investigation has been conducted in accordance with the Regulations on Trade Remedy Measures, and a public notice has been given, all interested parties have been given the opportunity to submit and make comments and an investigation by the Investigating Authority has led to the determination that all the pre-conditions to anti-dumping have been met, may a state begin to apply trade remedy measures.[72]

It must be noted, however, that determining whether or not a product is being dumped is often a difficult undertaking for the Investigating Authority, and though provided for within the Regulations, still involves many complex steps.[73] The Investigating Authority must conduct a thorough investigation into what the 'normal' value of the product is. This is often a complex economic problem, for which COMESA has adopted detailed regulations.[74] The costs are normally calculated by looking to the records kept by the exporter or producer which is under investigation.[75] The Investigating Authority will take into consideration all evidence on the allocation of costs when calculating costs on the basis of these records.[76] Other characteristics that an Investigating Authority may take into account are: the seasonality and cyclicality of the products, as well as the existence of special orders or customized sales.[77] The period of data collection for an investigation into dumping should be between six and twelve months, and in all cases the Investigating Authority should notify the interested parties in advance of the time covered by the data

67 Regulations on Trade Remedy Measures, P. III: Anti-Dumping, Reg. 16: Determination of Dumping, subs. 16.1.

68 *Ibid.* Reg. 16: Determination of Dumping; Reg. 17: Determination of Injury.

69 *Ibid.* 70 *Ibid.* 71 *Ibid.*, at subs. 17.5.

72 *Ibid.* Reg. 16: Determination of Dumping; Reg. 17: Determination of Injury; Reg. 18: Initiation and Subsequent Investigation.

73 See *Ibid.* Reg. 16: Determination of Dumping; Reg. 17: Determination of Injury; Reg. 18: Initiation and Subsequent Investigation; Reg. 19: Evidence.

74 *Ibid.* 75 *Ibid.* Reg. 16: Determination of Dumping, subs. 16.4. 76 *Ibid.*

77 *Ibid.*, at subs. 16.13.

collection, and of any deadlines for data collection and submissions that the Investigating Authority has set.[78]

When investigating whether dumping is taking place, a case may arise in which there may be no sale of a like product in the domestic market of the exporting state, or such a low volume of sales that it does not provide for a fair comparison. In this case, the Investigating Authority will determine the 'normal' price by comparing the price of a like product when exported to a third country.[79] All calculations of price are made in accordance with COMESA regulations, which take into account the cost of production in the country of origin, as well as administrative, selling, general costs and profit, the basis of which must be actual data pertaining to the trade of the like product under investigation.[80] When a comparison between prices requires a conversion of currencies, the conversion will be made using the rate of exchange on the date of the sales.[81]

An Investigating Authority may also face a situation in which products are not imported directly from the country of origin, but are instead sold from the place of origin to an intermediate Member State before reaching the importing Member State. In such a case, there are two ways in which the 'normal' price may be calculated.[82] In most cases the price at which the products are sold from the exporting member country to the importing Member State shall be compared with the price of the goods in the country of export.[83] However, the comparison may be made with the price of the country of origin if the products are merely transshipped through the exporting member country, or like products are not produced in the exporting Member State.[84]

If dumping is indeed taking place, the Investigating Authority must then also determine if the domestic market of the importing state has sustained or is faced with a threat of material injury.[85] A determination of injury must be based on positive evidence and an objective examination of both the volume of dumped imports and the effect of the dumped imports on the domestic market, as well as the impact of these imports on domestic producers of the product.[86] It must then be demonstrated that the dumped imports are in fact the cause of the material injury, or a threat thereof to the domestic market of the importing state.[87]

Anti-dumping duties may be imposed in the case of a threat of material injury to domestic industry; however, the Regulations require that when

78 *Ibid.*, at subs. 16.12. 79 *Ibid.*, at subs. 16.2. 80 See *ibid.*, at subs. 16.5.
81 *Ibid.*, at subs. 16.8. 82 *Ibid.* subs. 16.11. 83 *Ibid.*, at subs. 16.11.
84 *Ibid.*, at subs. 16.11. 85 *Ibid.* Reg. 17: Determination of Injury.
86 *Ibid.*, at subs. 17. 87 *Ibid.*, at subs. 17.5.

considering the application of anti-dumping measures to these cases, the Investigating Authority must make such a decision with special care.[88] A determination of threat of material injury cannot be based on mere 'allegations, conjecture or remote possibility', they must be based on facts.[89] According to Regulation 17, the state of things must be such that 'the change in circumstances which would create a situation in which the dumping would cause injury must be clearly foreseen and imminent'.[90]

The Investigating Authority must thus consider several factors in determining if there is a material injury and whether that injury has been caused by the dumping of the product.[91] The first factor to be examined is 'the volume of the dumped imports and the effect of the dumped imports on prices in the domestic market'.[92] With regard to volume, the Authority will consider whether there has been a significant increase in dumped imports, either absolute or relative to production or consumption of the importing state.[93] With regard to the effect of the dumped import on the domestic market, the Investigating Authority will consider whether there has been 'significant price undercutting by the dumped imports as compared to a like product of the importing member state'.[94] The Investigating Authority will also consider whether the effect of the imports is otherwise depressing prices, or preventing their increase to a significant degree.[95] It is also, however, recognized that a situation may arise where 'no one or several of these factors . . . [will] necessarily give decisive guidance', to the Investigating Authority.[96]

Another factor that must be considered is 'the consequent impact of these imports on domestic producers of such products'.[97] There is a long list of relevant economic factors that may be considered while examining the impact of dumped imports on the domestic industry concerned; it includes, but is not limited to: 'actual and potential decline in sales, profits, output market share, productivity, return on investments, or utilization of capacity, factors affecting domestic price, the magnitude of the margin of dumping, actual and potential negative effects on cash flow, inventories, employment, wages, growth, ability to raise capital or investments'.[98]

It must also be demonstrated simultaneously that there is a causal link between the dumping and the injury.[99] The Investigating Authority will examine all relevant evidence, and where appropriate should examine

88 *Ibid.*, at subs. 17.8. 89 *Ibid.*, at subs. 17.7(e). 90 *Ibid.*
91 See generally *ibid.* Reg. 17: Determination of Injury. 92 *Ibid.*, at subs. 17.1(a).
93 *Ibid.*, at subs. 17.2. 94 *Ibid.* 95 *Ibid.* 96 *Ibid.*
97 *Ibid.* Reg. 17: Determination of Injury, subs. 17.1. 98 *Ibid.*, at subs. 17.4.
99 *Ibid.*, at subs. 17.5; Reg. 18: Initiation and Subsequent Investigation, subs. 18.9.

any other known factors other than dumped imports which could be causing injury to the domestic market.[100] The Authority must differentiate between injury caused by the dumping and injury caused by other factors such as: 'contraction in demand, or changes in the pattern of consumption, trade restrictive practices of and competition between foreign and domestic producers, development in technology and the export performance and productivity of the domestic industry'.[101] Anti-dumping measures can only be applied if the dumping is the cause of the injury.[102]

Once it has been determined that dumping is indeed taking place and that the dumping is the cause of an injury or a threatened injury to the domestic market of a state, the decision of whether an anti-dumping duty will be imposed, and as to 'whether the amount of the anti-dumping duty . . . shall be the full margin of dumping or less' will be made by the Investigating Authority of the injured Member State.[103] The anti-dumping duties should only remain in force as long as they are necessary to counteract dumping which is causing material injury, which will be determined periodically by the Investigating Authority.[104]

3 *Subsidies and countervailing measures*

A subsidy exists when 'there is a financial contribution by a government or any public body within the territory of a foreign government'.[105] There are several government actions that are considered to be subsidies. Revenue that is otherwise due to a government but is not collected, are considered a subsidy.[106] Other examples of subsidies include: government provision of goods or services, government purchases of goods, government payments to a funding mechanism, or any other benefit conferred by the government on a private body.[107] There are several ways in which subsidies can illegally injure competitors. The subsidizing of an industry in an exporting state can hurt an importing state's domestic market.[108] Subsidies can also hurt rival exporters when the two states compete in a third

100 *Ibid.* Reg. 17: Determination of Injury, subs. 17.5. 101 *Ibid.* 102 See *ibid.*
103 *Ibid.* Reg. 22: Imposition and Collection of Anti-Dumping Duties, subs. 22.1.
104 *Ibid.* at Reg. 24: Duration and Review of Anti-Dumping Duties and Price Undertakings, subs. 24.1–24.2.
105 Regulations on Trade and Remedy Measures P. IV: Subsidies and Countervailing Measures, Reg. 26: Existence of a Subsidy, subs. 26.1.
106 *Ibid.* at subss. 26.1(i), 29.2. 107 See *ibid.*, at subs. 26.1(ii)(iii)(iv)(v).
108 COMESA Programmes, 'Trade Remedies and Safeguards, Damages that Subsidy Can Cause'.

state's markets.[109] Additionally, a domestic subsidy can hurt exporting states trying to compete in that state's market.[110] Thus, in order to protect its domestic market, a state may in some cases impose trade remedy measures.[111] The remedy against injurious subsidy is a countervailing duty, a process under which '[a] member can levy a countervailing duty equal to subsidization rate, after following the prescribed procedure'.[112]

Just as with other trade remedies, there are pre-conditions for imposing countervailing duties against subsidies.[113] For an investigation into subsidies to begin, an application must be submitted to the Investigating Authority which includes sufficient evidence that: there is a subsidy (and if possible, the amount of that subsidy), there has been an injury or a threat thereof and the causal link between the subsidization of imports and that injury.[114] Each factor must be substantiated by relevant evidence, and will be reviewed for accuracy and adequacy by the authorities.[115] The methods used to determine an injury associated with a subsidy is substantially similar to those used when investigating injuries associated with dumping.[116] After reviewing the evidence, if the authorities find that it is sufficient, an investigation may be initiated.[117] However, as soon as possible after an application has been accepted, and before the initiation of any investigation, states whose products may be subject to an investigation will be invited for consultations, the goal of which will be to clarify the situation and arrive at a mutual agreement.[118] If no such agreement can be reached, an investigation will be initiated, but Member States whose products are the subject of the investigation will continue to be afforded reasonable opportunities to continue consultations throughout the investigation.[119]

Once the investigation has been initiated all interested parties will be given an opportunity to present evidence.[120] Except when information is by nature confidential, authorities shall provide full disclosure of evidence to all interested parties.[121] The investigation may take many forms, depending upon what the authorities deem relevant and necessary. For example exporters, foreign producers and interested Member States may

109 *Ibid.* 110 *Ibid.*

111 Regulations on Trade Remedy Measures, P. IV: Subsidies and Countervailing Measures.

112 COMESA Programmes, 'Trade Remedies and Safeguards, Preconditions for Countervailing Duty Against Subsidy'.

113 Regulations on Trade Remedy Measures, P. IV: Subsidies and Countervailing Measures, Reg. 29: Initiation and Subsequent Investigation, subs. 29.2.

114 *Ibid.*, at subss 29.2(b), (c), (d). 115 *Ibid.*, at subs. 29.3.

116 See section, see also *ibid.* Reg. 33: Determination of Injury. 117 *Ibid.*

118 *Ibid.* Reg. 31: Consultations, subs. 31.1. 119 *Ibid.*, at subs. 31.2.

120 See generally, *ibid.* Reg. 30: Evidence. 121 See *ibid.*, at subss. 30.3, 30.5, 30.6.

be issued questionnaires to be returned promptly to the Investigating Authorities.[122] The Investigating Authorities may also carry out investigations in the territory of other Member States, provided there is no objection by that state.[123] Additionally, if the firm and state agree to it, the Investigating Authority may also carry out investigations on the premises of the firm and may examine its records.[124] Just as with anti-dumping measures, there are provisional measures which may be applied in some limited circumstances when the Investigating Authority judges such measures necessary to prevent injury being caused during the investigation.[125]

For the investigation to continue there are additional conditions which must be met. First, the subsidization cannot be *de minimis*, that is, it must be no less than a total of 2 per cent of the product's value when calculated on a per-unit basis.[126] Importation of a subsidized product must account for no less than 4 per cent of imports of the like product or not less than 9 per cent for supplying countries with market shares of less than 4 per cent.[127] If at any time during the investigation the authorities concerned determine that either of these conditions is not met, the investigation will be immediately terminated.[128] Before a final determination is made, the authorities will inform all Member States of the essential facts which form the basis for their decision, allowing the parties time to defend their interests.[129]

If no agreement is reached after reasonable efforts have been made to complete consultations, a Member State makes a final determination that the existence and amount of a subsidy, and the effect of that subsidy is causing injury, it may impose a countervailing duty in accordance with the COMESA Regulations (unless, of course, the subsidy is withdrawn).[130] Just as with anti-dumping duties, the decision of whether or not to impose such a measure, and the amount of the duty, is made by the Investigating Authorities of the importing Member State.[131] Regulation 32 provides methods by which the Investigating Authority shall calculate benefits to the recipient of the countervailing duties.[132] Countervailing duties shall

122 See *ibid.*, at subs. 30.2. 123 *Ibid.*, at subs. 30.11. 124 *Ibid.*

125 See *supra* Section C2; see also *Ibid.* Reg. 35: Provisional Measures, subs. 35.1.

126 *Ibid.* Reg. 29: Initiation and Subsequent Investigation, subs. 29.9.

127 *Ibid.* (There is, however, an exception to this if 'imports from Member States whose individual shares of total imports represent less than 4 per cent collectively account for more than 9 per cent of the total imports of the like product in the importing Member State'.)

128 *Ibid.*, at Reg. 37, subs. 29.9. 129 *Ibid.*, at Reg. 30: Evidence, subs. 30.13.

130 *Ibid.*, at Reg. 37, subs. 37.1. 131 *Ibid.* at subs. 37.2. 132 See *ibid.* Reg. 32.

only remain in force 'as long as, and to the extent necessary to counteract subsidization which is causing injury'.[133]

4 COMESA safeguards for Kenyan sugar and wheat industries

Over the past decade, Kenya has faced a trade problem coined by the press as 'the sugar wars':[134] Kenya has, since the year 2000, been enjoying a safeguard on sugar aimed at creating an environment in which the sugar industry can be competitive, to remedy import surges of sugar into Kenya.[135] This has provided Kenya with ten years in which to prepare its sugar sector for competition, the absolute maximum allowed under COMESA trade regulations.[136] When safeguards are lifted on 12 January 2012, COMESA will remove the safeguard measures and re-open the gates for other COMESA states to import sugar into Kenya.[137] It had been expected that the COMESA trade remedy measures would allow Kenya to continuously reduce its duty on sugar imports, so that by 2012 it would attract zero duty.[138] While the safeguards provided for by COMESA have been aiding Kenya temporarily, they have been unsuccessful in facilitating the adjustment of the Kenyan sugar industry. In June 2009, even at 120 per cent import duty, sugar brought into the country was still cheaper than the locally produced commodity.[139] Not only is the infrastructure to help the industry recover missing, but no structure has been established to handle a competitive environment. This may be a sign that there will be some industrial casualties even when trade remedies are used to their fullest extent, as COMESA moves towards its goal of a common market.[140]

The Kenyan wheat industry has also been adversely affected by COMESA trade liberalization over the last decade. Beginning around 2000, cheap imports of wheat flour from Egypt have contributed to a drop in local Kenyan producer prices and discouraged domestic wheat production.[141] Wheat farmers were said to have 'faced ruin as producer

133 *Ibid.*, at Reg. 39: Duration of Countervailing Duties and Undertakings, subss. 39.1, 39.2.

134 D. Maiko, 'No let-up In Sugar Wars', News From Africa, August 2004, www.newsfromafrica.org/newsfromafrica/articles/art&6508.html.

135 B. Namunane, 'Kenya: Team set up to Monitor Sugar Imports', AllAfrica.com, 5 Dec. 2008, allafrica.com/stories/200809060029.html.

136 C. Riungu, 'COMESA D-Day Shock For Kenya Sugar Firms', *The East African*, 1 June 2009, www.theeastafrican.co.ke/news/-/2558/604892/-/r316aoz/-/index.html.

137 *Ibid.* 138 *Ibid.* 139 *Ibid.* 140 See generally, *ibid.*

141 M. Raman, 'Liberalization And Interactions With The Market: a Survey Of Some Experiences Of Rural Produces In Developing Countries', Third World Network, Apr. 2006,

prices plummeted by 30 per cent'.[142] Beyond that, '[m]illers threatened to shut down and refused to purchase locally grown wheat, as they could not compete with imported flour. As a result, the government invoked special safeguards on COMESA wheat imports, and placed a 60 per cent duty.'[143] First granted in November 2001, safeguards for Kenyan wheat provided for by COMESA have been extended in 2003, 2004, 2005, 2006 and 2007.[144]

D Trade remedies available under the Protocol on the Establishment of the East African Customs Union

This section of the chapter examines the trade remedies available under the Protocol on the Establishment of the East African Customs Union, established by the East African Community (EAC). I will describe the three trade remedies available to members of the EAC, namely, safeguards, anti-dumping measures and subsidies, as well as detailing the pre-conditions for each of their use, and exploring some of the procedural rules which govern those three remedy areas.

1 *The EAC Committee on Trade Remedies*

Article 24 of the Protocol on the Establishment of the East African Customs Union ('the Protocol') established an East African Community Committee on Trade Remedies ('the Committee') to handle all trade remedy matters.[145] In addition to handling matters pertaining to safeguard measures, anti-dumping measures and subsidies and countervailing measures, the Committee also handles matters pertaining to rules of origin, dispute settlement and any other matter referred to the Committee by the EAC Council of Ministers.[146] The Committee is composed of members from each Partner State who are qualified in matters of trade, customs and

www.ivcs.org.uk/IJRS/April2007/Effects%20of%20market%20liberalisation%20on%20rural%20producers.pdf (extracts from the paper).

142 *Ibid.* 143 *Ibid.*

144 'Kenya: COMESA Grants Country Safeguards On Wheat And Sugar Imports', AllAfrica.com, 3 Dec. 2007.

145 Protocol on the Establishment of the East African Customs Union, P. E: Trade Related Aspects, Art. 24(1). Notably, the East African Common Market Protocol in Art. 43 makes provision for prohibited subsidies while Art. 48 provides for safeguard measures. No mention is made of dumping in the Common Market Protocol, perhaps because all of the trade remedy regimes already established in the community apply equally to the common market.

146 *Ibid.*, at Art. 24(1)(a), (b), (c), (d), (e), (f).

law.[147] Each Partner State nominates three members for the Committee, and the Committee has determined its own procedures.[148] Each Partner State is required to notify the Committee of the Investigating Authority within its territory which will initiate and conduct investigations on behalf of the Committee.[149]

The Committee has many functions pertaining to Trade Remedies. It functions to initiate, through the Investigating Authorities of Partner States, investigations on disputes under the EAC Customs Union Regulations.[150] The Committee also has the power to make affirmative or negative determinations on these investigations, as well as to recommend provisional measures to prevent injury to domestic industry when the Investigating Authority has reported an affirmative preliminary determination.[151] Additionally, the Committee undertakes consultations with Partner States and other countries on various matters.[152] The Committee must report to the EAC Council of Ministers on all determinations it makes, all matters submitted to it and decisions made by it.[153] It also provides advisory opinions to Partner States, issues public notices, facilitates consultations between Partner States and administers and manages the dispute settlement mechanisms.[154] The Committee must also annually review all implementations and operations related to its areas of functions, in addition to undertaking any function that the EAC Council of Ministers assigns to it.[155] The Committee also enjoys tremendous power with respect to dispute settlement, and in most cases its decisions on such matters are final.[156]

E Trade remedies available to EAC Customs Union partners

The three trade remedies that are available under the Protocol are safeguard measures, anti-dumping measures and countervailing measures.[157] The trade remedies are provided for briefly and generally by the Protocol on the Establishment of the East African Customs Union, and are then further provided for in detail by Annexes to the Protocol.[158]

147 *Ibid.*, at Art. 24(2)(a). 148 *Ibid.*, at Art. 24(2)(b), 6. 149 *Ibid.*, at Art. 24(3).
150 *Ibid.*, at Art. 24(4)(a). 151 *Ibid.*, at Art. 24(4)(b), (c). 152 *Ibid.*, at Art. 24(4)(d).
153 *Ibid.*, at Art. 24(4)(e). 154 *Ibid.*, at Art. 24(4)(f), (h), (i), (j).
155 *Ibid.*, at Art. 24(4)(g), (k). 156 *Ibid.*, at Art. 24(5).
157 See *ibid.*, at Art. 16: Anti-dumping Measures; Art. 18: Countervailing Measures; and Art. 19: Safeguard Measures.
158 See Protocol on the Establishment of the East African Customs Union, Annex IV: The East African Community Customs Union (Anti-Dumping Measures) Regulations; Annex V:

1 Safeguards

A safeguard measure is a 'protective measure taken by a Partner State to prevent serious injury to her economy'.[159] Article 19 of the Protocol provides the procedures for applying safeguard measures.[160] The Protocol provides that the Partner States agree to apply safeguard measures to situations in which 'there is a sudden surge of products imported into a Partner State, under conditions which cause or threaten to cause serious injury to domestic producers in the territory of like or directly competing products in the territory'.[161] Protocol Annex VI: The East African Community Customs Union (Safeguard Measures) Regulations provides for safeguard measures in more detail.[162]

The Safeguard Measures Regulations ('the Regulations') provide interpretations of key words, conditions for applying safeguards, protocol for investigations, protocol for the determination of serious injury or threat of serious injury, the application of safeguard measures and provisional safeguard measures, the duration and review of measures, as well as regulations on notification and consultations Partner States must make.[163]

There are two major conditions for the application of safeguard measures, the first being that when the measures are applied to a product they must be applied irrespective of that product's source.[164] The second condition is more complex. It requires that before applying safeguard measures, a Partner State must have determined that the product being imported into the territory of that Partner State is in such increased quantities (either absolute or relative to domestic production), and under such conditions that it is causing or threatening to cause injury to the domestic industry that produces like or directly competitive products.[165] If both of these conditions are met, then a state may apply safeguard measures to protect its domestic industry. However, in order to confirm that both these conditions are met, an investigation must take place.[166]

East African Community Customs Union (Subsidies and Countervailing Measures) Regulations, Annex VI: East African Community Customs Union (Safeguard Measures) Regulations.

159 Protocol on the Establishment of the East African Customs Union, Part A: Interpretation, Art. 1: Interpretation.

160 See *ibid.*, at P. E: Trade Related Aspects, Art. 19: Safeguard Measures. 161 *Ibid.*, (1).

162 See *ibid.*, at Annex VI, The East African Community Customs Union (Safeguard Measures) Regulations.

163 *Ibid.* 164 *Ibid.*, at Reg. 4: Conditions for Applying Safeguard Measures (1).

165 *Ibid.* Reg. 4: Conditions for Applying Safeguard Measures (2).

166 See *ibid.*, at Reg. 5: Investigation.

A Partner State can only apply safeguard measures following an investigation by that state's Investigating Authority.[167] Regulation 5 briefly provides the steps that must take place during the investigation.[168] The Investigating Authority must give public notice of the investigation to all interested parties.[169] The investigation will then include public hearings or procedures in which all interested parties are provided both an opportunity to present evidence and views, as well as an opportunity to respond to evidence and views given by other interested parties as to whether safeguard measures would be in the interest of the public.[170] Any information presented to the Investigating Authority which is by nature confidential will be treated as such. However, when such information is provided, the Investigating Authority may request that the party furnish a non-confidential summary of the information, or at the very least provide a reason why the information cannot be summarized in a non-confidential manner.[171] If a situation should arise in which the Investigating Authority finds that information a party wishes to be kept confidential is not of a confidential nature, it may disregard such information unless it can be demonstrated from appropriate sources that the information is indeed correct.[172] After the investigation is complete, the Investigating Authority will immediately publish a report setting out the finding and conclusions that it has reached on all pertinent issues of fact and law and giving a detailed analysis of the case and a demonstration of all the relevant factors examined.[173] In order for the Investigating Authority to conclude that safeguard measures are applicable, they must first determine that there has been a serious injury or threat thereof to the domestic industry of a Partner State.[174]

A serious injury is defined by the Regulations as 'a significant overall impairment in the position of the domestic industry of a Partner State, determined basing on facts'.[175] The Regulations define 'threat of serious injury' as 'serious injury that is clearly imminent, determined basing on facts and not merely on allegation, conjecture or remote possibility'.[176] When determining whether there has been a serious injury or threat thereof to the domestic market of a Partner State, the Investigating Authority will 'evaluate all relevant factors of an objective and quantifiable nature'.[177] In particular, this includes: 'the rate and amount of the increase

167 *Ibid.* at (1). 168 See generally *ibid.*, at Reg. 5: Investigation. 169 *Ibid.* at (2).
170 *Ibid.* 171 *Ibid.* at (3). 172 *Ibid.* at (4). 173 *Ibid.* at (5).
174 *Ibid.* Reg. 6: Determination of Serious Injury or Threat of Serious Injury.
175 *Ibid.* at (1)(a). 176 *Ibid.* at (1)(b). 177 *Ibid.* at (2).

in imports of the product concerned, the share of the domestic market taken by increased imports, changes in the level of sales, production, productivity, capacity utilization, profits and losses and employment'.[178] Additionally, to determine that there is serious injury or threat thereof, the investigation must demonstrate through objective evidence that there is a causal link between the increase in imports of the product concerned and the serious injury or threat thereof to the domestic industry.[179] However, even if all conditions are met and the Investigating Authority concludes that the Partner State may apply safeguard measures, there are still limitations on the application of the measures.[180]

A Partner State may only apply safeguard measures to the extent that they are necessary to prevent or remedy serious injury and to facilitate adjustment of the domestic industry, and measures must always be applied in a non-discriminatory manner.[181] Where quantitative restrictions are used as a safeguard, the measure should not reduce the quantity of imports below the level of a recent period.[182] That level will be determined by calculating the average imports of the last three representative years for which statistics are available, 'unless a clear justification is given that a different level is necessary to prevent or remedy serious injury'.[183] Additionally, when safeguards take the form of a quota allocated among supplying countries, the Partner State applying the restrictions may seek an agreement as to the allocation of shares in the quota with all other Partner States who have a substantial interest in supplying the product concerned.[184] If this method is not reasonably practicable under the circumstances, the Partner State concerned may use a previous representative period to calculate previous proportions and allot shares to Partner States with a substantial interest using those calculations. However, due account should be taken of any 'special factors which may have affected or may be affecting' trade of the product.[185]

The Safeguard Regulations also provide for certain emergency circumstances under which provisional safeguard measures can be taken.[186] Regulation 8 allows for a Partner State to 'take provisional safeguard measures pursuant to a preliminary determination that there is clear evidence that increased imports are threatening to cause serious injury to the domestic industry of that Partner State', in situations in which delay would cause damage which would be difficult to remedy.[187] The duration

178 *Ibid.* 179 *Ibid.* at (3). 180 *Ibid.* Reg. 7: Application of Safeguard Measures.
181 *Ibid.* at (1), (2). 182 *Ibid.* at (3). 183 *Ibid.* 184 *Ibid.* at (4).
185 *Ibid.* 186 *Ibid.* Reg. 8: Provisional Safeguard Measures. 187 *Ibid.* at (1).

of provisional measures, however, is limited to 200 days.[188] The provisional safeguard measures take the form of a tariff increase to be promptly refunded in the case that the subsequent investigation determines that the increased imports have not caused serious injury or a threat thereof to the domestic market.[189]

There is an additional Regulation for the duration and review of safeguard measures.[190] The major limitation on the application of safeguard measures is their duration; a Partner State may only apply safeguard measures for such a period as they are necessary to prevent or remedy serious injury and facilitate adjustment.[191] A safeguard may remain in force for a period of one year, but may be extended annually for three years by a decision of the EAC Council of Ministers, if the Partner State has proven that the measures continue to be necessary to prevent or remedy serious injury and there is evidence that the domestic industry is adjusting.[192] The total time period that a safeguard measure can be applied must not exceed three years.[193] When the expected duration of safeguard measures is less than six months, the Partner State applying the measure must progressively liberalize it at regular intervals in order to facilitate adjustment.[194] Where the duration of a measure exceeds one year, the Partner State applying the measure must review it no later than mid-term and where appropriate withdraw it or increase the rate of liberalization.[195] Additionally, a safeguard measure which has been extended cannot be more restrictive than it was at the end of its initial period of application, but should continue to be liberalized.[196] In certain circumstances, safeguard measures may be repeated. A safeguard measure with a duration of no more than 108 days may be applied again when at least one year has passed since the date of introduction of the measures, and the safeguard measure has not been applied on that same product more than twice in the three-year period immediately preceding the date the application of the safeguards began.[197]

When taking actions to investigate or apply safeguard measures, there are certain notifications a Partner State must make.[198] It must immediately notify the EAC Committee on Trade Remedies first, upon initiating an investigation into serious injury or threat thereof, and notify the Committee of the reasons for that investigation.[199] The Partner State must

188 *Ibid.* at (2). 189 *Ibid.* at (4).
190 *Ibid.* Reg. 9: Duration and Review of Safeguard Measures. 191 *Ibid.* at (1).
192 *Ibid.* at (2). 193 *Ibid.* at (3). 194 *Ibid.* at (4). 195 *Ibid.* at (5).
196 *Ibid.* at 6(a), (b). 197 *Ibid.* at (5).
198 *Ibid.* Reg. 10: Notification and Consultation. 199 *Ibid.* at (1)(a).

also notify the Committee if they make a finding of a serious injury or threat thereof caused by an increase in imports, and when and if they decide to apply or extend a safeguard measure.[200] When making these notifications, the Partner State intending to apply or extend the safeguard must provide the Committee with all the relevant information.[201] Information that should be reported to the Committee includes 'evidence of serious injury or threat of serious injury caused by increase in imports, a precise description of the product involved and the proposed safeguard measure, the proposed date of introduction, the expected duration and the timetable for progressive liberalization'.[202] In an instance where the Partner State is seeking to extend a safeguard measure, there must also be evidence that the industry concerned is adjusting.[203] The Committee may also request additional information that it considers necessary.[204] A Partner State must also notify and keep the Committee up to date on their laws, regulations and administrative procedures relating to safeguard measures and before taking provisional measures.[205]

A Partner State intending to apply or extend safeguard measures must also provide adequate opportunities for consultations with Partner States who have a substantial interest as exporters of the product concerned.[206] The purpose of such consultation is to exchange views on the measures and reach an understanding on ways in which to achieve the objectives of the safeguard.[207] In a case where provisional measures have been taken by a Partner State, consultations must be initiated immediately after the measures have been applied.[208] The results of all consultations should be immediately reported to the Committee by the Partner State concerned.[209]

2 *Anti-dumping measures*

The EAC recognizes anti-dumping measures as 'measures taken by the investigating authority of the importing Partner State after conducting an investigation and determining dumping and material injury resulting from dumping'.[210] According to the EAC Customs Protocol, dumping has occurred when a situation arises in which 'the export price of goods imported or intended to be imported into the Community is less than

200 *Ibid.* at (1)(b), (c). 201 *Ibid.* at (2). 202 *Ibid.*
203 *Ibid.* 204 *Ibid.* at (3). 205 *Ibid.* at (5), (7). 206 *Ibid.* at (4).
207 *Ibid.* 208 *Ibid.* at (5). 209 *Ibid.* at (6).
210 Protocol on the Establishment of the East African Customs Union, Part A: Interpretation, Art. 1: Interpretation.

the normal value of like good in the market of a country of origin'.[211] All anti-dumping actions must be taken in accordance with Annex IV of the Protocol, The East African Community Customs Union (Anti-dumping Measures) Regulations ('the Regulations').[212] Additionally, any time anti-dumping measures are taken by a Partner State, the EAC Secretariat must notify the WTO of the action.[213]

The Regulations provide conditions for the application of anti-dumping measures.[214] Anti-dumping measures may only be applied in the circumstances provided for in Article 16 of the Protocol, which provides that: 'dumping is prohibited if it causes or threatens to cause material injury to an established industry in any of the Partner States, materially retards the establishment of a domestic industry therein or frustrates the benefits expected from the removal or absence of duties and quantitative restrictions of trade between partners'.[215] If these circumstances occur, a Partner State may then apply an anti-dumping measure pursuant to an investigation initiated and conducted pursuant to the Regulations.[216] However, in order for the Investigating Authority to conclude that anti-dumping measures are applicable, they must first determine that a dumping has in fact taken place, and has resulted in material injury or threat thereof to the domestic market of a Partner State.[217]

The EAC Regulations on Anti-Dumping consider a product to have been dumped when it is imported into a Partner State at 'less than its normal value, and where the export price of such a product exported from another Partner State is less than the comparable price, in the ordinary course of trade for a like product . . . [consumed] in the exporting country'. Determining whether a dumping has taken place can often be a complex process involving multiple steps and difficult calculations.[218] Sales of a like product which is consumed in the domestic market of

211 *Ibid.*

212 Protocol on the Establishment of the East African Customs Union, P. E: Trade Related Aspects, Art. 16: Anti-dumping Measures (3).

213 *Ibid.* at (2).

214 *Ibid.*, Annex IV: The East African Community Customs Union (Anti-Dumping Measures) Regulations, Reg. 6.

215 *Ibid.* at Reg. 6(1); Protocol on the Establishment of the East African Customs Union, P. E: Trade Related Aspects, Art. 16: Anti-dumping Measures (1).

216 See *ibid.*, Annex IV: The East African Community Customs Union (Anti-Dumping Measures) Regulations, Reg. 6(1), (2).

217 See generally *ibid.*, at Reg. 7: Determination of Dumping; Reg. 8: Determination of Injury.

218 See *ibid.* at Reg. 7: Determination of Dumping.

the exporting country will be considered a sufficient quantity where sales constitute five per cent or more of the sales of the product to the importing state.[219]

A situation may arise, however, in which there are no sales of a like product in the domestic market of the exporting country, or where sales are so low in volume (less than 5 per cent of the amount sold to the importing country) that they do not permit a proper comparison. In such a case, the margin of dumping can be determined by comparison with a comparable price of a like product when exported to an appropriate foreign country provided, of course, that the price is representative.[220] The Investigating Authority must thus calculate costs to determine whether dumping has taken place.

When calculating costs, the Investigating Authority will normally do so on the basis of records kept by the exporter or producer under investigation, provided that such records are kept in accordance with accepted accounting principles of that state and reasonably reflect the costs associated with production and sale of the product.[221] When undertaking this investigation, the Authority should consider 'all available evidence on the proper allocation of costs, including that which is made available by the exporter or producer in the course of the investigation provided that the allocations have been historically utilized by that exporter or producer'.[222]

When calculating costs, the Investigating Authority may take into account the amounts for 'administrative, selling and general costs and profits', as long as these figures are based on actual data pertaining to the production and sales of a like product by the producer under investigation.[223] If a situation should arise in which the amounts cannot be determined on this basis, there is alternative data on which the amounts may be based, including the actual amount incurred and realized by that exporter or producer in the country of origin of a product in the same general category of products, the weighted average of the actual amounts incurred and realized by other exporters of a like product in the country of origin, or any other reasonable method 'provided that the amount for profit so established shall not exceed the profit normally realized by other exporters or producers on sales of products of the same general category in the domestic market of the country of origin'.[224]

In addition to the methods for calculating cost given above, there are also alternative means of calculating costs under certain circumstances

219 *Ibid.* at (2)(b). 220 *Ibid.* 221 *Ibid.* at (3)(a). 222 *Ibid.* at (3)(b). 223 *Ibid.* at (4). 224 *Ibid.* at (4)(a), (b), (c).

provided for in the Regulations.[225] The Regulations also provide in detail for situations in which the export price is unreliable, comparability has been affected, a conversion of currency is required, there is a fluctuation in exchange rates, or the products have not been directly imported.[226]

Simply proving that dumping has occurred, however, does not suffice to evidence a need to apply anti-dumping measures; the Partner State must also show that the dumping has caused, or is threatening to cause material injury to the domestic industry within its territory. The Investigating Authority must base their determination of injury on an objective examination of evidence.[227] Such evidence should include: 'the volume of the dumped imports, and the effect of the dumped imports on prices in the domestic market for like product; and the consequent impact of the dumped imports on the domestic producers of like products'.[228]

When examining the volume of the dumped imports, the Investigating Authority must consider whether there has been a 'significant increase in dumped imports in either absolute or relative terms to production or consumption in the importing Partner State'.[229] With regard to the effect of the dumped imports on prices, the Authority must consider whether there has been significant price-undercutting by the dumped imports when compared to the price of a like product of the importing state, or whether the effect of the dumped imports is otherwise depressing prices to a significant degree or preventing prices from increasing which otherwise would have.[230] While the totality of these factors will lead the Authority to a conclusion on the matter, 'no individual or several of these factors may give decisive guidance to the determination of injury'.[231]

In a situation in which imports of a product from more than one country are simultaneously being subjected to anti-dumping investigations, the Investigating Authority can only cumulatively assess the effects if it is determined that two factors are present.[232] First, the margin of dumping from each country must not be *de minimis*, that is, it must not be less than two per cent, when expressed as a percentage of the export price.[233] Then it must be determined that 'a cumulative assessment of the effects of the imports is appropriate in light of the conditions of competition between the imported products and the like domestic products'.[234]

When examining the impact of dumped imports on the domestic industry concerned, the Investigating Authority must evaluate all the

225 *Ibid.* at (3), (4), (5). 226 *Ibid.* 227 *Ibid.* Reg. 8(1). 228 *Ibid.* at (1)(a), (b).
229 *Ibid.* at (2). 230 *Ibid.* 231 *Ibid.* at (2), (3). 232 *Ibid.* at (4).
233 *Ibid.* Reg. 8(4); Reg. 10(8)(2). 234 *Ibid.* Reg. 8(4)(b).

relevant economic factors and indices which have a bearing on the state of the industry.[235] Such an examination should include an evaluation of: 'actual and potential decline in sales, profits, output, market share, productivity, return on investments, utilisation of capacity, factors affecting domestic prices, the magnitude of the margin of dumping, actual and potential negative effects on cash flow, inventories, employment, wages, growth, ability to raise capital or investments'.[236]

It must be demonstrated that the dumped imports are, through the effects of dumping, causing injury within the meaning of the Regulations.[237] The causal relationship between the dumped imports and the injury to the domestic market must be demonstrated on the basis of an examination of all relevant evidence available to the Investigating Authority.[238] However, the Authority must also examine any known factors other than the dumping of imports which may have, at the same time, injured the domestic industry, to ensure that any injury caused by other factors is not attributed to the dumped imports.[239]

A determination of a threat of material injury must be 'based on facts and not on allegation, conjecture or remote possibility'.[240] The Regulations require that '[t]he change in circumstances which would create a situation in which the dumping would cause injury shall be clearly foreseen and imminent'.[241] In determining whether or not the threat of material injury exists, the Investigating Authority will consider several factors: the rate of import, increase in capacity of the exporter taking into account the availability of other export markets and 'whether imports are entering at prices that will have significant or suppressing effect on domestic prices, and would likely increase demand for further imports; and inventories of the products being investigated'.[242] While these factors may not individually give decisive guidance, the totality of the factors considered will lead to a conclusion of whether or not further dumped exports are imminent and therefore injury will be imminent.[243]

When it comes to investigating instances of dumping, the definition of the term 'domestic industry', is very important, so important, in fact, that there is an entire regulation devoted to defining it precisely.[244] When the

235 *Ibid.* at (5). 236 *Ibid.*

237 *Ibid.* at (6); see *ibid.* at Reg. 3: Interpretation (defining 'injury' as 'material injury to a domestic industry, threat of material injury to a domestic industry or material retardation of the establishment of that industry').

238 *Ibid.* Reg. 8(6). 239 *Ibid.* 240 *Ibid.* at (8). 241 *Ibid.*

242 *Ibid.* at (8)(a)(b)(c)(d). 243 *Ibid.* at (9).

244 *Ibid.* Reg. 9: Definition of Domestic Industry.

Regulations refer to 'domestic industry', they are referring to 'the domestic producers as a whole of the like product or . . . those domestic producers whose collective output of the product constitutes a major portion of the total domestic production of those products'.[245] There are, however, two important exceptions to that definition.[246] The first exception is that if the producers of the product are related to the exporters or importers or are themselves importers of the allegedly dumped product, then the term 'domestic industry' may be referring to the rest of the producers of a like product.[247]

The second exception, which is only applicable in rare circumstances, is one in which the territory of the Partner State may be divided into two or more competitive markets (for the production of the product in question), and the producers within each market may be regarded as being separate industries.[248] However, such a division will not be made 'unless the producers within the competitive market sell all or almost all of their production of the product in question on the market; and the demand in that market is not at any substantial degree supplied by producers of the product in question located elsewhere in the territory'.[249] In these situations, 'injury may be found to exist even when a major portion of the total domestic industry is not injured, if there is a concentration of dumped imports into such an isolated market and provided further that the dumped imports are causing injury to the producers of all or almost all of the production . . .'[250] In these cases, however, anti-dumping duties may only be levied on products which are consigned for final consumption in that market.[251] Where the law of the importing Partner State does not permit anti-dumping duties to be levied on this basis, the importing Partner State may levy the duties without limitation if the exporters are given the opportunity to cease exporting at dumper prices, or where the anti-dumping duties cannot be levied only on specific producers which supply the market in question.[252]

The Anti-Dumping Regulations also provide a specific section on anti-dumping measures and duties which details the procedures for applying anti-dumping measures.[253] Included in this section are procedures and rules for initiating and conducting investigations, collecting relevant evidence, applying provisional measures and price undertakings, imposing

245 *Ibid.* 246 *Ibid.* at (1)(a)(b). 247 *Ibid.* at (1)(a). 248 *Ibid.* at (1)(b).
249 *Ibid.* at (1)(b)(i)(ii). 250 *Ibid.* at (1)(b)(ii). 251 *Ibid.* Reg. 9(2).
252 *Ibid.* at (2)(a)(b). 253 See *ibid.* Part III, Regs. 10–18.

and collecting anti-dumping duties and provisions for the duration and review of anti-dumping duties.[254]

An investigation into the existence and effect of dumped imports is initiated when a written application is made by or on behalf of the complaining domestic industry.[255] The application must include: evidence of a dumping, injury and causal link between the two, the identity of the applicant with physical and postal address and a description of the volume and value of the domestic production of the like product by the applicant.[256] The application must also include: 'A complete description of the allegedly dumped product, the name of the country of origin or export, the identity of each known exporter or foreign producer and a list of known persons importing the product in question', information on the prices at which the product in question is sold when consumed in the domestic market of the country of its origin, as well as information on the evolution of the volume of the allegedly dumped imports and their effect on the prices of like products in the domestic market of the importing state.[257] The Investigating Authority will then examine the evidence provided in the application, checking for accuracy and adequacy and then determine if sufficient evidence has been given to justify the initiation of an investigation.[258] An investigation cannot be initiated unless the application had been made by or on behalf of the domestic industry. The application will be considered to have been made by or on behalf of the domestic industry when 'it is supported by those domestic producers whose collective output constitutes more than fifty per centum of the total production of the like product produced by that portion of the domestic industry expressing either support for or opposition to the application'.[259] An investigation cannot be initiated where domestic producers supporting the application account for less than twenty-five per cent of the total production of the like product in the domestic industry.[260] Until a decision has been made to initiate an investigation, the Investigating Authority will refrain from publicizing the application or initiation of the investigation.[261]

After the Investigating Authority has received a sufficient application, and before it proceeds with the investigation, the Authority must notify the government of the exporting country concerned.[262] If, in a special circumstance, the Investigating Authority has decided to initiate an

254 See *ibid.* 255 *Ibid.* Reg. 10: Initiation and Subsequent Investigations (1).
256 *Ibid.* at (2)(a). 257 *Ibid.* at (2)(b)(c)(d). 258 *Ibid.* at (3).
259 *Ibid.* at (4). 260 *Ibid.* 261 *Ibid.* Reg. 10(5). 262 *Ibid.*

investigation without receiving an application, it must proceed only where it has sufficient evidence of dumping, injury and a causal link between the two.[263] Where an Investigating Authority decides to initiate, an investigation notice must be given to all known interested parties. Additionally, a public notice shall be issued containing such information as: the name of the exporting country, the initiation date of the investigation, the basis of the investigation, a summary of factors, addresses to which representations of interested parties may be made and time limits for representations.[264]

In both the decision of whether or not to investigate the situation and the decision of whether or not to apply provisional measures during the course of the investigation, the Authority must consider both the evidence of dumping and the evidence of injury simultaneously.[265] If at any time in the process the Investigating Authority is satisfied that there is not sufficient evidence of either dumping or injury, the application shall be rejected or the investigation shall be terminated.[266] The investigation will also be terminated in cases in which the Authority determines the margin of dumping to be *de minimis*, that is, less than 2 per cent, expressed as a percentage of the export price, or where the volume of dumped imports (actual or potential) is negligible.[267] The volume of exports will be considered negligible if it is less than three per cent of imports of the like product in the importing Partner State, unless multiple countries which each account for less than three per cent of the imports collectively account for more than seven per cent of the like products in the importing state.[268] Anti-dumping proceeding cannot hinder the procedures of customs clearance, nor should an investigation (except in special circumstance) exceed the duration of one year, and in any case last any longer than eighteen months from its initiation.[269]

Regulation 11 provides for the way in which evidence will be collected and the way in which information will be disclosed to parties involved in the matter.[270] The investigation, for the most part, upholds the ideal of transparency; the Investigating Authority must give notice of information to all interested parties, and give them ample opportunity to present in writing any evidence that they consider relevant to the investigation.[271] The Investigating Authority may issue questionnaires to exporters and

263 *Ibid.* at (6). 264 *Ibid.* Reg. 17: Public Notice and Explanation of Determinations (1).
265 *Ibid.* Reg. 10(7)(a)(b). 266 *Ibid.* at (8)(1). 267 *Ibid.* at (8)(2).
268 *Ibid.* at (8)(3). 269 *Ibid.* at (9), (10). 270 *Ibid.* Reg. 11: Evidence.
271 *Ibid.* at (1).

foreign producers which they will be given thirty days to complete and return.[272] At the outset of the investigation, the Authority must provide the full text of the application to known exporters involved and to the Investigating Authority of that exporting state, as well as upon request to other interested parties involved.[273] Except for information which is of a confidential nature, any evidence presented to the Authority shall be made available promptly to other interested parties participating in the investigation. If the information is provided to the Authority orally, it must be subsequently reproduced in a written form, or it cannot be taken into account by the Authority in the decision-making process.[274] Whenever it is practical to do so, the Authority should provide opportunities for all of the interested parties to access all information that is relevant to the case (except, of course, that which is confidential).[275] The Authority must also take steps to ensure the non-disclosure of information which would be of a significant competitive advantage to a competitor, or which would have a significant adverse effect on the party which has disclosed it, or which is provided in confidence to the Authority. In the case that such information is provided to the Authority, it should not be disclosed to any other parties without the specific permission of the submitting party.[276] Where information is of a confidential nature, the party submitting it will be requested to furnish a non-confidential version of the information which can be made available to the other parties.[277] In the case that a party feels that information is confidential but the Investigating Authority does not find the information to be confidential, the information must be disregarded by the Authority unless it can be shown to be correct by appropriate sources.[278] The Investigating Authority may conduct investigations in the territory of other Partner States in order to verify or obtain information, as long as it obtains prior consent from the firms involved, and the government of the Partner State does not object.[279] Any information obtained in such manner shall be made available to the firms to which they pertain.[280] In addition to the other transparency requirements, before a final determination is made by the Investigating Authority, it must inform all interested parties of the essential facts on which it has formed the basis of its determination. The disclosure should be made in sufficient time for the parties to defend their interests.[281] Part V of the Regulations provides additional guidance for the Investigating

272 *Ibid.* at (2)(1). 273 *Ibid.* at (2)(3). 274 *Ibid.* at (2)(4).
275 *Ibid.* at (5). 276 *Ibid.* Reg. 11(6). 277 *Ibid.* at (7)(1). 278 *Ibid.* at (7)(2).
279 *Ibid.* at (9)(1). 280 *Ibid.* at (9)(2). 281 *Ibid.* at (11).

Authority by 'Procedures for On the Spot Investigations', and 'Procedures for Obtaining Best Information Possible', which may be used by the Authority as a guide during investigations.[282]

The Investigating Authority must determine the individual margin of dumping for each known exporter or producer of the product under investigation. However, the Regulations recognize that the Authority has limited resources and therefore, in cases in which there is a large number of exporters or producers such as to make it burdensome or impractical to make a determination, the Authority may use statistically valid samples.[283] Likewise, the Regulations recognize difficulties that may be experienced by interested parties and therefore provide that the Authority should take due account of such difficulties, in particular those experienced by small companies.[284]

Just as in the case of safeguards, in circumstances where delay would cause injury, the Investigating Authority may apply provisional measures if there has been a preliminary determination of dumping linked to injury.[285] The provisional measures will take the form of a provisional duty or may be estimated on security by cash deposit, or bond equal to the amount of the duty (which cannot be higher than the estimated margin of dumping). Provisional measures cannot be applied within sixty days from the initiation of the investigation, must not exceed the duration of four months, or in special cases six months, and may be adjusted or terminated according to subsequent findings of the Authority.[286] A public notice setting out a sufficiently detailed explanation of the preliminary determinations, reasons for the imposition of provisional measures and details such as the product and the suppliers and countries involved, must also be released.[287]

In some cases, dumping may be remedied without applying anti-dumping duties. This is possible if the exporter voluntarily revises the prices of the product or ceases to export it at dumped prices to the area in question; this is called 'a voluntary price undertaking'.[288] Increases under price undertakings cannot be higher than necessary to eliminate the margin of dumping; neither can they be less than the margin of dumping

282 *Ibid.* First Sched. Procedures for on the Spot Investigation, Second Sched., Procedures for Obtaining Best Information Available.

283 Protocol on the Establishment of the East African Customs Union, Annex IV: The East African Community Customs Union (Anti-Dumping Measures) Regulations, Reg. 11(12).

284 *Ibid.* at (15).

285 *Ibid.* Reg. 12: Provisional Measures (1).

286 *Ibid.* at (2)(a)(b), (5).

287 *Ibid.* Reg. 17(4)(a)(b)(c).

288 *Ibid.* Reg. 13(1).

when the increases would be adequate to remove the injury to the domestic industry affected.[289] A price undertaking cannot be sought or accepted from an exporter unless the Investigating Authority has made a preliminary determination of dumping and injury caused by that dumping.[290] A price undertaking also cannot be accepted in instances where the Investigating Authority considers its acceptance impracticable, and in situations in which the undertaking is accepted, an investigation may nevertheless be completed if the exporter so desires or the Investigating Authority so decides.[291] A price undertaking can be suggested by the Investigating Authority, but an exporter must not be compelled to make such an offer.[292] The Investigating Authority may, however, require an exporter from whom a price undertaking has been accepted to provide information relevant to the fulfilment of that undertaking, and if the undertaking is violated the Authority may take action including the immediate application of provisional measures, or levying definitive duties on products.[293]

In cases in which all the requirements for the imposition of anti-dumping measures have been fulfilled, the decision to impose anti-dumping duties and the amount of those duties will be made by the EAC Trade Remedies Committee.[294] In cases in which the Committee decides to impose duties, there are procedures which must be followed.[295] The duty must be collected in the appropriate amount on a non-discriminatory basis.[296] The Investigating Authority must name the suppliers of the product concerned, or where that is impracticable, the name of the supplying country concerned.[297] The amount of an anti-dumping duty cannot exceed the margin of dumping, and the Investigating Authority should disregard any zero or *de minimis* margins.[298] Individual duties or normal values will apply to any exporter or producer who was not included in the examination and who has provided the necessary information during the investigation.[299] In certain instances anti-dumping measures may be taken retroactively; however, there are restrictions on the instances in which retroactive measures may be applied.[300]

289 *Ibid.* 290 *Ibid.* at (2). 291 *Ibid.* at (3), (4). 292 *Ibid.* at (5).
293 *Ibid.* at (6), (7)(a)(b).
294 *Ibid.* Reg. 14: Imposition and Collection of Anti-dumping Duties (1).
295 See *ibid.* Reg. 14: Imposition and Collection of Anti-dumping Duties.
296 *Ibid.* at (1). 297 *Ibid.* at (2). 298 *Ibid.* at (3), (6).
299 *Ibid.* at (6); see also *ibid.* at (7) (providing more complete details on the treatment of producers and exporters who were not involved in the investigation or did not import to the state in question during the investigation).
300 *Ibid.* Reg. 15: Retroactivity.

Anti-dumping Regulation 16 provides limitations for the duration and procedures for the review of anti-dumping duties and price undertakings.[301] An anti-dumping duty is limited in duration, and can 'only remain in force as long as and to the extent necessary to counteract dumping which causes injury'.[302] The Investigating Authority must review the need for the continuation of the anti-dumping duty, where warranted, either on its own initiative or if a reasonable time has passed since the imposition of the duty, at the request of any interested party who submits information substantiating the need for a review.[303] Any definitive anti-dumping duty must be terminated within five years of the date of its imposition or, in certain circumstances, five years from the date of the most recent review.[304] Additionally, the provisions of Regulation 11, regarding evidence and procedure, apply to reviews.[305] Reviews must also, in all cases, be carried out expeditiously and will under normal circumstances conclude within twelve months of their initiation.[306]

An application for anti-dumping action can also be made on behalf of a foreign country.[307] Such an application must be made by the authorities of the foreign country to the authority of a Partner State to which the request is made, and must be supported by: 'price information to show that imports are being dumped; and detailed information to show that the alleged dumping is causing injury to the domestic industry concerned in the foreign country'.[308] The government of the foreign country must also afford all assistance to the Investigating Authority of the Partner State in obtaining any further required information on the anti-dumping action.[309] The Investigating Authority of the Partner State will then consider the effects of the alleged dumping on the industry (as a whole) in that foreign country, and decide whether or not to proceed with an anti-dumping action on behalf of that country. If the Partner State decides to take action, it must first seek the approval of the EAC Council of Ministers through the EAC Committee on Trade Remedies.[310]

The Anti-dumping Regulations also provide for consultations and the settlement of any disputes which might arise under the Regulations between States.[311] The Regulations require that a Partner State 'afford fair

301 *Ibid.* Reg. 16: Duration and Review of Anti-Dumping Duties and Price Undertakings.
302 *Ibid.* at (1). 303 *Ibid.* at (2). 304 *Ibid.* at (3).
305 *Ibid.* at (4). 306 *Ibid.* at (3).
307 *Ibid.* Reg. 18: Anti-dumping Action on Behalf of a Foreign Country.
308 *Ibid.* at (1), (2)(1)(a)(b). 309 *Ibid.* at (2)(2). 310 *Ibid.* at (3), (4).
311 *Ibid.* Reg. 19: Consultation and Dispute Settlement.

consideration to, and adequate opportunity for consultation regarding representations made by another Partner State of a foreign country with respect to any matter relating to . . . [the] Regulations'.[312] Additionally, in situations in which a Partner State considers that a benefit accruing to it under the Regulations has been nullified or impaired, it can, with a view of reaching a mutually satisfactory resolution on the matter, request a consultation with the partner or foreign state concerned.[313] In certain cases the Committee may be asked to step in and take over these consultations.[314]

3 *Subsidies and countervailing measures*

Articles 17 and 18 of the Protocol provide briefly for countervailing measures in cases where subsidies are causing injury to a Partner State. However, Annex V of the Protocol, the East African Customs Union (Subsidies and Countervailing Measures) Regulations ('the Regulations') provides for countervailing measures in much greater detail.[315] The purpose of the Regulations is to implement the provisions found in the Protocol, and to ensure uniformity among the EAC Partner States in the application of subsidies and countervailing measures, and to ensure 'to the extent possible the process is transparent, accountable, fair, predictable and consistent with provisions of the Protocol'.[316]

A subsidy exists where there is a financial contribution by a government or any public body within the territory of a Partner State or foreign country and as a result of that contribution, a benefit has been conferred.[317] Some examples of subsidies include: a direct transfer of funds such as grants or loans, the forgoing of revenue that is due to the government, government-provided goods or services and payment by a government to a funding mechanism.[318] A subsidy exists where there is any form of income or price support and a benefit is conferred as a result.[319] If a Partner State gives or maintains a subsidy either directly or indirectly by favouring certain undertakings or the production of certain goods in

312 *Ibid.* at (2). 313 *Ibid.* 314 See *ibid.* Reg. 19.

315 See Protocol on the Establishment of the East African Customs Union, Annex IV: The East African Community Customs Union (Subsidies and Countervailing Measures) Regulations.

316 *Ibid.* Reg. 2: Purpose of the Regulations.

317 *Ibid.* Reg. 7, Definition of a Subsidy (1). 318 *Ibid.* at (1)(a)(b)(c)(d).

319 *Ibid.* at (2).

that state, it must notify all the other Partner States in writing.[320] This notification should contain: 'the extent and nature of the subsidization, the estimated effect of the subsidization, the quantity of the affected product or products exported to the Partner States and the circumstances making the subsidization necessary'.[321]

A countervailing measure is the term for 'actions taken to counteract the effect of injurious subsidies'.[322] The EAC may, for the purposes of offsetting the effect of a subsidy, levy a countervailing duty on any product of any foreign country imported into the customs union.[323] Just as with all trade remedies, there are conditions which must be satisfied in order for a Partner State to apply countervailing measures.[324] The countervailing duty must be 'equal to the amount of the estimated subsidy determined to have been granted directly or indirectly on the manufacture, production or export of that product in the country of origin or export'.[325]

Some kinds of subsidies are prohibited by the EAC.[326] Except for those which are provided for by the World Trade Organization Agreement on Agriculture, any subsidy which is contingent (in law or fact) solely or as one of several other conditions, on either the use of over imported goods, or upon export performance, shall be prohibited.[327] However, in the case of a subsidy based on export performance, the standard will only be met when the facts demonstrate that the granting of a subsidy is tied to actual or anticipated exportation or export earnings.[328] The mere fact that a subsidy has been granted to an enterprise which exports is not, alone, enough to be considered an export subsidy.[329]

Whenever a Partner State has reason to believe that a prohibited subsidy is being granted or is being maintained by another Partner State or by a foreign state, the Partner State may make a request for consultations

320 Protocol on the Establishment of the East African Customs Union, Art. 17: Subsidies (1).

321 *Ibid.* at (2). 322 *Ibid.*, Art. 1(1): Interpretation.

323 *Ibid.*, Art. 18: Countervailing Measures (1)(a).

324 Protocol on the Establishment of the East African Customs Union, Annex IV: The East African Community Customs Union (Subsidies and Countervailing Measures) Regulations, Reg. 6: Conditions for Applying Countervailing Measures.

325 Protocol on the Establishment of the East African Customs Union, Art. 18: Countervailing Measures (1)(b).

326 See Protocol on the Establishment of the East African Customs Union, Annex IV: The East African Community Customs Union (Subsidies and Countervailing Measures) Regulations, Reg. 9: Prohibited Subsidies.

327 *Ibid.* at (1)(a)(b). 328 *Ibid.* at (1)(a). 329 *Ibid.*

with that state.[330] The EAC Committee on Trade Remedies should be notified of the request, and the request should include a statement of the available evidence on the existence and nature of the subsidy.[331] Upon receiving the request the partner or foreign state believed to be granting the subsidy must enter into consultations as quickly as possible and clarify the fact of the situation to arrive at a mutually agreed solution.[332] Where no solution can be reached within 30 days, any Partner State party to the consultations can refer the matter to the Committee for consideration, and the Committee will immediately review the evidence and submit a final report within 90 days.[333] Where the Committee determines there is a prohibited subsidy, it will recommend that the subsidy be withdrawn.[334] Unless one of the parties disputes the Committee's report within 30 days or the Council of Ministers unanimously decides not to adopt the report, it will be adopted by the Council of Ministers.[335] When a report is appealed by a party, the Council of Ministers will decide if and what action is to be taken: where they do so by consensus, their decision will be issued in the form of a directive; where they fail to do so, the aggrieved party may refer the matter to the East African Court of Justice.[336] In cases '[w]here no reference is made within twenty days or where the parties do not implement the directive within the period specified by the Council, the Council shall grant authorisation to the complaining Partner State to take the appropriate counter measures'.[337]

Not all subsidies are actionable; actionable subsidies are ones which cause adverse effects to the interests of Partner States.[338] Adverse effects include: 'Injury to the domestic industry of a Partner State; nullification or impairment of benefits accruing directly or indirectly to other partner states under the General Agreement on Tariffs and Trade, 1994 . . . [and] serious prejudice [or threat thereof] to the interests of another state.'[339] 'Serious prejudice' exists when either the total '*ad valorem* subsidization of a product' exceeds five per cent, subsidies are being used to cover operating losses in the industry or an enterprise (except for one-time measures),

330 *Ibid.* Reg. 10: Remedies on Prohibited Subsidies (1). 331 *Ibid.* at (1), (2).
332 *Ibid.* at (3). 333 *Ibid.* at (4), (5), (6). 334 *Ibid.* at (7). 335 *Ibid.* at (8).
336 *Ibid.* Reg. 10: Remedies on Prohibited Subsidies (9), (1), (2), (3).
337 *Ibid.* at (10). 338 *Ibid.* Reg. 11: Adverse Effects (1).
339 This does not, however, apply to subsidies maintained on agricultural produce, as provided by Art. 13 of the WTO Agreement on Agriculture; Protocol on the Establishment of the East African Customs Union, Annex IV: The East African Community Customs Union (Subsidies and Countervailing Measures) Regulations, Reg. 12: Serious Prejudice (2)(a), (b), (c), (3), (4).

or the government is directly cancelling debts or issuing grants to cover debt repayment.[340] 'Serious prejudice' may arise when the effect of a subsidy is to displace or impede the import or export of a like product from a partner or foreign state, or significantly undercut the price of a like product.[341] Some subsidies are non-actionable under the Regulations. Assistance for research activities when they are conducted on a contract basis with firms, if they are for the enlargement of general science and technical knowledge and not for industrial or commercial objectives, and non-specific[342] assistance to disadvantaged regions when given pursuant to a general framework of regional development are non-actionable subsidies.[343] Also considered a non-actionable subsidy is assistance to promote adaptation of existing facilities to new environmental requirements imposed by law which result in greater constraints and financial burden on firms.[344] Where a Partner State has reason to believe that one of the above listed non-actionable subsidies, although in compliance with the Regulations, has resulted in serious adverse effects to its domestic industry and is causing damage that will be difficult to repair, it may request consultations in a process that is similar to that for actionable subsidies.[345]

When imposing a countervailing duty, a Partner State must take all necessary steps to ensure that it is doing so in accordance with Article 18 of the Protocol and Part VI of the Regulations.[346] Countervailing duties can only be imposed pursuant to an investigation initiated and conducted pursuant to the Regulations.[347] An investigation is initiated and conducted on the same basis as an investigation under Regulations for safeguard and anti-dumping measures, as is the process of consultations, determination of injury, imposition of provisional measures and the process for review.[348]

340 *Ibid.* (3)(a)(b)(c). 341 *Ibid.* Reg. 11: Adverse Effect.

342 See *ibid.* Annex V, Pt. II, Reg. 8.

343 *Ibid.* Pt. V, Reg. 14: Identification of Non-Actionable Subsidies (2)(a)(b).

344 This, however, must be a one-time measure, is limited to 20% of the cost of the adaptation, does not cover the cost of replacing and operating the assisted investment and must be available to all firms which can adopt new equipment and production processes: Reg. 14(c).

345 *Ibid.* Pt. V, Reg. 15: Consultations on Non-Actionable Subsidies.

346 *Ibid.* Pt. VI: Countervailing Measures, Reg. 16: Application of Art. 18 of the Protocol (1).

347 *Ibid.* at 16(2).

348 See *infra.* See also Union, Annex V: East African Community Customs Union (Subsidies and Countervailing Measures) Regulations, Reg. 17: Initiation and Subsequent Investigations; Reg. 18: Evidence; Reg. 19: Consultations on Countervailing Measures; Reg. 21:

In cases where a countervailing measure is to be imposed, the method used by the Investigating Authority to calculate the benefit conferred on the recipient must be provided for in the national legislation or implementing regulations of the Partner State concerned, and its applications must be transparent and adequately explained.[349] The Regulations also provide specific guidelines with which any method of calculation used must be consistent.[350] In situations where the subsidy is actionable, reasonable efforts have been made to complete consultations, and the subsidy has not been withdrawn, a Partner State may impose a countervailing measure.[351] The decision whether or not to impose countervailing duties, and the amount of the countervailing duty, are ultimately made by the Committee on Trade Remedies.[352] It is desirable that the imposition be permissive in the territory of all the Partner States and that the duty be less than the total amount of the subsidy, where it would be adequate to remove the injury; in any case, however, the duty cannot be in excess of the amount of the subsidy.[353] The duty will be levied in the appropriate amounts in each case and must be done on a non-discriminatory basis.[354]

Partner States must notify other Partner States of any specific subsidies granted or maintained within their territory no later than 13 June in each year.[355] The notification must be sufficient to enable other Partner States to understand and evaluate the effects of the subsidy.[356] The notification must thus include: the form of the subsidy, subsidy per unit or total amount, policy objective or purpose of the subsidy, the duration or any other limit on the subsidy and statistical data permitting an assessment of the trade effects of the subsidy.[357] Any Partner State may, at any time, request information on the nature and extent of a subsidy granted or maintained by a Partner State, and any Partner State who receives such a request must provide the information within 30 days of receiving the request.[358]

In some instances, special or differential treatment may be given for developing and lesser-developed Partner States; such treatment is

Determination of Injury; Reg. 22: Definition of Domestic Industry; Reg. 23: Provisional Measures; Reg. 28: Public Notice and Explanation of Determinations; Reg. 29: Duration and Review of Countervailing Duties and Price Undertakings.

349 *Ibid.* Reg. 20: Calculation of the Amount of a Subsidy in Terms of the Benefits to the Recipient.

350 See *ibid.* (a)(b)(c)(d).

351 *Ibid.* Reg. 25: Imposition and Collection of Countervailing Duties (1).

352 *Ibid.* at (2). 353 *Ibid.* at (2), (4). 354 *Ibid.* at (3).

355 *Ibid.* Pt. VII, Reg. 29: Notification (1)(2). 356 *Ibid.* at (3).

357 *Ibid.* at (3)(a), (b), (c), (d), (e). 358 *Ibid.* at (8), (9).

governed by Article 27 of the WTO Agreement as amended from time to time.[359]

4 Investigations of dumping, subsidies and application of safeguard measures

Article 20 of the Protocol provides a brief explanation of the way in which Partner States should cooperate in order to detect and investigate instances in which trade remedies may be applied.[360] The Protocol provides that all Partner States must cooperate in the detection and investigation of dumping, subsidies and sudden surges in imports and in the imposition of agreed measures to curb such practices.[361] Where there is evidence of a sudden surge of imports, dumping, or where subsidized imports from a Partner State are threatening or distorting competition within the Community, the affected Partner State may request the Partner State in whose territory the surge, dumping or subsidization is occurring to impose anti-dumping duties or countervailing duties or safeguard measures on such goods.[362] If the Partner State to which the request is made does not act within 30 days of the request, the requesting Partner State can then report to the appropriate customs union authority which shall take the necessary actions.[363]

F Southern African Development Community (SADC) trade remedies

The SADC Free Trade Area (FTA) was established by twelve of the fourteen SADC Member States and has been in effect since 2000.[364]

SADC allows Member States to manage trade by introducing temporary protection in order to safeguard an infant industry, if it is done in consultation with other Member States. SADC's trade remedies also include anti-dumping measures and countervailing measures.

359 Reg. 31: Special and Differential Treatment for Developing and Least Developed Partner States.

360 See Protocol on the Establishment of the East African Customs Union, Pt. E: Trade Related Aspects, Art. 20: Co-operation in the Investigation of Dumping, Subsidies, and Application of Safeguard Measures.

361 See *ibid.* at (1). 362 See *ibid.* at (2). 363 *Ibid.* at (3).

364 Handbook, *Free Trade Area, The South African Development Community Protocol on Trade*, 2008, 4 available at www.sadc.int/cms/uploads/SADC%20Free%20Trade%20Area%20Handbook%20-%20English.pdf.

1 Anti-dumping measures

Dumping is defined by the SADC as 'the introduction of a product into the commerce of another country at less than its normal value, if the price of the product exported from one country to another is less than the comparable price in the ordinary course of trade, for the like product when destined for consumption in the exporting country'.[365] When it comes to implementing anti-dumping measures, the SADC, in Article 18 of the Protocol, has adopted the WTO's approach, by simply stating that '[n]othing in this Protocol shall prevent any Member from applying anti-dumping measures which are in conformity with WTO provisions'.[366] This is an alternative approach to adopting the provisions; some organizations, like COMESA, simply copied the WTO provisions word-for-word into their own regulatory instruments.[367]

2 Subsidies and countervailing measures

The SADC has adopted the WTO's definition of a subsidy, a situation in which:

> there is a financial contribution by a government or any public body within the territory of a Member. For example where: a government practice involves a direct transfer of funds (e.g. grants, loans, and equity infusion), potential direct transfers of funds or liabilities (e.g. loan guarantees); government revenue that is otherwise due is foregone or not collected (e.g. fiscal incentives such as tax credits); a government provides goods or services other than general infrastructure, or purchases goods . . . or there is any form of income or price support . . . And a benefit is thereby conferred.

Under the Protocol, Member States must not grant subsidies which distort or threaten to distort competition in the region.[368] A Member State may, however, for the purposes of offsetting the effect of subsidies and subject to WTO provisions, levy countervailing duties on a product of another state.[369] A Member State may only introduce a new subsidy if it does not

365 Southern African Development Community (SADC) Protocol on Trade, Art. 1: Definitions, available at www.sadcstan.co.za/Secure/downloads/protocol.pdf.

366 *Ibid.*, Art. 18: Anti-Dumping Measures. See World Trade Organization Agreement on Implementation of Article VI of the General Agreement on Tariffs and Trade 1994 (the Anti-Dumping Agreement).

367 See COMESA Regulations on Trade Remedies.

368 SADC Protocol on Trade, Art. 19: Subsidies and Countervailing Measures, 1.

369 *Ibid.* at 3.

distort or threaten competition in the region, and it is in accordance with the WTO provisions.

3 *Safeguard measures*

Under the SADC Protocol on Trade, a Member State may apply a safeguard measure to a product only if that member has determined that such a product is being imported into its territory in such increased quantities (either absolute or relative to domestic production) and under these conditions has caused or is threatening to cause serious injury to the domestic industry that produces like or directly competitive products.[370] Whether or not the effect on the domestic market constitutes a 'serious injury' shall be determined in accordance with Article IV of the World Trade Organization Agreement on Safeguards.[371] A safeguard measure can be applied to a product being imported irrespective of its source within the region, and in applying these measures a Member State should give like treatment to all imports of originating goods.[372]

A Member State may only apply a safeguard measure to the extent and for such a period of time as necessary to prevent or remedy serious injury and facilitate adjustment. The Protocol's Article 20 mandates that this time period be in accordance with Article 7 of the World Trade Organization's Agreement on Safeguards, and thus the period should not exceed four years, unless the competent authorities of the importing Member State determine that the safeguard measure continues to be necessary to prevent or remedy serious injury and there is evidence that the affected industry is adjusting.[373] Notwithstanding this, the total period of time in which a safeguard measure is applied should not exceed eight (8) years.

4 *Protection of infant industries*

Upon the application by a Member State, the Committee of Ministers responsible for trade matters ('the CMT') may as a temporary measure in order to promote an infant industry, and subject to WTO provisions, authorize a Member State to suspend certain obligations of the Protocol in the respect of like goods imported from other Member States.[374] The CMT may, in taking such decisions, impose terms and conditions to which such authorization will be subject, for the purposes of preventing

370 *Ibid.* Art. 20: Safeguard Measures, 1. 371 *Ibid.* at 2. 372 *Ibid.* at 3 and 4. 373 *Ibid.* at 5. 374 *Ibid.* Art. 21: Protection of Infant Industries, 1.

or minimizing excessive disadvantages as those which may result in trade imbalances.[375] The CMT must, however, regularly review the protection of infant industries by a Member State applied under these terms.[376]

G Trade remedies under the Southern African Customs Union (SACU) Agreement

In 2002, SACU adopted a new Agreement in order to facilitate the cross-border movement of goods amongst the member territories of Botswana, Lesotho, Namibia, South Africa and Swaziland.[377] The further objective of the Agreement included ensuring equitable trade benefits, promoting conditions of fair competition, increasing investment opportunities and enhancing the economic development, diversification and industrialization and competitiveness of Member States.[378] The Agreement itself is a very brief document, only eleven pages in length and provides little detail; notably, the only mention of trade remedies is contained in the section of the Agreement which sets out the institutions of SACU.[379] In Article 8, the Agreement provides that 'The Council [of Ministers] shall approve . . . trade related remedies.'[380] There are, however, multiple annexes to the SACU Agreement which shed more light on trade remedies and their use under the Agreement.[381] In part 8 of Annex C, SACU adopts the substance law of the World Trade Organization Agreements on Trade Remedies, and then lays out the procedures by which that substantive law shall be applied.[382]

Annex C of the SACU Agreement 2002 provides for 'National Bodies', which are specialized, independent institutions entrusted with receiving request for tariff changes and other related SACU issues and which are established on the national level and designated by each Member State in accordance with the SACU Agreement.[383] Under Annex C there is a brief section entitled 'Consideration of Imposition of Trade Remedies'.[384]

375 *Ibid.* at 2. 376 *Ibid.* at 3.

377 Southern African Customs Union (SACU) Agreement 2002, Pt. One: Definitions and Objectives, Art. 2: Objectives.

378 See *ibid.* 379 *Ibid.* Pt. Three: Institutions, Art. 8: Council of Ministers (7).

380 *Ibid.*

381 See SACU Agreement 2002, Annex C: National Bodies, 8: Consideration of Imposition of Trade Remedies.

382 *Ibid.* 383 *Ibid.* Pt. Three: Institutions, Art. 14: National Bodies.

384 SACU Agreement 2002, Annex C: National Bodies, 8: Consideration of Imposition of Trade Remedies.

This section of the Annex provides the responsibilities of national bodies when considering the imposition of trade remedies.

Under Section 8 of Annex C, when considering and recommending duties or measures related to trade remedies, National Bodies must ensure that procedures followed and subsequent recommendations to the SACU Tariff Board are consistent with the General Agreement on Implementation of Article VI of the General Agreement on Tariffs and Trade 1994 (Anti-Dumping Agreement), the Agreement on Subsidies and Countervailing Measures and the Agreement on Safeguards concluded in the WTO, and any trade arrangement entered into by SACU and consistent with policy guidelines and procedures developed by the Council of Ministers in accordance with their duties.[385]

Section 8 also provides that whenever a National Body receives an application for remedial action such as anti-dumping, countervailing measures and safeguards, against the importation of goods into the SACU common customs area that are allegedly being dumped or subsidized, the National Body may decide whether or not it will initiate an investigation into the allegation.[386] If it decides in favour of an investigation, the National Body must notify the Secretariat of the application and its intention to investigate the matter.[387] The National Body shall also report to the Tariff Board through the Secretariat on the investigation and evaluation, and recommend that the request be approved, approved with amendments, or rejected.[388] The National Body must also ensure that reports, as well as the evaluation and recommendations, conform to the standards and requirements agreed on between the Member State and the Tariff Board from time to time.[389]

H Conclusion

This chapter shows that trade remedy regimes in African RTAs form a formidable array of legal rules – primarily borrowed from the WTO, with modifications in a variety of respects. The adoption of these WTO-based rules for countries like Ethiopia, which is a member of COMESA but not a WTO member yet, has the effect of binding Ethiopia to WTO disciplines as a matter of regional law even before it finally accedes to the WTO. The weakness of this massive legal edifice that is now part of many African RTAs is that it is seldom operationalized. Rare uses of

385 *Ibid.* at para. 8.1. 386 *Ibid.* at para. 8.2. 387 *Ibid.*
388 *Ibid.* at para. 8.2(a). 389 *Ibid.*, at para. 8.2(b).

this framework include Kenya's controversial use of COMESA sugar and wheat subsidies. While these regional rules are impressive in their detail, a majority of African countries have not incorporated them into their domestic legal systems, much less established the kind of institutional settings with trained personnel to oversee their implementation. The cost of putting in place such institutions and training personnel to oversee their implementation is a costly exercise. That is why pooling resources at the regional level may offer the best prospect for the enforcement of the trade remedy regimes of African RTAs.

IX

Monetary unions in Africa

A Introduction

This chapter examines monetary unions in Africa. These monetary unions are primarily in Central and West Africa. There are three of them: the Economic and Monetary Community of Central Africa (CEMAC); the West African Economic and Monetary Zone (UEMOA); and the West Africa Monetary Zone (WAMZ). This chapter discusses each of these experiments in monetary union in Africa and briefly appraises progress made in each of these groups.

B The Economic and Monetary Community of Central Africa

The Economic and Monetary Community of Central Africa (CEMAC), created in 1994, is a by-product of French colonial rule.[1] CEMAC's members are Cameroon, Central African Republic, Chad, Congo, Equatorial Guinea and Gabon.[2] The Central African Republic, Chad, Congo and Gabon signed a declaration creating the Union Douanière Equatoriale (UDE) in 1959.[3] In 1964, the UDE nations signed a treaty with Cameroon, creating the Customs and Economic Union of Central Africa (UDEAC).[4] The Central African Republic, Chad, Congo and Gabon were the four original members of what we know as CEMAC. Equatorial Guinea joined

1 The French created the Afrique Equitoriale Française (AEF) in 1910 comprising Chad, what we now know as the Central African Republic, Congo and Gabon. See A. Zafar and K. Kubota, 'Regional Integration In Central Africa: Key Issue', World Bank African Region Working Paper Series No. 52, June 2003, 1, available at www.worldbank.org/afr/wps/wp52.pdf.

2 *Ibid.*

3 See V. Essien, 'Regional Trade Agreements In Africa: A Historical and Bibliographical Account of ECOWAS And CEMAC', October 2006, available at www.nyulawglobal.org/globalex/CEMAC_ECOWAS.htm#_edn. (Both Chad and the Central African Republic are landlocked nations. This has added to the difficulty of regional integration in CEMAC.)

4 *Ibid.*

UDEAC in 1983.[5] The six nations, which include Cameroon, have a population of around 32 million, encompassing over 3 million square kilometers.[6] The two most dominant countries in the economic union are Cameroon and Gabon, which make up 50 per cent and 25 per cent respectively of the total GDP of the member nations, while the other four nations make up the remaining 25 per cent.[7] The CEMAC economies are heavily dependent on oil exports, and the region's economic stability tends to rise and fall with the price of oil.[8] In addition, all CEMAC members share the CFA franc as a common regional currency.[9] The Colonies Française d'Afrique (CFA) franc, now known as Coopération Financière Africaine, was established in 1945 to 'maintain exchange rates' with the AEF while France was devaluing the franc, and this relationship with France's monetary system stayed in tack even after independence from France.[10] The Bank of Central Africa (BEAC), is guaranteed full convertibility of the franc into the euro by the French Treasury, in exchange for the bank keeping 'at least 65 per cent of its foreign assets on account with the French Treasury, and maintain[ing] a foreign exchange cover of at least 20 per cent of its sight liabilities'.[11] The CFA franc has been pegged at a fixed rate to the euro since 1999: 656CFA =1 Euro.[12] CEMAC is included in the Economic Community of Central African States (ECCAS), which was established in 1983.[13]

The Central African Region contains vast amounts of natural resources such as petroleum, gold, forestry and iron ore, which give the region a strong incentive to further boost economic integration and to maximize

5 *Ibid.*

6 See 'CEMAC-Transport-Transit Facilitation Project', World Bank Organization Document, 25 May 2007, 50, available at www-wds.worldbank.org/external/default/WDSContentServer/WDSP/IB/2007/06/05/000020953_20070605105125/Rendered/PDF/38463.pdf.

7 See Zafar and Kubota, 'Regional Integration In Central Africa: Key Issues', 19.

8 See J. Wakeman-Linn, R. Portillo, P. Iossifov and D. Milkov, 'The International Financial Crisis and Global Recession: Impact on the CEMAC Region and Policy Considerations', IMF Staff Position Note, 22 July 2009, 4, available at www.imf.org/external/pubs/ft/spn/2009/spn0920.pdf.

9 *Ibid.* at 5. 10 *Ibid.* at 7.

11 See A. Gulde-Wolf, C. Tsagarides, C. Delechat, J. Christensen and F. Fischer, 'Central African Economic And Monetary Community: Selected Issues', IMF Country Report, 3 June 2005, 25, available at www.imf.org/external/pubs/ft/scr/2005/cr05390.pdf.

A sight deposit is a deposit that can be withdrawn immediately without notice or penalty.

12 *Ibid.* at 40, n. 39.

13 See Zafar and Kubota, 'Regional Integration In Central Africa: Key Issues', 9.

the region's ability to take full advantage of their natural resources in the global marketplace.[14] Under economic pressure prior to 1994, due to oil price volatility and currency fluctuation, the six member nations of the UDEAC sought to create a closer economic unit to better foster growth and prosperity.[15] Although UDEAC started out with the goal of increasing trade liberalization, this position changed when high commodity prices in the 1970s prompted nations to undertake protectionist measures to help their industries.[16] The high tariffs and taxation of goods produced within the UDEAC was the main reason for the nations to come together in 1994 to find a better solution.[17]

According to Ali Zafar and Keiko Kubota, 'the success of a regional policy depends on whether or not the large countries support it'.[18] They attribute the region's economic integration problems in part to Cameroon and Gabon adopting trade policies that were more 'inward looking', than 'outward looking', as well as France's resistance to more liberalized trade.[19] There has been rivalry between Cameroon and Gabon, as both are vying for regional superiority. This has hindered the cause of integration.[20]

1 Legal framework establishing CEMAC

The Treaty establishing the Central African Economic and Monetary Community was open for signature on 16 March 1994 in N'Djamena, Chad and came into force on 5 February 1998.[21] The Treaty's main objective is to 'promote the harmonious development of the Member States within the framework of a true common market'.[22] This objective is to be completed and carried through by the establishment of the Union Economique de l'Afrique Centrale (UEAC) (CEMAC's common market) and the Union Monétaire de l'Afrique Centrale (UMAC) (CEMAC's monetary union).[23] Through the economic and monetary union, the Treaty sets out to achieve several goals, including (1) oversight of fiscal and economic policies of the Member States, (2) guaranteeing a stable common currency, (3) maintaining a safe regional environment conducive to trade and harmony, and (4) creating a common economic union to

14 *Ibid.* at 6. 15 See Essien, 'Regional Trade Agreements In Africa' at n. 67.

16 See Zafar and Kubota, 'Regional Integration In Central Africa: Key Issues', 9.

17 *Ibid.* 18 *Ibid.* 19 *Ibid.* 20 *Ibid.* at 22.

21 The Treaty of CEMAC is available at www.aict-ctia.org/courts_subreg/cemac/cemac_docs.html.

22 See Essien, 'Regional Trade Agreements In Africa' at n. 68. 23 *Ibid.*

promote the free movement of trade and ideas.[24] The Treaty also established the Court of Justice of the Community, as well as the Parliament Communautaire.[25]

The Treaty establishing CEMAC also created several other bodies to further execute the objectives of the treaty. The Conference of the Heads of State (COHS) takes the lead in stipulating binding decisions to CEMAC institutions and Member States.[26] The Council of Ministers (COM) on its part carries out the policy decisions of the COHS.[27] The Ministerial Committee (MC) which is comprised of ministers of the Member States, takes primary responsibility in overseeing the activities of UMAC. It reviews the economic trends in the region and ensures that the Member States harmonize their monetary policies.[28] The COM, by contrast, is charged with directing the activities of UEAC. The President of COM comes from the Member State that heads the COHS that particular year. The presidency of the MC, by contrast, rotates annually among the member nations in alphabetical order.[29] The UEAC is headed by the Executive Secretary, who is responsible for the implementation of the UEAC's legislation.[30] The Bank of Central West Africa (BEAU), the Central African Banking Commission (in French, Commission Bancaire de l'Afrique Centrale, or COBAC) and the Institution of Financial Development are also established under the treaty.[31]

The COHS promulgates supplementary acts to the treaty, which are binding on the member nations, while the COM and MC issue 'regulations, directives, decisions, recommendations, or opinions'. The basic regulations that the COM and MC produce are only binding with respect to certain elements of the declaration, unlike plain regulations which are

24 *Ibid.*

25 See Zafar and Kubota, 'Regional Integration In Central Africa: Key Issues', 23.

26 See Essien, 'Regional Trade Agreements In Africa' at n. 71.

27 *Ibid.*

28 See CEMAC, 'Ministerial Committee', available at http://translate.google.com/translate?hl=en&sl=fr&u=http://www.cemac.int/&ei=gk1tTPC4KIHGlQfCsu2vDw&sa=X&oi=translate&ct=result&resnum=1&ved=0CBYQ7gEwAA&prev=/search%3Fq%3Dcemac.int%26hl%3Den.

29 *Ibid.*

30 See Intellectual Network for the South, 'Economic and Monetary Community of Central Africa', available at www.insouth.org/index.php?option=com_sobi2&sobi2Task=sobi2Details&sobi2Id=55&Itemid=.

31 See CEMAC Treaty, transl. available at http://translate.google.com/translate?hl=en&sl=fr&tl=en&u=http%3A%2F%2Fwww.worldtradelaw.net%2Ffta%2Fagreements%2Fcemacfta.pdf (original version in French available at www.worldtradelaw.net/fta/agreements/cemacfta.pdf).

binding on all Member States.[32] While the directives issued by the COM and MC are binding, Member States are free to implement them as they choose, as long as the objectives of the COHS are met.[33] The COM as MC also issue decisions, which are only applicable to and bind the specific Member States that are addressed.[34] When the COM and MC issue recommendations, they are just what they say they are – recommendations – and not binding on the Member States, but merely suggestions.[35] When the COHS supplements the treaty, or when MC issues regulations, these must all be published in the Official Bulletin of the Community.[36] If there is no date specified for commencement of the item in question, then the commencement date is the 20th day after publication in the Official Bulletin of the Community.[37] When the COM or MC issues a directive or decision, they come into effect on the subsequent date after the relevant parties are notified of the directive or decision.[38]

Following the ratification of the CEMAC Treaty, some of these new institutions created by the treaty were established in the various Member States.[39] The Judicial Court of the Community was established in Chad and the Inter-parliamentary Commission was established in Equatorial Guinea.[40]

Following the devaluation of 1994, certain reforms followed in UDEAC. These reforms were informed by fears that 'a liberalization of trade policy without devaluation would increase imports into the region and worsen the ongoing recession'.[41] As a result, UDEAC was transformed into what we now know as the UEAC under the CEMAC Treaty. The CEMAC Treaty was amended to reflect the transformed commitments in favour of liberalization, and in particular to address the problems of 'protectionism, low custom revenue, intra-regional distortions in production, and the low level of trade with the rest of the world'.[42] The reforms that addressed the problems above included (1) a uniform reduced tariff system, (2) the elimination of 'quantitative restrictions' on goods, (3) eliminating previous taxes on 'production and sales' and replacing them with a 'two-tier turnover tax which will be converted into a value added tax (VAT) plus an excise tax', (4) replacing taxes with a Common External Tariff (CET) on 'intra-regional trade', (5) a path towards the elimination of 'import tariffs and direct tax exemptions granted under national investment codes', and

32 *Ibid.* 33 *Ibid.* 34 *Ibid.* 35 *Ibid.* 36 *Ibid.*
37 See Essien, 'Regional Trade Agreements In Africa' at n. 91. 38 *Ibid.*
39 See Zafar and Kubota, 'Regional Integration In Central Africa: Key Issues', 23.
40 *Ibid.* 41 *Ibid.* 42 *Ibid.* at 24.

(6) an 'optional declining surtax' on goods that were previously under quota restrictions.[43]

2 *The Bank of Central Africa*

The Bank of Central Africa (BEAC) was established in 1972 and serves the member nations of CEMAC as a regional bank.[44] The BEAC was established by the CEMAC nations, with the exception of Equatorial Guinea, which joined in 1985.[45] It closely resembles the duties undertaken by the Central Bank of West African States, which is comprised of eight nations (Benin, Burkina Faso, Guinea Bissau, Ivory Coast, Mali, Niger, Senegal and Togo) that make up the West African Economic and Monetary Union (WAEMU).[46] These banks function in the same fashion as any central bank, by handling currency and demanding adequate reserves of funds from member nations.[47] Both BEAC and WAEMU have ties to the French Treasury, which sets the rules and regulations under which they operate.[48] In 1973, the BEAC, under the direction of the African nations, gained more autonomy, reduced French influence with respect to the policies followed by the bank and decided to pursue a growth rather than a stability policy.[49] In 1990, the BEAC introduced policy reforms to help strengthen the bank, as the previous decade had been filled with economic turmoil. As a result, it was pressured by the Member States not to devalue the currency.[50] COBAC was formed to oversee the BEAC.[51] A central objective of the BEAC is to help CEMAC meet its objectives by ensuring economic harmony and stability throughout the region.[52]

Despite the franc being tied to the euro and losing some autonomy in the process, the BEAC retains some control with respect to interest rate movements.[53] As John Wakeman-Linn, Rafael Portillo,

43 *Ibid.*; see also J. K. Martijn and C. G. Tsangarides, 'Trade Reform in the CEMAC: Developments and Opportunities', IMF Working Paper WP/07/137, 11, available at www.imf.org/external/pubs/ft/wp/2007/wp07137.pdf.

44 *Ibid.* at 8.

45 See Zafar and Kubota, 'Regional Integration In Central Africa: Key Issues', 8.

46 United States Department of Commerce Information on Central Africa, 'Brief on Central and West Africa', available at www.buyusa.gov/westafrica/en/79.html.

47 See Zafar and Kubota, 'Regional Integration In Central Africa: Key Issues', 8.

48 *Ibid.* 49 *Ibid.* 50 *Ibid.* at 23. 51 *Ibid.*

52 See Gulde-Wolf *et al.*, 'Central African Economic And Monetary Community: Selected Issues', 27.

53 See Wakeman-Linn, *et al.*, 'The International Financial Crisis And Global Recession', 4.

Plamen Iossifov and Dimitre Milkov point out, since the CEMAC region shares a common monetary and exchange rate framework, any monetary policies must address the entire region, and not just individual countries.[54]

While the BEAC's main purpose acting as a central bank is to limit economic volatility throughout the region, since reforms enacted in 1994, it has changed its monetary policy from 'direct controls to more market-based instruments, which include the gradual phasing out of advances to member governments, the development of an inter-bank money market, and the preparation of a government bond market'.[55] In fact, the 2002 conference in Gabon was held precisely to examine the viability of a bond market in the region.[56] Other reforms include the creation of a Central African Deposit Insurance Fund in 1998, which was implemented in 2004.[57] A stock exchange was also opened in Gabon. However, there is a competing stock exchange in Cameroon, and both exchanges would benefit from a more cooperative partnership, as opposed to one of stiff competition.[58] There is a delicate balance between the Member States and the organization of CEMAC, which divides the regional duties according to the treaty establishing the organization. CEMAC organizations have the authority over fiscal, monetary and trade matters, while the member nations have control over taxes, expenditures, investment and general governance.[59] Zafar and Kubota point out that the powers given to the CEMAC organizational structure are beneficial, because they are less likely to succumb to special interests that may potentially compromise them at the individual nation level.[60]

In 2000, the Heads of State of CEMAC agreed to strengthen the regional institutions by requiring member contributions from import fees. These fees would help further the integration of the region by allowing the organization to take on regional projects that would benefit the member economies.[61]

Notably, the Treaty for the Establishment of an African Economic Community which was discussed at fuller length in Chapter V, seeks the establishment of a 'single domestic market and a Pan-African Economic

54 *Ibid.* at 9. 55 *Ibid.* at 4.

56 See Zafar and Kubota, 'Regional Integration In Central Africa: Key Issues', 25.

57 *Ibid.*

58 'Gabon: Douala, Libreville – Need for Surgery', *The Cameroon Tribune*, 17 September 2009, available at http://allafrica.com/stories/200909170539.html.

59 See Zafar and Kubota, 'Regional Integration In Central Africa: Key Issues', 23.

60 *Ibid.* 61 *Ibid.*

and Monetary Union through the harmonisation of regional monetary zones, as well as the establishment of a Central Bank and single currency'.[62] Both the Treaty for the Establishment of an African Economic Community and the CEMAC Treaty share very similar goals on different levels.[63] Whereas the AEC Treaty seeks to create economic integration on a continent-based level, CEMAC seeks to achieve it on a regional level.[64] The AEC Treaty provides that members of regional economic communities should pursue 'all necessary measures aimed at progressively promoting increasingly closer co-operation among the communities, particularly through co-ordination and harmonisation of their activities in all fields or sectors in order to ensure the realization of the objectives of the community'.[65] The AEC Treaty prohibits the Member States of regional economic communities from enacting any legislation or fostering any activity that will hinder the free movement of trade.[66] The objectives set out in the AEC Treaty are similar to those listed in the CEMAC, such as reducing trade barriers and promoting economic integration, so as CEMAC achieves its goals, the AEC becomes one step closer to achieving its goals.[67]

The goal of the AEC is that regions like CEMAC would initially integrate regionally so as to eventually transform into a monetary union under the Treaty for the Establishment of an African Community.[68] Zafar and Kubota suggest that projects such as the Chad–Cameroon pipeline and the BEAC will help to further integrate the region,[69] which will in turn help to reach the goals of the AEC. The CEMAC region is densely populated with forests, yet it is faced with inadequate trade infrastructure such as working roads. This hinders integration. A project undertaken by the CEMAC Secretariat sought to connect all the capital cities of the Member States by 2010.[70] Lack of infrastructure, as well as an oil- and forestry-dominated market, has kept trade between the CEMAC countries substantially lower than their regional counterparts, at just around five per cent.[71]

62 *Ibid.*

63 See AEC Treaty, available at www.africa-union.org/root/au/Documents/Treaties/Text/AEC_Treaty_1991.pdf.

64 *Ibid.*

65 *Ibid.* at Chapter IV: Regional Economic Communities, Art. 28.

66 *Ibid.* at Chapter V: Customs Union and Liberalisation of Trade of the AEC Treaty, at Art. 5.

67 See Zafar and Kubota, 'Regional Integration In Central Africa: Key Issues', 19.

68 See AEC Treaty, 'Objectives', 8.

69 See Zafar and Kubota, 'Regional Integration In Central Africa: Key Issues', 29.

70 *Ibid.* at 30.

71 *Ibid.* at 10.

C The West African Economic and Monetary Union

The UEMOA was created by the Dakar Treaty on 10 January 1994.[72] The UEMOA originally comprised seven nations: Benin, Burkina Faso, Ivory Coast, Mali, Niger, Senegal and Togo.[73] On 2 May 1997, these seven nations were joined by Guinea-Bissau.[74] The UEMOA zone, which has a population of around 80 million people, shares the CFA franc as a common currency.[75]

1 Objectives of the UEMOA

The objectives of the UEMOA are set out in Article IV of the Dakar Treaty.[76] These objectives include:

(a) Enhancing the economic and financial competitiveness of Member States;
(b) Achieving economic performance and policy convergence among Member States through the institution of a multilateral monitoring procedure;
(c) Creating among the Member States a common market based on the free movement of persons, goods, services, capital and right of establishment; and
(d) Coordinating national sectoral policies in such areas as human resources, physical planning, transportation, telecommunications, the environment, agriculture, energy, industry, and mining.[77]

2 Organizational structure of the UEMOA

The UEMOA contains several organizations to help foster the objectives set out in Article IV of the Dakar Treaty.[78] These organizations include the Conference of Heads of State and Government, Council of Ministers, the Commission and Court of Justice among several others.[79] The Conference of the Heads of State, which meets at least once annually, is the

72 See United Nations Conference on Trade and Development, 'Voluntary Peer Review of Competition Policy: West African Economic and Monetary Union, Benin and Senegal' (New York, UN, 2007), available at www.unctad.org/en/docs/ditcclp20071overview_en.pdf.

73 *Ibid.* at 2. 74 *Ibid.* 75 *Ibid.* 76 *Ibid.* 77 *Ibid.* at 2–3.

78 See UN, 'Voluntary Peer Review of Competition Policy: West African Economic and Monetary Union, Benin and Senegal', 3.

79 *Ibid.*

supreme governing body of the UEMOA.[80] The Council of Ministers is tasked with undertaking monetary policy to protect the currency and to further develop businesses and the economy.[81] The Commission is tasked with developing the UEMOA's budget and plays an advisory role to the Council of Ministers and the Conference of the Heads of State.[82] The Court of Justice, which seats a judge from each Member State on it, is tasked with interpreting the UEMOA law, and acting as an intermediary between Member State disputes.[83]

These organizational structures act on 'two basic principles' when enacting legislation. First, such legislation becomes effective immediately in the Member States, and second, it takes precedence over any individual country's law in the event of a conflict.[84] The UEMOA functions from funds via a common external tariff, as well as outside help from organizations such as the European Union.[85]

3 The BCEAO and the payment system

The Central Bank of West African States (BCEAO) serves as the regional bank.[86] The Commission Bancaire de l'UEMOA, a supervisory banking agency headed by the Secretary General and the Governor of the BCEAO, was established in 1990 to help strengthen oversight of the bank.[87] According to Amanda N.R. Sy, the 1995 PARMEC law (Projet d'Appui à la Réglementation sur les Mutuelles d'Epargne et de Crédit) which regulated savings and credit institutions, 'paved the way for a regulatory framework for cooperative financial institutions in the region'.[88]

A new payment system was introduced by the BCEAO in response to the high costs of using cash.[89] The main goals in the new system are

80 UEMOA, 'The Organs of Management', English trans., available at www.microsofttranslator.com/BV.aspx?ref=BVNav&a=http%3A%2F%2Fwww.uemoa.int%2Forganes%2Fdirection.htm.

81 *Ibid.* 82 *Ibid.*

83 See UEMOA, 'UEMOA Commission', English trans., available at www.microsofttranslator.com/BV.aspx?ref=BVNav&a=http%3A%2F%2Fwww.uemoa.int%2Fuemoa%2FSchema_Fonctionnement.htm.

84 UN, 'Voluntary Peer Review of Competition Policy', 4. 85 *Ibid.*

86 A.N.R. Sy, 'Financial Integration in the West African Monetary Union', *Journal of Financial Transformation* (2009) 99, available at www.capco.com/files/pdf/65/02_LESSONS%20LEARNED/09_Financial%20integration%20in%20the%20West%20African%20Monetary%20Union.pdf.

87 *Ibid.* 88 *Ibid.*

89 BCEAO, 'The New Payment Systems in the West African Economic and Monetary Union (WAEMU)', 1 available at: www.bceao.int/internet/bcrsmp.nsf/pdf/newsystempaymentWAEMU.pdf/$FILE/newsystempaymentWAEMU.pdf.

to (1) reduce the cost and improve the efficiency of transactions throughout the zone, (2) minimize the use of cash as new methods of non-cash instruments are established, (3) increase population access to the bank and financial system, and to (4) consolidate policy through a Central Bank to facilitate the further integration of the regional market.[90] These goals are sought to be achieved in at least three ways.[91] First, the Automated Transfer and Settlement System within the UEMOA (STAR-UEMOA), created in 2004,[92] whose goal is to modernize the exchange and payment system by 'the establishment of a real-time gross settlement system for systemically important payments, particularly cash transfers, money market transactions, stock exchange transactions settlement, public [and] debt payment.'[93] Second, the Automated Interbank Clearing System, created in 2005,[94] within the UEMOA (SICA-UEMOA), whose goal is modernizing the small payment exchange through methods such as cheques, among others.[95] Lastly, the BCEAO is tasked with developing a regional interbank card-based system so as to further enhance integration.[96] The Payment Incidents Centre (CIP) was also established by the BCEAO with the main task of seeking public confidence in the banking sector.[97]

4 Legal framework governing the payment system

In order to enact the new payment system, the legal framework of the UEMOA had to be updated.[98] The WAEMU Council adopted this new legal framework in 2002.[99] The BCEAO's main goal under this framework is to 'ensure a proper functioning of payment systems on the WAEMU member states'.[100]

D The West African Monetary Zone

On 20 April 2000, six countries agreed to unite and create the West African Monetary Zone (WAMZ) with the intention that it be fully

90 *Ibid.* 91 *Ibid.*

92 BCEAO, 'Currency Issue and Payment Systems, Annual Report 2005', 35, available at: www.bceao.int/internet/bcweb.nsf/files/III%20-%20Currency%20issue%20and%20payment%20systems.pdf/$FILE/III%20-%20Currency%20issue%20and%20payment%20systems.pdf.

93 The New Payment Systems in the West African Economic and Monetary Union (WAEMU), *supra* n. 89 at 1.

94 See BCEAO, 'Currency Issue and Payment Systems', 2, available at: www.bceao.int/internet/bcrsmp.nsf/pdf/newsystempaymentWAEMU.pdf/$FILE/newsystempaymentWAEMU.pdf.

95 *Ibid.* 96 *Ibid.* 97 *Ibid.* 98 *Ibid.* 99 *Ibid.* at 5. 100 *Ibid.*

functional by 2003.[101] The six countries, Gambia, Ghana, Guinea, Liberia, Nigeria and Sierra Leone, created the WAMZ framework by signing the Accra Declaration during the Second Summit of the Heads of State and Government.[102] In addition to agreeing to the formation of WAMZ, they also enacted statutes regarding the West African Monetary Institute (WAMI), the West African Central Bank, and provisions relating to the Stabilization and Cooperation Fund (SCF).[103] The main objective of the WAMZ is to 'establish a common central bank that will issue and manage a common currency with a cooperative integration framework'.[104]

1 Organizational structure of the WAMZ

The WAMZ is made up of several organizations.[105] The Authority of the Heads of State, made up of Heads of State and Government of the member countries, is the main body that governs the WAMZ.[106] The Convergence Council, made up of Ministers of Finance, Integration and Foreign Affairs, and the Governors of Central Banks, is the supervisory authority to the WAMZ.[107] The Technical Committee, an advisory board made up of experts from the central banks, ministries of finance, foreign affairs and integration, work with the WAMI to achieve the goals and objectives of the WAMZ.[108] The WAMI is a multi-level organization[109] overseen by the Convergence Council of Ministers and the Governors of the Central Banks that was established in the interim leading up to the creation of a common bank among the WAMZ.[110] It is led by the Director General, and includes within its framework research, operations, finance and administration, internal audit and legal departments.[111] Once the Central Bank is created, it will be in charge of monetary policy for the WAMZ.[112] The SCF is the fund that gives low interest and easy access to financial aid to Member States in order to correct temporary deficiencies in these countries as a result of the formation of the WAMZ.[113]

101 'Introduction, West African Monetary Institute', available at: www.wami-imao.org (under Welcome Message).

102 *Ibid.* 103 *Ibid.*

104 See WAMI, 'Questions and Answers on the West African Monetary Zone', available at www.wami-imao.org/english/doc/q-and-a.htm (Question 11).

105 *Ibid.* (Question 12). 106 *Ibid.* 107 *Ibid.* 108 *Ibid.*

109 See App. 1 for WAMI organizational structure.

110 See WAMI, 'Questions and Answers on the West African Monetary Zone' (Question 12).

111 *Ibid.* 112 *Ibid.* (Question 55). 113 *Ibid.* (Question 49).

2 *The role of the WAMI*

The WAMI performs several functions to help foster the stability and transitioning of the WAMZ.[114] These functions include (1) monitoring and reporting on the state of macroeconomic convergence of the Member States to the Convergence Council; (2) equalizing regulations for all financial institutions and designing a single monetary policy for Member States; (3) 'promot[ing] a regional payment system in the second monetary zone';[115] (4) maintaining a common exchange and conversion rate system for member nations; (5) designing and preparing the new currency (called the ECO) including setting par value; and (6) introducing and gathering popular support for the new currency.[116]

Benchmarks, primary and secondary, have been established to monitor whether convergence standards are met, and which the WAMI uses to report to the Convergence Council.[117] There are four elements to the primary criteria, and six elements to the secondary criteria that the WAMI reviews to see if standards are being met.[118] The four elements of the primary criteria included checking to see if (1) inflation was below ten per cent and less than 5 per cent by 2004, (2) 'less than four per cent GDP/Deficit ratio', (3) 'central bank financing of government of less than ten per cent of previous year's tax revenue' and (4) 'import/reserves over three months'. There are six secondary criteria, which relate to (1) 'the prohibition of accumulation of domestic arrears';[119] (2) 'tax revenue/GDP ratio';[120] (3) 'wage bill/total tax ratio';[121] (4) 'public investment/tax revenue';[122] (5) a 'positive real interest rate'; and (6) 'stable real-exchange rates'.[123]

There is much value in promoting a regional payment system. The WAMI would organize a close association between the central banks of each member nation, as well as West African Bankers Association (WABA), to institute a convenient and efficient way to enact money transfers throughout the zone.[124] The payment system is a critical aspect of the WAMI activities, because the system 'frees funds that would have

114 See Official Page of the West African Monetary Institute, 'About WAMI: Roles and Functions'.

115 *Ibid.*

116 *Ibid*; see WAMI, 'Questions and Answers on the West African Monetary Zone'.

117 *Ibid.* 118 *Ibid.*, see footnote. 119 *Ibid.*

120 See Official Page of the West African Monetary Institute, 'About WAMI, Roles and Functions' (greater than 20%).

121 *Ibid.* (that is, over 20%). 122 *Ibid.* (that is, less than 35%).

123 *Ibid.* 124 *Ibid.*

been used to print and manage currency into productive sectors', therefore lowering the cost of currency management.[125] According to WAMI, by enabling these financial systems to reduce the amount of cash and increase the use of non-cash equivalents, the risk of loss due to moral hazards, theft and natural disasters all decrease, while speeding up the transaction processes.[126] There are several non-cash methods that are available to help increase the use of non-cash equivalents.[127] These methods include cheques, money orders, electronic transfers, ATM machines, and bank drafts amongst others.[128]

E The successes and challenges of the African monetary unions

One yardstick to measure the successes and challenges of monetary integration in Africa is to examine these integration initiatives against Optimum Currency Areas (OCAs).[129] OCAs can be defined as 'a region in which factors of production are internally mobile but internationally immobile, so as to facilitate the intraregional redistribution of resources in response to demand shifts'.[130] OCAs can be characterized by price and wage flexibility, and financial market integration.[131] Blocs of countries with close trade links and economic interests that are not OCAs may morph into a quasi-OCA by adopting a common currency.[132] Despite the CFA zone not being considered an OCA,[133] a monetary union is attractive if 'there are no reasonable alternatives'.[134] The WAMZ could turn into an OCA zone if there is the political will to give up some monetary policies to a supranational banking system.[135] This step seems logical, because WAEMU member countries have had greater economic growth and stability from 1990 to 2001 than non-WAEMU countries, although they had higher than average inflation, which is another reason why the member countries of the zone should continue to further their integration.[136]

The CEMAC zone had a 7.6 per cent growth rate from 1997 to 2005 and exceeded the African growth rate as well, making it one of the highest of the African regional unions.[137] The region also had the second-best level of inflation, at about 3.1 per cent, which was significantly lower than the

125 See WAMI, 'Questions and Answers on the West African Monetary Zone' (Question 24).

126 *Ibid.* 127 *Ibid* (Question 25). 128 *Ibid.*

129 O.J. Nnanna, 'Economic and Monetary Integration in Africa,' 5 available at www.g24.org/nnan0906.pdf (presented at G24 Meeting in Singapore, 14 Sept. 2006).

130 *Ibid.* 131 *Ibid.* at 5. 132 *Ibid.* at 6. 133 *Ibid.* at 7.

134 *Ibid.* 135 *Ibid.* at 12. 136 *Ibid.* at 8. 137 *Ibid.* at 18.

African average.[138] CEMAC also had the highest budget surplus of all the regions, 2.1 per cent of GDP.[139] Total investment and domestic savings of GDP were also greatest in this region during this period, in which the second-best performing region, ECOWAS, had a deficit.[140]

The primary problem for the CEMAC zone is that it is heavily dependent on oil exports. The region will experience significant economic turbulence directly tied to the price of oil, unless it can further integrate with another union, or wean its dependence on oil exports. When a country is heavily dependent on a good or service, there is a greater need for intra-regional diversification as a protection of economic shock due to price fluctuation for the traded commodity.[141] Countries with an economy dependency on one commodity would be better protected by forming monetary unions which are not dependent on the same commodity.[142]

The problem can be seen in a report prepared by the IMF. Despite GDP growth in 2004 hitting its highest level in a decade (driven primarily by the high price of oil), non-oil growth was disappointing.[143] The non-oil segment of the economy slowed from 3.6% in 2003 to 3.2% in 2004, which was the lowest in 5 years.[144] Furthermore, the Central African Republic is the region's only non-oil exporter, and their economic performance was weak, at less than 1% growth.[145]

In addition, low levels of capital availability in the regional banking system are a challenge and concern that must be addressed by the member nations.[146] However, due to favourable oil prices in 2004, all CEMAC oil exporting countries but for Equatorial Guinea were able to meet all of the criteria for the first time since the criteria were established in 1997.[147]

Another challenge facing CEMAC is the lack of implementation of the BEAC's policies, due to weak financial markets.[148] Because the bank cannot control the payment flows it receives, as well as the advances it makes to member countries, the liquid growth of the bank is limited.[149] The BEAC's ability to achieve price stability could potentially be hindered unless the region implements long-term debt instruments to free up liquidity.[150] The member countries have resisted this thus far, due to potential borrowing restraints that may affect them.[151]

138 *Ibid.* 139 *Ibid.* at 15. 140 *Ibid.* 141 *Ibid.* at 6. 142 *Ibid.*

143 Central African Economic and Monetary Community, 'Paper on recent developments and regional policy issues; public information notice on the executive board discussion; and statement by the executive director on recent developments and regional policy issues in the central African economic and Monetary Community', 6, available at www.imf.org/external/pubs/ft/scr/2005/cr05403.pdf.

144 *Ibid.* 145 *Ibid.* 146 *Ibid.* at 9. 147 *Ibid.* 148 *Ibid.* 149 *Ibid.* at 10.
150 *Ibid.* 151 *Ibid.*

The BEAC has generally been successful in its overall liquidity management as far as stabilizing liquidity through differentiated reserve requirements, short-term deposits and the convergence criteria.[152] However, challenges abound. For example, another potential challenge for the zone is the fact that many fiscal policies remain under the control of member countries, despite the need for further integration as one monetary union.[153]

1 WAMZ and WAEMU success and challenges

The WAMZ had the third-highest growth rate among African regional groupings, at 4.5 per cent – 1.2 per cent above the WAEMU during the 1997–2005 time frame.[154] However, the region had the third-highest inflation rate compared to other African regional groups, at 12.1 per cent, (significantly higher than the WAEMU's 2.1%), as well as the worst fiscal balance, at a 7.5 per cent deficit during the 1997–2005 period.[155] The 4.6 per cent deficit throughout the period was the worst performance of all the groups, followed by the WAEMU. The deficits were 8.2 and 5.2 per cent, respectively.[156] The WAMZ domestic savings to GDP was 11.6 per cent, 1.6 percentage points below WAEMU's and well below the African average of 21.1 per cent.[157]

Inflation in the WAMZ has been a problem in recent years, however, during the same time that deficits have narrowed.[158] The rising cost of oil was a big contributory factor to the inflation experienced in these countries.[159] However, both Ghana and Nigeria met the criteria of having 20 per cent tax revenue as a percentage of GDP in 2003, and Sierra Leone and Gambia increased their standing in this criterion as well.[160] Another success of the zone was that Gambia and Nigeria kept their wages and salaries below 35 per cent of their tax revenue.[161] Budget deficits are a challenge that the zone needs to address in order to create a stable environment for the monetary union to flourish, to achieve the ultimate goal of the common ECO currency.[162] According to the WAMZ, the zone has

152 *Ibid.* 153 *Ibid.* at 11.

154 Nnanna, 'Economic and Monetary Integration in Africa', p. 19, available at www.g24.org/nnan0906.pdf (presented at G24 Meeting in Singapore, 14 Sept. 2006).

155 *Ibid.* at 19. 156 *Ibid.* 157 *Ibid.* at 20.

158 M.O. Ojo, 'The Challenges of introducing the Eco Currency', West African Monetary Institute, 8 June 2004, available at www.wami-imao.org/english/doc/IntroducingEcoCurrency.pdf.

159 *Ibid.* at 4. 160 *Ibid.* 161 *Ibid.* at 5. 162 *Ibid.*

also faced challenges regarding the sensitization programme.[163] Member countries need to 'provide adequate funding for the sensitization program to ensure effective implementation by the national sensitization committees, which would result in the creation of a high level of awareness on the program'.[164] Member countries will be able to accomplish this task by allocation of funds to its goals.[165] Furthermore, the member countries need to contribute more to the Stabilization and Cooperation Fund, as it has not been adequately funded.[166] Member countries must also agree to the means and methods of accomplishing these goals, as there are several outstanding statutes that address the function of the organization that have not been ratified.[167]

The Vice President of Ghana has echoed sentiments decrying the lack of political will in the member countries for the WAMZ, as better integration might have shielded the zone more from the global economic downturns such as that of the late 2000s.[168] He specifically referred to the 'chronic non-observance of commitments undertaken within the respective agreement as well as the insufficient use of instruments set by these agreement among others constitute a huge challenge to efforts made at regional and economic integration'.[169] However, the Vice President did point out some highlights in Ghana's improvement, specifically pointing to economic growth and the lowering of inflation.[170]

2 *Challenges for the CFA franc zone*

One of the challenges that the CFA franc zone must overcome is the role that France plays in the region.[171] The requirements imposed by the French in exchange for their guarantees of convertibility have essentially 'taken sovereignty away from the Member States' and created inequality in the region.[172] For example, Chad and Ivory Coast have different economic needs, but their parity to the franc is the same.[173] Since the zone places a limit on deficit spending, the smaller country of Chad is running a

163 *Ibid.* at 7. 164 *Ibid.* 165 *Ibid.* 166 *Ibid.* 167 *Ibid.*

168 Modern Ghana, 'Vice President challenges Member States to meet WAMZ criteria' (1 Jan. 2010), available at www.modernghana.com/news/257141/1/vice-president-challenges-member-states-to-meet-wa.html.

169 *Ibid.* 170 *Ibid.*

171 M. Kavanagh, 'The 1994 Devaluation of the CFA Franc and the Changing Role of France in African Development', International Development Studies Working Paper Series, available at www.yale.edu/macmillan/iac/kavanagh.pdf.

172 *Ibid.* at 9. 173 *Ibid.*

surplus, while bigger economies such as Ivory Coast can still pursue deficit spending policies due to their access to private capital markets.[174] Michael Kavanagh concludes that this essentially allows the larger economies to 'hijack' the CFA operations by running up debt, a phenomenon he states occurred in the 1980s.[175] Furthermore, despite the regional banks having avoided being more intertwined in the global banking crisis, due to the fact that they hold no toxic international assets, the fact that they are subsidiaries to foreign banks puts them at more risk, which in turn makes it necessary for them to be completely independent institutions.[176]

3 Success of the 1994 devaluation

The growth in exports expanded significantly after the CFA franc currency devaluation of 1994.[177] This led to domestic products becoming more competitive as the devaluation helped trade terms, and the CFA franc zone being able to compete against other African and Asian countries also created trade improvement.[178] According to Kavanagh, the devaluation was a success, at least on a short-term level in spurring growth, increasing trade and increasing the GDP of member countries.[179] This may have been a mixed blessing, since the devaluation may have increased dependency on certain exports in the region.[180]

4 The euro crisis and Africa

The euro zone went through a crisis due to the global downturn of the late 2000s, and this certainly impacted the African Franc Zones of WAEMU and CEMAC.[181] Some commentators have argued that these African zones are 'de facto puppets' of the French Treasury, as they must maintain 'at least 65% of its foreign exchange reserves in an "operations account"

174 *Ibid.* 175 *Ibid.* at 10.

176 See J. Mueller, I. Yackovlev and H. Weisfeld, IMF Staff Position Note, 'The Global Financial Crisis: Impact on WAEMU Member Countries and Policy Options', International Monetary Fund Staff Position Note, 2 July 2009, 4, available at www.imf.org/external/pubs/ft/spn/2009/spn0916.pdf.

177 Kavanagh, 'The 1994 Devaluation of the CFA Franc and the Changing Role of France in African Development', 26, available at www.yale.edu/macmillan/iac/kavanagh.pdf.

178 *Ibid.* 179 *Ibid.* at 27. 180 *Ibid.*

181 G.K. Busch, 'The Euro Crisis and Africa', *Nigerian Village Square*, 17 May 2010, available at www.nigeriavillagesquare.com/index.php?option=com_content&view=article&id=15528&catid=181&Itemid=177.

held at the French Treasury, as well as another 20% to cover financial liabilities'.[182]

Furthermore, these banks impose caps on the credit that is available, which is 20 per cent of that country's public revenue in the previous year.[183] Dr. Busch further notes that the French treasury has the final say on any overdraft policies in the zone.[184] The fixed exchange rate of the franc 'draws its credibility from monetary agreements with France'.[185] In fact, according to Dr. Busch, the CFA banks are 'African in name only, but have no monetary policies of their own', as they do not know or are told how much of their pool of reserves being held by France belongs to them.[186]

F Conclusions

African monetary zones are works in progress. They offer much hope, but their links to the euro and French franc make them vulnerable to volatilities in the global economy, although some measure of stability in good times. The dependence of a lot of African countries in monetary unions on oil exports makes these countries more vulnerable to external shocks. However, the work being undertaken to build policy harmonization and convergence on monetary policies in these zones is something that needs emulation in the rest of Africa. The challenge here, as with the trade regimes studied in this book, is to transform into reality the very well intentioned and stated commitments on paper.

182 *Ibid.* 183 *Ibid.* 184 *Ibid.* 185 *Ibid.* 186 *Ibid.*

X

Intra-African regional trade integration

A Introduction

This chapter examines intra-African regional trade integration agreements, as well as examples of projects funded to realize such integration. The chapter begins by giving a brief overview of the African Economic Community (AEC), which is ultimately the goal of economic integration in the continent, as well as the various regional arrangements that are its pillars and that have been the subject of this book so far. The chapter shows that the treaties establishing each of these regional bodies, or RTAs as I have referred to them throughout this book, anticipate such cooperation between regions. The chapter then examines the importance of linkages between the regions in agriculture, which is of major importance to African economies, before examining the importance of links in communications, information and communication technology and air transport and surface transport (roads, rail, ports and maritime). The chapter ends with a discussion of the proposed COMESA-EAC-SADC FTA and the East Africa Migration Route Programme.

As the chapter shows, law remains an important feature of the continued integration in Africa. As an example, the chapter discusses the Yamoussoukro Decision, an ECOWAS-CEMAC agreement to cooperate in the liberalization of the air transport sector in that region. That Decision has already been extended to ECOWAS and COMESA and is supported by many international organizations, including the International Civil Aviation Organization (ICAO). This Decision provides that all inconsistent multilateral and bilateral agreements in force in the region are suspended as long as the Decision is in effect. The importance of the liberalization of African skies is evidenced by agreements like the Yamoussoukro Decision, which is only one of the several initiatives discussed in this chapter that gives a legal underpinning to the continuing integration agenda in Africa.

B The relationship between the African Economic Community and Regional Economic Communities

The AEC was established by the Heads of States and Governments of the Organization of African Unity (OAU) by signing the Abuja Treaty[1] in June 1991. The main purpose for establishing the AEC was to:

> mobilize and co-ordinate collective efforts and resources of the OAU Member States for the attainment of the economic and social integration through harmonization and rationalization of the activities of the various African Inter-governmental Organizations at all levels.[2]

Under the Abuja Treaty, the AEC will be established in six stages.[3] It encourages its Member States to strengthen existing Regional Economic Communities (RECs) (which I have referred to as RTAs throughout this book), and to establish new communities where none exist.[4] Furthermore, it specifically encourages regional integration among Member States through 'the co-ordination, harmonisation and progressive integration of the activities of [RECs]' to attain the vision of establishing the AEC.[5]

The eight pillars of the AEC are formed by eight RECs.[6] They are:

(a) Arab Maghreb Union (AMU/UMA);
(b) Community of Sahel-Saharan States (CEN-SAD);
(c) Common Market for Eastern and Southern Africa (COMESA);
(d) East African Community (EAC);
(e) Economic Community of Central African States (ECCAS/CEEAC);
(f) Economic Community of West African States (ECOWAS);
(g) Inter-Governmental Authority on Development (IGAD); and
(h) Southern African Development Community (SADC).

1 Assembly of Heads of State and Government of the Organization of African Unity meeting in its Twenty-seventh Ordinary Session in Abuja, Federal Republic of Nigeria, Resolution on the African Economic Community, June 1991, AHG Res. 205 (XXVII), www.africa-union.org/root/au/Documents/Decisions/hog/1HoGAssembly1991.pdf (last visited 21 Aug. 2010) (hereinafter AHG Res. 205).

2 *Ibid.* at para. 4.

3 Treaty Establishing the African Economic Community, 3 June 1991, art. 6.1, www.africa-union.org/root/au/Documents/Treaties/Text/AEC_Treaty_1991.pdf (last visited 21 Aug. 2010) (hereinafter 'AEC Treaty').

4 *Ibid.* at art. 28.1.

5 *Ibid.* at art. 88.1.

6 African Union, Status of Integration in Africa 2nd Edn, Apr. 2009, para. 419, www.africa-union.org/root/ua/conferences/2009/mai/ea/07–08mai/status%20of%20integration%20in%20africa%2027–04–09.pdf (last visited 21 Oct. 2010).

The Treaty establishing the AMU allows Member Countries to enter into agreements 'among themselves or with other States or groupings' provided that such a new agreement does not contravene provisions of the establishing treaty.[7] The Treaty establishing the COMESA provides that COMESA may enter into agreements with other RECs[8] with a view to realizing its regional integration goals. 'Council' refers to the Council of Ministers of the Common Market established under the Treaty.[9] The Treaty establishing the EAC also permits it to enter into cooperative arrangements with other regional and international organizations in order to accomplish its objectives.[10] Similarly, the Treaty establishing the ECCAS permits Member States to enter into agreements among themselves or with other non-Member States so long as the agreements are compatible with the objectives of the establishing Treaty.[11] Additionally, the Community may enter into cooperative agreements with non-Member States provided such agreements receive prior approval from the Conference[12] consisting of the Heads of State and Government.[13]

The Treaty establishing the ECOWAS provides that it may enter into agreements with other regional communities[14] if it receives prior approval by the Council.[15] Additionally, it may also enter into cooperation agreements with non-Member States and international organizations, upon prior approval by the Council.[16] 'Council' refers to the Council of Ministers of the Community established under the Treaty.[17] The IGAD Treaty also permits it to enter into agreements with other regional organizations, intergovernmental and non-governmental agencies and non-Member States, to realize its objectives.[18] The SADC Treaty also provides that

7 Treaty Instituting the Arab Maghreb Union, 17 Feb. 1989, art. 16 (hereinafter 'AMU Treaty').

8 Treaty Establishing the Common Market for Eastern and Southern Africa, art. 179.1, http://about.comesa.int/attachments/149_090505_COMESA_Treaty.pdf (last visited 9 July 2010) (hereinafter 'COMESA Treaty').

9 *Ibid.* at art. 2.

10 East African Community Treaty, 30 Nov. 1999, art. 130.3 (hereinafter 'EAC Treaty').

11 Treaty Establishing the Economic Community of Central African States, 18 Oct. 1983, art. 86.1 (hereinafter 'ECCAS Treaty').

12 *Ibid.* at art. 89.1. 13 *Ibid.* at art. 1(e).

14 Economic Community of West African States Revised Treaty, 24 July 1993, art. 79.1 (hereinafter 'ECOWAS Revised Treaty').

15 *Ibid.* at art. 79.2. 16 *Ibid.* at art. 83. 17 *Ibid.* at art. 1.

18 Agreement Establishing The Inter-Governmental Authority on Development, art. 18 (hereinafter 'IGAD Treaty'), www.gtz.de/en/dokumente/en-agreement-establishing-igad.pdf.

it may enter into agreements with other states, regional and international organizations, with compatible objectives.[19]

COMESA, EAC, Economic and Monetary Community of Central Africa (CEMAC, a subgroup of ECCAS), ECOWAS, IGAD and SADC are all involved in inter-regional integration efforts to promote the vision of the AEC. This chapter will discuss the inter-regional integration efforts adopted by these RECs, and by others that are not part of the AEC, by analysing them under the legal framework of the RECs to determine whether such efforts are permitted under their establishing treaties.

C Sources of support for intra-regional trade cooperation

1 Africa Development Bank

The Africa Development Bank (AfDB) was formed in 1964 by 23 African nations.[20] Its goal is to 'mobilize resources to finance economic development and social projects and programmes in its Regional Member Countries (RMCs)'.[21] It is also affiliated with the African Development Fund (ADF), established in 1972, and with the Nigeria Trust Fund (NTF), established in 1976.[22] In order to supplement its resources, the AfDB managed 25 bilateral trust funds totalling UA12.7m in 2009.[23]

The AfDB is a key player in inter-regional integration efforts. As of April 2010, about 683 ongoing projects received assistance from the bank and its affiliates; 198 of these were agriculture-related, while 89 were transport-related.[24] The AfDB also has an extensive project cycle with 8 components: country strategy paper and project identification; project preparation; project appraisal; loan negotiation; board approval; loan agreements; loan effectiveness; and finally, implementation.[25]

19 Treaty of the Southern African Development Community As Amended, 17 Aug. 1992, art. 24.1 (hereinafter 'SADC Treaty').

20 African Development Bank Group, 'AfDB in Brief', 3, available at www.afdb.org/en/documents/publications/afdb-in-brief (last visited 24 Feb. 2011) (hereinafter 'AfDB in Brief').

21 *Ibid.* at 3. 22 *Ibid.*

23 African Development Bank, 'Trust Funds Annual Report 2009, 15–17, available at www.afdb.org/fileadmin/uploads/afdb/Documents/Corporate-Procurement/Departmental_Annual_Reports/2009%20Trust%20funds%20AnnualReport.pdf.

24 African Development Bank Group, 'Project Portfolio', available at www.afdb.org/en/projects-operations/project-portfolio/ (last visited 21 Aug. 2010).

25 African Development Bank Group, 'Projects and Operations: Project Cycle', available at www.afdb.org/en/projects-operations/Project-cycle (last visited 24 Feb. 2011).

2 Foreign aid

As developing nations, African countries receive aid from the World Bank and other foreign donors to implement their regional integration programmes.[26] The World Bank created the Regional Integration Department to increase bank assistance to regional integration and bring it into the mainstream of country programmes.[27] Consequently, the World Bank attaches certain conditions to its aid. For example, the bank became involved in Chad's Chad–Cameroon pipeline project on the condition that Chad would spend a designated amount of its profits on social programmes.[28] However, Chad used its profits instead to prepay part of the $140m loan. As a result, the bank pulled out of its deal with Chad.[29]

The European Union (EU), too, has extended financial help, in the form of grants to support regional integration efforts.[30] The EU signed an agreement with IGAD, COMESA, EAC and Indian Ocean (IO) regions to provide financing worth $161m for a number of regional economic integration and development projects.[31] These projects are part of an allocation granted under the 10th European Development Fund (EDF).[32] The ESA-IO region has been allocated $645m for the period 2008 to 2013.[33] The four RECs, along with SADC and the European Commission (EC), facilitate the formulation, implementation and monitoring of the EU-funded projects through the Inter-Regional Coordination Committee (IRCC).[34]

Additional foreign involvement in regional integration programmes has come from middle-income countries like China and India. China is making major inroads in Africa through investment and aid programmes.[35] As a voracious consumer of natural resources such as

26 The World Bank, 'Sub-Saharan Africa Regional Integration Q&A', http://web.worldbank.org/WBSITE/EXTERNAL/COUNTRIES/AFRICAEXT/EXTREGINI/EXTAFRREGINICOO/0,,contentMDK:20655099~menuPK:1587625~pagePK:64168445~piPK:64168309~theSitePK:1587585,00.html (last visited 21 Aug. 2010).

27 *Ibid.*

28 L. Polgreen, 'World Bank Ends Efforts to Help Chad Ease Poverty', *New York Times*, 10 Sept. 2008, www.nytimes.com/2008/09/11/world/africa/11chad.html?_r=2&ref=world&oref=slogin (last visited 25 Oct. 2010).

29 *Ibid.*

30 A. Odhiambo, 'EU Grants $160m to Support Regional Integration', *Business Daily*, 16 Mar. 2010, available at www.tralac.org/cgi-bin/giga.cgi?cmd=cause_dir_news_item&cause_id=1694&news_id=83964&cat_id=1072 (last visited 25 Oct. 2010).

31 *Ibid.* 32 *Ibid.* 33 *Ibid.* 34 *Ibid.*

35 'World Bank President Attacks China Over African Lending Policy', *Global Insight*, www.globalinsight.com/SDA/SDADetail7292.htm (last visited 25 Oct. 2010).

oil and copper, China has strong trade ties with the African continent.[36] However, recently, former World Bank President, Paul Wolfowitz, criticized China for ignoring human rights and environment standards when lending to Africa.[37] India established a relationship with Africa through the Africa–India Forum Summit, as we saw in the previous chapter, which was perhaps a more tactful strategy than that of China, to capture the regional interests of all RECs by progressively strengthening its partnership with the African Union (AU) and the individual RECs.[38]

Perhaps a word about China's involvement in Africa would be appropriate here. Recent analysis on China's involvement in Africa have invoked alarmist rhetoric without much quantitative and qualitative support.[39] Such alarmist literature has invoked familiar tropes such as re-colonization and a new scramble for African resources.[40] While this book is not the place to examine these assertions, such accounts are skewed for a number of reasons. First, because the accounts are based on a very partial and incomplete analysis of Sino-African relations. For example, these accounts have tended to privilege seeing Africa's external relations from the perspective of either an exploited continent with no agency of its own to determine its future, or a continent that must necessarily pursue relations based on a particular development model promoted by western donors, which the Chinese do not buy into. As this book shows, African governments have a very strong sense of the objectives of their cooperation and integration schemes. While they do not always prevail at the negotiating table, it is inaccurate to think of Chinese investors in Africa as any more self-interested or even more righteous than other investors. The prudence with which African countries should treat any foreign investors applies equally to Chinese investors.

D The importance of linkages between RECs in agriculture

Agriculture is the cornerstone of economic development in many African countries. Eighty per cent of the population in Africa still relies heavily

36 *Ibid.* 37 *Ibid.*

38 India–Africa Forum Summit 2008, Delhi Declaration, Apr. 2008, para. 19, www.ibef.org/download/India_Africa.pdf (last visited 25 Oct. 2010).

39 See H. Broadman, *Africa's Silk Road: China and India's New Economic Frontier* (Washington, DC: The World Bank, 2007), 3; I. Taylor, *China and Africa: Engagement and Compromise* (New York: Routledge, 2006) (noting that compared to other area studies on Chinese foreign policy, the study of Sino-African relations has been sparse).

40 M.C. Lee, 'The 21st Century Scramble for Africa', *The Journal of Contemporary African Studies*, 24(3) (2006); J. Daniel, H. Melber and R. Southall (eds.), *A New Scramble? Imperialism, Investment and Development in Africa* (University of Kwazulu Natal Press; London: Merlin Press, 2009).

on the agricultural industry to support their economies.[41] Mr. Sindiso Ngwenya, Secretary General of COMESA, calls agriculture the 'engine for economic development'.[42] Sub-Saharan Africa still faces the sort of poverty and hunger experienced twenty years ago, with as much as 300 million people suffering chronic hunger. According to the CEO of the Food, Agriculture, and Natural Resources Policy Analysis Network, Dr. Lindiwe Majele Sibanda, investment in agriculture is the solution to these pressing issues.[43] The AU, too, re-emphasized the importance of agriculture to the African economy at the 13th AU Summit held in Tripoli, Libya, celebrating the Comprehensive Africa Agriculture Development Programme (CAADP) Day, under the theme of 'Investing in Agriculture for Economic Growth and Food Security'.[44]

CAADP is an agricultural development framework of the New Partnership for Africa's Development (NEPAD), a strategic framework adopted by the OAU for Africa's 'Renewal' seeking to address issues such as poverty and underdevelopment throughout the continent.[45] I examine NEPAD a little further below. Unlike the majority of the programmes discussed in this chapter, the CAADP is owned and led solely by African nations seeking to achieve economic growth through agriculture.[46] CAADP brings agriculture to the forefront of the development dynamics of African nations, by linking key players in national, regional and continental levels, and thus enabling the sharing of best practices, and promoting individual and joint efforts aimed at eliminating hunger and reducing poverty.[47] In order to achieve this end, African governments have promised to invest 10 per cent or more of their national budgets in agriculture, and to increase agricultural output by 6 per cent.[48] CAADP operates under the following four pillars:

41 African Union Commission, 'CAADP Day: African Union Promotes Agricultural Development in Africa', African Press Organization, Division of Communication and Information, 29 June 2009, available at: http://appablog.wordpress.com/2009/06/29/caadp-day-african-union-promotes-agricultural-development-in-africa/ (last visited 25 Oct. 2010) (hereinafter 'CAADP Press Release').

42 Speech by Mr. Sindiso Ngwenya, Secretary General, COMESA, at the Second Africa Agriculture Markets Programme Policy Seminar, David Livingstone Hotel, Livingstone, Zambia, 15 June 2009, at 2, http://about.comesa.int/attachments/161_090616AAMP_Secretary_General_speech_Livingstone.pdf (last visited 21 Aug. 2010) (hereinafter 'Ngwenya Speech').

43 M.S. Lindiwe, 'Put Farming First in Africa', *The Guardian*, 27 Apr. 2009, www.guardian.co.uk/society/katineblog/2009/apr/27/farming-in-africa (last visited 25 Oct. 2010).

44 CAADP Press Release.

45 NEPAD, 'About NEPAD', www.nepad.org/about (last visited 25 Oct. 2010).

46 CAADP, 'About CAADP', www.caadp.net/about-caadp.php (last visited 25 Oct. 2010).

47 *Ibid.* 48 *Ibid.*

Pillar 1 – Extending the area under sustainable land management.
Pillar 2 – Improving infrastructure and trade-related capacities for market access.
Pillar 3 – Increasing food supplies and reducing hunger.
Pillar 4 – Agricultural research, technology dissemination and adoption.[49]

The CAADP is not a one-size-fits-all programme; therefore, each REC, and the Member States within, follows different agendas within the framework of the four pillars to achieve the overall goals of CAADP.[50] National round-table processes form the platform for agreements between donors and governments and also focus on exploiting synergies, donor funding, monitoring and evaluating CAADP's progress, aligning state policies with regional priorities and the four pillars and developing financial commitments for agricultural investment programmes, in order to implement the CAADP uniformly. [51]

1 The AEC and NEPAD

After the AU was launched at the 38th OAU Summit in Lusaka, Zambia, 7–9 July 2001,[52] in a subsequent summit held in Abuja, Nigeria, on 23 October 2001, it mandated and launched its economic agenda, the New African Initiative, which was later re-named NEPAD. The New African Initiative was itself a merger of two prior drafts of an economic strategy for Africa: the Millennium Partnership for the African Recovery Programme (MAP) and the OMEGA plan.[53] These economic recovery plans were drawn against the backdrop of calls for renewing the OAU to meet the

49 CAADP, 'Implementing the CAADP Agenda', www.caadp.net/implementing-caadp-agenda.php (last visited 25 Oct. 2010).

50 CAADP, 'National Roundtables', www.caadp.net/national-roundtables.php (last visited 25 Oct. 2010).

51 *Ibid.*

52 The Constitutive Act of the Union entered in force on 26 May 2001. The Act establishing the Union establishes it in place of the Organization of African Unity (OAU). This new political, judicial and economic organization will have a variety of institutions including the Pan-African Parliament, the Court of Justice and the Central Bank. See Constitutive Act of the African Union, 11 July 2000, at www.africa-union.org/root/au/Aboutau/Constitutive_Act_en.htm. For further reading on the African Union, see C.A. Packer and D. Rukare, 'The New African Union and Its Constitutive Act', *Am. J. Int'l L.* 96 (2002) 365.

53 The New African Initiative, 'A Merger of the Millennium African Renaissance Partnership Programme (MAP) and The Omega Plan', July 2001, www.uneca.org/eca_resources/conference_reports_and_other_documents/nepad/nai.pdf. (This plan was approved at an OAU Heads of State Summit on 11 July 2001.)

challenges of peace, security, poverty and underdevelopment in Africa.[54] In addition, these plans were given impetus by South African President Thabo Mbeki's call for an African Renaissance in the new millennium.[55] The political support particularly in the area of economic recovery for Africa was critical, especially in light of the fact that no concerted programmatic or institutional vision had been given to the 1991 Treaty Establishing the African Economic Community up to that point.[56]

The inauguration of the AU as a successor to the OAU was in part a recognition of the need to give a renewed focus to issues of development and the economies of the continent. This move represented a shift in focus at the continental level from a focus almost exclusively on stability and security, to meeting the challenges of globalization. However, the NEPAD agenda, as I have argued elsewhere,[57] represented a move away from the inspirations of the Lagos Plan of Action and the goals of the African Economic Community. While the Lagos Plan in particular sought home-grown solutions to Africa's economic predicaments, the NEPAD Agenda adopts the view that a market-centred type of development narrowly tailored towards meeting economic growth by borrowing large sums of money from the west is the best way to develop Africa.[58] There is nothing wrong with pursuing economic growth. Yet, growth should not be pursued without regard to broader developmental goals or at the expense of ensuring that economic progress benefits more people than the captains of industry. In other words, development should not be defined solely by evidence of economic growth associated with high levels of industrialization, urbanization and growth in such areas as technical knowledge and capability without reference to the existence of poverty, inequality and environmental degradation, when they occur alongside increasing levels of aggregate economic growth and production.[59] NEPAD seems to

54 N.J. Udombana, 'How Should We Then Live? Globalization and the New Partnership for Africa's Development', *B.U. Int'l L.J.* 20 (2002) 293, 295.

55 Thabo Mbeki, 'Speech of the President of South Africa', at the launch of the African Renaissance Institute, 11 October 1999, available at www.au2002.gov.za/docs/speeches/mbeki991011.htm.

56 Treaty Establishing the African Economic Community, 3 June 1991, ILM 30 (1991) 1241.

57 J. Gathii, 'A Critical Appraisal of the NEPAD Agenda in Light of Africa's Place in the World Trade Regime in an Era of Market Centered Development', *Transnational Law and Contemporary Problems* 13 (2003) 179.

58 *Ibid.*

59 On this, see T. Banuri, 'Development and the Politics of Knowledge: A Critical Interpretation of the Social Role of Modernization Theories in the Development of the Third World', in F. Appfel-Marglin and S. Marglin, *Dominating Knowledge* (Oxford: Clarendon, 1990), 29.

surrender these broader goals of development to market forces, unlike under the Lagos Plan of Action and some of the immediate inspirations of the African Economic Community discussed above.

Thus, while economic integration has witnessed some renewed attention with the NEPAD Agenda, I would argue that there are strong tensions in the goals of the NEPAD Agenda and the objectives of establishing an African Economic Community. I do not think the fact that the NEPAD Agenda was defined to primarily placate Africa's donors, while the goal of an African Economic Community was inspired by the continent's own experience ought to necessarily derail either. Yet, both represent rather different strategies, with NEPAD looking outward and the African Economic Community inward as starting points. Undoubtedly, both represent two of the great challenges facing the continent – the poor state of intra-African trade evidenced by the fact, for example, that the continent exports as much oil as it imports, on the one hand, and the huge trade imbalances between Africa and her trading partners, on the other.

2 *Agricultural programmes in East and Southern Africa*

COMESA and ECOWAS are said to have achieved the most progress in the CAADP programme among the various RECs.[60] In the COMESA region, 17 of the 19 Member States have initiated national round table processes – which are officially in place once a focal point official is designated by the country to marshal the stakeholders – toward the implementation of the CAADP.[61] COMESA is also implementing certain key activities under each of the four pillars, such as: Climate Change Initiative and Irrigation Programme under Pillar 1; African Agricultural Markets Programme (AAMP) and Regional Agricultural Trade Expansion Support (RATES) project under Pillar 2; Alliance for Commodity Trade in Eastern and Southern Africa (ACTESA) under Pillar 3; and Regional Approach to Biotechnology and Bio-safety for Eastern and Southern Africa (RABESA II) under Pillar 4, among others.[62] A brief explanation of RATES, AAMP and ACTESA follows below.

60 CAADP, 'The Role of Regional Economic Communities', www.caadp.net/role-regional-economic-communities.php (last visited 25 Oct. 2010).

61 The Comprehensive Africa Agriculture Development Programme (CAADP), COMESA Programmes, COMESA, http://programmes.comesa.int/index.php?option=com_content&view=article&id=25&Itemid=42&lang=en (last visited 25 Oct. 2010).

62 *Ibid.*

3 *Regional Agricultural Trade Expansion Support (RATES) Programme*

RATES is a USAID-funded programme based in Nairobi and is intended to support commodity-specific regional trade initiatives through innovative private and public sector alliances.[63] Partners in the programme include COMESA, EAC and Cottonafrica.com, Eastern African Fine Coffees Association (EAFCA), among others.[64]

RATES consists of six programmes: coffee, maize, cotton, livestock, dairy and policy. The Coffee Programme is intended to help position EAFCA as a key player in the marketing and promotion of Eastern African coffees in both regional and global coffee markets and to enable its sustainability.[65] Key activities include supporting EAFCA's national and regional marketing campaigns and supporting EAFCA to further develop linkages with the international coffee industry.[66] The Maize Programme aims to improve the flow and availability of maize in order to contribute to regional market stabilization and food security.[67] RATES also initiated a joint private/public sector policy rationalization/harmonization initiative launched in 2003 with the support of COMESA and EAC.[68] The Cotton Programme aims to promote African cotton trade in both regional and international markets.[69] Cottonafrica.com is a key player in this programme, as it brings buyers and sellers together in an electronic

63 'Industry Associations: A Catalyst in Regional Integration', Eastern and Southern African Dairy Association, 22 Feb. 2008, available at: www.dairyafrica.com/news.asp?ID=41 (last visited 28 Oct. 2010).

The RATES programme has been succeeded by COMPETE, another USAID funded programme. Like RATES, this programme seeks to enhance trade in East and Central Africa by harmonizing regional trade and transit policies and procedures, developing financial markets and developing value chains in staple foods, coffee and textiles. COMPETE, 'About COMPETE', www.competeafrica.org/about.htm (last visited 31 Aug. 2010). Subject to USAID funding, the COMPETE contract is for a period of four years, from 11 February 2009 to 1 March 2013. *Ibid.* This programme also serves as a platform for countries seeking AGOA eligibility by providing targeted assistance in two areas: firm-level assistance and AGOA National Assistance. COMPETE, AGOA, www.competeafrica.org/agoa.htm (last visited 31 Aug. 2010).

64 'Industry Associations: A Catalyst in Regional Integration', Eastern and Southern African Dairy Association.

65 COMPETE, 'Specialty Coffee', www.competeafrica.org/components/building%20value%20chains/specialtycoffee.htm (last visited 28 Oct. 2010).

66 *Ibid.*

67 COMPETE, 'Staple Foods', www.competeafrica.org/components/building%20value%20chains/staplefoods.htm (last visited 28 Oct. 2010).

68 *Ibid.*

69 Cotton Africa, 'About Cotton Africa', www.cottonafrica.com/page.php?id=9 (last visited 6 July 2010).

trading forum and facilitates communication between traders.[70] The Livestock Programme was limited to supporting Djibouti complete a livestock holding facility accomplished in 2005.[71] The Dairy Programme recognized the need for free flow of milk products in the COMESA region, and aims to remove regional export market trade constraints and to promote intra-regional exports of dairy products through the Eastern and Southern African Dairy Association (ESADA).[72] RATES policy aims to increase COMESA's and EAC's capacity to better serve the trading community in commodities supported by RATES by identifying trade constraints and initiating policy changes through these RECs.[73] Key activities in this include facilitating incorporation of regional grain and dairy standards into national policy in the COMESA and EAC regions.[74]

4 *Competitiveness and Trade Expansion Programme*

The RATES programme has been succeeded by the Competitiveness and Trade Expansion Programme (COMPETE), another USAID-funded programme. Like RATES, this programme seeks to enhance trade in East and Central Africa by harmonizing regional trade and transit policies and procedures.

5 *Africa Agricultural Market Programme*

COMESA and Africa's Agriculture and Rural Development Unit (AFTAR) of the World Bank entered into a partnership to create the Africa Agricultural Market Programme (AAMP).[75]

This programme's core objectives include: strengthening institutional capacity to implement programmes in support of the CAADP; enhancing knowledge and providing information to national decision makers regarding agricultural market issues; and creating a regional network

70 *Ibid.*

71 RATES, 'Annual Performance Monitoring Report: October 2003–September 2004', Chemonics International Inc., 15 Oct. 2004, 4, http://pdf.usaid.gov/pdf_docs/PDACM138.pdf; RATES, 'Annual Progress Report: October 2004–September 2005', Chemonics International Inc., 15 Oct. 2005, 53, http://pdf.usaid.gov/pdf_docs/PDACM139.pdf.

72 *Ibid.*, 3, http://pdf.usaid.gov/pdf_docs/PDACM140.pdf.

73 RATES, 'Annual Performance Monitoring Report: October 2002–September 2003', Chemonics International Inc., 15 October 2003, 35, http://pdf.usaid.gov/pdf_docs/PDACM135.pdf.

74 *Ibid.*

75 Ngwenya Speech, at 3.

between ministries and private sector to allow dialogue regarding agricultural markets.[76]

6 *Alliance for Commodity Trade in Eastern and Southern Africa*

'Smallholders' produce the majority of agricultural output in Africa.[77] In the COMESA region, the average sale of a smallholder is between 500 and 1,500 kilos, while the market demand is between 10 and 100 metric tons.[78] The difference between the supply and demand is largely due to a lack of sufficient mechanisms to provide viable options and predictable prices to smallholders.[79] The Alliance for Commodity Trade in Eastern and Southern Africa (ACTESA) was adopted by COMESA to promote collaborative partnerships between public and private sector entities, in order to increase trade of staple crops within the region, by disseminating mechanisms to allow smallholders to become viable market participants.[80]

ACTESA has three main objectives: improve competitiveness through enhanced economic policies; improve and expand market facilities and services for staple foods; and increase commercial integration of staple food producers into the national and regional markets.[81] Existing programmes and projects with similar objectives, such as the AAMP, may integrate with ACTESA in countries where both programmes are present.[82]

E Agricultural programmes in West Africa

Like COMESA, ECOWAS too has achieved substantial progress in the implementation of CAADP.[83] Concept paper development for Pillars 1, 2 and 3 has begun, and an expert reference group has been initiated under Pillar 4.[84] Additionally, ECOWAS developed and adopted the West Africa Agricultural Policy (ECOWAP) in order to achieve the following goals: increase food security; reduce food dependence; involve producers in

76 *Ibid.*

77 Alliance for Commodity Trade in Eastern and Southern Africa (ACTESA), Design Plan, August 2008, s. 2, http://programmes.comesa.int/attachments/130_ACTESA%20Design%20Plan.pdf (last visited 25 Oct. 2010) (hereinafter 'ACTESA Design Plan').

78 *Ibid.* 79 *Ibid.* 80 *Ibid.* at s. 2.1. 81 *Ibid.* at s. 3. 82 *Ibid.* at s. 5.

83 CAADP, 'The Role of Regional Economic Communities', www.caadp.net/role-regional-economic-communities.php (last visited 25 Oct. 2010).

84 CAADP Implementation, 'Donor Platform', para. 9, www.donorplatform.org/content/view/101/147 (last visited 17 July 2009).

the market; create jobs; develop sustainable production systems; combat West African economic vulnerabilities by reducing regional instability and insecurity; and adopt suitable financing mechanisms.[85]

While some countries like Nigeria, Mali, Niger, Gambia and Sierra Leone have achieved CAADP's goal of 6 per cent increase in agricultural growth, others still have a long way to go.[86] Current trends indicate that progress in agriculture integration has decelerated in West Africa. This is mainly due to the fact that national governments are not living up to their promise to increase government expenditure on agriculture to a minimum of 10 per cent of their national budgets.[87] Clearly, it is not enough to emphasize the importance of agriculture to the African economy in national and international forums; governments should also match their words with actions by making agriculture a priority in their national budgets and economic policies.

F Agricultural programmes in North Africa

According to the Food and Agriculture Organization of the United Nations, agricultural integration has fared badly in North Africa.[88] The AMU in particular does not have a good record in the market for agricultural products.[89] Agricultural imports within the region are mostly provided by Algeria and Morocco, with some inter-regional trade with other RECs.[90]

G Challenges in agricultural integration and some solutions

The Commission on Sustainable Development met in 2009 in Windhoek, Namibia, and was attended by African and international ministers and

85 'Make Agriculture the Lever of Regional Integration', Regional Agricultural Policy for West Africa: ECOWAP, www.diplomatie.gouv.fr/fr/IMG/pdf/01_ANG-ComCEDEAO.pdf (last visited 25 Oct. 2010) (hereinafter 'ECOWAP').

86 Regional Dissemination Workshop on Agricultural Trends and Progress in Living Conditions in West Africa, 'Synthesis Report of the Main Conclusions and Recommendations', Accra, Ghana, 12 May 2009, http://resakss.files.wordpress.com/2009/06/ghanamay2009_conclusions.pdf (last visited 25 Oct. 2010).

87 *Ibid.*

88 Food and Agriculture Organization of the United Nations, 'Towards an African Common Market for Agricultural Products', Rome, Oct. 2007, at s. 3.2.4 (hereinafter 'FAO, African Common Market').

89 *Ibid.* AMU entered into various agreements, such as the Convention on Trade in Agricultural Products, and the Trade and Tariffs Agreement; the former was never implemented, and the latter was short-lived.

90 *Ibid.* AMU trades with ECOWAS/WAEMU and COMESA for rice and legumes, and with SADC for dairy products.

government representatives. Certain key challenges in African agriculture were identified, and solutions to make a 'sustainable green revolution' were recommended at this meeting.[91] Some of the challenges identified were: the financial crisis; the global food and energy crisis; environmental degradation such as droughts, desertification and land degradation; and climate change.[92]

The global food and energy crisis poses a serious threat to Africa's goal of eradicating poverty and hunger. Individual countries have taken measures to tackle this challenge by suspending customs duty, reducing or suspending VAT (value added tax) on some food items and subsidizing fuel and rice, among others.[93] The Commission makes a number of recommendations to alleviate this crisis, including, ensuring the availability of credit and other financial facilities to small-scale farmers and encouraging the formation of agricultural cooperatives to enhance farmers' earning power.[94]

Environmental degradation and climate change are undeniably significant risks in agricultural communities. The Commission recommended the implementation of National Action Plans (under the United Nations Convention to Combat Desertification) and National Adaptation Programmes of Action (under the United Nations Framework Convention on Climate Change) in order to adapt to climate change.[95]

Other challenges that hinder agricultural integration are technical in nature. Tariffs are a major impediment to trade. As individual RECs move towards establishing customs unions, tariff barriers within the RECs may become a thing of the past.[96] Non-tariff barriers such as quotas and price control mechanisms such as minimum prices and restraints on export prices also restrict trade within the RECs.[97] Individual RECs have different approaches to addressing this issue. For instance, COMESA opted to eliminate non-tariff barriers immediately, while ECOWAS and SADC have decided to do this gradually.[98]

Additional restrictions to trade include potential revenue loss and monetary constraints that may come with the formation of a customs union. Although liberalization of trade would prove beneficial to all concerned, it could result in loss in revenues from toll charges and import levies to

91 UN Economic and Social Committee (ECOSOC), Commission on Sustainable Development, 'Thematic Cluster for the Implementation Cycle 2008–2009' – Policy Session, E/CN.17/2009/14 (6 Mar. 2009) (hereinafter 'ECOSOC, Implementation Cycle').

92 *Ibid.* at para. 9. 93 ECOWAP, at 12.

94 ECOSOC, Implementation Cycle, at para. 31. 95 *Ibid.* at para. 31(p).

96 FAO, African Common Market, at s. 5.1. 97 *Ibid.* at s. 5.2. 98 *Ibid.*

individual countries.[99] However, such losses are expected to be nominal as intra-regional trade usually makes up only a fraction of total trade.[100]

H The importance of linkages between RECs in transport and communications

The African Economic Community can only be realized once individual RECs become viable trading blocs and compete in the global economy. For this to happen, it is necessary to establish linkages between each REC; particularly in the areas of transport and communications, as national programmes alone will not accomplish the 'growth rates needed to combat poverty'.[101]

Indeed, transport infrastructure and services are essential 'preconditions' for the facilitation of trade.[102] However, as one of the least developed continents, Africa has a huge infrastructural challenge to overcome. For instance, as of 2005, only 24.5 per cent of the continent's road network was tarred.[103] These roads are poorly maintained and overloaded with vehicles, thus reducing their lifespan.[104] However, some RECs are attempting to remedy this situation by entering into transport agreements to improve transport infrastructure and services within their areas.[105]

In order to compete with the rest of the world, Africa would not only have to be connected physically, by road, rail, air, or sea, but also through cyberspace. Africa has long lagged behind in the information age. Kenya's third president, H.E. Mwai Kibaki, emphasized this in 2007 when he stated that inadequate communication had been 'the

99 *Ibid.* at s. 5.3. 100 *Ibid.*

101 'What is the Rationale for Regional Integration?', World Bank, http://web.worldbank.org/WBSITE/EXTERNAL/COUNTRIES/AFRICAEXT/EXTREGINI/EXTAFRREGINICOO/0,,contentMDK:20655099~menuPK:1587625~pagePK:64168445~piPK:64168309~theSitePK:1587585,00.html (last visited 25 Oct. 2010).

102 ECOSOC, 'The Transport Situation in Africa', Economic Commission for Africa, para. 1, E/ECA/CTRCI/5/3 (7 Aug. 2007), www.uneca.org/crci/5th/The-transport-situation-Africa.pdf (last visited 25 Oct. 2010) (hereinafter 'ECOSOC, The Transport Situation in Africa').

103 *Ibid.* at para. 7. 104 *Ibid.* at paras 8–9.

105 G. Ikiara, Permanent Secretary Ministry of Transport and Communications (Kenya), 'EAC Common Market Protocol: Protocol on Transport', Paper presented at the National Retreat for Members and Key Stakeholders of the East African Common Market High Level Task Force, Utali Hotel, Nairobi, 12 May 2008 (EAC partner states agree to 'promote, facilitate and regulate international road transport services between and in transit through their respective territories').

weakest point in Africa's regional integration'.[106] In recent years, information and communication technology (ICT) has become a priority to African leaders. A prime example of this is the liberalization of telecommunication networks in Africa and the involvement of private international companies in the East African regions. The Treaty Establishing the EAC, to which Kenya, Tanzania, Rwanda, Burundi and Uganda belong, allows these countries to enter into agreements with international organizations in order to accomplish their ICT objectives.[107]

Following independence, African governments inherited existing telecommunications infrastructure and institutional framework that was only designed for a very small and elite business sector.[108] This infrastructure was woefully inadequate to serve the needs of the newly independent African countries and many governments did not do nearly enough after independence to build on and improve this colonial inheritance. Mismanagement of national institutions overseeing telecommunications and other infrastructure, as well as the debt crisis of the 1980s, catapulted the World Bank and International Monetary Fund to direct economic reforms referred to as structural adjustment.[109] Structural adjustment programmes, adopted in return for continued access to borrowings from these international institutions and from Wall Street, spurred the liberalization of the telecommunication networks, with mixed results in terms of service provisioning and cost.[110] As a result, the privatization of public-owned monopoly in the mobile segment dropped dramatically between 1995 and 2004, from 70 per cent to 10 per cent.[111] Consequently,

106 A. Wakama, 'World's First Borderless Mobile Network Expands Into Central Africa', IT News Africa, 7 June 2007, www.itnewsafrica.com/?p=119 (last visited 25 Oct. 2010).

107 COMESA Treaty, at Art. 2.

108 A. Keck and C. Djiofack-Zebaze, 'Telecommunications Services in Africa: The Impact of Multilateral Commitments and Unilateral Reform on Sector Performance and Economic Growth', World Trade Organization, Economic Research and Statistics Division s. 3, Staff Working Paper ERSD-2006–10 (Nov. 2006) available at: www.wto.org/english/res_e/reser_e/ersd200610_e.htm (last visited 25 Oct. 2010).

109 *Ibid.* See also, J. Gathii, 'Retelling Good Governance Narratives About Africa's Economic and Political Predicaments: Continuities and Discontinuities in Legal Outcomes Between Markets and States', *Vill. L. Rev.* 45 (2000) 971.

110 A lot of corruption has accompanied the privatization and liberalization of these sectors in almost every African country. In addition, privatization and liberalization were accompanied by programmes that cut massive amounts off public spending, see J. Gathii, 'Good Governance as a Counter-Insurgency to Oppositional and Transformative Social Agenda to Oppositional and Transformative Social Projects in International Law', *Buff. Human Rts L. Rev.* 5 (1999) 107.

111 Keck and Djiofack-Zebaze, 'Telecommunications Services in Africa'.

foreign telecommunication companies have firmly established themselves in Africa. One example is the Middle Eastern mobile company, Zain Group. Zain introduced Celtel, a 'borderless mobile network',[112] into Central Africa, allowing its customers in Kenya, Tanzania and Uganda to make and receive calls without roaming call surcharges and without having to pay for incoming calls.[113] Tanzania's President, H.E. Jakaya Kikwete, called Celtel's 'One Network' a 'federative tool' that would enable Africa to revive its common heritage between the people and incorporate it in their development dynamics.[114] In fact, deregulation of mobile phone services in Africa is said to offer huge potential for continental mobile phone links under Zain that may not have been possible even within Europe.[115]

I Information and Communication Technology (ICT)

1 ICT in North Africa

The North African coast is connected to the global fibre-optic network through the South East Asia–Middle East–West Europe (SEA-ME-WE) submarine cable system.[116] This system has 3 series with landing points in North African countries. SEA-ME-WE 2 has terminal stations in Egypt, Tunisia and Algeria, and SEA-ME-WE 3 has terminal stations in Djibouti, Egypt and Morocco.[117] The latest in the series, SEA-ME-WE 4, will also have terminal stations in Egypt, Tunisia and Algeria.[118] This project is expected to support telephone, internet, multimedia and various broadband data applications, thereby re-affirming North Africa's place in the information age.[119]

2 ICT in West Africa

The West African coast is also connected to the global fibre-optic network through a submarine cable system called the South Africa/West

112 Wakama, 'World's First Borderless Mobile Network Expands Into Central Africa'.

113 *Ibid.* 114 *Ibid.*

115 Sponsor Wire, 'Africa Abolishes Roaming as Celtel's One Network Expands', AllAfrica.com, 22 Nov. 2007 (quoting *The Economist*), http://allafrica.com/stories/200711230067.html (last visited 21 Aug. 2010).

116 Fiber Networks in Africa, 'ICTs in Africa', http://ictinafrica.com/ict/fiber.htm (last visited 20 July 2009) (hereinafter 'ICTs in Africa').

117 *Ibid.* 118 *Ibid.*

119 About SEA-ME-WE 4, para. 2, www.seamewe4.com/inpages/about_sea_me_we_4.asp (last visited 25 Oct. 2010).

Africa Submarine Cable/South Africa Far East (SAT3/WASC/SAFE) cable system.[120] This system has terminal stations in Senegal, Ivory Coast, Ghana, Benin, Nigeria, Cameroon, Gabon and Angola on the West African coast, in addition to La Reunion and Mauritius in the Indian Ocean.[121] It also has two terminal stations in South Africa.[122]

Unlike other fibre-optic cable systems in Africa, the SAT3/WASC/SAFE is funded entirely by individual countries.[123] It is currently owned by thirty-six countries with the majority of the terminal stations located in Africa.[124] As a result, the revenue generated by this cable system will be reinvested in African economies.[125]

3 ICT in East and Southern Africa

Individual countries are at different stages in ICT development. For example, South Africa, a member of SADC, is the twentieth largest consumer of IT products and services in the world and as such, has a superior ICT programme.[126] South Africa currently provides ICT products and services to most of the African continent. It has established itself as a call-centre destination for AOL and Virgin Mobile, among others, and has supplied fixed and wireless networks that have been established across the continent.[127]

East Africa was the only remaining inhabited coastal region in Africa that was not a part of the global fibre-optic network.[128] However, as private companies battle for the control of the East Africa broadband market,[129] it looks as though it will not be long before East African countries catch up with the rest of Africa. East Africa Marine System (TEAMS) project – a collaboration between the Kenyan government and private companies

120 ICTs in Africa.

121 SAT3/WASC/SAFE, 'SAT3WASC/SAFE Configuration', www.safe-sat3.co.za/ (last visited 21 Aug. 2010).

122 *Ibid.*

123 SAT3/WASC/SAFE, 'Homepage', www.safe-sat3.co.za (last visited 21 Aug. 2010).

124 *Ibid.* 125 *Ibid.*

126 'ICT and Electronics in South Africa', SouthAfrica.info, Oct. 2008, www.southafrica.info/business/economy/sectors/icte-overview.htm (last visited 25 Oct. 2010).

127 *Ibid.*

128 X. Rice, 'Internet: Last Piece of Fibre-Optic Jigsaw Falls Into Place As Cable Links East Africa To Grid', *The Guardian*, 18 Aug. 2008, www.guardian.co.uk/technology/2008/aug/18/east.africa.internet (last visited 25 Oct. 2010).

129 M. Malakata, 'Rival Fiber-Optic Cables Set For Battle in Africa', *Computerworld Zambia*, 18 June 2009, www.computerworld.co.ke/articles/2009/06/18/rival-fiber-optic-cables-set-market-battle-africa (last visited 25 Oct. 2010).

including Safaricom, Telkom Kenya, Kenya Data Network, Africa Fibre Net of Uganda and Etisalat of the United Arab Emirates[130] – and rival Sea Cable System (SEACOM) cable project are racing to connect Eastern and Southern Africa to the rest of the world by laying fibre-optic cable network throughout both regions.[131] Kenyan President Kibaki stated that readily accessible bandwidth will provide new opportunities in areas such as e-health, scientific research, and e-commerce, in addition to lowering telecommunication costs in the region.[132] Other countries like Rwanda are also following suit. Rwanda is negotiating a deal with Kenya to connect to the TEAMS cable.[133]

At the inter-regional level, COMESA, EAC and SADC agreed to initiate a programme to implement 'an accelerated, seamless inter-regional ICT Broadband Infrastructure network' as part of their plan to ultimately merge the three RECs into one.[134] The summit directed the RECs to put this programme in place within one year.[135] This ICT initiative is permitted by the COMESA,[136] EAC,[137] and SADC[138] treaties.

4 *Regional Information and Communication Technology Support Programme*

The Regional Information and Communication Technology Support Programme (RICTSP) is an inter-regional ICT initiative that was established by COMESA, EAC, IGAD and the Indian Ocean Commission (IOC) with funding from the 9th European Development Fund (EDF).[139] The distributions of the 9th EDF were intended to fund projects under the Cotonou Agreement.[140] The RICTSP was one of the projects funded to further communications development as required under the Agreement.[141]

130 *Ibid.* 131 *Ibid.* 132 *Ibid.* 133 *Ibid.*

134 Final Communiqué of the COMESA-EAC-SADC Tripartite Summit of Heads of State and Government, Kampala, Uganda, 22 October 2008, para. 16, www.tralac.org/cause_data/images/1694/FinalCommuniqueKampala_20081022.pdf (last visited 25 Oct. 2010) (hereinafter 'COMESA-EAC-SADC Final Communiqué').

135 *Ibid.* 136 COMESA Treaty, at Art. 84(c).

137 EAC Treaty, at Art. 89(d). 138 SADC Treaty, at Art. 21.

139 Regional ICT Support Programme, 'Home', http://rictsp.comesa.danishmanagement.dk/index.php?option=com_content&task=view&id=17&Itemid=22 (last visited 25 Oct. 2010).

140 Cotonou Agreement, 23 June 2000, Art. 61.5, available at http://ec.europa.eu/development/icenter/repository/agr01_en.pdf (last visited 21 Aug. 2010) (hereinafter 'Cotonou Agreement').

141 *Ibid.* at art. 43.5.

The main goal of the RICTSP is to improve regional integration by providing a more effective and efficient ICT environment that would ultimately lead to economic growth and reduced poverty through the reduction in costs of trade and investment.[142]

The RICTSP's activities aim to achieve the following results:

(a) The development and monitoring of implementation of ICT policy guidelines and strategies and monitoring of e-readiness status.
(b) Provision of high-speed internet connectivity to key regional stakeholders, and installation and use of ASYCUDA++ (customs management software), in selected countries.
(c) Improved and more efficient access to economic, commercial and practical information for the public and private sector through establishment of regional internet portals, information clearing houses and database-driven websites coupled with improved SME ICT skills.[143]

The RICTSP is critical for economic integration in each of the four RECs involved in this programme, and therefore, is compatible with the objectives of their individual establishing treaties. One of the main objectives enumerated under COMESA's Treaty is the cooperation in promoting research and adapting science and technology for development.[144] The RICTSP is compatible with this objective, and therefore, COMESA's agreement with the other RECs is permissible under its establishing treaty. The Treaty establishing the EAC encourages the development of programmes that would deepen cooperation among the Partner States in the areas of, among others, research and technology.[145] The RICTSP is consistent with this objective, and therefore, the EAC may enter into cooperative agreements with the other RECs. The establishing treaty of IGAD stresses the need for economic integration and harmonization of the policies of the Member States particularly in the areas of, among others, infrastructure development, trade, transport and communications.[146] The RICTSP

142 Regional ICT Support Programme, 'Home'.

143 IGAD, 'About the Economic Cooperation and Social Development – Transport & Communications', 11 Jan. 2010, http://igad.int/index.php?option=com_content&view=article&id=96&Itemid=147&limitstart=2 (last visited 25 Oct. 2010). ASYCUDA is an acronym for Automated SYstem for CUstoms DAta, a computerized management system which accelerates customs clearance and simplifies procedures, leading to decreased costs to businesses. UNCTAD, 'What is ASYCUDA?' www.unctad.org/templates/Page.asp?intItemID=3905&lang=1 (last visited 21 Aug. 2010). SME is an acronym for Small and Medium Enterprises.

144 COMESA Treaty, at Art. 3(c).

145 EAC Treaty, at Art. 5.1.

146 IGAD Treaty, at Art. 7(b) and (f).

is a crucial step in achieving this objective, and therefore, IGAD may enter into an agreement with the other RECs in accordance with its treaty.

J Air transport

1 The need for air transport liberalization and the Yamoussoukro Decision

Air transport markets were based on Bilateral Air Service Agreements (BASAs) with varying rules and regulations and differing standards of service and consumer rights.[147] Consequently, air transport is extremely costly, with poor connectivity, is not very competitive and has little impact on socio-economic development for most of the African people.[148] The Yamoussoukro Decision was adopted in order to counter the protectionist nature of BASAs that obstructed expansion of air transport services in Africa.[149] All multilateral and bilateral agreements that are inconsistent with the Yamoussoukro Decision are suspended as long as the Decision is in effect.[150]

2 Air transport policy in West Africa

In order to address poor air transport services in the region, ECOWAS and CEMAC, a sub-group of ECCAS, agreed on 14 November 1999, to cooperate in the implementation of the Yamoussoukro Decision.[151] The main objective of the ECOWAS-CEMAC collaboration is the liberalization of the air transport sector through reforms in air transport legal,

147 D. Kajange, 'Air Transport Market Liberalisation in Africa: The Yamoussoukro Decision Process', African Union, Infrastructure & Energy Department, April 2009, at 3, http://ec.europa.eu/transport/air/events/doc/eu_africa/session_1_air_transport_market_liberalisation_in_africa.pdf (last visited 25 Oct. 2010).

148 *Ibid.* at 4.

149 Ethiopia, 'Implementation of the Yamoussoukro Decision Progressing or Stalled?', ICAO/ATAG/WB Development Forum, 24–6 May 2006, available at www.icao.int/DevelopmentForum/Forum_06/Docs/YamoussoukroDecision.pdf (last visited 21 Oct. 2010).

150 ECOSOC, 'Decision Relating to the Implementation of the Yamoussoukro Declaration Concerning the Liberalisation of Access to Air Transport Markets in Africa', art. 2, Economic Commission for Africa, ECA/RCID/CM.CIVAC/99/RPT (13 Nov. 1999).

151 M. I. Chambas, ECOWAS, Annual Report of the Executive Secretary of ECOWAS, 'Fostering Regional Integration Through NEPAD Implementation', s. 10.6, ECW/CM/XLIX/2 (Dec. 2002), www.comm.ecowas.int/sec/fr/rapport/es_annual_report_2002.pdf (last visited 21 Aug. 2010).

economic and technical regulation.[152] Other key players in this project include Agency for Aerial Navigation Safety in Africa and Madagascar (L'Agence pour la Sécurité de la Navigation aérienne en Afrique et à Madagascar, ASECNA), West African Economic and Monetary Union (Union économique et monétaire ouest-africaine, UEMOA), United Nations Economic Commission for Africa (ECA), African Civil Aviation Commission (AFCAC), COMESA, African Airlines Association (AFRAA), Banjul Accord, International Civil Aviation Organization (ICAO), Federal Aviation Administration (FAA) as well as donors like the World Bank, EU, French Cooperation and Africa Development Bank, among others.[153]

The Decision is not inconsistent with ECOWAS's establishing treaty, because its objective of improving air transport services is compatible with the treaty's objective of promoting regional integration programmes in, among other areas, transport and communications.[154] Therefore, ECOWAS may enter into a cooperative agreement with CEMAC and other regional and international organizations without contravening the provisions of its establishing treaty.

3 Air transport policy in East and Southern Africa

Similarly, in 2001, COMESA, EAC and SADC decided to implement the Yamoussoukro Decision together.[155] At regional level, the Air Transport Liberalization Programme is permitted by the COMESA,[156] EAC[157] and SADC[158] treaties. The three RECs launched the Joint Competition Authority (JCA) on Air Transport Liberalization at the Tripartite Summit held in October 2008 in order to oversee the implementation of the Yamoussoukro Decision.[159]

To this end, SADC has also begun several regional integration initiatives, such as the regulatory capacity-building initiative known as the Cooperative Development of Operational Safety and Continuing Air

152 Third Meeting of the Coordination and Monitoring Committee for the Implementation of the Yamoussoukro Decision in West and Central Africa, Libreville, 29 Nov. 2004 at 3.

153 *Ibid.*

154 ECOWAS Revised Treaty, at Art. 3.2(a).

155 ICAO, 'Air Transport Liberalization Process in SADC', www.icao.int/icao/en/atb/meetings/2008/Sympo_Nigeria/Docs/SADC.pdf (last visited 25 Oct. 2010) (hereinafter 'SADC Air Transport Liberalization').

156 COMESA Treaty, at Art. 87.

157 EAC Treaty, at Art. 92.

158 SADC Treaty, at Art. 21.

159 COMESA-EAC-SADC Final Communiqué, at para. 16(i).

Worthiness Project (COSCAP).[160] Objectives of this programme include addressing deficiencies in oversight of safety aspects in civil aviation, as well as developing regional capacity in personnel licensing, airworthiness certification, surveillance and harmonization of regulations.[161]

Other regional integration initiatives in the SADC region include Aviation Security (AVSEC), whose objectives include application of uniform security measures and sharing of human resources for security audits and the like,[162] and operation capacity-building initiatives such as the Upper Air Space Control Centre (UACC) Project that is intended to consolidate air traffic control and navigation at regional and continental levels.[163]

Air transport services are crucial to trade and development in landlocked countries like Botswana in the SADC region, and Rwanda in EAC, because of the impracticality of other forms of transport, such as maritime. Liberalization of air transport services will make the Member States more accessible by the outside world and thereby increase trade and tourism, as well as to boost foreign direct investment in the region.[164]

K Surface transport – road, rail, ports and maritime

Surface transport is an integral part of the road to economic integration and regional trade among African countries. To achieve this end, several regional integration efforts have been put in place by individual countries, RECs and other African and international organizations.

1 Road and rail transport

Landlocked countries in Africa rely heavily on road transport systems for regional trade, and therefore it is vital for such countries to be properly connected to the rest of the continent in order to realize the vision of economic integration and the formation of the AEC.

However, the current road network status in Africa is inadequate, given that less than 25 per cent of the continent has tarred roads.[165] Inadequate

160 'Sub-Theme for Infrastructure Support on Regional Integration', SADC Consultative Conference, Windhoek, Namibia, 27 Apr. 2006, http://unpan1.un.org/intradoc/groups/public/documents/cpsi/unpan027121.pdf (last visited 21 Aug. 2010) (hereinafter 'SADC Consultative Conference').

161 *Ibid.* 162 SADC Air Transport Liberalization.

163 'Record', Integrated Committee of Ministers: Infrastructure and Services Cluster, SADC/ICM/1/2008/2.2a, 19 June 2008, www.madagascar-diplomatie.net/article.php?article_id=568.

164 SADC Air Transport Liberalization.

165 ECOSOC, 'The Transport Situation in Africa', at para. 7.

road transport facilitation leads to high transport costs, which in turn leads to increased price of exports for many African nations, particularly landlocked countries, leaving them at a disadvantage in the world market. It is estimated that transport and insurance costs of exports in landlocked Least Developed Countries (LDCs) comprises 32 per cent of the cost of export operations.[166]

In order to tackle this problem, several regional efforts have been put in place to develop intra-regional and inter-regional road network systems. For example, SADC has several projects in place to enable the establishment of transit development corridors among Member States, such as the Kazangula Bridge connecting Botswana, Zambia and Zimbabwe. The main objective of this project is to allow free flow of traffic by road and rail across the Zambezi River.[167]

Other regional transport integration initiatives include the Sub-Saharan Africa Transport Programme (SSATP), New Partnership for Africa's Development (NEPAD) and Almaty Action Plan initiated by the Office of the High Representative for Least Developed Landlocked Developing and Small Developing Island Countries (OHRLLS).[168]

The SSATP in particular is an excellent example of inter-regional integration in transport services involving multiple RECs and international organizations. The SSATP is made up of 15 public and private sector regional and sub-regional organizations and the following RECs: CEMAC, COMESA, EAC, ECCAS, ECOWAS, IGAD, SADC and UEMOA.[169] The main objective of the SSATP is to improve transport services in the partner states through policy reform and institutional transformation, in order to facilitate economic growth and reduce poverty in these countries.[170]

At regional levels, individual countries are also contemplating entering into agreements on customs and transport infrastructure. Recently, Tanzania sent a delegation to landlocked Uganda, to lobby Uganda to give Tanzania its container and goods logistics market which is currently handled through the port of Mombasa in Kenya. In the scenario that Tanzania would like to see, Uganda's transit goods would arrive at the port of Dar es

166 *Ibid.* at Table 5. 167 SADC Consultative Conference, at 31.

168 ECOSOC, 'The Transport Situation in Africa', at s. 4.

169 World Bank, 'Sub-Saharan Africa Transport Policy Program Partners', http://web.worldbank.org/WBSITE/EXTERNAL/COUNTRIES/AFRICAEXT/EXTAFRREGTOPTRA/EXTAFRSUBSAHTRA/0,,contentMDK:20625619~menuPK:1586428~pagePK:64168445~piPK:64168309~theSitePK:1513930,00.html (last visited 25 Oct. 2010).

170 ECOSOC, 'The Transport Situation in Africa', at s. 4.

Salaam, Tanzania, and be transported via the Southern Corridor by rail, water and road, to Kampala, Uganda.[171] This proposal might not seem cost-efficient, as the distance between Dar es Salaam and Kampala is 600 kilometres more than the original route between Mombasa, Kenya, and Kampala. However, after the disruption in transport following Kenya's disputed presidential election in 2007, Uganda may be wise to bear the additional cost in order to ensure continuing service through Tanzania.[172] This may no longer be true since in August 2010, Kenyans overwhelmingly passed a new constitution in a referendum. The new constitution addresses many of the problems that resulted in post-election violence in early 2008.

2 Ports and maritime transport

Maritime transport is one of the most important modes of transport in Africa and accounts for 92 to 95 per cent of Africa's international trade.[173] Therefore, it follows that it is vital for Africa's economy, and indeed the world, to ensure that a high quality of maritime transport is maintained to allow free flow of trade. Unfortunately, Africa's 80 major ports are plagued with problems ranging from inadequate or outdated equipment, safety and inadequate facilitation and technical capacity.[174] In addition, 80 per cent of the ships used are more than 50 years old, while the global average is only about 15 per cent.[175]

Although Africa has many inland waterways, they are seldom used for international navigation, with the exception of the Congo, the Nile and the Zambezi basins, owing to the fact that the depth of these waterways remains unpredictable and therefore cannot be developed.[176]

L Other areas of regional integration

1 COMESA-EAC-SADC Free Trade Area[177]

While the third of the six stages to establish the AEC calls only for the establishment of a free trade area (FTA) within each REC,[178] the Tripartite Summit of the Heads of State and Government of COMESA, EAC and

171 C. Kazooba, 'Dar Offers to Move Uganda Cargo in New Affront to KPA Monopoly', *The East African*, 6 July 2009, www.theeastafrican.co.ke/news/-/2558/619284/-/r2baj3z/-/index.html (last visited 25 Oct. 2010).

172 *Ibid.* 173 ECOSOC, 'The Transport Situation in Africa', at s. 4.

174 *Ibid.* 175 *Ibid.* 176 *Ibid.*

177 COMESA-EAC-SADC Final Communiqué. 178 AEC Treaty, at Art. 6.2.

SADC, have made commitments to plan to establish an FTA constituted by Member States of each of the three RECs.[179]

The main aim of the Tripartite Summit was to ultimately allow the three RECs to merge into a single REC through regional integration in the following areas: trade, customs and economic integration;[180] and infrastructure development, including a seamless upper airspace and inter-regional ICT Broadband Infrastructure Network.[181]

Member States have taken some affirmative steps towards regional integration by cooperating in areas such as customs and border control issues. Customs agencies from twenty countries in East and Southern Africa met in Mombasa, Kenya, in 2009 to identify ways of increasing surveillance at border posts in order to prevent smuggling and transport of hazardous products.[182] Members who are also part of the World Customs Organization (WCO) may also share information.[183]

The treaties establishing each of the three RECs involved in this programme permit them to enter into agreements with other RECs in order to promote their integration objectives, as we saw earlier in the chapter. The establishment of the COMESA-EAC-SADC FTA is therefore a first step in the direction of regional integration that would fast-track the establishment of the AEC. A task force has prepared a framework for the formation of the FTA.[184] This framework addresses a number of issues including rules of origin, development of infrastructure and creation of a working regime.[185] The COMESA-EAC-SADC FTA will cover the length of Africa, from Cape Town to Cairo, involve more than 527 million people and have an estimated combined gross domestic product (GDP) of $624 billion.[186] The FTA would therefore consist of economies of varying sizes and affluence.

179 COMESA-EAC-SADC Final Communiqué, at para. 14(i).

180 *Ibid.* at para. 14. 181 *Ibid.* at para. 16.

182 G. Kihara, 'Regional Customs Agencies Meet Over Border Surveillance', *Business Daily*, 10 July 2009, www.businessdailyafrica.com/-/539552/621756/-/567h5j/-/index.html (last visited 25 Oct. 2010).

183 *Ibid.*

184 'Roadmap for Grand Free Trade Area in Pipeline', *Tanzania Daily News*, 6 July 2010, www.tralac.org/cgi-bin/giga.cgi?cmd=cause_dir_news_item&cause_id=1694&news_id=89402&cat_id=1061 (last visited 25 Oct. 2010). In April 2008, the task force had raised over $1.3 billion for the formation of the FTA through a fund-raising event that had attracted international development agencies and organizations. *Ibid.*

185 *Ibid.*

186 A. Odhiambo, 'Kenya Proposes Ways of Merging Trade Blocs', *Business Daily*, 25 Feb. 2010, www.tralac.org/cgi-bin/giga.cgi?cmd=cause_dir_news_item&cause_id=1694&news_id=82768&cat_id=1074 (last visited 2 July 2010).

The more economically strong members of the FTA, such as South Africa and Egypt, are likely to be its leading beneficiaries.[187] To ensure that benefits of the FTA are equitably shared, a proposal has been floated that a flexible framework that would accommodate the needs of the individual countries participating in the grand FTA negotiations would be ideal.[188] There is also a proposal that transitional measures that take into account existing market access conditions among the countries of the three RECs, including Economic Partnership Agreements (EPAs) signed with the EU, help weaker economies to adjust to the adversity that may come with the formation of the grand FTA.[189] Such calls for flexibility, as we saw in the first three chapters of this book, are a central theme in regional integration initiatives in Africa.

2 *The East Africa Migration Route Programme*

The East Africa Migration Route Programme was created to address the challenges faced by the countries of origin, transit and destination with regard to migration management issues, especially illegal migration.[190] The Programme was created by IGAD, the African Union Commission (AUC) and the International Organization for Migration (IOM), with funding from the European Commission (EC) and the governments of Italy, Malta, Netherlands and the UK.[191] Although the focus is mainly on IGAD states, non-Member States – namely Chad, Egypt, Libya, Niger, Tunisia and Yemen – also participate in the Programme.[192]

The objectives of the Programme are to establish a Migration Resource Centre and to create a Regional Consultative Process (RCP) to exchange information and best practices of migration management.[193] The latter objective was accomplished with the establishment of the IGAD Regional

187 *Ibid.* 188 *Ibid.* 189 *Ibid.*

190 IGAD, 'The East Africa Migration Route: Building Co-operation, Information Sharing and Developing Joint Practical Initiatives Amongst Countries of Origin, Transit, and Destination', 27 July 2010, at 1, available at http://igad.int/index.php?option=com_content&view=article&id=231&Itemid=160 (last visited 25 Oct. 2010) (hereinafter 'East Africa Migration Route').

191 IGAD, 'Addressing Migration Challenges in Eastern Africa', 27 June 2008, http://igad.int/index.php?option=com_content&view=article&id=228:addressing-migration-challenges-in-eastern-africa-&catid=63:migration&Itemid=159 (last visited 25 Oct. 2010).

192 *Ibid.* 193 *Ibid.*

Consultative Process on Migration in May 2008.[194] The former objective was accomplished in May 2009, when IOM established a local office in Djibouti.[195]

Irregular migration poses many challenges including health and safety issues, human trafficking and overpopulation, particularly in countries of transit. Tackling illegal migration in a holistic approach by involving countries of origin, transit and destination will help to effectively address these challenges and promote regional integration and the objectives of the IGAD region as enumerated in its treaty. Therefore, IGAD's involvement in the East Africa Migration Route Programme, with other international organizations and non-Member States, is permitted under its establishing treaty.

M Conclusions

This chapter shows that trade integration between African RECs is picking up pace. The legal framework for cooperation between the regions already exists and the ultimate goal of an AEC is projected to be achieved by early in the fourth decade of the twenty-first century at the latest. To achieve that goal, African countries have put in place a variety of programmes and projects to cooperate in areas as diverse as air and road transport, as well as in agriculture. These programmes and projects are partly funded by African governments, but others are financed by external funders. Perhaps the most ambitious intra-regional trade initiative is the proposed EAC, SADC, COMESA FTA. Such an FTA would link three disparate RECs and potentially open up much of Africa to regional trade on an unprecedented scale.

194 'The Declaration of the Establishment of the IGAD Regional Consultative Process on Migration', Inter-State and Intra-Regional Cooperation on Migration Management Workshop Report, 14 May 2008, at 61.

195 IGAD, 'Djibouti/IOM Office Opens To Help Address Migration Challenges Along Strategic Route', 13 May 2009, http://igad.int/index.php?option=com_content&view=article&id=230:djibouti–iom-office-opens-to-help-address-migration-challenges-along-strategic-route-&catid=63:migration&Itemid=159 (last visited 21 Aug. 2009).

XI

African RTA relations with non-African RTAs

A Introduction

This chapter examines trade agreements between African regional trade areas and non-African trade areas. Some agreements are not finalized yet. Examples of agreement that are yet to be finalized include Economic Partnership Agreements between various African countries, either individually or as members of a regional group, on the one hand, and the European Union, on the other. In addition, there are free trade agreements (FTAgs) being negotiated between African regional groups like the East African Community, on the one hand, and the United States, on the other. Several agreements have been finalized and these will be discussed. There are several bilateral treaties, including those relating to investment signed between individual African countries and their non-African trading partners, including China and certain Latin American countries, among others. The goal of this chapter is to provide a sense of the types of trade agreements African regions have entered into or are entering into with their non-African trading partners. As the chapter shows, a common feature of these is that they often embody trade commitments in areas such as services and investment measures which are traditionally not areas in which intra-African trade agreements, until recently, have been concerned about. In addition, many of the agreements such as the Economic Partnership Agreements are moving away from preferential measures towards full reciprocity. Perhaps as an extreme example, some of the agreements now incorporate WTO-Plus obligations. The best example of this is the US–Morocco FTAg under which Morocco agreed to extremely broad protections of intellectual property rights beyond those it has committed itself under the TRIPS Agreement. An example of such a WTO-Plus protection includes data exclusivity protection that prevents generic competitors from using clinical trial data. Another example is the prohibition of registration of competing generics prior to the expiry of the period of patent protection.

While the US–Morocco FTAg illustrates the success of a non-African trading partner prevailing in enshrining its interests in an FTAg, SACU provides a contrasting example. Unlike Morocco, SACU declined to sign the standard US FTAg precisely because of the stringent intellectual property protections that the United States sought. These are some of the major issues highlighted in this chapter. Many of the issues that I address here are, however, moving targets, as negotiations particularly on the Economic Partnership Agreements, continue in many regions and the final outcome will not be known until these agreements have been signed, ratified and the commitments begin to be enforced.

B Trade Agreements between African RTAs and Europe

1 EU FTAg: The Cotonou Agreement and the dawn of Economic Partnership Agreements

Economic Partnership Agreements (EPAs) are FTAgs in the process of being negotiated between the European Union (EU) and Africa-Caribbean-Pacific (ACP) within the framework of the Cotonou Agreement.[1] As an essential part of the Cotonou Agreement,[2] EPAs have the following development objectives: poverty reduction, promotion of sustainable development and facilitating the integration of ACP countries into the global economy through trade.[3]

The EPAs are built around four pillars. The first is partnership. EPAs outline rights and obligations for both the EU and the ACP countries and their success is dependent upon compliance with the agreement by both sides. The second is regional integration initiatives in the ACP community, which are an essential step toward integration into the global economy. The third pillar is development, regarded as the central focus of EPAs. To do this, EPAs were to be designed to take into account the economic, social, and political limitations of the ACP countries, while ensuring their integration into the development policies of these countries. Lastly, EPAs were regarded as a springboard for the ACP countries to integration into the global economy through linkage to the World Trade Organization (WTO).

1 'International And Regional Trade Relation: EU-ACP, Economic Partnership Agreements', *Europa*, www.delbrb.ec.europa.eu/en/irtr/euacp_repa.htm (last visited 25 Oct. 2010) (hereinafter 'International and Regional Trade Relation').

2 Cotonou Agreement, 23 June 2000, art. 37.1, available at http://ec.europa.eu/development/icenter/repository/agr01_en.pdf.

3 International and Regional Trade Relation.

The EU and ACP countries agreed to negotiate EPAs pursuant to Article 36 of the Cotonou Agreement in 2000. The goal was to use the EPAs to design trading arrangements that were compatible with the rules of the WTO by progressively removing 'barriers to trade between them and enhancing cooperation in all areas relevant to trade'.[4] Since 2007 the negotiations of the EPAs in essence have sought to end non-reciprocal trade preferences that ACP countries enjoyed from the EU. These preferences are being ended, since the WTO waiver of the Most Favoured Nation norm that allowed their existence expired at the end of 2007.[5] EPA negotiations have not been concluded in many of the ACP regions.[6]

Since reciprocal trading relationships are the defining feature of EU-ACP negotiations, it is important to be cognizant of the experience of developing countries the last time they assumed broad ranging trade commitments. In 1994 at the conclusion of the Uruguay Round, several new trade treaties came into effect, including in the areas of intellectual property and trade in services. Research since then has shown that the cost of implementing these new treaties far outweighed the dynamic benefits the treaties would confer on developing countries.[7] Further, this research showed that the trade-liberalization mandates contained in these new trade treaties were working at cross-purpose with the World Bank's poverty reduction programmes.[8] Such an impact on new trade commitments made by ACP states would almost certainly adversely affect poverty elimination programmes and invariably make it harder for ACP countries to meet social and economic rights obligations to their citizens.

(a) EPA negotiations

The EPAs are being negotiated by ACP countries on a regional basis, although ratification will be on a bilateral level.[9] EPA negotiations have

4 Cotonou Agreement, at Arts 36(1) and 34(4).

5 Art. 37(1) provides that EPAs 'shall be negotiated during the preparatory period which shall end by 31 December 2007'.

6 Arts 35(2) and 37(5) provide a basis for conducting EPA negotiation with the regions rather than bilaterally as part of the Cotonou Agreement's goal of strengthening regionalism as a strategy of integrating ACP countries better within the international trading system.

7 J.M. Finger and P. Schuler, 'Implementation of Uruguay Round Commitments: The Development Challenge', 1, World Bank Working Paper No. 2215, 1 Oct. 1999 available at www.wds.worldbank.org/external/default/WDSContentServer/IW3P/IB/2001/02/10/000094946_01013005324822/Rendered/PDF/multi_page.pdf (last visited 25 Oct. 2010).

8 *Ibid.*

9 Article 35(2) of the Cotonou Agreement provides that 'economic and trade cooperation shall build on regional integration initiatives of ACP States, bearing in mind that regional integration is a key instrument for integration of ACP countries into the world economy'.

raised a number of issues, including: market access commitments in the EPAs; capacity building and technical support in the EPAs; human rights implications and incorporation of Singapore issues in the EPAs.

ACP countries have difficulties making market access commitments to the EU because of different interpretations of the obligation in Article XXIV of the WTO's General Agreement on Tariffs and Trade (GATT) (1994) to 'substantially liberalize all trade'.[10] ACP states are construing this provision in a manner that allows them not to make concessions on market access with respect to areas of their economies, like in agriculture and in particular sensitive products where they would not be able to compete effectively with the more superior EU agricultural sector. The argument of the ACP countries is that they are not ready to compete on a level playing field in areas of their economy that would essentially be decimated by EU competitors unless there is phased implementation of the commitments. The basis for this accommodation that the ACP countries are seeking is the commitment in Article 37(7) of the Cotonou Agreement, which obliges the EU 'to improve market access for ACP countries'. The EU has shown little inclination to give ACP countries more access. Lack of market access or reductions of levels of current market access for ACP countries after the expiry of the non-reciprocal arrangements is going to result in losses of revenue and export opportunities in a manner that will adversely impact the social and economic rights of those affected.

West African countries are fully aware of the advantages of gaining access to the EU market,[11] but are not willing to enter into an agreement that would be unfavourable to national interests.[12] While African countries may have gained political independence from their former colonial powers decades ago, some critics view the EPAs as a tool used by the EU to facilitate the *neo*-colonization of Africa.[13] Economic benefits of the

10 Final Report of the Meeting of Legal Experts of the ACP on EPA Negotiations, 9–11 Oct. 2007, ACP/00/051/07 Rev. 1, para. 4.3, available at www.africa-union.org/root/UA/Conferences/2007/octobre/TI/ 11%20oct 0005107%20Rev1%20Report%20ACP%20Legal%20Experts%20(3).doc (last visited 25 Oct. 2010) (hereinafter 'Meeting of ACP Legal Experts').

11 'We Won't Sign Bogus Trade Pacts', *Daily Graphic*, 22 July 2009, www.modernghana.com/news/228802/1/we-won039t-sign-bogus-trade-pacts.html (last visited 25 Oct. 2010), where the Ghanaian Minister of Trade and Industry, Ms. Hannah Tetteh, informed the press of the importance of having access to the EU market in the horticultural sector, the cocoa processing sector and canned fish and processed food products sector.

12 'EPA: A Carrot for Africa', *Daily Trust*, 31 July 2009, available at http://allafrica.com/stories/200907310388.html (last visited 25 Oct. 2010). Nigeria, constituting two-thirds of the continent's market, hesitated over signing a dubious and controversial EPA.

13 *Ibid.*

EPA are considered to be very one-sided, favouring the EU much more than Africa.[14] Many of the commitments are regarded as unlikely to fulfil the commitment to development which is a central pillar of the Cotonou Agreement.[15] For example, market liberalization under the EPA would result in lost income in import taxes, which is an important source of income for many West African countries. In addition, it is unlikely that African goods will be able to compete favourably in European markets, as they will have to compete with brands that already command consumer familiarity, confidence and taste, thus further potentially lowering the value of the EPA to West Africa.[16]

Negotiations in Central Africa have not fared better either. Despite concessions made by Central Africa in recent negotiations, the EU has remained inflexible on many issues being negotiated, particularly in the area of liberalization in trade of goods.[17] While Central Africa has offered to raise the percentage of market access liberalization from 60 per cent to 71 per cent over a 20-year period, the EU has refused to budge from its position of 80 per cent market access liberalization over a 15-year period.[18]

None of the draft EPAs contains binding commitments on capacity building and technical support, yet 'lack of capacity to conduct complex negotiations' within the tight time frame for concluding EPA negotiations[19] has been a major barrier in various ACP regions.[20] The right of the ACP to participate effectively in the EPA negotiations will therefore be undermined by their lack of capacity to effectively participate. This is also inconsistent with the right to participate in formulating policies relating to development anticipated in the Declaration on the Right to Development.[21]

14 *Ibid.* 15 *Ibid.* 16 *Ibid.*

17 Platform of Central African Non-State Actors, 'Why EPA Negotiations Have Slowed: A Central African Perspective', *Trade Negotiations Insights* 8(2) March 2009, http://ictsd.net/i/news/tni/42036/ (last visited 25 Oct. 2010).

18 *Ibid.*

19 J. Kelsey, 'Going Nowhere in a Hurry? The Pacific's EPA Negotiations with the European Union', *Wellington Law Review* 38 (2007) 81.

20 Meeting of ACP Legal Experts. Notably, capacity building in trade negotiations is an objective specified in Art. 34(3) of the Cotonou Agreement.

21 UN Human Rights Council, High Level Task Force on the Implementation of the Right to Development, Working Group on the Right to Development, 'The Cotonou Partnership Agreement Between European Union (EU) and African, Caribbean and Pacific (ACP) Countries', para. 1, UN Doc. A/HRC/8/WG.2/TF/CRP.6 (21 Dec. 2007) (prepared by James Thuo Gathii).

The EU has sought to include a set of new generation issues for trade known as the Singapore issues. These new issues that are currently not part of the multilateral treaty framework of the WTO are: rules regulating government procurement; rules regarding competition law in the WTO; rules regarding trade facilitation such as those aiming to ensure that ports effectively and efficiently process imports and exports; and rules relating to liberalizing foreign investment. Developing countries objected to expanding the trade agenda to these new areas before they had fully implemented their previous commitments following the end of the Uruguay Round in 1994. As such, in the context of the Doha Round of negotiations, developing countries managed to secure a commitment that these issues would be negotiated only if there was 'explicit consensus' to proceed with negotiations on these issues. ACP states regard the EU's pushing of these issues as trying to achieve in the context of EPAs a trade agenda that they cannot in the WTO. While negotiations on competition policy are contemplated in Article 45 of the Cotonou Agreement, negotiations on government procurement are not expressly contemplated as a negotiating item in the Agreement. Yet, there are ongoing negotiations on government procurement in the various EPAs. These additional commitments will, if included in the EPAs, cost ACP countries much more in the short term than any gains they may reap from these commitments. These additional costs will affect the ability of ACP states to provide budgetary support for sectors like education and health as well as other human rights obligations. Further, commitments in government procurement will require ACP states to source goods and services to corporations other than their own – thereby undermining their ability to support local companies and in effect keep their revenue to support the domestic economy.[22]

Although consultation of all stakeholders, including non-state actors, is anticipated in the Cotonou Agreement, this has been a source of concern. In Kenya, a suit was filed by a Small Scale Farmers Association and a human rights organization seeking to prevent the government from signing the East African (ESA) EPA, primarily on the basis that negotiations on the ESA EPA have not widely consulted all stakeholders.[23]

At an EPA negotiation meeting, one EU official argued that '[t]he European Commission's mandate is to negotiate a trade agreement, not a

22 This is inconsistent with the Declaration on the Right to Development's premise of self-determination in economic management. *Ibid.*

23 M. Agutu, 'Lobby Files Suit to Stop EU Pact', *Daily Nation*, 27 Oct. 2007.

cooperation for development agreement'.[24] Thus, although one of the primary negotiating pillars of EPAs is development, the EU has not always regarded development with the seriousness with which ACP countries have. As result, in the SADC region, Angola, Namibia and South Africa have emerged as a separate configuration known as ANSA in the EPA negotiations, united in their scepticism of the current provisions of the EPA.[25] Namibia has asked Europe to stop its '"bully" trade negotiations', and declared that it would not sign the interim agreement until contentious issues were resolved and the changes reflected in the agreement.[26] Some commentators have argued that the EPAs have become a new opportunity for Europe to give its large businesses another go at the African market.[27]

The process of negotiating EPAs among African countries has also been contentious. For example, the signing of an Interim Economic Partnership Agreement (IEPA) by three of the five SACU members – Botswana, Lesotho and Swaziland – could tear apart the oldest customs union on the continent.[28] The main reasons that these states chose to sign an interim agreement were (a) to diversify trade and investment, and (b) to move away from their dependence on South African subsidies.[29] Botswana and South Africa, especially, do not see eye-to-eye on issues such as 'foreign policy orientation'. This became increasingly evident under the Mbeki administration as tensions escalated regarding the policy toward Zimbabwe.[30] The EU's insistence on the Most Favoured Nation (MFN) clause has not helped the situation either. The MFN clause would require South Africa, and other African states, to offer identical market access terms that it offers to other emerging markets such as Brazil and India, to all EPA signatories as well.[31] South Africa Department of Trade (DTI) International Trade and Economic Development Deputy Director-General, Xavier Carim, also stated that unless differences in

24 Platform of Central African Non-State Actors, 'Why EPA Negotiations Have Slowed: A Central African Perspective'.

25 S. Johnstad (ed.), 'Namibia: Caught in Stand-Off Between South Africa and EU', Inter Press Service, 20 Aug. 2009, available at www.afrika.no/Detailed/18623.html (last visited 25 Oct. 2010).

26 M. Bakare, 'Europe's EPA Condemned as it Tears Africa Apart: Now Africans Are Hitting Back at Europe', *Afrik* (4 June 2009) available at http://en.afrik.com/article15771.html (last visited 25 Oct. 2010).

27 *Ibid.*

28 P. Draper and N. Khumalo, 'The Future of the Southern African Customs Union', *Trade Negotiations Insights* 8(6) (August 2009), available at http://ictsd.net/i/news/tni/52394/ (last visited 25 Oct. 2010).

29 *Ibid.* 30 *Ibid.* 31 *Ibid.*

the trade regimes, such as tariffs and rules of origin, between the South African FTA with the EU and the EPA, are addressed, 'SACU itself, and the coherence of SACU [will be] undermined.'[32]

(b) How is development incorporated in the EPAs?

ACP states have consistently noted that the EU has not shown adequate attention to the development chapters of the EPAs.[33] Many ACP states have expressed reservations at the heavy pressure of the EU on them to sign the EPAs, even while they may not represent the best interests of ACP countries.[34] The EPAs were scheduled to be implemented by 1 January 2008. However, due to lack of agreement in negotiations between the EU and the ACP, the EPAs were not concluded within the specified period and both parties decided instead to enter into 'interim agreements' that conformed to WTO rules dictating trade in goods.[35]

'Development' remains the major theme of the EPA negotiations for the ECOWAS region. When it became clear that an agreement would not be concluded by 31 December 2007, ECOWAS negotiators identified several areas including 'joint definition of the EPA support measures and their funding by the European Commission', as an area to be negotiated as a precondition for signing the EPA.[36] West African states argued they were committed to establishing support measures, such as the EPA Development Programme (PAPED), to enable the EPA to become 'a tool for development'.[37] PAPED would focus on the following five strategic areas: diversification and growth of production capacity; developing intra-regional trade and facilitating access to international markets; improvement and strengthening of trade-related infrastructure; carrying

32 C. Van Der Merwe, 'EU Trade Agreements Undermine Regional Integration, Says SA Official', *Engineering News*, 3 August 2009.

33 African Union, 'Addis Ababa Declaration on Economic Partnership Agreement Negotiations', Report of the Conference of Ministers of Trade of the African Union, 15–16 January 2007, Ext/Exp/Trade/Decl.(2) III, available at www.uneca.org/eca_resources/news/2007/EPA_Addis_Ababa_Ministerial_Declaration.pdf (last visited 21 Aug. 2010).

34 UN Conference on Ministers of Trade, 'Nairobi Declaration on Economic Partnership Agreements', TI/TIMIN/MIN/Decl.2 (IV), 14 Apr. 2006, available at www.africa-union.org/root/AU/Conferences/Past/2006/April/TI/Nairobi%20Declaration%20on%20EPAs.pdf (last visited 21 Aug. 2010).

35 Europa, 'Fact Sheet on the Interim Economic Partnership Agreements', http://trade.ec.europa.eu/doclib/docs/2009/january/tradoc_142188.pdf (last visited 25 Oct. 2010).

36 'EPA: A Carrot for Africa'.

37 CTA Agritrade, 'Executive Brief: EU-West Africa EPA Negotiations, March 2009', at 10, available at http://agritrade.cta.int/en/content/view/full/1790#31 (last visited 25 Oct. 2010).

out necessary adjustments and consideration of other trade-related needs; implementation and monitoring and assessment of the EPA.[38]

However, according to the President of the ECOWAS Commission, Mohammed Ibn Chambas, the EPA negotiations stalled partly due to the fact that a definite position on the sources of funding for PAPED could not be determined.[39]

Like West Africa, 'development' is the central theme around which the CEMAC-EU EPA negotiations are expected to continue; however, the negotiations have slowed down due to several reasons. The EU has moved back on several development aspects of the EPA.[40] For example, it has ignored the agreement of a 'roadmap for strengthening capacities and developing central African economies'.[41] The European Commissioners and Ministers have not signed this agreement either.[42] Additionally, while the two parties have agreed that the Central African countries should be compensated for lost tax revenue following the dismantling of tariff barriers, the EU has been reluctant to consider the individual economic and political situations of each country, despite Central Africa's efforts to provide a simplified method that would allow for such considerations.[43]

(c) The interim ESA–EC EPA

The interim Eastern and Southern Africa (ESA) EPA eliminates duties placed on goods originating in ESA states.[44] It also allows ESA states to maintain existing duties on goods originating in the EU.[45] ESA states are prohibited from instituting any new duties and the EU shall be granted the same treatment as those of MFNs in other trade agreements.[46] Under the agreement, the EU maintains safeguards that allow temporary suspension of preferential treatment to ESA states in the event that increased quantities of ESA goods pose a substantial threat to domestic industries in the EU.[47]

This interim EPA has provisions for the removal of any quantitative restrictions on trade.[48] It seeks to ensure that once EU goods enter ESA

38 *Ibid.*

39 'EPA: A Carrot for Africa'. The article incorrectly spells Dr. Chambas's last name as 'Chambers'.

40 Platform of Central African Non-State Actors, 'Why EPA Negotiations Have Slowed: A Central African Perspective'.

41 *Ibid.* 42 *Ibid.* 43 *Ibid.*

44 Interim Economic Partnership Agreement Between Eastern and Southern African States and European Community, 29 Aug. 2009, art. 11, www.investmauritius.com/download/ESA-EPA-INTERIM.pdf (last visited 25 Oct. 2010) (hereinafter 'ESA-EC IEPA').

45 *Ibid.* at art. 12. 46 *Ibid.* at arts 15–16.

47 *Ibid.* at arts 20–1. 48 *Ibid.* at art. 17.

states they are not subject to any indirect taxation and are granted the same treatment as domestic products.[49] Administrative cooperation is encouraged.[50] In the event that the provisions regarding administrative cooperation are not observed, the interim EPA allows the EU to temporarily suspend any preferential treatment.

The EPA recognizes that fisheries constitute a key economic resource in ESA states and strives to develop this sector of ESA economies.[51] The EPA has provisions for special and differential treatment to ESA fisheries and for preferential access into the international market.[52] Similar provisions encourage the development of marine fisheries and inland fisheries.[53] The EPA also aims to diversify ESA economies. It has provisions to encourage development in other areas of the private sectors.[54] For example, there are provisions for the development of industry and secure investment climates within ESA states.[55] It also seeks to promote mining and tourism services in these states.[56]

The interim EPA does contain some provisions concerning the development of innovations systems and modern standards of environmental protection. It addresses the production of renewable sources of energy in ESA states.[57] It seeks to promote the development of information and communications technologies.[58] Some consideration is given to bringing ESA states up to international standards with regard to environmental issues.[59]

(d) Status of EPA negotiations

EPA negotiations between the EU and West Africa (consisting of 16 countries) had commenced in 2003. By December 2007, Ivory Coast and Ghana agreed to an IEPA with the EU in order to prevent disruption in trade when the Cotonou Agreement expired that month.[60] The EPA negotiations with West Africa were expected to continue in two phases: the first phase, an agreement covering trade in goods, some trade rules and development cooperation were expected to

49 *Ibid.* at art. 18.
50 Interim Economic Partnership Agreement Between Eastern and Southern African States and the European Community at art. 22.
51 *Ibid.* at arts 25–6. 52 *Ibid.* at art. 29. 53 *Ibid.* at arts 30–5.
54 *Ibid.* at art. 39. 55 *Ibid.* at arts 40–1. 56 *Ibid.* at arts 43–4.
57 *Ibid.* at art. 47. 58 *Ibid.* at art. 48. 59 *Ibid.* at arts 49, 51.
60 Europa, Africa, Asia, Pacific Regional Negotiations of Economic Partnership Agreements, ec.europa.eu/trade/issues/bilateral/regions/acp/regneg_en.htm (last visited 25 Aug. 2010) (hereinafter 'Africa, Asia, Pacific Regional EPA Negotiations').

be finalized by October 2009, and the second phase, negotiations covering trade in services and other trade-related issues, that commenced in January 2010.[61]

Central Africa consists of the CEMAC trade bloc and São Tomé and Príncipe.[62] In February 2009, Cameroon and the EU entered into an IEPA.[63] Negotiations for a full EPA continue at the regional level, but have stalled for a number of reasons.[64] EPA negotiations between ESA and the EU began in 2004 and by April 2009, Seychelles, Zambia, Zimbabwe, Mauritius, Comoros, and Madagascar had signed interim agreements with the EU.[65] Ethiopia did not sign an IEPA and is still trading with the EU under the Everything But Arms (EBA) regime.[66] An EPA is not expected to be of any great advantage over the current EBA regime for Ethiopia.[67] However, negotiation for a full EPA with the ESA states was expected to be concluded by the end of 2009.[68]

The EU and the EAC, consisting of Kenya, Uganda, Tanzania, Rwanda and Burundi, signed an interim agreement in April 2009.[69] Negotiations for a full EPA were expected to be concluded in July 2009; however, they came to a halt when the EU introduced other voluntary trade-related issues including government procurement, environment and sustainable development to the negotiations.[70] The EAC is reluctant to enter into a final EPA before these issues are finalized under the WTO talks on trade.[71] The EAC is also dissatisfied with the development aspects of the agreement and is unwilling to proceed before these issues are addressed.[72]

61 *Ibid.* 62 *Ibid.*

63 EU–Cameroon Interim Economic Partnership Agreement, 2 Feb. 2009, eur-lex.europa.eu/LexUriServ/ LexUriServ.do?uri=OJ:L:2009:057:0002:0360:EN:PDF (last visited 25 Oct. 2010).

64 'Why EPA Negotiations Have Slowed: A Central African Perspective'. The Platform of Central African Non-State Actors (PANEAC) is a non-governmental organization (NGO).

65 'EPA Negotiations: Where Do we Stand? – Eastern and Southern Africa', 26 May 2009, available at www.acp-eu-trade.org/index.php?loc=epa/ (last visited 25 Oct. 2010) (hereinafter 'ESA EPA Negotiations').

66 'EPA Negotiation Issues Between ESA and EU', *CTA Agritrade*, April 2010, available at agritrade.cta.int/en/Resources/Agritrade-documents/Agriculture-Executive-briefs/EPA-negotiation-issues-between-ESA-and-the-EU (last visited 25 Oct. 2010).

67 *Ibid.* 68 Africa, Asia, Pacific Regional EPA Negotiations.

69 ESA EPA Negotiations.

70 G. Obulutsa, 'East Africa May Delay Trade Pact with EU', *The New Vision*, 29 July 2009, available at www.newvision.co.ug/D/1/10/689543 (last visited 25 Oct. 2010).

71 *Ibid.*

72 'EAC Right on Trade Deal', *Business Daily*, editorial, 4 Aug. 2010, available at www.businessdailyafrica.com/Opinion%20&%20Analysis/-/539548/634464/-/item/0/-/1425pex/-/index.html (last visited 25 Oct. 2010).

As of June 2009, four of the fifteen members of the SADC region – namely, Botswana, Lesotho, Swaziland, and Mozambique entered into IEPA agreements with the EU.[73] Namibia had initialled an IEPA, but it will not sign it until outstanding issues are ironed out.[74] Although the EU currently has trade regimes with Angola and South Africa in place – namely, the EBA initiative with Angola and the Trade and Development Cooperation Agreement (TDCA) signed in 1999 with South Africa – it is also working with these countries to resolve outstanding issues in order to sign IEPAs with them.[75]

The EU–SADC EPA could also potentially remove differences between TDCA and the other SACU members and thus bring the region closer to a single trade regime with the EU. Such an outcome would be 'conducive to regional integration and economic development'.[76] However, the negotiation process has been a bumpy ride for the EC and South Africa, with both parties having walked away from the negotiations at critical moments.[77]

At present, the EPA negotiations are taking place in five separate configurations in Southern Africa.[78] Namibian Permanent Secretary in the Ministry, Calle Schlettwein, states that the Europeans' tried and tested strategy of 'divide and rule' has not helped current regional integration efforts in Southern Africa.[79] Additionally, according to Mr. Schlettwein, these separate negotiation configurations have made establishing a common external tariff for the 2010 SADC customs union impossible.[80]

2 *European Free Trade Area (EFTA)–Southern African Customs Union (SACU) FTA*[81]

The EFTA signed an FTAg with SACU in 2006. It came into force in May 2008.[82] The EFTA is made up of four European countries that are not part

73 Africa, Asia, Pacific Regional EPA Negotiations.

74 M. Bakare, 'Europe's EPA Condemned as it Tears Africa Apart: Now Africans Are Hitting Back at Europe'.

75 Africa, Asia, Pacific Regional EPA Negotiations.

76 A. Walker, 'The EC-SADC EPA: The Moment of Truth for Regional Integration', *Trade Negotiations Insight* 8(6), Aug. 2009, available at http://ictsd.org/i/news/tni/52416/ (last visited 25 Oct. 2010).

77 *Ibid.*

78 Johnstad (ed.), 'Namibia: Caught in Stand-Off Between South Africa and EU'.

79 *Ibid.* 80 *Ibid.*

81 Free Trade Agreement Between EFTA and SACU, July 2006, www.sacu.int/docs/tradeneg/efta-fta2006.pdf (last visited 25 Oct. 2010) (hereinafter 'SACU–EFTA FTA').

82 EFTA, 'Free Trade Agreement Between EFTA and SACU', 5 May 2008, www.efta.int/free-trade/free-trade-news/2008–05–05-efta-sacu-fta-enters-into-force.aspx (last accessed 25 Oct. 2010). See SACU–EFTA FTA.

of the EU – namely, Iceland, Liechtenstein, Norway and Switzerland.[83] As noted in Chapter V, SACU comprises five Southern African nations that also belong to the SADC regional trade bloc – namely, Botswana, Lesotho, Namibia, South Africa and Swaziland.[84] The EFTA–SACU Agreement is intended to liberalize trade in goods as required by WTO rules on RTAs.[85] At present, EFTA has completely liberalized trade in all goods by removing tariffs on imports from SACU countries, upon enforcement of the agreement in 2008; SACU, on the other hand, will gradually dismantle tariffs on EFTA exports by the year 2014.[86]

In addition to trade in goods, the EFTA–SACU FTA covers several areas, including the following: competition; intellectual property; services, investments, and government procurement; economic cooperation and technical assistance, in line with the objective of the agreement to promote economic and social development in the SACU region; and institutional and procedural provisions.[87] Clearly, this agreement has commitments that go beyond those which developing countries have agreed to negotiate in the Doha Round of WTO negotiations. For example, government procurement and competition are currently not part of the Doha negotiations. These two areas, as well as trade facilitation and investment measures, are known as the Singapore issues. The Doha Ministerial Statement of 2001 required explicit consensus as a precondition for negotiations on these issues. Without such an explicit consensus, which does not exist so far, developing countries have argued more important issues of concern to them like making development a central negotiating item as well as resolving outstanding implementation issues is key for them.[88]

The SACU–EFTA FTA was negotiated at the same time that SACU was negotiating an FTA with the United States. In both negotiations, intellectual property provisions became the most contested issues and SACU refused to make commitments in this area. During the negotiations between SACU and EFTA, there was heavy lobbying by NGOs to prevent the inclusion of stringent intellectual property (IP) provisions that would

83 EFTA, 'About EFTA, Member States', www.efta.int/about-efta/the-efta-states.aspx (last visited 1 June 2010).

84 Southern African Customs Union (SACU) Agreement 2002, Preamble, www.sacu.int/main.php?include=docs/legislation/2002-agreement/main.html (last visited 1 June 2010).

85 SACU–EFTA FTAg. 86 *Ibid.* 87 *Ibid.*

88 See J. Gathii, 'The High Stakes of WTO Reform', *Mich. L. Rev.* 104 (2006) 1361 (book review); 'Process and Substance in WTO Reform', *Rutgers L. Rev.* 56 (2004) 885.

restrict access to healthcare.[89] In fact, fifty-seven NGOs sent a letter to the foreign ministers of EFTA Member States imploring them not to include any provisions in the FTA that would restrict access to medicines.[90]

The final FTA did not contain any of the contentious provisions.[91] The IP section in the EFTA does not contain any substantive provisions, rather, it merely states that 'the Parties shall grant and ensure adequate . . . protection of intellectual property rights, and provide for measures for the enforcement . . . in accordance with the provisions of this Article and the obligations set out in the international agreements to which they are parties'.[92] One of the international agreements referred to is the TRIPS Agreement, with regard to exemptions from obligations.[93] This FTA is an excellent example of what a few states can achieve collectively – prevailing in keeping out TRIPS-plus provisions from the FTA – that might make it harder for them to continue their programmes on access to affordable medicines to their populations.

C Trade Agreements between African RTAs and the United States

1 *African Growth and Opportunities Act 2000*[94]

The May 2000 African Growth and Opportunities Act (AGOA), which has been amended four times, encourages African countries to liberalize their economies and to undertake free markets, and in return they are given preferential access to the US market for designated goods.[95] Access to the US market under this Act is considered even more liberal than access for countries with which the United States has free trade agreements; for

89 Berne Declaration, 'NGOs request "EFTA countries shall not endanger public health and food security in Southern Africa"', 4 Nov. 2004, available at www.evb.ch/index.cfm?page_id=3220 (last visited 25 Oct. 2010).

90 *Ibid.*

91 Berne Declaration, 'Southern African countries have taken a firm stand against EFTA demands on Intellectual Property Rights in Free Trade Agreement', 4 March 2005, www.liberationafrique.org/spip.php?article456 (last visited 21 Oct. 2010) ('South Africa's approach to trade negotiations is to always seek the best possible benefits for the country and for SACU in all areas under negotiation . . . As SACU and EFTA have not been able to arrive at mutually beneficial outcomes in our IPR discussions, we have agreed to suspend negotiating any substantive commitments in this area. As a result the final agreement will contain none of the IPR obligations referred to in [the NGOs'] letter').

92 SACU–EFTA FTAg. 93 *Ibid.*

94 Africa Growth and Opportunities Act, 19 U.S.C. ss. 3701–47 (2000) (hereinafter 'AGOA').

95 AGOA, 'Summary of AGOA', www.agoa.gov/agoa_legislation/agoa_legislation.html (last visited 25 Oct. 2010).

example, the United States offers zero import duty under the Generalized System of Preferences (GSP) to more than 6,400 items of which AGOA is part, consisting mostly of textiles and apparels,[96] exported from Sub-Saharan Africa to the United States, compared to the norm of 4,600 items under typical US FTAgs.[97]

AGOA contains provisions for trade facilitation and technical assistance to African producers.[98] It also directs the organization of a US–Sub-Saharan Africa Trade and Economic Forum (known as the AGOA forum) to facilitate dialogue between the two parties on trade, economics and investment.[99] The forum met for the eighth time since its inception, on 4 August 2009, in Nairobi, Kenya,[100] and attracted government delegates, business leaders and civil society, from AGOA-eligible countries and the United States, including US Secretary of State, Hillary Clinton.[101] One of the main focuses of the eighth AGOA forum was how to achieve its full potential.[102] Secretary Clinton addressed this issue by urging African nations to dismantle trade barriers and promote trade within the African continent.[103] She told the forum that 'progress will depend on good governance and adherence to the rule of law',[104] citing mounting corruption, poor leadership and the failure to invest in infrastructure by African nations as factors that decelerate progress and development in the region.[105]

The AGOA programme also faces several other challenges. The following are some of the problems faced by AGOA due to both internal and external factors:

- Termination of Article 2 of the WTO's Agreement on Textiles and Clothing (ATC) in January 2005 resulted in a decrease in apparel exports under AGOA, believed to have been caused by the inability of African

96 *Ibid.* 97 *Ibid.*

98 M.S. Kimenyi, 'African Growth and Opportunity Act: a Case of Vanishing Benefits', The Brookings Institution, 30 July 2009, available at www.brookings.edu/opinions/2009/0730_agoa_kimenyi.aspx (last visited 25 Oct. 2010).

99 AGOA, 'Summary of AGOA'.

100 'Kenya: Give Real Meaning to AGOA', *All Africa*, editorial, http://allafrica.com/stories/200908040985.html (last visited 25 Oct. 2010).

101 J. Kisero, 'Kenya: Opening of Agoa By Clinton Reaffirms Kenya's Regional Status', 4 Aug. 2009, http://allafrica.com/stories/200908040792.html (last visited 25 Oct. 2010).

102 Kimenyi, 'African Growth and Opportunity Act: a Case of Vanishing Benefits'.

103 M. Xuequan, 'U.S. Urges Africa to Break Trade Barriers', *AJ News*, 6 Aug. 2009, www.ajnews.co.kr/uhtml/read.jsp?idxno=200908061411440240113&section=S1N4 (last visited 25 Oct. 2010).

104 *Ibid.* 105 *Ibid.*

producers to compete in the global market without the quota-free advantage afforded by the ATC.

- Diversification of AGOA exports resulted in the textile and manufacturing industries imports being dwarfed by AGOA imports from the petroleum and mining sectors. Unfortunately, the petroleum and mining industries do not provide much employment opportunities for African workers.
- Small Business Participation accounts for about 55 per cent of the US GDP; however, very few in the small business community are aware of the AGOA programme, and therefore, there is very little partnership between small businesses in America and businesses in Africa.[106]

AGOA eligibility standards have been controversial since its inception. There is a view that the eligibility requirements must be strictly enforced to make certain that reforms are adhered to, and that minimum eligibility terms must be increased in order to protect investments.[107] Under AGOA, the President of the United States is required to certify countries wishing to participate in the programme.[108] The eligibility criteria require that an AGOA candidate 'has established, or is making continual progress toward establishing', the following standards:

> (A) a market-based economy that protects private property rights;
> (B) the rule of law, political pluralism and the right of due process, a fair trial and equal protection under the law;
> (C) the elimination of barriers to United States trade and investment; . . .
> (D) economic policies to reduce poverty, increase the availability of health care and educational opportunities; . . .
> (E) a system to combat corruption and bribery[; and] . . .
> (F) protection of internationally recognized worker rights, including the right of association, [and] the right to organize and bargain collectively.[109]

Several countries have lost their AGOA eligibility, including Eritrea and the Central African Republic in 2003, Ivory Coast in 2004 and more recently, Mauritania in 2009.[110] Presently eligible countries have had their share of problems; labour organizations in Lesotho complain of working conditions in newly developed textile plants, while Swaziland has been

106 V.C. Jones, 'U.S. Trade and Investment Relationship with Sub-Saharan Africa: The African Growth and Opportunities Act' (Congressional Research Service, 24 July 2009), http://fpc.state.gov/documents/organization/128835.pdf (last visited 25 Oct. 2010) (hereinafter 'AGOA Report').

107 *Ibid.* 108 AGOA, at s. 106. 109 *Ibid.*, at s. 104. 110 AGOA Report.

warned by the US State Department for not meeting AGOA's human rights standards.[111]

AGOA has had its success, although its critics claim that its success is limited. African exports to the United States have increased by more than 50 per cent since the enactment of AGOA.[112] Kenya was one of the AGOA-eligible nations to benefit considerably. It attained a large increase in its apparel and garment industry at the height of the AGOA boom.[113] However, Africa has yet to fully exploit the immense potential of the AGOA market. For instance, apparel exports from Bangladesh, a non-AGOA Asian country, to the United States, was more than double the exports of Sub-Saharan Africa.[114] African countries will only be able to enjoy the extended trade benefits if 'their capacity to produce and supply the U.S. market is enhanced'.[115] In order to achieve this enhanced capacity, AGOA should be consistent with the industrialization strategies of these countries.[116] Such strategies often recommend a 'selective, rather than a full-scale market liberalization'.[117]

D Free Trade Agreements

1 US–Morocco FTAg

Morocco is the sole African country to sign an FTAg individually with the United States.[118] Unlike the arduous FTAg negotiations with SACU, the United States concluded its negotiations and finalized an FTAg with Morocco within a year of initiating the negotiations in January 2003.[119] The FTAg was marketed as mutually beneficial, since it involved eliminating tariffs on more than 95 per cent of bilateral trade between the two countries, with the remaining tariffs scheduled to end in nine years.[120]

The FTAg has commitments on market access, agriculture, textiles and apparel, government procurement, investment, financial services and

111 *Ibid.*

112 Kisero, 'Kenya: Opening of Agoa By Clinton Reaffirms Kenya's Regional Status'.

113 *Ibid.* 114 *Ibid.*

115 J.M.M. Akech, 'The African Growth and Opportunity Act: Implications for Kenya's Trade and Development', *N.Y.U. J. Int'l L. & Pol.* 33 (2001) 651.

116 *Ibid.* 117 *Ibid.*

118 'Morocco Gets US Free Trade Deal', BBC News, 23 July 2004, http://news.bbc.co.uk/2/hi/africa/3920489.stm (last visited 21 Oct. 2010).

119 Embassy of the United States, 'US Embassy, U.S. Policy & Issues, United States and Morocco Sign Historic Free Trade Agreement', http://rabat.usembassy.gov/fta.html (last visited 25 Oct. 2010).

120 'Morocco Gets US Free Trade Deal'.

intellectual property rights (IPR), among many others.[121] The US pharmaceutical industry was particularly pleased with the IPR chapter in the Agreement, calling it 'the most advanced . . . in any FTA negotiated so far' and a benchmark for future agreements.[122] Some of the enhanced IPR features include the following clauses: ensuring extended terms of protection for copyright works; requiring governments to take steps to prohibit the marketing of pharmaceutical products infringing patents and notifying when the infringement is to be challenged; and criminalizing software piracy, among others.[123]

The United States does not do much trade with Morocco;[124] so the question remains 'Why Morocco?' Critics cynical of the Bush administration's sudden interest in securing an FTAg with a Muslim country, particularly following on the heels of the September 11 attacks and the 'War On Terror', believe that this odd partnership is no coincidence; rather, it is considered to be a contrived 'friendship' in order to achieve the political objective of 'pull[ing] a friendly North African country deeper into [the United States'] "sphere of influence"' and thereby creating a 'wedge vis-a-vis the Arab world'.[125] The US–Morocco FTAg was lauded as a stepping stone towards a full-scale Middle East FTAg (MEFTA), an agreement which is expected to be signed by 2013 and used as a vehicle to promulgate economic and political reform in the region – as part of the US's agenda of fighting terrorism with trade.[126]

2 TRIPS v. US FTAgs – effect of stringent IPR standards

The US–Morocco FTAg and the US–SACU FTA negotiations took place roughly within the same period of time and yet yielded dramatically different results. The SACU states refused to compromise their position on

121 Office of the United States Trade Representative, 'Morocco FTA', www.ustr.gov/trade-agreements/free-trade-agreements/morocco-fta/final-text (last visited 25 Oct. 2010).

122 US Commercial Service, 'Frequently Asked Questions', www.buyusa.gov/morocco/en/96.html (last visited 25 Oct. 2010).

123 *Ibid.*

124 R.J. Ahearn, 'Morocco-U.S. Free Trade Agreement,' CRS Report for Congress, 26 May 2005, 3, http://ftp.fas.org/sgp/crs/mideast/RS21464.pdf (last visited 21 Aug. 2010).

125 Grain, 'Morocco's FTA Frenzy', Africa and the Middle East, www.bilaterals.org/IMG/pdf/fightingFTA-en-Hi-2-f-morocco-fta-frenzy.pdf (last visited 25 Oct. 2010).

126 *Ibid.*

IPRs in particular, citing oversight difficulties,[127] whereas the IPR section in the Morocco FTAg was declared to be a shining example by the US pharmaceutical industry.[128] This section will focus on IPR-related clauses in the US–Morocco FTAg and contrast it with IPR standards under the Trade-Related Intellectual Property Rights (TRIPS) Agreement, focusing especially on how stringent patent requirements affect access to medicines in developing nations.

A brief overview of the IPR sections in FTAgs negotiated by the United States including US–Chile (2003), US–Jordan (2000), US–Morocco (2004), US–Singapore (2003) and the US–Central America FTAg (CAFTA–2004), which includes the Dominican Republic, shows that all of the aforementioned FTAgs have similar IPR building blocks, while some have identical text for certain clauses. The IPR section in all FTAgs begin with General Provisions and then address individual areas such as trade marks, geographical indications, domain names on the internet, copyrights and related rights, protection of encrypted programs carrying satellite signals, patents, measures relating to certain regulated products, enforcement of IPR and final or transitional provisions. The IPR section of the oldest of the five FTAgs, the US–Jordan FTA, has a considerably shorter text than the other four, and does not contain sections pertaining to domain names on the internet or protection of encrypted programs carrying satellite signals.

All FTAg arrangements entered into by the members of the WTO have to comply with the Doha Declaration on Trade-Related Aspects of Intellectual Property Rights and Public Health, signed in November 2001 by the WTO members.[129] However, the standards imposed by the United States with regard to patents on pharmaceutical products are much higher than those required under WTO standards and may serve to cut off access to inexpensive medicines.[130]

Oxfam International conducted an analysis of the five FTAgs mentioned above and identified five specific clauses that would prevent access

127 R. Mukumbira, 'US-SACU Free Trade Talks Hit Snags', Islamonline.net, 15 May 2006, www.bilaterals.org/spip.php?article4712 (last visited 25 Oct. 2010).

128 US Commercial Service, 'Frequently Asked Questions'.

129 Oxfam International, 'Undermining Access to Medicines: Comparison of Five US FTAs', Oxfam Briefing Note, June 2004, at 1–2, www.twnside.org.sg/title2/FTAs/Intellectual_Property/IP_and_Access_to_Medicines/UnderminingAccessToMedicines.pdf (last visited 25 Oct. 2010) (hereinafter 'Oxfam Briefing Note'). See also, J. Gathii, 'The Legal Status of the Doha Declaration on TRIPS and Public Health Under the Vienna Convention of the Law of Treaties', *Harv. J.L. & Tech.* 15 (2002) 291.

130 Oxfam Briefing Note, at 1.

to inexpensive, generic medicines. Each of these five clauses requires more stringent IPR standards than those called for under TRIPS. Commentators have typically labelled these provisions as 'TRIPS-plus' provisions. However, as Peter K. Yu notes, in order to better understand the impact of each of these provisions, it is important to study them under three categories: 'TRIPS-plus', 'TRIPS-extra', and 'TRIPS-restrictive'.[131]

TRIPS-plus provisions seek to 'increase the commitments of less developed countries by increasing the protection stated in the TRIPS Agreement'.[132] One example of a TRIPS-plus provision is patent term extension required by the United States in FTAgs. While Article 32 of the TRIPS Agreement provides only for a 20-year patent protection, US FTAgs with Chile, Singapore and Central America all contain provisions that extend patent protection past the TRIPS period.[133] Specifically, these provisions extend the patent term in order to accommodate delays in regulatory review of the product.[134] This extension would ultimately result in a delayed introduction of affordable generic medicines. A delay in affordable medicines in turn restricts access to healthcare.

TRIPS-extra provisions on the other hand, 'add [new] commitments that are not covered by the TRIPS Agreement'.[135] Examples of these include provisions that demand data exclusivity and patent-linkage with drug registration and approval.

Although Article 39.3 of the TRIPS Agreement provides that Member States are required to protect clinical data from 'unfair commercial use', it does not specify how each state should prevent such use. The United States decided to take the guesswork out by including provisions in FTAgs that specifically prevent generic companies from using clinical trial data generated by brand name companies.[136] Like patent extensions, this too has the potential to delay or prevent generic competition, invariably leading to higher-cost drugs that are less accessible in the health care system.[137]

Even though there is no link between patent status and regulatory approval in the TRIPS Agreement, the second example of TRIPS-extra

131 P.K. Yu, 'The International Enclosure Movement', *Ind. L. J.* 82 (2007) 827, 867.

132 *Ibid.* 133 Oxfam Briefing Note, at 6–7. 134 *Ibid.*

135 Yu, 'The International Enclosure Movement', at 868.

136 Agreement on Trade-Related Aspects of Intellectual Property Rights, 15 Dec. 1993, Marrakesh Agreement Establishing the World Trade Organization, Annex 1C, Legal Instruments – Results of the Uruguay Round, vol. 31, 33 ILM 81 (1994), art. 39.3, available at www.wto.org/english/tratop_e/trips_e/t_agm0_e.htm (last visited 25 Oct. 2010) (hereinafter 'TRIPS Agreement'); Oxfam Briefing Note, at 13.

137 *Ibid.* at 2.

provisions prevents generic versions of drugs from being registered by national drug registration authorities before the patent expires.[138] Advocates of healthcare argue that 'separation is appropriate, given the different goals of regulatory authorities (safety of medicines) and patent authorities (enforcement of IP)'.[139]

Heightened standards in the US FTAgs may certainly be beneficial to the US pharmaceutical companies who seek to profit from their inventions for as long as possible; however, developing nations that have to battle poverty and poor health simultaneously are prevented from providing access to affordable generic medicines to their populace due to these stringent IPR clauses. Individual countries may be more willing to sign FTAgs with the United States to reap potential trade benefits, but in the long run a careful study of US FTAgs would most likely indicate that potential costs may outweigh potential benefits.

3 *IPR provisions: EPAs v. US FTAgs*

Unlike the United States, the EU does not typically pursue TRIPS-plus provisions with developing countries. Notwithstanding this relatively laid-back approach to IP protection, the EU does call for some additional patent-related commitments in proposed EPAs with the ACP countries. First, it requires ACP countries to accept the obligations imposed by the Patent Cooperation Treaty (PCT) and the Patent Law Treaty (PLT), whose primary goal is to facilitate obtaining patents in signatory countries.[140] This could potentially open the floodgates to increased numbers of patent filing for both pharmaceutical products and processes, which may in turn restrict and delay generic competition.[141]

Second, the EU is also attempting to include strict enforcement mechanisms in the Agreement under the framework of Intellectual Property Enforcement Directive. These provisions have a low evidentiary standard, requiring only '*reasonably* available evidence to support [a patent holder's] claims', while enforcement mechanisms may include harsh measures such as 'the physical seizure of the infringing goods, and, in appropriate cases,

138 *Ibid.* at 16. 139 *Ibid.*

140 F.M. Abbott and J.H. Reichman, 'The Doha Round's Public Health Legacy: Strategies for the Production and Diffusion of Patented Medicines Under the Amended TRIPS Provisions', *J. Int'l Econ. L.* 10 (2007) 921, 965.

141 'At the very least, it affords originators a 30-month priority period during which investors in generic products cannot readily enter local markets, even if no patent applications have been filed.' *Ibid.* at 966.

the materials and implements used in the production and/or distribution of these goods'.[142]

One consequence for developing countries that are party to both US FTAgs with TRIPS-plus provisions, and EPAs with additional patent-related commitments, is that these commitments will significantly restrict the introduction of generic products and as such 'provide a very strong market dominant position for pharmaceutical originator companies'.[143]

E Trade and Investment Framework Agreements between the United States and African states

Trade and Investment Framework Agreements (TIFAs) serve as a stepping stone to future FTAgs and Bilateral Investment Treaties (BITs) between the United States and other countries. TIFAs are also known by different names, such as TIDCA. There is, in fact, a TIDCA between the United States and SACU, as we saw above. The goals of a TIFA or TIDCA are the same as those of an FTAg or BIT: to enhance opportunities for trade and investment, particularly for the non-African countries, and to deepen cooperation in development support, particularly for African countries.[144]

1 US–SACU Trade, Investment and Development Cooperative Agreement

The United States and SACU entered into a Trade, Investment and Development Cooperative Agreement (TIDCA) in July 2008, following five years of negotiations.[145] The negotiations were initially aimed at the creation of an FTAg between the two parties; however, in May 2006, SACU refused to enter into a 'one-size-fits-all' FTAg favoured by the United States, because from SACU's perspective, the United States failed to recognize the level of economic development within the region was not

142 *Ibid.* 143 *Ibid.* at 967.

144 Office of the United States Trade Representative, 'Trade and Investment Framework Agreements', www.ustr.gov/trade-agreements/trade-investment-framework-agreements (last visited 25 Oct. 2010).

145 W. Hongjiang, 'U.S., African Countries Sign First Trade Agreement', Xinhuanet, 16 July 2008, http://news.xinhuanet.com/english/2008–07/17/content_8558376.htm (last visited 25 Oct. 2010).

commensurate with signing such an agreement.[146] As a result, the two parties agreed on the TIDCA as a compromise in November 2006.[147]

The initial FTAg negotiations were unsuccessful due to a number of reasons. As mentioned above, the SACU countries were not interested in signing a standard FTAg that the United States typically offered to developing countries. Both parties disagreed on several issues, namely, intellectual property, government procurement, investment and services provisions.[148] SACU states argued that given their economic development these standard provisions or 'golden standards'[149] set by the United States were simply too high and therefore sought to focus the negotiations on market access commitments, while having the aforementioned areas excluded from their negotiations.[150]

US negotiators were particularly unwilling to compromise on intellectual property. They were uncomfortable in exporting to countries with weak intellectual property rights citing the possibility of the piracy of US products warranted the inclusion of these provisions.[151] SACU states on the other hand, argued that the enforcement of these rights would not be easy and would compromise their ability to provide affordable essential medicines to their populations.[152]

SACU countries thought that they had little to lose and a lot to gain by refusing to agree to a standardized FTAg with the United States. As a region that reaped considerable rewards under the AGOA programme, negotiations for an FTAg with the United States may not have been top priority once Congress extended the AGOA benefits to 2015 through the AGOA Acceleration Act of 2004 (P.L.108–274).[153] The United States Trade Representative confirmed in 2009 that the United States and SACU members were continuing with negotiations to upgrade the TIDCA into an FTAg.[154]

146 Mukumbira, 'US-SACU Free Trade Talks Hit Snags'.

147 Hongjiang, 'U.S., African Countries Sign First Trade Agreement'.

148 D. Langton, 'CRS Report for Congress, United States-Southern African Customs Union (SACU) Free Trade Agreement Negotiations: Background and Potential Issues', 24 July 2008, at 5, http://fpc.state.gov/documents/organization/109530.pdf (last visited Aug. 21, 2010).

149 Mukumbira, 'US-SACU Free Trade Talks Hit Snags'.

150 Langton, 'CRS Report for Congress'.

151 Mukumbira, 'US-SACU Free Trade Talks Hit Snags'.

152 *Ibid.*

153 Langton, 'CRS Report for Congress'.

154 'US, SACU Anticipate Future Cooperation on Trade', *Bridges Weekly Trade News Digest* 13(20), 3 June 2009, http://ictsd.net/i/news/bridgesweekly/47834/ (last visited 25 Oct. 2010).

F Bilateral Investment Treaties between the United States and African states

The United States has an extensive BIT Program designed to 'protect private investment, to develop market-oriented policies in partner countries, and to promote U.S. exports'.[155] The BITs also provide several incentives to investors, including the following:

- investors and their 'covered investments' are given the 'most-favoured-nation' treatment for the duration of the investment;
- limitations on the expropriation of investments, including provision for prompt, adequate and effective compensation at the time of expropriation;
- free repatriation of investment-related funds at the market rate of exchange;
- restriction on performance requirements impositions, 'such as local content targets or export quotas, on investments';
- limitations on the imposition of trade-distorting or inefficient practices on US investments – including requirements in hiring; and
- right of submission of investment disputes to international arbitration.[156]

Currently, the United States has signed BITs with 40 countries worldwide, including the following African countries: Rwanda, the Republic of Congo, the Democratic Republic of Congo, Egypt, Cameroon, Morocco, Mozambique, Senegal and Tunisia.[157] The United States also launched Investment Treaty talks with Mauritius in August 2009.[158] US Trade Representative Ron Kirk called Mauritius 'one of the most economically successful and politically stable countries in Africa . . . [with] an impressive track record on democracy, economic growth, openness to foreign direct investment, economic diversification, and the expansion of trade'.[159]

155 Office of the United States Trade Representative, 'Bilateral Investment Treaties', www.ustr.gov/trade-agreements/bilateral-investment-treaties (last visited 25 Oct. 2010).

156 *Ibid.*

157 United States Department of State, 'United States Bilateral Investment Treaties', www.state.gov/e/eeb/ifd/bit/117402.htm (last visited 25 Oct. 2010).

158 Office of the United States Trade Representative, 'United States and Mauritius Launch Investment Treaty Talks', www.ustr.gov/about-us/press-office/press-releases/2009/august/united-states-and-mauritius-launch-investment-treaty (last visited 1 Aug. 2010).

159 *Ibid.*

Elsewhere I have noted concerns that arise from BITs, particularly in the context of investor-state arbitrations which are contrary to the public welfare of host states in Africa and elsewhere.[160]

G South–South trade – A survival strategy of trade between developing states?

Europe and the United States are not alone in the race to Africa. In the interests of promoting South–South cooperation and integration, Latin American and Asian states, too, have attempted to forge strong trade ties with African nations. China and India, two of the largest economies in Asia, are right at the centre of the African–Asian race for trade and investment agreements.[161] Although neither China nor India was a colonial power in Africa, international trade between these two countries and the African continent goes back a long way.[162] The Chinese investments in Africa date back to post-colonial times, particularly in the infrastructure sector such as railways, while the Indian trade link with East Africa has not only resulted in trade between the two regions, but also large expatriate Indian communities settling in the East African region.[163]

The Indian and Chinese economies have been dubbed as the 'emerging economic "giants"' and their burgeoning economies are creating a greater demand for natural resources, as well as light manufactured goods and other goods such as household consumer items.[164] Africa is a goldmine of natural resources as well as cheap labour; therefore, Africa perhaps is an obvious choice as a trade partner for India and China.

The Chinese and Indian Foreign Direct Investment (FDI) in Africa has traditionally been concentrated in the oil extraction and mining industries; however, in recent years, FDI flows between the two Asian countries and Africa has become more diversified, with FDI being made in the apparel industry and processed foods, as well as other sectors.[165] By

160 J. Gathii, *War, Commerce and International Law* (Oxford University Press, 2010) (esp. Ch. 5); see also Public Statement on the International Investment Regime, 31 Aug. 2010 available at www.osgoode.yorku.ca/public_statement/documents/Public%20Statement.pdf.

161 H.G. Broadman, 'Africa's Silk Road: China and India's New Economic Frontier', at 42, available at http://siteresources.worldbank.org/AFRICAEXT/Resources/Africa_Silk_Road.pdf (last visited 25 Oct. 2010).

162 *Ibid.* 163 *Ibid.* 164 *Ibid.* 165 *Ibid.*

contrast, FDI in Asia by African firms has been far less than that of Asian firms in Africa.[166]

1 *Indo-African trade*

Like Europe and the United States, India, too, has set out to claim a slice of the African market. To this end, India initiated several programmes to establish healthy and ongoing trade relations with Africa. In fact, Indo-African trade tripled in five years, with Indian exports increasing from $2 billion in 2000, to $6 billion in 2005, and African exports increasing from $3 billion to $4 billion during the same period.[167]

'Focus: Africa' is argued to be an illustration of success in Indo-African trade. The target countries for this programme were Mauritius, Kenya and Ethiopia.[168] Under this programme, India provided financial assistance in the form of market development assistance to various trade promotion organizations, export promotion councils and apex chambers.[169] The Exim Bank of India also extended lines of credit to the COMESA region for eligible export goods on a deferred payment basis, in the interests of promoting trade with COMESA.[170] The 'Focus: Africa' programme is said to have brought a 35 per cent increase worth $3.91 billion in bilateral trade between the two parties.[171]

Recently, India, South Africa and Brazil launched trade talks to increase trade flow amongst these regions from $10 billion to $25 billion by the year 2015.[172] These negotiations are taking place in the frameworks of the SACU, the Indian government and the Southern Common Market (MERCOSUR).[173] India and SACU have begun negotiations and the

166 *Ibid.* at 42–3.

167 S. Hopkins, 'India-Africa Trade Boom: New Summit Stokes Red-Hot Trade Growth', *Wealth Daily*, 7 April 2008, available at www.wealthdaily.com/articles/india-africa-trade/1246 (last visited 25 Oct. 2010).

168 'India – Boosting Trade with Africa', *Africa Business Pages*, Business Guide Internet Edition, available at www.africa-business.com/features/india_africa.html (last visited 25 Oct. 2010).

169 *Ibid.* 170 *Ibid.*

171 IANS, 'India's Focus: Africa Yields Encouraging Results', SiliconIndia, 23 September 2003, www.siliconindia.com/shownews/Indias_Focus_Africa_yields_encouraging_results__-nid-20870.html (last visited 1 June 2010).

172 'Brazil, India, S Africa to Boost Trade Ties Via Agreements', *Global Times*, 2 Sept. 2009, available at http://business.globaltimes.cn/world/2009–09/463314.html (last visited 25 Oct. 2010).

173 *Ibid.*

foreign ministers of the countries involved have approved preferential trade agreements between the regions.[174]

2 *India–Africa Forum Summit*

The India–Africa Forum Summit ('the Summit') is the official platform for Indo-African trade relations. The main objective of the Summit is to strengthen cooperation between the two regions in the following areas: economic; political; science, technology, research and development; social development and capacity building; tourism; infrastructure, energy and environment; and media and communication.[175]

The Summit's first meeting was held in New Delhi on 8–9 April 2008 and was attended by African Heads of States and Governments, Heads of Delegation representing the African Union and the Indian Prime Minister, Dr. Manmohan Singh.[176] The Summit also adopted two major documents: the Delhi Declaration and the Framework for Cooperation.[177] The Delhi Declaration is a political document covering 'issues of bilateral, regional and international interest to India and Africa, including [their] common positions on UN Reforms, climate change, WTO and international terrorism'.[178]

The Framework for Cooperation, on the other hand, discusses particular areas of cooperation agreed by the two parties, including the following: human resources and institutional capacity building; education; science and technology; agricultural productivity and food security; industrial growth; minerals; health sector; infrastructure; ICT; and 'the establishment of judicial systems with police and defence establishments under civilian control'.[179] The Summit agreed to develop a joint plan of

174 *Ibid.*

175 'Africa-India Framework for Cooperation' Africa-India Forum Summit, New Delhi, India, 9 April 2008, available at www.africa-union.org/root/au/Conferences/2008/april/India-Africa/India-Africa.html (last visited 25 Oct. 2010).

176 African Union, 'Africa-India Summit Forum Adopts Delhi Declaration and the Framework for Cooperation', 9 April 2008, available at www.africa-union.org/root/au/Conferences/2008/april/India-Africa/press_releases.htm (last visited 25 Oct. 2010) (hereinafter African Union, 'Delhi Declaration').

177 *Ibid.*

178 'PM to Unveil Delhi Declaration at Africa Summit', *Indian Express*, 7 April 2008, available at www.indianexpress.com/news/pm-to-unveil-delhi-declaration-at-africa-sum/293769/ (last visited 25 Oct. 2010).

179 *Ibid.*

action, without prejudice to India's current trade arrangements at the bilateral and regional levels, to implement the Framework for Cooperation at the continental level.[180] The Framework also has a provision for economic cooperation in regional integration in Africa, where the two parties agreed to provide financial assistance to 'mutually agreed integration programmes carried out by the African Union and the RECs' of 'inter-regional or continental importance'.[181] Dr. Singh also announced in his inaugural address that India will increase financial credit to Africa to $5.4 billion over the next five years, doubling the current credit limit, and provide preferential market access for exports from 34 least developed African countries.[182]

3 India–SACU Preferential Trade Agreement

In a bid to forge firmer trade ties between the two regions by liberalizing their respective markets, India and SACU sought to sign a Preferential Trade Agreement (PTA) – which is intended to be a stepping stone to a fully-fledged FTAg between the two regions. However, negotiations stalled early in 2010 due to a reluctance on the part of SACU to liberalize its market.[183] According to an Indian Commerce Ministry official, India wanted SACU to offer tariff concessions on 30–50 per cent of the total traded goods, but SACU was only willing to offer tariff concessions on 10 per cent of the total traded goods.[184]

South Africa offers a significant market for Indian goods. In fact, $7.5 billion of India's total trade of $7.7 billion with SACU was with South Africa alone.[185] The India–SACU PTA will also serve as an important link in the multilateral initiative between India, Brazil and South

180 African Union, 'Delhi Declaration'.

181 Africa Union, 'Africa-India Framework for Cooperation', Africa Forum Summit 2008, available at www.africa-union.org/root/au/Conferences/2008/april/ India-Africa/press_releases.htm (follow hyperlink 'Africa-India Framework for Cooperation') (last visited 25 Oct. 2010).

182 'India-Africa Summit Concluded in New Delhi', *China View*, 9 Apr. 2008, available at http://news.xinhuanet.com/english/2008–04/09/content_7947657.htm (last visited 25 Oct. 2010).

183 A.R. Mishra, 'India-SACU Trade Pact May Get Delayed', LiveMint.com, 1 Mar. 2010, available at www.tralac.org/cgi-bin/giga.cgi?cmd=cause_dir_news_item&cause_id=1694&news_id=82932&cat_ id=1079 (last visited 25 Oct. 2010).

184 *Ibid.* 185 *Ibid.*

Africa (IBSA) to promote South–South trade.[186] Despite reluctance by Botswana, Lesotho, Namibia and Swaziland, South Africa intends to pursue the India–SACU PTA with renewed vigour.[187]

4 *Sino–African trade*

China and Africa have enjoyed a long and fruitful trade relationship since the birth of 'New China' and the independence of the African states.[188] Over the past decade, trade between the two regions has expanded, with bilateral trade increasing from $10 billion in 2000 to a whopping $106.8 billion in 2008, constituting an average growth rate of 30 per cent per year for eight consecutive years.[189] Chinese exports to Africa constitute 3.6 per cent of Chinese global exports, valued at $50,869 million.[190] Imports to China from Africa are valued at $55,883 million.[191] While these numbers are a significant improvement and a sign of considerable growth, China is such a huge market for African goods and produce that there is much room for improvement. In order to realize the full potential of this trade relationship, China could very well extend 'its currently limited preferences for Africa into a more ambitious scheme', like AGOA.[192]

Notably, China has already established itself as South Africa's top trading partner and has signed several multi-million dollar trade deals with South Africa. The most recent of these was worth 2.3 billion South African Rands ($311 million), more than twice the amount of the last trade deal between the two states.[193]

186 *Ibid.*

187 'South Africa to Move Ambitiously on India PTA', *Economic Times*, 7 June 2010, available at www.tralac.org/cgi-bin/giga.cgi?cmd=cause_dir_news_item&cause_id=1694&news_id=88115&cat_ id=1079 (last visited 25 Oct. 2010).

188 W. Le, 'Sino-African Trade Has Broader Prospects', *China Daily*, 11 Feb. 2009, available at www.chinadaily.com.cn/china/2009–02/11/content_7463268.htm (last visited 25 Oct. 2010).

189 *Ibid.*

190 R. Sandrey, 'China-Africa Merchandise Trade for the December 2008 Year', Trade Law Center for South Africa (TRALAC) and the Centre for Chinese Studies, Stellenbosch University, South Africa, 1–17, available at www.tralac.org/cause_data/images/1694/WP07_SandreyCCS_ChinaAfrTrade_20090909.pdf (last visited 21 Aug. 2010).

191 *Ibid.* at 188.

192 *Ibid.*

193 L. Pinsloo, 'SA, China Sign Trade Deals Worth R2.3bn', Engineering News Online, 1 Apr. 2010, www.engineeringnews.co.za/article/sa-and-china-sign-trade-deals-worth-r2.3bn-2010–03–31 (last visited 25 Oct. 2010).

5 Forum on China–Africa Cooperation

The Forum on China–Africa Cooperation (FOCAC) was established by China and 'friendly' African countries to encourage collective consultation, promote political dialogue and economic cooperation between the two parties for mutual benefit and common development.[194] FOCAC's fourth Ministerial Conference was hosted by Egypt in 2010 from 8 to 9 November.[195] The Conference convened to review the implementation of the follow-up actions to the Beijing Summit of the Forum held three years previously and to discuss new ways to enhance Sino–African trade relations.[196] To this end, FOCAC adopted the Sharm El Sheikh Action Plan of the Forum on China–Africa Cooperation (2010–12) at the Conference.[197]

The Sharm El Sheikh Action Plan was intended to strengthen cooperation between the two parties in the following areas: political affairs and regional peace and security; international affairs; economic; social development; and cultural and people-to-people exchanges.[198] Recognizing the severe impact that the current global financial crisis has on developing nations, and the impracticability of attempting to achieve the UN's Millennium Development Goals under these conditions,[199] China has promised to extend $10 billion in preferential loans to African countries over the next three years to be used for infrastructure and social development projects.[200] The two parties have also agreed to increase cooperation between relevant financial institutions from both regions to support African regional integration efforts.[201]

6 China–SACU FTAg negotiations

China's industries have enjoyed a significant presence in Southern Africa. In 1997, China and Swaziland signed a Protocol on Technical

194 FOCAC, 'Characteristics of FOCAC', www.focac.org/eng/ltda/ltjj/t157576.htm (last visited 25 Oct. 2010).

195 Forum on China–Africa Cooperation, 'Declaration of Sharm El Sheikh of the Forum on China-Africa Cooperation', 12 Nov. 2009, available at www.focac.org/eng/zxxx/t626388.htm (last visited 25 Oct. 2010) (hereinafter 'Sharm El Sheikh Declaration').

196 *Ibid.* 197 *Ibid.*

198 Forum on China–Africa Cooperation, Sharm El Sheikh Action Plan (2010–2012), 12 Nov. 2009, available at www.focac.org/eng/zxxx/t626387.htm (last visited 25 Oct. 2010) (hereinafter 'Sharm El Sheikh Action Plan').

199 Sharm El Sheikh Declaration. 200 Sharm El Sheikh Action Plan, at art. 4.5.

201 *Ibid.* at art. 4.3.3.

Cooperation, whereby China would provide $10 million per year for development projects.[202] However, this agreement lapsed in 2007, and negotiations for renewal were expected to result in a new protocol for January 2008.[203] Through this protocol, Swaziland has benefited in more than fifty projects, including rural electrification, rural resettlement, agriculture and research and computers for schools and government ministries, among many others.[204]

SACU and China even began FTAg negotiations, but ultimately discontinued these negotiations because overall imports into the SACU region would have been higher than exports, and any gains in GDP were found to be marginal;[205] consequently, the proposed FTAg would have resulted in increased Chinese exports to the SACU region, which would have been more favourable for China than it would have been for SACU.

One commenter notes that it is necessary to view the deepening relationship between China and Africa with 'guarded optimism' rather than with 'paranoia'.[206] Even though South–South cooperation has ended the dependence of African states on the north for trade, it is equally important not to give in to trade arrangements with China or other developing states that 'threaten sustainable development on the continent or undermine respect for human rights and dignity'.[207] Some scholars also argue that an in-depth knowledge of the legal, social and political systems of China and their language is necessary to benefit from Sino–African trade.[208] China has a distinct edge over Africa, because French and English – two of the most widely spoken European languages in Africa – are already being taught in Chinese schools, whereas only a handful of African nationals can speak Chinese.[209]

7 *MERCOSUR–Africa trade*

Like India and China, the Latin American trade bloc, the MERCOSUR, consisting of Argentina, Brazil, Paraguay and Uruguay, too, have

202 Kingdom of Swaziland–European Community, 'Country Strategy Paper and National Indicative Programme for the Period 2008–2013', 24, http://ec.europa.eu/development/icenter/repository/scanned_sz_csp10_en.pdf (last visited 25 Oct. 2010).

203 *Ibid.* 204 *Ibid.*

205 R. Sandrey and H.G. Jensen, 'SACU, China and India: The Implication of FTAs for Botswana, Lesotho, Namibia, and Swaziland (BLNS)', TRALAC, January 2009, www.tralac.org/cause_data/images/1694/WP012009SACUChinaIndiaFTAImplSandrey.pdf (last visited 21 Oct. 2010).

206 U.E. Ofodile, 'Trade, Empire, and Subjects – China-Africa Trade: A New Fair Trade Arrangement or A New Scramble for Africa?', *Vand. J. Transnat'l L.* 41 (2008) 505, 510.

207 *Ibid.* at 511. 208 *Ibid.* at 582. 209 *Ibid.*

established strong trade ties with African nations. In December 2004, MERCOSUR signed a PTA with SACU to increase trade between the two regions as part of a greater scheme to create a fully-fledged FTAg.[210] The Agreement consisted of a main text and five annexes. The main text set out the principles, legal provisions and procedures for the PTA. It also established an institutional arrangement to manage the trade arrangement.[211] Annexes 1 and 2 set out MERCOSUR and SACU's respective tariff concessions covering around 1,000 products each way, with preference margins spread over 100–10 per cent.[212] The remaining annexes covered by the general rules of origin, safeguards and dispute settlement.[213] The Agreement contained provisions for continued negotiations between the two regions on several issues including rules of origin, Sanitary and Phytosanitary Standards and specific requests for additional trade preferences for specific products on both sides.[214] A final round of negotiations in April 2008 resolved outstanding technical issues and resulted in the conclusion of another PTA replacing the 2004 Agreement.[215]

MERCOSUR also expanded its reach to Northern Africa by finalizing an FTAg with Egypt.[216] Egypt's Minister of Trade, Rachid Rachid, hoped that the FTAg would result in the doubling of bilateral trade between the two regions over the course of ten years.[217] This FTAg is a prime example of what South–South trade seeks to achieve – the integration of trade between suppliers and consumers in developing states. Although Egypt is the world's biggest importer of wheat and Argentina is one of the largest exporters of grain, until recently Argentina had not exported wheat to Egypt.[218] MERCOSUR is also currently negotiating similar trade pacts with other Islamic states such as Morocco, Jordan and the Gulf Cooperation Council (GCC), which also includes Saudi Arabia and Qatar.[219]

210 Preferential Trade Agreement Between Southern Common Market (MERCOSUR) and Southern African Customs Union (SACU), 16 Dec. 2004, available at www.sice.oas.org/tpd/MER_SACU/MER_SACU_e.asp (last visited 25 Oct. 2010).

211 *Ibid.* 212 *Ibid.* at Annex I and II. 213 *Ibid.* at Annex III, IV and V. 214 *Ibid.*

215 'SACU Approves PTA with MERCOSUR', Mmegi, 9 July 2008, available at http://palapye.wordpress.com/2008/07/09/sacu-approves-pta-with-mercosur (last visited 25 Oct. 2010).

216 'Egypt Signs Free Trade Deal with MERCOSUR', M&C News, 3 Aug. 2010, www.monstersandcritics.com/news/business/news/article_1575165.php/Egypt-signs-free-trade-deal-with-Mercosur (last visited 25 Oct. 2010).

217 *Ibid.*

218 'Mercosur bloc signs free-trade deal with Egypt', Reuters, 3 Aug. 2010, www.bilaterals.org/spip.php?article17797 (last visited 21 Aug. 2010).

219 *Ibid.*

8 Legal regimes on counterfeit goods

One consequence of the expansions of imports into Africa is the large number of substandard and counterfeit goods. Counterfeit imports unfairly displace locally produced goods and may be dangerous to the end consumer. In June 2009, Kenya destroyed counterfeit Panadol Extra drugs worth 5 million Kenyan Shillings, and lost a total of $500 million in revenue to counterfeit goods.[220] A recent study on counterfeit goods claims that in Kenya alone, more than 30 per cent of medicines sold in the market are counterfeit.[221] Counterfeit drugs pose a threat not only to local businesses, but to the health of the consumers. Much like Kenya, Uganda, too, is a leading recipient of counterfeit goods in the region.[222] A study carried out by consultants contracted by the EAC Secretariat on counterfeiting and piracy found that counterfeit trade included trade in a range of consumer goods including fake drugs, adulterated cement and counterfeit electric cables, which lead to health risks, the collapse of buildings and fire outbreaks, respectively.[223] Unfortunately, unsophisticated consumers in Uganda tolerate such low-grade and hazardous goods due to their attractive prices.[224] Therefore, action must be taken at the political level to ensure the safety and well-being of a country's citizens.

In recent years, African governments have begun cracking down on counterfeits sold by both local and foreign businesses. East Africa, for instance, is attempting to combat trade in counterfeit goods by involving local landlords. A proposed law will require landlords to cancel leases of all businesses that sell counterfeit goods, for a start.[225] In Kenya, an Anti-Counterfeit Agency has been organized under the Ministry of Industrialization, to combat trade in counterfeit goods,[226] while in South Africa, businesses work with government agencies to combat trade in counterfeit goods. Recently, Bayer Healthcare seized nearly 1.5 million South African Rands' worth of Zam-buk tins believed to have been

220 J. Onyango, 'Eastern African Regions Loses $500 Million to Counterfeit Goods', *Business Daily*, 31 July 2009, www.businessdailyafrica.com/Company%20Industry/-/539550/632458/-/view/printVersion/-/qil155z/-/index.html (last visited 25 Oct. 2010).

221 *Ibid.*

222 H. Mukasa, 'Uganda Tops in Counterfeits', *The New Vision*, 13 July 2009, available at www.newvision.co.ug/D/8/13/687442 (last visited 25 Oct. 2010).

223 *Ibid.* 224 *Ibid.*

225 F. Ayeiko, 'East Africa: Landlords to be Used in War Against Counterfeits', 20 July 2009, http://allafrica.com/stories/200907201266.html_ (last visited 25 Oct. 2010).

226 P. Tayler, 'Kenya's Counterfeit Agency Starts Operations', Securing Pharma, 9 Dec. 2009, available at www.securingpharma.com/40/articles/312.php (last visited 25 Oct. 2010).

manufactured in China, and is collaborating with the South African Revenue Service (SARS), on the matter. Retailers and distributors involved in the sale of counterfeit goods are charged with criminal offences and fined, while expatriate entrepreneurs also face deportation as a consequence.[227]

H Conclusions

This chapter has examined trade and investment agreements between African and non-African RTAs. There is a broad range and array of such agreements with the European, American, Asian and even Latin American countries. While the purpose of the chapter was not to evaluate the stakes for Africa in these agreements, it is clear that Africa's external trading partners have invested heavily in negotiating the agreements. The slowdown in multilateral negotiations in the Doha Round has in part spurred the need to negotiate bilateral and regional agreements. In addition, Africa's external trading partners see these regional and bilateral agreements as offering opportunities to negotiate extensive commitments beyond those in current multilateral agreements. The legacy of these agreements for Africa has therefore to await further critical scrutiny to see whether the promise of mutual gains comes to fruition. At the moment, the mutuality of such gains in many of these agreements is not decidedly on the African side, as this chapter has demonstrated. It is therefore not surprising that there have been vigorous debates about the merits and demerits of these agreements in the negotiations.

227 'Business Strikes Back Against Counterfeits', *Volksblad*, 29 July 2009, http://jv.news24.com/Die_Volksblad/Express_Noordkaap/0,,5–2256_2542947,00.html (last visited 25 Oct. 2010).

BIBLIOGRAPHY

Articles

Abbott, F.M. and Reichman, J.H., 'The Doha Round's Public Health Legacy: Strategies for the Production and Diffusion of Patented Medicines Under the Amended TRIPS Provisions', *Journal of International Economic Law* **10**(4) (2007) 921–87.

Abbott, K. and Snidal, D., 'Hard and Soft Law in International Governance', *International Organization* **54** (2000) 421–56.

Abbott, K.W. *et al.*, 'The Concept of Legalization', *International Organization* **54** (2000) 401–19.

Abdoulahi, M., 'Progress Report on Regional Integration Efforts in Africa towards the Promotion of Intra-African Trade', African Trade Policy Centre, Dec. 2005, available at www.uneca.org/eca_programmes/trade_and_regional_integration/atpc/Work%20in%20progress/30.pdf.

Abedini, J. and Péridy, N., 'The Greater Arab Free Trade Area (GAFTA): An Estimation of the Trade Effects', Canadian Economics Association (2007), 1–21, available at http://economics.ca/2007/papers/0300.pdf.

'African Free Trade', *Business Daily*, 5 July 2010, available at www.tralac.org/cgi-bin/giga.cgi?cmd=cause_dir_news_item&cause_id=1694&news_id=89373&cat_id=1026.

Agu, V., Correia, A.N. and Behbehani, K., 'Strengthening International Health Co-Operation in Africa Through the Regional Economic Communities', *African Journal of Health Science* **14**(3–4) (2007) 104–13.

Agutu, M., 'Lobby Files Suit to Stop EU Pact', *Daily Nation*, 27 October 2007.

Akaoha, K., 'ECOWAS EPA – The Facts and the Fallacies', AllAfrica.com (21 Jan. 2008), available at www.bilaterals.org/article.php3?id_article=10985.

Akech, J.M.M., 'The African Growth and Opportunity Act: Implications for Kenya's Trade and Development', *N.Y.U. J. Int'l L. & Pol.* **33** (2001) 651–702.

Allain, L. and Loko, B., 'Fresh Impetus Toward Maghreb Integration', IMF Middle East and Central Asia Department (12 Sept. 2007), available at www.imf.org/external/pubs/ft/survey/so/2007/car0912b.htm.

Allen, R.L., 'Integration in Less Developed Areas', *Kyklos* **14** (1961) 315–36.

Alli, F., 'Nigeria: Common External Tariff Ready Jan. 2009', AllAfrica.com, available at http://allafrica.com/stories/200810130451.html.

Alusala, N., 'Is There Hope for ECCAS?', Institute for Security Studies, 19 Oct. 2007, available at www.iss.co.za/pgcontent.php?UID=27157.

Alvarez, J.E., 'How Not to Link: Institutional Conundrums of an Expanded Trade Regime', *Widener Law Symposium Journal* **7** (2001) 1–19.

Amdetsion, F., 'Scrutinizing the Scorpion Problematique: Arguments in Favor of the Continued Relevance of International Law and a Multidisciplinary Approach to Resolving the Nile Dispute', *Texas International Law Journal* **44** (2008) 1–43.

'Applications of Anti-dumping Measures and Safeguard Provisions under the COMESA Treaty', a Paper presented during the Workshop on Sugar Importers Forum held at the Holiday Inn Hotel, Westlands, 3–4 April 2002, available at www.kenyalink.org/sucam/documents/safeguards1.html (last visited 20 Oct. 2010).

Axline, W.A., 'Underdevelopment, Dependence and Integration: The Politics of Regionalism in the Third World', *International Organization* **31** (1977) 83–105.

Ayeiko, F., 'East Africa: Landlords to be Used in War Against Counterfeits', 20 July 2009, http://allafrica.com/stories/200907201266.html (last visited 1 Aug. 2010).

Bakare, M., 'Europe's EPA Condemned as it Tears Africa Apart: Now Africans Are Hitting Back at Europe', *Afrik* (4 June 2009) available at http://en.afrik.com/article15771.html (last visited 21 Aug. 2010).

Bartels, L., '"Interim Agreements" under Article XXIV GATT', *World Trade Review* **8**(2) (2009) 339–50.

Bearce, D., 'Grasping the Commercial Institutional Peace', *International Studies Quarterly* **47** (2003) 347–70.

Bell, A., 'Outrage as High Court Dismisses SADC Land Ruling', SW Radio Africa News (27 Jan. 2010), available at www.swradioafrica.com/news270110/outrage270110.htm.

Bensouiah, A., 'Stunted Growth of the Arab Maghreb Union', PANA Press (21 June 2002), available at www.panapress.com/newslatf.asp?code=eng008203&dte=21/06/2002.

Berne Declaration, 'NGOs request "EFTA countries shall not endanger public health and food security in Southern Africa"', bilateral.org, 4 Nov. 2004, available at www.evb.ch/index.cfm?page_id=3220 (last visited 25 Oct. 2010).

Berne Declaration, 'Southern African countries have taken a firm stand against EFTA demands on Intellectual Property Rights in Free Trade Agreement', 4 March 2005, available at www.liberationafrique.org/spip.php?article456 (last visited 21 Oct. 2010).

Berthelot, J., 'David and Goliath: Argument Against the EPAs between the European Union and African, Caribbean and Pacific Countries' (19 Dec. 2006), available at www.acp-eu-trade.org/library/files/Berthelot_EN_191206_Solidarite_David-Goliath-argument-against-the-EPAs.pdf.

Bhagwati, J. *et al.*, 'Trading Preferentially: Theory and Policy', *The Economic Journal* **108** (1998) 1128–48.

Biersteker, T.J., 'Self-Reliance in Theory and Practice in Tanzanian Trade Relations', *International Organizations* **34** (1980) 229–64.

Boutros-Ghali, B., 'The Addis Ababa Charter', *International Conciliation* **546** (1964) 19.

'Brazil, India, S Africa to Boost Trade Ties Via Agreements', *Global Times*, 2 Sept. 2009, available at http://business.globaltimes.cn/world/2009–09/463314.html (last visited 25 Oct. 2010).

Brown, A.J., 'Economic Separation Versus a Common Market in Developing Countries', *Yorkshire Bulletin of Economics and Social Research*, May and Nov. 1961.

Bursvik, E. *et al.*, 'Supporting Regional Integration in East and Southern Africa – Review of Select Issues', TRALAC, 28 Apr. 2010, available at www.tralac.org/cgi-bin/giga.cgi?cmd=cause_dir_news_item&cause_id=1694&news_id=86141&cat_id=1033.

Busch, G.K., 'The Euro Crisis and Africa', *Nigerian Village Square*, 17 May 2010, available at www.nigeriavillagesquare.com/index.php?option=com_content&view=article&id=15528&catid=181&Itemid=177 (last visited 21 Oct. 2010).

'Business Strikes Back Against Counterfeits', *Volksblad*, 29 July 2009, http://jv.news24.com/Die_Volksblad/Express_Noordkaap/0,,5–2256_2542947,00.html (last visited 25 Oct. 2010).

Castro, L., Kraus, C. and de la Rocha, M., 'Regional Trade Integration in East Africa: Trade and Revenue Impacts of the Planned East African Community Customs Union', World Bank Africa Region Working Paper Series No. 72, 29 Aug. 2004 (Washington, DC: World Bank).

Chacha, M., 'The New Community: Liberal Intergovernmentalism and East Africa Integration', APSA 2009 Toronto Meeting Paper, Toronto, Canada (Sept. 2009) 3–6, available at http://papers.ssrn.com/sol3/papers.cfm?abstract_id=1449277.

Charalambides, N., 'The Private Sector's Perspective, Priorities and Role in Regional Integration and Implications for Regional Trade Arrangements', ECDPM Discussion Paper **No. 66** (ECDPM, 2005).

Chhatbar, S., 'France and EAC Sign Lake Victoria Agreement', *The Arusha Times* (22 Mar. 2002), available at www.arushatimes.co.tz/2002/12/features_1.htm.

Chirinda, S., 'Land Seizures now SADC Issue – Tribunal', ReliefWeb (8 Feb. 2010), available at http://reliefweb.int/rw/rwb.nsf/db900SID/KHII-82G4S4?OpenDocument.

Cho, S., 'Defragmenting World Trade', *Northwestern Journal of International Law and Business* **27** (2006) 39–88.

Choi, W.M., 'Defragmenting Fragmented Rules of Origin of RTAs: A Building Block to Global Free Trade', *Journal of International Economic Law* **13** (2010) 111–38.

Cohen, M., 'Southern African Leaders Hold Summit to Rescue 100-Year-Old Customs Union', Trade Law Centre for Southern Africa (15 July 2010), available at www.tralac.org/cgi-bin/giga.cgi?cmd=cause_dir_news_item&cause_id=1694&news_id=89865&cat_id=1026.

'COMESA Finalises New Trade Regime', *The Herald*, Harare, Trade Law Centre for Southern Africa (29 July 2010), available at www.tralac.org/cgi-bin/giga.cgi?cmd=cause_dir_news_item&cause_id=1694&news_id=90513&cat_id=1026.

'COMESA May Miss Deadline for Duty-Free Trade', Trade Law Centre for Southern Africa (24 June 2010), available at www.tralac.org/cgi-bin/giga.cgi?cmd=cause_dir_news_item&cause_id=1694&news_id=88882&cat_id=1026.

Cooper, C.A. and Massell, B.F., 'Toward a General Theory of Customs Unions for Developing Countries', *Journal of Political Economics* **73** (1965) 461–76.

'Cotonou Infokit 2: The Cotonou Agreement at a Glance' (ECDPM, 2002), available at www.ecdpm.org/Web_ECDPM/Web/Content/Navigation.nsf/index2?readform&http://www.ecdpm.org/Web_ECDPM/Web/Content/Content.nsf/vwDocID/A68AE1325FBA33DCC1256C7500580251?OpenDocument.

Cropley, E., 'Southern Africa Grasps Trade Subsidy Nettle', Trade Law Centre for Southern Africa (19 July 2010), available at www.tralac.org/cgi-bin/giga.cgi?cmd=cause_dir_news_item&cause_id=1694&news_id=89969&cat_id=1026.

Dam, K., 'Regional Economic Arrangements and the GATT: The Legacy of a Misconception', *University of Chicago Law Review* **30** (1963) 615–65.

Davey, W.J. and Separ, A., 'The Soft Drinks Case: The WTO and Regional Agreements', *World Trade Review* **8** (2009) 5–23.

de Bendern, P., 'Gaddafi Urges Self-Reliance at Africa Summit', Reuters, 4 July 2005, available at www.int.iol.co.za/index.php?set_ id=1&click_id=68&art_id=qw1120478401298B261.

Desta, M.G., 'The Regulatory Framework for Trade in IGAD Livestock Products', IGAD Livestock Policy Initiative, IGAD LPI Working Paper No. 07–08.

Development Forum: Maximizing Civil Aviation's Economic Contribution: Safe, Secure and Sustainable Air Transport in Open Skies Challenges and Potential, Montreal, Canada, May 2006, www.icao.int/DevelopmentForum/Forum_06/Docs/YamoussoukroDecision.pdf (last visited 21 Aug. 2010).

Draper, P. and Khumalo, N., 'The Future of the Southern African Customs Union', *Trade Negotiations Insights* **8**(6) (August 2009), available at http://ictsd.net/i/news/tni/52394/ (last visited 21 Oct. 2010).

Dzirutwe, M., 'Mugabe Calls For Self-Reliance, End to Conflicts', Reuters, 7 June, 2009, available at http://in.reuters.com/article/businessNews/idINIndia-40138720090607.

'EAC Regional Integration: Can't Take Your Lawyer?', *Ratio Magazine*, 27 Jan. 2009, available at www.ratio-magazine.com/20090127392/EAC-Regional/EAC-Regional-Integration-Can-t-Take-Your-Lawyer.html.

'EAC Right on Trade Deal', *Business Daily*, editorial, 4 Aug. 2010, available at www.businessdailyafrica.com/Opinion%20&%20Analysis/-/539548/634464/-/item/0/-/1425pex/-/index.html (last visited 25 Oct. 2010).

Eagle, D.F., 'SA: Zimbabwe Tribunal Court Ruling Stands', *Metro Zimbabwe*, 6 Feb. 2010, available at www.zimbabwemetro.com/current-affairs/sazimbabwe-tribunal-court-ruling-stands/?utm_medium=newzimsituation&utm_source=newzimsituation.com.

'ECOWAS Leaders Approve New Common External Tariff Regime', *Afrique en Ligne*, available at www.afriquejet.com/news/africa-news/ecowas-leaders-approve-new-common-external-tariff-regime-2009062330285.html.

'ECOWAS Seeks Increased EU Funding', *African Business* (1 June 2003), available at www.thefreelibrary.com/ECOWAS+seeks+increased+EU+funding.+(Business+Briefs:+Funding)-a0102660558.

'Egypt Signs Free Trade Deal with MERCOSUR', *M&C News*, 3 Aug. 2010, www.monstersandcritics.com/news/business/news/article_1575165.php/Egypt-signs-free-trade-deal-with-Mercosur (last visited 25 Oct. 2010).

Enabulele, A.O., 'Reflections on the ECOWAS Community Court Protocol and the Constitutions of the Member States', *International Community Law Review*, **12** (Mar. 2010) 111–37.

'EPA: A Carrot for Africa', *Daily Trust*, 31 July 2009, available at http://allafrica.com/stories/200907310388.html (last visited 25 Oct. 2010).

Erasmus, G., 'Will SACU Have a Permanent Summit?', Trade Law Centre for Southern Africa (11 May 2010), available at www.tralac.org/cgi-bin/giga.cgi?cmd=cause_dir_news_item&cause_id=1694&news_id=86783&cat_id=1058.

Ethiopia, 'Implementation of the Yamoussoukro Decision Progressing or Stalled?', ICAO/ATAG/WB Development Forum, 24–6 May 2006 available at: www.icao.int/DevelopmentForum/Forum_06/Docs/YamoussoukroDecision.pdf (last visited 21 October 2010).

Felice, C.D., 'According to the World Bank, Maghreb is Key to EU Development', *Medibtikar* (13 April 2007).

Finaish, M. and Bell, E., 'The Arab Maghreb Union', IMF Working Paper WP/94/55.

Finger, J.M. and Schuler, P., 'Implementation of Uruguay Round Commitments: The Development Challenge', World Bank Working Paper No.

2215, 1 Oct. 1999 available at www-wds.worldbank.org/external/default/WDSContentServer/IW3P/IB/2001/02/10/000094946_01013005324822/Rendered/PDF/multi_page.pdf (last visited 21 Aug. 2010).

Frimpong, C.Y., 'Vice President challenges member states to meet WAMZ criteria,' *Modern Ghana*, 1 Jan. 2010 available at www.modernghana.com/news/257141/1/vice-president-challenges-member-states-to-meet-wa.html.

'Gabon: Douala, Libreville – Need for Surgery', *The Cameroon Tribune*, 17 Sept. 2009, available at http://allafrica.com/stories/200909170539.html.

Gathii, J., 'Process and Substance in WTO Reform', *Rutgers L. Rev.* **56** (2004) 885–925.

Gathii, J., 'Spat With Dar Over Trade Unnecessary', *Business Daily Africa*, 8 Feb. 2008, available at http://allafrica.com/stories/200802070871.html.

Gathii, J., 'The High Stakes of WTO Reform', *Mich. L. Rev.* **104** (2006) 1361–86.

Gathii, J., 'Kenya's Piracy Prosecutions', *Am. J. Int'l L.* **104** (2010) 416.

Gathii, J., 'The Legal Status of the Doha Declaration on TRIPS and Public Health Under the Vienna Convention of the Law of Treaties,' *Harv. J.L. & Tech.* **15** (2002) 291–317.

Gathii, J., 'A Critical Appraisal of the NEPAD Agenda in Light of Africa's Place in the World Trade Regime in an Era of Market Centered Development', *Transnat'l L. and Contemp. Prob.* **13** (2003) 179–210.

Gathii, J., 'Good Governance as a Counter-Insurgency to Oppositional and Transformative Social Agenda to Oppositional and Transformative Social Projects in International Law', *Buff. Human Rts L. Rev.* **5** (1999) 107–73.

Gathii, J., 'Retelling Good Governance Narratives About Africa's Economic and Political Predicaments: Continuities and Discontinuities in Legal Outcomes Between Markets and States', *Vill. L. Rev.* **45** (2000), 971–1035.

Geda, A. and Kebret, H., 'Regional Economic Integration in Africa: A Review of Problems and Prospects with a Case Study of COMESA', *Journal of African Economics* **17**(3) (2008) 357–94.

Gendrano, J., 'League of Arab States: The Greater Arab Free Trade Agreement', Rutgers Model United Nations (Institute for Domestic and International Affairs Inc. 2007) available at www.idia.net/Files/ConferenceCommitteeTopicFiles/149/PDFFile/U07-LAS-GreaterArabFreeTradeAgreement.pdf (last visited 21 Oct. 2010).

Grimett, L., 'Protectionism and Compliance with the GATT Article XXIV in Selected Regional Trade Agreements', Thesis, Rhodes University (1999), i, 223, available at http://eprints.ru.ac.za/208/01/grimett-thesis.pdf.

Guzman, A., 'A Compliance-Based Theory of International Law', *Calif. L. Rev.* **90** (2002) 1826–87.

Healy, S., Pearce, R. and Stockbridge, M., 'The Implications of the Uruguay Round Agreement on Agriculture for Developing Countries', Food and Agriculture

Organization of the United Nations (FAO, 1998), available at www.fao.org/docrep/004/w7814e/W7814E11.htm.

Heita, D., 'SACU Advocates Win-Win Solution on EPA Negotiations', Trade Law Centre for Southern Africa (20 July 2010), available at www.tralac.org/cgi-bin/giga.cgi?cmd=cause_dir_news_item&cause_id=1694&news_id=90029&cat_id=1026.

Helfer, L.R., 'Regime Shifting: The TRIPs Agreement and New Dynamics of International Intellectual Property Lawmaking', *Yale J. of Int'l L.* **29** (2004) 1–83.

Helfer, L.R., Alter, K.J. and Guerzovich, M.F., 'Islands of Effective International Adjudication: Constructing An Intellectual Property Rule of Law in the Andean Community', *Am. J. Int'l L.* **109** (2009) 1–55.

Hongjiang, W., 'U.S., African Countries Sign First Trade Agreement', *Xinhuanet*, 16 July 2008, http://news.xinhuanet.com/english/2008–07/17/content_8558376.htm (last visited 25 Oct. 2010).

Hopkins, S., 'India-Africa Trade Boom: New Summit Stokes Red-Hot Trade Growth', *Wealth Daily*, 7 April 2008, available at www.wealthdaily.com/articles/india-africa-trade/1246 (last visited 25 Oct. 2010).

Hoppe, M., 'Economic Partnership Agreements: Does Preferential Access of Non-LDC African Countries Increase?', World Bank Group, Trade Note No. 32 (12 July 2007), 1–10.

IANS, 'India's Focus: Africa Yields Encouraging Results', *SiliconIndia*, 23 September 2003, available at www.siliconindia.com/shownews/Indias_Focus_Africa_yields_encouraging_results__-nid-20870.html (last visited 1 June 2010).

'ICT and Electronics in South Africa', SouthAfrica.info, Oct. 2008, www.southafrica.info/business/economy/sectors/icte-overview.htm (last visited 25 Oct. 2010).

'ICTs in Africa', Fiber Networks in Africa, http://ictinafrica.com/ict/fiber.htm (last visited 20 July 2009).

'India-Africa Summit Concluded in New Delhi', *China View*, 9 April 2008, available at http://news.xinhuanet.com/english/2008–04/09/content_7947657.htm (last visited 25 Oct. 2010).

Islam, Md. Rizwanul and Alam, S., 'Preferential Trade Agreements and the Scope of GATT Article XXIV', *Netherlands International Law Review* **56** (May 2009) 1–34.

Jaidev, R., 'Governors Gloomy on Outlook for Pan-African Currency', Risk.net (7 July 2010), available at www.risk.net/risk-magazine/news/1721130/governors-gloomy-outlook-pan-african-currency.

Jakobeit, C. *et al.*, 'Overlapping Membership in COMESA, EAC, SACU and SADC: Trade Policy Options for the Region and for EPA Negotiations', (*Deutsche Gesellschaft für Technische Zusammenarbeit* (GTZ)) (2005), available at www.gtz.de/de/dokumente/en-epa-overlapping-memberships-2005.pdf.

Jarvis, S., 'Chinamasa Wrong on SADC Tribunal Pull Out', *The Standard – Zimbabwe* (3 October 2009), available at www.thestandard.co.zw/opinion/21583-chinamasa-wrong-on-sadc-tribunal-pull-out.html.

Johnstad, S. (ed.), 'Namibia: Caught in Stand-Off Between South Africa and EU', Inter Press Service, 20 Aug. 2009, available at www.afrika.no/Detailed/18623.html (last visited 25 Oct. 2010).

Karuhanga, J., 'EAC Judges Call for Stronger Judicial Systems', *The New Times* (10 December 2009), available at http://allafrica.com/stories/200912100297.html.

Kavanagh, M., 'The 1994 Devaluation of the CFA franc and the Changing Role of France in African Development', International Development Studies Working Paper Series, available at www.yale.edu/macmillan/iac/kavanagh.pdf.

Kazooba, C., 'Dar Offers to Move Uganda Cargo in New Affront to KPA Monopoly', *The East African*, 6 July 2009, www.theeastafrican.co.ke/news/-/2558/619284/-/r2baj3z/-/index.html (last visited 25 Oct. 2010).

Keck, A. and Djiofack-Zebaze, C., 'Telecommunications Services in Africa: The Impact of Multilateral Commitments and Unilateral Reform on Sector Performance and Economic Growth', World Trade Organization, Economic Research and Statistics Division, Staff Working Paper ERSD-2006–10 (Nov. 2006), available at www.wto.org/english/res_e/reser_e/ersd200610_e.htm (last visited 25 Oct. 2010).

Keck, A. and Piermartini, R., 'The Economic Impact of EPAs in SADC Countries', WTO Economic Research and Statistics Division Staff Working Paper No. 2005–04 (Aug. 2005).

Kelly, C. R., 'Enmeshment as a Theory of Compliance', *N. Y. U. J. Int'l L. and Pol.* **37** (2005) 303–56.

Kelly, R., 'WTO Compatibility and the Legal Form of EPAs: A Case Study of Eastern and Southern Africa', Working Paper No. 48–08, Inaugural Conference, Geneva (Society of International Economic Law, 15–17 July 2008), available at www.ssrn.com/link/SIEL-Inaugural-Conference.html.

Kelsey, J., 'Going Nowhere in a Hurry? The Pacific's EPA Negotiations with the European Union', *Wellington L. Rev.* **38** (2007) 81–103.

'Kenya Cancels Auction of Sugar Import Rights', Reuters, 10 March 2010, available at http://af.reuters.com/article/investingNews/idAFJOE6270CP20100308.

'Kenya: COMESA Grants Country Safeguards On Wheat And Sugar Imports', AllAfrica.Com, 3 December 2007.

'Kenya: Give Real Meaning to AGOA', AllAfrica, editorial, http://allafrica.com/stories/200908040985.html (last visited 25 Oct. 2010).

Khandelwal, P., 'COMESA and SADC: Prospects and Challenges for Regional Trade Integration', IMF Working Paper WP/04/227 (Dec. 2004), available at www.imf.org/external/pubs/ft/wp/2004/wp04227.pdf.

Kihara, G., 'Regional Customs Agencies Meet Over Border Surveillance', *Business Daily*, 10 July 2009, www.businessdailyafrica.com/-/539552/621756/-/567h5j/-/index.html (last visited 21 Aug. 2010).

Kikechi, B., 'Rwanda and Burundi Join the East African Community', 19 June 2007, available at http://allafrica.com/stories/200706181801.html (last visited 20 October 2010).

Kimenyi, M. S., 'African Growth and Opportunity Act: a Case of Vanishing Benefits', The Brookings Institution, 30 July 2009, available at www.brookings.edu/opinions/2009/0730_agoa_kimenyi.aspx (last visited 25 Oct. 2010).

Kisero, J., 'Kenya: Opening of Agoa By Clinton Reaffirms Kenya's Regional Status', 4 Aug. 2009, http://allafrica.com/stories/200908040792.html (last visited 21 August 2010).

Koh, H., 'How is International Human Rights Law Enforced?', *Ind. L. J.* **74** (1999) 1397–417.

Koh, H., 'On American Exceptionalism', *Stan. L. Rev.* **55** (2003) 1479–528.

Koh, H., 'Transnational Legal Process', *Neb. L. Rev.* **75** (1986) 181–206.

Kokutse, F., 'Trade: ECOWAS Delay on EPA Allows Ghana to Rethink', *Global Issues* (29 June 2009), available at www.globalissues.org/news/2009/06/29/1970.

Krishna, P. and Bhagwati, J., 'Necessarily Welfare Enhancing Customs Unions With Industrialization Constraints: The Cooper-Massell-Johnson-Bhagwati Conjecture', *Japan and the World Economy* **9** (1997) 441–6.

Kron, J., 'East African Countries Form a Common Market', *New York Times* (1 July 2010), available at www.nytimes.com/2010/07/02/business/global/02africa.html?src=busln.

Lang, R., 'Renegotiating GATT Article XXIV: a Priority for African Countries Engaged in North-South Trade Agreements', Working Paper No. 33, (African Trade Policy Centre, Feb. 2006), 12, available at http://uneca.org/atpc/Work%20in%20progress/33.pdf.

'Le Budget 2008 de la CEN-SAD Estimé à Plus de 10 Millions de Dollars', *African Manager* (15 June 2008), available at www.africanmanager.com/articles/117232.html.

Le, W., 'Sino-African Trade Has Broader Prospects', *China Daily*, 11 February 2009, available at www.chinadaily.com.cn/china/2009–02/11/content_7463268.htm (last visited 25 Oct. 2010).

Lee, M.C., 'The 21st Century Scramble for Africa', *The Journal of Contemporary African Studies*, **24**(3) (2006) 303–30.

Lipsey, R.G., 'The Theory of Customs Unions: Trade Diversion and Welfare', *Economica* **24**(93) (1957) 40–6.

Lipson, C., 'Why Are Some International Agreements Informal?', *International Organization* **45** (1991) 495–538.

Maiko, D., 'No let-up In Sugar Wars', News From Africa, August 2004, www.newsfromafrica.org/newsfromafrica/articles/art_6508.html.

Malakata, M., 'Rival Fiber-Optic Cables Set For Battle in Africa', *Computerworld Zambia*, 18 June 2009, www.computerworld.co.ke/articles/2009/06/18/rival-fiber-optic-cables-set-market-battle-africa (last visited 25 Oct. 2010).

Mansfield, E.D. and Bronson, R., 'Alliances, Preferential Trading Arrangements, International Trade', *American Political Science Review* **91**(1) (1997) 94–107.

Manyukwe, C., 'Gov't to Withdraw Judge from Tribunal', *Financial Gazette* (17 Sept. 2009), available at http://allafrica.com/stories/200909220904.html.

Marcedu, G. and Reiman, C., 'When and How is an RTA Compatible with the WTO?', *Legal Issues of Economic Integration* 28(3) (2001) 297–336.

Martijn, J.K. and Tsangarides, C.G., 'Trade Reform in the CEMAC: Developments and Opportunities', IMF Working Paper WP/07/137, available at www.imf.org/external/pubs/ft/wp/2007/wp07137.pdf.

Martinez, L., 'Algeria, the Arab Maghreb Union and Regional Integration', EuroMesco 59 (Oct. 2006), 6–43, available at www.euromesco.net/images/59_eng.pdf.

Masinga, W., '2002 SACU Deal to be Renewed', Trade Law Centre for Southern Africa (14 July 2010), available at www.tralac.org/cgi-bin/giga.cgi?cmd=cause_dir_news_item&cause_id=1694&news_id=89788&cat_id=1026.

Masinga, W., 'COMESA Members to Implement Agriculture Policies', Trade Law Centre for Southern Africa (21 July 2010), available at www.tralac.org/cgi-bin/giga.cgi?cmd=cause_dir_news_item&cause_id=1694&news_id=90109&cat_id=1026.

Mati, M., 'Kenya is Guilty of Judicial Interference', *The East African* (26 Feb. 2007), available at www.theeastafrican.co.ke/opOrEd/-/434748/253402/-/rbk891z/-/index.html.

Mavroidis, P., 'If I Don't Do it, Somebody Else Will (or Won't): Testing the Compliance of PTAs with the Multilateral Rules', Global Trade and Financial Architecture Research Paper, Yale Center for the Study of Globalization, available at www.ycsg.yale.edu/focus/gta/if_i_dont.pdf.

Meier, G.M., 'Effects of a Customs Union on Economic Development', *Social and Economic Studies*, March 1960.

Menya, W., 'Sugar Industry in Bitter Wars Ahead of COMESA Date', *Business Daily* (Apr. 2009), available at http://multimedia.marsgroupkenya.org/?StoryID=253746&page=4.

'Mercosur bloc signs free-trade deal with Egypt', Reuters, 3 Aug. 2010, available at www.bilaterals.org/spip.php?article17797 (last visited 21 Aug. 2010).

Michalopoulos, C., 'The Role of Special and Differential Treatment for Developing Countries in the GATT and the WTO', World Bank Policy Research Working Paper No. 2388 (July 2000), available at http://papers.ssrn.com/sol3/papers.cfm?abstract_id=630760.

Mishra, A.R., 'India-SACU Trade Pact May Get Delayed', LiveMint.com, 1 March 2010, available at www.tralac.org/cgi-bin/giga.cgi?cmd=cause_

dir_news_item&cause_id=1694&news_id=82932&cat_ id=1079 (last visited 25 Oct. 2010).

Mguni, M., 'Botswana Pioneers SACU Tariff Body', Trade Law Centre for Southern Africa (28 July 2010), available at www.tralac.org/cgi-bin/giga.cgi?cmd=cause_dir_news_item&cause_id=1694&news_id=90444&cat_id=1026.

'Morocco Gets US Free Trade Deal', BBC News, 23 July 2004, http://news.bbc.co.uk/2/hi/africa/3920489.stm (last visited 21 October 2010).

Mugomba, A., 'Regional Organizations and African Underdevelopment: The Collapse of the East African Community', *Journal of Modern African Studies* **16** (1978) 261–72.

Mukasa, H., 'Uganda Tops in Counterfeits', *The New Vision*, 13 July 2009, available at www.newvision.co.ug/D/8/13/6874424 (last visited 25 Oct. 2010).

Mukumbira, R., 'US-SACU Free Trade Talks Hit Snags', Islamonline.net, 15 May 2006, www.bilaterals.org/spip.php?article4712 (last visited 25 Oct. 2010).

Mushi, D., 'Why EAC Monetary Union Talks Should be Landed', *Daily News*, 25 Jan. 2011, available at www.dailynews.co.tz/feature/?n=16664&cat=feature.

Muwanga, D., 'COMESA to Address Power Shortage', Trade Law Centre for Southern Africa (22 July 2010), available at www.tralac.org/cgi-bin/giga.cgi?cmd=cause_dir_news_item&cause_id=1694&news_id=90181&cat_id=1026.

Mvogo, R., '6.41 Billion USD to Mobilize for the Tarring of Roads International Capitals', Emploi Service (20 March 2010).

Mytelka, L., 'The Salience of Gains in Third-World Integrative Systems', *World Politics* **25**(2) (1973) 236–50.

Naldi, G.J. and Magliveras, K.D., 'The African Economic Community: Emancipation For African States or Yet Another Glorious Failure?', *North Carolina Journal of International Law and Commercial Regulation* **24** (1999) 601–31.

Namunane, B., 'Kenya: Team set up to Monitor Sugar Imports', AllAfrica.com, 5 Dec. 2008, allafrica.com/stories/200809060029.html.

Njini, F., 'SADC Limps Towards a Common Market', Trade Law Centre for Southern Africa (13 Aug. 2010), available at www.tralac.org/cgi-bin/giga.cgi?cmd=cause_dir_news_item&cause_id=1694&news_id=91207&cat_id=1026.

Njoroge, E., 'East African States to Harmonize Blueprints', Trade Law Centre for Southern Africa (16 Aug. 2010), available at www.tralac.org/cgi-bin/giga.cgi?cmd=cause_dir_news_item&cause_id=1694&news_id=91259&cat_id=1026.

Njoroge, E., 'East African States Urged to Ease Trade Barriers', Trade Law Centre for Southern Africa (9 July 2010), available at www.tralac.org/cgi-bin/giga.cgi?cmd=cause_dir_news_item&cause_id=1694&news_id=89604&cat_id=1026.

Nkomo, N., 'South African High Court Approves Legal Action Against Harare in Land Case', Voice of America News (13 Jan. 2010), available at www1.voanews.com/zimbabwe/news/human-rights/Zimbabwe-South-African-Group-Granted-Right-to-Sue-Zimbabwe-13Jan10–81347412.html.

Nnanna, O.J., 'Economic and Monetary Integration in Africa', presented at G24 Meeting in Singapore, 14 September 2006, available at www.g24.org/nnan0906.pdf.

Obulutsa, G., 'East Africa May Delay Trade Pact with EU', *New Vision*, 29 July 2009, available at www.newvision.co.ug/D/1/10/689543 (last visited 25 Oct. 2010).

Odhiambo, A., 'Global Economies Rush to Strengthen Ties in EAC Market', Trade Law Centre for Southern Africa (13 Aug. 2010), available at www.tralac.org/cgi-bin/giga.cgi?cmd=cause_dir_news_item&cause_id=1694&news_id=91084&cat_id=1026 (last visited 20 Oct. 2010).

Odhiambo, A., 'EU Grants $160m to Support Regional Integration', *Business Daily*, 16 March 2010, available at www.tralac.org/cgi-bin/giga.cgi?cmd=cause_dir_news_item&cause_id=1694&news_id=83964&cat_id=1072 (last visited 25 Oct. 2010).

Odhiambo, A., 'Kenya Proposes Ways of Merging Trade Blocs', *Business Daily*, 25 Feb. 2010, www.tralac.org/cgi-bin/giga.cgi?cmd=cause_dir_news_item&cause_id=1694&news_id=82768&cat_id=1074 (last visited 2 July 2010).

Ofodile, U.E., 'Trade, Empire, and Subjects – China-Africa Trade: A New Fair Trade Arrangement or A New Scramble for Africa?', *Vand. J. Transnat'l L.* **41** (2008) 505–83.

Oh, H. and Weiss, E., 'Strengthening Compliance With International Environmental Accords: Preliminary Observations from a Collaborative Project', *Global Governance* **1** (1995) 119–48.

Okuye, J., 'COMESA Likely to Petition Kenya Over Safeguards on Sugar', *The East African Standard* (1 Dec. 2009), available at www.standardmedia.co.ke/mag/InsidePage.php?id=1144029312&cid=457&.

Oluoch, F., 'Bid to Let Regional Court of Justice Try Genocide and Human Rights Suspects', *East African* (12 Oct. 2009), available at http://allafrica.com/stories/200910120115.html.

Omondi, G., 'EAC Traders Take Tariffs War to Minister', *Business Daily*, 16 July 2010, available at http://allafrica.com/stories/201007160004.html.

Onyango, J., 'Eastern African Regions Loses $500 Million to Counterfeit Goods', *Business Daily*, 31 July 2009, www.businessdailyafrica.com/Company%20Industry/-/539550/632458/-/view/printVersion/-/qil155z/-/index.html (last visited 25 Oct. 2010).

Oyuke, J., 'Dawn of an Era for East Africans', *The Standard*, 1 July 2010, available at www.standardmedia.co.ke/InsidePage.php?id=2000012871&cid=4.

Oyuke, J., 'EAC Intensify Co-operation in Infrastructure Development', *The Standard*, 9 July 2010, available at www.standardmedia.co.ke/InsidePage.php?id=

2000013439&cid=464&story=EAC%20intensify%20co-operation%20in%20infrastructure%20development.

Oyuke, J., 'EAC Judges Call for a Harmonized Judiciary', *The Standard*, 3 Jan. 2010, available at www.standardmedia.co.ke/InsidePage.php?id=2000000137&cid=14&j=&m=&d.

Packer, C.A. and Rukare, D., 'The New African Union and Its Constitutive Act', *Am. J. Int'l L.* **96** (2002) 365–79.

Panagariya, A., 'Preferential Trade Liberalization: The Traditional Theory and New Developments', *Journal of Economic Literature* **38**(2) (2000) 287–331.

Panagariya, A., 'The Regionalism Debate: An Overview', *World Economy* **22** (1999) 455–76.

Pibasso, A.M., 'ECCAS: 8000 Billion FCFA for Roads', BusinessinCameroon.com (25 Nov. 2009), available at www.businessincameroon.com/real-estate-and-constructions-news/eccas-8000-billion-fcfa-for-roads.

Pinsloo, L., 'SA, China Sign Trade Deals Worth R2.3bn', Engineering News Online, 1 April 2010, www.engineeringnews.co.za/article/sa-and-china-sign-trade-deals-worth-r2.3bn-2010–03–31 (last visited 25 Oct. 2010).

Platform of Central African Non-State Actors, 'Why EPA Negotiations Have Slowed: A Central African Perspective', *Trade Negotiations Insights* **8**(2) March 2009, http://ictsd.net/i/news/tni/42036 (last visited 25 Oct. 2010).

'PM to Unveil Delhi Declaration at Africa Summit', *Indian Express*, 7 April 2008, available at www.indianexpress.com/news/pm-to-unveil-delhi-declaration-at-africa-sum/293769 (last visited 25 Oct. 2010).

Polgreen, L., 'World Bank Ends Efforts to Help Chad Ease Poverty', *New York Times*, 10 Sept. 2008, www.nytimes.com/2008/09/11/world/africa/11chad.html?_r=2&ref=world&oref=slogin (last visited 25 Oct. 2010).

Powers, K.L., 'International Institutions, Trade and Conflict: African Regional Trade Agreements From 1950–1992', Ph.D Dissertation, Ohio State University (2001).

Pressly, D., '"Disappointing" SACU Talks Fail to Resolve Disunity over EU Deals', Trade Law Centre for Southern Africa (20 July 2010), available at www.tralac.org/cgi-bin/giga.cgi?cmd=cause_dir_news_item&cause_id=1694&news_id=90030&cat_id=1026.

Raman, M., 'Liberalization and Interactions with the Market: A Survey of Some Experiences of Rural Producers in Developing Countries', Third World Network, April 2006, www.ivcs.org.uk/IJRS/April2007/Effects%20of%20market%20liberalisation%20on%20rural%20producers.pdf (extracts from the paper).

Raustiala, K., 'Compliance and Effectiveness in International Regulatory Cooperation', *Case Western Reserve J. Int'l L.* **32** (2000) 387–440.

Rice, X., 'Internet: Last Piece of Fibre-Optic Jigsaw Falls Into Place As Cable Links East Africa To Grid', *The Guardian*, 18 Aug. 2008, www.guardian.co.uk/technology/2008/aug/18/east.africa.internet (last visited 25 Oct. 2010).

Riungu, C., 'COMESA D-Day Shock For Kenya Sugar Firms', *The East African*, 1 June 2009, www.theeastafrican.co.ke/news/-/2558/604892/-/r316aoz/-/index.html.

'Roadmap for Grand Free Trade Area in Pipeline', *Tanzania Daily News*, 6 July 2010, www.tralac.org/cgi-bin/giga.cgi?cmd=cause_dir_news_item&cause_id=1694&news_id=89402&cat_id=1061 (last visited 21 Aug. 2010).

Robson, P., 'Regional Integration and the Crisis in Sub-Saharan Africa', *Journal of Modern African Studies* **23** (1985) 609.

Roessler, F., 'Domestic Policy Objectives and the Multilateral Trade Order: Lessons from the Past', *Univ. Penn. J. Int'l Econ. L.* **19** (1998) 513–34.

Rugumamu, S., 'Africa's Search for Regional Cooperation and Integration in the Twenty-First Century', African Foundation for Capacity Building Paper No. 3 of 2004, available at www.acbf-pact.org/knowledge/documents/ACBF%20WORKING%20PAPER%20NO.%203.pdf.

'Rwanda and Burundi Join EAC Customs Union', e-EAC Newsletter Issue No. 30, 15 July 2009.

'SACU Approves PTA with MERCOSUR', Mmegi, 9 July 2008, available at http://palapye.wordpress.com/2008/07/09/sacu-approves-pta-with-mercosur (last visited 25 Oct. 2010).

'SADC Fails to Meet Deadline', Botswana Press Agency, Gaborone, Trade Law Centre for Southern Africa (19 Aug. 2010), available at www.tralac.org/cgi-bin/giga.cgi?cmd=cause_dir_news_item&cause_id=1694&news_id=91465&cat_id=1026.

Sander, A., 'Africa Should Seize Control of Its Development', AllAfrica.com, 29 May 2009, available at http://allafrica.com/stories/200905290267.html (last visited 21 Oct. 2010).

Sandrey, R., 'China-Africa Merchandise Trade for the December 2008 Year', Trade Law Centre for South Africa (TRALAC) and the Centre for Chinese Studies, Stellenbosch University, South Africa, 1–17 available at www.tralac.org/cause_data/images/1694/WP07_SandreyCCS_ChinaAfrTrade_20090909.pdf (last visited 21 Aug. 2010).

Sandrey, R. and Jensen, H.G., 'SACU, China and India: The Implication of FTAs for Botswana, Lesotho, Namibia, and Swaziland (BLNS)', Trade Law Centre for South Africa (TRALAC), January 2009, www.tralac.org/cause_data/images/1694/WP012009SACUChinaIndiaFTAImplSandrey.pdf (last visited 21 October 2010).

Sasa, M., 'SADC Tribunal Does Not Exist', *The Herald – Zimbabwe*, 10 August 2009, available at http://allafrica.com/stories/200908100127.html.

Sibanda, L.M., 'Put Farming First in Africa', *The Guardian*, 27 April 2009, www.guardian.co.uk/society/katineblog/2009/apr/27/farming-in-africa (last visited 25 Oct. 2010).

Sifile, V. and Dube, J., 'Farm Invasions Illegal – SA', *The Standard – Zimbabwe*, 28 Nov. 2009, available at www.thestandard.co.zw/local/22423-farm-invasions-illegal–sa.html.

'South Africa to Move Ambitiously on India PTA', *Economic Times*, 7 June 2010, available at www.tralac.org/cgi-bin/giga.cgi?cmd=cause_dir_news_item&cause_id=1694&news_id=88115&cat_ id=1079 (last visited 25 Oct. 2010).

'Southern Africa Region Makes Progress on EPA', International Centre for Trade and Sustainable Development, **13**(1) (March 2009), available at http://ictsd.org/i/news/bridges/44186.

Sponsor Wire, 'Africa Abolishes Roaming as Celtel's One Network Expands', AllAfrica.com, 22 Nov. 2007, http://allafrica.com/stories/200711230067.html (last visited 21 Aug. 2010).

Staff reporter, 'Germany Tops Up EAC Commitment with Euro 6m', *The Arusha Times*, 1 Aug. 2008, available at www.arushatimes.co.tz/2008/29/local_news_4.htm

Staff writer, 'AfriForum gets Green Light to Sue Zim', *Farmers' Weekly*, 29 Jan. 2010, available at www.farmersweekly.co.za/index.php?p[IGcms_nodes][IGcms_nodesUID]=8e3a0284a973f3576d1560e65712a69f.

Staff writer, 'BIPPA Goes Against SA Law – Legal Consultants', *Zimbabwe Independent*, 26 Nov. 2009), available at www.theindependent.co.zw/local/24475-bippa-goes-against-sa-law–legal-consultants.html.

Staff writer, 'Commitment Now Needed', *The Financial Gazette*, 4 Dec. 2009, available at www.financialgazette.co.zw/index.php?option=com_content&view=article&id=2165:commitment-now-needed&catid=30:comment&Itemid=13.

Staff writer, 'Kibaki Rails at EAC Court as Rwanda, Burundi Join Up', *The East African*, 4 Dec. 2006, available at www.theeastafrican.co.ke/news/-/2558/252342/-/t6awg5z/-/index.html.

Sy, A.N.R., 'Financial Integration in the West African Monetary Union', *Journal of Financial Transformation* (2009) 91–103, available at www.capco.com/files/pdf/65/02_LESSONS%20LEARNED/09_Financial%20integration%20in%20the%20West%20African%20Monetary%20Union.pdf (last visited 20 Oct. 2010).

Tayler, P., 'Kenya's Counterfeit Agency Starts Operations', Securing Pharma, 9 Dec. 2009, available at www.securingpharma.com/40/articles/312.php (last visited 1 Aug. 2010).

Thompson, C.B., 'African Initiatives for Development: The Practice of Regional Economic Cooperation in Southern Africa', *Journal of International Affairs* **46** (1992) 125–44.

Thorp, T., 'Challenges of Incorporating the Economic Acquis Communautaire of the East African Community in a New Common Market', Working Paper No. 2010/14 (Society of International Economic Law, 29 June 2010), available at http://papers.ssrn.com/sol3/papers.cfm?abstract_id=1632439.

'Towards an African Common Market for Agricultural Products', Food and Agriculture Organization of the United Nations, Rome, Oct. 2007, at s. 3.2.4.

Udombana, N. J., 'How Should We Then Live? Globalization and the New Partnership for Africa's Development', *B.U. Int'l L.J.* **20** (2002) 293–354.

'US, SACU Anticipate Future Cooperation on Trade', *Bridges Weekly Trade News Digest* **13**(20), 3 June 2009, http://ictsd.net/i/news/bridgesweekly/47834/ (last visited 21 Aug. 2010).

Vaitsos, C.V., 'Crisis in Regional Economic Cooperation (Integration) Among Developing Countries: A Survey', *World Development* **6** (1978) 719–69.

Van Der Merwe, C., 'EU Trade Agreements Undermine Regional Integration, Says SA Official', *Engineering News*, 3 August 2009.

Wa Mutua, M., 'Why Redraw the Map of Africa: A Legal and Moral Inquiry', *Michigan Journal of International Law* **16** (1995) 1113–76.

Wakama, A., 'World's First Borderless Mobile Network Expands Into Central Africa', IT News Africa, 7 June 2007, www.itnewsafrica.com/?p=119 (last visited 25 Oct. 2010).

Walker, A., 'The EC-SADC EPA: The Moment of Truth for Regional Integration', *Trade Negotiations Insight* **8**(6) Aug. 2009, available at http://ictsd.org/i/news/tni/52416 (last visited 25 Oct. 2010).

Walker, P., 'Niger Guilty in Landmark Slavery Case', *The Guardian*, 27 Oct. 2008, available at www.guardian.co.uk/world/2008/oct/27/niger-slave-court.

Wang, J., 'What Drives China's Growing Role in Africa?', International Monetary Fund Working Paper No. 07/211 (2007).

'We Won't Sign Bogus Trade Pacts', *Daily Graphic* (22 July 2009), www.modernghana.com/news/228802/1/we-won039t-sign-bogus-trade-pacts.html (last visited 21 Aug. 2010).

Weiler, J.H.H., 'The Transformation of Europe', *Yale L. J.* **100** (1991) 2403–83.

Wood, R.N., 'The East African Common Market: A Reassessment', *Oxford University Bulletin of Economics and Statistics* **28**(4) (1966) 273–9.

Woolfrey, S., 'South Africa's Concerns over the Interim Economic Partnership Agreement', Trade Law Centre for Southern Africa, 7 Oct. 2009, available at www.tralac.org/cgi-bin/giga.cgi?cmd=cause_dir_news_item&cause_id=1694&news_id=75268&cat_id=1058.

'World Bank President Attacks China Over African Lending Policy', *Global Insight*, www.globalinsight.com/SDA/SDADetail7292.htm (last visited 21 Aug. 2010).

Xuequan, M., 'U.S. Urges Africa to Break Trade Barriers', AJ News, 6 Aug. 2009. www.ajnews.co.kr/uhtml/read.jsp?idxno=200908061411440240113&section=S1N4 (last visited 25 Oct. 2010).

Yahia, M., 'Tunis forum targets Maghreb unity as solution to economic crisis', Magharebia, 14 May 2009, www.magharebia.com/cocoon/awi/xhtml1/en_GB/features/awi/features/2009/05/14/feature-03.

Yang, Y., 'Africa in the Doha Round: Dealing with Preference Erosion and Beyond', IMF Policy Discussion Paper No. 05/8 (2005).

Yang, Y. and Gupta, S., 'Regional Trade Arrangements in Africa: Past Performance and the Way Forward', IMF Working Paper No. 05/36 (2005), 5.

Yu, P. K., 'The International Enclosure Movement', *Indiana Law Journal* **82** (2007) 827–907.

Zafar, A. and Kubota, K., 'Regional Integration In Central Africa: Key Issue', World Bank African Region Working Paper Series No. 52, June 2003, available at www.worldbank.org/afr/wps/wp52.pdf.

Zartman, I.W., 'Africa as a Subordinate State System in International Relations', *International Organization* **21**(3) (1967) 545–64.

Books

Adésínà, J.O., Graham, Y. and Olukoshi, A. (eds), *Africa and Development Challenges in the New Millennium: the NEPAD Debate* (London: Zed Books, 2006).

Akanle, O., 'The Legal and Institutional Framework of the African Economic Community', in M.A. Ajomo and O. Adewale (eds), *African Economic Community Treaty: Issues, Problems and Prospects* (Nigerian Institute of Advanced Legal Studies, 1993).

Alvarez, J., *International Organizations as Lawmakers* (Oxford University Press, 2005).

Anderson, B., *Imagined Communities: Reflections on the Origin and Spread of Nationalism* (London: Verso, 1991).

Andic, F., Andic, S. and Dosser, D., *A Theory of Economic Integration for Developing Countries, Illustrated by Caribbean Countries*, vol. I (London: Allen & Unwin, 1971).

Asante, S.K.B., 'ECOWAS/CEAO: Conflict and Cooperation in West Africa', in R.I. Onwuka and A. Sesay (eds.), *The Future of Regionalism in Africa* (London: Macmillan Education, 1985).

Asante, S.K.B. *et al.*, *Towards An African Economic Community* (Africa Institute of South Africa, 2001).

Bach, D., 'Foreword', in *Regionalisation in Africa: Integration and Disintegration* (Oxford: James Currey, 1999), xvii–xix.

Balassa, B., *The Theory of Economic Integration* (Homewood, IL: R.D. Irwin, 1961).

Banuri, T., 'Development and the Politics of Knowledge: A Critical Interpretation of the Social Role of Modernization Theories in the Development of the Third World,' in F. Apffel-Marglin and S. Marglin, *Dominating Knowledge* (Oxford: Clarendon, 1990), 29.

Bhagwati, J., 'US Trade Policy: The Infatuation with Free Trade Agreements', in J. Bhagwati and A.O. Krueger (eds.), *The Dangerous Drift to Preferential Trade Agreements* (Washington, DC: AEI Press, 1995).

Bhagwati, J., *The World Trading System at Risk* (Princeton University Press, 1991).

Broadman, H., *Africa's Silk Road: China and India's New Economic Frontier* (Washington, DC: The World Bank, 2007), 3, available at: http://siteresources.worldbank.org/AFRICAEXT/Resources/Africa_Silk_Road.pdf (last visited 25 Oct. 2010).

Bye, M., 'Structural Changes Required by Growth', in R. Harrod and D. Hague (eds.), *International Trade Theory in a Developing World* (London: Palgrave Macmillan, 1963).

Cass, D., *The Constitutionalization of the World Trade Organization* (Oxford University Press, 2005).

Cervenka, Z., *The Unfinished Quest for Unity: Africa and the OAU* (London: Julian Friedmann, 1977).

Charterjee, P., *Nationalist Thought and the Colonial World: A Derivative Discourse* (Minneapolis: University of Minnesota Press, 1993).

Chayes, A. and Chayes, A.H., *The New Sovereignty: Compliance with International Regulatory Agreements* (Cambridge, MA: Harvard University Press, 1995).

Collier, P., *Wars, Guns and Votes: Democracy in Dangerous Places* (New York: HarperCollins, 2009).

Cottier, T. and Foltea, M., 'Constitutional Functions of the WTO and Regional Trade Agreements', in L. Bartels and F. Ortino (eds.), *Regional Trade Agreements and the WTO Legal System* (Oxford University Press, 2006), 43–76.

Daniel, J., Melber, H. and Southall, R. (eds.), *A New Scramble? Imperialism, Investment and Development in Africa* (University of Kwazulu Natal Press; London: Merlin Press, 2009).

Deutsch, K., *The Analysis of International Relations* (New Jersey: Prentice Hall, 1988).

Dominguez, J., 'International Cooperation in Latin America: The Design of Regional Institutions by Slow Accretion', in A. Acharya and A. Johnson (eds.), *Crafting Cooperation: Regional Interdependence in Comparative Perspective* (Cambridge University Press, 2007).

Edel, M., 'Regional Integration and Income Distribution: Complements or Substitutes?', in R. Hilton (ed.), *The Movement Toward Latin American Unity* (New York: F.A. Praeger, 1969).

Elago, P. and Kalenga, P., 'Whither the SADC Customs Union', in *Monitoring Regional Integration Yearbook 2007* (TRALAC, 2008), available at www.garnet.sciencespobordeaux.fr/Garnet%20papers%20PDF/ELAGO%20Paulina%20&%20KALENGA%20Paul.pdf.

Essien, V., 'Regional Trade Agreements In Africa: A Historical and Bibliographical Account of ECOWAS And CEMAC', October 2006, available at www.nyulawglobal.org/globalex/CEMAC_ECOWAS.htm#_edn.

Estrella, A.T. Gobbi and Horlick, G.N., 'Mandatory Abolition of Anti-Dumping, Countervailing Duties and Safeguards in Customs Unions and Free Trade Areas Constituted between WTO Members', in Bartels and Ortino (eds), *Regional Trade Agreements and the WTO Legal System*, 109–48.

Evans, G., 'Lawmaking under the Trade Constitution: A Study in Legislating by the WTO', *Studies in Transnational Economic Law* (The Netherlands: Kluwer Law International, 2000), 14.

Ezenwe, U., *ECOWAS and the Economic Integration of West Africa* (London: Palgrave Macmillan, 1983).

Franck, T.M., *East African Unity Through Law* (Yale University Press, 1964) citing D. Apter, *The Political Kingdom of Uganda* (Princeton University Press, 1961).

Fredland, R. (ed.), *Integration and Disintegration in East Africa* (Lanham: University Press of America, 1980).

Gat, A., *War in Human Civilization* (Oxford University Press, 2006).

Gathii, J., 'Third World Approaches to International Economic Governance', in R. Falk, B. Rajagopal and J. Stevens (eds.), *International Law and the Third World: Reshaping Justice* (Abingdon: Routledge-Cavendish, 2008), 255–68.

Gathii, J., *War, Commerce and International Law* (Oxford University Press, 2010).

Green, R.H. and Seidman, A., *Unity or Poverty: The Economics of Pan-Africanism* (London: Penguin Books, 1968).

Grossman, G. and Sykes, A., 'A Preference for Development: The Law and Economics of GSP', in G. Bermann and P. Mavroidis (eds), *WTO Law and Developing Countries* (Cambridge University Press, 2007).

Haas, E., 'The Study of Regional Integration: Reflections on the Joy of and Anguish of Pre-Theorizing', in L.N. Lindberg and S. Scheingold (eds), *Regional Integration: Theory and Research* (Cambridge, MA: Harvard University Press, 1971).

Haas, E., *The Uniting of Europe* (Stanford University Press, 1958).

Hazlewood, A., 'Problems of Integration Among African States', in A. Hazlewood (ed.), *African Integration and Disintegration* (Oxford University Press, 1967).

Hazlewood, A., 'The Economics of Federation and Dissolution in Central Africa', in Hazlewood (ed.), *African Integration and Disintegration.*

Hazlewood, A., *Economic Integration: The East African Experience* (New York: St. Martin's Press, 1975).

Hazlewood, A., 'Economic Instrumentalities of Statecraft and the End of the EAC', in C. Potholm and R. Fredland (eds), *Integration and Disintegration in East Africa* (Lanham: University Press of America, 1980).

Henderson, R.D.A., 'The Southern African Customs Union: Politics of Dependence', in R.I. Onwuka and A. Sesay (eds), *The Future of Regionalism in Africa* (London: Macmillan Education, 1985).

Hettne, B., 'Globalization, Regionalism and the New Third World', in N. Poku and L. Pettiford (eds), *Redefining the Third World* (New York: St. Martin's Press, 1998).

Hilpold, P., 'Regional Integration According to Article XXIV GATT – Between Law and Politics', in *Max Planck Yearbook of United Nations Law* 7 (2003) 219–60, available at www.mpil.de/shared/data/pdf/pdfmpunyb/hilpold_7.pdf.

Hufbauer, G.C. and Brunel, C., *Maghreb Regional and Global Integration: A Dream to be Fulfilled* (Washington, DC: Peterson Institute, 2008).

Isaken, J., 'Prospects for SACU After Apartheid', in B. Oden (ed.), *Southern Africa After Apartheid: Regional Integration and External Resources* (Uppsala: Nordiska Afrikainstitutet, 1993), 182–200.

Jackson, J., *The World Trading System: Law and Policy of International Economic Relations* (Cambridge, MA: MIT Press, 1989).

Jawara, F. and Kwa, A., *Behind the Scenes at the WTO: The Real World of Trade Negotiations: The Lessons of Cancun XV* (London: Zed Books, 2004).

Kessie, E., 'The Legal Status of Special and Differential Treatment', in Bermann and Mavroidis (eds), *WTO Law and Developing Countries.*

Krasner, S. (ed.), *International Regimes* (Utica, NY: Cornell University Press, 1983).

Krasner, S., 'Structural Causes and Regime Consequences; Regimes as Intervening Variables', in S. Linder, *Trade and Trade Policy for Development* (New York: Praeger Series on International Economics and Development, 1967).

Krueger, A.O., 'Problems with Overlapping Free Trade Areas', in O. Takatoshi and A.O. Krueger (eds.), *Regionalism Versus Multilateral Trade Arrangements* (University of Chicago Press, 1997), 9–23.

Kufuor, K., *The Institutional Transformation of the Economic Community of West African States* (Aldershot: Ashgate Publishing Ltd., 2006).

Kumar, U., 'Economic Dominance and Dependence: The Case of the Southern African Customs Union', in O. Saasa (ed.), *Joining the Future: Economic Integration and Co-operation in Africa* (Nairobi: African Centre for Technology Studies, 1991).

Lyakurwa, W., Mckay, A., Ng'eno, N. and Kennes, W., 'Regional Integration in Southern Africa: A Review of Experiences and Issues', in A. Oyejide, I. Elbadawi and P. Collier (eds), *Regional Integration and Trade Liberalization in Subsaharan Africa: Framework Issues and Methodological Perspectives* (London: Palgrave Macmillan, 1997).

Maphanyane, E.M., 'SADCC-Future Challenges', in Oden (ed.), *Southern Africa After Apartheid: Regional Integration and External Resources*, 174–81.

Mathis, J., 'Regional Trade Agreements and Domestic Regulation', in L. Bartels and F. Ortino (eds.), *Regional Trade Agreements and the WTO Legal System* (Oxford University Press, 2006), 79–108.

Mathis, J.H. and Bhagwati, J., *Regional Trade Agreements in the GATT/WTO: Article XXIV and the Internal Trade Requirement* (The Netherlands: T.M.C. Asser Press, 2002).

McCarthy, C., 'Regional Integration in SubSaharan Africa: Past, Present and Future', in A. Oyejide, B. Ndulu and D. Greenway (eds), *Regional Integration and Trade Liberalization in SubSaharan Africa, vol. IV: Synthesis and Review* (London: Palgrave Macmillan, 1999).

McMillan, J., 'Does Regional Integration Foster Open Trade?', in K. Anderson and R. Blackhurst (eds), *Regional Integration and the Global Trading System* (New York: Harvester Wheatsheaf, 1993).

Meade, J.E., *The Theory of Customs Unions* (Westport, CT: Greenwood Press, 1955).

Mengisteab, K., *Globalization and Autocentricity in Africa's Development in the 21st Century* (Trenton, NJ: Africa World Press, 1996).

Mikesell, R.F., 'The Movement Towards Regional Trading Groups in Latin America', in A.O Hirschman. (ed.), *Latin American Issues: Essays and Comments* (New York: The Twentieth Century Fund, 1961), 125–51.

Mikesell, R.F., 'The Theory of Common Markets as Applied to Regional Arrangements Among Developing Countries', in R. Harrod and D. Hague (eds.), *International Trade Theory in a Developing World* (London: Palgrave Macmillan, 1963).

Mortimer, R.A., 'The Arab Maghreb Union: Myth and Reality', in Y. H. Zoubir (ed.), *North Africa in Transition: State, Society, and Economic Transformation in the 1990s* (Gainesville, FL: University Press of Florida, 1999), 177–91.

Mutai, H.K., *Compliance With International Trade Obligations: The Common Market for Eastern and Southern Africa* (Boston: Kluwer Law International, 2007).

Mwaura, C. and Schmeidl, S. (eds), *Early Warning and Conflict Management in the Horn of Africa* (Lawrenceville, NJ: The Red Sea Press, Inc., 2002).

Myrdal, G., *Economic Theory and Underdeveloped Regions* (New York: Harper & Row, 1957).

Nkurumah, K., *Africa Must Unite* (London: Panaf Books, 1963).

Nwachukwu, I., *Nigeria and the ECOWAS Since 1985: Towards a Dynamic Regional Integration* (Nigeria: Fourth Dimension Publishing Co., 1991).

Nye, J., *Pan-Africanism and East African Integration* (Cambridge, MA: Harvard University Press, 1965).

Nye, J., 'Comparing Common Markets: A Revised Neo-Functionalist Model', in L.N. Lindberg and S. Scheingold (eds), *Regional Integration: Theory and Research* (Cambridge, MA: Harvard University Press, 1971).

Nyerere, J.K., *Ujamaa-Essays on Socialism* (Oxford University Press, 1968).

Ogan, C.A., 'The International Personality of the African Economic Community', in M.A. Ajomo and O. Adewale, *African Economic Community Treaty: Issues, Problems and Prospects* (Lagos: Nigerian Institute of Advanced Legal Studies, 1993), 52–3.

Ohlson, T. and Stedman, S.J., 'Towards Enhanced Regional Security in Southern Africa?', in Oden (ed.), *Southern Africa After Apartheid: Regional Integration and External Resources*, 87–107.

Oshodi, A.O., 'The Legal Framework of the A.E.C.', in Ajomo and Adewale, *African Economic Community Treaty: Issues, Problems and Prospects.*

Ostergaard, T., 'Classical Models of Regional Integration – What Relevance for Southern Africa?', in Oden (ed.), *Southern Africa After Apartheid: Regional Integration and External Resources*, 27–47.

Philip, A., 'Preface' to F. Kahnert *et al.*, *Economic Integration Among Developing Countries* (Paris: OECD Development Centre, 1969).

Poku, N., *Regionalization and Security in Southern Africa* (London: Palgrave Macmillan, 2001).

Ravenhill, J., 'The Future of Regionalism in Africa', in Onwuka and Sesay (eds), *The Future of Regionalism in Africa* (London: Macmillan Education, 1985).

Ravenhill, J., 'The Theory and Practice of Regional Integration in East Africa', in Potholm and Fredland, *Integration and Disintegration in East Africa.*

Rivas, J.A., 'Do Rules of Origin in Free Trade Agreements Comply with Article XXIV GATT?', in Bartels and Ortino (eds), *Regional Trade Agreements and the WTO Legal System*, 149–72.

Robson, P., 'Economic Integration in Equatorial Africa', in Hazlewood (ed.), *African Integration and Disintegration.*

Robson, P., 'Problems of Integration Between Senegal and Gambia', in A. Hazlewood (ed.), *African Integration and Disintegration.*

Robson, P., *Economic Integration in Africa* (Evanston, IL: Northwestern University Press, 1968).

Robson, P., *Integration, Development, and Equity: Economic Integration in West Africa* (London: Unwin Hyman, 1968).

Roessler, F., 'The Relationship between Regional Integration Agreements and the Multilateral Trade Order', in Anderson and Blackhurst (eds), *Regional Integration and the Global Trading System.*

Rosenau, J.N. and Czempiel, E.O., *Governance Without Government: Order and Change in World Politics* (Cambridge University Press, 1992).

Rothchild, D. and Curry, Jr., R.L., *Scarcity, Choice and Public Policy in Middle Africa* (Berkeley: University of California Press, 1978).

Saasa, O.S., 'Background to Regional Integration in Africa', in O.S. Saasa (ed.), *Joining the Future: Economic Integration and Co-operation in Africa* (Nairobi: African Centre for Technology Studies Press, 1991).

Saasa, O.S., 'Economic Cooperation and Integration Among Developing Countries', in Saasa (ed.), *Joining the Future.*

Saasa, O.S., 'SADCC Industrial Co-Operation and Donor Support', in Saasa, (ed.), *Joining the Future.*

Shaw, T.M., 'Towards a Political Economy of Regionalism in Africa', in Onwuka and Sesay (eds), *The Future of Regionalism in Africa.*

Sonarajah, M., *The International Law on Foreign Investment* (Cambridge University Press, 2004).

Taylor, I., *China and Africa: Engagement and Compromise* (New York: Routledge, 2006).

Vaitsos, C.V., 'The Role of Transnational Enterprises in Latin American Economic Integration Efforts: Who Integrates With Whom, How and for Whose Benefit?', in M.N. Jovanovic (ed.), *Economic Integration And Spatial Location Of Firms And Industries*, 3 vols (Cheltenham: Edward Elgar, 2007), vol. III.

Viner, J., *The Customs Union Issue* (New York: Carnegie Endowment for International Peace, 1950).

Wionczek, M.S., 'Introduction – Present Status and Prospects of Economic Integration Movements in Developing Countries: Political Atomization and Economic Backwardness of the Southern Hemisphere', in M.S. Wionczek, *Economic Cooperation in Latin America, Africa and Asia* (Cambridge, MA: MIT Press, 1969).

World Trade Organization, *The Results of The Uruguay Round of Multilateral Trade Negotiations* (Cambridge University Press, 2000).

Reports

'Addis Ababa Declaration on Economic Partnership Agreement Negotiations', African Union, Report of the Conference of Ministers of Trade of the African Union, 15–16 January 2007, Ext/Exp/Trade/Decl.(2) III, available at www.uneca.org/eca_resources/news/2007/EPA_Addis_Ababa_Ministerial_Declaration.pdf (last visited 21 Aug. 2010).

African Peer Review Mechanism, 'Kenya Progress Report on the Implementation of the African Peer Review Mechanism (APRM) National Programme of Action', available at www.nepadkenya.org/Documents/progress_report_jan06.pdf.

African Peer Review Mechanism, 'South African Country Review Report No. 5', (2007), available at www.aprm.org.za/docs/ SACountryReviewReport5.pdf.

African Union, 'Status of Integration in Africa', 2nd edn, April 2009, available at www.africa-union.org/root/ua/conferences/2009/mai/ea/07–08mai/status%20of%20integration%20in %20africa%2027–04–09.pdf.

African Union, 'The Report of the Committee of Heads of State and Government on the Proposals of the Great Socialist Peoples' Libyan Arab Jamahiriya', 13 June 2005.

Ahearn, R. J., 'Morocco-U.S. Free Trade Agreement,' CRS Report for Congress, 26 May 2005, http://ftp.fas.org/sgp/crs/mideast/RS21464.pdf (last visited 21 Aug. 2010).

'Brief on COMESA', High Commission of India (Aug. 2010), available at http://meaindia.nic.in/foreignrelation/23fr01.pdf.

CRTA, 'Examination of the EC-Jordan Euro-Mediterranean Agreement – Note on the Meeting of 29 March 2004', WT/REG141/M/1 (28 April 2004).

East African Community, 'The Lake Victoria Basin Commission', available at www.eac.int/lvbc.pdf.

'EBID in Brief', ECOWAS Bank for Investment and Development, no author, no date, available at www.bidc-ebid.org/en/documentation.php.

ECA Policy Research Report, 'Assessing Regional Integration in Africa' (Addis Ababa: United Nations Economic Commission for Africa, 2004), available at http://www.uneca.org/aria1/ARIA%20English_full.pdf.

ECA Policy Research Report, Assessing Regional Integration in Africa II: Rationalizing Regional Economic Communities (Addis Ababa: United Nations Economic Commission for Africa, 2004), available at http://www.uneca.org/aria2/full_version.pdf.

ECA Policy Research Report, Assessing Regional Integration in Africa III: Towards Monetary and Financial Integration in Africa (Addis Ababa: United Nations Economic Commission for Africa, 2008), available at www.iss.co.za/uploads/ARIA3NOV08.PDF.

ECA Policy Research Report, Assessing Regional Integration in Africa IV: Enhancing Intra-African Trade (Addis Ababa: United Nations Economic Commission for Africa, 2010), available at www.uneca.org/eca_resources/Publications/books/aria4/ARIA4Full.pdf.

Economic Commission for Latin America, 'The Latin American Common Market', UN Publication No. 59.II.G.4 (New York, 1959).

EPA Negotiations: 'Where Do we Stand? – Eastern and Southern Africa', 26 May 2009, available at www.acp-eu-trade.org/index.php?loc=epa (last visited 25 Oct. 2010).

'EPA Negotiation Issues Between ESA and EU', CTA Agritrade, April 2010, available at: http://agritrade.cta.int/en/Resources/Agritrade-documents/Agriculture-Executive-briefs/EPA-negotiation-issues-between-ESA-and-the-EU (last visited 25 Oct. 2010).

Europa, Fact Sheet on the Interim Economic Partnership Agreements, http://trade.ec.europa.eu/doclib/docs/2009/january/tradoc_142188.pdf (last visited 25 Oct. 2010).

'ICEG, Free Trade Agreements and Rules of Origin', Policy Brief No. 0012, Middle.

Imani Development, 'Inventory of Regional Non-Tariff Barriers: Synthesis Report' (July 2007), available at http://ntb.africonnect.com/media/ntb_synthesis_2007_final.pdf.

'Implementation of the Great Arab Free Trade Agreement: The Case of Syria', Working Paper No. 8, National Agriculture Policy Center of the Ministry of Agricultural and Agrarian Reform, available at www.napcsyr.org/dwnld-files/working_papers/en/08_gafta_en.pdf.

International Center for Economic Growth, East Africa Program, no author, no date.

Jones, V.C., 'U.S. Trade and Investment Relationship with Sub-Saharan Africa: The African Growth and Opportunity Act' (Congressional Research Service, 24 July 2009), available at http://fpc.state.gov/documents/organization/128835.pdf (last visited 25 Oct. 2010).

Kahnert, F. *et al.*, *Economic Integration Among Developing Countries* (Paris: OECD Development Centre, 1969).

'Lagos Plan of Action for Economic Development of Africa 1980–2000'. Organization for African Unity (OAU, Addis Ababa, 1980).

Lahcen ACHY, 'Trade in North Africa: Assessing Regional Integration Potential in North Africa', UN Economic Commission for Africa, ECA-NA/RABAT/ICE/XXI/3/I (April 2006), available at www.uneca.org/sros/na/documents/Trade.pdf.

'Lake Victoria Fisheries Organization: An Institution of East African Communities' (no author, no date), available at www.lvfo.org.

Langton, D., 'United States-Southern African Customs Union (SACU) Free Trade Agreement Negotiations: Background and Potential Issues', CRS Report for Congress, 24 July 2008, available at http://fpc.state.gov/documents/organization/109530.pdf (last visited 21 Oct. 2010).

Lebale, N. *et al.*, 'Economic Development in Africa: Report 2009: Strengthening Regional Economic Integration for Africa's Development', United Nations Conference on Trade and Development (United Nations, 2009).

Maluwa, T., 'The Move From Institutions? Examining the Phenomenon in Africa', Proceedings of the Annual Meeting (American Society of International Law), 100 (2006) 294–8.

Mugisa, E., 'An Evaluation of the Implementation and Impact of the East African Community Customs Union', Final Report, EAC Secretariat, (Mar. 2009).

'Non-Tariff Barriers Monitoring Mechanism', Regional Trade Facilitation Programme, no author, no date, http://ntb.africonnect.com.

Obasanjo, O., 'Study on An African Union Government: Towards the United States of Africa, presented to the Seventh Session of the Assembly of the Heads of States of the African Union in Banjul' (July 2006), available at www.africa-union.org/Doc/study_on_ AUGovernment_june2006.pdf.

Paper on the Establishment of an African Common Market, No. E/CN.14/STC/20 (13 Oct. 1963), no author.

'Quantitative Restrictions on Trade', presented at the Seventh Trade Policy Coordinating Meeting of CAREC, 6 Sept. 2007, no author, available at www.adb.org/Documents/Carec/QRStudy.pdf.

'Regional Dissemination Workshop on Agricultural Trends and Progress in Living Conditions in West Africa, Synthesis Report of the Main Conclusions and Recommendations', Accra, Ghana, 12 May 2009, http://resakss.files.wordpress.com/2009/06/ghanamay2009_conclusions.pdf (last visited 25 Oct. 2010), no author.

'Regional Economic Outlook: Middle East and Central Asia', IMF (Sept. 2006), available at www.imf.org/external/pubs/ft/reo/2006/ENG/02/mreo0906.pdf.

'Regional Integration for Global Competitiveness', World Bank, available at http://siteresources.worldbank.org/INTMENA/Resources/EDP2008_Chap_2.pdf.

Report of the Committee of Heads of State and Government on the Proposals of the Great Socialist Peoples' Libyan Arab Jamahiriya, 13 June 2005, available at www.africa-union.org/Doc/Report_of_the_Committee_of_Heads_of_State_and_Government_on_the_Proposals_of_Libya.doc.

Scollay, R., '"Substantially All Trade": Which Definitions are Fulfilled in Practice?', Report for the Commonwealth Secretariat, 15 Aug. 2005, available at www.thecommonwealth.org/shared_asp_files/uploadedfiles/54198A83–736D-4D36-B484–27400E267BCE_SATPaperforComsecCompleteJano6.pdf.

'Secretariat's Report on Coverage, Liberalization Process and Transition Periods in Regional Trade Agreements', WTO Doc. No. WT/REG/W/46, 5 Apr. 2002.

Short Term Consultancy on the Status of Implementation of Overload Control and other Trade Facilitation Instruments in the IGAD Region, IGAD (June 2010), available at http://igad.int/attachments/221_TOR_FOR_A_SHORT_CONSULTANCY_OF_the_WB%5B1%5D%5B1%5D.pdf.

Sub-Committee Report on Annex II of the Protocol on the Establishment of the East African Common Market.

'Supporting Regional Integration in East Africa through Strengthening CSO's Regional Approaches and Capacities', EAC/GTZ Programme 'Support to the Integration Process', available at www.eacgermany.org/index.php/eac-gtz-programme.

The Seventh EU-ECOWAS Ministerial Troika Meeting, Luxembourg, 18 May 2005, available at www.europa-eu-un.org/articles/en/article_4706_en.htm.

United Nations Economic Commission on Africa, 'European Integration and African Trade', UN Pub. No. E/CN.14/STC/4 (23 Aug. 1964).

United Nations Economic Commission on Africa, 'Background Paper on the Establishment of an African Common Market', No. E/CN.14/STC/20 (13 Oct. 1963).

US Department of State, Bureau of Public Affairs, *Background Notes: Sierra Leone* (09/10), http://www.state.gov/r/pa/ei/bgn/5475.htm.

Vienna Convention on the Law of Treaties (signed 23 May 1969, entered into force 27 Jan. 1980).

Official Documents

2002 Southern African Customs Union (SACU) Agreement (21 Oct. 2002), Art. 34, available at www.sacu.int/main.php?include=docs/legislation/2002-agreement/part7.html.

2002 Southern African Customs Union (SACU) Agreement, Preamble, http://www.sacu.int/main.php?include=docs/legislation/2002-agreement/main.html (last visited 1 June 2010).

About COMESA, 'History of COMESA', about.comesa.int/lang-en/component/content/article/1-general/14-history-of-comesa.

Accra Declaration of the African Union Summit Meeting (3 July 2007), available at http://ausummit-accra.org.gh/index1.php?linkid=242&page=2&sectionid=303.

ACP's WTO submission, Doc. No. TN/RL/W/155, 26 Apr. 2004.

African Development Bank Group, AfDB in Brief, available at www.afdb.org (last visited 9 July 2010).

African Development Bank Group, Project Portfolio, available at www.afdb.org/en/projects-operations/project-portfolio (last visited 21 Aug. 2010).

African Growth and Opportunities Act, 19 U.S.C. ss 3701–3747 (2000), available at www.agoa.gov/agoa_legislation/agoa_legislation.html (last visited 21 Aug. 2010).

African International Courts and Tribunals Website, 'ECOWAS CCJ', available at www.aict-ctia.org/courts_subreg/ecowas/ecowas_home.html.

African Union Commission, 'CAADP Day: African Union Promotes Agricultural Development in Africa', African Press Organization, Division of Communication and Information, 29 June 2009, available at http://appablog.wordpress.com/2009/06/29/caadp-day-african-union-promotes-agricultural-development-in-africa/ (last visited 25 Oct. 2010).

African Union, Status of Integration in Africa 2nd edn, Apr. 2009, www.africa-union.org/root/ua/conferences/2009/mai/ea/07–08mai/status%20of%20integration%20in%20africa%2027–04–09.pdf (last visited 21 Aug. 2010).

AGOA, 'Summary of AGOA', www.agoa.gov/agoa_legislation/agoa_legislation.html (last visited 25 Oct. 2010).

Agreed Conclusions on Preferences in UNCTAD, 24 Apr. 1985, available at www.chasque.net/frontpage/suns/trade/areas/develope/unctad/04240085.htm.

Agreement Establishing the Inter-Governmental Authority on Development, Intergovernmental Authority on Drought and Development Assembly of Heads of State and Government (adopted 21 March 1996, into force 25 Nov. 1996), at Art. 14(a).

Agreement Establishing The Inter-Governmental Authority on Development (IGAD), available at http://www.gtz.de/en/dokumente/en-agreement-establishing-igad.pdf.

Agreement on Rules of Origin, Preamble, available at www.wto.org/english/docs_e/legal_e/22-roo_e.htm.

Agreement on Trade-Related Aspects of Intellectual Property Rights, 15 Dec. 1993, Marrakesh Agreement Establishing the World Trade Organization, Annex 1C, Legal Instruments – Results of the Uruguay Round, vol. 31, 33 ILM 81 (1994), art. 39.3, available at www.wto.org/english/tratop_e/trips_e/t_agm0_e.htm (last visited 25 Oct. 2010).

Alliance for Commodity Trade in Eastern and Southern Africa (ACTESA), Design Plan, August 2008, http://programmes.comesa.int/attachments/130_ACTESA%20Design%20Plan.pdf (last visited 25 Oct. 2010).

Annual Report of the Executive Secretary of ECOWAS, Fostering Regional Integration through NEPAD Implementation, ECW/CM/XLIX/2, (2002), available at www.sec.ecowas.int/sitecedeao/english/rapport/es_annual_ report_2002.pdf.

Arab Maghreb Union – Request for Observer Status, 'Communication from the Arab Maghreb Union', L/7548 (2 Nov. 1994), available at www.wto.org/gatt_docs/English/SULPDF/91820125.pdf.

Assembly of Heads of State and Government of the Organization of African Unity meeting in its Twenty-seventh Ordinary Session in Abuja, Federal Republic of Nigeria, Resolution on the African Economic Community, June 1991, AHG Res. 205 (XXVII), www.africa-union.org/root/au/Documents/Decisions/hog/1HoGAss embly1991.pdf (last visited 21 Aug. 2010).

'Assessing Regional Integration in Africa III', UN Economic Commission on Africa, African Union (2008), available at www.iss.co.za/uploads/ARIA3NOV08.PDF.

'Assessing Regional Integration in Africa IV', UN Economic Commission on Africa, 14–15, available at www.uneca.org/eca_resources/Publications/books/aria4/ARIA4Full.pdf.

BCEAO, 'Currency Issue and Payment Systems, Annual Report 2005', available at: www.bceao.int/internet/bcweb.nsf/files/III%20-%20Currency%20issue%20and%20payment%20systems.pdf/$FILE/III%20-%20Currency%20issue%20and%20payment%20systems.pdf.

BCEAO, 'The New Payment Systems in the West African Economic and Monetary Union (WAEMU)', available at www.bceao.int/internet/bcrsmp.nsf/pdf/newsystempaymentWAEMU.pdf/$FILE/newsystempaymentWAEMU.pdf.

CAADP Implementation, Donor Platform, www.donorplatform.org/content/view/101/147 (last visited 17 July 2009).

CAADP, 'Implementing the CAADP Agenda', www.caadp.net/implementing-caadp-agenda.php (last visited 21 Aug. 2010).

CAADP, 'National Roundtables', www.caadp.net/national-rountables.php (last visited 21 Aug. 2010).

CAADP, 'The Role of Regional Economic Communities', www.caadp.net/role-regional-economic-communities.php (last visited 25 Oct. 2010).

'CEMAC-Transport-Transit Facilitation Project', A Document of the World Bank Organization, 25 May 2007, available at www-wds.worldbank.org/external/default/WDSContentServer/WDSP/IB/2007/06/05/000020953_20070605105125/Rendered/PDF/38463.pdf.

Central African Economic and Monetary Community – 'Paper on recent developments and regional policy issues; public information notice on the executive board discussion; and statement by the executive director on recent developments and regional policy issues in the Central African Economic and Monetary Community', available at www.imf.org/external/pubs/ft/scr/2005/cr05403.pdf.

Chambas, M. I., 'ECOWAS, Annual Report of the Executive Secretary of ECOWAS, Fostering Regional Integration Through NEPAD Implementation', s. 10.6, ECW/CM/XLIX/2 (Dec. 2002), www.comm.ecowas.int/sec/fr/rapport/es_annual_report_2002.pdf (last visited 21 Aug. 2010).

'COMESA Court of Justice to Improve its Visibility' (30 May 2010), available at www.comesa.int/lang-en/component/content/article/34-general-news/382-comesa-court-of-justice-to-improve-its-visibility.

COMESA Regulations on Trade Remedy Measures adopted at The Twelfth Meeting of the Council of Ministers in Lusaka, Zambia, on 30 November, 2001, available at http://programmes.comesa.int/index.php?option=com_content&view=article&id=54&Itemid=63&lang=en

COMESA Rules of Origin Protocol, Rule 2(1)(a), available at http://about.comesa.int/attachments/059_Protocol_on_the_Rules_of_Origin.pdf.

COMESA, 'COMESA Court of Justice', available at http://about.comesa.int/lang-en/institutions/court-of-justice.

Common Declaration with regard to Preferential Rules of Origin, Annex II of the Agreement on Rules of Origin, para. 2, available at www.wto.org/english/docs_e/legal_e/22-roo_e.htm.

Communication from the EC, Doc. No. TN/TF/W/37, 29 Apr. 2005.

Communiqué, IGAD–EU Ministerial Troika Meeting, available at www.igad.int/index.php?option=com_content&view=article&id=141:communique-igad-eu-ministerial-troika-meeting&catid=47:communique&Itemid=149.

Communiqué of the 12th Ordinary Summit of the Heads of State and Government of IGAD, available at www.igad.int/index.php?option=com_content&view=article&id=107:communique-of-the-12th-summit-of-heads-of-state-and-government-of-igad-&catid=47:communique&Itemid=149.

Communiqué of the 10th Extraordinary Summit of the Heads of State of the East African Community (29 Apr. 2009).

Communiqué of the 12th Summit of the COMESA Heads of State and Government, 22–3 May 2007.

Constitutive Act of the African Union, 11 July 2000, at www.oau.oua.org/LOME2000/introductory_note.htm.

Cotonou Agreement, 23 June 2000, available at http://ec.europa.eu/development/icenter/repository/agr01_en.pdf (last visited 1 June 2010).

'Country Strategy Paper and National Indicative Programme for the Period 2008–2013', Kingdom of Swaziland–European Community, http://ec.europa.eu/development/icenter/repository/scanned_sz_csp10_en.pdf (last visited 25 Oct. 2010).

Crawford, J. and Fiorentino, R., 'The Changing Landscape of Regional Trade Agreements', Discussion Paper No. 8 (Geneva: WTO Secretariat, 2005), available at www.wto.int/english/res_e/booksp_e/discussion_papers8_e.pdf.

CTA Agritrade, 'Executive Brief: EU–West Africa EPA Negotiations', March 2009, available at http://agritrade.cta.int/en/content/view/full/1790#31 (last visited 25 Oct. 2010).

Decisions and Declarations, 8th Assembly of the African Union, Assembly/AU/Dec. 154 (VIII) (30 Jan. 2007).

Decisions and Declarations, 2nd Assembly of the African Union, Assembly/AU/Decl.6 (II) (12 July 2003).

Decisions and Declarations, 2nd Assembly of the African Union, AHG/Dec. 31 (II) (12 July 2003).

Decisions and Declarations, 2nd Assembly of the African Union, AHG/Dec. 8 (II) (12 July 2003).

Decisions and Declarations, 2nd Assembly of the African Union, AHG/Dec. 8(4) (II) (12 July 2003).

Decisions and Declarations, 2nd Assembly of the African Union, AHG/Dec. 7 (II) (12 July 2003).

Decisions and Declarations, 12th Executive Council, EX.CL/Dec. 378 (XII) (29 Jan. 2008).

Decisions and Declarations, 12th Executive Council, EX.CL/Dec. 379 (XII) (29 Jan. 2008).

Decisions and Regulations of the 69th Ordinary Session of the Council of Ministers, CM/Dec.437 (LXIX) (23 March 1999).

Declarations and Resolutions as Adopted by the 21st Ordinary Session of the Assembly of Heads of State and Government, AHG/Decl.1(10) (XXI) (20 July 1985).

Declarations and Resolutions Adopted by the 31st Ordinary Session of the Assembly of Heads of State and Government, CM/Res.1580 (LXII) (23 June 1995).

Decisions, Declarations, Message of Congratulations and Motion, 12th Assembly of the African Union, Assembly/AU/Dec. 208 (XII) (3 Feb. 2009).

Decisions, Declarations, Message of Congratulations and Motion, 14th Assembly of the African Union, Assembly/AU/Dec.287 (XIV) (3 Feb 2010).

Decisions, Declarations and Resolution, 5th Assembly of the African Union, Assembly/AU/Dec. 89 (V) (5 July 2005).

Decisions, Declarations and Resolution, 5th Assembly of the African Union, Assembly/AU/Dec. 88 (V) (5 July 2005).

Decisions, 8th Extraordinary Session of the Executive Council, Ext/EX.CL/Dec.1 (VIII) (19 Jan. 2006).

Decisions, 11th Executive Council, EX.CL/Dec.371 (XI) (29 June 2007).

Decisions, 3rd Assembly of the African Union, Dec.47 (III) (8 July 2004).

Decision No. A/Dec. 1/5/83 relating to the adoption and the implementation of a single trade liberalization scheme for industrial products originating from member states (30 May 1983), available at www.sec.ecowas.int/sitecedeao/english/adec010583.htm.

Decision No. C/DEC.3/5/8.

Decision No. A/DEC.1/5/81of the Authority of Heads of State and Government, available at www.comm.ecowas.int/sec/index.php?id=adec010581&lang=en.

Decision No. A/DEC.1/5/83 of the Authority of Heads of State and Government, available at www.comm.ecowas.int/sec/index.php?id=adec010583&lang=en.

Decision No. A/DEC.6/6/89 of the Authority of Heads of State and Government, available at www.comm.ecowas.int/sec/index.php?id=adec060689&lang=en.

Decision No. A/DEC.6/7/92 of the Authority of Heads of State and Government, Preamble, available at www.comm.ecowas.int/sec/index.php?id=adec060792&lang=en.

Decision No. A/DEC.6/7/92 of the Authority of Heads of State and Government, available at www.comm.ecowas.int/sec/index.php?id=adec060792&lang=en.

Decisions, 8th Extraordinary Session of the Executive Council Ext/EX.CL/Dec.2 (VIII) (19 Jan. 2006).

Decisions, 7th Executive Council, EX.CL/Dec. 217 (VII) (2 July 2005).

Decisions, 13th Executive Council, EX.CL/Dec.423(5) (XIII) (28 June 2008).

Decisions, 3rd Assembly of the African Union, Dec.47 (III) (8 July 2004).

Decisions of the 76th Ordinary Session, OAU Council of Ministers and 11th Ordinary Session of the AEC, CM/Dec. 652 (LXXVI).

Decisions of the 4th Ordinary Session of the Executive Council (16 March 2004).

Declarations and Resolutions as Adopted by the 21st Ordinary Session of the Assembly of Heads of State and Government, AHG/Decl.1 (XXI) (20 July 1985).

EAC Development Strategy 2006–2010, Executive Summary, available at www.eac.int/home.html.

East African Community Common Market (Free Movement of Workers) Regulations, Annex II to the East African Community Common Market Protocol, Reg. 5(2).

East African Community Customs Management Act 2004.

East African Community Customs Union (Rules of Origin) Rules, available at www.tralac.org/unique/tralac/pdf/20060629_Rules_of_Origin.pdf.

East African Community, 'East African Court of Justice – Role of the Court', Corporate Communications and Public Affairs Department, available at www.eac.int/organs/eacj.html?start=2.

East African Community Web Site, 'East African Court of Justice – Review of Judgments', Corporate Communications and Public Affairs Department, available at www.eac.int/organs/eacj.html?start=5.

Economic Community of West African States Revised Treaty, 24 July 1993.

ECOWAS Community Court of Justice, Protocol A/P.1/7/91 (adopted 6 July 1991, into force 5 Nov. 1996, amended by Supplementary Protocol A/SP.1/01/05 in 2005), at Art. 9(1).

ECOWAS Vision 2020, available at: http://www.pambazuka.org/aumonitor/comments/2194/

EFTA, 'About EFTA, Member States', www.efta.int/about-efta/the-efta-states.aspx (last visited 1 June 2010).

Electronic Transactions Act 2000 (Act No 23 of 2000) (1 Aug. 2001), available at http://programmes.comesa.int/attachments/128_Electronic%20Transaction%20Act.pdf.

Eleventh Meeting of the COMESA Council of Ministers, 20–1 May 2001.

EU–Cameroon Interim Economic Partnership Agreement, 2 Feb. 2009, http://eur-lex.europa.eu/LexUriServ/ LexUriServ.do?uri=OJ:L:2009:057:0002:0360:EN:PDF (last visited 25 Oct. 2010).

Europa, Africa, Asia, Pacific Regional Negotiations of Economic Partnership Agreements, http://ec.europa.eu/trade/issues/bilateral/regions/acp/regneg_en.htm (last visited 25 Oct. 2010).

Europa, 'International And Regional Trade Relation: EU–ACP, Economic Partnership Agreements', www.delbrb.ec.europa.eu/en/irtr/euacp_repa.htm (last visited 21 Aug. 2010).

European Commission, 'Clarification and Improvement to GATT Art. XXIV Provisions', Second Submission on Regional Trade Agreements by the European Communities (26 Apr. 2005), 3, available at http://trade.ec.europa.eu/doclib/docs/2005/may/tradoc_123424.pdf.

European Commission, 'The Cotonou Agreement', available at http://ec.europa.eu/development/geographical/cotonouintro_en.cfm (providing an overview of the Agreement).

Final Communiqué of the 26th Meeting of the ECOWAS Heads of State and Government (31 Jan. 2003).

Final Communiqué of The COMESA-EAC-SADC Tripartite Summit of Heads of State and Government, Kampala, Uganda, 22 Oct. 2008, www.tralac.org/cause_data/images/1694/FinalCommuniqueKampala_20081022.pdf.

Final Communiqué of the 11th Summit of the COMESA Heads of State and Government (1 Dec. 2006).

Final Communiqué of the 13th Summit of the COMESA Authority of Heads of State and Government (8 June 2009).

Final Report of the Meeting of Legal Experts of the ACP on EPA Negotiations, 9–11 October 2007, ACP/00/051/07 Rev. 1, available at www.africa-union.org/root/UA/Conferences/2007/octobre/TI/ 11%20oct/ 0005107%20Rev1%20Report%20ACP%20Legal%20Experts%20(3).doc (last visited 21 Aug. 2010).

Forum on China–Africa Cooperation, 'Declaration of Sharm El Sheikh of the Forum on China–Africa Cooperation', 12 Nov. 2009, available at www.focac.org/eng/zxxx/t626388.htm (last visited 25 Oct. 2010).

Forum on China-Africa Cooperation, 'Sharm El Sheikh Action Plan (2010–2012)', 21 Nov. 2009, available at www.focac.org/eng/zxxx/t626387.htm (last visited 25 Oct. 2010).

Free Trade Agreements and Rules of Origin, International Center for Economic Growth Policy Brief No. 0012, available at www.atdforum.org/IMG/pdf/Policy_Brief_RoO.pdf (last visited 26 Oct. 2010).

Free Trade Agreement between EFTA and SACU, July 2006, www.sacu.int/docs/tradeneg/efta-fta2006.pdf (last visited 25 Oct. 2010).

'Free Trade Agreement Between EFTA and SACU', EFTA, 5 May 2008, www.efta.int/free-trade/free-trade-news/2008–05–05-efta-sacu-fta-enters-into-force.aspx (last visited 25 Oct. 2010).

GATT Article XI(1), available at www.wto.org/english/docs_e/legal_e/gatt47_01_e.htm#articleXI.

General Council, 'Decision on a Transparency Mechanism for Regional Trade Agreements of 16 Dec. 2006', WT/L/671, adopted 18 Dec. 2006.

Gulde-Wolf, A. *et al.*, 'Central African Economic And Monetary Community: Selected Issues', IMF Country Report, 3 June 2005, available at www.imf.org/external/pubs/ft/scr/2005/cr05390.pdf.

'Handbook: Free Trade Area', The South African Development Community Protocol on Trade, 2008, 4 available at www.sadc.int/cms/uploads/SADC%20Free%20Trade%20Area%20Handbook%20-%20English.pdf.

ICAO, 'Air Transport Liberalization Process in SADC', www.icao.int/icao/en/atb/meetings/2008/Sympo_Nigeria/Docs/SADC.pdf (last visited 25 Oct. 2010).

'Implementation of the Yamoussoukro Decision Progressing or Stalled?', ICAO/ATAG/WB Development Forum: Maximizing Civil Aviation's Economic Contribution: Safe, Secure and Sustainable Air Transport in Open Skies Challenges and Potential, Montreal, Canada, May 2006, www.icao.int/DevelopmentForum/Forum_06/Docs/YamoussoukroDecision.pdf (last visited 21 Aug. 2010).

India–Africa Forum Summit 2008, Delhi Declaration, Apr. 2008, www.ibef.org/download/India_Africa.pdf (last visited 25 Oct. 2010).

'Industry Associations: A Catalyst in Regional Integration', Eastern and Southern African Dairy Association, 22 Feb. 2008, available at www.dairyafrica.com/news.asp?ID=41 (last visited 28 Oct. 2010).

Interim Economic Partnership Agreement Between Eastern and Southern African States and the European Community, 29 Aug. 2009, art. 11, www.investmauritius.com/download/ESA-EPA-INTERIM.pdf (last visited 21 Aug. 2010).

International Plant Protection Convention, available at www.ippc.int/index.php?id=1110589&L=0 (follow 'Core Activities' hyperlink; then 'Commission (CPM)' hyperlink).

Kajange, D., 'Air Transport Market Liberalisation in Africa: The Yamoussoukro Decision Process', African Union, Infrastructure & Energy Department, April 2009, http://ec.europa.eu/transport/air/events/doc/eu_africa/session_1_air_transport_market_liberalisation_in_africa.pdf (last visited 25 Oct. 2010).

Mbeki, T., 'Speech of the President of South Africa, Thabo Mbeki, at the launch of the African Renaissance Institute, 11 October 1999', available at www.au2002.gov.za/docs/speeches/mbeki991011.htm.

'Mission, Vision, Objectives & Role of UIA', Uganda Investment Authority, available at www.ugandainvest.com/uia.php?uhpl=mission&&uhpl1=Mission.

Monrovia Declaration of Commitment on the Guidelines and Measures for National and Collective Self-Reliance in Economic and Social Development for the Establishment of a New International Economic Order, 17–20 July 1979, available at www.africa-union.org/root/au/Documents/Decisions/hog/pHoGAssembly1979.pdf.

Mueller, J., Yackovlev, I. and Weisfeld, H., 'The Global Financial Crisis: Impact on WAEMU Member countries and Policy Options', International Monetary Fund Staff Position Note, 2 July 2009, available at www.imf.org/external/pubs/ft/spn/2009/spn0916.pdf.

Negotiating Group on Rules, 'Compendium of Issues Related to Regional Trade Agreements', Doc. No. TN/RL/W/8/Rev.1 (1 Aug. 2002).

'Non-Tariff Barriers Monitoring Mechanism', Regional Trade Facilitation Programme, available at http://ntb.africonnect.com.

Observer Status for the Community of Sahel-Saharan States in the General Assembly, 'Explanatory Memorandum: Annex 1 to the Letter Dated 24 July 2001 from Permanent Representative of Sudan to the United Nations addressed to the Secretary-General', A/56/191, 2, available at www.un.org/documents/ga/docs/56/a56191.pdf.

Official Gazette of the Common Market for Eastern and Southern Africa (COMESA), vol. 15, No. 1, Part III, Art. 7 (9 June 2009), available at http://about.comesa.int/attachments/062_2009%20Gazette%20Vol.%2015%20No1.pdf.

Ojo, M.O., 'The Challenges of introducing the Eco Currency', West African Monetary Institute, 8 June 2004, available at www.wami-imao.org/english/doc/IntroducingEcoCurrency.pdf.

Organization for African Unity, Lagos Plan of Action for the Economic Development of Africa 1980–2000, adopted at the OAU Meeting in its 2nd Extraordinary Session, Preamble, para. 3(iii), 28–9 April 1980.

Organization for African Unity Charter, First Assembly of Heads of State and Government (25 May 1963), at Art. III(1).

Oxfam International, 'Undermining Access to Medicines: Comparison of Five US FTAs', Oxfam Briefing Note, June 2004, available at www.twnside.org.sg/title2/FTAs/Intellectual_Property/IP_and_Access_to_Medicines/ UnderminingAccessToMedicines.pdf (last visited 25 Oct. 2010).

Preferential Trade Agreement Between Southern Common Market (MERCOSUR) and Southern African Customs Union (SACU), 16 Dec. 2004, available at www.sice.oas.org/tpd/MER_SACU/MER_SACU_e.asp (last visited 25 Oct. 2010).

Procedures Manual on the Implementation of the Protocol on the Rules of Origin for Products to be traded between the Member States of the Common Market for Eastern and Southern Africa (Nov. 2002), available at http://about.comesa.int/attachments/059_Revised_Procedures_Manual.pdf.

'Profile: Economic Community of West African States (ECOWAS)', African Union, available at www.africa-union.org/root/au/recs/ECOWASProfile.pdf.

Protocol on the Establishment of the East African Community Common Market, signed 20 Nov. 2009, available at www.eac.int/advisory-opinions/cat_view/68-eac-common-market.html.

Protocol on the Establishment of the East African Customs Union, 30 Nov. 1999, available at www.eac.int/customs/index.php?option=com_content&view=article&id=2:customs-union-protocol&catid=3:key-documents&Itemid=141.

Protocol on Tribunal and the Rules of Procedure Thereof, South African Development Community (adopted 7 Aug. 2000).

Protocol Relating to the Application of Compensation for Loss of Revenue Incurred by ECOWAS Member States as a Result of the Trade Liberalisation

Scheme, May 2002, available at www.ehu.es/ ceinik/tratados/ 11TRATADOSSOBREINTEGRACIONYCOOPERACIONENAFRICA/ 111ECOWAS/IC11121.pdf.

Protocol Relating to the Assessment of Loss of Revenue by Member States, 5 Nov. 1976 available at www.ehu.es/ceinik/tratados/11TRATADOSSOBR EINTEGRACIONYCOOPERACIONENAFRICA/111ECOWAS/IC1113.pdf.

Protocol Relating to the Fund for Co-operation, Compensation and Development of the Economic Community of West African States, 5 Nov. 1976, available at www.comm.ecowas.int/sec/ index.php?id=ap051176 fund&lang=en.

Regional Agricultural Policy for West Africa: ECOWAP, 'Make Agriculture the Lever of Regional Integration', www.diplomatie.gouv.fr/fr/IMG/pdf/ 01_ANG-ComCEDEAO.pdf (last visited 25 Oct. 2010).

Report of the 6th Ordinary Meeting of the Executive Council, 22–3 August 2001, available at www.uneca.org/CEN-SAD/reportofthe6thordinary-sessionoftheEC.htm.

Resolutions Adopted by the 47th Ordinary Session of the Council of Ministers, CM/Res. 1130 (XLVII) (27 Feb. 1988).

Resolutions Adopted by the 52nd Ordinary Session of the Council of Ministers, CM/Res.1279 (LII) (8 July 1990).

Resolutions Adopted by the 59th Ordinary Session of the Council of Ministers, CM/Res. 1480 (LIX) (4 Feb. 1994).

Resolutions Adopted by the 60th Ordinary Session of the Council of Ministers, CM/Res.1514 (LX) (11 June 1994).

Resolutions Adopted by the 61st Ordinary Session of the Council of Ministers, CM/Res. 1555 (LXI) ANNEX (27 Jan. 1995).

Resolutions Adopted by the 61st Ordinary Session of the Council of Ministers, CM/Res. 1556.

Resolutions Adopted by the 61st Ordinary Session of the Council of Ministers, CM/Res. 1580 (LXI).

Resolutions Adopted by the 63rd Ordinary Session of the Council of Ministers, CM/Res. 1617 (LXIII) (28 Feb. 1996).

Resolution No. 6/11/2000 Relating to the Capital Expenditure Budget of the ECOWAS Fund for the 2001 Financial Year, ECOWAS Council of Ministers, Resolution No. 6/11/2000 (14 Nov. 2000).

Resolution No. 5/11/2000 Relating to the Operational Budget of the ECOWAS Fund for the 2001 Financial Year, ECOWAS Council of Ministers, Resolution No. 5/11/2000 (14 Nov. 2000).

Revised Treaty of the Economic Community of West African States (ECOWAS), 24 July 1993, 35 ILM 660 (1993).

Rwanda Investment Promotion Agency, Law No. 14/98 of 18 Dec. 1998.

SADC Regional Indicative Strategic Development Plan, available at www.sadc.int/ index/browse/page/319.

SACU, 'History of SACU', available at www.sacu.int/about.php?include=about/history.html.

SACU Web Site, 'Trade Facilitation: An Overview', available at www.sacu.int/tradef.php?include=about/tradef/overview.html.

SACU Web Site, 'Trade Facilitation: SACU-WCO Customs Development Programme', available at www.sacu.int/tradef.php?include=about/tradef/customs.html.

South African Customs Union Agreement (SACU), signed 21 Oct. 2002, available at www.sacu.int/main.php?include=docs/legislation/2002-agreement/part5.html.

'Southern Africa: Towards Economic Liberation: A Declaration by the Governments of Independent Africa Made at Lusaka on the 1st of April 1980', in *Record of the Southern African Development Coordination Summit Conference* (Lusaka, 1980) 35.

Speech by Mr. Sindiso Ngwenya, Secretary General, COMESA, at The Second Africa Agriculture Markets Programme Policy Seminar, David Livingstone Hotel, Livingstone, Zambia, 15 June 2009, http://about.comesa.int/attachments/161_090616AAMP_Secretary_General_speech_Livingstone.pdf (last visited 21 Aug. 2010).

Stevens, C., 'Economic Partnership Agreements (EPAs): Where We Are', ODI Briefing Paper (June 2006).

'Sub-Theme for Infrastructure Support on Regional Integration', SADC Consultative Conference, Windhoek, Namibia, April 2006, http://unpan1.un.org/intradoc/groups/public/documents/cpsi/unpan027121.pdf (last visited 25 Oct. 2010).

Supplementary Protocol, A/SP.1/01/05 Amending the Preamble and Articles 1, 2, 9, 22 and 30 of Protocol A/P.1/7/91 Relating to the Community Court of Justice and Article 4 Paragraph 1 of the English Version of Said Protocol', 28th Session of the Authority of Heads of State and Government (19 Jan. 2004).

Sutherland, P. *et al.*, 'The Future of the WTO: Addressing Institutional Challenges in the New Millennium', Report by the Consultative Board to the Director-General, Supachai Panitchpakdi (WTO, 2005), available at www.wto.org/english/thewto_e/10anniv_e/future_wto_e.pdf.

The Comprehensive Africa Agriculture Development Programme (CAADP), COMESA Programmes, COMESA, http://programmes.comesa.int/index.php?option=com_content&view=article&id=25&Itemid=42&lang=en (last visited 25 Oct. 2010).

'The Declaration of the Establishment of the IGAD Regional Consultative Process on Migration', Inter-State and Intra-Regional Cooperation on Migration Management Workshop Report, 14 May 2008.

The East African Community Council of Ministers, http://security.eac.int.

The General Agreement on Tariffs and Trade (GATT) 1948, 30 Oct. 1947, Art. 1, available at www.wto.org/english/docs_e/legal_e/gatt47_e.pdf.

The South African Development Community (SADC) Protocol on Trade, August 1996, available at www.sadc.int.

The Trade Act 1974, as amended, 19 U.S.C. 2251 *et seq.* (2006).

The Trade Act 2002, 19 U.S.C. s. 2102 *et seq.* (2006).

The World Bank, 'Sub-Saharan Africa Regional Integration Q&A', http://web.worldbank.org/WBSITE/EXTERNAL/COUNTRIES/AFRICAEXT/EXTREGINI/EXTAFRREGINICOO/0, contentMDK:20655099~menuPK:1587625~pagePK:64168445~piPK:64168309~theSitePK:1587585,00.html (last visited 21 Aug. 2010).

The World Bank, 'Sub-Saharan Africa Transport Policy Program Partners', http://web.worldbank.org/WBSITE/EXTERNAL/COUNTRIES/AFRICAEXT/EXTAFRREGTOPTRA/EXTAFRSUBSAHTRA/0, contentMDK:20625619~menuPK:1586428~pagePK:64168445~piPK:64168309~theSitePK:1513930,00.html (last visited 25 Oct. 2010).

Third Meeting of the Coordination and Monitoring Committee for the Implementation of the Yamoussoukro Decision in West and Central Africa, Libreville, 29 Nov. 2004.

Treaty Establishing the African Economic Community (AEC), 3 June 1991, available at http://www.africa-union.org/root/au/Documents/Treaties/Text/AEC_Treaty_1991.pdf.

Treaty Establishing the Common Market for Eastern and Southern Africa (COMESA), signed 5 Nov. 1993, available at http://about.comesa.int/attachments/ 149_090505_COMESA_Treaty.pdf.

Treaty Establishing the East African Community (adopted 30 Nov. 1999, into force 7 July 2000), 2144 UNTS 255.

Treaty Establishing the Economic Community of Central African States (ECCAS), 19 Oct. 1983, 23 ILM 945 (1984).

Treaty Establishing the Economic Community of West African States (ECOWAS), signed 28 May 1975, available at www.comm.ecowas.int/sec/index.php?id=treaty&lang=en.

Treaty Establishing the Southern African Development Community (adopted and into force 17 Aug. 1992, amended 14 Aug. 2001), at Arts 1(g) and 16(1).

Treaty for East African Co-operation, Art. 87, Kenya–Uganda–Tanz., 6 June 1967, 6 ILM 932.

Treaty for the Establishment of the African Economic Community, signed 3 June 1991, 30 ILM 1241 (1991).

Treaty for the Establishment of the East African Community, chs 11–27, signed 30 Nov. 1999, available at www.eac.int/ (click on 'About EAC' tab and follow 'Treaty Establishing the EAC' hyperlink).

Treaty Instituting the Arab Maghreb Union (adopted 17 Feb. 1989, into force 1 July 1989).

Treaty of Lisbon Amending the Treaty on European Union and the Treaty Establishing the European Community, Art. 43 and 43(b), 13 Dec. 2007, 2007 OJ (C 306) 1.

Treaty of the CEMAC is available at www.aict-ctia.org/courts_subreg/cemac/cemac_docs.html.

Treaty of the Southern African Development Community (SADC) As Amended, 17 Aug. 1992.

Uganda Export Promotion Board, 'COMESA, COMESA Trade Remedies', www.ugandaexportsonline.com/comesa.htm.

UN Conference on Ministers of Trade, Nairobi Declaration on Economic Partnership Agreements, TI/TIMIN/MIN/Decl.2 (IV), 14 Apr. 2006, available at www.africa-union.org/root/AU/Conferences/Past/2006/April/TI/Nairobi%20Declaration%20on%20EPAs.pdf (21 Aug. 2010).

UN Conference on Trade and Development, 'Current Problems of Economic Integration: The Distribution of Benefits and Costs of Integration Among Countries', UN Doc. No. TD/B/394 (New York, 1973).

UN Conference on Trade and Development, 'Voluntary Peer Review of Competition Policy: West African Economic and Monetary Union, Benin and Senegal' (New York, 2007), available at www.unctad.org/en/docs/ditcclp20071overview_en.pdf.

UN Economic and Social Council Commission on Sustainable Development, 'Thematic Cluster for the Implementation Cycle 2008–2009 – Policy Session', E/CN.17/2009/14 (6 Mar. 2009).

U.N. Econ. & Soc. [ECOSOC], Economic Commission for Africa, 'Decision Relating to the Implementation of the Yamoussoukro Declaration Concerning the Liberalisation of Access to Air Transport Markets in Africa', art. 2, ECA/RCID/CM.CIVAC/99/RPT (13 Nov. 1999).

U.N. Econ. & Soc. [ECOSOC], Economic Commission for Africa, 'The Transport Situation in Africa', E/ECA/CTRCI/5/3 (1 Aug. 2007), www.uneca.org/crci/5th/The-transport-situation-Africa.pdf (last visited 25 Oct. 2010).

UN Human Rights Council, High Level Task Force on the Implementation of the Right to Development, Working Group on the Right to Development, The Cotonou Partnership Agreement Between the European Union (EU) and African, Caribbean and Pacific (ACP) Countries, UN Doc. A/HRC/8/WG.2/TF/CRP.6 (21 Dec. 2007) (prepared by James Thuo Gathii).

Understanding on the Interpretation of Article XXIV of the GATT 1994, Preamble, available at www.wto.org/english/docs_e/legal_e/10–24_e.htm.

United States Department of Commerce Information on Central Africa, 'Brief on Central and West Africa,' available at www.buyusa.gov/westafrica/en/79.html.

Wakeman-Linn, J., Portillo, R., Iossifov, P. and Milkov, D., 'The International Financial Crisis and Global Recession: Impact On The CEMAC Region and Policy Considerations', IMF Staff Position Note, 22 July 2009, available at www.imf.org/external/pubs/ft/spn/2009/spn0920.pdf.

World Trade Organization (WTO), *Agreement on Safeguards*, www.wto.org/english/tratop_e/safeg_e/safeint.htm.

WTO, *Understanding the WTO* (2007), available at www.wto.org/english/thewto_e/whatis_e/tif_e/understanding_e.pdf.

WTO, 'Legal Texts: the WTO Agreements', available at www.wto.org/english/docs_e/legal_e/ursum_e.htm#iAgreement.

WTO, 'Non-Tariff Barriers: Red Tape, etc.', available at www.wto.org/english/thewto_e/whatis_e/tif_e/agrm9_e.htm#origin.

WTO, 'Work of the CRTA', available at www.wto.org/english/tratop_e/region_e/regcom_e.htm.

WTO, 'Regional Trade Agreements Notified to the GATT/WTO and in Force', available at www.wto.org/english/tratop_e/region_e/type_e/xls.

WTO, 'Trade Policy Review: Report by the Secretariat: Southern African Customs Union', Doc. No. WT/TPR/S/222 (30 Sept. 2009), at 1, para. 1, available at www.wto.org/english/tratop_e/tpr_e/tp322_e.htm.

WTO, 'GATT and Goods Council', available at www.wto.org/english/tratop_e/gatt_e/gatt_e.htm.

WTO Secretariat, 'Standard Format for Information on Regional Trade Agreements', WTO Doc. No. WT/REG/W/6 (Aug. 1996).

www.usig.org/countryinfo/laws/Uganda/East%20African%20Community%20customs%20Management%20Act%202004.pdf.

Other Sources

'About SEA-ME-WE 4', SEA-ME-WE 4, www.seamewe4.com/inpages/about_sea_me_we_4.asp (last visited 25 Oct. 2010).

About the Economic Cooperation, IGAD, and Social Development – Transport & Communications, 11 Jan. 2010, http://igad.int/index.php?option=com_content&view=article&id=96&Itemid=147&Limitstart=2 (last visited 25 Oct. 2010).

'ACP Member States', The Secretariat of the African, Caribbean and Pacific Group States, available at www.acpsec.org/en/acp_states.htm.

'Addressing Migration Challenges in Eastern Africa', IGAD, 27 June 2008, http://igad.int/index.php?option=com_content&view=article&id=228:addressing-migration-challenges-in-eastern-africa-&catid=63:migration&Itemid=159 (last visited 21 Aug. 2010).

'Africa–India Framework for Cooperation', Africa–India Forum Summit, New Delhi, India, 9 April 2008, available at www.africa-union.org/root/au/

Conferences/2008/april/India-Africa/India-Africa.html (last visited 25 Oct. 2010).

African Union, 'Africa Forum Summit 2008', available at www.africa-union.org/root/au/Conferences/2008/april/India-Africa/press_releases.htm (last visited 25 Oct. 2010).

African Union, 'Africa–India Summit Forum Adopts Delhi Declaration and the Framework for Cooperation', 9 April 2008, available at www.africa-union.org/root/au/Conferences/2008/april/India-Africa/press_releases.htm (last visited 25 Oct. 2010).

African Union, 'Economic Community of Central African States: Profile', 2, available at www.africa-union.org/Recs/ECCASoverview.pdf. See also Chapter II for more on UDEAC.

African Union, 'The New Partnership for African Development' (October 2001), available at www.nepad.org/home/lang/en (follow the NEPAD Framework link).

African Union, 'Regional Economic Communities, Community of Sahel-Saharan States', available at www.africa-union.org/root/au/recs/cen_sad.htm.

AGOA, 'Resource on the African Growth and Opportunities Act', available at www.agoa.info.

Agreement Establishing the WTO, Preamble, available at www.wto.org/english/docs_e/legal_e/04-wto.pdf.

Akiwumi, A.M., 'Towards an Independent and Effective Judiciary in Africa', Speech given at the African Development Forum Conference, 'Governance for a Progressing Africa', held in Addis Ababa (11–15 Oct. 2004), available at www.uneca.org/adfiv/documents/speeches_and_presentations/speech_akiwumi.htm.

Arab Maghreb Union, *Encyclopedia of Business* (2nd edn), available at www.referenceforbusiness.com/encyclopedia/A-Ar/Arab-Maghreb-Union.html.

Arab Maghreb Union, 'History', available at www.maghrebarabe.org/en/uma.cfm.

CAADP, 'About CAADP', www.caadp.net/about-caadp.php (last visited 21 Aug. 2010).

CEMAC official site, 'Ministerial Committee,' available at http://translate.google.com/translate?hl=en&sl=fr&u=http://www.cemac.int/&ei=gk1tTPC4KIHGlQfCsu2vDw&sa=X&oi=translate&ct=result&resnum=1&ved=0CBYQ7gEwAA&prev=/search%3Fq%3Dcemac.int%26hl%3Den.

CEN-SAD, '11th Ordinary Session of the Conference of Leaders and Heads of State', available at www.cen-sad.org/new/index.php?option=com_content&task=view&id=282&Itemid=236.

CEN-SAD Web Site, 'About CEN-SAD', available at www.cen-sad.org/new/index.php?option=com_content&task=view&id=33&Itemid=76.

CEN-SAD Web Site, 'Trade Sector', available at www.cen-sad.org/new/index.php?option=com_content&task=view&lang=en&id=150.

COMESA Programmes, 'Infrastructure', available at http://programmes.comesa.int/index.php?option=com_content&view=article&id=110&Itemid=50&lang=en.

COMESA Programmes, 'Investment Promotion and Private Sector Development', available at http://programmes.comesa.int/index.php?option=com_content&view=article&id=82&Itemid=66&lang=en.

COMESA Programmes, 'COMESA Customs Union', available at http://programmes.comesa.int/index.php?option=com_content&view=article&id=119&Itemid=73&lang=en.

COMESA Programmes, 'The COMESA Customs Union: Status on Sensitive Products and Implementation of the Transition Period', available at http://programmes.comesa.int/attachments/119_comesa_customs_union_status_03%2006%202010.pdf.

COMESA Programmes, 'Trade Facilitation', available at http://programmes.comesa.int:80/index.php?option=com_content&view=article&id=55&Itemid=63&lang=en.

COMESA Programmes, 'Trade Remedies and Safeguards, Initiation of Safeguard Measures or Actions Against Subsidy and Dumping', available at http://programmes.comesa.int//index.php?option=com_content&view=article&id=54%20.

COMESA, 'COMESA Strategy', available at http://about.comesa.int/lang-en/overview/comesa-strategy.

COMESA, 'History of COMESA', available at http://about.comesa.int/lang-en/overview/history-of-comesa.

COMESA, 'Overview', available at http://about.comesa.int/lang-en/overview.

COMPETE, 'About COMPETE', http://www.competeafrica.org/about.htm (last visited 31 Aug. 2010).

COMPETE, 'Staple Foods', http://www.competeafrica.org/components/building%20value%20chains/staplefoods.htm (last visited 28 Oct. 2010).

COMPETE, 'Specialty Coffee', www.competeafrica.org/components/building%20value%20chains/specialtycoffee.htm (last visited 28 Oct. 2010).

Constitutive Act of the African Union, 11 July 2000, at www.africa-union.org/root/au/Aboutau/Constitutive_Act_en.htm.

Cotton Africa, 'About Cotton Africa', www.cottonafrica.com/page.php?id=9 (last visited 6 July 2010).

'Country Strategy Paper and National Indicative Programme for the Period 2008–2013', Kingdom of Swaziland–European Community, 24, http://ec.europa.eu/development/icenter/repository/scanned_sz_csp10_en.pdf (last visited 25 Oct. 2010).

Department of International Relations and Cooperation of the Republic of South Africa, 'Arab Maghreb Union', available at www.dfa.gov.za/foreign/Multilateral/africa/amu.htm.

Differential and more Favourable Treatment, Reciprocity and Fuller Participation of Developing Countries, Decision of 28 Nov. 1979, GATT Doc. L/493, available at www.wto.org/english/docs_e/legal_e/enabling1979_e.htm.

'Djibouti/IOM Office Opens To Help Address Migration Challenges Along Strategic Route', IGAD, 13 May 2009, http://igad.int/index.php?option=com_content&view=article&id=230:djibouti–iom-office-opens-to-help-address-migration-challenges-along-strategic-route-&catid=63:migration&Itemid=159 (last visited 21 Aug. 2009).

EAC, 'Towards the EAC Political Federation', available at www.eac.int/summit/201-towards-the-eac-political-federation.html.

East African Community, 'East African Community – Kenya, Uganda, Tanzania, Rwanda, Burundi', available at www.eac.int.

FOCAC, 'Characteristics of FOCAC', www.focac.org/eng/ltda/ltjj/t157576.htm (last visited 25 Oct. 2010).

'Frequently Asked Questions', US Commercial Service, www.buyusa.gov/morocco/en/96.html (last visited 25 Oct. 2010).

Grain, Africa and the Middle East, Morocco's FTA Frenzy, www.bilaterals.org/IMG/pdf/fightingFTA-en-Hi-2-f-morocco-fta-frenzy.pdf (last visited 21 Aug. 2010).

'IGAD Profile', African Union, available at www.africa-union.org/Recs/IGAD_Profile.pdf.

IGAD Strategy, s. 1.3.1.

IGAD, 'About Us', available at http://igad.int/index.php?option=com_content&view=article&id=93&Itemid=124.

IGAD, 'Roadmap for Regional Integration' (19 Mar. 2009), available at http://igad.int/index.php?option=com_content&view=article&id=161:roadmap-for-regional-integration-plan&catid=44:economic-cooperation&Itemid=127.

Ikiara, G., Permanent Secretary Ministry of Transport and Communications (Kenya), 'EAC Common Market Protocol: Protocol on Transport', Paper presented at the National Retreat for Members and Key Stakeholders of the East African Common Market High Level Task Force, Utali Hotel, Nairobi, 12 May 2008.

'India – Boosting Trade with Africa', Africa Business Pages, Business Guide Internet Edition, available at www.africa-business.com/features/india_africa.html (last visited 25 Oct. 2010).

Intellectual Network for the South, 'Economic and Monetary Community of Central Africa,' available at www.insouth.org/index.php?option=com_sobi2&sobi2Task=sobi2Details&sobi2Id=55&Itemid=.

'International Trade Agreements – Brief guide to Importers and Exporters', Zambia Revenue Authority, Leaflet No. 10, available at www.zra.org.zm/publications/TradeAgreement.pdf.

Mutai, H., 'The Regulation of Regional Trade Agreements: Harnessing the Energy of Regionalism to Power a New Era in Multilateral Trade', (PhD thesis, School of Graduate Studies (Law), University of Melbourne, July 2005).

Nalo, DSO, Permanent Secretary, Ministry of East African Community on Kenya National Consultation Workshop for the Study on the Establishment of the East African Community Development Fund, Statement at the Grand Regency Hotel (6–7 Oct. 2008), at 2, available at www.meac.go.ke (follow 'Permanent Secretary's Speeches' hyperlink).

NEPAD, 'About NEPAD', www.nepad.org/about (last visited 25 Oct. 2010).

Office of the High Representative for the Least Developed Countries, 'Landlocked Developing Countries and the Small Island Developing States, Least Developed Countries: Criteria for Identification of LDCs', available at www.unohrlls.org/en/ldc/related/59.

Office of the United States Trade Representative, 'Bilateral Investment Treaties', www.ustr.gov/trade-agreements/bilateral-investment-treaties (last visited 25 Oct. 2010).

Office of the United States Trade Representative, 'Morocco FTA', www.ustr.gov/trade-agreements/free-trade-agreements/morocco-fta/final-text (last visited 25 Oct. 2010).

Office of the United States Trade Representative, 'Trade and Investment Framework Agreements', www.ustr.gov/trade-agreements/trade-investment-framework-agreements (last visited 25 Oct. 2010).

Office of the United States Trade Representative, 'United States and Mauritius Launch Investment Treaty Talks', www.ustr.gov/about-us/press-office/press-releases/2009/august/united-states-and-mauritius-launch-investment-treaty (last visited 1 Aug. 2010).

Opening Statement by Nana Akufo-Addo, Minister for Foreign Affairs of the Republic of Ghana and Chairperson of the Executive Council of the African Union at the 11th Ordinary Session of the Executive Council, 28–29 June 2007, available at www.africa-union.org/root/au/conferences/2007/june/summit/9thAUSummit.htm.

Osoro, G., 'An Overview of the Elimination of Non-Tariff Barriers' (23 April 2009), available at www.mcci.org/photos/ntbs.ppt.

PAIDF fund manager website at www.harith.co.za/investors/index.html.

Powers, K.L., 'Why Do States Pursue Water Cooperation through Regional Trade Agreements?' Trade, Environment and Security Linkages in International River Basins (1 Sept. 2005) (unpublished manuscript, on file with the American Political Science Association).

President of the East African Court of Justice, H.R. Nsekela, 'The Role of the East African Court of Justice in the Integration Process', Presentation during the 3rd East African Community Media Summit (22 Aug. 2009).

President Thabo Mbeki, 'Address of the President of South Africa to the Joint Session of the Parliament of Namibia' (30 October 2007), available at www.polity.org.za/article/sa-mbeki-parliament-of-namibia-joint-session-30102007–2007–10–30.

Press Release, 'Council Chairperson Assures Community on Ratification of Common Market Protocol' (26 Apr. 2010), available at www.eac.int/news/index.php?option=com_content&view=article&id=226:ratification-of-common-market-protocol&catid=48:eac-latest&Itemid=69.

Press Release, 'Council Commends Secretariat and Organs for Receiving Unqualified Accounts', East African Community, 22 Oct. 2010.

Press Release: 'East African Court Takes Justice Closer to the People' (13 Aug. 2010), available at http://news.eac.int/index.php?option=com_content&view=article&id=276:eacj-closer-to-the-people&catid=48:eac-latest&Itemid=69.

Press Release, 'Heads of Human Rights Commissions Recommend Draft EAC Bill of Rights to Council of Ministers' (EAC Department of Corporate Communications and Public Affairs, 4 June 2010), available at www.news.eac.int/index.php?option=com_content&view=article&id=253:nhrcs-recommend-bill-of-rights&catid=48:eac-latest&Itemid=69.

Press Release, 'Heads of Human Rights' Commissions Review EAC Draft Bill of Rights' (EAC Department of Corporate Communications and Public Affairs, 1 June 2010), available at www.news.eac.int/index.php?option=com_content&view=article&id=250:heads-of-human-rights-commissions-review-eac-draft-bill-of-rights&catid=48:eac-latest&Itemid=69.

Press Release, 'Negotiations on the Annexes to the EAC Common Market Protocol Ongoing in Kigali, Rwanda' (8 June 2009).

Press Release, 'Secretary General, Japanese Delegation Discuss Common Market', 5 July 2010, available at www.eac.int/component/content/461.html?task=view.

Press Release, 'Status and Meaning of Ratification of SADC Treaty and Tribunal Protocol', Zimbabwe Human Rights NGO Forum (6 Sept. 2009), available at www.zimbabwedemocracynow.com/2009/09/06/status-and-meaning-of-ratification-of-sadc-treaty-and-tribunal-protocol.

'Profile: Arab Maghreb Union', African Economic Community website, available at www.africa-union.org/Recs/AMUOverview.pdf.

Public Statement on the International Investment Regime, 31 Aug. 2010, available at www.osgoode.yorku.ca/public_statement/documents/Public%20Statement.pdf.

RATES, 'Annual Performance Monitoring Report: October 2002–September 2003', Chemonics International, Inc., 15 October 2003, 35, http://pdf.usaid.gov/pdf_docs/PDACM135.pdf.

RATES, 'Annual Performance Monitoring Report: October 2003–September 2004', Chemonics International, Inc., 15 October 2004, http://pdf.usaid.gov/pdf_docs/PDACM138.pdf.

RATES, 'Annual Performance Monitoring Report: October 2004–September 2005', Chemonics International, Inc., 15 October 2005, http://pdf.usaid.gov/pdf_docs/PDACM140.pdf.

RATES, 'Annual Progress Report: October 2004–September 2005', Chemonics International, Inc., 15 October 2005, http://pdf.usaid.gov/pdf_docs/PDACM139.pdf.

'Record', Integrated Committee of Ministers: Infrastructure and Services Cluster, SADC/ICM/1/2008/2.2a, 19 June 2008, www.madagascar-diplomatie.net/article.php?article_id=568.

Regional ICT Support Programme, 'Home', http://rictsp.comesa.danishmanagement.dk/index.php?option=com_content&task=view&id=17&Itemid=22 (last visited 25 Oct. 2010).

SADC FTA Brochure, available at www.sadc.int/fta.

SADC FTA Leaflet, available at www.sadc.int/fta.

SADC FTA website, available at www.sadc.int/fta.

SADC Protocol on Trade Pt. 2, Art. 3(1), available at www.sadc.int.

SADC, 'Profile', available at www.sadc.int/index/browse/page/52.

SADC, 'SADC Tribunal', available at www.sadc.int/tribunal.

SAT3/WASC/SAFE, www.safe-sat3.co.za (last visited 21 Aug. 2010).

'The East Africa Migration Route: Building Co-operation, Information Sharing and Developing Joint Practical Initiatives Amongst Countries of Origin, Transit, and Destination', IGAD, 27 July 2010, available at http://igad.int/index.php?option=com_content&view=article&id=231&Itemid=160 (last visited 25 Oct. 2010).

The New African Initiative, A Merger of the Millennium African Renaissance Partnership Programme (MAP) and The Omega Plan, July 2001, http://www.uneca.org/eca_resources/conference_reports_and_other_documents/nepad/nai.pdf.

The Third Extraordinary Summit of the Heads of State of the EAC, Joint Communiqué, 29–30 May 2005).

UEMOA, 'The Organs of Management', (English trans.), available at www.microsofttranslator.com/BV.aspx?ref=BVNav&a=http%3A%2F%2Fwww.uemoa.int%2Forganes%2Fdirection.htm.

UEMOA official site, 'UEMOA Commission', (English trans.), http://www.microsofttranslator.com/BV.aspx?ref=BVNav&a=http%3A%2F%2Fwww.uemoa.int%2Fuemoa%2FSchema_Fonctionnement.htm.

UNCTAD, 'What is ASYCUDA?', available at www.unctad.org/templates/Page.asp?intItemID=3905&lang=1 (last visited 25 Oct. 2010).

United Nations, 'World Population Prospects Population Database', available at http://esa.un.org/unpp/definition.html.

United States Department of State, 'United States Bilateral Investment Treaties', www.state.gov/e/eeb/ifd/bit/117402.htm (last visited 21 Aug. 2010).

US Commercial Service, 'Frequently Asked Questions', www.buyusa.gov/morocco/en/96.html (last visited 21 Aug. 2010).

'US Embassy, U.S. Policy & Issues, United States and Morocco Sign Historic Free Trade Agreement', Embassy of the United States, http://rabat.usembassy.gov/fta.html (last visited 21 Aug. 2010).

'West African Monetary Institute', available at www.wami-imao.org.

West African Monetary Institute official website, 'Questions and Answers on the West African Monetary Zone', available at www.wami-imao.org/english/doc/q-and-a.htm.

World Bank, 'What is the Rationale for Regional Integration?', http://web.worldbank.org/WBSITE/EXTERNAL/COUNTRIES/AFRICAEXT/EXTREGINI/EXTAFRREGINICOO/0,,contentMDK:20655099~menuPK:1587625~pagePK:64168445~piPK:64168309~theSitePK:1587585,00.html (last visited 25 Oct. 2010).

INDEX